MONSTROUS
AMERICAN CAR
SPOTTER'S GUIDE
1920-1980

TAD BURNESS

Motorbooks International
Publishers & Wholesalers Inc.
Osceola, Wisconsin 54020, USA ®

First published in 1986 by Motorbooks International Publishers & Wholesalers Inc, PO Box 2, 729 Prospect Avenue, Osceola, WI 54020 USA

This book consists of three individual works first published separately in paperback as follows: *American Car Spotter's Guide 1920-1939*, published in 1975; *American Car Spotter's Guide 1940-1965* (revised edition), published in 1978; *American Car Spotter's Guide 1966-1980* published in 1981

Printed and bound in the United States of America

Library of Congress Cataloging-in-Publication Data
Burness, Tad
  Monstrous American car spotter's guide 1920-1980.

    1. Automobiles—United States. 2. Automobiles—United States—Pictorial works. 3. Automobiles—United States—Identification. I. Title.
TL23.B83   1986   629.2'222'0973   86-12754
ISBN 0-87938-223-6

Cover photo taken by Tim Parker
Cover car, 1973 Firebird SD-455, owned by Jack Janney

Contents

Page numbers run numerically through each part only because this book is compiled from three individual works. Separate contents pages for each part are available at the start of each part.

Introduction to Part One

Part One, the early years from 1920 to 1939, was written after Part Two (1940-1965) although obviously it now comes first. My "preface" at that time appeared as follows:

"In the 1940-1965 edition of *American Car Spotter's Guide*, I refer to automobiles as "four-wheeled friends." One may laugh at this analogy, but in many ways old cars are like old friends. Surely you remember your first car with fondness, even if it was a klunker.

"My first car was a 1932 DeSoto Airstream sedan. It was already old and tired when I saw it advertised at the bottom of a newspaper's classified column of low-priced 'transportation specials'—FREE. Even though I was not yet sixteen, I still could hardly believe that any car lot would give away its merchandise. A trip verified the ad. The car was free; but to be awarded to the winner of a straw drawing contest. My straw was a loser but a friend drew the right one—the car was mine. And with a total expenditure of fifteen dollars I was on wheels!

"During the years that followed, I bought many other old cars, mostly from the twenties and thirties. These years were, to many, the most fascinating era in automotive history. There are many cars which have been forgotten but now are able to live again in this book.

"A considerable amount of information and technical detail has been included with the pictures to help you identify and familiarize yourself with each model. Your personal favorites should be here, along with pictures of many hundreds of cars both well-known and obscure.

"I welcome any questions or comments from readers of this book. Inquiries accompanied with a self-addressed, stamped envelope sent to me in care of the publisher will be personally answered."

Acknowledgements

I am very grateful to my wife and daughter for their patience with me while I was involved with this part.

My special thanks go to Keith Marvin for his help in compiling a list of many of the forgotten and unsuccessful cars of the twenties.

Also, special thanks are due to Walter F. 'Frank' Robinson, Jr., who was kind enough to make many library trips to photocopy pages from early automotive journals.

Thanks are due to the following individuals for pictures, catalogs or technical details: Bill Adams, David Allen, Roger Allen, Ray E. Amundsen, Warren Baier, Swen H. Carlson, Will Carter, Mike Concordia, John A. Conde, Howard DeSart, Jim Evans, Fred K. Fox, R. C. Freitag, Norm Frey, Bruce Gilbert, Percy R. Gilbert, Dick Grove, Phil Hall, Stanley Hanenkratt, David Lindsay Heggie, Larry C. Holian, Dr. Earl G. Huwatschek, C. E. Jones, Mike Lamm, June Larson, Dick Laue, Scott Lewandoske, William B. Lewis, Larry W. Mauck, John B. McKean, Carl Mendoza, Al Michaelian, Elsa Montgomery, H. Morrison, Harold C. Nauman, Al Newman, Doug O'Connell, Mark Oppat, Everette J. Payette, Raymond B. Petersen, Isadore Rabinovitz, Evan L. Richards, Fred H. Rust, B. F. Schroeder, Wayne Sisk, Kirk Slater, Paul A. Stover, Tom Terhune, Walt Thayer, Bruce Thompson, R. J. Walton, Gates Willard, Ken Wilson, Kenneth 'Butch' Wilson, and R. A. Wawrzyniak.

Thanks are due as well to the following corporations and organizations for either making little-known facts public or for making direct contributions of pictures and/or information: Airflow Club of America, American Motors Corp., Antique Automobile Club of America, Chrysler Corp., Contemporary Historical Vehicle Assn., DeSoto Club of America, Automotive History Collection-Detroit Public Library, Ford Motor Company, General Motors Corp., Harrah's Automobile Collection (and Jim Edwards), Horseless Carriage Club, Society of Automotive Historians, Studebaker Driver's Club, Veteran Motor Car Club of America, Willys-Knight Registry and the W.P.C./Chrysler Product Restorer's Club.

Part One: Ace to Yellow Cab 1920-1939

TOURING CAR or PHAETON

COACH (2-DOOR SEDAN)

COUPE

ROADSTER →

CONVERTIBLE SEDAN

RUMBLE-SEAT

CONVERTIBLE COUPE (CABRIOLET)

TOWN CAR (SOMETIMES KNOWN AS A "CABRIOLET")

TRUNK RACK

CLOSE-COUPLED SEDAN

VISOR — COWL VENT — SURCINGLE (SADDLE BAND)

COWL LAMP — HOOD LOUVRES

RADIATOR SHELL

TIE BAR

CAT-WALK

HOOD

BELT

SPARE TIRE

FENDER

LUG NUTS

RUNNING BOARD

DUST (OR CHASSIS) APRON

(1929-30 WHIPPET 6)

BRAKE DRUM

BODY KEY

TIRE KEY

(SHOWS PRE-1929 OUTER SIZE AT LEFT; POST-1929 (RIM) SIZE FOLLOWS)

Pre-1929	Post-1929	Pre-1929	Post-1929	Pre-1929	Post-1929	Pre-1929	Post-1929
25 × 3.75	= 3.75 × 18	30 × 4.50	= 4.50 × 21	31 × 7.00	= 7.00 × 17	33 × 6.75	7.00 × 21
28 × 3.00	22"	30 × 4.75	4.75 × 21	31 × 7.50	7.50 × 17	33 × 7.00	7.00 × 19
28 × 4.40	4.75 × 20	30 × 4.95	5.00 × 21	32 × 4	24"	33 × 7.50	7.50 × 19
28 × 4.75	4.75 × 19	30 × 5.00	5.00 × 20	32 × 4½	23"	34 × 4	26"
28 × 5.25	5.25 × 18	30 × 5.25	5.25 × 20	32 × 5.00	5.00 × 22	34 × 4½	25"
28 × 5.50	5.50 × 18	30 × 5.50	5.50 × 20	32 × 5.77	6.00 × 22	34 × 6.00	6.00 × 22
29 × 4.40	4.40 × 21	30 × 5.77	6.00 × 20	32 × 6.00	6.00 × 20	34 × 7.00	7.00 × 20
29 × 4.50	4.50 × 20	30 × 6.00	6.00 × 18	32 × 6.20	6.50 × 20	35 × 5	25"
29 × 4.75	4.75 × 20	30 × 6.20	6.50 × 18	32 × 6.50	6.50 × 20	35 × 6.00	6.00 × 23'
29 × 4.95	5.00 × 20	30 × 6.50	6.50 × 18	32 × 6.75	7.00 × 20	35 × 7.00	7.00 × 21
29 × 5.00	5.00 × 19	30 × 6.75	7.00 × 18	32 × 7.00	7.00 × 18	36 × 4	28"
29 × 5.25	5.25 × 19	31 × 4.95	5.00 × 22	32 × 7.50	7.50 × 18	36 × 4½	27"
29 × 5.50	5.50 × 19	31 × 5.00	5.00 × 21	33 × 4	25"	37 × 5	27"
29 × 6.00	6.00 × 17	31 × 5.25	5.25 × 21	33 × 4½	24"	38 × 4½	29"
29 × 6.50	6.50 × 17	31 × 6.00	6.00 × 19	33 × 5.77	6.00 × 23		
30 × 3.00	24"	31 × 6.20	6.50 × 19	33 × 6.00	6.00 × 21		
30 × 3½	23"	31 × 6.50	6.50 × 19	33 × 6.20	6.50 × 21		
		31 × 6.75	7.00 × 19	33 × 6.50	6.50 × 21		

ACE
(1920-1922)

APEX MOTOR CORP., YPSILANTI, MICH.
USED 4-CYL. GRAY-BELL OR
6-CYL. HERSCHELL-SPILLMAN
AND CONTINENTAL ENGINES.

BECAME A PART OF AMERICAN
MOTOR TRUCK CO., NEWARK, OHIO.

('21)
MODEL L (6 CYL.)

ALLEN
(1914-1922)

ALLEN MOTOR CO.,
FOSTORIA, OHIO

(MODEL "43" ALL-NEW FOR 1920)
110" W.B., 4-CYL., 192.4 C.I.D.
4.63 GEAR RATIO
32 x 4" TIRES

20-22 MODEL "43"

AMCO (1920)

AMERICAN MOTORS, INC., N.Y.C.
with 4 CYL. G.B. and S. ENGINE
DESIGNED FOR EXPORT ONLY
RIGHT HAND DRIVE AVAILABLE
114" wheelbase

AMERICAN

AMERICAN MOTORS CORPORATION
Factory and General Offices: Plainfield, N.J.
AMERICAN SOUTHERN MOTORS CORPORATION,
Greensboro, N.C.

(1916-1924)

20

(DRUM HEADLIGHTS
and NICKEL TRIM IN '23)

WITH HERSCHELL-SPILLMAN
6-CYL. ENGINE

(NO RADICAL
CHANGES FOR 1920,
BUT COLUMBIA
REAR AXLE IS NEW.)

7

AMERICAN STEAMER

22 (ONLY MODEL YEAR)

(1922-1924) AMERICAN STEAM TRUCK CO., CHICAGO and ELGIN, ILL.

2-CYLINDER COMPOUND ENGINE

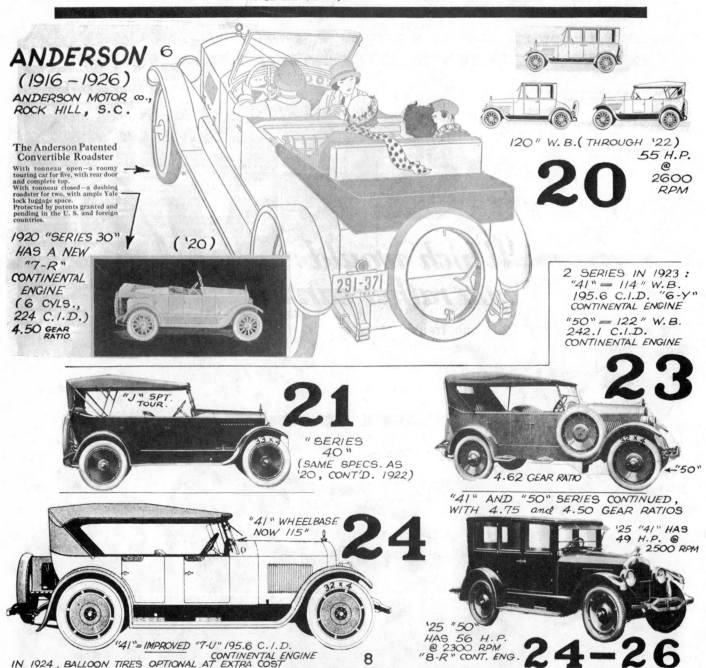

ANDERSON 6
(1916-1926)
ANDERSON MOTOR CO., ROCK HILL, S.C.

The Anderson Patented Convertible Roadster

With tonneau open—a roomy touring car for five, with rear door and complete top.
With tonneau closed—a dashing roadster for two, with ample Yale lock luggage space.
Protected by patents granted and pending in the U. S. and foreign countries.

1920 "SERIES 30" HAS A NEW "7-R" CONTINENTAL ENGINE (6 CYLS., 224 C.I.D.) 4.50 GEAR RATIO

('20)

291-371

120" W.B. (THROUGH '22)

20

55 H.P. @ 2600 RPM

2 SERIES IN 1923 :
"41" = 114" W.B. 195.6 C.I.D. "6-Y" CONTINENTAL ENGINE
"50" = 122" W.B. 242.1 C.I.D. CONTINENTAL ENGINE

"J" SPT. TOUR.

21

33 X 4

"SERIES 40" (SAME SPECS. AS '20, CONT'D. 1922)

23

4.62 GEAR RATIO

←"50"

"41" AND "50" SERIES CONTINUED WITH 4.75 and 4.50 GEAR RATIOS

"41" WHEELBASE NOW 115"

24

33 X 4

32 X 4

"41" = IMPROVED "7-U" 195.6 C.I.D. CONTINENTAL ENGINE

IN 1924, BALLOON TIRES OPTIONAL AT EXTRA COST

'25 "41" HAS 49 H.P. @ 2500 RPM

'25 "50" HAS 56 H.P. @ 2300 RPM "8-R" CONT. ENG.

24-26

8

APPERSON BROS. AUTOMOBILE CO. (1902-1926)
Kokomo, Indiana

APPERSON

331.8 C.I.D. V-8

THE EIGHT WITH EIGHTY LESS PARTS

STANDARD MODEL

130" WHEELBASES
(8-CYL., THROUGH '26)

20
"ANNIVERSARY" MODEL (NOTE DIFFERENT RADIATOR DESIGN)

"ANNIVERSARY"

4.25 GEAR RATIOS

34 × 4½

33 × 4

1922 = FIRST YEAR WITH SQUARE-BACK AND SQUARE-EDGED BODIES. DRUM HEADLIGHTS ON LATER MODELS OF "BEVERLY" SPORTSTER.

THE SELECTOR

EMERGENCY BRAKE CONTROL

GEARSHIFT and HAND-BRAKE CONTROLS MOVED AWAY FROM FLOOR in 1923.

'23 INTERIOR

('24)(6)

21
331.8 C.I.D. V-8 AVAILABLE THROUGH '25; (REPLACED BY LYCOMING 276 C.I.D., 65-H.P. STRAIGHT-8 FOR '25-26)

23
NEW 207.1 C.I.D. SIX ALSO AVAIL.

BALLOON TIRES AND 4-WHEEL BRAKES OPTIONAL.
'25 CLOSED CARS SIMILAR, BUT HAVE VENTILATING EAVES. 6, 8, V-8 IN '25.)

ARGONNE FOUR

128" WHEELBASE, 32 × 4 TIRES, 12-VOLT ELECTRICAL SYSTEM

ARGONNE MOTOR CAR CO., JERSEY CITY, N.J.
(1919* – 1920)

*(ALL CARS 1920 MODELS)

DUESENBERG-DESIGNED "OWN" 4-CYL. ENGINE

(3¾" × 5⅛" BORE + STROKE)

9

AVBURN Beauty-SIX

AUBURN AUTOMOBILE COMPANY, Auburn, Indiana

(1900 - 1937)*

*- 1936 MODEL IS FINAL AUBURN

"BEAUTY SIX" DESIGNATION RETAINED THROUGH 1922.

BLACK HARD-RUBBER (METAL-BOUND) OUTSIDE DOOR HANDLES REPLACE BRIGHT METAL TYPE IN 1922.

(DRUM HEADLIGHTS IN 1922)

19-22

33 × 4

"6-39" HAS 120" W.B., 224 C.I.D. 6-CYL. CONTINENTAL ENGINE, 4.66 GEAR RATIO (1920) "6-51" IS 1922 MODEL WITH 121" W.B., 5.00 GEAR RATIO; "8-R" REPLACES "7-R" CONTINENTAL ENGINE IN LATER MODELS.

NEW MODELS ON JAN. 1, 1923, BUT "6-51" STILL AVAILABLE UNTIL 3-23.

"6-43" HAS 114" W.B., 195.6 C.I.D. CONTINENTAL "6-Y" ENGINE   31 × 4 TIRES
SAME SIZE "7-U" CONTINENTAL ENGINE IN 1924, STARTS 9-1-23.

"6-63" HAS 122" W.B., 248.9 C.I.D. AUBURN O.H.V. ENGINE.* 32 × 4½ TIRES
*- Weidely spec.

23-24

"6-43" AND "6-63" (6 CYL.)

EARLIEST 1925 MODELS (9-24 TO 12-24) (8 CYL.) SIMILAR IN STYLE. (6 CYL. CONTINUED)

4.63 GEAR RATIO ('24) "6-43" (1924) FIRST YEAR WITH CHAIN CHECKS ON DOORS.

"6-43" "ENGLISH COACH" OFFERED '24 - EARLY '25.

"6-43"

"SPORT CAR" ("6-63")

AUBURN

8·88 ROADSTER

21-171 OHIO-1926

COMPLETELY RESTYLED EARLY IN 1925.

25-27

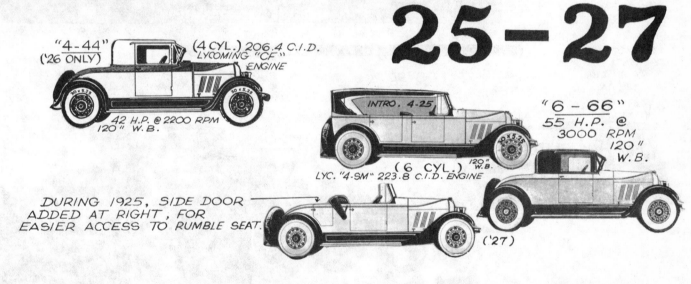

"4-44" ('26 ONLY) (4 CYL.) 206.4 C.I.D. LYCOMING "CF" ENGINE

42 H.P. @ 2200 RPM 120" W.B.

INTRO. 4-25

(6 CYL.) LYC. "4-SM" 223.8 C.I.D. ENGINE

"6-66" 55 H.P. @ 3000 RPM 120" W.B.

('27)

DURING 1925, SIDE DOOR ADDED AT RIGHT, FOR EASIER ACCESS TO RUMBLE SEAT.

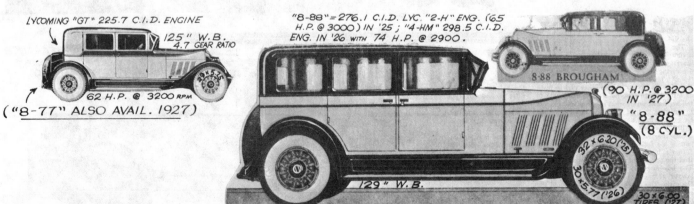

LYCOMING "GT" 225.7 C.I.D. ENGINE

125" W.B. 4.7 GEAR RATIO

62 H.P. @ 3200 RPM

("8-77" ALSO AVAIL. 1927)

"8-88" = 276.1 C.I.D. LYC. "2-H" ENG. (65 H.P. @ 3000) IN '25; "4-HM" 298.5 C.I.D. ENG. IN '26 WITH 74 H.P. @ 2900.

8-88 BROUGHAM

(90 H.P. @ 3200 IN '27)

"8-88" (8 CYL.)

129" W.B.

32 × 6.20 ('25) 30 × 5.77 ('26) 30 × 6.00 TIRES ('27)

AUBURN

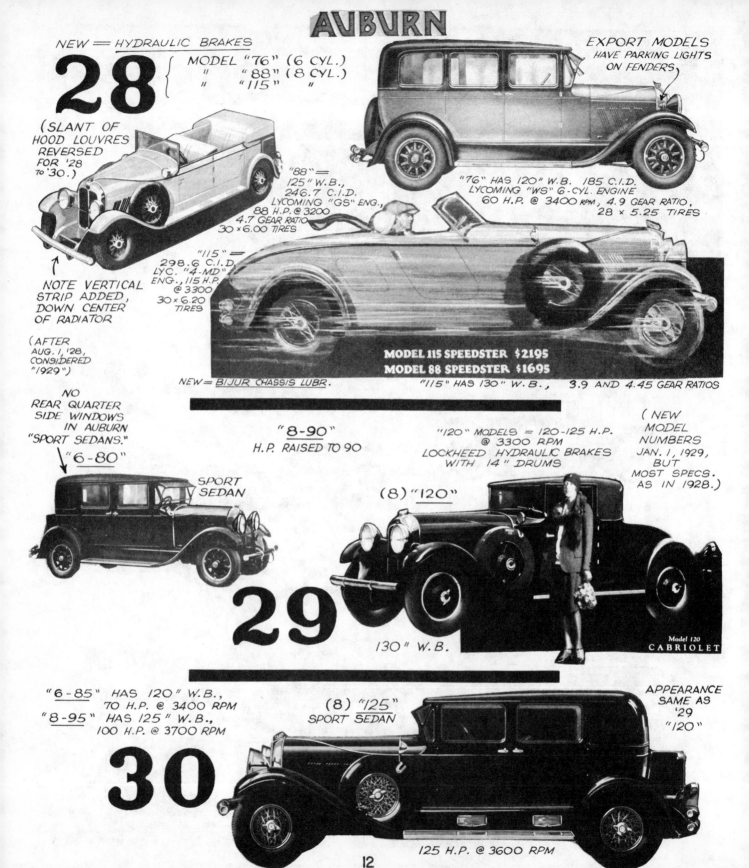

NEW = HYDRAULIC BRAKES

28
MODEL "76" (6 CYL.)
" "88" (8 CYL.)
" "115" "

EXPORT MODELS HAVE PARKING LIGHTS ON FENDERS

(SLANT OF HOOD LOUVRES REVERSED FOR '28 TO '30.)

"88" = 125" W.B., 246.7 C.I.D. LYCOMING "GS" ENG., 88 H.P. @ 3200 4.7 GEAR RATIO 30 x 6.00 TIRES

"76" HAS 120" W.B. 185 C.I.D. LYCOMING "WS" 6-CYL. ENGINE 60 H.P. @ 3400 RPM, 4.9 GEAR RATIO, 28 x 5.25 TIRES

NOTE VERTICAL STRIP ADDED, DOWN CENTER OF RADIATOR

"115" = 298.6 C.I.D. LYC. "4-MD" ENG., 115 H.P. @ 3300 30 x 6.20 TIRES

(AFTER AUG. 1, '28, CONSIDERED "1929")

MODEL 115 SPEEDSTER $2195
MODEL 88 SPEEDSTER $1695

NEW = BIJUR CHASSIS LUBR.   "115" HAS 130" W.B., 3.9 AND 4.45 GEAR RATIOS

NO REAR QUARTER SIDE WINDOWS IN AUBURN "SPORT SEDANS."

"6-80"

SPORT SEDAN

"8-90" H.P. RAISED TO 90

"120" MODELS = 120-125 H.P. @ 3300 RPM LOCKHEED HYDRAULIC BRAKES WITH 14" DRUMS

(NEW MODEL NUMBERS JAN. 1, 1929, BUT MOST SPECS. AS IN 1928.)

(8) "120"

29

130" W.B.

Model 120 CABRIOLET

"6-85" HAS 120" W.B., 70 H.P. @ 3400 RPM
"8-95" HAS 125" W.B., 100 H.P. @ 3700 RPM

(8) "125" SPORT SEDAN

APPEARANCE SAME AS '29 "120"

30

125 H.P. @ 3600 RPM

AUBURN

COMPLETELY RESTYLED FOR 1931!

('31½)   "8-98-A"

4.45 GEAR RATIO

126" W. B.
286.6 C.I.D. LYCOMING "GU"
STRAIGHT-8 ENGINE.
98 H.P. @ 3400 RPM
(THROUGH '32)

2-DOOR BROUGHAM

31-32

"8-98" ONLY MODEL AVAILABLE IN 1931. IN 1932, A CHOICE OF "8-100" OR "12-160." "A" AFTER '32 MODEL NO. DENOTES CUSTOM SERIES WITH "DUAL RATIO" 2-SPEED DIFFERENTIAL.

"8-100" HAS **4.7** GEAR RATIO, 127 OR 136" W. B.

6.00 × 17 TIRES IN 1932

V-12 LYCOMING "BB" 391 C.I.D. ENGINE
160 H.P. @ 3400 RPM   132" W. B.
4 TO 1 GEAR RATIO

V-12 HAS "12" ON BUMPER

V-12 (1932)

33

8

SPEEDSTER

V-12 "SALON" SERIES

13

AUBURN

"850"

6 — 6-CYL. AUBURNS AVAILABLE AGAIN, FOR FIRST TIME SINCE '30.
119" W.B. "652"
85 H.P. @ 3500
4.60 GEAR RATIO

8

34

THIS NEW STYLING RETAINED JUST 1 YEAR.

1933 SALON-STYLE "12-165" CONTINUED INTO 1934.

COUPE

4.50 G.R. ON '35 "851"

35-36

6 OR 8 CYL.

120" W.B.   127" W.B.

4.44 G.R. ON 6

INTERIOR (COUPE)

WITH RIGID TOP FITTED TO OPEN-STYLE BODY.

"851" ('35) and "852" ('36) HAVE 279.9 C.I.D. LYCOMING "GG" ENGINE, 115 H.P. @ 3600, 6.50 × 16 TIRES

'35 "653" and '36 (FINAL) "654" 6-CYL. MODELS HAVE 85 H.P. @ 3500 RPM, 209.9 C.I.D. LYCOMING "WF" ENGINE, 120" W.B.
5.50 × 17 TIRES ON '35 "653," 6.00 × 16 ON '36 "654"

SUPERCHARGED '36 "SC-852" HAS 150 H.P. @ 4000 RPM 4.08 GEAR RATIO ON '36 8s.

SPEEDSTER (8)

REAR

NO 1937 AUBURNS, BUT CORD V-8 and DUESENBERG 8 AVAIL. IN 1937 (FINAL YEAR.)

14

AUSTIN 4

(AFTER 1936, ALSO KNOWN AS "AMERICAN BANTAM")

(BLT. 1930-1941 AT BUTLER, PA.)

"BANTAM" CAR

(SLANTING WINDSHIELD and VERTICAL HOOD LOUVRES INTRODUCED FOR ('33.)

V- WINDSHIELD ← ON ROADSTER SINCE '31

75" W.B. (THROUGH '41)

33-34

"2-75" SERIES

(1935 HAS SLANTING LOUVRES)
13 H.P. @ 3200 RPM (1932 THROUGH '36)

30-32

12½ H.P. @ 3000 RPM (THROUGH '31)

4 CYLS., 45.6 C.I.D.
5.25 GEAR RATIO (THROUGH '41)
3.75 × 18 TIRES (THROUGH '36)

39

"62"

37

38

"60"

20 H.P. @ 4000 RPM (THROUGH '39)

(DURING '39, HOOD LOUVRES SHORTENED, THEN ELIMINATED.)

Bantam

BALBOA

BALBOA MOTOR CORP. FULLERTON, CALIF.

(1923 - 1925)

KESSLER STRAIGHT-8 ENGINE   178 C.I.D.
SUPERCHARGED   100 H.P. @ 4000 RPM

BAY STATE

R. H. LONG CO., FRAMINGHAM, MASS.

(1922 -1924)

(CONTINENTAL 6-CYL. ENGINE)

BEGGS

20

BEGGS MOTOR CAR CO., KANSAS CITY, MO.
(1918 – 1923)
6 - CYL. CONTINENTAL ENGINE

120" WHEELBASE

15

BELL

BELL MOTOR CAR CO., YORK, PA.
(1915—1921)

20-21

BIDDLE

BIDDLE MOTOR CAR
CO., PHILADELPHIA, PA.
(1915—1923)

121" W.B., 32 × 4" TIRES
4-CYLINDER DUESENBERG OR
BUDA ENGINE

4.5 GEAR RATIO

BIRCH   (1917—1923)

BIRCH MOTOR CARS, INC., CHICAGO
(SOLD BY MAIL ORDER, 4 and 6 CYL.)

"SUPER 4"   **20**

BIRMINGHAM

BIRMINGHAM MOTORS, JAMESTOWN, N.Y.
(1920—1924)

6-CYL. CONTINENTAL "7-R" engine
124" W.B., 32 × 4 TIRES

WILSON BODY, MADE OF "HASKELITE"
PLYWOOD, COVERED WITH DUPONT FABRIKOID

22

(ONLY YEAR MODEL
IN
PRODUCTION)

4-WHEEL
INDEPENDENT
SUSPENSION

BOUR — DAVIS
(1915—1922)

BUILT AT CHICAGO, ILL.; SHREVEPORT, LA.; also DETROIT
(COMPANY CHANGED LOCATIONS, KNOWN AS BOUR-DAVIS CO.
AND <u>ALSO</u> AS LOUISIANA MOTOR CAR CO.)

125" WHEELBASE

20

NEW FOR 1920:
WESTINGHOUSE STARTING + LIGHTING,
13-DISC CLUTCH, AND NEW CARBURETOR.

224 C.I.D. CONTINENTAL
ENGINE, 4.75 GEAR RATIO

BREWSTER
(BREWSTER-KNIGHT)
BREWSTER + CO., LONG ISLAND CITY, N.Y.
(1915 - 1925)

"41" TOWN LANDAULETTE

6-PASS. DOUBLE ENCL. DRIVE

BREWSTER-FORD
(CUSTOM BODY ON FORD V-8 CHASSIS)

SPRINGFIELD MFG. CO., SPRINGFIELD, MASS.

(1934 TO 1936)

BRIGGS AND STRATTON

1-CYLINDER AIR COOLED ENGINE

BRIGGS AND STRATTON, MILWAUKEE, WIS.

(1919 - 1923)

BRISCOE

"4-34"

LATE '21 = NAME CHANGED TO EARL

BRISCOE MOTOR CORP., JACKSON, MICH.

(1914 - 1921)

(109" W.B.)

NEW "BEVEL-LINE" STYLING FOR 1920.

20-21

4 CYLS.

4.18 GEAR RATIO, 31 x 4 TIRES

BROOKE-SPACKE
(1920 - 1921)

SPACKE MACHINE and TOOL CO., INDIANAPOLIS, INDIANA

(1921 = MORE COMPLETE BODY)

(2 CYL.)

BROOKS STEAMER
26

MFD. IN CANADA, 1923 - 1926. OPERATIONS MOVED TO BUFFALO, N.Y., 1926.

(FABRIC-COVERED BODY)

BRYAN STEAMER

BRYAN STEAM MOTORS, PERU, INDIANA
(1918 – 1923)   (TOURING CARS ONLY)

4.0 GEAR RATIO

BUICK

BUICK MOTOR COMPANY, FLINT, MICHIGAN
Division of General Motors Corporation
Canadian Factories: McLaughlin-Buick, Oshawa, Ontario

ESTABLISHED 1903; A G.M. PRODUCT SINCE 1908.

6 CYLINDERS OVERHEAD VALVES (241.6 C.I.D. THROUGH '23)

19-20

21-22

1922 CLOSED CARS HAVE HEATER.

1922 SIX and NEW FOUR AVAILABLE AUGUST, 1921.

4.08 G.R. ('21)

1922 GEAR RATIOS = 4.66 (4, THROUGH '23) 4.60 ; 4.90 (6)

TRUNK DETAILS

23

NEW COWL VENT

BUICK 4 HAS 170 C.I.D., 35 H.P.

"4-36" COUPE

"4-38" TOURING SEDAN (2-DOOR COACH)

'23 HAS DRUM-TYPE LAMPS; ALUMINUM HOOD BEADING ON 6.

4

"6-45"

6

4.40 G.R. (6)

18

"6-54"

7-PASS.

"6-50"

BUICK

4 (FINAL 4-CYL. BUICK)

NEW 4-WHEEL BRAKES

(FRONT BRAKE DETAILS)

"4-37" SEDAN

24

NEW STYLING, NEW RADIATOR DESIGN

"4-34" ROADSTER

"4-33" 4-PASS. COUPE

"4-35" TOURING

PAINTED RADIATOR SHELL ON 4-CYL. MODELS

$\frac{4}{6}$

6

HAS LONGER HOOD AND NICKEL-PLATED RADIATOR

"6-44" 2-PASSENGER ROADSTER

"6-54" SPORT ROADSTER

FIRST YEAR THAT 6-CYL. ENGINE HAS DETACHABLE CYLINDER HEAD.
255 C.I.D. 65 H.P. @ 2600 RPM

Buick TRADITIONAL EMBLEM

BUICK

"6-45" 5-PASS. TOURING

24 (CONT'D.)

"DOUBLE SERVICE" 5-PASS. SEDAN
"6-41"

A LOW-PRICED SEDAN WITH SQUARE-EDGED REAR PANELS.

"6-49" 7-PASS. TOURING

"6-47" 5-PASS. SEDAN

"6-55" 4-PASS. SPORT TOURING

"6-50" 7-PASS. SEDAN

"6-48" 4-PASS. COUPE

"6-51" BROUGHAM

(EARLIEST '24 BROUGHAM HAS SEMI-RECTANGULAR-STYLE REAR QUARTER WINDOWS INSTEAD OF OVAL AS ILLUSTRATED.)

25

ALL MODELS 6-CYLINDERS

WITH "SEALED CHASSIS"

MASTER 6
255 C.I.D.
70 H.P.
@ 2800 RPM

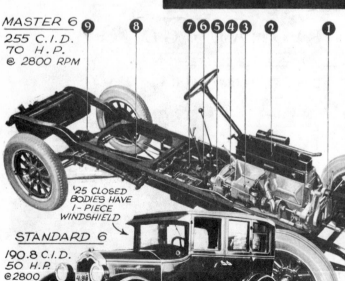

'25 CLOSED BODIES HAVE 1-PIECE WINDSHIELD

STANDARD 6
190.8 C.I.D.
50 H.P.
@ 2800 RPM

Here are the vital points at which Buick engineering provides this extra protection:

❶ = FAN HUB
❷ = ENGINE
❸ = STARTER-GENERATOR (IN 1 UNIT)
❹ = FLYWHEEL
❺ = CLUTCH
❻ = TRANSMISSION
❼ = UNIVERSAL JOINT
❽ = TORQUE TUBE (ENCLOSING DRIVESHAFT)
❾ = DIFFERENTIAL

NEW BALLOON TIRES. DUCO FINISH ON ALL MODELS BEGINNING JANUARY, 1925.

2-DOOR COACHES AVAILABLE AFTER NOV., '24.

(32 × 5.77 TIRES ON MASTER 6)

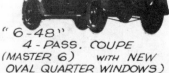

"6-48" 4-PASS. COUPE (MASTER 6) WITH NEW OVAL QUARTER WINDOWS)

BUICK

STANDARD 6
207.1 C.I.D.
60 H.P. @ 2800 RPM
114 3/8" W.B.

MASTER 6
274.2 C.I.D.
75 H.P. @ 2800 RPM
120" OR 128" W.B.

26

(INTRODUCED AUG. 1, 1925)

PUROLATOR OIL FILTER ON ALL MODELS.

CLOSED CARS WITH NEW DOUBLE-BEAD BELT MOLDINGS.

"54-C" COUNTRY CLUB COUPE

MASTER 6

"27" SEDAN

STANDARD 6

"48" 4-PASS. COUPE

31 × 5.25 TIRES ON STANDARD, 33 × 6.00 " ON MASTER (THROUGH '28)

WHEN BETTER AUTOMOBILES ARE BUILT — BUICK WILL BUILD THEM

"128" HAS INSIDE WATER TEMPERATURE GAUGE AND ORNAMENTAL RADIATOR CAP.

ONE-PIECE WINDSHIELD ON OPEN CARS

(STARTS AUG. 1, 1926)

27

"115" = 63 H.P.

"120," "128" = 77 H.P.

SERIES # INDICATES WHEELBASE, EXCEPT "115" HAS 114½" W.B.

Body by Fisher

21

BUICK

ASSIST CORD

"115," "120" and "128" SERIES AGAIN

(MINOR RESTYLING)

28

"115" has
31 × 5.25 TIRES, 5.1 G.R.
"120" and "128"
have 33 × 6.00 TIRES, 4.9 G.R.

(MODELS AND SPECS. SIMILAR TO 1927)

UPPER RADIATOR PAN IS DEEPER FOR 1928.

IGNITION AND STEERING LOCK

NEW BOWL-SHAPED HEADLIGHTS

NEW RADIATOR MASCOT

WATER TEMP. GAUGE ON ALL 1928 MODELS.

STANDARD GEARSHIFT PATTERN ADOPTED.

LANDAUS WITH NEW STYLE QUARTER WINDOWS

The Silver Anniversary **BUICK**

4.9 GEAR RATIO ("116;") 4.8 ON OTHERS

29 (COMPLETELY RESTYLED)

(INTRODUCED SATURDAY, JULY 28, 1928)

29½ MODELS HAVE COLORFUL HUB CAPS OF NEW DESIGN (RED and BLACK, ON SILVER.)

EARLY TYPE HUB CAP (PLAINER STYLE)

SILVER ANNIVERSARY BUICK—FIVE PASSENGER SEDAN

"51" CLOSE-COUPLED SEDAN

BECAUSE OF ITS ODD, BULGING SIDE-PANELS, THE 1929 MODEL WAS SOON NICKNAMED "THE PREGNANT BUICK."

239.1 C.I.D., 74 H.P. @ 2800 OR 309.6 C.I.D. WITH 90½ H.P. @ 2800

new FUEL PUMP ON ALL '29 BUICKS.

"26"

"20" SERIES 116" W.B.
40 " 121 "
50 " 129 "
30 × 5.50 OR 32 × 6.50 TIRES

"54-CC"

NEW DASH HAS BLACK CIRCULAR GAUGES IN A ROW.

23

BUICK

1930 — 6 CYL.
1931 — 8 CYL.

(COMPLETELY RESTYLED)
('30 MODEL INTRO. JULY, 1929)

new "ROAD-SHOCK ELIMINATOR"
new NON-GLARE WINDSHIELD (SLANTED 7°)

VALVE-IN-HEAD
Buick
MOTOR CARS

5.50 OR 6.50 × 19 TIRES

1930 INSTRUMENT PANEL

3 SERIES FOR '30 →	"40"	118" W.B.	80½ H.P.
	50	124	98
	60	132	"

NEW STRAIGHT-8 1931 ENGINES REPLACE ALL 1930 SIXES

30-31

1931 MODEL HAS ALL-NEW INSTRUMENT PANEL. →

FINAL BUICK ROADSTER

4 1931 BASIC MODEL SERIES

"50"	114" W.B.	77 H.P.	220.7 C.I.D.
60	118	90	272.6
80	124	104	344.8
90	132	"	"

TIRES = 5.25 × 18 (50,)
5.50 × 19 (60,)
OR 6.50 × 19 (80 and 90 SERIES)

1931 HAS SYNCHRO-MESH TRANSMISSION.

WINGED "8" → ON RADIATOR CAP OF 1931 MODEL.

24

32 BUICK
with WIZARD CONTROL

NEW STYLE
SWEEP-HAND
SPEEDOMETER

SPEEDOMETER

DASH GAUGES
MOVED TO *LEFT SIDE*

DETAILS OF
FRONT
END

"50" HAS
230.4 C.I.D.,
78 H.P. @
3200 RPM,
114" W.B.
5.50 × 18 TIRES

"60" HAS
272.5 C.I.D.,
90 H.P. @
3000 RPM,
118" W.B.
6.00 × 18 TIRES

"80" AND "90" HAVE
344.7 C.I.D.,
104 H.P. @ 2900 RPM,
126" AND 134" W.B.
7.00 × 18 TIRES

H.P. INCREASED '33
(@ 3200 RPM)
TO 86 ("50,")
97 ("60,")
113 ("80", "90")

NEW 6.00 × 17, 6.50 × 17, 7.00 × 17 TIRE SIZES ('33 ONLY)

WHEELBASES OF 119, 127, 130, 138"

33

BUICK

NEW 16" WHEELS ON ALL.

INTERIOR →

93, 88, 100 OR
88 TO 116 H.P. @ 3200 RPM
233, 235.3, 278.1 OR
344.8 C.I.D.; 4.33,
4.8, 4.7 OR 4.36 G.R.
"AUTOMATIC STARTING"

'34

34-35

"40," "50," "60" and
"90" SERIES
("40"
STARTS
5-34)

117", 119"   128", 136" W.B.

6.50 × 16, 7.00 × 15,
7.00 × 16 OR
7.50 × 16 TIRES
(THROUGH '39)
4.44, 3.9,
4.22 OR
4.55 G.R.

"40" HAS 233 C.I.D.
(AS SINCE '34)
OTHERS HAVE
320.2 C.I.D.
"40" HAS 93 H.P.
OTHERS HAVE 120
(@ 3200 RPM)

ROADMASTER

The ROADMASTER, series 80 six-passenger Sedan

118," 122"
131" and 138"
WHEELBASES

STARTING 1936,
NAMES GIVEN TO
MODELS

36

"40" = SPECIAL
"60" = CENTURY
"80" = ROADMASTER
"90" = LIMITED

INTERIOR ←

The BUICK LIMITED, Series
90 four-door six passenger

BUICK

"SPECIAL" has 100 H.P. @ 248 C.I.D. 3200 RPM (THROUGH '49)

320.2 C.I.D. ON OTHERS (TO '52, EXCEPT "SUPER", WHICH STARTS '40.)

1937

37

130 H.P. @ 3400 RPM ON "CENTURY 60" and up.

4.4, 3.9, 4.22 (1937 WHEELBASES: 122", 126", 131", 138") OR 4.62 G.R.

"LIMITED"

7.50 × 16

SPECIAL = 122" W.B. 107 H.P. @ 3400 RPM

CENTURY = 126" W.B. 141 H.P. @ 3600 RPM, AS ON LARGER MODELS.

ROADMASTER = 133" W.B.

LIMITED = 140" W.B.

(SAME FIGURES THROUGH '40, EXCEPT "SPECIAL" W.B.)

4.44, 3.9, 4.18 OR 4.56 G.R. (THROUGH '39)

"LIMITED"

SINCLAIR

"ROADMASTER"

USA 1938

38

DELCO-REMY IGN. (SINCE '27) FISHER BODIES, AS BEFORE

← DASH

39

DIRECTIONAL SIGNALS

BUICK EIGHT

1939

"SPECIAL" WHEELBASE SHORTENED TO 120."

"LIMITEDS" have OLDER STYLE BODIES.

BUSH
(1916-1924)

BUSH MOTOR CO., CHICAGO

4 OR 6 CYLS.

LYCOMING, RUTENBER, OR CONTINENTAL ENGINES

('19-20)

"E.C. 4" has 192.4 C.I.D. LYCOMING ENGINE. "E.C. 6" has 230.1 C.I.D. RUTENBER ENGINE. BOTH have 116" W.B., 33 × 4 TIRES ('21 SPECIFICATIONS)

CADILLAC
DIVISION OF GENERAL MOTORS CORPORATION

(ESTABLISHED 1902; JOINED G.M. 1909)

V-8 ENGINE

20-21

TYPE 59

35 × 5" TIRES IN 1920; 34 × 4½", 1921.

314.4 C.I.D. (1915 THROUGH '27)
60 H.P. @ 2700 RPM (TO '23)
125" OR 132" W.B. (THROUGH '21)

4.44 GEAR RATIO

4-PASS. ('21)

'21 IS FINAL MODEL with TILTING STEER. WHEEL.

TRADITIONAL EMBLEM AND MOTTO

Standard of the World

4.5 and 2 OTHER GEAR RATIOS

STEERING-COLUMN QUADRANT REPLACED BY SMALLER FINGER-GRIPS FOR SPARK and THROTTLE CONTROLS. SUPPLEMENTARY TRANSMISSION LOCK.

22-23

TYPE 61

new '22 TYPE 61 STEERING WHEEL RIM, SPOKES, and HORN BUTTON are all made of WALNUT.
LARGER COWL VENT.

WITH AMES CUSTOM BODY ('23)
(MOST BODIES BY FISHER, BUT IN CALIFORNIA, CUSTOM BODIES ARE AVAILABLE BY DON LEE.)

VICTORIA COUPE CONTINUED, with DOORS HINGED at REAR. NEW FOR 1922 IS 5-PASS. COUPE (ILLUSTRATED,) with DOORS HINGED AT FRONT, AND with LONGER CAB SECTION.

RADIATOR IS HIGHER FOR 1922.

132" W.B. ONLY OPTIONAL GEAR RATIOS

33 × 5 TIRES (THROUGH '25)

NEW '22 "61" has DELCO SWITCHES AT CENTER OF DASH

new BAUSCH and LOMB OPTICAL LENSES

INTERIOR

SPEEDOMETER AND CLOCK

CADILLAC

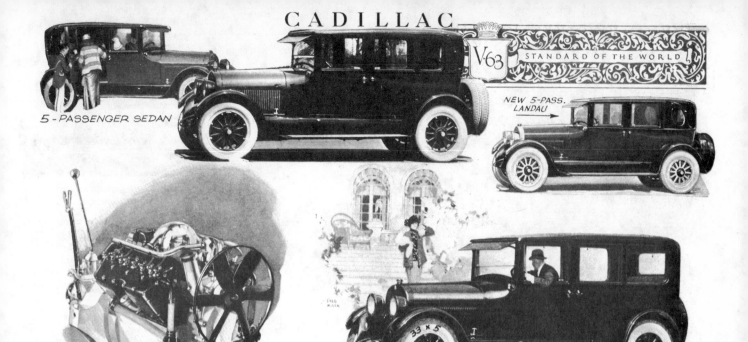

V-63

STANDARD OF THE WORLD

5 - PASSENGER SEDAN

NEW 5-PASS. LANDAU →

STANDARD OF THE WORLD

THE NEW V-63 SUBURBAN

DASH

24

NEW "V-63"

AS FITTED WITH DUAL SPARE TIRES

INTERNAL-EXPANDING FRONT-WHEEL BRAKES (EXTERNAL-CONTRACTING ON REAR WHEELS.)

72 H.P. @ 3000 RPM (THROUGH '25)

132" WHEELBASE

33 × 5

C A D I L L A C

25

COACH INTRO. JAN., 1925

STANDARD W.B. = 132"
* CUSTOM BUILT LINE " = 138"
*- aluminum bodies

4.91 GEAR RATIO

FROM 1926 TO 1935,
MODEL NUMBER
INDICATES DISPL.
OF ENGINE, (EXCEPT
FOR FRACTION-OF-
INCH DIFFERENCES.)

26

33 × 6.75
BALLOON TIRES
(THROUGH '27)

"314" (INTRO. 7-30-25)
(314.4 C. I. D.)
87 H.P. @ 3000 RPM
(THROUGH '27)

VERTICAL
RADIATOR
SHUTTERS

STANDARD · OF · THE · WORLD

(CUSTOM ROADSTER ON 132" W.B.)   HORN IS UNDER LEFT HEADLAMP

SINCE 1-26, CUSTOM
CLOSED MODELS HAVE THIS
TYPE OF WINDSHIELD.

50 BODY STYLES
AND TYPES;
500 COLOR
AND UPHOLSTERY
COMBINATIONS!

4.91
GEAR
RATIO

27 (STARTS
7-15-26)

NEW 1-PIECE
FRONT FENDERS

"314"

BATTERY and
TOOL BOX CONCEALED
BEHIND DUST SHIELD

7-PASS.
CUSTOM SUBURBAN

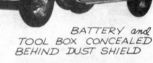

LIGHT SWITCH ON STEERING QUADRANT

STARTING 1-27, DISTRIBUTOR
MOVED, FROM REAR, TO FRONT, OF ENGINE.

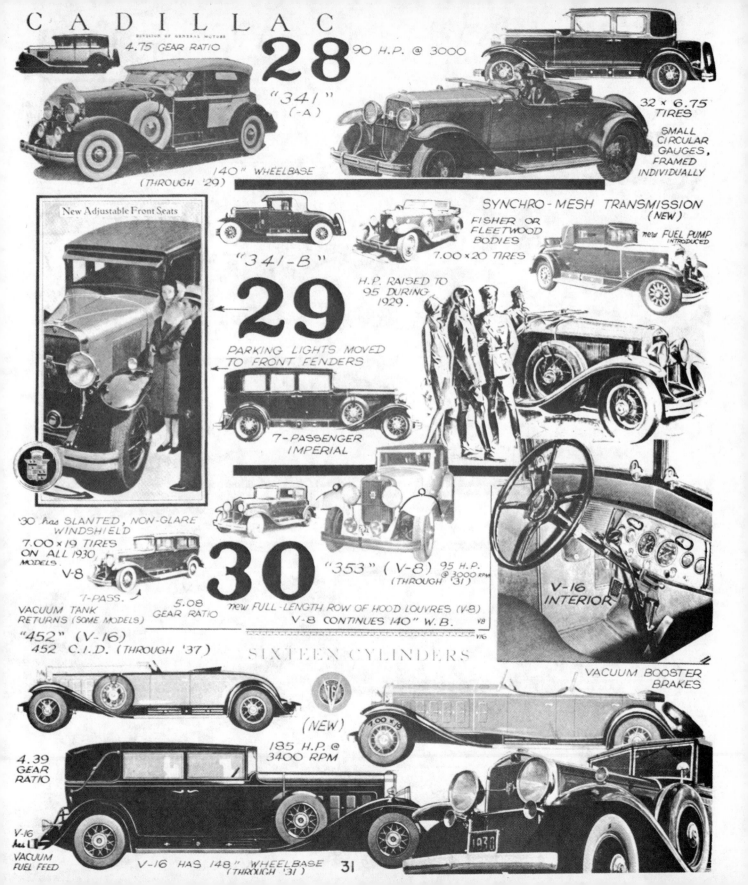

C A D I L L A C

DIVISION OF GENERAL MOTORS

4.75 GEAR RATIO

28

90 H.P. @ 3000

"341" (-A)

32 × 6.75 TIRES

SMALL CIRCULAR GAUGES, FRAMED INDIVIDUALLY

140" WHEELBASE

(THROUGH '29)

New Adjustable Front Seats

"341-B"

29

SYNCHRO-MESH TRANSMISSION (NEW)

FISHER OR FLEETWOOD BODIES

new FUEL PUMP INTRODUCED

7.00 × 20 TIRES

H.P. RAISED TO 95 DURING 1929.

PARKING LIGHTS MOVED TO FRONT FENDERS

7-PASSENGER IMPERIAL

'30 has SLANTED, NON-GLARE WINDSHIELD

7.00 × 19 TIRES ON ALL 1930 MODELS.

V-8

30

"353" (V-8)

95 H.P. @ 3000 RPM (THROUGH '31)

7-PASS.

5.08 GEAR RATIO

new FULL-LENGTH ROW OF HOOD LOUVRES (V-8)

V-16 INTERIOR

VACUUM TANK RETURNS (SOME MODELS)

V-8 CONTINUES 140" W.B.

V-8

V-16

"452" (V-16)

452 C.I.D. (THROUGH '37)

SIXTEEN CYLINDERS

VACUUM BOOSTER BRAKES

(NEW)

185 H.P. @ 3400 RPM

7.00 × 19

4.39 GEAR RATIO

V-16 HAS WB

VACUUM FUEL FEED

V-16 HAS 148" WHEELBASE (THROUGH '31)

31

CADILLAC

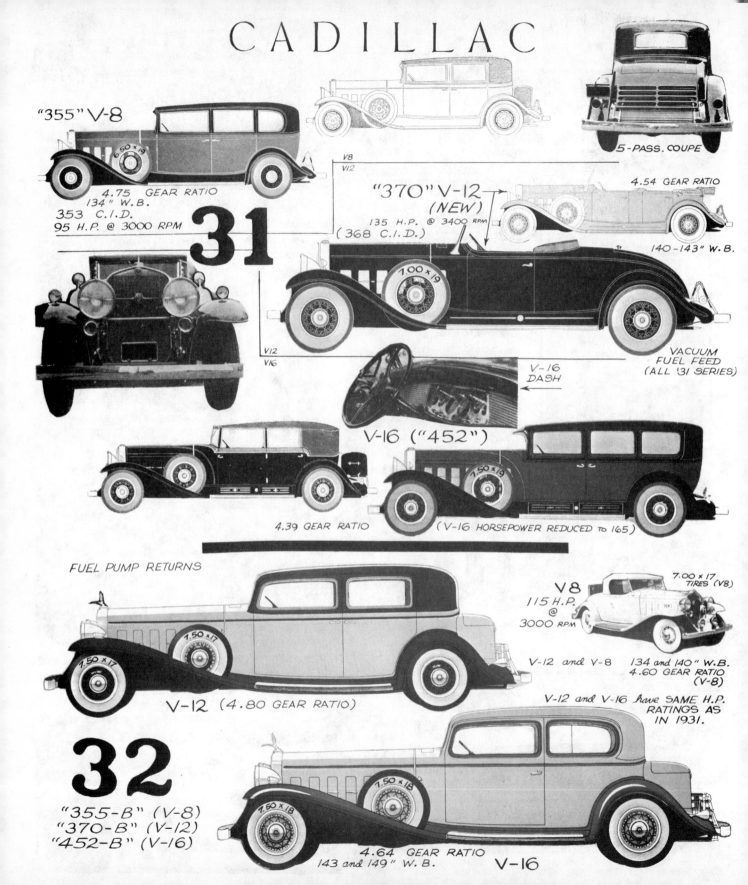

"355" V-8

4.75 GEAR RATIO
134" W.B.
353 C.I.D.
95 H.P. @ 3000 RPM

31

5-PASS. COUPE

"370" V-12
(NEW)
135 H.P. @ 3400 RPM
(368 C.I.D.)

V8
V12

4.54 GEAR RATIO

140-143" W.B.

7.00 x 19

VACUUM
FUEL FEED
(ALL '31 SERIES)

V12
V16

V-16
DASH

V-16 ("452")

4.39 GEAR RATIO

(V-16 HORSEPOWER REDUCED to 165)

FUEL PUMP RETURNS

7.50 x 17

V-12 (4.80 GEAR RATIO)

V8
115 H.P.
@
3000 RPM

7.00 x 17
TIRES (V8)

V-12 and V-8   134 and 140" W.B.
4.60 GEAR RATIO
(V-8)

V-12 and V-16 have SAME H.P.
RATINGS AS
IN 1931.

32

"355-B" (V-8)
"370-B" (V-12)
"452-B" (V-16)

7.50 x 18

4.64 GEAR RATIO
143 and 149" W.B.   V-16

C A D I L L A C

33

7.00×17" TIRES ON V-8
(THROUGH '35)

"355-C" (V-8)
"370-C" (V-12)
"452 C" (V-16)

SAME H.P.
RATINGS AS
IN 1932.

V-12

V-12

7.50×17 TIRES
on V-12 and V-16
(THROUGH '35)

V-16 ENGINE

CHICAGO WORLD'S
FAIR SHOW CAR

V-16

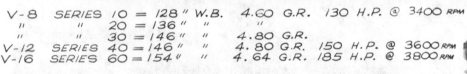

V-8	SERIES 10 = 128" W.B.	4.60 G.R.	130 H.P. @ 3400 RPM
"	" 20 = 136" "	"	
"	" 30 = 146" "	4.80 G.R.	
V-12	SERIES 40 = 146" "	4.80 G.R.	150 H.P. @ 3600 RPM
V-16	SERIES 60 = 154" "	4.64 G.R.	185 H.P. @ 3800 RPM

(V-8)

8 J 18 88

34

"355-D" (V-8)
"370-D" (V-12)
"452-D" (V-16)

TEARDROP
HOOD LOUVRES ON V-16

CADILLAC

7.50 x 17
TIRES (V-16)
(ALSO V-12)

V-16

(SOLID BUMPERS
MORE TYPICAL DURING '35.)

V-8

35
(INTRO.
JAN., 1935)

1935 INTERIOR
(PLAIN UPHOLSTERY REPLACES PLAITED)

7.00 x 17
TIRES (V-8)

"355-E" (V-8) "370-E" (V-12)
"16-62" (V-16)

TWO V-8s FOR 1936 : "60" HAS 322 C.I.D. ENGINE
(125 H.P. @ 3400 RPM) (USED IN La SALLE, 1937-1940 ;)
"70" and "75" HAVE 346 C.I.D. ENGINE
(135 H.P. @ 3400 RPM)

60

85

90

FLEETWOOD V-12

"60," "70," "75" (V-8)   "80," "85" (V-12)   "90" (V-16)

(HYDRAULIC
BRAKES ON
V-8 and V-12)

36
(STARTS OCT., 1935)

CADILLAC

60
(V-8)

(FINAL V-12 CADILLAC)
85

"60" NOW SHARES 346 C.I.D.
V-8 ENGINE WITH "70" and "75"

37
(STARTS
OCT., 1936)

FLEETWOOD V 8·12·16

FINAL YEAR FOR OVERHEAD VALVES IN
V-16 ENGINE

V-16 HAS HYDRAULIC
VACUUM BOOSTER BRAKES, RETAINS TEARDROP HOOD LOUVRES, 154"
W.B., 7.50 × 17 TIRES

V-8

V-16 (L-HEAD)
4.31
G.R.

38
(STARTS OCT., 1937)

V-16 HAS NEW ENGINE OF 431 C.I.D.,
175 H.P. @ 3600 RPM

35

CADILLAC

38 (CONT'D.)

"75" RATED AT 140 H.P. WHILE OTHER V-8 MODELS RATED AT 135.

"SUNSHINE ROOF," NEW TO U.S.A. IN '38, AVAILABLE ON SOME '39 MODELS OF CADILLAC, LA SALLE, BUICK AND OLDSMOBILE.

"60 - SPECIAL" = (WITHOUT RUNNING BOARDS) HAS ITS OWN UNIQUE STYLING.

127" W.B. ON "60-S" (THROUGH '40)

7.00 x 16

60-SPECIAL (FRONT DETAILS)

FLEETWOOD V·8 and 16

126" W.B. ON "61," 141" W.B. ON "75" and V-16

V-16

(V-16 DISCONTINUED DURING 1940) 185 H.P. @ 3600 RPM FOR 1939-1940 V-16s.

39 (STARTS OCT., 1938)

36

75

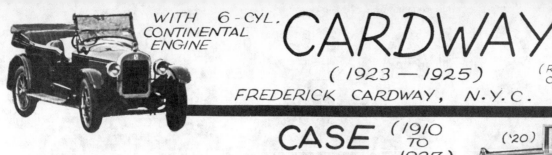

WITH 6-CYL. CONTINENTAL ENGINE

CARDWAY

(1923 — 1925)   (REPORTEDLY, ONLY 6 BUILT)

FREDERICK CARDWAY, N.Y.C.

CASE (1910 TO 1927)

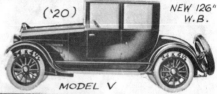

('20)   NEW 126" W.B.

J.I.C. CASE CO., RACINE, WIS.

MODEL V

NEW BODIES FOR 1920, AND NEW 1-PIECE FRONT SEAT IN TOURING. 6 CYL. CONTINENTAL ENGINE (303.1 C.I.D.) RAYFIELD CARB., DELCO IGNITION, AND NEW ALEMITE LUBRICATION SYSTEM.

132" W.B.

SCHEB. CARB. ('26 ON)

32 x 4½

('24) MODEL "Y"

(REPLACES MODEL "W," AUG. 1, '23)
(MODEL "X" ALSO)
(LIKE "JIC") "JAY EYE CEE" 6
(122" W.B.)

('25) (HYDRAULIC BRAKES)

'25 "J.I.C." 122" WB 4.9 G.R.
6 CYL. (241.6 CID)
56 H.P. @ 2300
'25 "Y"
132" WB 4.45 G.R.
6 CYL. (234.8 CID;
331.3 IN '26-'27)
70 H.P. @ 2400
34 x 7.30 TIRES ('26-7)
FEW CHANGES THR. '27.

CHALMERS (1908-1924)

CHALMERS MOTOR CAR CO., DETROIT, MICH.
CHALMERS MOTOR CO. OF CANADA, LTD., WINDSOR, ONTARIO
32 x 4 OR   33 x 4½ TIRES

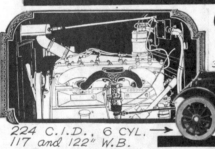

224 C.I.D., 6 CYL.
117 AND 122" W.B.

REMY IGN.

"35-C" (5-PASS.)

20-21   4.75 and 5.18 GEAR RATIOS

22-23

KNOWN AS "NEW SERIES" ('22) "IMPROVED" ('23)

32 x 4

5.12 GEAR RATIO
(MOST OTHER SPECS. SAME AS 1920)

STROMBERG CARB. (THROUGH '25)

23½

24

(PRODUCED DURING LATTER MONTHS OF 1923.)

HYDRAULIC BRAKES AVAILABLE
5.10 GEAR RATIO

REPLACED BY CHRYSLER

new AUTO-LITE IGN.

NEW RIBBED WHEELS

37

(1913-1929)

CHANDLER 20

6 CYLINDERS
288.6 C.I.D.
THROUGH '28

RAYFIELD CARB.

4.40 GEAR RATIO
THROUGH '22

123" W.B.
(THROUGH 1926)

7-PASS. SEDAN

CHANDLER SIX
Famous For Its Marvelous Motor

21
The Chandler Dispatch

The Royal Dispatch, a new sport model of utmost distinction and ultra-smart style

ROYAL DISPATCH HAS 34 x 4½ TIRES

FIRST YEAR WITH VISOR, COWL LIGHTS, COWL VENT, DRUM-TYPE HEADLIGHTS.

22
(NEW BODY LINES)

CYLINDERS NOW CAST EN BLOC (1923)

METROPOLITAN
5-PASS. SEDAN (NEW)
STARTS 6-22

NEW 32 x 4 TIRES *
and STROMBERG CARBURETOR
NEW 4.45 GEAR RATIO

23

✱ = 33 x 4½ ON CLOSED CARS, ROYAL DISP.

38

The New Pike's Peak Motor
Built by Chandler

CHANDLER

CAR OF THE YEAR

ALUMINUM BEAD BETWEEN HOOD and COWL

32 × 4 OR 33 × 4½ TIRES (BALLOONS OPTIONAL)

"CHUMMY"
(5-PASSENGER)

24

with the
TRAFFIC TRANSMISSION

(The Traffic Transmission is built complete in the Chandler plant under Campbell patents.)

NEW CONSTANT-MESH TRANSMISSION ELIMINATES CLASHING AND DOUBLE-CLUTCHING.

MODEL 32-A
("SS")

ALL OPEN MODELS HAVE ALUMINUM KICK PADS ON RUNNING BOARDS.

7-PASS. TOURING

SCHEBLER CARBURETOR
33 × 6 TIRES

25

"33" and "33-A"

49 H.P. @ 2100 RPM
4-WHEEL BRAKES OPTIONAL

OVERALL HEIGHT OF CLOSED CARS REDUCED TO LESS THAN 6 FEET.

COACH IMPERIAL

at exactly Touring Car price →

Body by Fisher

$1595

The Greatest Success
in Ten Years of Succeeding

39

CHANDLER

26 NEW VERTICAL RADIATOR STRIPS →

MODEL "SS-35"
55 H.P. @ 2800 RPM

7-PASS. SEDAN

20TH CENTURY SEDAN

The New Royal Eight BY CHANDLER

314 C.I.D.   80 H.P. @ 3000 RPM
124" W.B.

27½

STANDARD 6

TILLOTSON CARBURETOR ON STD. 6, SCHEBLER ON OTHERS.

27

BIG 6

METROPOLITAN SEDAN
(EARLY '27 TYPE)

STANDARD 6
MODEL "31" (108½" W.B.)
180.2 C.I.D., 45 H.P.
BIG 6 "35" (124" W.B.)
289 C.I.D., 55 H.P. @ 2100 RPM
SPECIAL 6 "43" = 218.6 C.I.D., 60 H.P. @ 2600 RPM
115" W.B.

SPECIAL 6   (ALSO "BIG 6")

196 C.I.D.   45 H.P. @ 2600 RPM

1928

EARLY SERIES (DRUM HEADLIGHTS)

ROYAL 8

28
(JOINS HUPMOBILE)

28½

195.5 C.I.D. "6-65"
55 H.P. @ 3000 →

"BIG 6" CONT'D. FROM 1928, 331.3 C.I.D. 83 H.P.

29

CHANDLER'S FINAL CARS

ROYAL 8 "75" →

"85" = LARGER 8

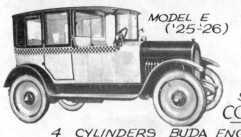

MODEL E ('25-'26)

CHECKER

MODEL F ('26 '27)

CHECKER CAB MFG. CO., KALAMAZOO, MICH. (SINCE 1923)

SUCCEEDS THE COMMONWEALTH CAR

4 CYLINDERS BUDA ENG. 117" W.B.

6-CYL. MODEL G IN '27-'28

MODEL K ('29-'30)

4.9 G.R. (K)

VARIETY OF MODEL M (INTRO. 1931) 122" W.B.

5.09 G.R.

6.50 x 18 TIRES

MODEL M 126" W.B. ('32) (VARIATION)

127" W.B., 7.00 x 18 TIRES MANY VARIATIONS ON EACH MODEL!

MODEL T ('33) (NEW PORTHOLES IN HOOD DOORS)

MODEL Y ('36-'39)

HAS 228.1 C.I.D. BUDA 6-CYL. "JC-214" ENG.

NO PRIVATE CARS AVAIL. UNTIL 1959.

"490"

30 x 3½ OR 31 x 4 TIRES
26 H.P. @ 1800 RPM

CHEVROLET

(ESTABLISHED NOV., 1911; JOINED G.M. MAY, 1918.)

ASSEMBLY AT FLINT, MICH. (MAIN PLANT)

"FB" 110" W.B.

Chevrolet Motor Co., Detroit, Michigan
Division of General Motors Corporation

"490" has 4-CYL.
ENGINE 170.9 C.I.D.
102" W.B.
3.63 G.R.
GRAVITY FUEL FEED

"490" SEDAN

20-21

(FB 50)
37 H.P. @ 2000 RPM
"FB" HAS 4-CYL., 224.3 C.I.D. ENGINE
4.62 G.R.
VACUUM FUEL FEED

'22 MODEL IS FIRST "490" WITH HAND-OPERATED EMERGENCY BRAKE

LOWER WINDSHIELD

"490" (32 H.P.)

STEEL FELLOE WHEELS

FRONT SEAT CUSHION LOWERED 4½" TO PROVIDE HIGHER SEAT BACK.

SHORTER STEERING COLUMN.

22

GYPSY-TYPE SIDE CURTAINS

GAS TANK ENLARGED TO 10 GALLONS.

3.66 G.R.

MODEL "FB 42" SEDAN

32 x 4 TIRES ADOPTED DURING '22 (FB)

CHEVROLET

SUPERIOR" (B)
WHEELBASE INCREASED TO 103"
ON ALL.

(759 AIR-COOLED SERIES C, M
CHEVROLETS ALSO BLT.,
JAN.,'23 TO MAY, '23.
RECALLED BY FACTORY, JUNE '23.
4 CYL., 134.7 C.I.D., 4.44 G.R.)

23

1923 4-Passenger Sedanette

3.77 G.R. (THROUGH '24)

EARLY
"B" TYPE
(9-23 TO
1-24)

CURVED
FRONT AXLE AND
CABLE-OPERATED
BRAKES.

24

"SUPERIOR" NAME
CONT'D.
THROUGH '26.

(24½)

26 H.P. @ 2000 RPM
(THROUGH '27)

FINAL YEAR WITH
CONE CLUTCH

24½ DE LUXE
(NICKEL TRIM)

LATER ("F")
TYPE has
STRAIGHT
FRONT AXLE
and
BRAKE RODS.

29 x 4.40 BALLOON TIRES (CLOSED
MODELS)

8-25:
new
KLAXON
HORN,
new
STEER.
WHEEL
WITH
CORRUG-
ATED
WALNUT
FINISH
RIM

1-PC.
"VV"
(VERTICAL
VENTILATING)
WINDSHIELD
(ON
CLOSED
CARS.)

3.82 G.R. (THROUGH '31)

25

(K)
INTRO.
1-3-25

NEW RADIATOR DESIGN

42

30 x 3½ TIRES ON OPEN MODELS

CHEVROLET

for Economical Transportation

AIR CLEANER INTRODUCED

26 (V) (INTERIOR)

NEW TIE-BAR BETWEEN HEADLIGHTS
29 × 4.40 TIRES (THROUGH '27)

GENERATOR MOVED FROM RIGHT TO LEFT SIDE OF ENGINE ('26.)

FROM '23 TO '26, CHEVROLET CARS BLT. SEPT. or LATER ARE SOMETIMES CLASSIFIED AS FOLLOWING YEAR'S MODEL, THOUGH ACTUAL MODEL CHANGE (DURING THESE YEARS) OCCURS IN JANUARY.

COACH HAS GREEN CORDUROY UPHOLSTERY.
SEDAN HAS BLUE CORDUROY.
BROWN "PLUSH" IN COUPE.

('27½)

new SPARE TIRE CARRIER →

TOURING CAR

IMPERIAL LANDAU (INTRODUCED MAY, 1927)

CO-INCIDENTAL STEERING and IGNITION LOCK

new "BULLET" HEADLIGHTS →

NEW RADIATOR DESIGN

27 (AA) "CAPITOL"

new AC OIL FILTER, AC AIR CLEANER

ROADSTER

43 *new* 1-PC. FULL-CROWN FENDERS

for Economical Transportation
CHEVROLET

(FINAL 4-CYL. MODEL)

57376

28

(AB)
"NATIONAL"

Bigger and Better

HORSEPOWER
INCREASED TO
35 @ 2200 RPM

WHEELBASE INCREASED
TO 107"

NEW RADIATOR
DESIGN AGAIN

for Economical Transportation
CHEVROLET

INTERIOR

4 - WHEEL BRAKES

30 x 4.50 TIRES

NEW CHEVROLET SIX

ALL-NEW 1929 ENGINE →

29

(AC) "INTERNATIONAL"

COMPLETELY *RESTYLED*

new FUEL PUMP

193.9 C.I.D.

46 H.P. @ 2600 RPM

FISHER BODIES, AS BEFORE

'29 DASH HAS 3 UPRIGHT OVALS WITHIN HORIZONTAL OVAL PANEL. ('30 DASH HAS SMALL CIRCULAR INSTRUMENTS.)

CHEVROLET for Economical Transportation

1929 IS FINAL CHEVROLET WITH FUEL GAUGE LOCATED OUTSIDE, ON TANK.

4.50 x 20" TIRES

3.81 G.R. = (ACCORDING TO CERTAIN SOURCES; 3.82 OTHERWISE.)

45

REAR TOP OF
CONVERTIBLE LANDAU
CAN BE FOLDED

29
(CONT'D.)

30

"UNIVERSAL" (AD)

New Dash Gasoline Gauge

NEW DARK-FACED, CIRCULAR GAUGES

The Chevrolet Special Sedan is a de luxe creation in every sense of the word. Standard equipment includes six wire wheels with fender wells, bumpers front and rear, robe rail, dome light, silk assist cords, etc.

THE ROADSTER

THE SPORT ROADSTER

50 H.P. @ 2600 RPM

THE SPORT COUPE

THE COUPE

THE SEDAN

(CABRIOLET SUSPENDED FOR 1930; RE-INTRODUCED JANUARY, 1931.)

THE PHAETON

4.75 × 19" TIRES (THROUGH '31) AND NEW, SLIGHTLY SLANTED NON-GLARE WINDSHIELD →

THE CLUB SEDAN

(30 ½ MODEL HAS *Landau Irons*.) →

A.75 × 19

47   THE COACH

CHEVROLET

31

NEW 109" WHEELBASE

2 NEW BODY TYPES IN '31

STANDARD '31s DO NOT HAVE THE NEW RADIATOR STONE GUARD.

(AE) "INDEPENDENCE"

THE STANDARD COACH

DASH ('31)

HORN BUTTON
OIL PRESSURE GAUGE
SPEEDOMETER
CHOKE BUTTON
THROTTLE GAUGE
GASOLINE GAUGE
AMMETER
WATER TEMPERATURE INDICATOR
SPARK BUTTON
LIGHTING SWITCH
GEARSHIFT LEVER
IGNITION LOCK
CLUTCH PEDAL
BRAKE PEDAL
HEAD LAMP DIMMER SWITCH
ACCELERATOR
STARTING PEDAL
HAND BRAKE LEVER
ACCELERATOR FOOT REST

'32 HAS NEW SYNCHRO-MESH TRANSMISSION

DASH ('32)

FREE WHEELING BUTTON
HORN BUTTON
OIL PRESSURE GAUGE
SPEEDOMETER
CHOKE BUTTON
HEAT CONTROL BUTTON
THROTTLE BUTTON
GASOLINE GAUGE
AMMETER
WATER TEMPERATURE
SPARK BUTTON
LIGHTING SWITCH
GEARSHIFT LEVER
IGNITION LOCK
CLUTCH PEDAL
BRAKE PEDAL
HEAD LAMP DIMMER SWITCH
ACCELERATOR
STARTING PEDAL
HAND BRAKE
ACCELERATOR FOOT REST

"CONFEDERATE" (BA)

32

60 H.P. @ 3000 RPM

"FREE WHEELING" (New)

4.1 G.R.

5.25 x 18" TIRES

THE SPORT ROADSTER

107" W.B.
4.3 GEAR RATIO

5.25 x 17" TIRES

CHEVROLET

33

MASTER *and* EAGLE "CA"

STARTS 12-32

181 C.I.D. 60 H.P. @ 3000 RPM

206.8 C.I.D. 65 H.P. @ 2800 RPM

STANDARD "CC"
(WITH HOOD LOUVRES)
STARTS 3-33

5.25 x 18" TIRES

DASH

(110" W.B.)
ACCELERATOR CONTROLS STARTER

4.11 GEAR RATIO (THROUGH '36)

NEW "KNEE ACTION" INDEPENDENT FRONT WHEEL SUSPENSION (WITH FRONT COIL SPRINGS) ON "MASTER" (DA) SERIES.

CHEVROLET MASTER SIX COUPE

CHEVROLET MASTER SIX SPORT COUPE

34

"STANDARD" (DC)
SERIES INTRODUCED LATE
(SPRING, 1934) WITH 107" W.B.,
5.25 x 17" TIRES,
181 C.I.D. ENGINE WITH
60 H.P. @ 3000 RPM

"MASTER" HAS 112" W.B.,
5.50 x 17" TIRES,
206.8 C.I.D. ENGINE
WITH 80 H.P. @ 3300 RPM

DASH

49

CHEVROLET

"STANDARD" MODEL (EC) RESEMBLES 1934 BUT HAS PAINTED HEADLIGHT SHELLS. DASH GAUGES MOVED TO CENTER.

"MASTER" (EA and ED)

"ED" SERIES AVAIL. W/O "KNEE ACTION"

35

(ALL MODELS NOW HAVE THE 80-H.P. "BLUE FLAME" ENGINE.)

3-WINDOW SPORT COUPE WITH RUMBLE SEAT

(5-WINDOW BUSINESS COUPE ALSO AVAILABLE) NEW 113" W.B. (MASTER) (STD. RETAINS 107" W.B.)

H.P. REDUCED TO 79 @ 3200 RPM, FOR '36

"EXPEDITER" COUPE AVAIL. WITH PICKUP BOX

(FC)
STANDARD ═══ 109" W.B.
MASTER ═══ 113" W.B.
(FA and FD)
"KNEE ACTION" OPTIONAL (FA)

36

'36 DASH

NEW 216.5 C.I.D. 1937 ENGINE (85 H.P. @ 3200 RPM)

37

NEW STYLING ALSO

"GB" ═══ MASTER (3.73 G.R.)
"GA" ═══ MASTER DE LUXE WITH "KNEE ACTION" (4.22 G.R.)

112¼" W.B. ON ALL (THROUGH 1939)

6.00 × 16" IS NOW THE TIRE SIZE ON ALL MODELS.

'37 DASH

50

CHEVROLET

"HB" = MASTER
"HA" = MASTER DE LUXE

38

ASH TRAY IN MASTER DE LUXE MODELS

'38 DASH

CHROME TRIM, GRILLE AND OUTSIDE DOOR HANDLES HAVE DECORATIVE VERMILLION-RED STRIPES IN HORIZONTAL GROOVES.

"JB" = MASTER
"JA" = MASTER DE LUXE
85 H.P. @ 3200 RPM,
AS BEFORE.

FISHER BODIES, AS BEFORE

NEW STEERING COLUMN GEARSHIFT CONTROL IS OPTIONAL. HAND BRAKE LEVER HUNG AT LEFT, BELOW DASH.

THE MASTER DE LUXE FOUR-PASSENGER COUPE

39

'39 INTERIOR

51

CHRYSLER (DETROIT)

(REPLACES
'24 CHALMERS
12 - 23
INTRO. 1-24)

IMPERIAL
SEDAN

PHAETON

NEW
HIGH-
COMPRESSION
(4.6 TO 1)
ENGINE

OPEN CARS
CAPABLE OF
70 M.P.H.

24

(MODEL B)
6 CYL.
201.5 C.I.D.
68 H.P.
@
3200 RPM

112 3/4" W.B.

29 x 4.50
TIRES

BROUGHAM

Roadster

HYDRAULIC BRAKES

DASH

NEW
ROYAL COUPE
HAS OPENING
REAR WINDOW,
RUMBLE SEAT

(CHRYSLER CORP. REPLACES MAXWELL-
CHALMERS)

Six (B)

25

(TO 7-25)

GEAR-
SHIFT
LEVER
LONGER
FOR
1925.

IMPERIAL

30 x 5.77
TIRES

ROADSTER HAS WIDER DOORS FOR 1925.

COACH

CHRYSLER SALES CORPORATION, DETROIT, MICHIGAN
CHRYSLER CORPORATION OF CANADA, LIMITED, WINDSOR, ONT.

CHRYSLER FOUR

25½

NEW
4 - CYL.
SERIES

(REPLACES
1925 MAXWELL)
"C")

"F - 58"
SERIES
(JUNE, 1925 TO
APRIL, 1926)

HYDRAULIC BRAKES
OPTIONAL ON SOME
4 - CYLINDER CHRYSLERS (ON WHICH
2 - WHEEL MECHANICAL BRAKES WERE
SOMETIMES FEATURED.) HYD. BRAKES
STANDARD ON OTHER CHRYSLERS.

185.8 C.I.D.
38 H.P. @ 2200 RPM
109" W.B.

53

CHRYSLER

"58" (F) 30 × 5.25 TIRES 4-CYL.

(FEDCO SERIAL NUMBERS ADOPTED DURING 1925, FOR 1926 SEASON; CONT'D. TO EARLY 1930.)

6-CYL. 218.6 C.I.D. 68 H.P. @ 3000 RPM

58 / 70

"70" (G)

(7-25 TO 9-26)

DASH →

30 × 5.77 TIRES

26

70 / 80

"70" Royal Sedan.

MODEL NUMBERS OF 1926-30 CHRYSLERS (RANGING FROM "50" TO "80,") INDICATED GUARANTEED TOP SPEED.

The New

IMPERIAL

(E-80)

The Imperial 4-passenger Coupe

The Imperial 2-4-passenger Roadster

6 CYL., 288.7 C.I.D. 92 H.P. @ 3000 RPM

120, 127, 133" WHEELBASES

The Imperial 7-passenger Sedan

The Imperial Phaeton

(STARTS DEC., 1925)

54

CHRYSLER
"50 - 60 - 70 - 80"
CHRYSLER MODEL NUMBERS MEAN MILES PER HOUR

LEATHER UPH. IN COUPE →

"50"
(I)
(7-26 TO 7-27)

106" W.B.   4 CYL.
170.3 C.I.D., 38 H.P. @ 2200 RPM

ALL-STEEL Budd BODIES AVAILABLE ON SOME "50" MODELS.

"50" DASH
↓ "60"

50

60

"60"
(H)

109" W.B.

(6-26 TO 6-27)
6 CYL., 180.2 C.I.D.
54 H.P. @ 3000 RPM

28 × 5.25

45-100

27
STARTING 8-26 BUDD-MICHELIN DISC WHEELS AVAIL. ON ALL SERIES OF EARLY '27 CHRYSLERS.

60
70 DASH

NEW CO-INCIDENTAL LOCK

FINER 70
(G)
(9-26 TO 10-27)

68 H.P. @ 3000 RPM

30 × 6.00 TIRES

112 3/4" W.B.

4-PASS. COUPE (NEW)

70

80

IMPERIAL "80"
(E)

FRANK QUAIL

NEW 30 × 6.75 TIRES

SAME SPECS. AS 1926

372-90A

55

CHRYSLER

"52" IS FINAL 4-CYL. MODEL WHICH SOMETIMES OFFERS 2-WHEEL MECHANICAL BRAKES.

"52" CHRYSLER BODIES HAVE COMPOSITE WOOD INNER FRAMEWORK, AS ON MOST OTHER PRE-1930 CHRYSLERS.

"52" HAS 4.7 GEAR RATIO

"52" (I)

28

"62" HAS 4.6 GEAR RATIO
28 × 5.25 TIRES

"62" (M)

52
62

"52" AND "62" INSTRUMENTS FRAMED SEPERATELY IN INDIVIDUAL PANES.

DASH ("52")

MODEL "52" IS FINAL 4-CYLINDER CHRYSLER, WITH 170.3 C.I.D., 45 H.P. @ 2800 RPM, 106" W.B.

PRODUCED JULY, 1927 TO JUNE, 1928. REPLACED BY THE CHRYSLER-PLYMOUTH CAR. (SEE: "PLYMOUTH")

CHRYSLER "RED HEAD" ENGINES (WITH HIGH-COMPRESSION CYLINDER HEAD) REQUIRED ETHYL GASOLINE WHEN NEW.)

YOUR FAVORITE ETHYL GASOLINE

Great New Chrysler "62" Coupe (with rumble seat), $1245
(108 ¾" W.B.)
(JUNE, 1927 TO JUNE, 1928)

"62" GIVES 54 H.P. @ 3200 RPM WITH STANDARD 5.2-COMPRESSION "Silver Dome" HEAD. 6.2-COMPRESSION "Red Head" GIVES 60 H.P.

DASH

Two-Passenger Coupe

CHRYSLER

THE ILLUSTRIOUS NEW
"72" (J)
(7-27 TO 6-28)

Four-Passenger Coupe

Royal Sedan, $1595

Crown Sedan

(118 3/4" W. B.)
30 x 6.00 TIRES

28

(CONT'D.)

NEW
248.9
C.I.D.
ENGINE

CLOSE-COUPLED SEDAN $1695

"72" GIVES 75 H.P. @ 3200 RPM
WITH STD. 5.1-COMPRESSION HEAD.
6.2-COMPRESSION "Red Head"
GIVES 85 H.P.

1928 IS FINAL YEAR
THAT CHRYSLER
USES ANY
FISHER BODIES.

ILLUSTRIOUS NEW "72"
TOWN CABRIOLET
BODY BY LE BARON

EARLY MODEL

(COWL LIGHTS, AFTER
JAN., 1928)

LATE MODEL

"72" and "80"
INSTRUMENTS BEHIND
LONG GLASS PANEL.

D = DIETRICH BODY
L = LE BARON "

"72" HAS 4.3 GEAR RATIO

LATE "72" ROADSTER HAS COWL LIGHTS,
NEW WINDSHIELD, NEW SIDE MOULDING.

72
80

NEW 309.6
C.I.D.
ENGINE

112 H.P.
@
3000
RPM

WITH "Red Head" 6 TO 1
COMPR.

(STD.
HEAD =
100 H.P.)
4.75
COMPR.

(11-27 TO 6-28) Imperial "80"

L "80" (L-80)

136"
W.B.

L

IMPERIAL "80" HAS
4.08 GEAR RATIO

L

RT. DOOR
FOR RUMBLE
SEAT

30 x 6.75 TIRES

INSTRUMENT PANEL

NO RADIATOR EMBLEM
ON '28 "80."

New 112 h.p. Imperial "80"
Town Sedan, $2995

Locke Touralette

57

CHRYSLER

CHRYSLER MOTORS PRODUCT

65 H.P. @ 3200 RPM.   195.6 C.I.D.

"65"
(P)

5-WINDOW COUPE HAS RUMBLE SEAT

5.2 STD. COMPR.
6.0 COMPR. "RED HEAD" GIVES 70 H.P.

"75" VICTORIA COUPE (RARE!)

112 3/4" W.B.
5.50 × 18 TIRES
(IGNITION KEY-HOLE REPLACES SWITCH)

(6-28 TO 6-29)

(3-WINDOW BUSINESS COUPE ALSO IN "65" SERIES.)

65
75

"65" INSTRUMENT PANEL ARRANGEMENT GENERALLY SIMILAR TO "62" BUT HAS "WOODGRAIN" TRIM ABOVE.

6.00 × 18 TIRES

"75" (R)

FEDCO I.D. PLATE

ALL GAUGES BEHIND LONG GLASS PANEL
DARK-FACED GAUGES ON SOME EARLY "75" MODELS; LIGHT-FACED ON LATER MODELS.

ROYAL SEDAN

INTERIOR

(6-28 TO 6-29)
121" W.B.
FIRST CHRYSLER TO FEATURE BUILT-IN RADIATOR SHUTTERS.

← REAR

(SAME ENGINE SPECS. AS LATE "72")

(HIGH-COMPRESSION "RED HEAD" OPTIONAL THROUGH 1933, AND OPTIONAL ALUMINUM HEAD FROM 1934 THROUGH 1941.)

29

75

(TO 1928)

IMPERIAL

'29-30 IMPERIAL HAS SAME SPECS. AS '28 MODEL

(SIDE DOOR FOR RUMBLE SEAT)

(1930 IMPERIAL 6 SIMILAR TO 1929, BUT HAS 4-SPEED "MULTI-RANGE" TRANSMISSION AND SMOOTH, NON-CORRUGATED BUMPERS.)

7.00 × 18 TIRES ('29 AND '30)

IMPERIAL CHRYSLER

(L)

(STARTS OCTOBER, 1928)

EARLIEST MODEL HAS NO LOWER COWL MOLDING.

Custom Roadster

New Imperial 7-passenger Sedan, illustrated. Also available in 5-passenger Sedan.

CHRYSLER 30

SOME "66" MODELS WITH SPLIT GROUP OF HOOD LOUVRES DURING 1930

3-SPEED TRANS. ON "66"

68 H.P. @ 3000 RPM

5.50 x 18 TIRES

NEW "66"

DASH (EXPORT MODEL)

(7-29 TO 5-30)

WOOD WHEELS STANDARD. (WIRE WHEELS OPTIONAL)

(ALL 6-CYL. MODELS)

new FUEL PUMP INTRODUCED (ON ALL BUT THE IMPERIAL 6.)

(CC)

218.6 C.I.D. ("66" and EARLY "70")

112 3/4" W.B.

66
70

= HOOD "PENNON" LOUVRES ON 70 (and 77) BLT. BEF. 1-30.

116 9/16" W.B.

EARLY MODEL

"70" DASH

5.50 x 18 TIRES

EARLY 70 (and 77) HAS PARK. LIGHTS HUNG FROM VISOR (CLOSED CARS)

4. The chromium plated sconce-type parking lights, metal cadet visor, tandem windshield cleaner, and the chromium window architraves are new features of design.

5. The concave moulding on the Roadster and Phaeton reflect originality of design.

NEW "70" (V)

75 H.P. @ 3200 RPM

LATE MODEL 11-29 = "77" ENGINE USED

70
77

70
77

MULTI-RANGE 4-SPEED TRANS.

CHRYSLER BLDG. (N.Y.) BUILT 1929-30 (77 STORIES)

93 H.P. @ 3200 RPM

268.9 C.I.D.

NEW "77" (W)

124 9/16" W.B.

77
IMPERIAL

LATER "70" AND "77" has VERTICAL HOOD LOUVRES.

1. The Futura Design Instrument Panel, designed by Chrysler, executed by Cartier (Paris-New York.)

1930 "IMPERIAL" RESEMBLES ILLUSTRATED 1929 STYLE. DIFFERENCES LISTED IN '29 IMPERIAL SECTION. (6-CYLINDER IMPERIAL DISCONTINUED IN JUNE, 1930.)

CHRYSLER

NEW 195.6 C.I.D. ENGINE

UPPER RADIATOR TANK MATCHES CORE ON "CJ" SERIES (LATEST MODEL CJ CONSIDERED "EARLY '31")

30½ SIX

MODEL "CJ" (STARTS MARCH, 1930)

ACCESSORY SHAFT IS INCLINED AND THE OIL PUMP IS EXTERNALLY MOUNTED ON THE LEFT SIDE OF THE ENGINE

has FUEL PUMP

FIRST CHRYSLER 6-CYL. ENGINE TO HAVE 4 MAIN BEARINGS INSTEAD OF 7.

(DE SOTO INTRODUCED WITH A 4-BEARING 6 FOR 1929. DODGE OFFERED ONE FOR LATER '30 SEASON.)

BUSINESS COUPE (SIDEMOUNT SPARE TIRES OPTIONAL)

"Royal" RUMBLE-SEAT COUPE ALSO AVAILABLE.

"CJs" BUILT AFTER JULY 20, 1930 SOMETIMES CONSIDERED "EARLY 1931" MODELS.

109" W.B.

62 H.P. @ 3200 RPM
4.7 GEAR RATIO
4.75/5.00 × 19 TIRES

AS ON OTHER PRE-1931 CHRYSLER CORP. CARS, WOOD WHEELS WERE STANDARD EQUIPMENT. (WIRE WHEELS OPTIONAL) STEEL BODY FRAME

FEDCO I.D. PLATE ON EARLIEST MODELS, BISECTING GRAIN STRIP.

CONVERTIBLE COUPE

THE "CJ" SIX WAS THE FIRST CHRYSLER SINCE 1925 WHICH DID NOT BEAR A "TOP SPEED" MODEL NO. (TOP SPEED OF "CJ" = 62.)

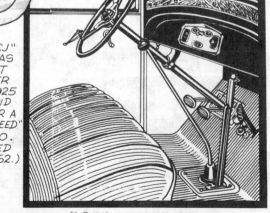

ROADSTER, TOURING CAR, ALSO AVAIL. IN THIS "CJ" SERIES.

(LATE MODEL "CJ" INTERIOR HAD POSITION OF KEY and SPEEDOMETER REVERSED.)

CHRYSLER

1931 "CM" SIX BEGINS JAN., 1931. 8-CYL. '31 MODELS INTRODUCED JULY, 1930.

217.8 C.I.D. 78 H.P. @ 3400 RPM

Six Sedan—$895

SIX (CM)

116 3/8" W.B.
5.25 x 19 TIRES

← EARLY 6 SEDAN = (NO VISOR)

(NEW STYLING) V - GRILLE

WIRE WHEELS STANDARD ON '31 SIX.

31

"70" (6 CYL.) (TO MAY, 1931)

"70" Business Coupe—$1245   "70" Royal Coupe—$1295

268.9 C.I.D. 93 H.P. @ 3200 RPM

WIRE WHEELS OPTIONAL

"70" Brougham—$1245

116 9/16" W.B.
5.50 x 18 TIRES

"70" Royal Sedan—$1295

EIGHT (CD) (7-30 TO 4-31)

EARLY "CD" HAS 240.3 C.I.D. AND 80 H.P. @ 3400 RPM. (LATER "CD" HAS 260.8 C.I.D. AND 88 H.P. @ 3400 RPM, AS OF JAN., 1931.)

CHRYSLER EIGHT SPORT ROADSTER

SEDAN

CHRYSLER'S FIRST 8s (1930 De Soto AND DODGE OFFERED A STRAIGHT - 8 ENGINE PRIOR TO CHRYSLER.)

124" W.B. 5.50 x 18 TIRES

(REPLACED BY DE LUXE 8s, SPRING, '31)

EIGHT COUPE $1495, F. O. B. FACTORY

Roadster—$1545

Convertible Coupe—$1585

DLX. 8

De Luxe Eight

(CD DELUXE) (4-31 TO 11-31)

282.1 C.I.D. 100 H.P. @ 3400 RPM

124" W.B.

Eight De Luxe Five-Passenger Coupe—$1565

(INTERIOR)

CHRYSLER

DUAL - COWL PHAETON
(BODY BY LE BARON)

(7-30
TO
10-31)

IMPERIAL EIGHT (CG)

VICTORIA
(CUSTOM BODY BY WATERHOUSE)

145" WHEELBASES ON
1931 IMPERIALS

(BODY BY LE BARON)

SEDAN

ROADSTER

31 (CONT'D.)

7.50 × 17

CLOSE - COUPLED SEDAN
384.8 C.I.D., 125 H.P. @
3200 RPM (THROUGH '32)

FUEL PUMP ON ALL MODELS.

'32 MODELS HAVE "FLOATING POWER" FLEXIBLE ENGINE MOUNTS,
AUTOMATIC CLUTCH, FREE - WHEELING.

5.50 × 18 TIRES
224 C.I.D.
82 H.P. @
3400

Chrysler Six Sedan

116 3/8" W.B.   (CI)

(12-31 TO 11-32)

$\frac{6}{8}$

SIX 32

DASH

100 H.P. @
3400
RPM   (CP)

298.7 C.I.D.
125" W.B.

EIGHT (CP)

(12-31 TO 11-32)
298.7 C.I.D., 100 H.P.
@ 3400 RPM

6.50 × 17 TIRES

Chrysler Eight Sedan

IMPERIAL EIGHT,

7.00 × 17 TIRES

LENGTHENED HOOD
WITH VENT DOORS

135" W.B. (CH)
Imperial Eight Sedan

7.50 × 17 TIRES

146" W.B. (CL)
Imperial Custom Eight Close-Coupled Sedan

CHRYSLER SIX SEDAN $785 (CO)

Chrysler

CHRYSLER ROADSTERS DISCONTINUED IN 1933.

6

SIX (CO) HAS 116½" W.B.,
224 C.I.D., 83
OR 89 H.P. @
3400 RPM

126" W.B.

(CT)
ROYAL 8
119½" W.B.
273.8 C.I.D.
90 H.P. @ 3400 RPM

(12-32 TO 12-33)

33

IMPERIAL 8 (CQ)
298.7 C.I.D.
100 OR 108 H.P.
@ 3400 RPM, WITH
5.2-COMPRESSION
"SILVER DOME" OR
6.2-COMPRESSION
"RED HEAD"

HIGH-COMPRESSION "RED HEAD"
ENGINES AVAILABLE ON CHRYSLERS
OF 1928 THROUGH 1933.

(CUSTOM IMPERIAL "CL"
SERIES RUNS FROM
2-33 TO 12-33.)
146" W.B.
384.8 C.I.D.
125 OR
135 H.P.
@
3200

Custom
IMPERIAL
8
(CL)

(CL)
INTERIOR

FOR 1934,
"AIRFLOW" BODIES ON ALL 8s

122 H.P. @ 3400
RPM

34

130 H.P. @ 3400 RPM

128" W.B.
AIRFLOW IMPERIAL (CV)   323.5   C.I.D.

241.6 C.I.D.
93 H.P. @
3400
RPM

6 (CA, CB)
117" W.B., 121"
WB

AIRFLOW 8 (CU)
298.7
C.I.D.

122 13/16" W.B.

CW = 150 H.P.
146½" W.B.

(CX)

1934 CHRYSLER AIRFLOW CUSTOM IMPERIAL CW)

63

(C-6) = 6
(CZ) = 8

AIRSTREAM *Chrysler*

35

AIRFLOW 8 (C-1, C-2, C-3, CW)

H.P. RANGE = 93 (6) TO 150 (CW IMPERIAL AIRFLOW)

36

(C-7 REAR)

(C-8)

(C-10)

INTERIORS

BEAUTIFUL NEW AIRFLOWS

NEW SIX (C-7)
DeLUXE EIGHT (C-8)

NOTE DIFFERENCES IN HOOD LOUVRE DESIGNS

8 CYL. AIRFLOWS (C-9, C-10, C-11, CW)

Chrysler

ROYAL 6 (C-16)

AIRFLOW 8 (C-17)

37

C-15 CUSTOM IMPERIAL NO LONGER AN "AIRFLOW"

IMPERIAL 8 (C-14) ↗

ROYAL 6 (C-18)
119" W.B. (THROUGH '39)
241.5 C.I.D. (THROUGH '41)
95 H.P. @ 3600 RPM

38

RICH NEW INTERIORS!

110 - H.P.
NEW YORK SPECIAL
and IMPERIAL (C-19)
8

Custom
130-H.P. IMPERIAL 8
(C-20)
323.5 C.I.D.
('34-50)

LIGHT-COLORED
STEERING
WHEEL

144" W.B.
(THROUGH '39)

NEW V-WINDSHIELD, "WATERFALL" LOWER GRILLE, SUNKEN HEADLIGHTS FOR 1939

ROYAL 6 (and Windsor)
(C-22)

100 H.P.
@
3600

39

NEW YORKER 8
and Saratoga 8 (C-23)
" Imperial 8

(C-24)

Custom Imperial 8

65

CLEVELAND SIX

(INTRODUCED JULY, 1919)
112" W.B. and 190.8 C.I.D.
(THROUGH '22)

MODEL 40
("41" = '22)

Cleveland Automobile Company
Cleveland, Ohio

BUILT BY

CLEVELAND

CHANDLER

19 – 22

FOR '21, GRAY AND DAVIS IGNITION IS
REPLACED BY BOSCH (THROUGH '26)
4.45 GEAR RATIO (THROUGH '22)

1921 = OUTSIDE DOOR HANDLES ON OPEN CARS
1922 = DRUM HEADLIGHTS

5-PASS. 2-DR. SEDAN
(INTRO. 1923)

FISHER BODY

31 × 4

112½" W.B., 4.9 GEAR RATIO

23 – 24

MODEL 42
'24 HAS CHASSIS APRON
PLATES (ALUMINUM KICK PADS,)
BOSCH AUTOMATIC SPARK
CONTROL, AND THIS NEW
RADIATOR
DESIGN →
('24 ONLY)

"ONE-SHOT" CHASSIS
LUBRICATION

25 – 26

MODEL 31 (STANDARD)

"31"
108½" W.B.
30 × 4.75 TIRES
165.5 C.I.D. ('25)
180.1 " ('26)
45 H.P. @ 2800 ('26)

"43"
115" W.B.
31 × 5.25 TIRES
218.6 C.I.D.
60 H.P. @
2800 RPM

MODEL 43 (SPECIAL 6)
HAS ALUMINUM KICK PADS
AND NICKEL TRIM

1926 MODEL HAS INTAKE MANIFOLD
ABOVE EXHAUST MANIFOLD.

AUGUST, 1926 = BECAME
CHANDLER STANDARD and
SPECIAL SERIES.

CLIMBER

(K) = 4 CYLS., 192.4 C.I.D., 4.0 G.R., 33 × 4 TIRES, 117" W.B.
(S) = 6 CYLS., 248.9 C.I.D., 4.75 G.R. (THROUGH '22)
32 × 4½ TIRES, 125½" W.B. (230.1 C.I.D., 4.0 G.R. IN '23)

('20)   ('23)

(1919 – 1923)
CLIMBER MOTOR CORP.,
LITTLE ROCK, ARK.
4 OR 6 - CYL.
HERSCHELL-SPILLMAN ENG.

COATS
(1922 - 1923)

COATS
STEAM
MOTORS,
SANDUSKY,
OHIO

COLE MOTOR CAR CO., INDIANAPOLIS (1909 – 1925)

Tourster

Cole Aero-Eight

NORTHWAY V-8 (346.3
C.I.D.) ENGINES
(THROUGH '25)

NEW FOR 1920: 1-PIECE
REAR AXLE HOUSING,
('20) JOHNSON CARB.,
ADJUSTABLE
STORM-PROOF
WINDSHIELDS
ON MODELS
"884" + "885."

NEW BRAKE
ADJUSTER

127" W.B.
and 4.45 G.R. (TO '22)
33 × 5 TIRES (THROUGH '24)

20 "870" SERIES

21

"884"
TOUROSINE
(7-PASS.)

'22 IS 1ST YEAR WITH
SPLIT FRAME
ENDS,
4.1
G.R.

22
NEW "890" SERIES IN '22.

"SPORTOSINE"

'23 MODELS have DRUM-TYPE
HEADLIGHTS, COWL VENT,
and STATIONARY LOWER
HALF of WINDSHIELD.

23
DISC WHEELS
ALSO
AVAILABLE.

SOME '23
COLES have 3/4
RUNNING BOARDS
and SIDEMOUNTS.

127¼" W.B. (DURING '22,
and THROUGH '25.)

"897"
BROUETTE

"MASTER"
SERIES

24
FULL-LENGTH
RUNNING BOARDS
FOUND ON ALL
COLES AGAIN,
IN 1924.

1925 MODEL SIMILAR TO
'24, BUT BALLOON TIRES
STANDARD INSTEAD OF
OPTIONAL (34 × 7.30)
76-80 H.P. @
2600 RPM
(3.5 TO 3.6 COMPR.)
"892-A"
5 - PASSENGER
AERO-VOLANTE

'25 has 2-PC. REAR
"BUMPERETTES"

COLE
INDIANAPOLIS

Columbia Six

COLUMBIA MOTORS COMPANY, DETROIT, U.S.A.

(1916-1924)

RADIATOR SHUTTERS WERE CONTROLLED BY A THERMOSTAT.

19-22 115" W.B. (THROUGH '24)

COLUMBIA SIX

The Columbia Six Five Passenger Touring Car

2 - PASS. ROADSTER AND 4 PASS. COUPE ARE NEW MODELS FOR 1920. CHASSIS SPECS. GENERALLY SIMILAR TO 1919. 6 CYL., 224-C.I.D. CONTINENTAL ENGINE. (TO '22)

50 H.P. LIGHT 6 HAS 7-U CONTINENTAL 195.6 C.I.D. ENGINE. BIG 6 HAS 8-R CONT. 241.6 C.I.D. ENGINE

22½-24

1924

COMET (1917-1922)

125" W.B.

6 - CYL. CONTINENTAL ENGINE 303.1 C.I.D. (THROUGH '22) 4.66 GEAR RATIO

COMET AUTOMOBILE CO., DECATUR, ILL.

33 x 4½ TIRES ON '21 "C-53" MODEL AND '22 "C-53-2" MODEL.

20

COMMONWEALTH

COMMONWEALTH MOTORS CO., JOLIET, ILLINOIS (1917-1922)

REPLACES PARTIN-PALMER CAR, 1917.

"4-40"

117" W.B.

32 x 4

'20 HAS 4-CYL. LYCOMING 192.4 C.I.D. ENGINE INSTEAD OF 6-CYL. AS IN 1919.

"4-45" ('21)

EVOLVED INTO THE CHECKER TAXI.

CONTINENTAL (1933-1934)

CONT. AUTO. CO., DETROIT 1933 MODELS: "BEACON" 4, "FLYER" 6, AND "ACE" 6 (V-WINDSHIELD ON "ACE")

CONTINENTAL ENGINES

MODEL "41" ('34) 4.33 G.R.

143.1 C.I.D. 4-CYL. 38 H.P. @ 2600 RPM

101½" W.B.

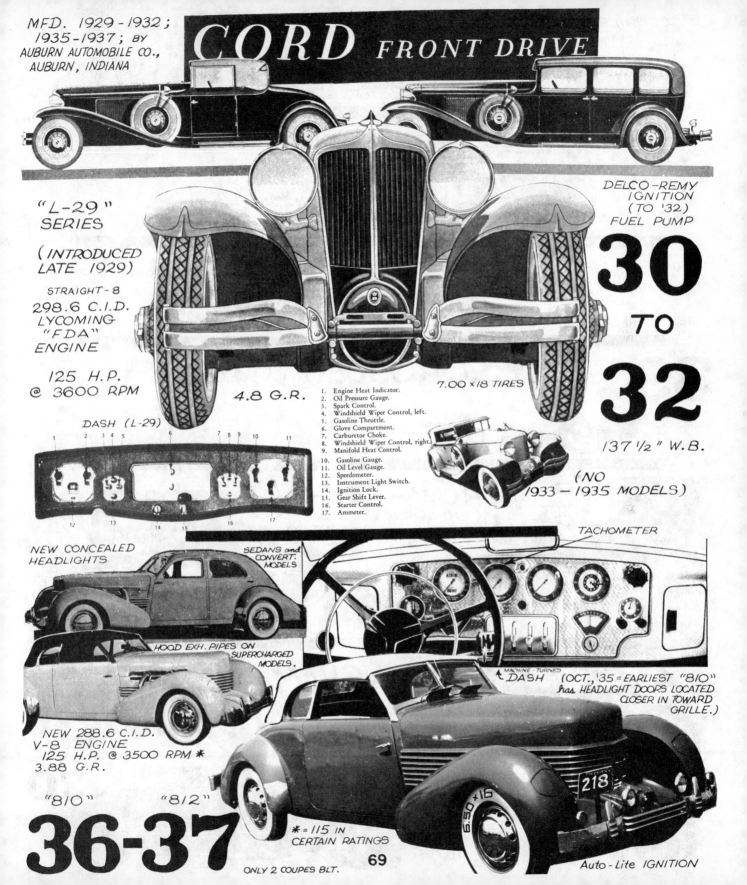

MFD. 1929-1932;
1935-1937; BY
AUBURN AUTOMOBILE CO.,
AUBURN, INDIANA

CORD FRONT DRIVE

DELCO-REMY
IGNITION
(TO '32)
FUEL PUMP

30 TO 32

137½" W.B.

(NO
1933 - 1935 MODELS)

"L-29"
SERIES

(INTRODUCED
LATE 1929)

STRAIGHT-8
298.6 C.I.D.
LYCOMING
"FDA"
ENGINE

125 H.P.
@ 3600 RPM

4.8 G.R.

7.00 x 18 TIRES

DASH (L-29)

1. Engine Heat Indicator.
2. Oil Pressure Gauge.
3. Spark Control.
4. Windshield Wiper Control, left.
5. Gasoline Throttle.
6. Glove Compartment.
7. Carburetor Choke.
8. Windshield Wiper Control, right.
9. Manifold Heat Control.
10. Gasoline Gauge.
11. Oil Level Gauge.
12. Speedometer.
13. Instrument Light Switch.
14. Ignition Lock.
15. Gear Shift Lever.
16. Starter Control.
17. Ammeter.

NEW CONCEALED
HEADLIGHTS

SEDANS and
CONVERT.
MODELS

TACHOMETER

HOOD EXH. PIPES ON
SUPERCHARGED
MODELS.

MACHINE - TURNED
DASH (OCT., '35 = EARLIEST "810"
has HEADLIGHT DOORS LOCATED
CLOSER IN TOWARD
GRILLE.)

NEW 288.6 C.I.D.
V-8 ENGINE
125 H.P. @ 3500 RPM *
3.88 G.R.

"810"   "812"

36-37

* = 115 IN
CERTAIN RATINGS

ONLY 2 COUPES BLT.

69

Auto-Lite IGNITION

COURIER MOTOR CO.,
SANDUSKY, OHIO

COURIER
(1922-1924)

116" W.B. 6-CYL., OVERHEAD-VALVE
5 to 1 G.R. 195.6 C.I.D. FALLS ENGINE
32 × 4 TIRES ATWATER-KENT IGNITION

(REPLACES
MAIBOHM)

('22)

6
CYL.

CRANE-SIMPLEX (1915-1924)

SIMPLEX AUTOMOBILE
CO.,
NEW BRUNSWICK, N.J.,
L.I. CITY, N.Y.

CRAWFORD

(CRAWFORD AUTOMOBILE CO., HAGERSTOWN, MD.)
(1905-1923)

SEE ALSO "DAGMAR"

('20)

MINOR CHANGES ONLY FOR '20.
6 CYL. CONTINENTAL ENG.
122½" W.B.

39

2
CYLINDERS

CROSLEY (1939-1952)

WEIGHT= ONLY 925 LBS.!
MECH. BRAKES
4.25 × 12" TIRES

5.14 GEAR RATIO

117" W.B.

CROW-ELKHART
(1909-1924)
CROW ELKHART
MOTOR CAR CO.

21

4.25
G.R.

"L-55" ('19-20)
4 CYL. 192.4 C.I.D.
LYCOMING OR
HERSCHELL-SPILLMAN
ENGINE

6
CYL.
RUTENB.
ENGINE
ALSO (H SERIES)

19-20

"S-67" 6 CYL.
7-PASS.

"L" CONT'D. AS 4-CYL. MODEL.

248.9 C.I.D.
HERSCH.-SP.
6-CYL.
ENGINE
ADOPTED
DURING '21
ON "S."

"V-4"

21

4.08
G.R.

CUNNINGHAM

JAS. CUNNINGHAM SON + CO.,
ROCHESTER, N.Y.
(1907-1933)
V-8 ENGINES
441.7 C.I.D.

24

"82-A"
INSIDE-DRIVE 6-PASS.
LIMOUSINE

132"-142"
W.B.

"125-A"

"LANDAULET" 7-PASS.

23

30

"V-9"

110 H.P. @ 2500 RPM

DAGMAR (1922-1927)

CRAWFORD AUTOMOBILE CO.;
M.P. MÖLLER CAR CO.,
HAGERSTOWN, MD.
(EARLY "CRAWFORD-DAGMAR"
has 138" W.B.)
6-CYL. CONTINENTAL OR LYCOMING ENGINES

LATER MODEL has 120" W.B.

DANIELS (1915-1924)

DANIELS MOTOR CAR CO., READING, PA.

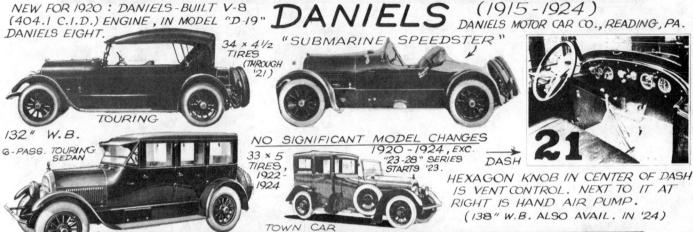

NEW FOR 1920: DANIELS-BUILT V-8
(404.1 C.I.D.) ENGINE, IN MODEL "D-19"
DANIELS EIGHT.

"SUBMARINE SPEEDSTER"

34 × 4½ TIRES (THROUGH '21)

TOURING

132" W.B.
6-PASS. TOURING SEDAN

33 × 5 TIRES, 1922-1924

NO SIGNIFICANT MODEL CHANGES 1920-1924, EXC. "23-28" SERIES STARTS '23.

DASH

TOWN CAR

21

HEXAGON KNOB IN CENTER OF DASH IS VENT CONTROL. NEXT TO IT AT RIGHT IS HAND AIR PUMP.
(138" W.B. ALSO AVAIL. IN '24)

DAVIS (1908-1929)

"Built of the Best"

GEORGE W. DAVIS MOTOR CAR CO. RICHMOND, IND., U.S.A.

FEW CHANGES on "51" FOR 1920. HAS 224 C.I.D. "7-R" CONTINENTAL 6 CYL. ENGINE, (THROUGH '22) STROMBERG CARB., 120" W.B. (THROUGH '23)

"71" SERIES ADDED DURING '22, with 115" W.B. 6-CYL., 195.6 C.I.D. "7U" CONTINENTAL ENG. (THROUGH '24, KNOWN AS "90" IN '25) 5.1 G.R. (THROUGH '25)

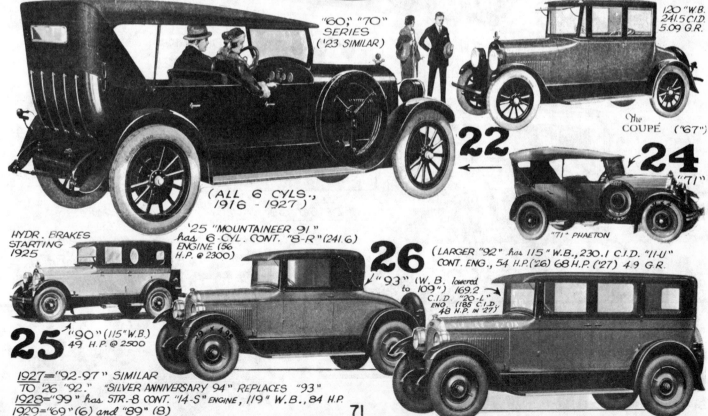

"60," "70" SERIES ('23 SIMILAR)

22

(ALL 6 CYLS., 1916-1927)

"60" SERIES (63-65)

23

120" W.B. 241.5 C.I.D. 5.09 G.R.

The COUPÉ ('67)

24

"71"

"71" PHAETON

HYDR. BRAKES STARTING 1925

'25 "MOUNTAINEER 91" has 6-CYL. CONT. "8-R" (241.6) ENGINE (56 H.P. @ 2300)

26

(LARGER "92" has 115" W.B., 230.1 C.I.D. "11-U" CONT. ENG., 54 H.P. ('26) 68 H.P. ('27) 4.9 G.R.

"93" (W.B. lowered to 109") 169.2 C.I.D. "20-L" ENG. (185 C.I.D. 48 H.P. IN '27)

25 "90" (115" W.B.) 49 H.P. @ 2500

1927="92-97" SIMILAR TO '26 "92." "SILVER ANNIVERSARY 94" REPLACES "93"
1928="99" has STR.-8 CONT. "14-S" ENGINE, 119" W.B., 84 H.P.
1929="69" (6) and "89" (8)

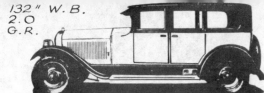

132" W.B.
2.0
G.R.

DELLING STEAM CAR
(1923 – 1927)
DELLING STEAM MOTOR CO.,
W. COLLINGWOOD,
N.J. and
PHILADELPHIA

2 CYLINDERS   "126" has HYDR. BRKS., ALUM.
BODY, 32 × 6.20 TIRES ('26 SPECS.)

IGNITION :
DELCO : TO 2-1-29
NORTHEAST : AFTER
2-1-29

174.9 C.I.D.
6 CYLINDERS

Section through the engine showing diagonal location of distributor and oil pump drive

55 H.P. @ 3000 RPM
5.2 COMPR.

(1928 – 1961)
DE SOTO SIX
A CHRYSLER-MOTORS PRODUCT

4.75/5.00 × 19

109" WHEELBASE
STROM. CARB.

29 MODEL K
JULY, 1928
TO
MAY, 1930

Four-door, five-passenger de luxe sedan

Business coupe with rear deck for luggage

(DE SOTO CARS
PRODUCED FROM
7-28 TO 12-60
FINAL CAR :
1961 V-8)

(ALL DE SOTOS HAVE HYDRAULIC BRAKES,
'28 - '61)

HAYES BODIES
ON SOME
"K" MODELS

has VACUUM TANK

SOME "K" MODELS HAVE
"De Soto Six" IN
CHROME-PLATED
SCRIPT, FASTENED
TO RADIATOR
CORE. (ALSO
IN '30)

De luxe coupe with rumble seat

Five-passenger, two-door sedan

EARLY '30 "K" LIKE '29, BUT HAS A FEW FALSE HOOD LOUVRES.   72

DE SOTO SIX

(DETAILS OF ROADSTER)

5.00 x 19

CARTER CARB. REPLACES STROMBERG.

Front Compartment

1—Windshield regulator handle
2—Ignition switch and lock
3—Throttle control hand lever
4—Horn push-button
5—Light control hand lever
6—Door remote control handle
7—Door window regulator handle
8—Gearshift lever
9—Windshield wiper control valve
10—Clutch pedal
11—Brake pedal
12—Rear view mirror

13—Fuel gauge
14—Choke control button
15—Oil gauge
16—Ammeter
17—Speedometer
18—Steering post support bracket
19—Release button
20—Transmission brake hand lever
21—Starter pedal
22—Accelerator pedal
23—Accelerator foot rest

Finer De Soto Six

(CK) STARTS 5-30
(AVAIL. TO 11-30)

NEW DISPL. OF 189.6 CU. IN.
60 H.P. @ 3400 RPM

$\frac{6}{8}$ **30** $\frac{6}{8}$

AFTER 11-30, "CF" has "NARROW PROFILE" RADIATOR SHELL. (SEE 1931)

DeSoto STRAIGHT EIGHT

(CF) INTRO. 1-30

5.25 x 19

← STYLE OF '30, with THICK RADIATOR SHELL.

207.7 C.I.D.

114" W.B.
STROMBERG CARB. ON "CF"

DASH

70 H.P. @ 3400 RPM
FUEL PUMP ADDED

EIGHT SEDAN

EIGHT CONVERTIBLE COUPE

DE SOTO

NEW DASH (SA) HAS GAUGES BEHIND OVAL GLASS PANEL.

RUMBLE-SEAT DETAILS (8)

6 "SA"

109 3/8" W.B.

205.3 C.I.D.
72 H.P. @ 3400 RPM
(6)

8 "CF"

6
8

31

(STARTS 12-30)

(8) 114" W.B. 220.7 C.I.D.
77 H.P. @ 3400 RPM

FUEL PUMP

"CF" AVAIL. TO 2-32

31½ – EARLY **32**

("SA" and "CF" BLT. 7-23-31 and AFTER ARE SOMETIMES KNOWN AS "EARLY 1932.")

(SA)

"SA"
OUTER VISOR RESTORED
"Free-Wheeling" AVAIL., and
"EASY-SHIFT" TRANSMISSION (SA or CF)

"SA" AVAIL. TO 3-32

(12-31 to 10-32)

B+B CARB. (THROUGH '35)

112 3/8" W.B.

CHROMED RADIATOR SHELL ON EARLY MODELS.

211.4 C.I.D.
75 H.P. @ 3400 RPM
NEW 5.25 x 18 AND OTHER TIRES.

32 "SC"
6 CYL. ONLY

Custom Roadster De Luxe

Custom 5 Passenger Sedan De Luxe

Custom Convertible Sedan De Luxe

Standard Coupe

Standard 2 Door Sedan

DE SOTO

(11-32 TO 10-33)

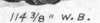

33

("SD")   6

114 3/8" W.B.   86 H.P. @ 3400 RPM

NEW 6 TO 1 COMPR.   NEW 5.50 × 17
217.8 C.I.D.   AND OTHER TIRES.

WHAT—NO HAND-STRAPS!   "WALK RIGHT IN" THESE DOORS

34

(SE) (1-34 TO 10-34)

THE WHEEL IS WHERE YOU WANT IT   RIDE INSIDE THE FRAME...NOT ON IT

ALL-NEW, STREAMLINED "AIRFLOW" (2 OR 4-DOOR)
IS ONLY MODEL OF DE SOTO AVAILABLE
FOR 1934.

115 1/2" W.B.
NEW 6.50 × 16 TIRES
(ON 1934 THROUGH 1936 "AIRFLOW")

241.5 C.I.D.   100 H.P. @ 3400 RPM   6.2 COMPR.

AIRSTREAM 6 (SF)

116" W.B.
6 TO 1 COMPR.
93 H.P. @ 3400 RPM

AIRFLOW 6 (SG)

6.5 COMP.
100 H.P. @ 3400

35

(STARTS 11-34)

115 1/2" W.B.

6.25 × 16 TIRES (ON 1935 and 1936 "AIRSTREAM")

AIRFLOW 6 (S-2)

115 1/2 WB

(NEW CARTER CARB.) (BOTH SERIES)   118" W.B.

AIRSTREAM CUSTOM 6 (S-1)

AIRSTREAM ALSO AVAIL WITH 1-PC. WINDSHIELD

36

(STARTS 9-35)

75

SAME ENGINES AS 1935

DE SOTO

116" W.B.

All Seat Edges Padded.

Safety-height Instrument Panel.

All Panel Controls are Flush.

DISPLACEMENT REDUCED TO 228.1 CU. IN.
6.5 COMPR.   93 H.P. @ 3600 RPM
CARTER B + B CARBURETOR
(THROUGH '38)

37
(S-3)
(9-36 TO 8-37)

6.00 x 16

38 (S-5)
(9-37 TO 7-38)

DASH

6.00 x 16 OR
6.50 x 16 TIRES
(THROUGH '40)

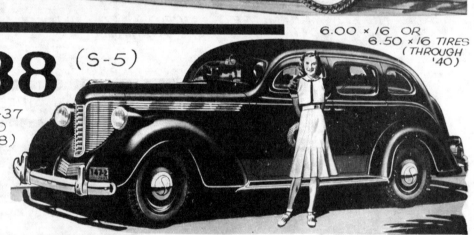

CARTER CARB.

('38 - 39 SPECIFICATIONS
SAME AS 1937)

39 (S-6)
(8-38 TO 7-39)

SPEED INDICATOR
CHANGES COLORS

COLUMN SHIFT

76

DETROIT AIR-COOLED
(1923)

DETROIT AIR-COOLED CAR CO., DETROIT, MICH.
(ALSO KNOWN AS "D.A.C" CAR, 1922-1923)
V-6 AIR-COOLED ENGINE

DETROIT ELECTRIC
(1907-1938)
DETROIT ELECTRIC CAR CO., DETROIT

FALSE "RADIATOR" TRIED BRIEFLY

20

"88" 5-PASS. BROUGHAM

MOST LATER MODELS BUILT TO ORDER, AS IS THIS 1931 MODEL "99" →

21 100" W.B.

32 × 4½

DETROIT STEAM
ORIGINAL NAME: TRASK-DETROIT

(1922-1923)
DETROIT STEAM MOTORS CORP., DETROIT

DE VAUX
31 **32**

DE VAUX-HALL MOTOR CORP., GRAND RAPIDS, MICH. and OAKLAND, CALIF.
(1931-1932)
6-CYL. 214.7 C.I.D. CONTINENTAL-HALL engine

"6-75" 65 H.P. @ 3400 RPM 4.4 G.R.

113" W.B. 5.00 × 19 TIRES

"80"

70 H.P. and 3.9 G.R. IN '32

DIANA
('26)

SUBSIDIARY OF MOON MOTOR CAR CO., ST. LOUIS, MO.

INTRO. 6-25 AS 1926 MODEL. DISCONTINUED 1928.

'27 HAS ARROWHEAD HOOD MOLDING

STRAIGHT-8, CONTINENTAL ENGINE 12-z

HYDRAULIC BRAKES

('27) 5.1 G.R.

32 × 6.00

240.2 C.I.D. 72 H.P. @ 2950 RPM

125½" W.B.

20-21 DIXIE FLYER
(1916-1922)

"H-S-60" 50

DIXIE
Kentucky Wagon Mfg. Co.
Louisville   Kentucky

4-CYL. HERS.-SPLMN. ENGINE (165.9 C.I.D. IN '20)

IN 1922, DIXIE FLYER ABSORBED BY NATIONAL

22 4.75 G.R.

4.72 G.R. (THROUGH '21)
32 × 4 TIRES

192.4 C.I.D. (SINCE '21)

112" W.B. ("HS-70" STARTS '21)

DOBLE STEAM

('25)

('29-32)

FORMERLY "DOBLE-DETROIT"

('31-32)

EST. 1914,
DOBLE STEAM MOTORS
MOVED TO EMERYVILLE,
CALIF. IN 1924 ; IN
BUSINESS UNTIL 1932.

MURPHY BODY

DODGE BROTHERS

(SINCE NOV., 1914)
DODGE BROS., DETROIT
(A PRODUCT OF
CHRYSLER CORP. SINCE MID-1928.)

20

4-DOOR SEDAN

(2-19 TO 7-21)

4 CYLINDER,
212.3 C.I.D.
ENGINE
(1915 TO 1927)

35 H.P. @ 2000 RPM

(4 TO 1 COMPRESSION
(THROUGH 1926)

7-19 TO 6-20

114 " WHEELBASE (1916-1923)

32 × 3½ TIRES (THROUGH 1921)

21-22

7-1-20 TO 5-23-22

JULY, 1921 ===
BUDD-MICHELIN
STEEL DISC WHEELS
INTRODUCED ON
SOME DODGES;
SEDAN 4" LOWER.
32 × 4" TIRES
(1922 THROUGH 1925)

DODGE BROTHERS

32 x 4 STEEL DISC
BUDD - MICHELIN
WHEELS AVAIL.

5-24-22
TO
6-28-23

22½

TO

BUSINESS
SEDAN
(ANNOUNCED 9-22)

SPEC.
SUBURB.
SEDAN

BUSINESS
COUPE
(AVAILABLE
SUMMER, 1922)

23

CANTRELL
BODY

BABCOCK
BODY

2-PASS.
BUSINESS
CPE.

(4-PASS.
CPE. ALSO
AVAILABLE)

7-1-23 TO
← 11-1-24

24

NEW 116"
WHEELBASE

BUSINESS SEDAN

TYPE A

1924 Model Cantrell Suburban Body for Latest Type Dodge Brothers Chassis

79

DodgeBrothers

TYPE-A SEDAN

25

NEW
COACH

26

JAN., '25

SPECIAL=
HAS NICKEL RADIATOR
SHELL

SPECIAL
TYPE-B SEDAN

(EARLY '26)
SEDANS

SPECIAL
TYPE-A SEDAN

1-PIECE WINDSHIELD
ON LATER MODELS.

SPECIAL

26½

80

DODGE BROTHERS

EARLY MODEL (TO FEB., '27)
MODEL 126

31 × 5.25 TIRES

27

4 CYL.

FEB., '27
MODEL 124 ROOF-VISOR
NEW 4.1 TO 1 COMPR.

IN 1927, DODGE BROS. CARS ABANDON 12-VOLT ELECTRICAL SYSTEM IN FAVOR OF CONVENTIONAL 6-VOLT SYSTEM. ELECTRICAL SYSTEM CHANGED FROM ONE-UNIT TO 2-UNIT (STARTER + GENERATOR SEPERATED.)

"126"

SPARK and THROTTLE LEVERS MOVED TO TOP OF STEERING WHEEL.

40 H.P. @ 2400 RPM

SENIOR 6
MODEL 2249
224 C.I.D.
6 CYL.
60 H.P. @ 2800 RPM
5.3 COMPR.
(FIRST 6-CYL. DODGE)
INTRO. 6-27

27½
(108" W.B.)

FAST 4 "128"
INTRO. 7-27, CONT'D. TO 1928 SEASON
29 × 5.00 TIRES

6-CYLINDER DODGES FOR 1928

The VICTORY SIX
BY DODGE BROTHERS

(INTRO. 1-5-28)
MODEL 130, 131

STD. 6 and VICTORY 6 HAVE 208 C.I.D., 5.2 COMPR. and 58 H.P. @ 3000 RPM with 29 × 5.00 TIRES

(MECHANICAL BRAKES)
STANDARD 6
MODEL 140 141

110" W.B.

112" W.B.
4.45 GEAR RATIO

HYDRAULIC BRAKES

VICTORY 6

The DeLuxe Sedan

8 FT

RT. HAND DRIVE - EXPORT MODEL

SENIOR 6 MODEL 2251

28
78 H.P. @ 3000 RPM
241.5 C.I.D.
5.2 COMPR.

31 × 6.00 TIRES

NEW 120" W.B.

81

DODGE BROTHERS

CHRYSLER MOTORS PRODUCT

6 (DA)

"DA" HAS SAME SPECS. AS VICTORY 6. BUILT 1-29 TO 3-30
BUDD BODIES, AS BEFORE

29

DA VIC.

('29 MODEL STARTS 8-28)

HYDRAULIC BRAKES, INTRODUCED TO DODGE ON '27-8 "SENIOR" and '28 "VICTORY 6," ARE STANDARD ON ALL DODGES FROM 1929 ON.

DA SR.

NEW VICTORY SIX
'29 "VICTORY 6" HAS HIGHER, LONGER BODY THAN '28. SEDAN DOORS WIDENED 3". SEAT CUSHIONS AND BACKS ARE DEEPER.

MURRAY BODIES ON "SENIOR 6" ONLY.

"FROSTED SILVER" INST. PANEL

SENIOR 6

MODEL 2252 SR. 6 BUILT 7-28 TO 6-29

(CONT'D. TO 6-30, AS "DB" series)
COMPRESSION INCREASED TO 5.5

CHRYSLER PURCHASED DODGE BROS. IN SPRING, 1928. 1929 AND LATER DODGES ARE CHRYSLER PRODUCTS.

6.00 × 19" TIRES

82

DODGE   BROTHERS

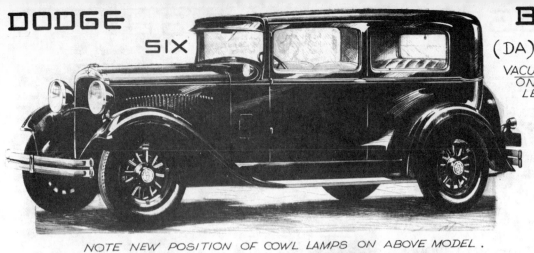

SIX

(DA) TO 3-30

VACUUM TANK RETAINED ON "DA" SIX, AS ON LEFTOVER MODELS OF "SENIOR SIX."

NAME SHORTENED TO <u>DODGE</u> DURING 1930.

NOTE NEW POSITION OF COWL LAMPS ON ABOVE MODEL.

30

NEW 8 (DC) HAS 114" W.B., 220.7 C.I.D., 5.4 COMPR., 75 H.P. @ 3400 RPM
4.6 GEAR RATIO
new FUEL PUMP

(DC)

EIGHT

60 H.P. @ 3400 RPM   189.8 C.I.D.   DODGE SIX (PRODUCTION STARTS 12-29)

109" W.B.

"DD" INTERIOR

new RADIATOR DESIGN

30½

TO MAY, 31

(DD)

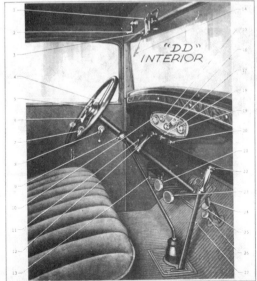

224·928
MICHIGAN 1930

HAS FUEL PUMP

4.9 GEAR RATIO   83

DODGE SIX AND EIGHT

New Dodge Six $815 to $845, New Dodge Eight $1095 to $1135; Standard Six $735 to $835, Standard Eight $995 to $1095. Prices f.o.b. factory

6 (DH)

31

113 5/8" W.B. 4.66 G.R.
211.5 C.I.D. 5.35 COMPR. 74 H.P. @ 3400 RPM

NEW DODGE SIX SEDAN 1931

"Standard" MODELS ARE CONTINUATIONS OF 1930 "DD" 6 AND "DC" 8.

THE LAST DODGE ROADSTER UNTIL 1949 →

8 (DG)
118" W.B.
240.3 C.I.D.
5.4 COMPR.
84 H.P. @
3400 RPM
5.50 × 18 TIRES
4.60 GEAR RATIO

5.50 × 18 TIRES
4.6 GEAR RATIO (DL) 6

217.8 C.I.D.
79 H.P. @ 3400 RPM
6.35 COMPR. OPTIONAL

6 and 8 COUPES and CVT. CPES. HAVE 4.3 (6) and 3.91 (8) GEAR RATIOS

114 3/8" W.B.

32

4.1 GEAR RATIO
6.00 × 18 TIRES
282.1 C.I.D.
5.2 OR 6.2 COMPR.
90 OR 100 H.P. @ 3400 RPM

8 (DK)

CONVERTIBLE SEDAN (NEW)

122 3/8" W.B.

84

33

DODGE

REDUCED TO 201.3 C.I.D. 5.5 OR 6.2 COMPR. 75 OR 81 H.P. @ 3600 RPM

6 (DP)

REAR DETAILS

115" W.B.

The big, new Dodge "6" Sedan—$675 f. o. b. factory, Detroit, special equipment extra

'33 DASH GAUGES IN CENTER

6
8

HOOD ON "8" DOES NOT CONCEAL COWL AS IT DOES ON "6."

DODGE "8"
WITH FLOATING POWER

An Aristocrat From Bumper to Bumper

(DO)=(*Final Dodge straight-8*)

"8" HAS COWL LAMPS

Dodge "8"
122" w.b.

OPTIONAL "RED HEAD" ON 8 GIVES 6.5 COMPRESSION.

'34 DASH GAUGES AT LEFT

92 OR 100 H.P. @ 3400 RPM (8)

217.8 C.I.D. 5.6 OR 6.5 COMPR.

82 OR 87 H.P. @ 3600 RPM

117" W.B.

34
(DR)

LUGGAGE CARRIED BEHIND REAR SEAT-BACK.

85

6.5 COMPRESSION
ALUMINUM HEAD
STANDARD ON
"DS"

DODGE

(DS) SPECIAL
121" WHEELBASE

6.25 × 16 TIRES

34½

(FEWER HOOD LOUVRES)

34

(CONT'D.)

"DRXX"
MODEL WAS
LOW-PRICED
1934½ SERIES,
WITHOUT
BUILT-IN VENT
WINDOWS.

217.8 C.I.D. CONTINUED
THROUGH 1941

REAR
DETAILS

The New Dodge Touring Sedan
Four-Door—with Trunk

Convertible Coupe

35

(DU)

Sedan

WITHOUT
TRUNK

DASH

The New Dodge Touring Sedan
Two-Door—with Trunk

SEDAN INTERIOR

NEW
HORN GRILLES
BELOW LIGHTS

87 H.P. @ 3600 RPM
(THROUGH 1940)

6.5
COMPRESSION
(THROUGH
1941)

WHEELBASE NOW
116" (AS ALSO
IN 1936)

Coupe with Rumble Seat

6.00 × 16 IS
STANDARD TIRE SIZE
UNTIL LATE 1940s.

Coupe

DODGE

Two-Door Sedan

STEEL
TIRE-COVER
AVAILABLE

DODGE (D-2)

DASH

36

37 (D-5)

WESTCHESTER SUBURBAN WAGON

NEW "HIGH-SAFETY" INTERIOR

PULL-DRAWER RECESSED KNOBS ON EARLY MODELS.

NEW HORIZONTAL GRILLE MOTIF

115" WHEELBASE IN 1937 and 1938

WINDSHIELDS DO NOT OPEN ON '38 CHRYSLER-BUILT CARS.

38 (D-8)

'39 ENGINE

INTERIOR

LIGHTED SPEED INDICATOR

FAST BACK

117" WHEELBASE

39 (D-11)

87

DORRIS
(1905–1926)

21 132" W.B. WESTINGHOUSE IGNITION (THROUGH '21)

"6-80" 7-PASS.

DORRIS MOTOR CAR CO. ST. LOUIS, MO.
OWN 377 C.I.D., O.H.V. 6-CYL. ENG.

22 NEW BOSCH IGNITION "6-80"

(NO NEW PRODUCTION AFTER 1923.)

DORT
(1915–1924)

Quality Goes Clear Through

DORT

Dort Motor Car Company
Flint, Mich.

21 "17-A" OR "17-12" MODELS

NEW, ANGULAR STYLING FOR 1921, NEW 108" W.B.

Top and curtains up
When the storm beats down

20

(4) 4 CYL. 192.4 C.I.D. LYCOMING ENGINE

105½" W.B.

MODEL "15" TOURING FEW CHANGES FROM 1919.

1922 "19-14" MODEL LIKE 1921.

23 "HARVARD SEDAN"

(6)

31 x 4 TIRES

NEW 1923
MODEL 18-23 HAS 108" W.B., LYCOMING ENGINE AS BEFORE, 4.60 GEAR RATIO
MODEL 25-20 HAS 115" W.B., NEW 195.6 C.I.D., 6-CYL. FALLS ENGINE, 4.66 GEAR RATIO 45 HORSEPOWER (INTRO. 11-22)

"27-C" "3-DOOR COUPE" IS A SEDAN WITH JUST ONE DOOR ON LEFT SIDE.

FALLS ENGINE (6 CYL., O.H.V.) 207.1 C.I.D.

24 MODEL 27 NEW RADIATOR DESIGN (THE FINAL DORT)

21 (97.4 CID) 4 CYLS. 104" W.B. 4.75 G.R.

DRIGGS
(1921–1923)

DRIGGS ORDNANCE AND MANUFACTURING CO., NEW HAVEN, CONN. AND N.Y.C.

22-23

OWN ENG. 30 x 3½ TIRES

DUESENBERG STRAIGHT 8

8

(1920-1937)
DUESENBERG
MOTOR CO.,
INDIANAPOLIS, IND.

"A" SERIES
259.7 C.I.D.
STRAIGHT-8 ENGINE
100 H.P. @ 3600 RPM ('26 RATING)

HYDRAULIC BRAKES
STANDARD EQUIPMENT
90 MILES PER HOUR

DASH

PRESSURE FUEL FEED
IN '26.

134" W.B.

21-28

(JOINED AUBURN
IN 1926)

('27-'28 MODEL "X")

29-37

AVAIL. WITH PRESSURE
FUEL FEED ('32)

HAS FUEL PUMP ('29)

"J" SERIES
STRAIGHT-8
420 C.I.D.
265 H.P. @ 4200
RPM

MURPHY BODY

"SJ"
(SUPERCHARGED)
(NOTE THE
EXHAUST
PIPES
THROUGH
HOOD.)

BARKER
BODY
142½"-153½"
WHEELBASES

DASH

RENOWNED
COACHBUILDERS SUPPLIED
MANY VARIETIES OF CUSTOM
BODIES.

"J"
(UN-SUPERCHARGED)

20 "A" MODEL   **DU PONT**

DUPONT MOTORS, INC. WILMINGTON, DEL. (ALSO MOORE, PA.)

(1920-1932)

124" W.B. (THROUGH '26)

16" BRAKE DRUMS, WATER TEMP. GAUGE ON DASH, CONCAVE BODY SIDES. OWN 4-CYL., 249.6 C.I.D. ENGINE (TO '23) 2-WH. MECH. BRAKES and 4.45 G.R. (THROUGH '24)

21

5-PASS. TOURING CAR

23

24 (6-CYL.)

('24 HAS 6-CYL. HERSCHELL-SPILLMAN "90" ENGINE) (288.6 C.I.D.)

MODEL C 57 H.P.

5-PASS. TOURING SEDAN

25

MODEL D (1925-1926) HAS NEW O.H.V. WISCONSIN 6-CYL. "Y" ENGINE (268.3 C.I.D. 75 H.P. @ 3000 RPM NEW HYDRAULIC BRAKES

4.7 GEAR RATIO 32 × 6.20 BALLOON TIRES (THROUGH '29)

MODEL E **28**

MODEL E RUNS FROM 1927 TO 1929. MODEL F ALSO, IN '28.

6-CYL. WISC. "Y" ENGINE 268.3 C.I.D., 75 H.P. @ 3000 RPM 32 × 6.20 TIRES MODEL E = 125" W.B., 4.7 GEAR RATIO MODEL F = 136" " 4.45 " "

29-30 MODEL G

140-H.P. SPEEDSTER

125" W.B.

NARROW "WOOD-LITES"

30-32 MODEL G (MERRIMAC BODY) 141" W.B.

MODEL G HAS STRAIGHT-8 CONTINENTAL "12-K" ENGINE (322 C.I.D.) WITH 114 H.P. @ 3200 RPM (GETS FUEL PUMP, '29)

LEFTOVER CARS STILL AVAIL. IN 1933.

MODEL H ('31-32) HAS 146" W.B.

H.P. INCREASED IN 1932, TO 130 @ 3200 RPM

The DU PONT

DURANT

(1921–1932)
DURANT MOTORS, INC.
(OFFICES IN N.Y.C.)

6-CYL. "B-22" HAS SQUARE-EDGED HOOD. 6 DISCONTINUED MID-1924. (PHOTO AT UPPER RIGHT.)

('24)

"B-22" 6 CYL. ('22)

ANSTED ENG.

FOUR

"A-22"

21-25

('21-'22 HAS WOOD WHEELS. DISC WHEELS ALSO, STARTING 1923.)

('25)

LATE '25 SOMETIMES CALLED "1926."

28

4 and 6 CYLS.

(EARLY '28 4-CYL. = "DURANT-STAR")

CONTINENTAL ENGINES USED (THROUGH '32) DURANT PRODUCTION SUSPENDED 1926-7, BUT STAR CAR CONTINUED.

HAYES-HUNT BODIES

"4-40" ("M")

29

OTHER 6-CYL. MODELS: "55," "60," "65," "6-60," "6-66"

("6-63" CONSIDERED AN EARLY '30 MODEL.)

(M SERIES (REPLACES STAR)

"6-70" DE LUXE SEDAN

119" W.B.

(65 H.P., 4-SPEED TRANS.)

BUDD ALL-STEEL BODIES ON SOME '30 DURANTS. NOTE NEW EMBLEM

30

'30 "6-14" has NEW FUEL PUMP.

"6-17" GETS IT IN '31

DURANT

EARLY '32 IS "6/9"

"621," "622" also, in '32 (71 H.P.)

31
"610," "612" (4) (6) VERTICAL HOOD LOUVRES; SOME MODELS HAVE RADIATOR SHUTTERS and SEATS THAT CONVERT TO A BED.

32
FINAL DURANT

5.00 or 5.50 × 19

"6-14" = 58 H.P., 199 CID
"6-17" = 70 H.P., 248 CID

SOME '30s HAVE VERTICAL HOOD LOUVRES.

('31)

DYMAXION

(ONLY 3 PILOT MODELS)
DESIGNED BY
BUCKMINSTER FULLER

33-34

SINGLE REAR WHEEL!

FORD V-8 REAR ENGINE

TOURING CARS ONLY

EAGLE

WITH 6-CYLINDER, 195.6 C.I.D.
CONTINENTAL ENGINE (Auto-Lite IGN.)

23-24

BUILT, BRIEFLY, BY
DURANT MOTORS

115" W.B.   4-WHEEL BRAKES
30 x 3½ TIRES   4.77 G.R.

REPLACES BRISCOE

The EARL

EARL MOTORS, INC.

JACKSON   MICHIGAN

21-24

"Cabriole"

4 CYL.   112" W.B.
('22 MODEL INTRO. 1921)

KNOWN AS
"BROUGHAM" UNTIL MID-'22

ELCAR

(1915-1931)

ELCAR MOTOR CO.,
ELKHART, INDIANA

116" W.B. IN '20

NEW STYLING FOR 1921
LYCOMING 4 CYL.
(192.4 CID) ('21)

(NEW STRAIGHT-LINE ROOF)

DRUM HEADLIGHTS ON 1922 MODELS, 118" W.B.

"4-40" ('23-24)   112" W.B.

Three-Door Four Cylinder

(6 CYL MODELS w 224 CID CONT. ENG. ALSO)
117" W.B. IN '21 (4+6)

"6-60" IS 6-CYL., 118" W.B.

NEW PEAKED RADIATOR FEATURED, MID-1924.

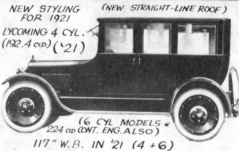

EMBLEM
A WELL BUILT CAR

'26 INTRODUCES LIGHT CONTROL ON STEERING WHEEL

26

MODEL "8-81"

25

"8-80" 7-PASS.

127" W.B.

FIRST YEAR FOR ELCAR STRAIGHT-8 (254.4 LYCOMING "H" ENG.)

63 H.P. @ 3000

FROM 1926 ON, LYCOMING ENGINES USED IN 6-CYL. MODELS also.

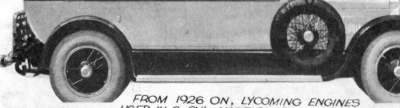

27

"8-90"

(4 CYL. MODEL DISCONTINUED JAN., 1927)

28

29

"PRINCESS"
NEW ROUNDED EDGE ON '29 RADIATOR

ELCAR-LEVER WAS AN ELCAR ENTRY IN 1930 AUTOMOBILE SHOW. IT HAD A POWELL-LEVER ENGINE WITH JOINTED CONNECTING RODS.

MODEL K
('20-21)

(1916 - 1924)

ELGIN MOTOR
CAR CORP.,
ELGIN and
ARGO,
ILL.

Elgin

(195.6 CID,
1922 ON)

4-WH.
BRKS.
ON
SOME
'24s

118" W.B.
(THROUGH '24)
(DISC WHEELS ON SPT. TOURING)

NEW FOR 1920 :
COLUMBIA AXLES . 10"
BORG + BECK CLUTCH REPLACES 8" TYPE.
6-CYL., O.H.V.
FALLS ENGINE

('24)
(NEW STYLING)

ERSKINE 6

CONTINENTAL "8-F" 6-CYL., L-HEAD
ENGINE

27

The Little
Aristocrat
40 H.P.
@ 3200

(1927 TO 1930)
PRODUCT OF STUDEBAKER

146.1
C.I.D.
IN
1927

28 x 4.40

4-WHEEL
BRAKES

STROM.
CARB.

'27 DASH

5.13
G.R.

107" W.B. (THROUGH '28)

"AMERICAN 6"
SERIES

107" W.B.

new
SCHEBLER
CARB. (THROUGH
'30)

MODEL "51"
(STARTS
1-1-28)

28

CONT. "9-F" ENG.
(THROUGH '29)
DOES NOT HAVE FENDER BOXES,
AS SEEN ON '27 ERSKINE.

(160.37 C.I.D.)
42 H.P.

4.78 G.R.

29 x 4.75
TIRES

'28
(DASH GAUGES
GROUPED BEHIND
GLASS PANEL.)

20 x 4.75
TIRES

29

SOME SEDANS HAVE
BUDD BODIES.

DELCO-REMY IGNITION
(1927 THROUGH '30)

MODEL "52"   43 H.P. @ 3000 RPM

109" W.B.
new 109" W.B.

(STARTS 7-9-28. CARS
BUILT AFTER 8-5-29 CONSIDERED "EARLY 1930.")

"DYNAMIC NEW" SERIES
"53"

30

(STARTS
12-26-29)
70 H.P.

(OWN
ENGINE)

30½ STUDEBAKER 6
LOOKS THE
SAME AS
THIS
MODEL.

HAS FUEL PUMP
(NEW ENGINE
SIZE :
205.3 C.I.D.)

NAME
CHANGED TO
STUDEBAKER 6

ERSKINE

STUDEBAKER BUILT

5.25 - 19

93

4.78 G.R. (SINCE '28)
new 114" W.B., 5.25 x 19 TIRES

ESSEX

INTRODUCED 1919, BUILT BY HUDSON

1919-21

108½" WHEELBASE (THROUGH '23)

4 CYLINDERS
178.9 C.I.D.
55 H.P.
5.09 GEAR RATIO (THROUGH '20)
4.66 GEAR RATIO (THROUGH '23)

OIL CUPS INSTEAD OF GREASE CUPS

Coach (NEW)

new DRUM HEADLIGHTS and FLANGED CROWN FENDERS in 1922.

22-23 (FINAL 4 CYLINDER ESSEX IN 1923)

(1924 NEW ENG., SIX RADIATOR SHELL)

NEW 6-CYL. 129.9 C.I.D. ENGINE OF 50 H.P. IN EARLY 1924.

144.7 C.I.D., 55 H.P. (THROUGH '27)

BALLOON 31 × 5.20 TIRES ('25) 30 × 4.95 TIRES ('26)

JUNE 23, 1924: BALLOON TIRES and LARGER ENGINE

NEW 110½" W.B. (THROUGH '29)

NEW 5.6 G.R.

24-25 (RECTANGULAR WINDSHIELD)

25½-26 →

ESSEX 26½

NEW STEEL BODIES WITH CURVED UPPER BACK.
LONG PIANO-TYPE DOOR HINGES = JULY, 1926

NICKEL-PLATED
RADIATOR = JULY, 1926

Speedabout

27

"SUPER 6"
(RESTYLED)

30 × 4.75

OR 31 × 5.00

STARTER
CONTROL
ON DASH

JULY,
1927 =

ENGINE STROKE 1/4"
LONGER. NEW 30 × 5
TIRES. REAR TIRE
CARRIER CHANGED FROM
BUCKET TYPE TO HOOP
TYPE (LIKE HUDSON.)

5.4 G.R.

ALUMINUM
BODY PANELS OVER
HARDWOOD
FRAME

"POLISHED EBONY"
INSTRUMENT BOARD

28

153.2 C.I.D.

BENDIX 4-WHEEL
MECHANICAL BRAKES

160.4 C.I.D.   55 H.P. @
3600 RPM

29   "THE
CHALLENGER"

30 × 5.00

(5.00 × 30)

"CHASE SILVERED"
INSTRUMENT PANEL

95

ESSEX

A uniform modernistic design has been carried into the details of Essex door handles, window lifts, lights and other appointments.

ESSEX SUPER SIX

5.40 GEAR RATIO

30

NEW 113" WHEELBASE
(THROUGH '32)

60 H.P. @ 3600 RPM

31

60 H.P. @ 3300 RPM

(NEW ENGINE SIZE OF 175.3 C.I.D.)

5.1 OR 5.4 GEAR RATIOS

ESSEX

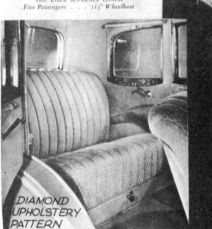

New triple-sealed in a new-type housing that retains the oil intact over thousands of miles, the famous Hudson-Essex oil cushion clutch adds a new standard of saving and trouble free operating to its long-established standard of durability and efficiency.

1932 ESSEX SUPER-SIX COACH
Five Passengers . . . 113" Wheelbase

FREE-WHEELING CONTROL
IN CENTER OF
GEARSHIFT LEVER KNOB

WINDSHIELD
OPENER

DIAMOND
UPHOLSTERY
PATTERN

NOTE NEW WARNING LIGHTS ON DASH

32

NEW "RIDE CONTROL" ADJUSTS SHOCK ABSORBERS
FROM INSIDE THE CAR.

5.25 x 18" TIRES
5.10 and 4.64 GEAR RATIOS

REAR VIEW OF 1932 ESSEX

FOR 1932, ENGINE SIZE AGAIN INCREASED (TO 193.1 C.I.D.) 70 H.P. @ 3200 RPM

IN SUMMER OF 1932, THE ESSEX WAS REPLACED BY THE ESSEX-TERRAPLANE.

6 CYL. 106" W.B.
NEW 8 CYL. 113" W.B.

6

8

The New SEVENTY HORSEPOWER ENGINE *of the* 1932 ESSEX SUPER-SIX

32½ TO 33

SEE ALSO "TERRAPLANE"

FALCON

115" W.B., 4.88 G.R.
32 × 4 TIRES
OWN 4 OR 6-CYL.
ENGINES —
LIGHT 4
192.4 C.I.D.
SIX
230.1 C.I.D.
(NOT IN FULL PROD.)

22

HALLADAY MOTORS
CORP.,
NEWARK, OHIO

REPLACES THE
HALLADAY CAR, 1922

ROOF-VISOR
ON 1927
CLOSED
MODELS

Falcon-Knight
(1927-1928)

27

FALCON MOTORS CORP., ELYRIA, O.; DETROIT
(WILLYS-KNIGHT AFFILIATE)

1927 — 109½" W.B. (MODEL "10")
30 × 5.00 TIRES
5.11 GEAR RATIO ('28 ALSO)
156.6 C.I.D. 4.6 COMPRESSION
45 H.P. @ 3000 RPM ('28 ALSO)
DASH GAUGES UNDER SINGLE GLASS PANE

6-CYL. SLEEVE-VALVE ENGINE

1928 — 109½" W.B. (MODEL "12")
29 × 5.50 TIRES
"FUMER" WARMS CARBURETOR
HARD-RUBBER-COVERED STEERING WHEEL
INDIVIDUAL DASH GAUGES (INCL. GAS
GAUGE)

28

FARGO

(1929 ON, BUILT BY
CHRYSLER CORP.)

29

(PRIMARILY COMMERCIAL
VEHICLES)

(6 CYL.)
HYDRAULIC BRAKES

1921

FERRIS

20-22

OHIO MOTOR VEHICLE CO., CLEVELAND
(1920-1922)
130" W.B.
6-CYL. 303.1 C.I.D. CONTINENTAL ENG.
4.08 G.R. 32 × 4½ TIRES
BECOMES MODEL "60" IN 1922;
1922 MODEL "70" ALSO, with 325.1
C.I.D., 6-CYL. CONTINENTAL ENGINE.

BUILDERS OF HIGH GRADE MOTOR CARS

FLINT SIX

120"
W.B.

23

CONTINENTAL
ENGINES
6 CYLS.

FLINT MOTOR COMPANY
FLINT, MICHIGAN
(1923-1927)
AFFILIATED WITH
DURANT AND
LOCOMOBILE

268.4 C.I.D.

32
×
4½
TIRES

70 H.P. @ 2500 RPM
4.7 GEAR RATIO

FLINT 24 SIX

4.78 G.R.
MODEL E

120" W.B.

(E) 55

120" W.B.

MODEL "FIFTY-FIVE" 268.4 C.I.D., 64½ H.P. @ 2400 RPM

BROUGHAM

FLINT

25

(E) 55

32 x 6.20

Model "55" Five Passenger Sedan

(MODEL "40" ALSO AVAIL.)'24-5
WITH 115" W.B., 196 C.I.D., 49 H.P. @ 2500)

"60" COUPE - ROADSTER ('27)

'27 "60" MODELS
BEGIN AT # 18776

The New Flint "SIXTY"
5-Passenger Sedan

60

FLINT

"60" HAS 230 C.I.D.,
56 H.P. @ 2600

30 x 5.77

The New Flint "EIGHTY" 268.4 C.I.D.
5-Passenger Sedan
65 H.P. @ 2400
120" W.B.

80

115" W.B.

"Z-18"
"FLINT JUNIOR" COACH ('26-7) 110" W.B.

HAS 6-CYL.
169.3 C.I.D. ENGINE
40 H.P. @ 2300 RPM
2-WHEEL BRAKES
'26 = #100-1911
'27 = #1912 and up

'27 "80" MODELS BEGIN
AT # 20103

26-27

JR.

30 x 5.77

4.875 TO 1 GEAR RATIO

NOTE DIFFERENCES IN HOOD LOUVRE PANEL
AND PLACEMENT OF HOOD LATCH ON
'26 and '27 "60" MODELS ILLUSTRATED.

100

CENTER-DOOR SEDAN

Ford THE UNIVERSAL CAR

FORD MOTOR CO., DEARBORN, MICH. (PRODUCTION BEGINS 1903)

MODEL "T"

(FIRST INTRODUCED LATE 1908, REPLACING MODEL "S.")

17-22

MINOR IMPROVEMENTS DURING COURSE OF PRODUCTION

OWN IGN. SYSTEM

4 CYLINDERS, 176.7 C.I.D. ENGINE 20 HORSEPOWER (THROUGH '27)

100" WHEELBASE 30 x 3½" tires

FORD USES OWN BRAND OF BATTERY, BUT EXIDE ALSO USED ON SOME 1924 MODELS (ACC. TO *Automotive Industries*, 2-21-24.)

23-25

RESTYLED '23 MODELS START AUGUST, 1922. CHOICE OF 2-DOOR OR 4-DOOR SEDANS.* CLOSED CARS HAVE RECTANGULAR REAR WINDOWS.

(BALLOON TIRES ON '25 MODELS.)

* = OTHER BODY TYPES ALSO.

Ford

IMPROVED '26 MODEL T HAS FUEL TANK IN COWL.

PLANETARY TRANSMISSION A MODEL T CHARACTERISTIC.

THE RUNABOUT

TOURING

26-27

WIRE WHEELS AVAILABLE ON 1927 MODEL T.

COUPE

29 × 4.40 BALLOON TIRES STANDARD EQUIPMENT IN 1927; BALLOON TIRES OPTIONAL DURING 1926.

1927 = FINAL MODEL T

MODEL "A" 28-29 Ford

(INTRO. 12-2-27)

NEW 200.4 CUBIC-IN. DISPL., 4-CYL. ENGINE 40 H.P. @ 2200 RPM

EARLY '28 OPEN MODEL As HAVE NO OUTSIDE DOOR HANDLES.

MODEL "A" AN ALL-NEW CAR FOR 1928.

STANDARD TYPE SLIDING-GEAR TRANSMISSION ADOPTED.

new 4-WHEEL MECHANICAL BRAKES (THROUGH '38)

SPORT COUPE (RIGID FABRIC TOP)

STATION WAGON ('29)

TAXI ('29)

103½" W.B.

'28 HAS REDDISH-COLORED STEERING WHEEL.

21" (4.50 x 30) TIRES IN '28-29 3.7 GEAR RATIO

BRIGGS OR MURRAY BODIES

EARLIEST MODELS HAVE BRAKE LEVER AT LEFT.

TUDOR SEDAN

"LINCOLN" STYLING

"Ford" IN SCRIPT ON NEW BLUE-and-WHITE OVAL RADIATOR EMBL.

TOWN CAR ('29)

Ford

30 (INTRO. 12-28-29)

MODEL "A" (IMPROVED)

NEW STAINLESS STEEL BRIGHTWORK

NEW, ENLARGED RADIATOR AND HOOD

3.77 GEAR RATIO

LATE '30, '31 MODELS have HORIZONTAL RIBS ON INSTRUMENT PANEL.

4.75 × 19" TIRES ON 1930-31 MODEL As.

MODEL "A" **31**

VICTORIA (PADDED TOP)

VICTORIA (METAL BACK)

"A-400" 2-DR. CONVT. SEDAN

SLANT-WINDSHIELD 31½

LEFTOVER MODEL As WERE SOLD EARLY IN 1932.

MODEL B- 4 CYL. **FORD**
V8 - 8 CYL . (221 C.I.D.)
106" W.B.

new DASH WITH 3 CIRCULAR GAUGES SET ON AN OVAL PANEL.

HENRY FORD I with the FIRST FORD V-8 ENGINE

32 "18" SERIES

V-8 HAS EMBLEM ON TIE-BAR.

BOTH 3-WINDOW AND 5-WINDOW COUPES AVAILABLE FROM 1932 TO 1936.

(FIRST FORD V-8 ASSEMBLED MARCH 9, 1932.)

STARTING '32, BOTH 3-WINDOW (new) and 5-WINDOW COUPES ARE AVAILABLE (THROUGH '36)

"40" SERIES **33** (4 and V-8) 3.77 G.R. (4) 4.33 (V-8)

(STARTS 2-33)

112" W.B.

5.50 x 17 TIRES (THR. '34)

WIRE WHEELS STD. (THROUGH '35)

(50-H.P. MODEL "4-40" IS RARE 4-CYL. SERIES.)*

OPTIONAL-STYLE SM. WHEELS

* = OFFICIALLY, A CONTINUATION OF MODEL B, BUT WITH 1933 STYLING.

3-WINDOW COUPE

DASH

HEAVIER GRILLE FOR 1934

5-WINDOW COUPE

PHAETON (AVAIL. THROUGH '36)

1934 MODEL HAS 2 HANDLES ON EACH SIDE OF HOOD.

CONT'D. 112" W.B. (THROUGH '40) 4.11 G.R.

34 "40" SERIES (STARTS 12-33)

(V-8s EXCLUSIVELY)

Ford

FINAL YEAR WITH WIRE WHEELS. 4.11 G.R.

35 "48" SERIES (STARTS 12-34)

'35 DASH RESEMBLES ILLUSTRATED '36 VIEW, BUT CENTER VERTICAL CHROME STRIPS ON '35 ARE FARTHER APART.

"68" SERIES (STARTS OCT., 1935) new POINTED GRILLE and STEEL ARTILLERY WHEELS. 4.11 OR 3.54 G.R.

NOW 3 HORIZ. STRIPS ACROSS HOOD LOUVRES, (INSTEAD OF 4 AS IN '35.)

36

FORD'S FINAL ROADSTER

5-PASS. CLUB CABRIOLET (NEW)

new "60" KNOWN AS MODEL 74, has 4.44 G.R.

85-H.P. 221-C.I.D. V-8 CONT'D., AND A NEW ECONOMY "60" SERIES ADDED (WITH 135.9 C.I.D. 60-H.P. SMALL V-8 ENGINE.)

new ALL-STEEL TOP

37 (STARTS NOV., 1936)

DAD and ME (AGE 4) and OUR '37 FORD

"85" KNOWN AS MODEL 78, has 3.78 G.R.

FORD

60 H.P. = "82-A"
85 H.P. = "81-A"

STANDARD 85 and 60 H.P.

STD.

DLX.

DE LUXE 85 H.P.

38

(STARTS NOV., 1937)

FROM 1938 THROUGH 1940, FORD'S STANDARD MODELS SOMEWHAT RESEMBLED (BUT WERE NOT IDENTICAL WITH) THE PREVIOUS YEAR'S DE LUXE MODEL.

112" W.B. (SINCE '33) SAME GEAR RATIOS SINCE '37.

DASH

STD. 85 and 60 H.P.

60 H.P. = "92-A"

85 H.P. = "91-A"

DE LUXE 85 H.P.

FORD BATTERIES and IGNITION ARE CHARACTERISTIC.

new HYDRAULIC BRAKES

39

(STARTS OCT., 1938)

"1924" MODEL (BUILT 1923)

FOX (1921-1923)

FOX MOTOR CO., PHILADELPHIA, PA.

6 CYLINDER, 50 H.P. AIR-COOLED, OVERHEAD VALVE, OVERHEAD CAM ENGINE

132" wheelbase
32 × 4½ TIRES
4.9 G.R.

DISPLACEMENT INCREASED FROM 248.9 TO 268.3 FOR 1923.

107

FRANKLIN

(1902-1934)

FRANKLIN
AUTOMOBILE COMPANY
SYRACUSE NEW YORK

17-20

SERIES 9

115" W.B.   4.33 GEAR RATIO

AIR-COOLED
6-CYL. OVERHEAD-VALVE ENGINE (199.1 C.I.D. THROUGH '27)

32 × 4

('21)   NEW "RADIATOR"

21-22

"DEMI-SEDAN" (below, left) AVAILABLE EARLY 1922.
(SERIES 10-A STARTS 9-1-22)

23-25

SERIES 10

"10-B" (1923) DASH GAUGES IN 3 RECTANGULAR PANELS

"DEMI-SEDAN"
1924 "10-B" HAS SIROCCO FAN. BALLOON TIRES OPTIONAL.
EARLY 1925 "10-C" STARTS JULY, 1924, WITH ALEMITE GASCOLATOR

STROMBERG CARBURETOR. 60 MILES PER HOUR

108

FRANKLIN

INTRODUCING
NEW DESIGNS *by de Causse*

25½-26

SERIES 11
(INTRODUCED MARCH, 1925)

COUPÉ

'25½ TO '28 MODELS
FREQUENTLY KNOWN AS
"DE CAUSSE" FRANKLINS.

STARTING LATE 1926, CLOSED
FRANKLINS HAVE NARROW FRONT
CORNER POSTS WITH "CLEAR VISION"
WINDSHIELD.

VICTORIA
COUPE

26-STYLE
COUPÉ CONTINUED ALSO

27

SERIES 11-B
TIRE SIZE CHANGED
FROM 31 x 5.25 TO
32 x 6.
NEW SWAN
MANIFOLD WITH SQUARE CORNERS.

(INTRODUCED JANUARY,
1927)

SPORT SEDAN

*The 25th
Anniversary
Franklin*

109

FRANKLIN

4 - WHEEL
LOCKHEED
HYDRAULIC BRAKES
WITH 14" DRUMS.

new 236.4 C.I.D.
46 H.P. @
2500 RPM

28

SERIES
12 - A
(INTRODUCED
OCT., 1927)

AIRMAN
"5" and "7"
HAVE, RESPECTIVELY,
119" and 128"
WHEELBASES.
(32 × 6 and
31 × 6.20
TIRES)

AIRMAN
S E R I E S

The new Franklin
AIRMAN LIMITED

SERIES 12-B
28½

WITH FENDER MIRRORS AND HEADLIGHT FOOT CONTROL

(INTRODUCED JULY, 1928)

WALKER BODIES,
AS
BEFORE

AC FUEL PUMP

FENDER
PARKING
LAMPS

29

"130," "135,"
"137"
(120, 125 and
132 - INCH
WHEELBASES)

1929 has SMALLER
CIRCLE ON
"RADIATOR"
TRIM

50 OR 60 - H.P. ENGINES

110

PRESSED STEEL CHASSIS FRAME

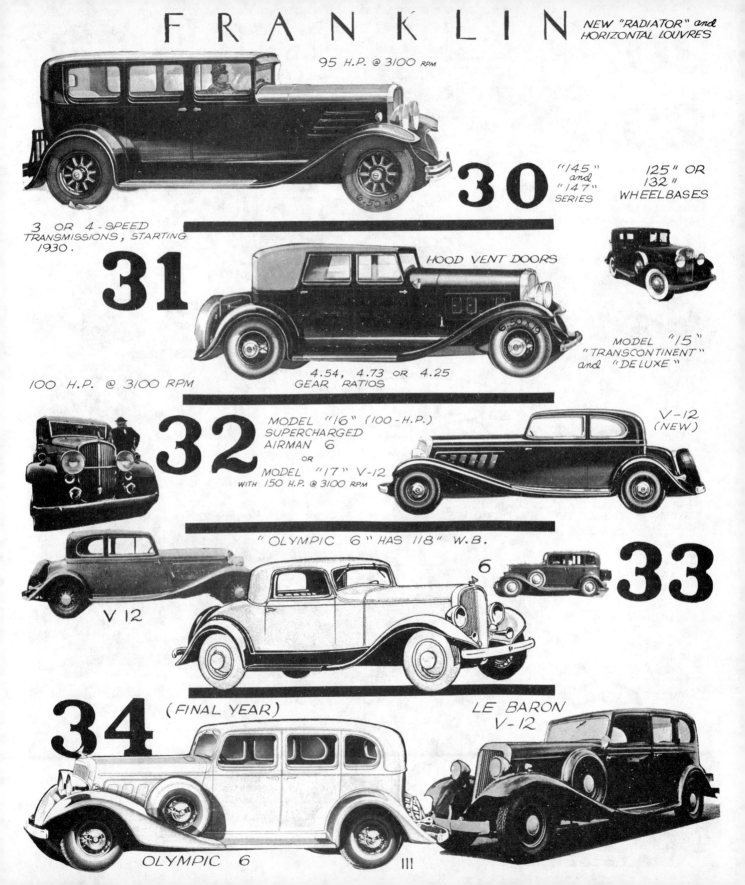

FRANKLIN

NEW "RADIATOR" and HORIZONTAL LOUVRES

95 H.P. @ 3100 RPM

30

"145" and "147" SERIES

125" OR 132" WHEELBASES

3 OR 4-SPEED TRANSMISSIONS, STARTING 1930.

31

HOOD VENT DOORS

MODEL "15" "TRANSCONTINENT" and "DELUXE"

100 H.P. @ 3100 RPM

4.54, 4.73 OR 4.25 GEAR RATIOS

32

MODEL "16" (100-H.P.) SUPERCHARGED AIRMAN 6
OR
MODEL "17" V-12 WITH 150 H.P. @ 3100 RPM

V-12 (NEW)

"OLYMPIC 6" HAS 118" W.B.

6

33

V 12

34 (FINAL YEAR)

LE BARON V-12

OLYMPIC 6

III

GARDNER
(1919-1931)

20 TO 23

112" W.B. "LIGHT 4"

32 × 3½

192.4 C.I.D.
35 H.P. @ 1800 RPM
4-CYLINDER LYCOMING ENGINE

NEW STYLE OF TOP BRACING IN '22, and 4.44 GEAR RATIO

32 × 4 TIRES AND 4.8 GEAR RATIO ON 1923 MODEL "5".

25

"8-A"

2-DOOR BROUGHAM

254.4 C.I.D.
63 H.P. @ 3000 RPM
NEW STRAIGHT-8 MODELS
FOR 1925 (ILLUSTRATED)
NEW 6-CYL. "6-A" ALSO (57 H.P.)
4-CYL. "5-C" CONTINUED with
44 H.P. @ 2200 RPM.

NEW 213.6 C.I.D. LYCOMING 4-CYL. '23 ENGINE HAS 5 (INSTEAD OF 2) MAIN BEARINGS. HAND BRAKE NOW CONTRACTS ON DRIVESHAFT. 43 H.P. @ 2150 RPM

"5-C" (4 CYL.)

24

"RADIO SPECIAL" SEDAN
(RADIO SPECIAL IN '23 WAS SPORT TOURING CAR.)

CARS BUILT 8-25 OR LATER ARE CONSIDERED "1926" MODELS, AND HAVE HOOD SUPPORT ROD.

6-CYL. LYCOMING ENG. HAS 207.1 C.I.D. ('25) 223.8 C.I.D. ('26-27)

27

"8-80"   "8-90"

26

'26 COUPE WINDSHIELD   NO MORE 6-CYL. GARDNERS UNTIL 1930 "136" MODEL.

"6-B" and "8-B" MODELS BEGIN JAN., '26 THESE MODELS, IF BUILT BETWEEN 8-26 AND 12-26, ARE "EARLY '27s."

WESTINGHOUSE IGNITION THROUGH 1924 (DELCO) REMY IGNITION 1925 and on

RADIATOR CAP MASCOT

28

(ALL 8-CYL.) LYCOMING ENG.

29

(INTRO. 9-28)

"120," "125," "130" HAVE 65, 85, 115 H.P.

"75"   225.7 C.I.D., 65 H.P.
"85"   246.7 " , 74 "
"95"   298.6 C.I.D. 115 H.P.

GARDNERS BUILT DURING LATTER MONTHS OF A YEAR ARE USUALLY CONSIDERED TO BE EARLY SERIES OF FOLLOWING YEAR'S MODELS.

'29 RADIATOR HIGHER, NARROWER THAN '28. BODIES BY CENTRAL

SPEED · STAMINA

GARDNER

6-CYL.
80 H.P.

FRONT-WHEEL-DRIVE MODEL ('30) WITH SLOPING FRONT END

"136" = 6 CYL., 185 C.I.D.
70 H.P. @ 3500 RPM
"140" = 8 CYL., 246.6 C.I.D.
90 H.P. @ 3300 RPM
"150" = 8 CYL., 298.6 C.I.D.
126 H.P. @ 3300 RPM

31

MODELS "136" "148" and "158"

30

"136" = 122" W.B.
"140" = 125 "
"150" = 130 "

ONLY THE FRONT-WHEEL-DRIVE MODEL HAS THE ABOVE UNIQUE RADIATOR DESIGN.

6 CYL. CONTINENTAL "11-E" ENGINE (248 C.I.D.) USED. LYCOMING "WR," "GR," "MDG" ENGINES IN 3 OTHER MODELS.

MECHANICAL SPECIFICATIONS AS BEFORE

"148" HAS 100 H.P.

MESH-TYPE CHROMED STONE GUARD IN FRONT OF RADIATOR.

GEARLESS STEAM CAR
(1921 - 1923)

GEARLESS MOTOR CORP., PITTSBURGH, PA.

GERONIMO

122" W.B. (1917 - 1921)

TOURING CAR ("6-A-45") ('20)
'20 MODEL BASICALLY UNCHANGED.
GERONIMO BUILT OWN BODIES STARTING 1919.

(6)

GERONIMO MOTOR CO., ENID, OKLA.
(LYCOMING ENGINE) ('18)
(230.1 C.I.D. RUTENBER ENGINE ALSO) DELCO IGN.

GLOBE

with "SUPREME" ENGINE
4 CYL., 178.9 C.I.D.
DELCO IGNITION

MODEL "B-10"
115" W.B., 4.9 G.R.
32 × 4 TIRES

(1921 - 1922)
GLOBE MOTORS CO., CLEVELAND, OHIO

GRAHAM-PAIGE

(1928 TO 1941, INCLUDING GRAHAM)

THE 3 GRAHAM BROTHERS PICTURED ON EMBLEM.

"614"

"619"

REPLACES *PAIGE*, JANUARY, 1928   HYDR. BRAKES NORTHEAST IGNITION SYSTEM

"610" IS LOWEST-PRICED SERIES, has 110½" W.B., 29 × 5.00 TIRES, 4.45 GEAR RATIO, 6 CYLS., 175 C.I.D., 52 H.P. @ 3100 RPM

"614" has 114" W.B. 29 × 5.25 TIRES, 3.9 G.R., 6 CYLS., 207 C.I.D., 71 H.P. @ 3200 RPM

28

"619" has 119" W.B., 29 × 5.50 TIRES, 6 CYLS., 288 C.I.D., 97 H.P. @ 3200 RPM

(AUG., 1928 — "EARLY 1929s" SIMILAR, BUT NO LONGER HAVE VERTICAL SEAMS ON BACKS OF BODIES.)

"629"

"629" has 129" W.B., 3.65 G.R., 31 × 6.00 TIRES, SAME ENGINE AS "619."

"835" has 135" W.B., 31 × 6.20 TIRES, 3.65 G.R., STRAIGHT-8 ENGINE, 322 C.I.D.

ALL BUT "610" have 4-SPEED TRANSMISSION; (AVAIL. ON ALL BUT SMALL MODELS THROUGH '31.)

ALL MODELS HAVE FUEL PUMP.

114

"835"

GRAHAM-PAIGE

"612" has
29 × 5.00 TIRES, 4.7
G.R., 190.8 C.I.D.,
62 H.P. @ 3200 RPM

BRIGGS BODY

"621"

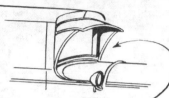

BEGINNING 1929,
DELCO-REMY
IGNITION ON ALL
GRAHAM-PAIGE
and GRAHAM CARS
TO FOLLOW.

VISOR BRACKETS
ON "612" and "615"

"615" has 5.50 × 19
TIRES, 3.9 G.R., 224 C.I.D.,
76 H.P. @
3200 RPM

"621" has 6.00 × 19 TIRES,
3.6 G.R., 288.6 C.I.D.,
97 H.P. @ 3200 RPM

AS IN '28,
MODEL NUMBERS
INDICATE NO. OF
CYLINDERS, and
WHEELBASE.

29

new THINNER
HOOD LOUVRES

"827" has
3.6 G.R.

"837" has
3.9 G.R.

"827"

"827" and "837"
have 6.50 × 19 TIRES,
STRAIGHT-8 ENGINES OF
322 C.I.D., 120 H.P. @ 3200
RPM

ROBBINS BODIES

(JULY 29, 1929, TO JANUARY, 1930)

EARLY **30**

3-SPOKE STEERING
WHEEL
NEW GLASS SUN VISOR

AFTER EARLY 1930,
"PAIGE" NAME RETAINED
ONLY FOR TAXIS AND
COMMERCIAL CARS.
JAN., 1930 = NEW STD. or
SPEC. 6, STD. or SPEC. 8, CUSTOM 8s

JAN., 1930 = 115, 122, 127, 137" W.B.,
66, 76, 96 (8-CYL.) or 120 H.P. (8-CYL.)

GRAHAM **30½**

QUALITY IS THE BEST POLICY

GRAHAM

STD. 6 (VISOR ON '31 MODEL)

8 HAS DOOR-TYPE
HOOD VENTS, FENDER
PARKING LIGHTS.

GRAHAM

31

(CHROME – PLATED WIRE WHEELS AVAILABLE ON 6 and 8- CYL. '31½ MODELS EXCEPT "PROSPERITY 6," THE '31½ ECONOMY MODEL OF 113" W.B., 207 C.I.D., 70 H.P.

(EARLY '32 MODELS BEGIN JULY, 1931, RESEMBLE '31 - 31½ GRAHAMS, BUT have OPTIONAL FREE – WHEELING.)

1932 SIX has 113" W.B. 5.50 × 17 TIRES, 207.1 C.I.D., 70 H.P. @ 3200 RPM, 4.45 G.R.

DASH (1932 Blue Streak)

The car is WIDER than it is high ('33)

224 C.I.D., 85-H.P. 6 IN 1933 ; 8-CYL. SPECS. LIKE '32.

32 - 33

'32 STD. and DLX. 8 SPECS. ALSO

'32 "BLUE STREAK" 8 (123" W.B.) HAS 1-PIECE BUMPER, 245.4 C.I.D., 90 H.P. @ 3400 RPM, 4.3 G.R., 6.00 × 17 TIRES

4.27 GEAR RATIO ON 1933 TO 1935 GRAHAMS.

34

6 = 116" W.B., 6.25 × 16 TIRES, 224 C.I.D., 85 H.P. @ 3400 RPM

8 = 123" W.B., 6.50 × 16 TIRES, 245.4 C.I.D., 95 H.P. @ 3400 RPM

CUSTOM 8 = 123" W.B., 7.00 × 16 TIRES, 265.4 C.I.D., 135 H.P. @ 4000 RPM (Supercharger avail.)

STD. 6 "74" = 111" W.B., 5.25 × 17 TIRES, 169.6 C.I.D., 70 H.P. @ 3500 RPM
SPECIAL 6 "73" = 116" W.B., 6.00 × 17 TIRES, 224 C.I.D., 85 H.P. @ 3400 RPM

35

(GRAHAM 8 HAS 2-PIECE REAR WINDOW.)

8 "72" = 123" W.B., 6.50 × 16 TIRES, 245.4 C.I.D., 95 H.P. @ 3400 RPM
Supercharged 8 "75" = 123" W.B., 7.00 × 16 TIRES, 265.4 C.I.D., 140 H.P. @ 4000 RPM

NO MORE 8-CYL. GRAHAMS AFTER 1935.

ALL 1935 GRAHAMS HAVE HORIZONTAL HOOD LOUVRES.

116

GRAHAM

6-CYLINDER MODELS ONLY (THROUGH '41)

36

"CRUSADER"

"80" CRUSADER 111" W.B., 6.00 × 16 TIRES 4.55 G.R., 169.6 C.I.D., 70 H.P. @ 3500 RPM

"90 CAVALIER" 115" W.B., 6.00 × 16 TIRES, 4.2 G.R., 217.8 C.I.D., 85 H.P. @ 3300 RPM
("90-A" STARTS 3-36, has 4.45 G.R., 199.1 C.I.D.)

"110" Supercharged 115" W.B., 6.25 × 16 TIRES, 4.2 G.R., 217.8 C.I.D. 112 H.P. @ 4000 RPM

"85 CRUSADER" 111" W.B., 5.25 × 17 or 6.00 × 16 TIRES, 4.55 G.R., 169.6 C.I.D., 70 H.P. @ 3500 RPM (INDIVIDUAL HOOD PORTS with TRIANGLE CHROME GRILLES)*

(1936-1937 "CRUSADERS" RETAIN 1935 BODY STYLING.)

"95 CAVALIER" 116" W.B., 6.00 × 16 TIRES, 4.45 G.R., 199.1 C.I.D., 85 H.P. @ 3800 RPM

37

* '37 "CRUSADER" HOOD LOUVRES DO NOT EXTEND INTO GRILLE AS ON '36.

"116 SUPERCHARGER" 116" W.B., 6.25 × 16 TIRES, 4.27 G.R., 199.1 C.I.D., 106 H.P. @ 4000 RPM

"120 CUSTOM SUPERCHARGER" 120" W.B. (COUPES - 116") 4.27 G.R., 217.8 C.I.D. 116 H.P. @ 4000

6.25 × 16 TIRES (6.00 × 16 ON '39 "96" SERIES)

38-39

STD. and SPEC. "96" have 90 H.P. @ 3600 RPM

SUPERCHARGED CLUB SEDAN ('39)

('38)

RUNNING-BOARDS NOT FEATURED ON 1939 GRAHAMS.

FLOOR OR STEERING-COLUMN GEARSHIFT CONTROL IN '39.

6 CYLS., 217.8 C.I.D. 120" W.B., 4.27 G.R. (ALL '38s - 39s)

"SPIRIT OF MOTION" STYLING

SPEC. and CUSTOM **"97" SUPERCHARGER** have 116 H.P. @ 4000 RPM

GRANT 6

(OWN 6-CYL. O.H.V. ENG. (198.9 C.I.D., IMPROVED FOR '20.)

GRANT MOTOR CAR CORP., FINDLAY, OHIO (1913-1922)

21

('20 MODEL MECH. RE-DESIGNED FROM '19. '20 SEDAN DOES NOT HAVE COWL LIGHTS AS ON '21 MODEL SHOWN.) →

22

(1922-1926)
GRAY MOTOR CORP., DETROIT

22

4 CYLINDERS (OWN ENGINE)
165.1 C.I.D.
21 H.P. @ 1500 RPM ('25 RATING)

SAN FRANCISCO TO NEW YORK
OFFICIAL ECONOMY TEST
SANCTION AMERICAN AUTOMOBILE ASSOCIATION

100" WHEELBASE (THROUGH '23)
30 x 3½ TIRES (THROUGH '25)
3.9 GEAR RATIO
WESTINGHOUSE IGNITION (THROUGH '25)

23

100" OR 103½" W.B. IN '24
TOP SPEED ONLY 46 MILES PER HOUR

24

"N" OR "O" MODELS

'25 AND '26 SIMILAR-LOOKING TO '24, BUT LATE '24 GRAY HAS FUEL TANK AT REAR. BALLOON TIRES AVAIL. ON '25 MODEL, AND 104" W.B. (MODEL "O")

(105" WHEELBASE, 29 x 4.40 BALLOON TIRES, 4-WHEEL BRAKES ON '26 GRAY (MODEL "S" WITH Auto Lite IGN.)

GRAY LIGHT CAR

(NOT AFFILIATED WITH GRAY CAR ILLUSTRATED ABOVE.)

LONGMONT, COLO. (1920)
ONLY 2 CARS COMPLETED.

1 AND 2-CYL. HARLEY-DAVIDSON MOTORCYCLE ENGINES

HALLADAY

1921 = 116" W.B., 6 CYL. RUT. ENG.

1922 = 115" W.B., 4 + 6 CYLINDERS

HALLADAY MOTORS CORPORATION
NEWARK, OHIO, U.S.A.

(1918 — 1922)

4.9 G.R., 32 × 4½ TIRES ON ALL '21-'23 MODELS

Handley-Knight

EARLY '23 7-PASS.

**HANDLEY MOTORS, INC.,
KALAMAZOO, MICH.
(1921 — 1923)**
NAME SHORTENED TO HANDLEY DURING '23.
NEW MODEL →

'23 "6-60" HAS 125" W.B., 268.4 MIDWEST ENG.

6 CYL. O.H.V. ('23)

125" W.B.

('22 = ALUMINUM REPL. LINOLEUM ON RUNNING BOARDS)

240.6 C.I.D., 4-CYL. KNIGHT ENG. (THROUGH '22 "B" SERIES)

21-23

'23 "6-40" HAS 195.6 FALLS ENG., 115" W.B.

23½

1920 MODEL "54" has 119" W.B.

121" W.B., 1921-1924

HANSON 6

**HANSON MOTOR CO.,
ATLANTA, GA.
(1917 - 1923)**

(32 × 4 TIRES, 4.66 G.R.)

MODEL "66" (1923-1924) HAS CONTINENTAL "8-R" ENGINE (241.6 C.I.D.)

EMBLEM →

HANSON

('20)

('21)

MODEL "60" (1921-1922) HAS 224 C.I.D., 6-CYL. CONTINENTAL ENGINE.

FINAL '24 MODEL (INTRO. 1923)

HARRIS 6

WISCONSIN AUTOMOTIVE CORP., MENASHA, WIS.

23 ONLY

HAYNES 20

THE HAYNES AUTOMOBILE COMPANY,

Kokomo, Indiana

IN PRODUCTION 1904 — 1925

ORIGINALLY "HAYNES-APPERSON"

1920 GEAR RATIOS : 4.42 ("45") 4.06 ("46")

'20 BATTERY UNDER FLOOR (INSTEAD OF UNDER SEAT AS IN 1919.)

127" W.B.

HAYNES-BUILT ENGINES : "45" 6-CYL. 288.6 C.I.D. (L-HEAD) OR "46" V-12 356.4 C.I.D. (O.H.V.)

HAYNES

21

NEW, LOWER-PRICE "50" has 121" W.B.

"47" has 132" W.B., 4.77 G.R., 34 x 4½ TIRES

BOTH "50" and "47" have 6-CYL., 288.6 C.I.D. ENGINES (THIS DISPL. RETAINED ON '22-'23 "55.")

22

3/4 RUNNING BOARDS AND SIDE-MOUNT SPARES ARE NEW ON "55." ("75" GETS THEM 6-15-22.)

"55" has 121" W.B., 33 x 4 TIRES, 4.11 G.R., 50 H.P., STARTER BUTTON ON DASH.
"75" has 132" W.B., 34 x 4½ TIRES, 16" BRAKE DRUMS, 4.60 G.R., 299 C.I.D., 75 H.P. @ 2500 RPM

EARLY '22 MODEL = HAS BOWL-SHAPED HEADLIGHTS, LONG RUNNING BOARDS

"75" 7-PASS. SEDAN

DRUM HEADLIGHTS INTRODUCED DURING 1922 SEASON. (2-22)

4-PASSENGER TOURISTER

ALUMINUM BODIES

"75" 2-PASSENGER BLUE RIBBON SPEEDSTER (TOP SPEED: 75)

5-PASS. BROUGHAM

"75" HAS NEW 3-PIECE REMOVABLE CYL. HEAD.

7-PASS. TOURING CAR

120

"MOTOR AGE" MAGAZINE LISTED A V-12 MODEL "48" (132" W.B.) IN SPRING, 1922.

23 HAYNES ("55" and "75" REPLACED BY "57" and "77" DURING 1923.)

The New, 1923 Haynes 55 Sport Coupelet, 3 Pass.

The New, 1923 Haynes 55 Sport Roadster, 2 Passengers

32 × 4½ TIRES CHANGED TO 33 × 5.77 DURING 1924.

"60" METROPOLITAN SEDAN

"60" IS ONLY SER. FOR 1924-1925.)

"60" TOURING (STARTS 8-23)

24

21" W.B., 274.2 C.I.D. 6 CYLS.

4.41 G.R.

50 H.P. @ 2400 RPM (MOST SPECS. AS IN '24)

25

120" W.B. ON 4-CYL. CARS

H.C.S. MOTOR CO., INDIANAPOLIS

H.C.S. (1920-1925)

126"-W.B. 288.6 C.I.D. 6-CYL. ALSO AVAIL., 1923-25 (MIDWEST ENG. IN EARLY MODELS.)

277.1 C.I.D., 4-CYL., O.H.V. WEIDELY ENGINE WITH LANCHESTER VIBRATION DAMPENER

SERIES 3 (1920-1922)

SERIES 6

5-PASS. TOURING

SERIES 4 (1922-1925)

HEINE-VELOX V-12 (SAN FRANCISCO, 1921)
148" W.B.

DRIVURSELF

HERTZ YELLOW CAB MFG. CO., CHICAGO (1925-1928)

BUILT FOR RENTAL USE

Hertz Drivurse'f, successor to the old-time livery stable.

('25)

MODEL "D-1" has 114" W.B., 31 × 4 TIRES ('25) 30 × 5.77 ('26 ON) 4.72 GEAR RATIO 195.6 C.I.D. (230.1 C.I.D., '27) 6-CYLINDER CONTINENTAL ENGINE 49 H.P. @ 2500 (61 H.P. @ 2600 RPM, '27) DELCO IGNITION

(REPLACES 1924 AMBASSADOR "D-1")

HOLMES
CANTON, OHIO (1918-1923)

126" W.B. 4.9 G.R. **21-23**

OWN AIR-COOLED ENGINE 6 CYLINDERS, O.H.V. (259.8 C.I.D.)

20

34 × 4½ TIRES

EISEMANN IGN. (THROUGH '23)

SERIES 4 (RESTYLED FOR 1921)

121

(1909 – 1957)

HUDSON

HUDSON MOTOR CAR COMPANY
DETROIT, MICHIGAN

Look for the White Triangle

HUDSON SUPER SIX

(6 CYL., 288.6 C.I.D. ENGINE, 1914 - 1929)

76 H.P. (SINCE '16)

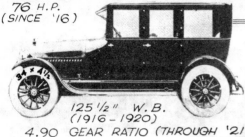

20-21

125 ½" W.B. (1916 - 1920)

4.90 GEAR RATIO (THROUGH '21

126" W.B. (1921 THROUGH 1924)

76 H.P. @ 2450 RPM

76 H.P. @ 2400 RPM

new 4.81 GEAR RATIO
FRONT APRONS EXTEND TO
FRONT END OF SPRING HANGERS;
SPLASH APRON BETWEEN
SPRING HORNS.

(PRESSED STEEL DOOR JAMBS REPLACE WOOD.)

22

The Coach (NEW)

MAY 1, 1922 = DRUM HEADLIGHTS, FLAT EDGE ON BODY, BOSCH DISTRIBUTOR, CURTAINS IN DOORS.

BLUE UPHOLSTERY IN COACH UNTIL SEPT. 1922; THEN CHANGE TO GRAY UPH.

(9-22: 7-PASS. SEDAN has SLANTED WINDSHIELD)

4.45 GEAR RATIO (THROUGH '28)
75 H.P. @ 2450 RPM (THROUGH '24)

LATE '23 COACHES UPHOLSTERED IN BROWN.

HUDSON'S WHITE TRIANGLE INSIGNIA IS EASY TO IDENTIFY.

SPECIAL SPEEDSTER

(4-PASS. SPEEDSTER IS SPORT TOURING.)

23

4-PASS. and 7-PASS. TOURING CARS

7-PASS. SEDAN BLT. FIRST HALF OF '23
5-PASS. SEDAN   "   LAST   "   "

ALUMINUM BODY BY BIDDLE and SMART

122

THE FINEST HUDSON EVER BUILT

HUDSON

15½" BRAKE DRUMS

34 × 4½ TIRES

INTERIOR ("CABRIOLET" COUPE) ←

24

117-615

NEW RIDGED FENDERS

LIMOUSINE

7- PASS. →

25

33 × 6.20
(BALLOON TIRES)

76 H.P. @ 2800 RPM
(THROUGH '26)

25½-26
(NEW WINDSHIELD)

The Brougham
(A NEW HUDSON MODEL)

HAS ALUMINUM BODY PANELS, LEATHER-COVERED REAR QUARTER SECTIONS.

26½ BROUGHAM HAS ROOF-VISOR →

33 × 6

123

HUDSON

COACH

F-HEAD ENGINE ; 4-WHEEL BRAKES

27

95 H.P. @ 3100 RPM

BROUGHAM

WHEELBASES
118" = STANDARD ; 127½" = CUSTOM

33 × 6 TIRES

JULY 1, 1927 = '27½
MODELS . REDESIGNED
CYL. HEAD, ETC.

31 × 6.00 TIRES

CONVERTIBLE
LANDAU SEDAN

RADIATOR SHUTTERS NOW VERTICAL.

ALL GAUGES UNDER
ONE LONG PANEL,
INDIRECTLY
LIGHTED.

GEAR RATIOS
4.08 (S)
4.45 (O)

28

MODELS "S" and "O"
80-90 H.P.

31 × 6.00 TIRES

(MURPHY BODY)

(BRIGGS BODY)

WIRE WHEELS STANDARD
ON LONG -
WHEELBASE
MODELS.

122½" OR 139" WHEELBASE
92 H.P. @ 3200 RPM

DASH

7-PASS. SEDAN

29

"THE
GREATER
HUDSON 6"

(BODY BY
HUDSON)

4.08 GEAR RATIO
TOP SPEED = OVER 80

5-PASS. CLUB SEDAN
(BODY BY
BIDDLE and SMART)

124

30 HUDSON

8 CYLS., 213.8 C.I.D.
84 H.P. @ 3400 RPM

(ALL MODELS HAD NEW
STRAIGHT-8 ENGINE.)

RADIATOR
FILLER
UNDER
HOOD

119" WHEELBASE

MODERNISTIC DASH
4.63 GEAR RATIO (THROUGH '32)
5.50 × 18 TIRES (THROUGH '31)

119" OR 126" W.B. (THROUGH '32)
233.7 C.I.D.

87 H.P. @ 3600 RPM

31

SOME 1931s
HAVE 1930-STYLE
HEADLIGHTS,
COWL LIGHTS and
WHEELS.

1931 7-PASS. PHAETON
HAS 1930-STYLE DASH.

DASH

CLUB SEDAN

31½

HUDSON

HUDSON EIGHT COACH
Five Passengers . . . . 119" Wheelbase
$1025 F. O. B. DETROIT

HUDSON EIGHT BUSINESS COUPE
Two Passengers . . . . 119" Wheelbase
$995 F. O. B. DETROIT

HUDSON EIGHT TOWN SEDAN
Five Passengers . . . . 119" Wheelbase
$1050 F. O. B. DETROIT

32

'32 INTERIOR

HUDSON EIGHT STANDARD SEDAN
Five Passengers . . . . 119" Wheelbase
$1095 F. O. B. DETROIT

HUDSON EIGHT SUBURBAN
Five Passengers . . . . 126" Wheelbase
$1275 F. O. B. DETROIT

HUDSON EIGHT SEDAN
Seven Passengers . . . . 132" Wheelbase
$1595 F. O. B. DETROIT

NEW GRILLE

PACEMAKER—Hudson Eight Standard Sedan for five passengers $1095 F. O. B. Detroit

254.4 C.I.D.   101 H.P. @ 3600 RPM   (THROUGH '33)

"STANDARD," "STERLING," and
"MAJOR" SERIES   (119, 126, 132" W.B.)

Hudson bodies, strong, smart and luxuriously finished, are built in Hudson's own $15,000,000 body plant. They realize in full those qualities which make steel the modern material for all structural duty in this day of high-power engine capacities and improved highways inviting to speed and demanding safety. The entire front and framework of the Hudson-built body shown here is welded into a single rattle-proof unit of unusual strength.

17 x 6.00 TIRES   (17 x 6.50 ON "MAJOR")   126

HUDSON

VACUUM CLUTCH
FREE WHEELING

SUPER 6 = ('33 ONLY) 193.1 C.I.D. 4.64 G.R. (6 OR 8)
73 H.P. @ 3200 RPM
5.25 × 18 TIRES 113" W.B.

PACEMAKER
EIGHT = 119" OR 132" W.B.
6.00 × 17 TIRES
"MAJOR" HAS 6.50 × 17 TIRES

33 →

'34 DASH SIMILAR TO '35, BUT ASH TRAY IS ON GLOVE-BOX DOOR (PLUS OTHER MINOR DIFFERENCES)

"LTS" CHALLENGER ECONOMY MODEL STARTS JUNE, 1934, WITHOUT "AXLEFLEX" SPRINGING, DRAFTLESS VENTILATION, OR INSIDE SUN VISORS.

34

(8-CYL. ONLY;
NO HUDSON 6
IN 1934.)
108 H.P. @ 3800 RPM

6.25 OR 6.50 × 16 TIRES

116" OR 123" WHEELBASE
"LT" = STD. "LL" = STD.
"LU" = DLX. "LLU" = DLX.

DELUXE MODELS HAVE RADIO

"GH" BIG 6 HAS 212 C.I.D., 93 H.P. @ 3800 RPM (THROUGH '36)

BIG 6 HAS 116" W.B.

4.11 GEAR RATIO (THROUGH '38)

35

8 = 113 H.P. @ 3800 (THROUGH '36)

NEW, OPTIONAL "ELECTRIC HAND" GEARSHIFT on STEERING COLUMN

8

"HT" SPECIAL 8
and
"HU" DELUXE 8
have 117" W.B.

"HHU"
CUSTOM 8
has 124" W.B.,
AS DO "HTL"
and "HUL"

DASH

IGNITION LOCK — WINDSHIELD REGULATOR — RADIO — STARTER BUTTON — GLOVE BOX
GENERATOR SIGNAL
LIGHTING SWITCH OR SIGNAL — FLOOD LAMP SWITCH
AUTOMATIC CLUTCH CONTROL — ASH TRAY — COWL VENTILATOR CONTROL — INSTRUMENT LAMP CONTROL AND SWITCH

127

HUDSON

NEW BODY

6 HAS 120" W.B.

36

8 HAS 120" OR 127" W.B.

" W.B.

HYDRAULIC BRAKES

OVAL SPEEDOMETER
IN CENTER OF DASH

"CUSTOM" STEERING
WHEEL HAS 3 SETS OF
4 CHROME-PLATED SPOKES.

6 HAS 101 H.P.
@ 4000 RPM
(THROUGH '39)
122" W.B.
(THROUGH '39)

8 HAS 122 H.P.
@ 4200 RPM
(THROUGH '39)
122" OR 129"
← 8   W.B.
(THROUGH
'39)

COUNTRY CLUB
8

37

New **HUDSON** *Eight*
122 AND 129-INCH WHEELBASE . . . 122 HORSEPOWER

HUDSON
TERRAPLANE

HUDSON
SIX

'38
"112"
HAS
83 H.P.

38

"112" HAS FRONT-HINGED
HOOD. →

OFFICIAL AAA CAR
HUDSON 112

128

HUDSON

LOWER - PRICED "112" MODELS HAVE SEPERATE HEADLIGHTS AND DIFFERENT GRILLE. →

"112" (112" W.B.) ("90" SERIES)

6 CYLS., 175 C.I.D.
86 H.P. @ 4000 RPM

"PACEMAKER 91" and "92"

6 = 118" W.B.
96 H.P. @ 3900 RPM

COUNTRY CLUB 6 = ("93")
122" W.B., 101 H.P. @ 4000 RPM

NEW DASH-LOCKING SAFETY HOOD

HOOD HINGED AT FRONT... WIND CAN'T LIFT IT ...

LOCKED BY LEVER INSIDE CAR: BATTERY AND ENGINE PARTS THEFT-PROOF

39

NEW DASH AND STEERING COLUMN GEARSHIFT ←

NEW CARRY-ALL LUGGAGE COMPARTMENT

DASH (IN "COUNTRY CLUB" model)

4.1 GEAR RATIO

NEW AIRFOAM CUSHIONS

Airfoam is standard in new Hudson Country Club and Convertible models, optional at small cost in all other 1939 Hudsons.

also
8 - CYLINDER
"95" COUNTRY CLUB
"97" CUSTOM
COUNTRY CLUB
122" or 129" W.B.

6

Huffman 6

(1920-1925)

HUFFMAN BROS. MOTOR CO., ELKHART, INDIANA

$1895
f. o. b. Elkhart

6 - CYL., 224 C.I.D.
CONTINENTAL ENGINE

120" W.B.

1921 = MODEL "R"

1923 = 241.5 C.I.D., 4.5 G.R

FINAL HUFFMANS HAVE HYDRAULIC BRAKES, DISC WHEELS.

MODEL "W" ('20)

129

HUPMOBILE

Hupp Motor Car Corporation
Detroit, Michigan

(1908 – 1940)

4 CYL.
182.5 C.I.D.
(THROUGH '25)

112" W.B. and
4.87 G.R. (THROUGH '24)

HIGHER RADIATOR AND
LOWER RUNNING-BOARDS
THAN ON 1919 MODEL.

20

"R-3"

32 × 4
TIRES
(THROUGH '24)

Hupmobile

5-PASSENGER
TOURING CAR

OPEN CARS
NOW FEATURE
OUTSIDE DOOR HANDLES

2-PASSENGER
ROADSTER

21

CLOSED CARS ADOPT SUN VISORS
WINDSHIELD WIPERS ADDED IN 1921

OLD-
STYLE
TAIL-LIGHT
RE-INTRODUCED.

FIRST YEAR WITH STEWART SPEEDOMETER.
EARLY MODELS HAVE TAN-LINED TOP AND
HAND ADJUSTMENT OF HEADLIGHT FOCUS.
LATER MODELS HAVE TWEED-LINED TOP
AND SCREWDRIVER
ADJUSTMENT OF
HEADLIGHT
FOCUS.

ROADSTER-COUPÉ

(INTRO.
DEC.,
1921)

22

FIRST YEAR FOR WINDOW
CRANKS IN CLOSED CAR DOORS.

COUPE TRUNK
DETAILS

23

"SPECIAL" MODELS HAVE NICKEL PLATING,
DRUM HEADLIGHTS, DELUXE EQUIPMENT

FRONT RIGHT SEAT FOLDS
UNDER
DASH
WHEN
NOT
IN USE.

Coupe Model RY · Two-Passenger

Special Roadster Model RRS

Coupe Model RK · Four-Passenger

HUPMOBILE

24

NEW 115" WHEELBASE

DRUM HEADLIGHTS ON __ALL__ MODELS

3 DOOR CLUB SEDAN ('24 and '25)

ONLY 1 DOOR ON LEFT SIDE.

"R-14" **4**

(FINAL 4-CYL. MODEL (R-14) HAS 4.9 G.R.) 31 x 5.25 TIRES)

FOURS AND EIGHTS

25

STRAIGHT-8 IS NEW FOR 1925.

"E-1" **8**

118¼" W.B.   4.63 G.R. 246.7 C.I.D.

HYDRAULIC BRAKES ON NEW 8.

"A-1" # SIX

114" W.B. (THROUGH '30)

195 C.I.D. 50 H.P. @ 3000 RPM

30 x 5.25 TIRES

FRENCH-STYLE ROOF VISOR NOW AVAILABLE ON __ALL__ CLOSED HUPMOBILES.

26

"E-2" EIGHT

"E-2" 8 BERLINE SIMILAR TO ILLUS. SEDAN, BUT HAS LIMOUSINE-TYPE CLEAR GLASS (PARTITION) BACK OF DRIVER'S SEAT.

NEW 268.7 C.I.D. 63 H.P. @ 2700 RPM NEW 125" W.B.

HUPMOBILE

"A-2" (8-26)
"A-3" (I-27, WITH DASH GAUGES IN ONE CENTER PANEL)

MODEL A SERIES
6 CYLS. 195.6 C.I.D.

4.9 GEAR RATIO
114" W.B.

27

7-PASS.

125" W.B.

MODEL E
8 CYLS. 268.7 C.I.D.
67 H.P. @ 2800 RPM
4.63 GEAR RATIO

CUSTOM BODIES USUALLY BY DIETRICH. SPECIAL BODIES HAVE ADVANCE STYLING.

BROUGHAM

30 × 5.25 TIRES

(8-27= "A-5" CONSIDERED "EARLY '28," has TRANSMISSION LOCK LIGHT.)

LATE MODELS HAVE IMPROVED "HYPER-EXPANSION" ENGINES.

27½

NEW 6 STARTS OCTOBER, 1927

NEW EMBLEM

ENGINE (6)

Six
(A-6)

28

NEW BODIES BY MURRAY

(COMPLETELY RESTYLED)

"CENTURY" MODELS (A, M)

("E-4" RETAINS 1927 STYLING AND ROOF-VISOR,) BUT HAS DOUBLE INTAKE MANIFOLD.)

211.6 C.I.D.
57 H.P.

4.73 GEAR RATIO

29 × 5.50

DISC WHEELS AVAILABLE, AS WELL AS WOOD OR WIRE WHEELS.

(M) 8
268.6 C.I.D.
80 H.P.

31 × 6.00

8-CYL. "M-8" INSTRUMENT PANEL

4.36 G.R.

120" W.B.

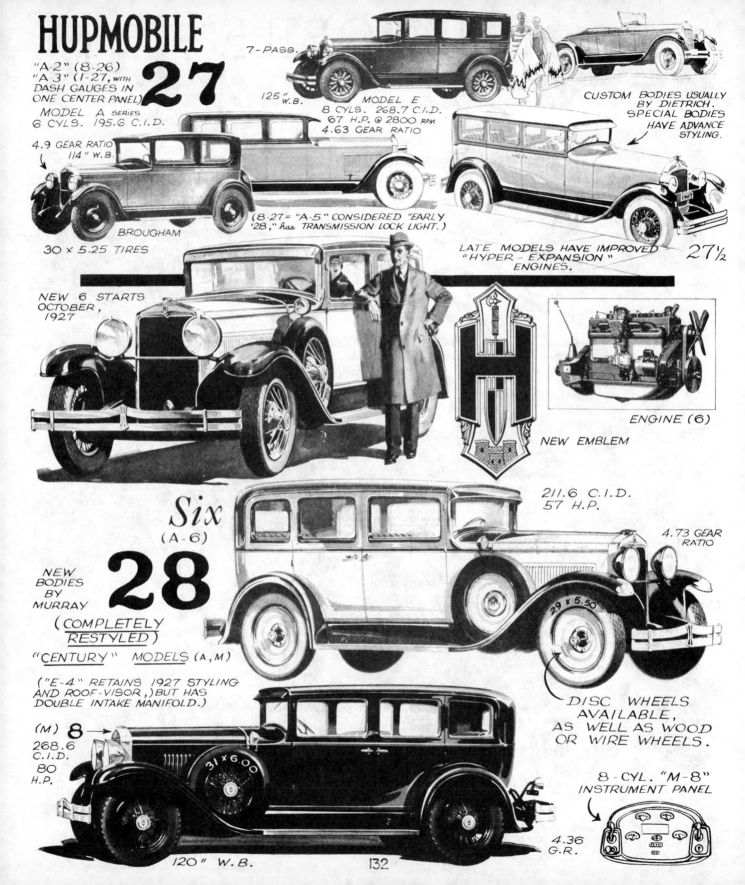

132

HUPMOBILE
1929 "CENTURY"
SIX & EIGHT

BODIES BY MURRAY,
EXCEPT FOR
BAKER-RAULANG
BODIES ON "M"
TOWN SEDAN, 7-PASS.
SEDAN, and LIMOUSINE.

29

CURVED AND
GROOVED FRONT SPLASH GUARD
EXTENDS OVER
SPRING HORNS.

SPECIFICATIONS SIMILAR
TO 1928, BUT 1929
SIX HAS 4.7 and other
GEAR RATIOS; "M" has 4.4

INSTRUMENT PANEL

BRONZE ("M")   SILVER ("A")
OXIDIZED-FINISH

HUPMOBILE

EXAGGERATED ARTIST'S RENDERING

CENTURY·SIX

MODEL "S"
70 H.P. @ 3200
4.7 G.R.
211.6 C.I.D.
5.25 × 19 TIRES
(BEGINS 8-10-29)

6
WOOD, WIRE, OR DISC WHEELS AS BEFORE

The 1930 Hupmobile Eight Coupe showing new peaked deck and top

Instrument Panel

EARLY "S" SIX, WITH DISC WHEELS, LOW-PLACED HOOD LOUVRES

8

Radiator Cap   Outside Door-Handle

Inside Light

Inside Door Molding

30

MODEL "C"
8 CYL.
100 H.P. @
3200 RPM
268.6 C.I.D.
4.55 G.R.
6.00 × 19 TIRES
(SUPERSEDES "M," 9-18-29)

MODEL "H"
8 CYL.
133 H.P. @
3400 RPM
365.6 C.I.D.
4.07 G.R.
125" W.B.
6.50 × 19 TIRES

Fender Parking Light   Smoking Set

Inside Door-Handles

137"-W.B. MODEL "U" HAS ENGINE LIKE MODEL "H."

NO VISOR

EIGHT

CENTURY 6

'31 SPECS. SIMILAR TO '30, BUT NEW "L" has 8-CYL., 240.2 C.I.D., 90 H.P. @ 3200 RPM

31

wheelbases:
"S-2" CENT. 6   113½
"L"   " 8   118
"C"   121
"H"   125
"U"   137

(FREE-WHEELING AVAIL. IN ALL MODELS AS OF 1-31.)

134

HUPMOBILE

STARTING '32, 1ST DIGIT OF MODEL NO. INDICATES YEAR; OTHER 2 DIGITS ARE W.B.

"2/6" (B)

6 CYL., 228.1 C.I.D.
75 H.P. @ 3200 RPM
4.54 G.R.

FREE-WHEELING AVAIL.

32

"222" (F)
8 CYL., 250.7 C.I.D.
93 H.P. @ 3200 RPM

8 DIFFERENT MODEL SERIES!

OTHER 1932 MODELS:

"214" (S) 6
(211.5 C.I.D., 70 H.P.)

"218" (L) 6
(240.2 C.I.D., 90 H.P.)

"221" (C) 8
(268.6 C.I.D., 100 H.P.)

"225" (H) 8
(365.6 C.I.D., 133 H.P.)

"226" (I) 8
(279.9 C.I.D., 103 H.P. ------ and "237" (U) 8 (SAME BIG ENGINE AS "225")

GEAR RATIOS VARY FROM 3.92 TO 4.7

SHORT FRONT FENDERS, NEW STYLING

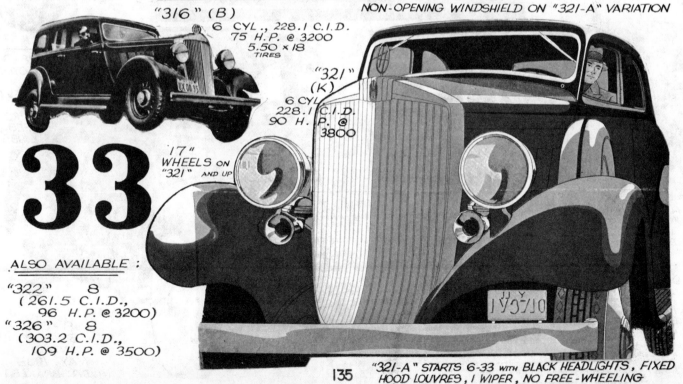

"316" (B)
6 CYL., 228.1 C.I.D.
75 H.P. @ 3200
5.50 × 18 TIRES

NON-OPENING WINDSHIELD ON "321-A" VARIATION

"321" (K)
6 CYL.
228.1 C.I.D.
90 H.P. @ 3800

33

"17" WHEELS ON "321" AND UP

ALSO AVAILABLE:

"322" 8
(261.5 C.I.D., 96 H.P. @ 3200)

"326" 8
(303.2 C.I.D., 109 H.P. @ 3500)

"321-A" STARTS 6-33 WITH BLACK HEADLIGHTS, FIXED HOOD LOUVRES, 1 WIPER, NO FREE-WHEELING

HUPMOBILE

34

ACTUAL PHOTO

STANDARD 6

GLAMORIZED ADVERTISING ILLUSTRATION

ENGINES RANGE FROM 224 C.I.D. 6 (80 H.P.) TO 303.2 C.I.D. 8 (115 H.P.)

"421-J"

MODELS "417-W," "KK-421-A," "K-421," "421-J," (SIXES) "422," "426," "427-T" (EIGHTS)

(1ST and 2ND SERIES)

NEW "AERODYNAMIC" MODELS ARE STREAMLINED.

35

"518-D" 6 CYLS.

118" W.B.

INTRO. FEB., 1935

REAR VIEW OF "518-D" (WITH HYDRAULIC BRAKES)

91 TO 120 H.P. 4.5 G.R. ON MOST

(MECHANICAL BRAKES ON (MODELS INTRO. OCT., 1934 : "517-W" (6) "521-J" (6) "527-T" (8)

8-CYL. "521-O" INTRO. MAY, 1935 (HYDR. BRAKES)

HUPMOBILE
35 (CONT'D.)

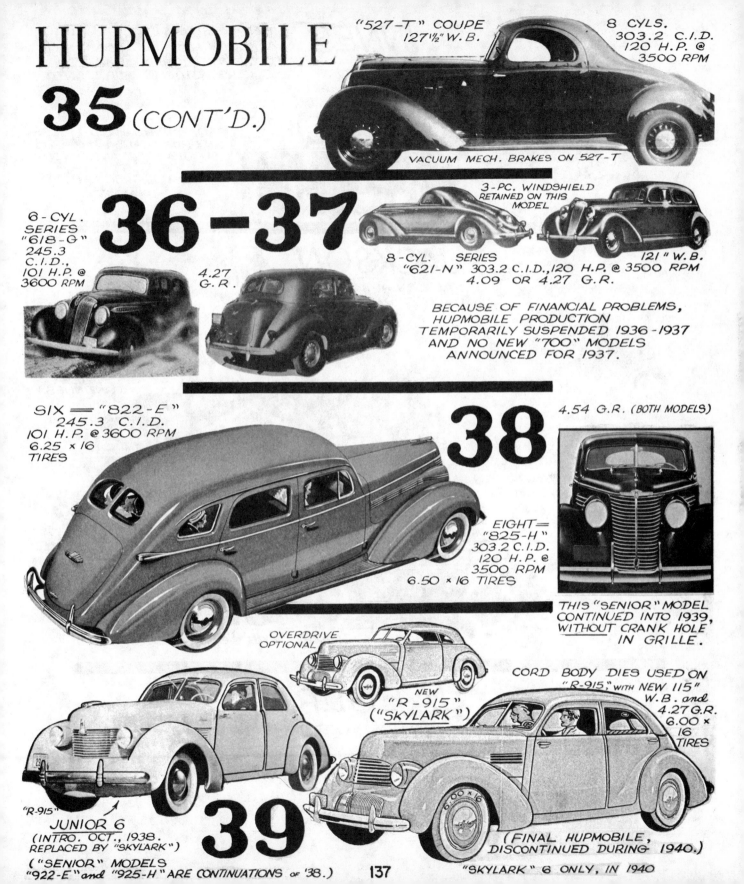

"527-T" COUPE 127½" W.B.

8 CYLS. 303.2 C.I.D. 120 H.P. @ 3500 RPM

VACUUM MECH. BRAKES ON 527-T

36-37

6 - CYL. SERIES "618-G" 245.3 C.I.D., 101 H.P. @ 3600 RPM

4.27 G.R.

3-PC. WINDSHIELD RETAINED ON THIS MODEL

8-CYL. SERIES "621-N" 303.2 C.I.D., 120 H.P. @ 3500 RPM 4.09 OR 4.27 G.R.

121" W.B.

BECAUSE OF FINANCIAL PROBLEMS, HUPMOBILE PRODUCTION TEMPORARILY SUSPENDED 1936-1937 AND NO NEW "700" MODELS ANNOUNCED FOR 1937.

38

SIX = "822-E" 245.3 C.I.D. 101 H.P. @ 3600 RPM 6.25 × 16 TIRES

4.54 G.R. (BOTH MODELS)

EIGHT = "825-H" 303.2 C.I.D. 120 H.P. @ 3500 RPM 6.50 × 16 TIRES

THIS "SENIOR" MODEL CONTINUED INTO 1939, WITHOUT CRANK HOLE IN GRILLE.

OVERDRIVE OPTIONAL

NEW "R-915" ("SKYLARK")

CORD BODY DIES USED ON "R-915" WITH NEW 115" W.B. and 4.27 G.R. 6.00 × 16 TIRES

39

"R-915" JUNIOR 6 (INTRO. OCT., 1938. REPLACED BY "SKYLARK")

("SENIOR" MODELS "922-E" and "925-H" ARE CONTINUATIONS of '38.)

(FINAL HUPMOBILE, DISCONTINUED DURING 1940.)

"SKYLARK" 6 ONLY, IN 1940

137

INNES
(1921)

HENRY L. INNES,
JACKSONVILLE, FLORIDA
(COMPANY FORMED IN 1920, BUT
NO CARS ACTUALLY BUILT UNTIL
1921.)

with 4-CYLINDER
178.9 C.I.D.
SUPREME ENGINE
(3 3/8" × 5")

CHOICE OF
BATTERY OR MAGNETO
IGNITION.

ROADSTERS or 5-PASS.
TOURING CARS, *each with*
RIGID "PERMANENT TOP."

SMALL TRUCK ALSO
(PLANNED)

JACKSON

JACKSON AUTOMOBILE CO.,
JACKSON, MICH. (1903-1923)

'20 "SPORT CAR" ("6-38")
HAS UNUSUAL TOP STYLE.

6-CYL., 3 1/4" × 5" (248.9 C.I.D.)
HERSCHELL-SPILLMAN
ENGINE ALSO LISTED,
DURING SPRING, 1922.
("6-38" SERIES
CONTINUES)

20 "6-38"
6-CYLINDER,
224 C.I.D.
CONTINENTAL
ENGINE (TO '23)
121" W.B. (TO '23)
32 × 4 TIRES
REMY IGNITION
(AUTO-LITE LOCK)

'21 "6-38"
SEMI-SPORT

21

32 × 4 1/2 TIRES, 4.75 GEAR RATIO (TO '23)

JAEGER
(1931 — 1933)

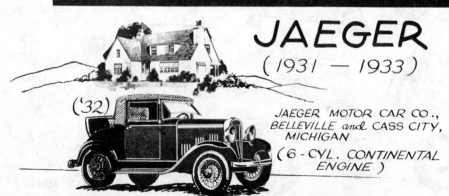

('32)

JAEGER MOTOR CAR CO.,
BELLEVILLE *and* CASS CITY,
MICHIGAN

(6-CYL. CONTINENTAL
ENGINE)

138

JEWETT

A Thrifty Six JEWETT *Built by Paige*

JEWETT'S 6-CYL. ENGINE IS A DEVELOPMENT FROM THE 1921 PAIGE "6-44" ENGINE, AND HAS THE ADDITION OF FORCE-FEED OILING.

22
"6-50"
12" BRAKE DRUMS

ATWATER KENT IGNITION

112" WHEELBASE (THROUGH '24)

248.9 C.I.D. (THROUGH '25)

50 HORSEPOWER (THROUGH '24)

FIRST YEAR WITH NO SECTOR ON SPARK OR THROTTLE HAND CONTROL.

23
"6-50"
14" BRAKE DRUMS

50 HORSEPOWER

24
"6-50"

De Luxe Sedan BODY COLOR = "LOTUS BLUE"

CARB. ON LEFT SIDE OF ENGINE. DISTRIBUTOR PUMP and GENERATOR ON RIGHT SIDE.

NICKEL TRIM ON DELUXE MODELS

3-PASS. BUSINESS MAN'S CPE. INTRO. ABOUT 2-24. DURING 1924, AND 4-PASS. CPE. DROPPED. NEW 2-DR. BROUGHAM SEATS CONVERT TO A BED.

AUTUMN, 1924 = 32 × 4.95 BALLOON TIRES, AND "AUTUMN GREEN" SATIN BODY COLOR (MOST MODELS)

JEWETT SIX

PAIGE BUILT

25

"6-50"
112" W.B.

STROMBERG CARB.
ATW. KENT IGNITION
LIGHT SWITCH
ON DASH

DE LUXE
BROUGHAM

(STD. BROUGHAM
has PAINTED RADIATOR,
NO LANDAU IRONS.)

LOCKHEED
HYDRAULIC
4 WHEEL
BRAKES
AVAILABLE
(SINCE
1924)
($40
EXTRA)

HIGHER
HOOD
AND
LOWER
RUNNING-
BOARDS

new
"SATIN
LACQUER"
FINISH

LATER IN YEAR, EARLY
1926 "6-55" MODEL
HAS LOCKING STEERING
WHEEL. WHEELBASE
CHANGED FROM
112" TO
115", with LIGHT
SWITCH ON STEER. WH.

63 H.P.
@
2800 RPM

(ONLY 55 H.P.
CLAIMED EARLY
IN SEASON.)

CARB. MOVED
TO RIGHT SIDE
OF ENGINE,
FOR '25.

31 x 5.25

31 x 5.25

TOP SPEED = 65 MILES PER HOUR

COACH ($1260.) (LOW-PRICED MODEL of CLOSED CAR. STARTS 4-25. HAS
DOORS 3' WIDE.)

The New-Day
JEWETT SIX

(STARTS DEC., 1925)

THE
ONLY JEWETT WITH
NEW, NARROW
CORNER POSTS

INTERIOR

SERIES "6-40"

"NEW-DAY"
MODEL HAS
SHORTENED
109"
W.B.

(A VERY SCARCE MODEL)

26

NICKELED RADIATOR SHELL
ON DE LUXE MODELS

NEW CONTINENTAL
ENGINE HAS 169.2 C.I.D.
and 40 H.P. @ 2400 RPM
JOHNSON CARB., REMY IGN.

FINAL JEWETT (1927 MODEL)
WAS INTRODUCED SEPTEMBER, 1926.
ON JANUARY 3, 1927, ITS NAME WAS CHANGED TO
THE PAIGE "6-45," APPEARANCE WAS SAME.
(SEE PAIGE, 1927 FOR PICTURE.)

JONES 6

('20-21 MODEL)

1920 MODEL 28 HAS IMPROVED RADIATOR, HIGH SHIFTING LEVER.

CONTINENTAL ENGINE (303.1 C.I.D.)

(1915 - 1920)

JONES MOTOR CAR CO., WICHITA, KANSAS

"SPEEDSTER" TOURING

126" W.B.
4.5 G.R.
AUTO-LITE IGNITION

JORDAN MOTOR CAR COMPANY, Inc., *Cleveland, Ohio*

JORDAN

('21)

224 C.I.D., 120" W.B. (1916 - 1931)

1920 "M" FEATURES ONLY MINOR IMPROVEMENTS. NEW 4-DOOR SEDAN. LIGHTWEIGHT ALUMINUM BODIES.

"F" SERIES HAS 303.1 C.I.D. ENGINE AND 127" W.B. (THROUGH '22)

"Silhouette" TOURING

Delco IGNITION (THROUGH '24 and on 6-CYL. '25)

6-CYL. CONTINENTAL ENGINES
32 × 4 TIRES (M)
32 × 4½ " (F)

PRE-1922 JORDANS *have* SCREW-ON (THREADED) GAS TANK CAP, AND STARTER SWITCH ON FLOOR NEAR FRONT SEAT.

NEW INSTRUMENT BOARD IN 1922, *with* ALL GAUGES UNDER ONE GLASS.

4.66 GEAR RATIO (M)
4.08 " " (F)

2-DOOR BROUGHAM

20-23

"M" and "F" SERIES
("M" BECOMES "MK" IN 1922)

(1920-1923 STYLE; '16-19 MODELS HAD REAR "TURTLEBACK" DECK LIKE VICTORIA COUPE.)

"F" REPLACED BY "H" SERIES IN 1923, WITH 124½" W.B. BOTH 1923 MODELS HAVE 245.6 C.I.D. (AS "MK" CHANGED TO, IN '22.)

JORDAN

"*Playboy*" SPT. ROADSTER

4-DOOR BROUGHAM
(INTRODUCED 1923)

EARLY TYPE HAS DASH GAUGES AT RIGHT SIDE

DISC WHEELS AVAILABLE ON 1923 "PLAYBOY"

JORDAN

"MX-6" TOURING CAR (5-PASS.)

REAR DETAILS AND TRUNK ON "BLUE BOY" PHAETON (AS OF 11-24)

24

"MX," "H" "L" MODELS

120" W.B.

4.42 G.R.

"PLAYBOY"

(Am. Bosch IGN., 125½" W.B. ON 8)

BREWSTER-STYLE WINDSHIELD ON 1925 JORDAN CLOSED MODELS

25

4.45 G.R. (K)
4.64 G.R. (A, L)

"A," "K," "L" MODELS

SERIES A "Great Line 8" (new)
268.6 C.I.D. STRAIGHT-8 ENGINE (74 H.P. @ 3000)
56 H.P. @ 2400 RPM 6-CYL. STILL AVAIL.)(K or L)

26

8 CYL. ONLY "A" and "J" MODELS

(American-Bosch IGNITION ON 8s THROUGH '27)

NEW "J" HAS 116" W.B.
246.5 C.I.D.
64 H.P. @ 3000 RPM

8-CYL. MODEL "J" (J-1)

SAME SPECS. AS IN '26

new 6-CYL. MODEL "R" "LITTLE JORDAN"

199 C.I.D.
62 H.P. @ 3000 RPM
Auto-Lite IGN.

27

SERIES "A" CONT'D. AS "AA"

107" W.B.

4.6 G.R.

The Sport Salon

"R" and "J-1" HAVE SAME SPECS. AS IN '27

"LITTLE TOMBOY"

28

FRONT END

SHORTER '28 HEADLIGHT SHELLS

NEW 268.7 C.I.D. MODEL "JE" "AIR LINE 8" HAS 4.45 G.R., CADET-TYPE VISOR, 116" W.B., 80 H.P. @ 3200 RPM

Auto-Lite IGNITION on ALL BUT "J-1"

NEW 1929 RADIATOR SHUTTERS AND HORIZONTAL HOOD LOUVRES

"E" (6 CYL.) HAS 116" W.B., 248.3 C.I.D. 70 H.P. @ 3000 RPM

29

Auto-Lite IGN. (THROUGH '32) new FUEL PUMP

"G" (8-CYL.) HAS 125" W.B., 268.6 C.I.D., 85 H.P. @ 3200 RPM 4.45 G.R.

142

MURRAY or OHIO BODIES

(NO 6-CYL. JORDAN AFTER 1929)

8 - CYL. "SPEEDWAY ACE"

114 H.P. @ 3200
322.2 C.I.D.

JORDAN

MODEL "Z" 145" W.B.

OTHER 1930 JORDAN 8s:
"70-U" { 80 H.P.
"80" { 246.7 c.i.d.
"90" 85 H.P.
268.6 c.i.d.

31-32

SERIES "90" 125" W.B.

STREAMLINED SERIES
WITH BUILT-IN RADIO!

30

"SPEEDBOY" PHAETON
(1929 TO 1932 TYPE ALSO AVAIL. DURING '30.)

SERIES "80" (120" W.B.) ALSO

JULIAN (1922)

JULIAN BROWN,
SYRACUSE, N.Y.

RADIAL ENGINE AT REAR

6 CYLS. (1921)
4 " (1922 ON)

EARLIEST KELSEYS HAVE "OWN ENGINE" (FALLS 195.6 CID)

116" W.B.

KELSEY

KELSEY MOTOR CO.,
NEWARK and
BELLEVILLE, N.J.
(1921 - 1924)

FRICTION DRIVE

32 × 4 TIRES FOR '24, 206.4 CID LYCOMING REPLACES 192.4 CID G-B ENGINE.

(FACTORY IN MISHAWAKA, IND.)

KENWORTHY

KENWORTHY MOTORS OF
NEW ENGLAND; BOSTON, MASS.

(1920 - 1922)

"8-90" OWN STRAIGHT-8
296.9 C.I.D. (3" × 5¼")
"LINE-O-EIGHT" ENGINE
130" W.B.   4.08 G.R.
32 × 4½ TIRES

21

('22 SIMILAR)

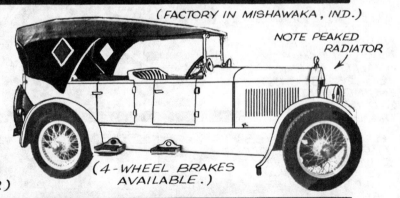

NOTE PEAKED RADIATOR

(4-WHEEL BRAKES AVAILABLE.)

V-8 ENGINE (INTRO. 2-15)

KING

KING MOTOR CAR CO., DETROIT
(1910 - 1923)
(PRODUCED IN BUFFALO, N.Y.,
1923 - 1924)

('22)

20

21-23 →

SEDANETTE (4-PASS.)

KISSEL

KISSEL MOTOR CAR CO.
HARTFORD, WISCONSIN
(1906-1931)

The Custom Built Car

SPEEDSTER

4-DR. COACH-SEDAN
(INTRO. 1-8-21)

3.62 G.R. REPLACED
BY 4.25 G.R. IN '21.

BOSCH IGNITION ('20)
REMY IGNITION
('21 ON)

4-PASS. COUPE

4-PASS. TOURSTER

124" W.B.
(THROUGH '23)
OWN 6-CYL.,
284.4 C.I.D. ENGINE
(THROUGH '23)
32 × 4 TIRES
(THROUGH '23)

19-22

'22 IS FIRST YEAR WITH SELF-LUBRICATING BRONZE BUSHINGS
ON BRAKE MECHANISM.

POPULARLY KNOWN
AS "GOLD BUG"

DRUM HEADLIGHTS, 1-PC.
WINDSHIELDS

23-24

'24= OIL TEST
GAUGE
ROD ON
LEFT
SIDE
OF
ENG.

4.4 G.R.
IN '23

1923 "45" SERIES IS
JOINED BY
NEW "55" SERIES
NEW 121" W.B.,
SMALLER 6-CYL.
265 (264.8) C.I.D.
ENGINE (USED ON
6-CYL. CHASSIS
THROUGH '27)

BROUGHAM

6-CYL. 1925 "55" IS
FINAL KISSEL TO OFFER
2-WHEEL MECHANICAL
BRAKES.

70 M.P.H.
"6-55"

25-26

OIL TEST GAUGE ROD
IS ELIMINATED (1925)

"8-75"
STRAIGHT-8
MODEL INTRODUCED
JANUARY, 1925.
(HAS HYDR. BRAKES)
287.3 CID, 63 H.P. @ 2400 ('25)
310 CID, 71 H.P. @ 3100 ('26)

75 M.P.H. TOP SPEED

50
H.P.
@
2800 RPM
(53 @ 2300 IN '26)

Body by Kissel

2ND KICK PAD ON
8-CYL. BROUGHAM

144

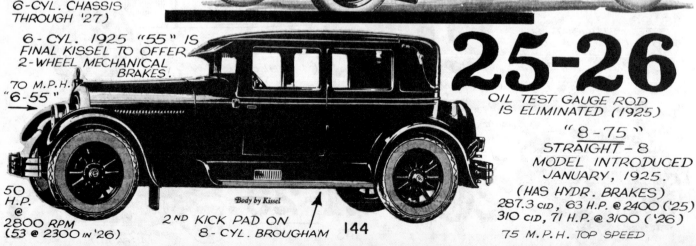

KISSEL

HYDRAULIC BRAKES ON
ALL '26-'27 KISSELS.

27

4.6 G.R. ("8-65")   HEAVIER WHEEL SPOKES
'27 ENGINES CUSHIONED IN RUBBER

8

"6-55"   124-131" W.B.
264.8 C.I.D. 61 H.P. @ 2300

"8-65"   125-132"
W.B., NEW SMALL 8
(246.5 C.I.D.)(THROUGH '31)
65 H.P. @ 2000 RPM

"8-75" 131" W.B.,
287.8 C.I.D., 71 H.P. @ 3000 RPM
(139" W.B. ALSO AVAIL.)

---

new, SMALL 185 C.I.D. 6
IN 117" W.B. "6-70"
52 H.P. @ 2905 RPM
(THROUGH '29)
4.63 G.R. 30 x 6.00 TIRES

28

(8-80) "SMALL 8" 4-DOOR
BROUGHAM
(REPLACES 8-65,
BUT HAS 70 H.P. @ 2900,
4.6 G.R., 31 x 6.20 TIRES)

HYDRAULIC BRAKES
CONTINUED
(THROUGH '31)

"8-80-S" has
125" W.B., 30 x 6.00 TIRES,
4.8 G.R.

1928 = NEW BODIES AND
ILCO-RYAN HEADLIGHTS ; WATER
TEMP. GAUGE
ON DASH.

"8-90"

"8-75"
BECOMES "8-90" FOR '28,
WITH 85 H.P. @ 3100 RPM,
4.89 G.R., 30 x 6.75 TIRES
131" OR 139" W.B.

SPEEDSTER

VACUUM-
TANK FUEL FEED
CONTINUED
ON ALL MODELS
(TO '31)

125-132" W.B.

"95" COUPE-ROADSTER
(8 CYL.)
246.5 C.I.D.
95 H.P. @ 3200 RPM
4.8 G.R. (5.1 IN '30)
6.00 x 18 TIRES (ALSO
ON "6-73")

132-139" W.B.
30 x 6.75
TIRES
('29)

"126"
BROUGHAM
(8 CYL.)

298.6 C.I.D. 126 H.P.
4.89 G.R. (4.8 IN '30)
7.00 x 16 TIRES IN '30)

29-31

"WHITE EAGLE"
MODELS
(BEGIN AUG. 15, 1928)

1931
MODEL
IS FINAL
KISSEL.

MODEL "73" = 6 CYL. (185 C.I.D.)
52 H.P. @ 2900 ('29)   117" W.B.
75 H.P. @ 3500 ('30-31)
4.6 G.R. (5.3 IN '30)

145

STARTS 7-1-30

KLEIBER MOTOR CO. (CARS = 1924-1929) ALSO BUILT TRUCKS

Kleiber

11th and Folsom Sts. SAN FRANCISCO

1800 E. 12th St. OAKLAND

11th and San Pedro Sts. LOS ANGELES

'27 (6)

'29 (8)

CONTINENTAL "8-R" 6-CYL. 241.6 C.I.D. ENGINE
55 H.P. @ 2300 RPM
122" W.B., 32 x 6.20 TIRES

'29 DASH →
(INSTRUMENTS SET IN BLACK WOOD PANEL; OUTDATED STYLE FOR 1929!)

KLINE KAR
(1910 - 1923)

SINCE 1912, BLT. BY KLINE MOTOR CAR CORP., RICHMOND, VA.

20-22

"6-55" 121" W.B. 224 C.I.D.
6-CYL. CONTINENTAL ENGINE

"6-60" (1923) HAS 241.5 C.I.D.

20

LAFAYETTE
(1919 to 1924)

21
4.5 G.R.

LaFAYETTE MOTORS CORPORATION
Milwaukee, Wisconsin

V-8 ENGINE 100 H.P.
132" W.B. 348.4 C.I.D.
(THROUGH '24)

The Four-Door Coupe (new)

(COMPANY ORIGINATED AT INDIANAPOLIS, INDIANA)

22-23

33 x 5 TIRES ON ALL

THOUGH NEW BODY TYPES APPEARED, THE MODEL "134" DIDN'T FEATURE NOTEWORTHY CHANGES BETWEEN 1920 AND 1924.

NEW PULL-TYPE HOOD FASTENERS and COWL BELT, LATE 1923

4.58 G.R.

CO. ABSORBED BY NASH. LAFAYETTE NAME APPEARS AGAIN IN 1934, ON LOW-PRICED CAR.

FRONT END, SHOWING RADIATOR SHUTTERS

24

LAFAYETTE

NASH BUILT

34

113" W.B. (THROUGH '36)

217.8 C.I.D. (THROUGH '36)
75 H.P. @ 3200 RPM
(THROUGH '35)
4.7 GEAR RATIO (THROUGH '35)

COUPE (ACTUAL PHOTO)

NEW 6.00 x 16 TIRES
AUTOMATIC STARTER WITH
CLUTCH PEDAL CONTROL.
3 HORIZONTAL LOUVRES
(INSTEAD OF VENT DOORS
ON HOOD)

CHASSIS

35

→

COUPE
(GROSSLY
EXAGGERATED
ARTIST'S
CONCEPTION
OF 1935.)

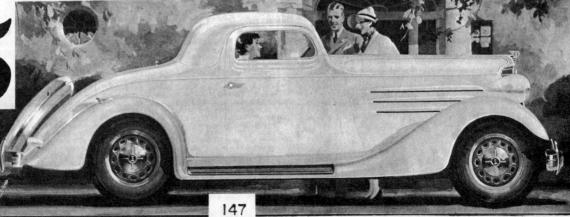

LaFAYETTE

ENGINE (7-BEARING)

NOTE HOW ENTIRE TRUNK BULGE OPENS, ON SEDAN

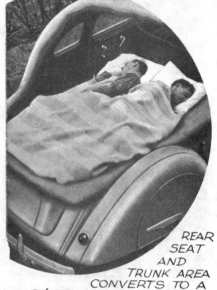

REAR SEAT AND TRUNK AREA CONVERTS TO A 6' DOUBLE BED (IN LAFAYETTE OR NASH "400" SEDANS)

REAR SEAT, SHOWING UPHOLSTERY PATTERN

36

SEAMLESS ALL-STEEL TOP (ON LAFAYETTE OR NASH "400")

NEW = HYDRAULIC BRAKES
4.4 GEAR RATIO

LATE MODELS HAVE DIE-CAST GRILLE.

FENDER SKIRTS AVAIL.

37

117" WHEELBASE AND SPECIFICATIONS SIMILAR TO '36 NASH "400."

4.11 GEAR RATIO

BECAME THE NASH-LAFAYETTE "400"

LaSalle

INTRO.
MARCH
1927

V-8
L-HEAD
ENGINE
(all years
except
'34 THROUGH
'36)

303 C.I.D.
(THROUGH '28)

27

MODEL
"303"

SEPT., 1927 = ELECTRO
LOCK ON DASHBOARD
REPLACES
TRANSMISSION
LOCK.

OPAQUED
GLASS VISOR

28

"303"
NEW,
NARROWER
HOOD LOUVRES

"HEAT ON AND OFF" CONTROL LEVER
ADDED ON LEFT SIDE OF DASH.

80 H.P. @ 3000 RPM
4.8 COMPRESSION

4.54 or 4.91 GEAR RATIO
(THROUGH '29)

125" OR 134" WHEELBASE (THROUGH '29)

CHROME-PLATING ON ALL BRIGHTWORK
PARKING LAMPS MOVED TO
FRONT FENDERS

FISHER OR
FLEETWOOD
BODIES

327.7 C.I.D.
86 H.P. @ 3000 RPM
5.3 and other COMPRESSION RATIOS

INSTRUMENT PANEL DESIGN
SIMILAR TO CADILLAC'S.

SYNCHRO-MESH TRANSMISSION
(ALSO ON CADILLAC)

29

"328"

REAR SECTION OF
TOP FOLDS DOWN

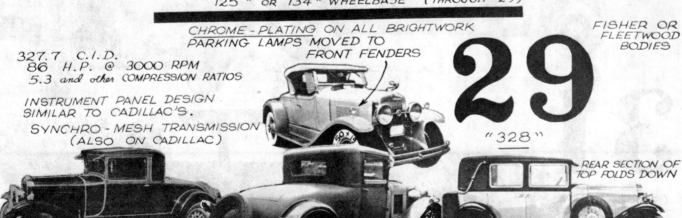

(FUEL PUMP USED DURING '29)

LaSalle

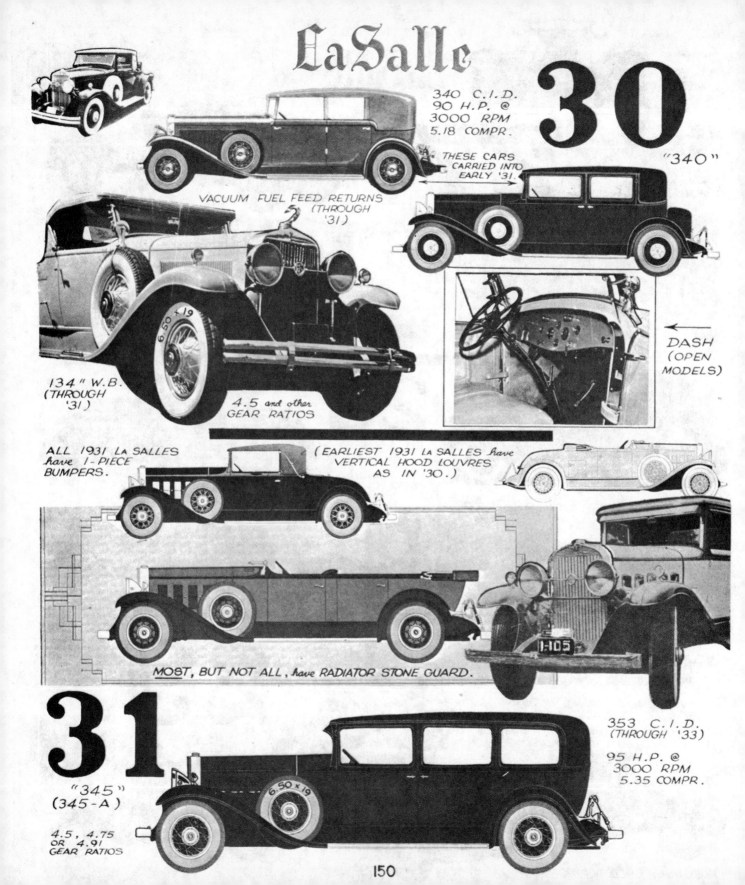

**340 C.I.D.
90 H.P. @
3000 RPM
5.18 COMPR.**

30
"340"

THESE CARS CARRIED INTO EARLY '31.

VACUUM FUEL FEED RETURNS (THROUGH '31)

134" W.B. (THROUGH '31)

4.5 and other GEAR RATIOS

DASH (OPEN MODELS)

ALL 1931 La SALLES have 1-PIECE BUMPERS.

(EARLIEST 1931 La SALLES have VERTICAL HOOD LOUVRES AS IN '30.)

MOST, BUT NOT ALL, have RADIATOR STONE GUARD.

31
"345"
(345-A)

4.5, 4.75 OR 4.91 GEAR RATIOS

**353 C.I.D.
(THROUGH '33)

95 H.P. @
3000 RPM
5.35 COMPR.**

LaSalle

4.6 GEAR RATIO (THROUGH '33)

FUEL PUMP RETURNS

32 "345-B"

115 H.P. @ 3000 RPM (THROUGH '33)

5.38 COMPR.

7.00 X 17

130" and 136" W.B. (THROUGH '33)

'33 DASH

"HERON" RADIATOR MASCOT with FILLER UNDER HOOD

33 "345-C"

BENDIX POWER BRAKES

5.40 COMPR.

GRACEFUL NEW STREAMLINING HYDRAULIC BRAKES 119" W.B.

34

MODEL "350"

7.00 x 16 TIRES (THROUGH '40)

STRAIGHT-8 ENGINE REPLACES V-8 (THROUGH '36)

240.3 C.I.D. 90 H.P. @ 3700 RPM

6.50 or 5.75 COMPR.

COUPE WITH BOTH RUMBLE-SEAT AND TRUNK

4.78 GEAR RATIO ('34 and '35)

35

"50" SERIES (CONT'D. TO '40)

(PUSH-BUTTON STARTER)

120" W.B. ('35 and '36)
105 H.P. @ 3600 RPM ('35 and '36)
6.50 or 5.75 COMPR.

V-WINDSHIELD, STEEL TOP

4.55 GEAR RATIO

36

HAND-BRAKE LEVER AT LEFT SIDE OF COWL.

6.25 or 5.75 COMPR. (THROUGH '40)

V·8 LaSalle

NEW ENGINE has 322 C.I.D. (THROUGH '40) 125 H.P. @ 3400 RPM (THROUGH '39)

37

3.92 GEAR RATIO (THROUGH '40)

'38 INTERIOR

38

HOOD HINGED AT REAR, EXTENDS TO GRILLE WHICH IS 2" WIDER FOR 1938.

39

SLIDING "SUNSHINE ROOF" OPTIONAL (2-DR. and 4-DR. SEDANS)

NUVO CORD OR RIBBED BROADCLOTH UPHOLSTERY

LEACH

(1920–1923)

LEACH MOTOR CAR CO., LOS ANGELES, CALIF.

CONTINENTAL 6-CYL. 303.1 C.I.D. ENGINE IN '20 and '21

126½" W.B. ('20)
128" W.B. ('21)

BEAR RADIATOR EMBLEM

(LEACH-BILTWELL)

('22)   134" W.B.

OWN "POWER PLUS 6" O.H.C. engine (347.9 CID) DELCO IGN. IN '22-'23 MODEL "999"

32 × 4½ TIRES

(FEATURED NEW "CALIFORNIA TOP" WITH SLIDING WINDOWS.)

LEON RUBAY

118" W.B.

5.10 G.R.

(1922–1924)
RUBAY CO., CLEVELAND, OHIO

OWN 122 C.I.D. 4-CYL. O.H.C. engine

(4-WHEEL BRAKES)

BOSCH IGNITION

32 × 4

LEXINGTON (1909–1928)

20

6 CYL. L-HEAD 224 C.I.D. CONTINENTAL ENGINE

= NO NEW MODEL LISTED AFTER 1926.

"Minute Man Six" ("S")

120" W.B.

LEXINGTON MOTOR CO., CONNERSVILLE, INDIANA (ORIGINATED IN LEXINGTON, KY.)

123"-W.B. "U" SERIES STARTS 1-22

"MINUTE MAN" JOINED BY NEW "CONCORD" SERIES IN 1924,

WITH 232.7 C.I.D. ANSTED O.H.V. 6-CYL. ENGINE

119" W.B., 32 × 4 TIRES

new '21 SERIES "T"

128" W.B.

(NEW ANSTED 6 CYL. O.H.V. ENGINES)

"Lark" MODEL 1921½-1922 (MODEL "S" CONTINUED)

FOLDED IN MID-20s, TAKEN OVER BY AUBURN

('21)

('23 = ABSORBED BY COLUMBIA)

117" W.B.

"10-C" OWN 6-CYL., 230.1 CID L-HEAD ENG. (Wagner IGN.)

LIBERTY SIX

('20)

Liberty Motor Car Company, Detroit   (1916–1924)

DRUM HEADLIGHTS IN 1922

'22 SERIES "10-D"

4.66 G.R.

LIBERTY

4.8 G.R. IN '23-'24

32 × 4 TIRES

153

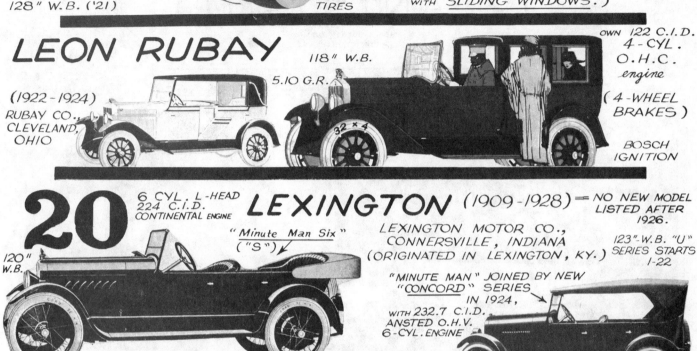

Henry M. Leland
President

and
FOUNDER

LINCOLN
MOTOR CARS

LELAND-BUILT

LINCOLN MOTOR COMPANY
DETROIT, MICH.

Wilfred C. Leland
Vice-Pres. and Gen. Mgr.

V-8
(357.8 C.I.D.)
(THROUGH 1927)

OWN
CARBURETOR
FOR 1921

7- PASS.
TOURING CAR

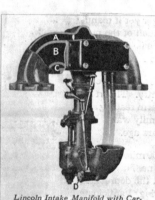

Lincoln Intake Manifold with Carburetor and Electro-Fog Producer

In the illustration, the intake manifold is shown in section. The upper passage (A) is for hot water; the lower passage (C) for hot exhaust gases, and the passage between (B) for intake gas mixture. The retort where fuel is converted into fog is shown at "D"

5- PASS.
TOURING
CAR

21
(STARTS AUTUMN, 1920)

130 " WHEELBASE

(136" W. B. ON LIMOUSINE
AND TOWN CAR)
4.45 GEAR RATIO

DELCO IGNITION
(THROUGH '27)

70 MILES PER HOUR

LINCOLN

LELAND-BUILT

21 (CONT'D.)

STANDARD WHEELBASE 136"
(THROUGH '30)

new STROMBERG
CARBURETOR
90 H.P.

22

SEVEN-PASSENGER SEDAN

I-22 = FORD
MOTOR CO.
PURCHASES
LINCOLN MOTOR CO.

4-PASS.
SEDAN

DRUM HEADLIGHTS
ON MOST 1923
LINCOLNS.

33 × 5

7-PASS. TOURING CAR

33 × 5 TIRES CONT'D. (THROUGH '27)

23

JUDKINS COUPE
(A SIMILAR COUPE WITH 1921-STYLE
"REVERSED" REAR FENDERS ALSO AVAIL.)

95 H.P. @ 2800 RPM
(THROUGH '24)

7-PASS. SEDAN

LINCOLN

MODEL "124"

24

VERTICAL
RADIATOR SHUTTERS

25

LINCOLN

MODEL "124"

JUDKINS THREE-WINDOW BERLINE

90 H.P.
@ 2800 RPM
(THROUGH '27)

LINCOLN

SPORT PHAETON
(LOCKE BODY)

7-PASS.
LIMOUSINE

JUDKINS 2-PASS.
COUPE

LE BARON
4-PASS. SEDAN

26

"124-A"

"CABRIOLET" (LANDAULET) WITH
COLLAPSIBLE
REAR QUARTER

TOWN CAR   ('26½)

4-WHEEL
BRAKES
NOW
ON ALL
MODELS.

GEAR RATIO 4.58 (THROUGH 1940)

27   "124-B"

90-
100
H.P.

33 x 5
TIRES

Four Passenger Two Window Sedan

157

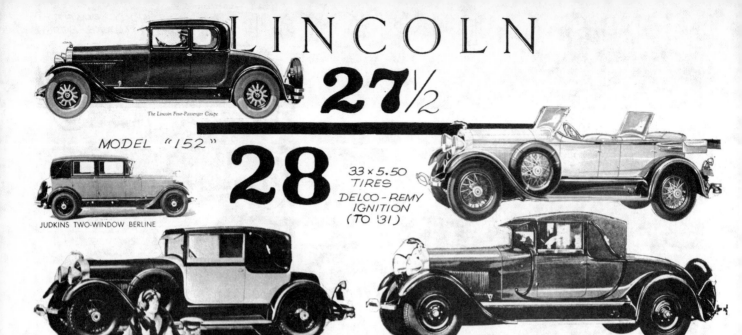

LINCOLN

27½

The Lincoln Four-Passenger Coupe

MODEL "152"

28

33 × 5.50 TIRES

DELCO - REMY IGNITION (TO '31)

JUDKINS TWO-WINDOW BERLINE

Club Roadster

29

7.00 × 20" (32 × 6.75) TIRES

BODIES BY
JUDKINS
DIETRICH
WILLOUGHBY
BRUNN
HOLBROOK
CENTRAL
LE BARON
ETC.

1929 — LE BARON AERO-PHAETON

90 H.P. @ 2800 RPM (THROUGH '30)

TOWN BROUGHAM

TOWN SEDAN

LINCOLN

1930 — BRUNN CABRIOLET

30

MODEL "169-B"

7.00 x 20
TIRES

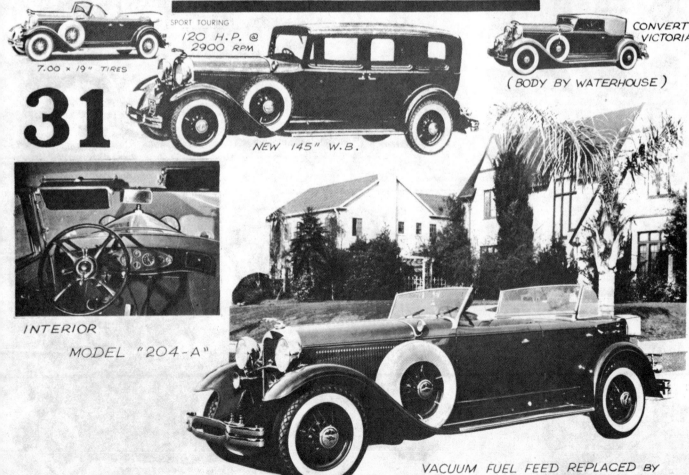

7.00 x 19" TIRES

31

SPORT TOURING

120 H.P. @
2900 RPM

NEW 145" W.B.

CONVERT.
VICTORIA

(BODY BY WATERHOUSE)

INTERIOR

MODEL "204-A"

VACUUM FUEL FEED REPLACED BY
NEW FUEL PUMP

LINCOLN

4-PASSENGER PHAETON

V-8

120-125 H.P. @ 2900 RPM

7.00 x 18" TIRES ON V-8

"2-WINDOW TOWN SEDAN"

V-12 (NEW)

136" W.B. ON V-8 "234-B"

32

WILLOUGHBY LIMOUSINE

V-12

145" W.B. ON V-12 "235"
V-12 HAS 447.9 C.I.D. ENGINE, WITH 150 H.P. @ 3400 RPM

7.50 x 18

(V-12) K-B

TOWN CAR

INT.

AUTO-LITE IGN.

160

DUAL-COWL PHAETON

LINCOLN

136" and 145" WHEELBASES

33

2-TONE
HORNS
BEHIND GRILLE

381.7-C.I.D. and 447-C.I.D. V-12 ENGINES (125 and 150 H.P. @ 3400 RPM)

ALL MODELS ADOPT SAME
TYPE OF 150-H.P. (@ 3400)
V-12 ENGINE.
(414 C.I.D.)
THIS ENGINE USED WITH
SAME SPECS. IN ALL LARGE ("K")
LINCOLNS FROM 1934 THROUGH
1940.)

HOOD VENT DOORS
THERMOSTATICALLY
CONTROLLED

LeBARON CONVERTIBLE ROADSTER

custom-built types by Judkins,
Brunn, Willoughby, Dietrich and Le Baron.

7.50 × 18 TIRES ON
145"-W.B. CUSTOM
200 SERIES

THE TWO-WINDOW TOWN SEDAN

34

136" and 145" W.B.
(THROUGH '40)
7.00/7.50 × 18 TIRES
(AS IN '33) (500 SER.)
4.58 GEAR RATIO
(THROUGH '40 "K")

MECHANICAL
VACUUM BOOSTER
BRAKES

THE FIVE-PASSENGER CONVERTIBLE SEDAN-PHAETON

JUDKINS
LIMOUSINE

FRONT-DOOR ARM-RESTS

RADIATOR FILLER
UNDER HOOD

HAND BRAKE
LEVER UNDER
DASH

VACUUM
POWER
BRAKES

35

5-PASS.
"2-WINDOW
SEDAN"

7.50 × 17

161

FENDERWELLS STD. EQUIP.
DURING '35.

LINCOLN

Lincoln Zephyr V-12

(NEW)

BLUE EMBLEM
ON GRILLE

ZEPHYR OF 1936
THROUGH 1936 HAS
267.3 C.I.D. V-12
ENGINE (110 H.P.
@ 3800 - 3900 RPM)

4.33 GEAR RATIO, 122" W.B. (THROUGH '37)
7.00 × 16" TIRES (THROUGH '41)

BRUNN
"CABRIOLET"

7.50 × 17

36

BRUNN
CVT. VICTORIA

MECHANICAL BRAKES (all)

BRIGHT METAL
SPOKES ON
STEERING WHEEL

37

ENTIRE LUGGAGE / TIRE COMPART.
NOW ACCESSIBLE THROUGH
THE TRUNK DOOR.

RED EMBLEM
ON GRILLE

ZEPHYR

new QUIETER FAN has ALTERNATE LONG and
SHORT BLADES.
MECHANICAL BRAKES

new V-SHAPED WINDSHIELD (K)

LINCOLN

37

(CONT'D.)

2-WINDOW BERLINE

BRUNN TOURING CABRIOLET

LIMOUSINE (WILLOUGHBY BODY)

HEADLIGHTS SUNKEN IN FENDERS →

7.50×17

VACUUM BOOSTER ON MODEL "K" BRAKES

ZEPHYR HAS NEW 125" W.B. AND 4.44 GEAR RATIO

38

LE BARON CONVERTIBLE SEDAN

ZEPHYR (RESTYLED)

The LINCOLN

7.50×17

STROMBERG CARB. (SINCE '22)

ZEPHYR HAS OWN IGNITION SYSTEM (SINCE '36)

ZEPHYR

CONTINUED USE OF AUTO-LITE IGNITION and 7.50×17" TIRES ON LARGE LINCOLNS

LARGE "K" TYPE DISCONTINUED AFTER '40

ZEPHYR GETS HYDRAULIC BRAKES

39

163

LOCOMOBILE

LOCOMOBILE CO.
OF AMERICA, INC.
BRIDGEPORT, CONN.
(1899 - 1929)

SPECIAL LOCOMOBILE SEDAN

"GUNBOAT" ROADSTER

17-29

(6 CYL.) MODEL "48"
OWN T-HEAD ENG.

SPECIAL GROWLER COUPE
A type adapted from the old London Four Wheeler

TYPICAL
HEADLIGHTS →

524.8 C.I.D.
(THROUGH '29
103 H.P. @ 2100 RPM ('25-'26)
105 " ('27 ON)

NO DRASTIC MODEL CHANGES IN MODEL "48"
DURING MOST YEARS IT WAS AVAILABLE, BUT
GRADUAL REFINEMENTS WERE INCORPORATED.
THE "48" WAS LOCOMOBILE'S LARGEST CAR.
142 " W.B.

AFTER EARLY 1920s, ('22)
DRUM HEADLIGHTS
USED FREQUENTLY →

('23)

('24) CUSTOM
EXHAUST
AND BRAKES

4 - WHEEL
MECHANICAL BRAKES
ON ALL MODELS,
STARTING 1925.

('25)

3.5 GEAR RATIO ('24 ON)
BERLING IGN. REPLACED BY DELCO ('23 ON)
("48")

LATE "48s", LOWER - PRICED
MODELS ON
FOLLOWING PAGE.

Locomobile Junior Eight

OWN STRAIGHT-8, L-HEAD
181.5 C.I.D. ENGINE   5.12 G.R.
63 H.P. @ 2800 RPM   124" W.B.

25

30 × 5.77

"J-6" ALSO AVAIL.   6 CYL. OWN ENG.,
195.6 C.I.D.   4.77 G.R.
115" W.B.   30 × 5.77 TIRES

DE JON IGNITION USED ON
MOST '25-29 LOCOMOBILES (EXCEPT
"48")

26-27

JUNIOR 8 KNOWN
AS
"LOCOMOBILE
STRAIGHT 8"
IN 1927.

"90" has OWN
L-HEAD, 371.5 C.I.D.
ENGINE
86 to 90 H.P.
138" W.B.
4.5 and other G.R.s
(THROUGH '29)

33 × 6.75 TIRES
ON "90"

MODEL "90"
(INTRO. LATE 1925)
NOTE UNUSUAL STYLING
OF FRONT
PILLARS.

"48"
SPORTIF
(1927)

LYCOMING
STRAIGHT-8
ENGINES ON
'27-'29 "8-80"
AND '29 "8-88"

124" W.B.
"8-66 IS
AVAIL.'27 (63 HP)
OWN O.H.V. ENG.

246.7 C.I.D., 4.77 G.R.
70 H.P. @ 3000

28

1928 "8-80" HAS WINDSHIELD
PILLARS AKIN TO MODEL 90.

130" W.B.
"8-80"   298.5 CID
90 H.P. @ 3200
4.81 G.R.
32 × 6.00 TIRES
(THROUGH '29)

CONTINENTAL-ENGINED
1928 "8-70" HAS ROOF-VISOR, 122" W.B.
DRUM HEADLIGHTS, HOOD LOUVRES
LIKE 1927 "8," BUT RADIATOR SHAPED LIKE '29 (BUT WITH RADIMETER.)

LOCOMOBILE OR
CENTRAL BODIES
"8-88"
130" W.B.

SHOWN WITH OWNER:
GEO. BANCROFT (FILM STAR)

"6-90"

115 H.P. @ 3300 RPM

29 (FINAL YEAR)

7-PASSENGER
SUBURBAN

SERIES 8
"48"

165

LORRAINE
(1920 – 1922)

LORRAINE MOTORS CORP.,
GRAND RAPIDS, MICH.; DETROIT

114" W.B.

4-CYL., 192.4 C.I.D. HERSCHELL-SPILLMAN ENGINE

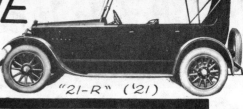

"21-R" ('21)

Maibohm

BUILT BY MAIBOHM, SANDUSKY, OHIO
(1916 to 1922)

6-CYL.
195.6 C.I.D.
FALLS ENGINE

20-22

MODEL "B"
116" W.B.

(REPLACED
BY
COURIER)

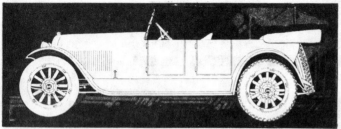

(1902 – 1933) MARMON

16-21

NORDYKE and MARMON, INDIANAPOLIS

136" W.B. (THROUGH '28)

MODEL "34"
(THROUGH '24)

('20)

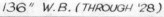

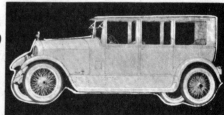

DELCO IGNITION on ALL

6-CYL., O.H.V., 339.7 C.I.D.
(THROUGH '28)

3.75 G.R. and 32 × 4½ TIRES (THROUGH '23)

MODEL "34"
CONTINUES
FROM 1916.

EARLY '22 == DOES NOT
HAVE DRUM
HEADLIGHTS

22-23

HOOD LOUVRES
(INTRODUCED
DURING 1921.)

MARMON

24

FINAL YEAR OF "34" SERIES

7-PASS. PHAETON

4-WHEEL BRAKES
OPTIONAL, IF DESIRED

NEW 4.10 GEAR RATIO (TO '26)
32 × 4½ OR 33 × 5 TIRES
(BALLOON TIRES AVAILABLE)

DURING LATE FEBRUARY, 1926,
MANUFACTURER CHANGED NAME TO
MARMON MOTOR CAR CO.

'25 HAS 82 H.P.
@ 2650 RPM

25-26

"74" SERIES

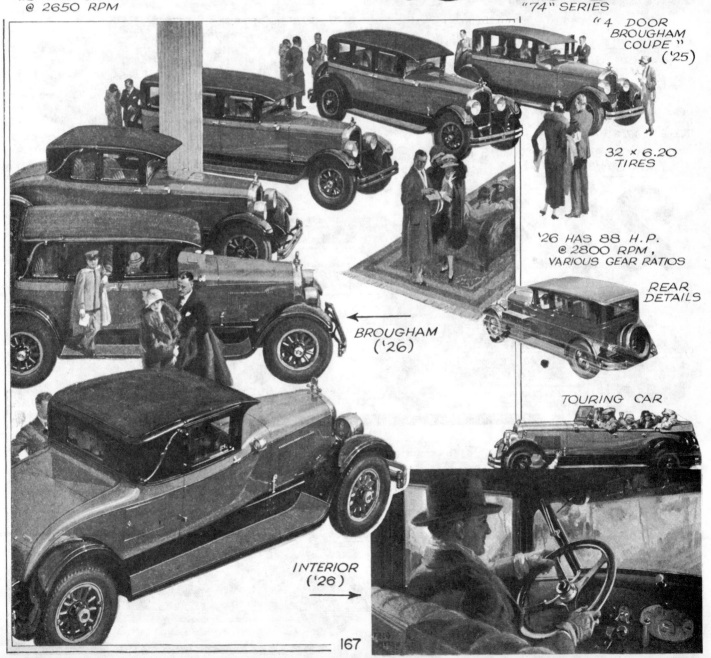

"4 DOOR
BROUGHAM
COUPE"
('25)

32 × 6.20
TIRES

'26 HAS 88 H.P.
@ 2800 RPM,
VARIOUS GEAR RATIOS

REAR
DETAILS

← BROUGHAM
('26)

TOURING CAR

INTERIOR
('26) →

167

the little MARMON 8
AMERICA'S FIRST TRULY FINE SMALL CAR

(INTRO. JAN., 1927)

COUPE (WITH RUMBLE SEAT)

2-DOOR SEDAN

4-DOOR SEDAN

COLLAPSIBLE COUPE-ROADSTER (WITH R.S.)

29 x 5.25

4-PASS. SPEEDSTER (PHAETON)

new STRAIGHT-8, O.H.V. 190.1 C.I.D. ENGINE
64 H.P. @ 3200 RPM
116" W.B. 5.1 G.R.
70-75 MILES PER HOUR

2-PASS. SPEEDSTER (WITH RUMBLE SEAT)

HYPOID GEAR DRIVE

FEDCO I.D. NUMBERS

ELECTRIC CLOCK

27

4-WHEEL BRAKES ON BOTH SERIES —

8

6

32 x 6.75 TIRES 4.1 G.R.

84 H.P. @ 2700 RPM ('27)

LATE '27s FEATURED UNUSUAL MARMON-VALENTINE "JEWEL COLORS."

COUPE-ROADSTER (NEW)

THIS 339.7 C.I.D. "E-75" 6-CYL. MODEL CONT'D. INTO 1928, BUT WITH LOWER H.P. RATING OF 75 @ 2800.

28

"68"
L-HEAD STR.-8
201.9 C.I.D.
72 H.P. @ 3200 RPM

114" W.B.

29 x 5.25 TIRES

4.9 GEAR RATIO

"78" O.H.V. STR.-8
216.8 C.I.D.
86 H.P. @ 3400 RPM

120" W.B., 29 x 5.50 TIRES

168

MARMON

THE NEW MARMON 68
THE NEW MARMON 78

"68" DASH

"68" DISPLACEMENT UP TO 211.2 , H.P. UP TO 76.
29 × 5.50 TIRES (29 × 6.00 ON "78")

"78" DASH has CLOCK AT LEFT CENTER (BY SPEED-OMETER)

"68"

29

(STRAIGHT—8 ENGINES ONLY)
MOST SPECS. AS IN 1928
HORIZONTAL HOOD LOUVRES
HAYES BODIES

"8-69" = 118" W.B.
211.2 C.I.D.
84 H.P. @ 3400 RPM
4.9 G.R.   5.50 × 19 TIRES

"8-79" = 125" W.B.
303.2 C.I.D.
110 H.P. @ 3400 RPM
4.45 G.R.
6.00 × 19 TIRES

NEW HOOD VENT DOORS

30

ALL 1930 MARMONS HAVE STRAIGHT-8 , L-HEAD ENGINES.

"BIG 8" =
136" W.B.
315.2 C.I.D., 125 H.P.
@ 3400 RPM, 4.45 G.R.
6.50 × 19 TIRES

8
('31)
"8-69" BECOMES "70"
"8-79"
"BIG 8" BECOMES "88" DURING 1931.

(8 - CYL. SERIES DROPPED DURING 1932.)
'32 "8-125" has 130-136" W.B., 315.2 C.I.D., L-HEAD ENG. 125 H.P. @ 3400 RPM

NOTE V-GRILLE ON '32 "8-125"

31-33

200 - H.P.
V-16
490.8 C.I.D., OHV, 145" W.B.

7.00 × 18 TIRES

3.69 G.R. IN '31;
3.78 ('32 ON)

"1934"
MODEL AL90

169

Marquette 30

BUILT ONE YEAR ONLY BY BUICK MOTOR CO., FLINT, MICH. (DIVISION OF GENERAL MOTORS)

6 - CYLINDER
L - HEAD
ENGINE
212.8 C.I.D.
3 1/8" × 4 5/8"
BORE and STROKE
67 1/2 HORSEPOWER
@ 3000 RPM

MARVEL CARBURETOR
DELCO - REMY IGNITION

INTRODUCED SATURDAY,
JUNE 1, 1929.

114" WHEELBASE   4.54 GEAR RATIO
5.25 × 18 TIRES

BODY BY FISHER

MASTERBILT 6 (1926)
(AIR COOLED)

GOVRO - NELSON CO.,
DETROIT

ENGINEERED BY VICTOR GAVREAU,
FORMERLY CHIEF ENGINEER OF THE
PAN CAR.

MAINLY AN EXPERIMENT.
NO DEALERSHIPS KNOWN TO
HAVE EXISTED.

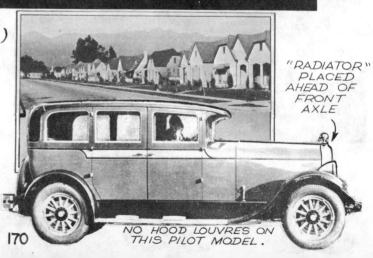

"RADIATOR"
PLACED
AHEAD OF
FRONT
AXLE

NO HOOD LOUVRES ON
THIS PILOT MODEL.

170

MAXWELL
(1904 – 1925)

MAXWELL MOTOR COMPANY, INC.,

Maxwell

DETROIT, MICHIGAN

4 CYLS.
25 H.P.

(NEW CASTLE,
INDIANA
PLANT)

185.8
C.I.D.
(THROUGH
1925)

109"
WHEELBASE
(THROUGH
1925)

30 x 3½

20-21

MODEL "25"

('21)

The Good Maxwell

NEW SERIES STARTS
11-21

22-24

CLUB COUPE

HORSEPOWER:
25 @ 1800 ('22)
30 @ 2150 ('23)
34 @ 2000 ('24)

EAGLE CARB. ('22)
STEWART
CARB. ('23
THROUGH
'25)

NEW
EMBLEM

Maxwell

PHANTOM VIEW,
SHOWING
WOODEN
BODY
FRAME

The
CLUB
SEDAN
('24)

31 x 4

4.56 GEAR RATIO ('22)
4.6 ('23 – '25)

REMY IGNITION

58 MILES PER HOUR

25

NICKELED RADIATOR
SHELL. ROOF-VISOR

L

GASOLINE

MAXWELL

The New Good
MAXWELL

3.9
COMPRESSION

38 H.P. @ 2200 RPM
30 x 5.25 TIRES

REPLACED 6-25 BY
CHRYSLER
4.

171

Mac DONALD (1923-1924)

(STEAMER) "BOBCAT" ROADSTER

Mac DONALD STEAM AUTOMOTIVE CORP., GARFIELD, OHIO

Mc FARLAN
(1910-1928)

McFARLAN MOTOR CAR CO., CONNERSVILLE, IND.

7-PASS. SUBURBAN SEDAN

TYPE "157" "T.V." 6 ('22)

6-CYL. T-HEAD
572.5 C.I.D.
ENGINE
140" W.B.
3.5 G.R.

(SV)"LIGHT 6" ALSO AVAIL.
IN 1924, WITH 127" W.B.
268.4 C.I.D. WISCONSIN ENG.
5.10 G.R.

'25 TOWN CAR

STRAIGHT-8
LYCOMING
ENGINE
70 H.P. ('26)
79 H.P. ('27)

'26-7
8-IN-LINE "872"
TOWN COUPE
131" W.B.

4-PASS. SPORTING

132" W.B.   ('23)

MERCER
(1910-1925)

MERCER AUTOMOBILE CO., TRENTON, N.J.

SERIES 5 = 4 CYLS. (298.2 C.I.D.)
LARGER SERIES 6 (331.3 C.I.D.,
6 CYL.) JOINS SERIES 5 IN '23

(2 1931 MERCER 8s
BUILT BY ELCAR.)

RACEABOUT ('21)

SPORTS ROADSTER ('22)

MERCURY 8

(BEGINS WITH 1939 MODEL)

A PRODUCT OF THE [ ] R COMPANY
FORD MOTOR CO

239 C.I.D. V-8

116" W.B.

39 95 H.P. @ 3600 RPM

REAR DETAILS (TRUNK OPEN)

MERCURY

METEOR

(1914-1930)
SHELBYVILLE, IND. and PIQUA, O.

('21)

METEOR MOTOR CAR CO.
Meteor
PIQUA, OHIO, U.S.A.

MILBURN
ELECTRIC

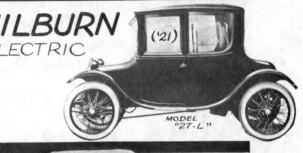

('21)

MODEL "27-L"

(1914-1922) MILBURN WAGON CO.,
TOLEDO, OHIO

MILLER

(CUSTOM-BUILT)
V-8 OR
V-16

FRONT-WHEEL
DRIVE
SPEEDSTER

HARRY A. MILLER
(RELLIMAH, INC.)
LOS ANGELES,
CALIF.

31

"SPECIAL"

NEW, SLANTED
STYLING

MITCHELL
20-21

(1903-1923)

MITCHELL MOTORS CO.,
RACINE, WIS.
(MFR. NAME AS OF 1916-1923)

120" W.B.

"F-40" 6-CYL., 248.9 CID
L-HEAD ENGINE   4.41 G.R.

FINAL "50" MODELS HAVE
CONVENTIONAL STYLING.

MONITOR

(1915-1922)

MONITOR MOTOR CAR CO.,
COLUMBUS, OHIO

20

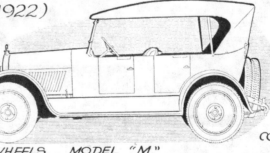

"B-50" and
"B-52" MODELS
IN 1921 (SAME
121" W.B.,
CONTINENTAL ENG.)

6-CYL. CONTINENTAL
"7-R" ENGINE
121" W.B. DISC WHEELS MODEL "M"

20

MONROE
FLINT, MICH.

(1914-1924)

(4 CYL.)

(CONTROLLED BY
PREMIER,
1923-24)

24

111" W.B.   ('24)

('20)

MOON (1905-1929)

Built by Moon Motor Car Company, St. Louis, U.S.A.

MOON HOOD LOUVRES ARE PUNCHED INWARD. CHARACTERISTIC PEAKED RADIATOR, 1919 THROUGH 1926

Moon's Ten Proven Units

1. Continental Red Seal Motor.
2. Delco Starter and Ignition.
3. Timken Axles.
4. Spicer Universal Joints.
5. Brown-Lipe Transmission.
6. Borg & Beck Clutch.
7. Rayfield Carburetor.
8. Exide Battery.
9. Fedders Radiator — Nickel-Silver.
10. Gemmer Steering Gear.

20

"6-48" VICTORY 122" W.B. 224 C.I.D. (THROUGH '22) 4.75 G.R.

32 × 4 TIRES   4.75 G.R.

"6-68" 125" W.B. 303.1 C.I.D. 33 × 5 TIRES 4.45 G.R.

(6-CYL. ONLY, UNTIL 1928)

21-22

('21 = DRUM HEADLIGHTS)

"6-75" ('22 ONLY) HAS 135" W.B., 325.1 C.I.D., 32 × 4½ TIRES 4.45 G.R.

"6-40" (115" W.B.)

(46 - H.P. "6-40" STARTS 2-22)

"6-48" →

Actual Photograph of the Six-48 Touring

23-24

("6-58" STARTS AUG., 1922 HAS 128" W.B. 241.6 C.I.D. "8-R" ENGINE (TO '26)

('24)

115" W.B. "6-40" (U) STARTING 8-23, REPLACES 195.6 C.I.D. "6-Y" ENG. WITH 195.6 C.I.D. "7-U" ENG. 5.10 G.R.

("6-50" INTRO. DURING '24)

60 M.P.H.

25-26

(HYDRAULIC BRAKES, NEW ROOF-VISOR)

NEW "A" SERIES INTRODUCED 1924 LOCKHEED HYDRAULIC 4-WHEEL BRAKES ALSO AVAILABLE (OPTIONAL). ("A" CONT'D. INTO '28)   113" W.B.

6-40 "NEWPORT" ('25) 50 H.P. @ 2600 RPM
6-50 "METROPOLITAN" ('25) 52 H.P. @ 2600 RPM
6-58 "LONDON" 56 H.P. @ 2300 RPM

('26 HAS HIGHER, NARROWER RADIATOR, CROWN FENDERS.)

One of the Moon innovations of the year is this new Cabriolet roadster. The deck lid opens up a fully upholstered rear seat "a deux." With the lid down the car is a closed roadster. Concealed compartment for golf bag and other luggage. Rear window may be lowered for communication between passengers.   (Patents applied for)

27

RADIATOR DESIGN IS NEW. USED 1 YEAR ONLY.

"NEW "BULLET" HEADLAMPS

"A" HAS 113" W.B. CONTINENTAL "7-Z" ENG. 50 H.P. @ 2600 RPM 30 × 5.25 TIRES

HAS 110" W.B. 185 C.I.D. CONTINENTAL "26-L" ENG. 47 H.P. @ 2600 RPM 29 × 4.75 TIRES (CONT'D. INTO 1928)

"6-60" (new)

FINAL "A" ('28) SOMETIMES KNOWN AS 6-A

28

6 OR 8 CYL.

new "6-72" (ROYAL) HAS OLD-STYLE BODY AND ROOF-VISOR BUT NEW RADIATOR DESIGN.

NEW STRAIGHT-8 "8-80" HAS 125" W.B., 268.6 C.I.D. CONTINENTAL ENG., 86 H.P. @ 3200 RPM, 31 × 6.20 TIRES, 4.63 G.R.

STARTING AUGUST, 1928, A RE-STYLED "6-72" CONT'D. INTO '29 WITH SAME 120" W.B., 214.7 C.I.D. "11-E" CONTINENTAL ENG., 66 H.P. @ 3150 RPM, 29 × 5.50 TIRES, 4.9 G.R.

('29-'30 WINDSOR CARS ALSO)

"6-72"

"AEROTYPE" 8-80 (DISC. LATE '28)

29

PETITE SEDAN

BODY BY UNION CITY

FOR 1920, 8 HOOD LOUVRES ON EACH SIDE, LARGER RADIATOR

MOORE (1916-1921)
MOORE MOTOR VEH. CO., DANVILLE, ILLINOIS

20

MODEL "F-30"
106" W.B.

4-CYL. GOLDEN, BELKNAP and SCHWARTZ ENGINE *
3¾" × 4¼" B.+S. 22 H.P.
4.25 G.R.
*-NEW TURNER and MOORE ENGINE ALSO.

FOR EXPORT TO ENGLAND

BRITISH BODIES INSTALLED ON MOST.

114" W.B.
4 CYL.

MORRISS - LONDON (1919-1925)
CROW-ELKHART MOTOR CAR CO.; CENTURY MOTOR CO., ELKHART, IND.

NASH (1917-1957)

THE NASH SIX

THE NASH MOTORS COMPANY, KENOSHA, WISCONSIN

("685" COUPE) ('20)

"SPORT"

"681" SERIES = 261.3 C.I.D.
(MODELS 681-687)

19-20

('20)

(6 CYL.)

"681" 6 CYL. O.H.V.
248.9 C.I.D.
55 H.P. @ 2400 RPM
121" WHEELBASE
4.50 GEAR RATIO

33 × 4

7 - PASS. SEDAN

(NOTE THINNER HOOD LOUVRES)

"41"

112" WHEELBASE

4 -CYL. SERIES
(INTRODUCED LATE IN 1920, CONTINUED INTO 1924.)
'21 = 165.9 C.I.D., 35 H.P. @ 2200 RPM
LATER = 178.9 C.I.D., 37 H.P. @ 2800 RPM

22½ ('23)

21-22

(1922 6-CYL. SERIES BEGINS OCT., 1921, WITH MODELS "691" THROUGH "698;"
GAS GAUGE ON DASH; NEW, MORE POWERFUL EMERGENCY BRAKE ON TRANSMISSION.)

(NOTE NEW DRUM HEADLIGHTS)

The New Five Passenger Six Cylinder Sedan

NASH

Nash Leads the World in Motor Car Value

23-24

NASH

(LARGER BRAKE DRUMS.)

"CARRIOLE" (INTRODUCED 1922)

← 4 CYL →

STEP-PLATES IN 1924

6-CYL. 4 PASS. VICTORIA (1924 STYLE)

The Nash Model 694 Sedan

(1924 MODELS END JULY 31, 1924.)

25

SPECIAL 6 112" W.B.

4.88 GEAR RATIO

Coffee Shop

AJAX HAS 169.7 C.I.D., 40 H.P. @ 2400 RPM 108" W.B.

21 × 4.75 TIRES

AJAX SIX NASH-BUILT

NEW L-HEAD ENGINE

(INTRODUCED MAY 26, 1925)

(WITH 4-WHEEL MECHANICAL BRAKES)

207.1 C.I.D. 46 H.P. @ 2200 RPM

176

SPECIAL SIX SEDAN

NASH

Leads the World in Motor Car Value

25 (CONT'D.)

"4-DOOR COUPE"

4-Wheel Brakes

ADVANCED SIX

OVERHEAD-VALVE, 6 CYLS.
248.9 C.I.D.
60 H.P. @ 2400 RPM

33 x 6

127-inch Wheelbase
Five Passengers
121" W.B. ON SOME BODY TYPES
4.50 GEAR RATIO

26

Light Six
4-Door Sedan

LIGHT 6
(REPLACES AJAX)

The New Special Six Series

112½" W.B.

31 x 5.25

New Special Six Sedan
(JULY, 1925)

The New Advanced Six Series

"4-DOOR COUPÉ"

177

NASH

Leads the World in Motor Car Value

27

108" W.B.
170 C.I.D.
40 H.P. @
2400

LIGHT 6

4.77
GEAR RATIO

DELUXE LIGHT 6
(WITH BUMPERS)

SPEC. 6 WITH
CONVENTIONAL
ROOFLINE →

4.67 GEAR RATIO   112½" W.B.

SPECIAL 6
224 C.I.D. (THROUGH '29)
52 H.P. @ 2600

CAVALIER
SEDAN
(WIRE WH.
AVAIL.)

"241"

New Nash Attractions

7-bearing crankshaft motor —world's smoothest type— powers all new Nash models.

New-type crankcase "breather" which prevents crankcase dilution.

Rubber insulated motor supports—(standard Nash practice for some time).

New-design motor muffler deepening operative quietness.

Motor heat control by new thermostatic water regulator.

Oil screen "agitator" preventing oil coagulation in coldest weather.

And many other new improvements.

A NEW Instrument Board

and Greater Front Compartment Convenience

27
(CONT'D.)

69 H.P. @ 2500 RPM

ADVANCED 6

VICTORIA
127" W.B.

AMBASSADOR

AMBASSADOR

AMBASSADOR
(ADVANCED 6)
and
CAVALIER
(SPECIAL 6)
SEDANS INTRODUCED
AT CHICAGO AUTOMOBILE
SHOW, JANUARY 29, 1927.

NASH

EMBLEM AND MASCOT (ABOVE)

LIGHT 6 REPLACED BY
STANDARD 6 ("321")
108 1/4" W.B. 4.77 GEAR RATIO
184.1 C.I.D. 30 × 5.00
45 H.P. @ 2600 TIRES (THROUGH '29)

"325" COUPE

SPECIAL 6 ("331")
HAS 224 C.I.D.
52 H.P. @ 2600 RPM
4.88 GEAR RATIO (THROUGH '29)
112 3/4" (TIRES = 30 × 5.25)
W.B.

28

ADVANCED 6 "SEDAN FOR 5"
(COACH) RESEMBLES ABOVE CAR (AND
ALSO HAS SAME FRENCH ROOF-LINE.)

32 × 6.00 TIRES' (THROUGH '29)
("361" SERIES)
ADVANCED 6 HAS 70 H.P.
@ 2400 RPM

"AMBASSADOR" →
("367")

184.1 C.I.D.
50 H.P. @
2800 RPM
112¼" W.B.
4.77 G.R.

STANDARD 6
(30 × 5.00 TIRES)

THE WORLD

HAS A NEW AND FINER

MOTOR CAR

Advanced Six Coupe

SPECIAL 6
(DUAL ROWS OF
HOOD LOUVRES)
65 H.P. @ 2900 RPM
116" W.B. 29 × 5.50 TIRES

ADVANCED 6
78 H.P. @ 2900 RPM

29

ADVANCED 6 AMBASSADOR

NASH RADIATOR,
FITTED WITH USEFUL
ACCESSORY "ALLEN
VERTICAL SHUTTERS"
(SOLD SEPERATELY.)

BODIES BY NASH
OR SEAMAN

new = 2 SPARK PLUGS PER CYLINDER

Advanced Six Sedan

TWIN IGNITION
MOTOR

29½ NASH

(MAY, 1929)

FINAL YEAR
FOR VACUUM
FUEL FEED.

FINAL YEAR
OF 6-CYL. NASH
CHOICES ONLY.

NEW "400" ROADSTER

STARTER CONTROL ON DASH

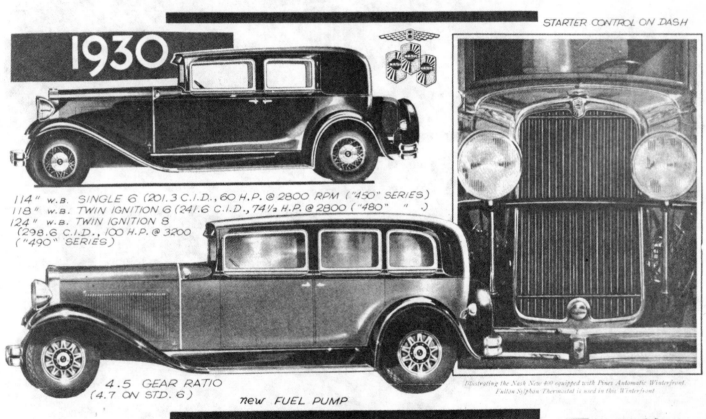

1930

114" w.b. SINGLE 6 (201.3 C.I.D., 60 H.P. @ 2800 RPM ("450" SERIES)
118" w.b. TWIN IGNITION 6 (241.6 C.I.D., 74½ H.P. @ 2800 ("480" ".)
124" w.b. TWIN IGNITION 8
(298.6 C.I.D., 100 H.P. @ 3200
("490" SERIES)

4.5 GEAR RATIO
(4.7 ON STD. 6)

new FUEL PUMP

Illustrating the Nash New 400 equipped with Pines Automatic Winterfront.
Fulton Sylphon Thermostat is used in this Winterfront

5.1, 5.1, 4.45, 4.5 RESPECTIVE
GEAR RATIOS ON
"6-60," "8-70," "8-80" and
"8-90" SERIES

(INTRO. 10-30)

31

JAN., '31 = NEW "CONVERTIBLE SEDAN" (871 or 881)

"8-70"

6-60 = 6 CYL., L-HEAD
201.3 CID   65 H.P.
114¼" WB, 5.00 x 19
TIRES (SPECS. THROUGH
EARLY '32 "960")

new
L-HEAD
STRAIGHT-8 "8-70"
227.2 CID   78 H.P.
(SPECS. THR. '32 "970")

116¼" WB
5.25 x 19
TIRES

8 TWIN IGN.
8-80 = STRAIGHT-8, O.H.V.
240.3 CID   87 H.P. @ 3400
121" WB,   5.50 x 18 TIRES
(94 H.P., 6.00 x 18 TIRES ON '32 "980")

TWIN IGN.
"8-90" = STRAIGHT-8, O.H.V.
298.6 CID, 115 H.P. @ 3600 RPM
124-133" WB,   6.50 x 19 TIRES
(SPECS. THROUGH EARLY '32 "9 90")

NASH

NEW "V" GRILLE →

(INTRODUCED JUNE 28, 1931)

31½-32

EARLY '32s IN "900" MODEL SERIES

new SILENT-2ND SYNCHRO-SHIFT TRAN. and FREE-WHEELING

AMBASSADOR 8

32½

NEW BODY DESIGNS

STANDARD 8

INTRODUCED SATURDAY, FEB. 27, 1932

Beavertail Back of the new Nash Slip-Stream Body

RIDE CONTROL AVAIL.

5 NEW SERIES NAMES (AS IN '33)

EARLY '33 LOW-PRICED MODELS HAVE VERTICAL HOOD LOUVRES

IN 5 SERIES:

BIG 6 == 116" WB, 75 H.P. @ 3200 RPM (217.8 CID)
STANDARD 8 == 116" WB, 80 H.P. @ 3200 RPM (247.4 CID)
SPECIAL 8 == 121" WB, 85 H.P. @ 3200 RPM " "
ADVANCED 8 == 128" WB, 100 H.P. @ 3400 RPM (260.8 CID)
AMBASSADOR 8 == 142" WB, 125 H.P. @ 3600 RPM (322 CID)
(OR '133")

33

MODEL "1194"
AMB. 8
7-PASS.

142" W.B.

NASH

34

88-H.P.
BIG 6
(234.8 C.I.D.)

IN ABOVE INTERIOR VIEW NOTE THE GROSS EXAGGERATION OF HOOD LENGTH (FROM AN ORIGINAL ADVERTISEMENT.)

AMBASSADOR

new HYDRAULIC BRAKES

35

BIG 6 BECOMES ADVANCED 6 :

6.25 x 16 TIRES
120" W.B.
(EARLY MODELS = 88 H.P. @ 3200 R.P.M.)
4.4 G.R. (AS IN '34)

Super-Hydraulic Brakes
Automatic Cruising Gear
All-Steel, One-Piece Bodies
Synchronized Springing
Ball-Bearing Steering
Mid-Section Seating
Balanced Ride

Aeroform Design
Flying Power (Developed from Twin Ignition)

ADVANCED SIX VICTORIA $895	ADVANCED EIGHT VICTORIA $1115	AMBASSADOR EIGHT VICTORIA $1240
120" Wheelbase — 90 Horsepower	125" Wheelbase — 102 Horsepower	125" Wheelbase — 102 Horsepower

(EARLY MODELS OF ADV. 8, AMB. 8 100 H.P. @ 3400 RPM)

STARTING 1935, 1ST TWO DIGITS OF MODEL NO. INDICATES YEAR, BEGINNING WITH 3500 SERIES FOR 1935. SYSTEM USED ON NASH AND SUBSEQUENT AMERICAN MOTORS CARS.

183

NASH 36 ENGINE

NASH 400

NEW!

NASH 400 MONITOR-SEALED MOTOR $675

EARLIEST "400" MODELS (STARTING AT # C-1001) ARE SOMETIMES LISTED AS LATE 1935 MODELS.

4.1 GEAR RATIO

"400"

has 6.00 x 16 TIRES

("400" (STARTS MAY, 1935)

"400" HAS 117" W.B. 6 CYL. 234.8 C.I.D., 90 H.P. @ 3400 RPM

L-HEAD ENGINE ON "400"

"400" DELUXE

60½ IN

SAME C.I.D. ON "400" and AMB. 6

ADVANCED 6 BECOMES AMBASSADOR 6

6.25 x 16 TIRES ON AMBASSADOR 6;

6.50 x 16 ON 8

NASH AUTOMATIC CRUISING GEAR!
Available at slight extra cost. Reduces engine revolutions about ⅓ at high speeds. Gives you an entirely new ride sensation. Saves 15% to 25% in gasoline; as much as 50% in oil!

AMBASSADOR 6 : 93 H.P. @ 3400 RPM

260.8 C.I.D. AMBASSADOR 8 : 102 H.P. @ 3400 RPM

125" W.B. ON AMBASSADOR 6 OR 8

184

NASH 37

"LAFAYETTE" GRILLE MEMBERS ARE HORIZONTAL.

"3713" 2-DOOR

"3788"

"3782"

AMBASSADOR

CHAS. W. NASH (FOUNDER)

"3781" CONVERTIBLE

BABE RUTH

"LAFAYETTE" BECOMES A 117"-W.B. SERIES OF NASH, (1937 THROUGH '40) (L-HEAD)

7.00 × 16 TIRES ON AMBASSADOR 8 (THROUGH '39)

"3815"

95 H.P. @ 3400 RPM (AS ON '37 AMB. 6)

117" W.B.

"LAFAYETTE"

AMBASSADOR 6

105 H.P. @ 3400 RPM (AS ON '37 AMB. 8) 4.11 G.R. (SINCE '37)

NASH World's FIRST CAR With CONDITIONED AIR For Winter Driving

38

JAN. 4, 1938: 1ST ANNIVERSARY OF 1937 NASH-KELVINATOR MERGER

OPTIONAL VACUUM SHIFT HAS CONTROL LEVER PROTRUDING FROM CENTER OF DASH.

← AMBASSADOR 8

115 H.P. @ 3400 RPM (4.1 G.R. (THROUGH FINAL STRAIGHT-8 SINCE '35) NASH OF 1942)

LAFAYETTE has 99 H.P. @ 3400 RPM (THROUGH '40)

39

LAST STOP for GAS

AMBASSADOR = 121" W.B. ON 6; 125" ON 8 (SINCE '37)

new 4.1 G.R. ON 6s, 4.4 ON AMBASSADOR 8.

185

The NATIONAL SEXTET

NATIONAL MOTOR CAR
and VEHICLE CORP.,
INDIANAPOLIS

(1900 - 1924)

OVERHEAD-VALVE
6-CYLINDER 301.3 C.I.D.
ENGINE NEW
FOR 1920;
REPLACES THE
FORMER L-HEAD
6-CYL. and V-12 TYPES.

DASH

130" W.B.,
32 x 4½ TIRES,
4.08 GEAR RATIO
ON "SEXTET" (BB)
(THROUGH '24)

FIVE CUSTOM BUILT BODY STYLES

FRONT END ('23)

20-24

WITH
TOP DOWN

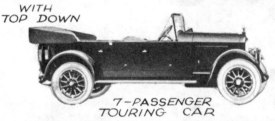

7-PASSENGER
TOURING CAR

NOTE THE
UNUSUALLY
LONG
REAR
QUARTER
WINDOWS →

7-PASSENGER
SEDAN

IN '23, 112"-W.B. "6-31" and 121"-W.B. "6-51" MODELS ALSO,
WITH 155 CID (OWN) and 241.6 CID (CONT.) ENG. "6-71" IS BB SERIES.

MODEL "D" UNCHANGED
FROM 1919
            104" W.B.
OWN 4-CYL., O.H.V.
145.7 C.I.D. ENGINE
4.25 G.R.
12-VOLT BOSCH IGNITION

32 x 4 TIRES

NELSON

(1917 — 1921)

E.A. NELSON
MOTOR CAR CO.,
DETROIT

(WITH DOUBLE-DROP
FRAME!)

NOMA 6   (1919 - 1923)

NOMA MOTORS CORP., N.Y.C.
224 CID CONTINENTAL OR BEAVER ENGINES

('22)

32 x 4½ TIRES, 128" W.B.

("3-C")

(364.5 CID, "1-D")

186

Oakland Motor Car Company,
Pontiac, Michigan (1907-1931)

OAKLAND
SENSIBLE SIX
"34-C"

20-21

6-CYL.
O.H.V.
177
C.I.D.
ENGINE

MARVEL
CARB.
(THROUGH '23)

4.50
GEAR
RATIO

44 H.P. @ 2600 RPM
(THROUGH 1924)

"34-C"
SERIES

W.B. INCREASED FROM
112" TO 115" FOR 1920.
115" W.B. CONT'D.
THROUGH 1923.

BOSCH IGN. ('20) REMY ('21)

22

"34-D"
SERIES
(6-44)

DRUM-TYPE HEADLIGHTS.
WALNUT STEERING WHEEL.
WALNUT INSTRUMENT BOARD WITH
SILVER-FACED, GLASS-COVERED
INSTRUMENTS.

32 × 4 TIRES
REMY IGNITION CONTINUED (THROUGH '26)

"6-44" SERIES

23

The New
Oakland
Six

NEW
4.66
GEAR
RATIO

1923 "6-44" IS THE
FINAL OAKLAND TO HAVE AN
OVERHEAD VALVE ENGINE.

187

OAKLAND
PRODUCT OF GENERAL MOTORS

(STARTS 9-8-23)

113" W.B. (THROUGH 1927)

BLUE DUCO ON BODIES

The True Blue

Six

24

"6-54" SERIES
(ADOPTS L-HEAD
VALVE ARRANGEMENT)

Oakland
PRODUCT OF GENERAL MOTORS

4-WHEEL BRAKES

STROMBERG CARB. (THROUGH '26)

'24
DASH GAUGES ON DARK
RECTANGULAR PANEL, BEHIND
GLASS PANE.

COUPE WITH LANDAU IRONS
AND OVAL QUARTER WINDOWS

25 "6-54"

HEADLIGHT
TIE-BAR
ELIMINATED

185 CU. IN. DISPL.
5 TO 1 COMPRESSION

4.7 GEAR RATIO

44 H.P. @ 2600 RPM
5 TO 1 COMPRESSION   60 M.P.H.

O A K L A N D
PRODUCT OF GENERAL MOTORS

EARLIEST LANDAU SEDANS
HAVE OVAL REAR QUARTER
WINDOWS. IN AUTUMN,
1925, WINDOW STYLE IS
LIKE '27.

DASH
(RADIO,
WATER
TEMP.
GAUGE
NOT
ORIG.)

26 "OS"

(INTRO. 7-25)

45 H.P. @ 2600 RPM
(THROUGH '27)
new HARMONIC BALANCER
AIR CLEANER
5.0 COMPR.

4.8 COMPR.
MARVEL CARB.
(THROUGH '31)

27 "OS"

(INTRO. 7-26)

DELCO-
REMY
IGNITION
(THROUGH
'31)

FROM JULY 29, 1926 TO JAN. 9, 1927, THIS
'27 "GREATER OAKLAND 6" WAS RUN (IN DETROIT)
CONTINUOUSLY ON A TREADMILL, ON PUBLIC
DISPLAY, FOR A 100,000-MILE ENDURANCE
TEST. AVG. SPEED 25.49 M.P.H.,
AVG. 34.09 MILES PER GALLON.

COMPARE THE ACTUAL PHOTO ABOVE
WITH THE GLAMOURIZED ADVERTISING
ILLUSTRATION AT LEFT!

4.7 G.R.   FOOT-DIMMER FOR HEADLIGHTS
"RUBBER-SILENCED" CHASSIS   189   NATURAL-FINISH WOOD WHEELS

OAKLAND MOTOR CAR COMPANY, PONTIAC, MICHIGAN

OAKLAND
ALL-AMERICAN SIX
PRODUCT OF GENERAL MOTORS

NEW 117" WHEELBASE
211.5 C.I.D.
60 H.P. @ 2800 RPM
4.8 COMPRESSION
4.41 GEAR RATIO

The Cabriolet
Body by Fisher

28
"212" SERIES

FUEL PUMP REPLACES VACUUM TANK

Body by Fisher

Body by Fisher

2-DOOR SEDAN

OAKLAND

SMOOTH GLOSS-BLACK
INSTRUMENT PANEL WITH
SMALL, INDIVIDUAL CIRCULAR
BLACK-FACED GAUGES.

DASH/MAP
LIGHTS

INDIRECT LIGHTING ALSO

ROADSTER and PHAETON
have BODY BY OAKLAND.
FISHER BODY ON
OTHERS.

117" W.B.

4.72 GEAR RATIO
228.1 C.I.D.   68 H.P. @ 3000 RPM

OAKLAND'S FINAL "ALL-AMERICAN SIX"

29

THE MOST RELIABLE AND
DURABLE OF OAKLANDS.
MORE 1929s HAVE SURVIVED
THAN ANY OTHER YEAR MODEL
OF THIS MAKE.

CONVERTIBLE
LANDAU SECTION

29 x 5.50 TIRES

NEW
MOLDINGS
ON
INSTRUMENT
PANEL

30

EIGHT
(V-8)

117" WHEELBASE,
251 C.I.D.
(THROUGH
1931)

82 H.P. @ 3000 RPM
4.42 GEAR RATIO

5.50 x 18 TIRES
(1930 and 1931)

85 H.P. @ 3400 RPM
4.55 GEAR RATIO

31

(THE FINAL
OAKLAND)

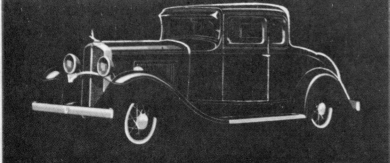

MAKING NEW FRIENDS AND KEEPING THE OLD

OGREN (1915-1923)

OGREN MOTOR CAR CO.,
MILWAUKEE, WIS.

(NICKELED RADIATOR SHELL ON '22 MODEL.)

BOSCH IGNITION

6-CYL. CONTINENTAL ENGINE
(325.1 C.I.D.)
('22-'23)
80 - 90 H.P.
TOP SPEED = 68 M.P.H. (ROADSTER, 90 MPH)

134" W.B.
33 × 5
TIRES

RAYFIELD CARB.

20 TO 23

OLDS MOTOR WORKS, LANSING, MICH. (EST. 1897)

Product of GENERAL MOTORS SINCE '09

Oldsmobile

6
MODEL "37-A"
112" W.B.
6 CYLS. (O.H.V.)
177 C.I.D.
4.58 GEAR RATIO
32 × 4" TIRES
44 H.P. @ 2600 RPM

JOHNSON CARB.

6-CYL.
OR
V-8
(SINCE '17) 8

20

MODEL "45-B"
122" W.B.
V-8 (T-HEAD)
246.7 C.I.D.
4.91 GEAR RATIO
33 × 4½" TIRES
58 H.P. @ 2600 RPM
BALL CARB.

4 (NEW)
"43-A"
224.3 C.I.D., 43 H.P., 115" W.B.
REMY IGN.
4.66 GEAR RATIO
ZENITH CARB.

21

"46"
V-8
SIMILAR
SPECS. AS
'20 "45-B"
BUT HAS
58 H.P.
@ 2510 RPM

"8"

"47"
STARTS March, 1921

192

OLDSMOBILE

REMY IGN. ON "43-A"
DELCO IGN. (OTHERS)

22

"46" V-8,
122" w.b., 4.93 GEAR RATIO
"43-A" = 4-CYL.,
115" w.b., 4.66 G.R.
"47" = V-8,
115" w.b., 5.10 G.R.
(THROUGH 1923)

4-CYL.
Semi-Sport
44 H.P. @ 2000 RPM

CARBURETORS:
"43-A" ZENITH
"47" JOHNSON
"46" BALL + BALL
(SAME IN '23)

"47" HAS 233.7 C.I.D.
V-8 ENGINE WITH
60 H.P. @ 2710 RPM

(FINAL YEAR
FOR 4 and
V-8)

The Four Cab—2 passengers—

The Four Sedan—5 passengers—

4-CYL. "43-A" HAS 4.70 GEAR RATIO, 40 H.P. @ 1800 RPM

"47"
(V-8) 63 H.P. @
2710 RPM

The Four Coupe—4 passengers—

23

PHANTOM VIEW
OF
"4" Brougham (AVAIL. 9-22)

4.92 G.R. ON
V-8 "46"

ALL MODELS have
DELCO IGN. (THROUGH '26)

PRODUCT OF GENERAL MOTORS

SPORT
TOURING

SIX 24

MODEL
"30"

STD. TOURING

(FROM '24 THROUGH '31,
6 CYL. ONLY)
(3-WINDOW BUSINESS COUPE
KNOWN AS "CAB.")

42 H.P. @
2600 RPM

110" W.B. (1924
and 1925)
ZENITH CARB. (THROUGH '25)

169.3 C.I.D. (THROUGH
'26)

31 x 4 TIRES IN
1924 and 1925, AS
WELL AS 5.10 GEAR RATIO

The Refined

OLDSMOBILE SIX

PRODUCT OF GENERAL MOTORS

New Beauty outside — but same good chassis 40,000 owners know!

25

MODEL "30"

41 H.P. @ 2600 RPM (THROUGH '26)

DISC WHEELS AVAIL.

new RADIATOR DESIGN (THROUGH '27)

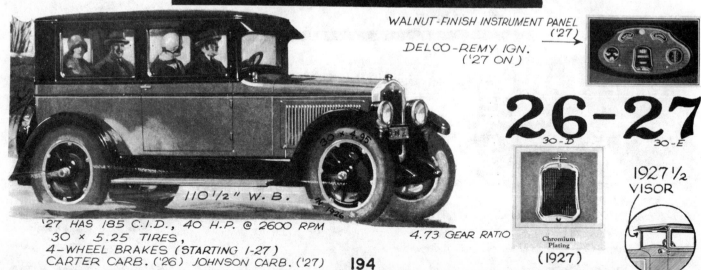

WALNUT-FINISH INSTRUMENT PANEL ('27)

DELCO-REMY IGN. ('27 ON)

26-27

30-D   30-E

1927½ VISOR

Chromium Plating (1927)

4.73 GEAR RATIO

110½" W.B.

30 × 4.95

30 × 5.25

'27 HAS 185 C.I.D., 40 H.P. @ 2600 RPM
30 × 5.25 TIRES,
4-WHEEL BRAKES (STARTING 1-27)
CARTER CARB. ('26) JOHNSON CARB. ('27)

OLDSMOBILE
28

55 H.P. @ 2700 RPM
(THROUGH '29)

MODEL "F-28"

113½"
WHEELBASE and
197.5 C.I.D.
(THROUGH
1931)

28 x 5.25 TIRES IN 1928 and 1929
4.41 GEAR RATIO IN 1928 and 1929
SCHEBLER CARB. (THROUGH '29)

LATE MODEL =
NOTE LONGER ROW
OF HOOD LOUVRES

ON '28 OLDSMOBILES,
FUEL PUMP REPLACES VACUUM TANK

This emblem identifies
the new 1929 Oldsmobile

(ON RADIATOR)

29
MODEL
"F-29"

195

OLDSMOBILE
PRODUCT OF GENERAL MOTORS

30
"F-30"

62 H.P. @ 3000 RPM
JOHNSON CARB.

DASH

GAUGES, LEFT TO RT. :
AMMETER, WATER TEMP.,
SPEEDOMETER-ODOMETER,
OIL PRESSURE, GASOLINE

5.25 x 18 TIRES IN
1930 and 1931

4.54 GEAR RATIO

31
"F-31"

65 H.P. @ 3350 RPM

STROMB.
CARB.
(THROUGH
'35)

4.56
GEAR RATIO
(THROUGH '33)

'31 DASH

6.00 x 17 TIRES, 116½" W.B.

6 HAS 213.3 C.I.D.
and 71 H.P.
@ 3200 RPM

6 "F-32"

32

8
(NEW)
"L-32"

STRAIGHT-
8 HAS
240.3 C.I.D.
and 82
H.P. @
3200 RPM

196

DASH

OLDSMOBILE

33

4.56 GEAR RATIO

240.3 C.I.D. CONTINUED ON 8 (THROUGH '36)

8 HAS 90 H.P. @ 3350 RPM (THROUGH '34)

119" W.B. (THROUGH '34)

6 INCREASED TO 221.4 C.I.D. FOR '33 ONLY. 80 H.P. @ 3200 115" WHEELBASE

5.50 × 17 TIRES ON 6, 6.00 × 17 ON 8

THE NEW EIGHT . . . THE NEW SIX . . . TWO GENERAL MOTORS VALUES

34

6 HAS 5.50 × 17 TIRES, 8 HAS 7.00 × 16 TIRES, 4.56 GEAR RATIO
4.78 GEAR RATIO
213.3 C.I.D., 84 H.P. @ 3250

HYDRAULIC BRAKES

"F-34" (114" W.B.) 6

"L-34" 8

WOOD-GRAINED dash

'34 DASH

'35 DASH

8 HAS 100 H.P. @ 3400 RPM (THROUGH '36)

"L-35" 8

"F-35" 6

6 HAS 213.3 C.I.D. and 90 H.P. @ 3400 RPM (THROUGH '36)

7.00 × 16 TIRES (8)

121" W.B. (THROUGH '36)

35

6.25 × 16 TIRES ON 6

115" W.B. (THROUGH '36)

OLDSMOBILE

TOURING SEDAN (W. TRUNK)

INTERIOR

6 "F-36"

GAS FILLER LOCATED HIGHER ON RT. REAR FENDER.

3-WINDOW SPORT COUPE

FRONT DOORS NOW HINGED AT FRONT.

8 "L-36"

36

8 has FENDER PARKING LIGHTS, and 5 HORIZONTAL CROSS-MEMBERS VISIBLE IN GRILLE.

CARTER CARB. (BOTH MODELS, STARTING '36)

7.00 x 16 TIRES ON OLDSMOBILE 8 FOR 1936 and 1937

6 HAS 229.7 C.I.D. (THROUGH '40) and 95 H.P. @ 3400 (THROUGH '38)

TAIL-LIGHTS MOVED UP TO SIDES OF BODY

6   117" W.B. (THROUGH '38)

8 NOW USES 257.1 C.I.D.

110 H.P. @ 3600 RPM

8

37

198

124" W.B. (THROUGH '38)

THE SIX

6 HAS 6.50×16 TIRES

OPTIONAL = AUTOMATIC TRANSMISSION!

38

THE EIGHT

OLDSMOBILE

6-CYL. "60" HAS 215.8 C.I.D.
and 90 H.P. @ 3200 RPM

NEW "60" 4-DOOR SEDAN

39

"F-39" and "G-39" (6)
"L-39" (8)

1-PIECE REAR WINDOW →

6

6-CYL. "60" and "70"
SERIES
115" and 120" W.B.

6-CYL. "70"
HAS 229.7 C.I.D. and
95 H.P. @ 3300 RPM

8

8-CYL.
"80"
HAS
257.1 C.I.D. and
110 H.P. @ 3500 RPM

200

Series 80

120" W.B.

Overland (1903-1926) (1939 ALSO*)

* - SEE **WILLYS**

WILLYS-OVERLAND, INC., TOLEDO, OHIO
Sedans, Coupes, Touring Cars and Roadsters
Willys-Overland, Limited, Toronto, Canada
The John N. Willys Export Corporation, New York

20-21

(4 CYLS.,
143.1 C.I.D.)
27 H.P.
4.5 GEAR
RATIO

100" W.B. CONT'D.
THROUGH '26 (ON 4-CYL.)

with NEW, DIAGONALLY-MOUNTED
"TRIPLEX" SPRINGS

REAR
DETAILS

HOOD LOUVRES
NEW FOR
1920

30 x 3½

Rides as if Every Bump Had Springs

22 27 H.P. @ 2400 RPM

22½

23

27 H.P. @ 2200 RPM

30 × 3½ TIRES
AND TRIPLEX SPRINGS
UNTIL 1926 (ON
4-CYL. SERIES)

24

NEW 153.9 C.I.D. and
30 H.P. (THROUGH '26)
@ 2400 RPM

SPRING-SUMMER, 1924 =
"BLUE BIRD" SPECIAL TOURING
HAS NICKEL TRIM; DISC WHEELS
OPTIONAL.

SPECIAL MODEL "92"
"RED BIRD" TOURING
HAS OWN 106" W.B.
INTRO. MAY, 1923
(NICKEL RADIATOR
ON EARLY MODELS.)

"CHAMPION" 3-DOOR SEDAN
INTRODUCED OCT. 6, 1923.

COUPE

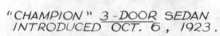

CHAMPION

THE Overland

"91"

OVERLAND

BUDD
(LIGHTWEIGHT, ALL-STEEL
BODIES ON 4-CYL.
MODELS, STARTING
AUGUST,
1924)

MODEL "91"

25

4

4 "91"

BUDD-BODIED 1925
"91s" ARE EASILY IDENTI-
FIED BY NARROW
WINDSHIELD CORNER-POSTS.
(ON COUPES and SEDANS.)

MODEL
"93"

new
OVERLAND SIX

NEW
'25 and '26 MODEL "93" 6-CYLINDER
OVERLANDS HAVE 169.6 C.I.D. ENGINE
WITH 38 H.P. @ 2800 RPM (30 × 5.25 TIRES)
and 112 3/4" W.B.

1926 4-CYL.
"91"
HAS BODY
SIMILAR TO 6.

26

The seats are wider, the windows larger, the doors
much broader than other cars of this size and price

203

REPLACED BY
WHIPPET

OWEN MAGNETIC—
(1914 – 1922)
THE CAR OF A THOUSAND SPEEDS

OWEN MAGNETIC MOTOR CAR CORPORATION, BROADWAY AT 57TH STREET, NEW YORK

(AND WILKES-BARRE, PA.)

19 – 21

142" WHEELBASE
6-CYL. WEIDELY ENGINE
(4" x 5½" BORE and STROKE)

CLOSE-COUPLED ('20)
(NOT LISTED EARLY IN SEASON.)

HAD A UNIQUE *ELECTRO-MAGNETIC* GEAR-SHIFT, CONTROLLED FROM QUADRANT ON STEERING WHEEL.

(KNOWN AS THE "CROWN MAGNETIC" FOR 1922 SEASON)

204

PACKARD

V-12
75 H.P. @ 2000 RPM
424.1 C.I.D.
136" W.B.
4.36 GEAR RATIO
35 × 5" TIRES

PACKARD MOTOR CAR COMPANY, *Detroit*

"*Ask the Man* *Who Owns One*"

DELCO IGN.
(THROUGH '27)
OWN CARB.
(THROUGH '29,
31-32)

(1899-1958)

("3-25" MODELS HAVE
128" W.B.)

18 TO 20

TWIN 6
(V-12)

SOME MODELS WITH 136" W.B.

21

SINGLE 6 (NEW)
(STARTS OCT., 1920)

NEW SINGLE SIX *has*
6-CYL., L-HEAD
241.6 C.I.D. ENGINE *with*
52 H.P. @ 2600 RPM (THROUGH '22)

TWIN 6
(85 H.P.)

SINGLE
6
↔

116" W.B. ON 6,
AS IN 1921

22

TWIN 6
(DISCONTINUED
DURING
1923)

85 H.P.
@ 2600
RPM

THE
TWIN-SIX
SPECIAL

205

PACKARD

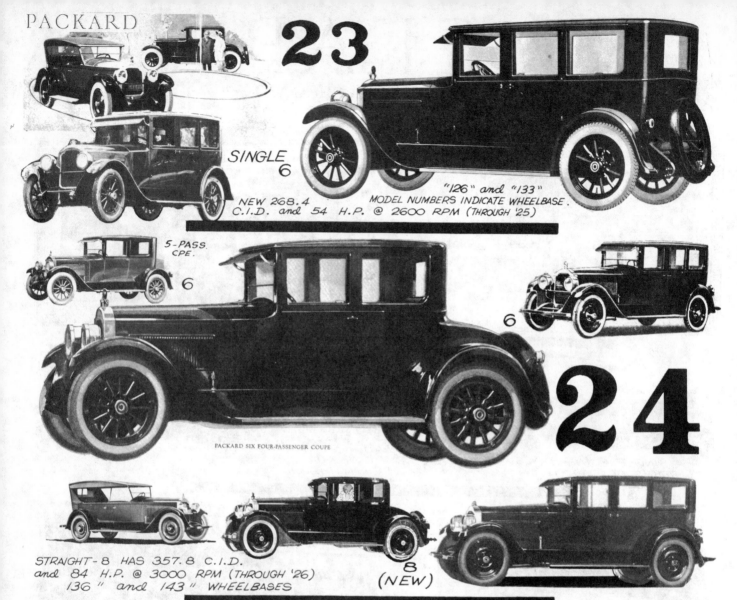

23

SINGLE 6

NEW 268.4 C.I.D. and 54 H.P. @ 2600 RPM (THROUGH '25)

"126" and "133" MODEL NUMBERS INDICATE WHEELBASE.

5-PASS. CPE. 6

PACKARD SIX FOUR-PASSENGER COUPE

6

24

STRAIGHT-8 HAS 357.8 C.I.D. and 84 H.P. @ 3000 RPM (THROUGH '26) 136" and 143" WHEELBASES

8 (NEW)

70 M.P.H. TOP SPEED OF 1925 "8" (4.7 GEAR RATIO)

ONLY PACKARD CAN BUILD A PACKARD

CHICAGO

8

25

6

8 7-PASS.

206

75 M.P.H. 4.66 GEAR RATIO

PACKARD SIX and EIGHT
the man who owns

PACKARD

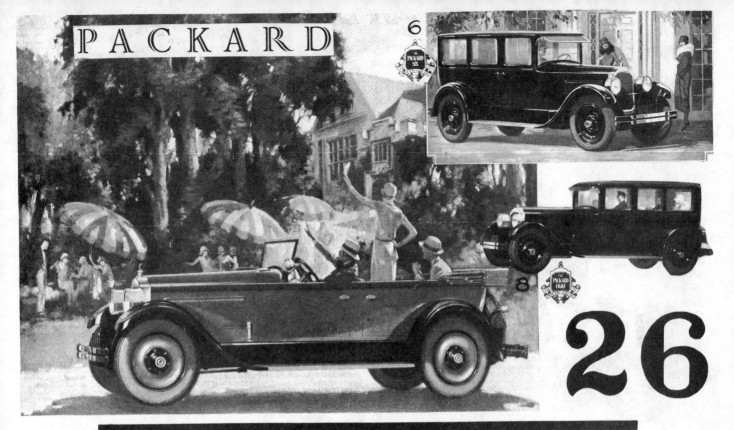

26

"426" and "433" are 6-CYL. MODELS
WITH
288.6 C.I.D., 82 H.P. @ 3200

27

"336" and "343" STRAIGHT-8
INCREASED TO 384.8 C.I.D.
and 106 H.P. @ 3200 RPM

(27½)

PACKARD

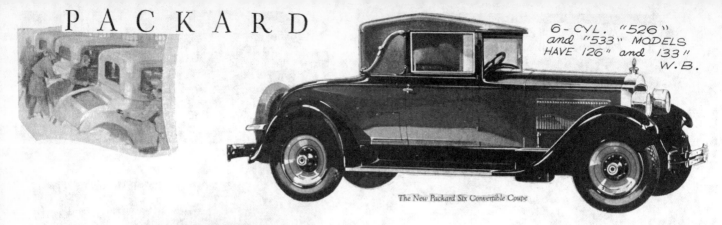

6-CYL. "526" and "533" MODELS HAVE 126" and 133" W.B.

The New Packard Six Convertible Coupe

UNTIL 1937, THE "526" and "533" OF 1928 WERE PACKARD'S FINAL 6-CYL. MODELS. 288.6 C.I.D., 82 H.P. @ 3200 RPM

28

(FINAL YEAR FOR DRUM HEADLIGHTS.) DELCO-REMY IGN.

6

LIMOUSINE

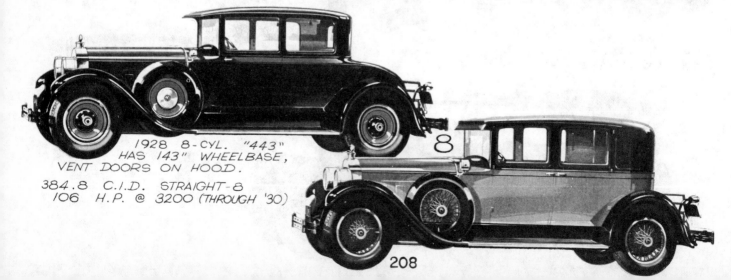

1928 8-CYL. "443" HAS 143" WHEELBASE, VENT DOORS ON HOOD.

384.8 C.I.D. STRAIGHT-8 106 H.P. @ 3200 (THROUGH '30)

8

208

PACKARD
ASK · THE · MAN · WHO · OWNS · ONE

EARLY '28

LATER '28

28 8-CYL. (CONT'D.)

ALL-WEATHER
TOWN CAR

8 CYL.
"626," "6-33" = 319.2 C.I.D. (THROUGH '39)
90 H.P. @ 3200 RPM (THROUGH '30)
"640," "645" = 384.8 C.I.D. (THROUGH
'36) 106 H.P. @ 3200 RPM
(THROUGH '30)

8 - CYLINDER PACKARDS ONLY IN 1929.
NO MORE PACKARD SIX CARS UNTIL '37
MODEL.

EARLIEST '29
PACKARDS HAVE NO
RADIATOR EMBLEM

29

NEW BOWL-SHAPED
HEADLIGHTS

126, 130, 140, 145" W.B.

209

P A C K A R D

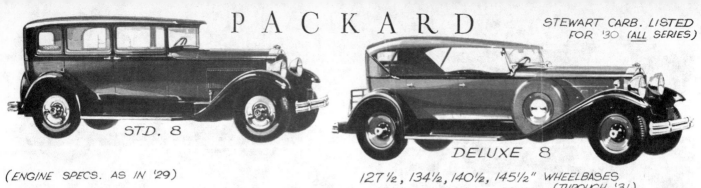

STD. 8

STEWART CARB. LISTED
FOR '30 (ALL SERIES)

DELUXE 8

(ENGINE SPECS. AS IN '29)

127½, 134½, 140½, 145½" WHEELBASES
(THROUGH '31)

30

"726," "733," "740," "745"
MODELS

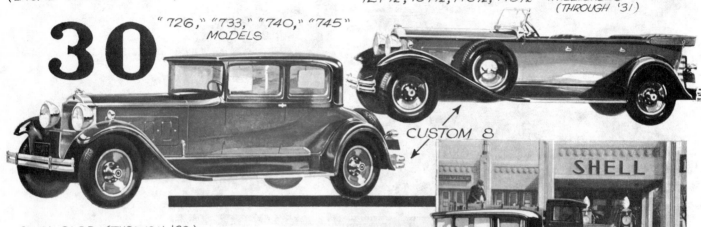

CUSTOM 8

SHELL

OWN CARB. (THROUGH '32)

NEW MECHANICAL FUEL PUMP
REPLACES VACUUM TANK.

31

"826," "833,"
"840," "845"
MODELS

100 OR
120 H.P. @
3200 RPM

31½
NEW
SERIES
(CONTINUES
INTO
1932)

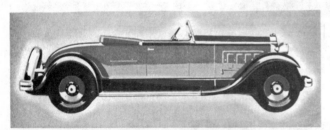

210

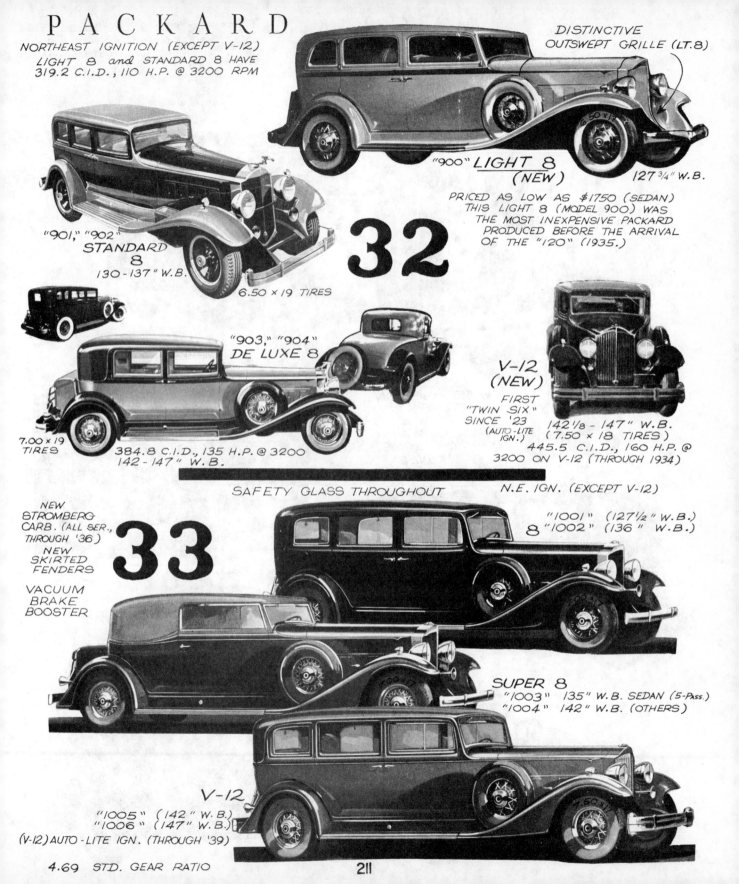

PACKARD

NORTHEAST IGNITION (EXCEPT V-12)
LIGHT 8 and STANDARD 8 HAVE
319.2 C.I.D., 110 H.P. @ 3200 RPM

DISTINCTIVE
OUTSWEPT GRILLE (LT.8)

"900" LIGHT 8
(NEW)   127 3/4" W.B.

PRICED AS LOW AS $1750 (SEDAN)
THIS LIGHT 8 (MODEL 900) WAS
THE MOST INEXPENSIVE PACKARD
PRODUCED BEFORE THE ARRIVAL
OF THE "120" (1935.)

"901," "902"
STANDARD
8
130-137" W.B.

6.50 × 19 TIRES

32

"903," "904"
DE LUXE 8

V-12
(NEW)

FIRST
"TWIN SIX"
SINCE '23
(AUTO-LITE
IGN.)

142 1/8 - 147" W.B.
(7.50 × 18 TIRES)

7.00 × 19
TIRES

384.8 C.I.D., 135 H.P. @ 3200
142 - 147" W.B.

445.5 C.I.D., 160 H.P. @
3200 ON V-12 (THROUGH 1934)

SAFETY GLASS THROUGHOUT

N.E. IGN. (EXCEPT V-12)

NEW
STROMBERG
CARB. (ALL SER.,
THROUGH '36)
NEW
SKIRTED
FENDERS

VACUUM
BRAKE
BOOSTER

33

8

"1001" (127 1/2" W.B.)
"1002" (136" W.B.)

SUPER 8
"1003" 135" W.B. SEDAN (5-PASS.)
"1004" 142" W.B. (OTHERS)

V-12
"1005" (142" W.B.)
"1006" (147" W.B.)
(V-12) AUTO-LITE IGN. (THROUGH '39)

4.69 STD. GEAR RATIO

PACKARD

4.69 STANDARD GEAR RATIO ON 8s

8 HAS CHROME-PLATING ON RADIATOR SHELL. →

SUPER 8 "1103" and "1104" have 384.8 C.I.D. and 145 H.P. @ 3200 RPM

NORTHEAST IGN. (EXCEPT V-12)

34

135", 142", 147" WHEELBASES ON SUPER 8s. 147"-W.B. "1105" SUPER 8 AVAILABLE with DIETRICH or LE BARON BODIES.

DASH

V-12

4.41 OR 4.69 GEAR RATIOS ON V-12

142 OR 147" W.B. ON V-12

PACKARD

HYDRAULIC BRAKES ON "120" ONLY.

"120". HAS 8-CYL. 257.1 C.I.D. ENGINE, 110 H.P. @ 3850 RPM 120" W.B. 4.36 GEAR RATIO

NEW LOW-COST 120

"120" IS LOWEST-PRICED PACKARD EVER, AT ONLY

$980 to $1095

"120" SEDAN

"1203," "1204," "1205" HAVE 132, 139, 144" W.B.

35

SUPER 8 →

SUPER 8 HAS 384.8 C.I.D., 150 H.P. @ 3200 RPM 4.41 G.R.

EIGHT ("1200," "1201," "1202") HAS 127, 134, 139" W.B., 319.2 C.I.D., 130 H.P. @ 3200 RPM 4.69 GEAR RATIO

"1207" 139" W.B. "1208" 144" W.B. 4.41 GEAR RATIO

← V-12

V-12 has NEW 473.3 C.I.D. WITH 175 H.P. @ 3200 RPM

new AUTO-LITE IGN. ON "120" and "V-12" (THROUGH '39) OTHERS have NORTHEAST IGN. (FINAL YEAR)

PACKARD SKIPPED 1300 SERIES AND MOVED ON TO 1400 MODEL NUMBERS IN '36.

213

PACKARD

"120" B

NEW 282 C.I.D.
120 H.P. @
3800 RPM
(THROUGH
'38
"1601")

36

SUPER 8

SU. 8 has
DELCO-REMY IGN.
(THROUGH '37)

V-12

MECHANICAL "POWER"
BRAKES ON LARGE 8s
AND V-12.

HYDRAULIC BRAKES ON ALL MODELS.

37

DE LUXE "120-CD"
and "138-CD" (138" W.B.)
HAVE AUTOMATIC RADIATOR SHUTTERS,
OTHER SPECIAL FEATURES.

NEW 6 HAS 236.7 C.I.D.
100 H.P. @ 3600 RPM

SIX

(NEW)
MODEL
115-C

115" W.B.
4.36 GEAR RATIO

6 has DELCO-REMY
IGN. (THROUGH '38)

120
C

120" W.B.
(CARTER CARB. ON
'37 "120")

"1500" (127" W.B.),
"1501" (134" W.B.) and
"1502" (139" W.B.) ARE SUPER 8
MODELS, WITH 319.2 C.I.D.
and 130 H.P. @ 3200 RPM
4.69 G.R., 7.50 x 16 TIRES
STROMBERG CARB.

6.50 x 16

214

V-12
STROMBERG CARB.

PACKARD
38

NEW 245.3 C.I.D.,
STILL RATED AT 100 H.P.
@ 3600 RPM

6

122" W.B.

MODEL
"1600"

8
"120" REPLACED
BY THIS "1601"
(127" W.B.) MODEL.

"1602" HAS 148"
W.B.

STROMBERG CARB. (ALL SERIES
EXCEPT 6)

SUPER 8

12

BODIES BY BRUNN

1938
MODEL NUMBERS
IN 1600 SERIES.

215

PACKARD

38
12 (CONT'D.)

AUTO-LITE IGN. ON
ALL '38 MODELS EXCEPT
6.

SIX

6 has CHANDLER-GROVES CARB.
(SINCE '37)

39
"CONTROLLED
OVERDRIVE"
OPTIONAL
ON ALL
MODELS.

1939 MODEL NUMBERS IN 1700 SERIES

120

EIGHT
"1701" and
"1702"
(127" and
148" W.B.)

319.2 C.I.D. ENGINE (SINCE '29)
130 H.P. @ 3200 RPM
(SINCE 1935 "EIGHT")

SUPER-8

AUTO-LITE IGN. ON
ALL 1939 PACKARDS.

216

12

(FINAL V-12)

PAIGE

(1909 – 1930)

PAIGE-DETROIT MOTOR CAR COMPANY, DETROIT, *Michigan*

Manufacturers of Paige Motor Cars and Motor Trucks

19-20

PAIGE TRUCK

"LARCHMONT" 4-PASS.

"GLENBROOK" 5-PASS.

"6-42" = 119" W.B. = OWN 6-CYL., 230.1 C.I.D. ENG.
"6-55" = 127" W.B. = 303.1 C.I.D. 6-CYL. CONTINENTAL ENG.

"6-66" 7-PASS. SEDAN

On January 21st, the Paige, Daytona Model, 6-66 broke every stock car record for speed when it covered a measured mile in 35.01 seconds—a speed of 102.8 miles an hour.

119"-W.B. "6-42" CONTINUED IN 1921; IS "6-44" IN 1922.

21-22

1922-STYLE TOP BOWS

"6-66" 131" W.B. 70 H.P.

331.4 C.I.D. CONT. ENG. (THROUGH '25)

JULY, 1922 = new series "6-66" has NEW CLUTCH AND TRANSMISSION THAT PERMITS DOWN-SHIFTING FROM HIGH to 2ND GEAR AT 35 M.P.H.

23 "6-66" BECOMES "6-70" IN 1923.

PAIGE

"6-70" DASH

131" WHEELBASE

"6-70"

24

NIGHT VIEW OF PAIGE FACTORY

4.6 GEAR RATIO

331.4 C.I.D.
6 - CYLINDER
CONTINENTAL
"10-A" ENGINE
73 H.P. @ 2400 RPM
131" W.B.

TOP SPEED = 75 M.P.H.

NOTE DIFFERENT QUARTER - WINDOW STYLE

MODEL "21-24"
4.9 G.R.

25

The New Paige Standard Brougham

('25½)

PAIGE

26

MODEL
"24-26"
6 CYL.
248.8 C.I.D.
63 H.P. @
2800 RPM
HYDRAULIC BRAKES

125" W.B.

32 × 6.00 TIRES

The Most Beautiful Car in America

HYDRAULIC BRAKES

4.9 GEAR RATIO
109" W.B.

185 C.I.D.
CONTINENTAL
SPECIAL ENGINE
43 H.P.
@
2600
RPM

"6-45"
COUPE

MODEL
"6-45"
(FORMERLY
"JEWETT")

27

4.45 GEAR RATIO
115"
W.B

"6-65"
249 C.I.D., 63 H.P. @
2800 RPM

"6-75"
268 C.I.D., 68 H.P.
@ 3000 RPM
4.82 GEAR RATIO
125" W.B.

[There are in the new Paige line 20 charming body types and color combinations on 4 chassis from $1095 to $2795—all prices f. o. b. Detroit]

STRAIGHT-8
"8-85"
298.6
C.I.D. LYC.
ENG.
80 H.P.
@ 3000

4.82 G.R.

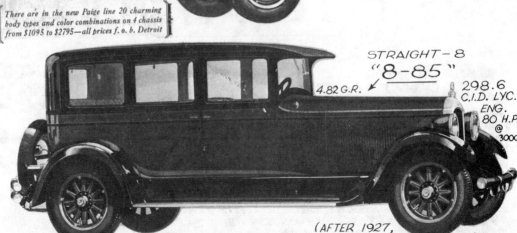

1927
INSTRUMENT PANEL

NEW NAME FOR
1928 :
GRAHAM-PAIGE

(AFTER 1927,
PAIGE NAME USED FOR TRUCKS, ETC.)

108" W.B.
MODEL "A"

PAN (1918-1922)

4 CYL., 165.9 C.I.D.
OWN O.H.V. ENGINE
33 × 4 TIRES
4.9 G.R.   (SEATS COULD BE
FOLDED, TO FORM
A BED.)

PAN MOTOR CO.,
ST. CLOUD, MINN.

125" W.B.
32 × 4 TIRES

PARENTI
(1920-1922)

OWN AIR COOLED V-8

PARENTI MOTORS CORP., BUFFALO, N.Y.

2 3/4" × 4 1/4" BORE and STROKE

PATERSON 6
W. A. PATERSON CO., FLINT, MICH.
(1908 - 1923)

('21)

22 "22-6-52"

32 × 4 1/2 TIRES
(THROUGH '23)
298.2 C.I.D.

4.5 G.R.
120" W.B. **21** "6-50"
6-CYL. CONTINENTAL ENGINE
(THROUGH '23)
224 C.I.D. (ALSO ON
'20 "6-47")

DELCO IGNITION (THROUGH '23)

('23)

23 "23-6-52"
242 C.I.D.

PEERLESS

7-PASS. SEDAN
SERIES 7
↓ (V-8) ('21)

(1900-1932) PEERLESS MOTOR CAR COMPANY, CLEVELAND, OHIO
Peerless Eight

MODEL "56"
('20)

19-22 "56-7"
CONT'D.
INTO 1922.

125" W.B. (THROUGH '22)
AUTO-LITE IGNITION AND 4.54 G.R. (THROUGH '20)
ATWATER-KENT IGNITION ('21-'22)
4.9 G.R. (TO '26)

OWN 331.8 C.I.D., V-8 L-HEAD ENGINE
(THROUGH '28)
34 × 4 1/2 TIRES (THROUGH '22)

220

PEERLESS

MODEL "66"

23 (INTRODUCED AUGUST, 1922)

NEW 128" W.B. (THROUGH '25, ON V-8)

TOWN COUPE (4-PASS.)

DELCO IGN. (ON 8s, THROUGH '29)

33 × 5 TIRES

24 6 CYL. "70"
V8 = "66"

PAINTED RADIATOR SHELL

new "70" has OWN 288.6 C.I.D. ENGINE (USED THROUGH '29) 126, 133" W.B. (THROUGH '26) 4.63 G.R., 32 × 4½ TIRES

("EQUIPOISED 8")
V-8 "67"

BALLOON TIRES, HYDRAULIC BRAKES

(INSTRUMENTS IN 3 OVALS, 2 GLASSED-IN)

70 H.P. @ 2500 RPM (THROUGH '26)

NEW RADIATOR DESIGN

25

(STYLE OF 6-CYL. "70" SIMILAR TO 1924)
70 H.P. @ 2500 RPM (THROUGH '29)
4.45 G.R.
33 × 6.20 TIRES

65 MILES PER HOUR

PEERLESS

6 - CYL., 230.2 C.I.D.
CONTINENTAL "8-U"
ENGINE ON NEW "6-80"
Auto - Lite IGNITION
30 × 5.77 TIRES ('26)
32 × 6.00 ('27)

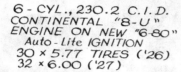

The Remarkable Six ~ 80
$1395 to $1795

116" W.B.
54 H.P. ('26)
63 " ('27)

26-27

FRENCH - STYLE
ROOF VISOR
(IN VOGUE ON
MANY AMERICAN
CARS OF 1925
TO 1928.)

The Powerful Six ~ 72
$1895 to $2995

126" W.B.
70 H.P.

DELCO IGN.
ON 6-72, 8-69

288.5 C.I.D.
70 H.P. @ 2500
(120" W.B. "6-90"
7 - WINDOW LANDAULET
SEDAN (WITH CONVERTIBLE
REAR QUARTERS) ALSO
AVAIL. IN 1927.

SMALL REAR QUARTER
WINDOWS ON MOST
PEERLESS COUPES
OF LATE 1920s.

The 90° V-type Eight-69
$2995 to $3795

133½" W.B. 70 H.P. ('26)
80 " ('27)

6 - 90
(NEW FOR 1927)

116" - W.B. "6-60" IS NEW FOR '27, has 199.1 C.I.D. CONTINENTAL ENG.,
52 H.P. @ 3000 RPM

EARLY 1928 MODELS : "6-60"   "6-80"
"6-90"   "8-69" (V-8)

28 (EARLY)

← MODEL   "6-60"
(INTRODUCED EARLY
SUMMER, 1927, WITH
ROOF-VISOR AS ON
'27 MODELS.)

62 H.P. @ 3000 RPM
(ALSO ON '29-30 "6-61")

222

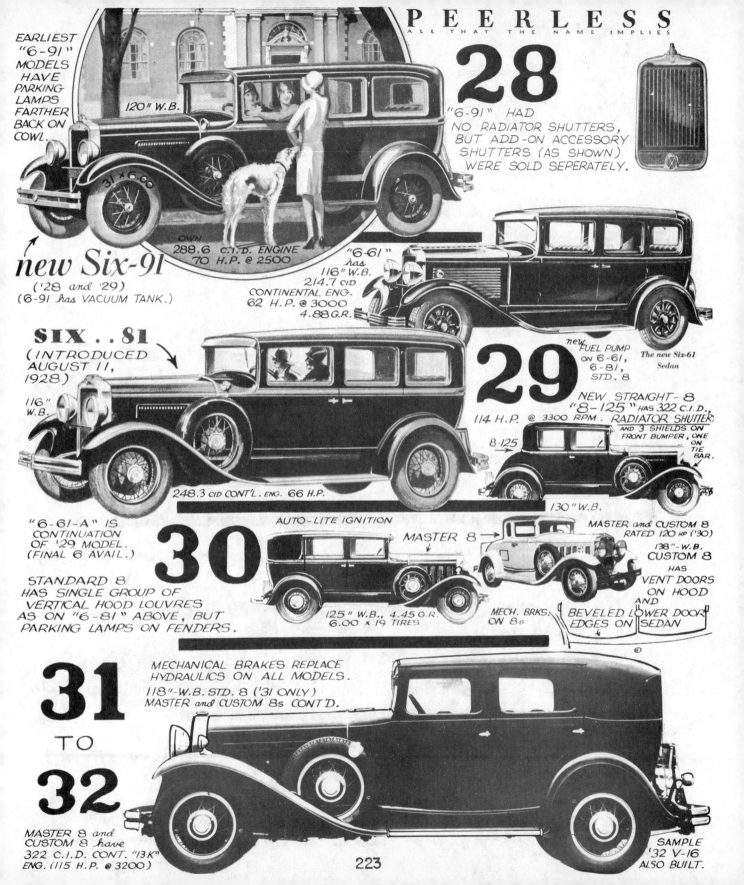

PEERLESS
ALL THAT THE NAME IMPLIES

EARLIEST "6-91" MODELS HAVE PARKING LAMPS FARTHER BACK ON COWL.

120" W.B.

31 x 6.00

OWN 288.6 C.I.D. ENGINE 70 H.P. @ 2500

new Six-91
('28 and '29)
(6-91 has VACUUM TANK.)

28

"6-91" HAD NO RADIATOR SHUTTERS, BUT ADD-ON ACCESSORY SHUTTERS (AS SHOWN) WERE SOLD SEPERATELY.

"6-61" has 116" W.B. 214.7 CID CONTINENTAL ENG. 62 H.P. @ 3000 4.88 G.R.

SIX .. 81
(INTRODUCED AUGUST 11, 1928)

116" W.B.

248.3 CID CONT'L. ENG. 66 H.P.

new FUEL PUMP ON 6-61, 6-81, STD. 8

The new Six-61 Sedan

29

NEW STRAIGHT-8 "8-125" HAS 322 C.I.D., 114 H.P. @ 3300 RPM. RADIATOR SHUTTER AND 3 SHIELDS ON FRONT BUMPER, ONE ON TIE BAR.

8-125

130" W.B.

"6-61-A" IS CONTINUATION OF '29 MODEL. (FINAL 6 AVAIL.)

STANDARD 8 HAS SINGLE GROUP OF VERTICAL HOOD LOUVRES AS ON "6-81" ABOVE, BUT PARKING LAMPS ON FENDERS.

30

AUTO-LITE IGNITION

MASTER 8

125" W.B., 4.45 G.R. 6.00 x 19 TIRES

MECH. BRKS. ON 8s

MASTER and CUSTOM 8 RATED 120 HP ('30)

138" W.B. CUSTOM 8 HAS VENT DOORS ON HOOD AND BEVELED LOWER DOOR EDGES ON SEDAN

31
TO
32

MECHANICAL BRAKES REPLACE HYDRAULICS ON ALL MODELS.
118"-W.B. STD. 8 ('31 ONLY)
MASTER and CUSTOM 8s CONT'D.

MASTER 8 and CUSTOM 8 HAVE 322 C.I.D. CONT. "13K" ENG. (115 H.P. @ 3200)

223

SAMPLE '32 V-16 ALSO BUILT.

The
PETERS
AUTOMOBILE
"Everybody's Car"

Peters Motor Corporation
Trenton   New Jersey

(1921–1922)

BUDDY MODEL   90" W.B.

IN 1919, PEAKED
RADIATOR AND
LOUVRELESS HOOD
ADOPTED, IN
ROLLS-ROYCE
STYLE.

PHIANNA
NEW SERIES
The Highest Type of Motor Car Construction

('19 -'21)

(1916–1922)
(PHIANNA MOTORS CO.,
NEWARK, N.J. ═══ TO 1918

M. H. CARPENTER,
LONG ISLAND CITY, N.Y. ═══ 1919 ON)

"1922" PHIANNAS BUILT FROM 1921 PARTS ON HAND.

(1917–1922) PIEDMONT
PIEDMONT MOTOR CAR CO.,
LYNCHBURG, VA.

Piedmont
MOTOR CAR CO. INC.
LYNCHBURG VIRGINIA

MODEL E

THE PIERCE-ARROW MOTOR CAR COMPANY, *Buffalo, N.Y.*

PIERCE-ARROW

(1901 TO 1938)

"38"
134" W.B.

20
(RIGHT-HAND
DRIVE)

"48"
142" W.B.

1921 ═══ NEW MODEL "33" (138" W.B.)
REPLACES 2 PREVIOUS
MODELS

LEFT-HAND DRIVE

DUAL-VALVE
ENGINE

6 CYLS.,
414.7
C.I.D.

21-23

4.28 G.R.

224

('23)

PIERCE-ARROW

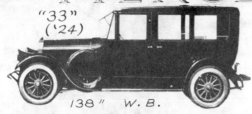

"33"
('24)

138" W. B.

"33" ('25)

100 H.P. @ 2600

24-26

LOWER-PRICED SERIES "80"
INTRODUCED
MID-1924.

Body by Pierce-Arrow   Series 80

1925-6
"80"
HAS 288.6
C.I.D., 6 CYLS.,
70 H.P. @ 2600 RPM
130" W. B.

COACH
('25½)

27

"80"
(130" W.B.)

"36"
(138" W.B.)

PIERCE-ARROW

28

"81" REPLACES "80"

"36"
7-PASSENGER TOURING CAR
4.29 G.R.

"6-81" INSTRUMENT PANEL

75 H.P. @ 3200 RPM
130" W.B.
4.45 G.R.

29

"143" (HOOD VENT DOORS)

NEW STRAIGHT-8 ENGINE
365 CU. IN. DISPL.
125 H.P. @ 3200 RPM
new FUEL PUMP

INSTRUMENT PANEL

143" W.B.

"133"
(7 GROUPS OF VERTICAL HOOD LOUVRES)

133" W.B.

30

4.08 and 4.42 G.R.

"B"

340, 366 and 385 C.I.D. STRAIGHT-8s,
DEVELOPING 115, 125, 132 H.P.
@ 3000 RPM

132³/₈, 134, 139, 144" W.B.

31

"43"=125 H.P.
134-7" W.B.
"42," "41"=
132 H.P.
142-7 W.B.

PIERCE ARROW

"54" STRAIGHT-8 HAS 366 C.I.D., 125 H.P. @ 3000

"53" V-12 = 140 H.P. @ 3100
"52," "51" V-12 = 150 H.P. @ 3100

4.42 GEAR RATIO

32

8

V-12 (NEW) 398 and 429 C.I.D.

7.00 × 17 TIRES
7.50 × 17 ON LARGE V-12.

"836"
136-9" W.B.

135-H.P. 8

POWER BRAKES
"1236" = 136"
OR 139" W.B.
"1247," "1242" =
137" OR 142" W.B.

33

"SILVER ARROW" HAS SMALL REAR WINDOW

429 and 462-C.I.D. V-12s (160 and 175 H.P.)

"SILVER ARROW" AND ITS INTERIOR

34

"836-A"
DIFFERENT GRILLE,
NO HOOD VENTS.*
(LOWER-PRICED
MODEL,
STARTS APRIL, 1934.)

* = HOOD VENTS
OPTIONAL ON SOME
"836-A" MODELS.

8 = 385 C.I.D.,
140 H.P. @ 3400

V-12 = 462 C.I.D.,
175 H.P. @ 3400

"836-A" DASH

"1240-A"

MODIFIED "SILVER
ARROW" OFFERED
FOR 1934.

PIERCE-ARROW

35

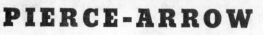

CHOICE OF STR. 8 V-12, CONT'D. THROUGH '38.

"845," "1245," OR "1255"

17" WHEELS AS BEFORE, CONT'D. THROUGH '38.

36

"1601" STRAIGHT-8 HAS 139" OR 144" W.B., 150 H.P. @ 3400 RPM

"1602," "1603" V-12s HAVE 139", 144", 147" W.B., 185 H.P. @ 3400 RPM

← BACK SEAT OF 1936 MODEL

MECHANICAL BRAKES STILL RETAINED.

37-38

'37 = 1700 SER.

'38 = 1800 SER.

DISCONTINUED 1938

PILOT (1909-1924)

PILOT MOTOR CAR CO., RICHMOND, IND.

120" W.B. (THROUGH '20)

"6-45" (SINCE '16) HAS TEETOR 6-CYL. ENG. (230.1 CID)

('19-21)

126" W.B., 6-CYL., 248.9 C.I.D. HERSCH.-SPLM. ENGINE (IN '21)

('22)

126" W.B. ('21 THROUGH '24)

('23)

"6-50" CUSTOM SEDAN 6-CYL. HERSCH.-SPLM. "E" ENGINE 288.6 C.I.D.

('24)

"6-56"

228

CHRYSLER PLYMOUTH

PLYMOUTH

EARLY EMBLEM (CHRYSLER PLYMOUTH) MODEL "Q"

IN JAN, 1929, MODEL "U" BEGINS, WITH THE ABOVE EMBLEM

PLYMOUTH
A CHRYSLER
MOTORS PRODUCT

"NARROW PROFILE" RADIATOR SHELL

STARTS JUNE, 1928 (MODEL Q)

29

REPLACES 1928 CHRYSLER "52" (4 CYLS.)

MODEL "Q"

(170.3 C.I.D.)

(4.6 COMPR.)

45 H.P. @ 2800 RPM

ROADSTER

BUSINESS COUPE (METAL BACK)

GAS GAUGE ON TANK

109" WHEELBASE
4.3 GEAR RATIO

FEDCO I.D. PLATE

DASH

SOFT-TOP COUPE IS VERY SCARCE.

MODEL "U" STARTS 1-29, with IMPROVED 175.4 C.I.D. ENGINE (HAS NEW SQUARED-OFF CORNERS ON CYLINDER HEAD.)

SPORT COUPE

(EARLY '30 is SIMILAR TO '29 MODEL.)

DELCO-REMY IGNITION (THROUGH '34)

30
LATE MODEL

STARTS APRIL, 1930 (EARLY '31 SIMILAR)

"NEW FINER" series

4.33 GEAR RATIO

EARLY TYPE WITH RECTANGULAR REAR WINDOW

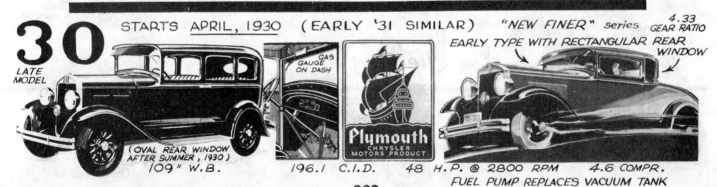

(OVAL REAR WINDOW AFTER SUMMER, 1930)
109" W.B.

GAS GAUGE ON DASH

Plymouth
CHRYSLER MOTORS PRODUCT

196.1 C.I.D.   48 H.P. @ 2800 RPM   4.6 COMPR.
FUEL PUMP REPLACES VACUUM TANK

PLYMOUTH

COWL VENTS ARE DELUXE EQUIPMENT

NEW GRILLE

31½ - 32

MODEL "PA"

STARTS JUNE, 1931

109 3/8" W.B.
56 H.P. @
2800 RPM
NEW 4.9 COMPRESSION

"NEW Floating Power"

FLEXIBLE ENGINE MOUNTS, "EASY-SHIFT" CONSTANT-MESH TRANSMISSION, AND FREE WHEELING

SCREEN-TYPE STONE GUARD IS OPTIONAL

NEW SHIELD-SHAPED RADIATOR EMBLEM, NEW MASCOT, NEW HUB CAPS

NEW CIRCULAR DASH GAUGES (5 IN A ROW)

INTERIOR ("PA")

WIRE WHEELS STANDARD EQUIPMENT

"PA" "THRIFT" SEDANS (WITH ONLY 3 DASH GAUGES) AVAILABLE AFTER "PB" MODELS INTRODUCED.

WALTER P. CHRYSLER (FOUNDER OF CHRYSLER CORP.) SHOWING 1932 PLYMOUTH MASCOT

32½

MODEL "PB"

INTRODUCED APRIL, 1932

FINAL 4-CYLINDER SERIES
NEW 112 3/8" WHEELBASE
65 H.P. @ 3400 RPM

INTERIOR ("PB")

COUPE SEAT BACK FOLDS, FOR EXTRA STORAGE

(5.6 - COMPRESSION "Red Head" OPTIONAL)

NEW BODY DOORS HINGED AT REAR

230

33

(FIRST 6-CYL. PLYMOUTH)

PLYMOUTH

"PC" MODEL
(10-32 TO
3-33)
CHROME ON
RADIATOR
SHELL
107"
W.B.

NEW 4.38
GEAR RATIO

189.8 C.I.D.
70 H.P. @ 3600 RPM
WITH 5.5 - COMPR. "SILVER DOME"
HEAD,
OR 76 H.P. @ 3600 RPM WITH
6.5 - COMPRESSION "Red Head"

33½

(3-33 TO 12-33. PAINTED RADIATOR SHELL)

"PD"

STD. 107 3/4 " W.B.
DE LUXE 113½" W.B.

34

new 201.3 C.I.D.
(THROUGH
1941)

NEW
VENT
WINDOWS
ROLL
DOWN
INTO
DOORS.

"PF" "PG"
MODELS
107 3/4"
W.B.

"PE"
DE
LUXE
has
113½" W.B.

77 H.P. @
3600 RPM
with 5.8
COMPRESSION
OR
82 H.P.
@
3600
with 6.5
ALUMINUM
CYL. HEAD

4.11 GEAR RATIO

HOOD
VENT DOORS
NOT ON STD.
MODELS.

DIP IN BUMPER

4.13 GEAR RATIO

35

"PJ"

LATE '35
MODEL

(EARLY '35s
[SHOWN AT
LEFT] HAVE
CHROMED
HOOD
"PORT-
HOLES.")

113" W.B.
85 H.P. @ 3600 RPM

6.7 COMPR. (THROUGH '41)

231

AUTO-LITE IGNITION REPLACES
DELCO-REMY.

PLYMOUTH

82 H.P. @ 3600 RPM (THROUGH 1939)

P-1 = "BUSINESS"
P-2 = "DE LUXE"

36

4.125 GEAR RATIO

X 54724

4.1 GEAR RATIO

SAFETY INTERIOR—Nothing protrudes on instrument panel

P-3 "BUSINESS" (STD.) MODEL

37

X 82678

P-4 DE LUXE MODELS HAVE BUTTERFLY VENT WINDOWS, GRAINED EFFECT on DASH.

LATE '37 DOES NOT HAVE DRAWER-TYPE SAFETY KNOBS ON DASH.

112" W.B. (1937 and 1938)

1938 WINDSHIELDS DO NOT OPEN

(1937 TO 1939 SEDANS HAVE 2-PC. REAR WINDOW; 1-PIECE ON COUPES.)

"ROADKING" (STD.)
P-5

38

3.9 OR 4.1 GEAR RATIO

HAND-BRAKE UNDER DASH

REGISTERED REST ROOM

309 816

232

"DE LUXE" P-6

PLYMOUTH

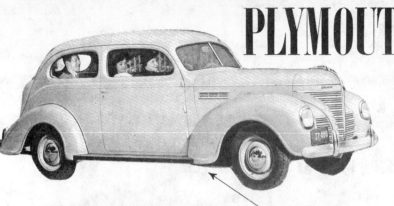

NEW AMOLA STEEL Coil Springs...

3.9, 4.1, OR 4.3 GEAR RATIO

PERFECTED Remote Control Shifting with new All-Silent Auto-Mesh Transmission.

NEW "SAFETY SIGNAL" SPEEDOMETER

Indicator Light shows green up to 30 miles per hour...from 30 to 50, amber ...above 50, a warning red.

NEW "ROADKING" (P-7)
NEW "DELUXE" (P-8)

NEW 114" W.B.

39

TURN A SWITCH AND THE TOP GOES UP OR DOWN — BY ITSELF!

AN "ECONOMY" ENGINE WITH 5.2 COMPR. and 65 H.P. WAS AVAIL. IF DESIRED, FROM 1935 THROUGH 1940.

PONTIAC SIX

CHIEF · OF · THE · SIXES

PONTIAC INTRODUCED 1926, BY GENERAL MOTORS, AS A LOWER-PRICED COMPANION TO OAKLAND CAR.

EARLIEST PONTIACS OF 1926 AVAILABLE ONLY WITH 2-DOOR COACH OR COUPE BODIES.

COACH

"STEP-UP" IN BELT MOULDING (CONT'D. ON EARLY '27 COUPE AND COACH)

26

6 CYLINDERS
186.6 C.I.D.
36 H.P. @ 2400 RPM (THROUGH '27)

110" WHEELBASE (THROUGH 1930)

4.18 GEAR RATIO (THROUGH 1929)

27

FINAL YEAR WITH 2-WH. BRAKES and VACUUM TANK.

H.P. INCREASED TO 37 @ 2400

28

new "TRI-CLUSTER" DASH

new = FUEL PUMP

new = 4-WHEEL BRAKES

ACTUAL '28 ROOFLINE IS NOT AS LOW AS THIS ORIGINAL ADVERTISEMENT SUGGESTS.

234

PONTIAC

EARLY SERIES 29

(HORIZONTAL → HOOD LOUVRES)

RDSTR. and PHAETON have BODY BY OAKLAND-PONTIAC. FISHER BODY ON OTHERS.

200.4 C.I.D. (THROUGH '32)
57 H.P. @ 3000 RPM
OVAL REAR WINDOW

← **29½**

(VERTICAL HOOD LOUVRES)

29 × 5.00 TIRES

60 H.P. @ 3000 RPM (THROUGH '31)

4.42 GEAR RATIO

30 "6-B"

SLIGHTLY SLANTED WINDSHIELD

5.00 × 19

4.55 GEAR RATIO

112" W.B.
5.00 × 19 TIRES

31 "6-401"

PONTIAC 32

CHIEF OF VALUES

(6 HAS INDIAN HEAD MASCOT, V-8 HAS BIRD.)

251 C.I.D.
V-8 (1 YEAR ONLY)

65 H.P. @ 3200 (6)

85 H.P. @ 3400 (V-8)

"6-402" OR "8-302"

6 CYL. OR V-8

5.25 × 18 TIRES (6)
6.00 × 17 TIRES (V-8)

114" W.B. (6)
117" W.B. (V-8)

4.55 (6) OR 4.22 (8) GEAR RATIOS

(NO 6-CYLINDER PONTIACS FOR 1933 OR 1934)

MODEL "8-601"

33
(STRAIGHT-8)

223.4 C.I.D. (THROUGH 1935)

75 H.P. @ 3600 RPM

115" WHEELBASE
4.44 GEAR RATIO

5.50 × 17 TIRES ('33)

6.00 × 17 TIRES ('34)

34
(STRAIGHT-8)
"8-603"

84 H.P. @ 3600 RPM

117 1/4" W.B.
4.55 GEAR RATIO

PONTIAC

8 HAS LEAPING FIGURE
HOOD ORNAMENT; 6 HAS
INDIAN HEAD IN CIRCLE.

(INTRODUCED DEC. 29, 1934)

35

STARTING 1935,
6 HAS 6.00 × 16 TIRES,
8 HAS 6.50 × 16

6-CYL. MODEL
AVAILABLE ONCE AGAIN.
STRAIGHT-8 CONTINUED.

HYDRAULIC BRAKES

TAIL / STOP LIGHT ON LEFT SIDE
OF TRUNK DOOR.

1935 MODEL
WAS FIRST TO USE
FAMOUS "SILVER
STREAK" BANDS
OF CHROME ALONG
CENTER OF HOOD
(A PONTIAC
TRADEMARK
UNTIL MID-'50s.)

Pontiac's ridged Silver Streak
and "V" windshield diffuse
and deflect sun-glare.

"6-701"
OR
"6-AB" (6)
112" W.B.
208 C.I.D.*
80 H.P. @ 3600*

"8-605" OR
"8-AA" (8)
116 5/8" W.B.
84 H.P. @ 3800

* - THROUGH '36

PONTIAC

DE LUXE 8
COUPE

6 = "BB" OR "6-BA"
                    DE LUXE
8 = "BA"

36

FRONT DOORS HINGED AT FRONT

SIMPLIFIED STARTING WITH AUTO-
MATIC CHOKE

BUILT-IN LUGGAGE AND SPARE TIRE
COMPARTMENT

6
SEDAN

THE MOST BEAUTIFUL THING ON WHEELS

NO CHOKE   NO SPARK

238

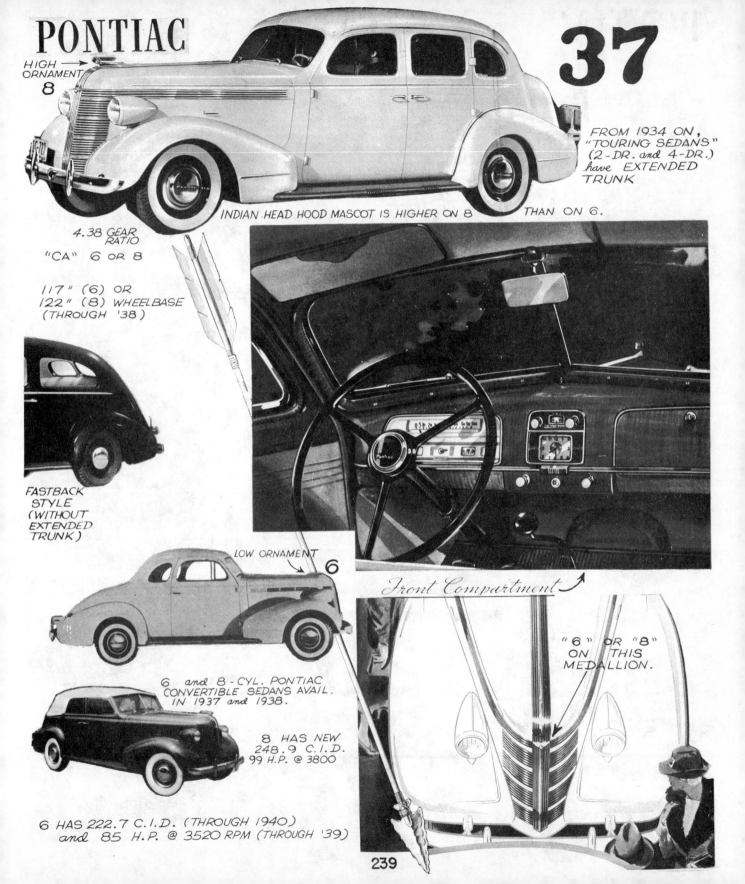

PONTIAC

37

HIGH ORNAMENT 8 →

FROM 1934 ON, "TOURING SEDANS" (2-DR. and 4-DR.) have EXTENDED TRUNK

INDIAN HEAD HOOD MASCOT IS HIGHER ON 8 THAN ON 6.

4.38 GEAR RATIO

"CA" 6 OR 8

117" (6) OR 122" (8) WHEELBASE (THROUGH '38)

FASTBACK STYLE (WITHOUT EXTENDED TRUNK)

LOW ORNAMENT 6

Front Compartment ↗

"6" OR "8" ON THIS MEDALLION.

6 and 8-CYL. PONTIAC CONVERTIBLE SEDANS AVAIL. IN 1937 and 1938.

8 HAS NEW 248.9 C.I.D. 99 H.P. @ 3800

6 HAS 222.7 C.I.D. (THROUGH 1940) and 85 H.P. @ 3520 RPM (THROUGH '39)

PONTIAC

38 6

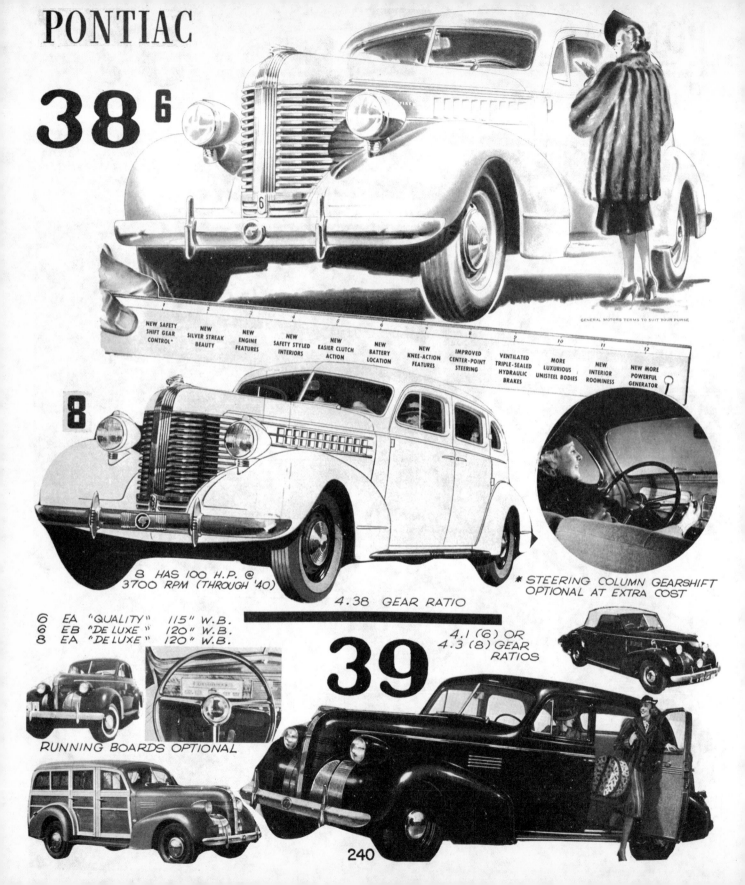

1 NEW SAFETY SHIFT GEAR CONTROL*
2 NEW SILVER STREAK BEAUTY
3 NEW ENGINE FEATURES
4 NEW SAFETY STYLED INTERIORS
5 NEW EASIER CLUTCH ACTION
6 NEW BATTERY LOCATION
7 NEW KNEE-ACTION FEATURES
8 IMPROVED CENTER-POINT STEERING
9 VENTILATED TRIPLE-SEALED HYDRAULIC BRAKES
10 MORE LUXURIOUS UNISTEEL BODIES
11 NEW INTERIOR ROOMINESS
12 NEW MORE POWERFUL GENERATOR

8

8 HAS 100 H.P. @ 3700 RPM (THROUGH '40)

4.38 GEAR RATIO

* STEERING COLUMN GEARSHIFT OPTIONAL AT EXTRA COST

6 EA "QUALITY" 115" W.B.
6 EB "DE LUXE" 120" W.B.
8 EA "DE LUXE" 120" W.B.

RUNNING BOARDS OPTIONAL

39

4.1 (6) OR 4.3 (8) GEAR RATIOS

PORTER
MODEL "45" ('20)

OWN 4-CYL.,
478.4 C.I.D. ENGINE
125 H.P.
12-VOLT ELECTRICAL SYS
3.0 GEAR RATIO
142"
WHEELBASE

MODEL "46"
(3.25 G.R.) ('21)

PREMIER (1903 - 1925)

MOTOR CORP
INDIANAPOLIS—USA
THE ALUMINUM SIX WITH MAGNETIC
GEAR SHIFT

EASILY IDENTIFIED BY V-SHAPED
RADIATOR AND STREAMLINED
COWL LAMPS.

32 × 4½

EXHAUST (RT.) SIDE
OF PREMIER'S OWN
ALUMINUM ENGINE (295.3 C.I.D.,
THROUGH 1925)

CUTLER-HAMMER MAGNETIC GEARSHIFT
CONTROLLED FROM STEERING WHEEL

('20)
"6-D"

126 ¾"
WHEELBASE
(THROUGH
1925)

STARTING 1922, CLOCK
and SPEEDOMETER ARE
COMBINED, AND C-H
MAGNETIC GEARSHIFT
BECOMES OPTIONAL,
AT $200. EXTRA.

('21)(6)

"6-D" 7-PASS.
CLOSED CAR

6 CYL.

"NEW SERIES"
"D-24"
('24)

7-PASSENGER SED.

R+V KNIGHT

SLEEVE-VALVE
KNIGHT ENGINES

(1920-1924)

R.+V. MOTOR CO.,
EAST MOLINE,
ILLINOIS

('21)

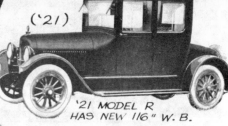

'21 MODEL R
HAS NEW 116" W.B.

(LENGTH EXAGGERATED)

('20)

MODEL R = 4 CYL. (220.9 C.I.D.)
115" W.B.

MODEL J = 6 CYL. (259.8
C.I.D.) 127" W.B.

(FORMERLY KNOWN AS
MOLINE KNIGHT and
MOLINE DREADNOUGHT)

MODEL J
SPORT CAR

('23-'24)

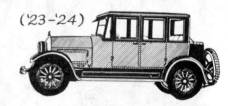

RAUCH + LANG ELECTRIC

(1905-1928)

BAKER, RAUCH and LANG,
CLEVELAND, OHIO (UNTIL '22)
CHICOPEE FALLS, MASS. (TO '28)

also known as
"R + L" OR
"RAULANG"

('21)
"C-55"

('20 MODEL
IS SIMILAR)

('24-25)

6-CYLINDER
ENGINES
(THROUGH '30)

"THE GOLD STANDARD OF VALUES"

REO

2-WHEEL MECH. BRAKES (THROUGH '25)
4.66 G.R. (THROUGH '21)
33 × 4 TIRES
(THROUGH
'22)

(AUTOMOBILES = 1904-1936)

REO MOTOR CAR COMPANY, Lansing, Mich.

SEDAN AND
VICTORIA COUPE
HAVE SLANTING
WINDSHIELD.

20-21

"T-6" SERIES
6 CYL. F-HEAD ENGINE,
239.4 C.I.D., and
120" W.B. (THROUGH 1926)

NORTHEAST IGNITION (THROUGH '26)

REO 22

"(B) T-6"
and
"U-6" MODELS LISTED
DURING 1922.

"T-6" has 50 H.P. @ 2000 RPM,
33 × 4
TIRES

New 4-Passenger Coupe

New Business Coupe

4.7 G.R. (TO '26)

ALSO NEW : "LIGHT 7"
SMALL 7-PASS. TOURING

"T-6"

23·24

33 × 4½ TIRES
ALSO AVAILABLE IN 1924.
(BALLOON TIRES OPTIONAL)

32 × 4

25

"T-6"

50 H.P. @
2000 RPM
(THROUGH '26)

32 × 6.20 BALLOON TIRES
(THROUGH '26)

25½
Series G SEDAN

1-PC. WINDSHIELD, FULL-LENGTH BELT MOLDING

NEW
ROOF-
VISOR

50 H.P.

26

"T-6"

COUPE WITH
WEDGE-SHAPED
QUARTER WINDOWS
AND DECORATIVE
LANDAU IRONS

4-WHEEL MECHANICAL BRAKES

243

REO
FLYING CLOUD

SEDAN · VICTORIA
BROUGHAM
SPORT COUPE

27

SPORT COUPE

VICTORIA

NEW "A" SERIES

6 CYLS.   121" WHEELBASE
249 CUBIC IN. DISPLACEMENT
65 H.P. @ 2800 RPM
4.58 GEAR RATIO

30 x 6.20

HYDRAULIC BRAKES
(THROUGH '36)

COACH
DASH
27½

WOLVERINE

INTRO. MAY 5, 1927

FINAL
"1929" (Summer, '28)
MODELS HAVE MILITARY-
STYLE PILLARS,
CADET VISOR.

114" W.B.
4.45 G.R.

28

"FLYING CLOUD" has 6-CYL., 249 C.I.D.
OWN ENGINE   DELCO-REMY IGNITION
73 H.P. @ 2800 RPM   121" W.B.
4.58 and other GEAR RATIOS

FLYING CLOUD

WOLVERINE has
6-CYL.   28 x 5.25 and other TIRES
199 C.I.D.
CONTINENTAL "15-E" ENGINE
NORTHEAST IGNITION   50 H.P. @ 2400 RPM

244

30 x 6.20 TIRES

REO

"MATE" EASILY IDENTIFIED BY THIS UNIQUE CURVED MOLDING.

MATE →

4.45 G.R., 30 × 6.00 TIRES (Mate)

FLYING CLOUD "MATE"
(REPLACES "WOLVERINE" DECEMBER , 1928.)
"MATE" HAS MURRAY BODY,
115" W.B., 6-CYL., 214.7 C.I.D.
CONTINENTAL "16-E" ENGINE
65 H.P. @ 2800 RPM
new FUEL PUMP

29

1929 "FLYING CLOUD" RADIATOR, FITTED WITH OPTIONAL

MASTER

ALLEN SHUTTERFRONT

MASTER →

Delco-Remy IGNITION ON BOTH "MATE" and "MASTER" and on cars that follow.

121" W.B.
OWN 6-CYL.
268.3 C.I.D. ENGINE
(USED ON CERTAIN MODELS THROUGH '35)
80 H.P. @ 3200 RPM

1929 ("MASTER") REO ANNOUNCED MARCH, 1928 !
"MASTER" RETAINS VACUUM TANK.

FLYING CLOUD ("MASTER" AS OF DEC., 1928.)

30 × 6.20 TIRES

MASTER "FLYING CLOUDS" have BUDD OR HAYES-IONA BODIES.

4.42 G.R.

30

"25" has 124" W.B., VACUUM TANK
OWN 6-CYL.,
268.3 C.I.D.
ENGINE
80 H.P. @
3200 RPM
4.42 G.R.,
6.50 × 18 TIRES

"15" has 115" W.B.
SAME 65-H.P. CONT.
"16-E" ENG. AS '29 Mate
4.25 GEAR RATIO
6.00 × 18 TIRES
(SAME TIRES ON "20")
FUEL PUMP

MODEL "20" SPORT COUPE →
(SAME ENGINE as "25")
120" W.B., 4.07 G.R.

245

FLYING CLOUD 8

(6 ALSO) **REO**

6-CYL. "25-N" has 125" W.B., 268.3 C.I.D., 85 H.P. 4.42 G.R. 6.50×17 TIRES

FLYING CLOUD "8-21" CUSTOM SEDAN

(SOME FLYING CLOUDS HAVE ROYALE-STYLE AERODYNAMIC BODIES AND V-SHAPED GRILLES, BUT RETAIN EARLY '31 HOOD LOUVRES AS SHOWN ABOVE AND AT RIGHT.)

"8-21" SERIES CONT'D. (STD. MODEL HAS MESH V-GRILLE, PARK. LIGHTS ON FENDERS ONLY.) CONT'D INTO '32 (INSTRUMENT PANEL)

1931½ "15" SERIES has 116" W.B., 4.27 G.R.

THE *Reo-Royale* EIGHT

1931 ROYALE 8 "N-35" (INTRODUCED OCTOBER, 1930.) has 135" W.B., STRAIGHT-8 357.8 C.I.D. ENG. 125 H.P. @ 3300 RPM (THROUGH '34) 4.07 G.R. 6.50×18 TIRES

31

ROYALE INTERIOR

ROYALE VICTORIA

"N-30" EIGHT has SAME ENGINE, TIRES, G.R. as "ROYALE," BUT has 130" W.B.

ROYALE CABRIOLET INTRODUCED APRIL, 1931.

STRAIGHT-8 REO ENGINES AVAILABLE 1931 THROUGH 1934.

REO

"6-21," "6-25" have
268.3 C.I.D., 85 H.P.
@ 3200 RPM, 4.07 G.R.
6.00 × 17 TIRES

"8-21," "8-25" have
268.6 C.I.D., 90 H.P.
@ 3300 RPM, 4.42 G.R.
6.00 × 17 TIRES

"8-31," "8-35" have
357.8 C.I.D., 125 H.P.
@ 3300 RPM, 4.07 G.R.
6.50 × 18 TIRES

FLYING CLOUD
MODEL "S"

32

REO FLYING CLOUD '8-25' COUPE

REO-ROYALE 8-35 SEDAN

REO-ROYALE 8-31 VICTORIA

(6 CYL
"S"
HAS OUTSWEPT
GRILLE)

1932 MODEL NUMBERS INDICATE NO. OF CYLINDERS, and WHEELBASE

1933 "S" has SAME ENGINE SPECS., SAME TIRE SIZE as '32 "6-21,"
but has 117½" W.B., 4.3 G.R. (STARTS 1-33, as "S-2;"
FREE-WHEELING.) ("8-131" also STARTS 1-33.)

"8-131"
"ROYALE" 8 has SAME
ENGINE SPECS., SAME TIRE
SIZE as PREVIOUSLY. 131" W.B.
4.42 G.R.   DELUXE MODELS
KNOWN as "ELITE" SERIES

* "SELF-SHIFTER"
AUTOMATIC TRANSMISSION
INTRODUCED BY
REO IN SPRING, 1933.
(AVAIL. FOR BOTH 6 and 8.)

AN AMAZING NEW INVENTION*

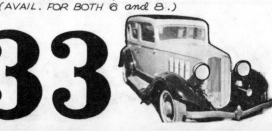

33

247

34 REO

NO GEARSHIFT LEVER
33⅓% easier to drive

2 LARGE, ROUND DASH INSTRUMENTS at CENTER

SIX (S-6) has 118" W.B., 268 C.I.D., 85 H.P. @ 3200 RPM, 4.3 G.R., 6.00×17 TIRES ("S-4" STARTS 12-33, HORIZONTAL LOUVRES.)

"ROYALE" 8 (N2-1) has SAME SPECS. as '33 MODEL; REO'S FINAL STRAIGHT-8.

131" W.B., but "CUSTOM" MODELS have 135" W.B.

MODELS ABOVE SERIAL NO. 5S-28677 START 7-34, CAN BE CONSIDERED "EARLY 1935."

NEW STREAMLINED MODELS START 2-35.

35

6 CYLINDER CARS ONLY; NO MORE CONVERTIBLES.

REO SELF SHIFTER OPTIONAL IN 1935 REOS

FLYING CLOUD "6-A" 228 C.I.D. 90 H.P. @ 3400 RPM 115" W.B.

DASH GAUGES MOVED TO LEFT.

6.25 × 16 TIRES ON "FLYING CLOUD" (1935 and 1936)

("6-75") ROYALE "S-7" 268 C.I.D. 95 H.P. @ 3200 RPM 118" W.B. 6.50 × 16 TIRES BOTH SERIES have 4.3 G.R.

COUPES AVAIL., BUT ONLY IN THE Royale '35 SERIES.

NO MORE COUPES, ONLY ONE REMAINING 1936 "FLYING CLOUD" SERIES

6 CYL. 228 C.I.D. 90 H.P. @ 3400

115" W.B. 4.27 G.R.

(STARTS 11-35)

36

AFTER 1936, REO TRUCKS ONLY.

REVERE (1917-1926)

('20) MODEL "C"

4-CYL. DUESENBERG ENGINE (TO '23)

32 × 4½ TIRES ON "C" and "M" SERIES

131" W.B. (THROUGH '26)

"M" SERIES ('24-'26) has 4-CYL., 360.8 C.I.D. MONSEN/REVERE O.H.V. ENG., 2-WHEEL BRAKES

"25" SERIES ('25-'26) has 6-CYL., 331.4 C.I.D. CONT'L. "6-J" 70-H.P. ENG., and 4-WHEEL BRAKES (32 × 6.20 BALLOON TIRES)   BOSCH IGNITION (ALL MODELS)

RICHELIEU (1922-1923)

(NOTE SIMILARITY TO REVERE CAR, ABOVE LEFT. RICHELIEU DESIGNED BY N. VAN ZANDT, FORMERLY WITH REVERE.)

RICHELIEU MOTOR CAR CORP., ASBURY PARK, N.J.

131" W.B.
32 × 4½ TIRES
2-WHEEL BRAKES

4-CYLINDER ROCHESTER-DUESENBERG 340.4 C.I.D. ENGINE
78 H.P. @ 2500 RPM   EISEMANN IGNITION

Rickenbacker
A · CAR · WORTHY · OF · ITS · NAME

Rickenbacker Motor Company
Detroit   Michigan

(1922-1927)

(FLYWHEEL AT EACH END OF CRANKSHAFT.)

('23) "HAT-IN RING" EMBLEM

'22 has 6-CYL., 218 C.I.D. ENGINE, 58 H.P. @ 2800 RPM, 4.63 G.R., 32 × 4 TIRES, 4-WHEEL BRAKES, 117" W.B.

IGNITION:
AUTO LITE ('22)
ATW. KENT ('23)
BOSCH ('24-'27)
DELCO ('25-'27)

('23)

The only 4-door Coach-Brougham on the American Market

('25)

('25)

"D" = 6 CYL., 236.4 CID 70 HP @ 3000
"8" = STRAIGHT-8 268.6 CID
BOTH HAVE 70 HP @ 3000, 117" WB

117"-WB
"E-6"
OR
121½"-WB
"B-8"
IN
'26

'27 SPECS.
"6-70" = 118½"WB
   236.4 CID
   70 HP @ 3000
"8-80" = 119½"WB
   268.5 CID
   80 HP @ 3000
"8-90" = 136"WB, 315.2 CID, 95 HP @ 3000

6-CYL. ONLY (THROUGH '24)

AM. BOSCH (6-70) OR DELCO-REMY ('27) IGNITION

ROAMER (1916-1930)   BARLEY MOTOR CAR CO., KALAMAZOO, MICH.

4-CYL. ROCH.-DUES. ENG. ALSO

128"-WB "6-54" ('20)

6-CYLINDER, 303.1 CID CONT'L. ENGINE

('22) "6-54"

LYCOMING STRAIGHT-8 ENGINES
('27)

4-PASS. CLUB SEDAN
"8-78" (120"WB)   "8-88" (136"WB)

ROCKNE 6
(1932-1933)
BY
(STUDEBAKER)

"6-10" IS 1933 MODEL.

"65" (110" W.B.)
189.9 C.I.D., 65
H.P. @ 3200 RPM
4.27 G.R.

"75" (114" W.B.)
205.3 C.I.D., 72
H.P. @ 3200 RPM
4.73 G.R.

(AUTO-LITE IGN. ON ALL)

('32)

5.25 × 18 TIRES (5.50 ON "75")

SPECS. AS '32 "65",
BUT H.P. UP TO
70 @ 3200

ROLLIN (LATE '23 TO 1925)

ROLLIN MOTORS CO.,
CLEVELAND, OHIO
IGNITION = O.D. ('24) CONNECT. ('25)

31 × 5.20 TIRES   4-WHEEL BRKS.

COUPE DETAILS
('24)

W.B. = 112"   5.1 G.R.,
149.3 C.I.D., 41 H.P. @ 2750 RPM (THROUGH '25)

('25)

6 CYL. ALSO

60 M.P.H.

'25 BELT MOLDING
RUNS FULL LENGTH OF CAR.

ROLLS-ROYCE

BEST CAR IN THE WORLD

('23)

6 CYL., 453 C.I.D.,
143½" W.B. ('25)

BUILT
IN
ENGLAND
SINCE 1904.

AMERICAN
FACTORY AT
SPRINGFIELD, MASS.
(1920 - 1931)

144¾" W.B.

('30)

"PHANTOM"
MODEL

'25 HAS
80 H.P. @
1800 R.P.M.,
3.25 GEAR RATIO,
73 M.P.H.
SPEED

"SILVER GHOST"
MODEL

("SILVER GHOST"
SUPERSEDED 1927
BY "PHANTOM")

7.00 × 20

THIS
1931 MODEL
"DERBY (BREWSTER)
SPEEDSTER" PHAETON
IS THE
FINAL AMERICAN-BUILT
ROLLS-ROYCE.

6 CYLINDERS (468 C.I.D.)
OVERHEAD VALVES (SINCE '29)
100 H.P. @ 2250 RPM

146½" WHEELBASE
3.72 GEAR RATIO
DE JON IGNITION

250

Roosevelt

MARMON-BUILT

A CAR FOR ALL (1929-1930*)

NAMED FOR THEODORE ROOSEVELT, PRESIDENT OF U.S.A. FROM 1901 TO 1909.

DELCO-REMY IGN.

STRAIGHT 8 engine.

201.9 C.I.D.
77 H.P. @ 3400
5.50 × 19 TIRES
4.9 GEAR RATIO

* = LISTED AS MARMON, '30-'31

RUGBY (1927)

BUILT BY DURANT, PRIMARILY FOR EXPORT. COMPARABLE TO STAR.

NOTE THE RIGHT-HAND DRIVE

RUXTON (1929-1931)

(NEW ERA MOTORS, N.Y.C. "IN COOPERATION WITH" MOON and KISSEL.)

PHAETON, FITTED WITH TYPICAL "WOOD-LITES"

RAINBOW-COLORED BANDS OF PAINT →

FRONT-WHEEL-DRIVE STRAIGHT-8 CONTINENTAL ENGINE (268.6 C.I.D. "18-S" with 100 H.P. @ 3400 RPM)
130" or 140" W.B.   4.4 G.R.

SEDAN, FITTED WITH CONVENTIONAL-STYLE HEADLIGHTS

SEDAN has BUDD BODY
RDSTR." BAKER RAULANG BODY
PHAETON " KISSEL BODY
CUSTOM MODELS ALSO

6.00 × 19 TIRES
HYDRAULIC BRAKES
Auto-Lite IGNITION

SAXON (1913-1923)

FOR 1922, 178.9 C.I.D., O.H.V. 4-CYL. ROOT and VAN. ENG. REPLACED BY 192.3 C.I.D. GRAY ENGINE. WAGNER IGNITION

('21-23) "125" SERIES

SAXON MOTOR CAR CO., DETROIT, MICH. and YPSILANTI, MICH.

(6 CYLS. IN 1920)

SAXON-DUPLEX   4 CYL. "BLACKSTONE" (5-PASS.) →

32 × 4 TIRES

4.75 G.R.

SAYERS 6 (1917-1924)

DELCO IGNITION STROMBERG CARB. ('21)

"AVONDALE" 5-PASS.

118" W.B. (THROUGH '23) 6-CYL. 224 C.I.D. CONTINENTAL ENGINE (THROUGH '22) 241.6 C.I.D. IN '23

(SAYERS and SCOVILL CO., CINCINNATI, OHIO)

FOR 1924, NAME CHANGED TO

S. + S. (1924-1930)

'25 and '26 "ELMWOOD" SIMILAR TO '24, BUT HAS OVAL REAR QTR. WINDOWS, LANDAU IRONS (34 × 7.30 TIRES IN '26)

new 136" W.B. (TO '27) new 33 × 5 TIRES (THROUGH '25) ('24)

('24)

S+S "BRIGHTON" 8 PASS. (6 CYL.)

new 331.4 C.I.D. CONT'L. 6-CYL. "6-J" ENG. (TO '27)

MILITARY CADET VISOR and BOWL HEADLIGHTS FOR 1929

('29)

"42" SUPERLINE 8-PASS. "LAKEWOOD" SEDAN

STR.-8 ENGINE new 3⅜" × 4½ B.+S.

new 143" W.B.

FOR '28, "Washington 8" S.+S. HEARSE has 141" W.B., STR.-8 ENG. (3" × 4¾" B.+S.) ROOF-VISOR, DRUM ILCO-RYAN LITES, 33 × 6.20 TIRES

SCHULER (1924)

(2 CYL.)

SCHULER MOTOR CAR CO. MILWAUKEE, WIS.

78" W.B.

6-CYL., 177 C.I.D. NORTHWAY F-HD. 40 H.P. ENGINE Marvel CARB. 4.5 G.R. CHANGED TO 4.87 for '21. SINCE '19, CHASSIS SIMILAR TO OAKLAND.

"B-39" TOURING ('20-'21) 115" W.B. 32 × 4 TIRES

SCRIPPS-BOOTH (1913-1922)

SCRIPPS-BOOTH CO., DETROIT

(BECAME A G.M. PRODUCT IN 1918.)

SEVERIN 6 (1920-1922)

('20)

122" W.B., 6-CYL. CONTINENTAL 303.1 C.I.D. ENGINE

SEVERIN MOTOR CAR CO., KANSAS CITY, MO.

TOURING-SPORTSTER

33 × 5 TIRES (33 × 4 ON LOWEST-PRICED MODELS.)

SHAW (1920-1921)

('21) V-12

WALDEN W. SHAW LIVERY CO., CHICAGO (FORMERLY BUILT TAXIS)

WEIDELY V-12 ENGINE REPLACED 4-CYL. ROCHESTER-DUESENBERG ENGINE, 1921. LATER BECAME "AMBASSADOR."

SHERIDAN (1920-1921)

A PROJECT BEGUN UNDER G.M., SHERIDAN WAS ACQUIRED BY WM. C. DURANT WHEN HE LEFT G.M., AND IT EVOLVED DURING '21 INTO THE 4-CYL. and 6-CYL. DURANT CARS.

SHERIDAN MOTOR CAR CO., MUNCIE, IND.

116 OR 132" W.B., 4-CYL. OR V-8 NORTHWAY ENGINES

4 CYL. "B-41" 35 H.P.

33 × 4 OR 33 × 5 TIRES

SINGER MOTOR CO., INC.,
MT. VERNON, N.Y.

(REPLACED THE
PALMER-SINGER CAR)

SINGER
(1915 – 1920)
3.77 GEAR RATIO   33 × 5
TIRES

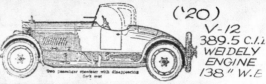

('20)
V-12
389.5 C.I.D.
WEIDELY
ENGINE
138" W.B.

ROADSTER
ALSO
AVAIL.

"35"
SERIES
('21)

CONNECTICUT IGN.
CARTER CARB.

SKELTON 4
SKELTON MOTOR CAR CO., ST. LOUIS, MO.
(1920 – 1922)
112" W.B.

4 - CYLINDER
192.4 C.I.D., L-HEAD LYCOMING ENGINE
32 × 3½ TIRES

STANDARD EIGHT
STANDARD STEEL CAR COMPANY
Automotive Dept.   Pittsburgh, Pa
(1912 – 1923)

(V-8)
OWN L-HEAD, 331.8 C.I.D. ENGINE (THROUGH '23)

127" W.B.
4.45 G.R.
ZENITH CARB.
34 × 4½
TIRES
(THROUGH '23)

('20)

('22)

SPLITDORF
IGNITION
REPLACES
CONNECTICUT
FOR '22 and
'23.

STANLEY
STEAM CAR
(1897 – 1927)
MANUFACTURER, IN
1924, CHANGED NAME
FROM STANLEY MOTOR
CARRIAGE CO. TO
STANLEY VEHICLE CORP.
OF AMERICA
NEWTON, MASS.

130"
W.B.
('21)

32 × 4½ TIRES
1.50 GEAR RATIO ON
'23 "740" SERIES;
32 × 5.77 TIRES,
122" W.B. and
HYDRAULIC BRAKES ON
FINAL "252" SERIES

34 × 4½ TIRES
('21)

2 CYL. STEAM ENGINE
(4" × 5" CYLINDERS)

(1920-1922)
STANWOOD
MOTOR CAR CO.,
ST. LOUIS, MO.

STANWOOD 6

"A" TOURING CAR
118" W.B.   ('21)
ATW. KENT
IGN.
6-CYLINDER CONTINENTAL ENGINE   STROMBERG CARB.
224 C.I.D.   33 × 4 TIRES   4.5 G.R.

253

Low-cost Transportation
Star ✦ Cars

DURANT MOTORS, Inc., NEW YORK CITY

(SHOWN WITH WM. C. DURANT, FOUNDER OF DURANT MOTORS)

22-23

(STARTS 6-22)

30 x 3½ TIRES

WAGON ('23)

102" W.B. and 4 - CYLINDER CONTINENTAL 130.4 C.I.D. ENGINE (THROUGH '25)

FOUR GREAT PLANTS AT ELIZABETH, N. J. o LANSING, MICH. o OAKLAND, CAL. o TORONTO, ONT,

24

For Your All-Weather Car Get a Sedan STAR

"SPECIAL" MODELS HAVE NICKEL TRIM and OPTIONAL DISC WHEELS.

The Coupster
TRADE MARK

25

(LEFT SIDE)
ENGINE
(RIGHT SIDE)

"4-M" (158 C.I.D.) 103" w.b.
30 H.P. @ 2200 RPM
"6-R" (169.2 C.I.D.) 107" w.b.
40 H.P. @ 2400 RPM

IMPROVED 4

26-27

NEW 6-CYL. MODEL

('27 HAS BOWL-
SHAPED LAMPS.)

CABRIOLET

COUPE
(6 CYL.)

1928 MODEL KNOWN TEMPORARILY AS
"DURANT-STAR," LATER AS DURANT 4.

Stearns-Knight
Motor Cars of Quality

(1899 – 1930, ORIGINALLY STEARNS)

F.B. STEARNS CO., CLEVELAND, OHIO

4 CYLS., 248.5 CID (THROUGH '26)

12-VOLT IGNITION (THROUGH '27) ATW. KENT IGN. ON ALL (THROUGH '24) 34 × 4½ TIRES (THROUGH '23)

20-21

125" W.B. (THROUGH '23) 4.5 G.R. (CONT'D. TO '29 ON SOME)

7-PASS. SEDAN ('21).

RADIATOR OUTLINED IN WHITE

"SKL-4" SERIES CONT'D.

22

RAYFIELD CARB. REPLACES SCHEBLER

DASH GAUGES BEHIND GLASS PANEL

new DRUM HEADLIGHTS

4-CYL. "SKL-4" IS JOINED BY NEW 6-CYL. SERIES (130"WB) 268 C.I.D., REDUCED TO 248.5 IN '24.

NEW 6 has 4.7 G.R.

23-24

33" TIRES ('24) SCHEBLER CARB. ('24)

4-CYL. WHEELBASE REDUCED TO 119" IN '24.

"B" (4), "C" (6) and "S" (6) SERIES

25-26

new JOHNSON CARB. ON SIXES

119", 121" and 130" W.B. (HYDR. BRAKES OPTIONAL IN '26.)

'26 VISOR and WINDSHIELD

'26 "S" SPORT SEDAN has REAR-HINGED DOORS and new PANEL DIVIDING COWL FROM BODY.

DE JON IGNITION ON BOTH MODELS, INTRO. ON 1925-1926 SIXES
NEW 137" W.B. ON BOTH MODELS.
NEW TILLOTSON CARBURETOR (TO '30)

NEW STRAIGHT-8 "G-8" SERIES has 385 C.I.D., 100 H.P. @ 2600 RPM, 4-WHEEL BRAKES (NEW), 4.5 G.R.
288.5 CID 6 CONT'D. (80 H.P. @ 2600 RPM) 5.1 G.R.
NEW 32 × 6.75 TIRES (TO '30)

27

new SMALL GROUPS OF HOOD LOUVRES IN '27-28.

ALL STEARNS CARS SINCE 1911 USE KNIGHT SLEEVE-VALVE ENGINE DESIGN.

NEW 6-VOLT IGNITION
ALL MODELS NOW HAVE 4-WHEEL BRAKES.

28

new BOWL HEADLIGHTS

"F6-85" CONT'D. NOW with 82 H.P., 5.0 G.R. (RETAINS VACUUM TANK)

"H8-85" has 112 H.P. @ 2800 RPM, 4.5 G.R., NEW FUEL PUMP.

'28 and later 8 has NEW FUEL PUMP.

"6-80"

29-30

126-134" W.B., 255 C.I.D., 70 H.P. @ 3200 RPM AUTO-LITE IGN.

"8-90" (H, J MODELS)

137-145" W.B. 120 H.P. @ 2800 DE JON IGN.

(M, N MODELS) VACUUM TANK RETAINED ON 6.

('29)

BODIES BY ROBBINS BAKER PHILIPS

OUT OF BUSINESS JAN., 1930

STEPHENS

STEPHENS MOTOR WORKS *of Moline Plow Company* · Freeport, Illinois

(1916-1924)

Salient Six

17-22

Salient "That which is strikingly manifest or catches the attention at once." —Webster

6 CYL. O.H.V. 224 C.I.D. ENGINE (THROUGH '24)

122" W.B. (THROUGH '22)

('20)

33 × 4½ TIRES (THROUGH '24, EXC. '23-'24 117" W.B. MODELS)

('22)

('21) CONNECTICUT IGNITION REPLACES Auto-Lite.

with Artcraft Top

57 H.P. IN 1922

STEPHENS

NO MAJOR CHANGES BETWEEN 1917 and 1922.

23-24

'23 RESTYLED, WITH MODERN "LIGHTNING" INSIGNIA.

STEPHENS

FOR '23, DELCO IGN. REPLACES CONNECTICUT IGN., AND STROMBERG CARB. REPLACES TILLOTSON.

32 × 4 TIRES, 4.66, 5.1 G.R. ON 117"-W.B. "10."

NEW 117" and 124" W.B. "10," "20" models

STERLING-KNIGHT 6

6-CYL., 230.2 C.I.D. SLEEVE-VALVE ENGINE

B-6   125" W.B.

(1923-1925) STERLING-KNIGHT MOTORS CO., CLEVELAND and WARREN, OHIO

WESTINGHOUSE IGN. 32 × 4½ TIRES

STROMBERG CARB. 4.66 G.R. (TO '24)

56 H.P. @2400 RPM and 5.09 G.R. ('25)

STEVENS-DURYEA

(1902-1927)

('21)

138" W.B. (TO '27)

"E-6" 6-PASS. 3.94 G.R. (TO '24)

STEVENS-DURYEA (MOTORS) CO. CHICOPEE FALLS, MASS.

6-CYL., 510.4 CID, L-HEAD ENGINE (TO '27)

VESTIBULE LIMO.

35 × 5

BOSCH IGNITION REPLACES BERLING IGNITION (AFTER '24)

('22)

90 H.P. @ 2000 RPM

35 × 5

33 × 5 TIRES ('23 ON)

STOUT "SCARAB" (1934-1939)

WM. B. STOUT ENGINEERING CO., DEARBORN, MICH.

FORD V-8 ENGINE (AT REAR)

('35-'36)

257

WAGNER IGNITION STROM. CARB. ON MOST MODELS

STUDEBAKER

CARS (1902-1966)

Detroit, Michigan   South Bend, Indiana   Walkerville, Canada
Address all Correspondence to South Bend

(CO. ORIGINATED 1852)

BIG 6 (EG)
353.8 C.I.D. (THROUGH '27)
126" W.B. (THROUGH '24)

112" W.B.

(EH, EU) **SPECIAL 6**

LIGHT 6 (EJ) ('21)
207.1 C.I.D.
45 H.P. @ 2000 RPM
4.55 G.R. (THROUGH '24)

288.6 C.I.D. (THROUGH '27)
51 ('20) 55 ('21) H.P. @ 2000 RPM
4.33 G.R. (THROUGH '24)

119" W.B. (THROUGH '24)

65 H.P. @ 2000

BIG 6 has BALL + BALL CARB. (THROUGH '27)

3.71 G.R. (THROUGH '24)

20-21

EARLY '22

('23) **LIGHT 6**
(has 31 x 4 TIRES, '23-'24)

(WOOD WHEELS and PAINTED RADIATOR SHELL)

1-PC. WINDSHIELD ON SPECIAL 6 and BIG 6 TOURING CARS.

COUPE INTERIOR

SPECIAL 6 ('23½)

NEW "5-PASS. COUPE"

22-24

WAGNER, REMY IGNITION (THROUGH '25)

BIG 6

TYPE OF '24

"EL" SPECIAL 6

"SPEEDSTER" PHAETON

STUDEBAKER

new STANDARD 6
has 241.6 C.I.D.,
50 H.P. @ 2200 RPM
(TO '28) new 113" W.B. (THROUGH '29 "DICTATOR")
new 4.18 G.R.

STD. 6 "DUPLEX" →

25

COMPLETELY
RESTYLED

(INTRO. FALL '24)

31 x 5.25

STANDARD 6
FRONT VIEW
←

STD. 6

new *Duplex*

OPEN MODELS with
RIGID, STEEL-REINFORCED
TOPS.

("DUPLEX" MODELS avail. THROUGH '27.
1928 "DICTATOR" SERIES INCLUDES
"DUPLEX" PHAETON.)

2-WHEEL MECHANICAL
BRAKES ON ALL 3
SERIES, with 4-WH.
HYDRAULIC BRAKES
OPTIONAL
(THROUGH '26)

"DUPLEX"
ROADSTER,
with DETAILS of
PULL-DOWN
CURTAINS

SPECIAL 6 "DUPLEX" ——

WITH CURTAINS
OPEN →

WITH
SIDE CURTAINS CLOSED

SPECIAL 6
has new 4.36 G.R. (THROUGH '27)
65 H.P. @ 2400 RPM
(THROUGH '27)
32 x 6.20 TIRES (THROUGH '26)
120" W.B. (THROUGH '28, '30
"COMMANDER")

SPECIAL 6 CONTINUES ITS UNIQUE
FLUTED RADIATOR SHELL

BIG 6
"5-PASS.
COUPE"

(COACH-STYLE,
UNLIKE
STUDEBAKER
4-PASS.
VICTORIA CPES.
WHICH HAVE
REAR DECK.)

BIG 6
has 75 H.P. @ 2400 RPM (THROUGH '27)
34 x 7.30 TIRES (THROUGH '26)
127" W.B. (THROUGH '27)   4.36 G.R.

259

STUDEBAKER

25½

STANDARD 6 "DUPLEX"

BIG 6

STANDARD 6 BROUGHAM

BROUGHAM

A NEW, CAPPED VISOR IDENTIFIES THESE TRANSITIONAL MODELS OF SPRING, 1925.

31 × 5.25 TIRES CONT'D. ON STD. 6 (THROUGH '27)

COUPE TOP

LE BARON "PRINCE OF WALES" SEDAN

(ONE OF A GROUP OF NEW CUSTOM-BODY TYPES.)

26

STD. 6

(NEW RADIATOR DESIGN and PAINT, 6-25)

NEW FRENCH-STYLE ROOF-VISOR (TO EARLY '28)

KEYS SOMETIMES PRESENTED IN GIFT-STYLE BOX, DURING 1920s.

DELCO-REMY IGNITION ON ALL MODELS (THROUGH '33)

STD. 6 and BIG 6 have 4-WH. MECH. BRAKES. (SPEC. 6 has 2-WH. MECH. BRAKES with 4-WH. HYDRAULICS OPTIONAL.

STD. 6   BIG 6

BIG SIX SEDAN

(new 32 × 6.20 TIRES AVAIL.)

27

FINAL YEAR FOR VACUUM-TANK FUEL FEED.

32 × 6.75

260

PRESIDENT IS A DELUXE SEDAN IN '27 BIG 6 LINE, REPLACES BIG 6 WITH NEW LINE FOR '28.

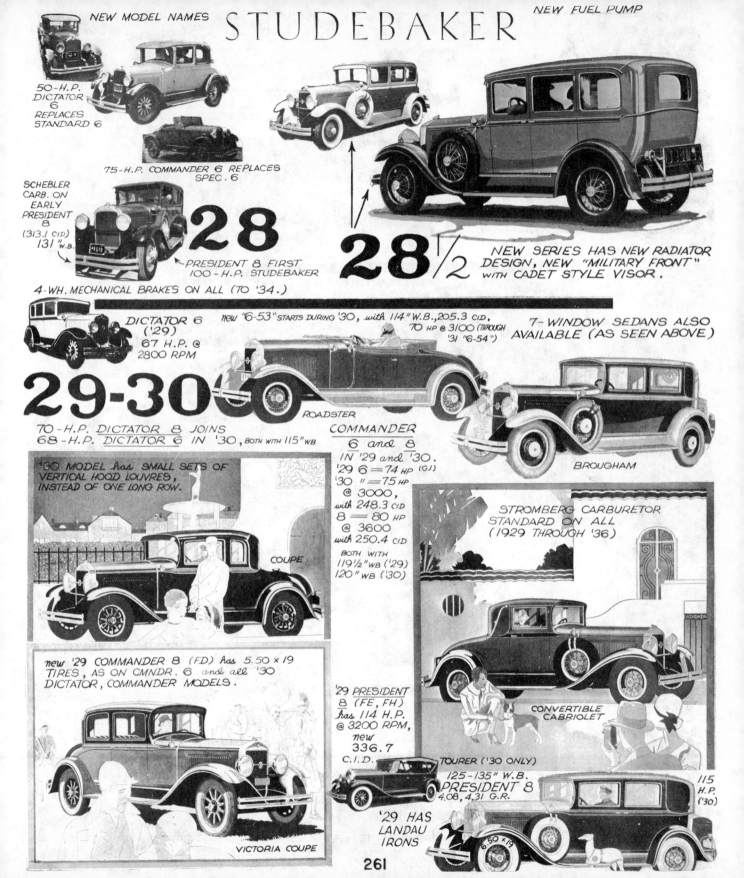

STUDEBAKER

NEW MODEL NAMES

NEW FUEL PUMP

50-H.P. DICTATOR 6 REPLACES STANDARD 6

75-H.P. COMMANDER 6 REPLACES SPEC. 6

SCHEBLER CARB. ON EARLY PRESIDENT 8 (313.1 CID) 131" W.B.

28

PRESIDENT 8 FIRST 100-H.P. STUDEBAKER

28½

NEW SERIES HAS NEW RADIATOR DESIGN, NEW "MILITARY FRONT" WITH CADET STYLE VISOR.

4-WH. MECHANICAL BRAKES ON ALL (TO '34.)

DICTATOR 6 ('29) 67 H.P. @ 2800 RPM

new "6-53" starts during '30, with 114" W.B., 205.3 CID, 70 HP @ 3100 (THROUGH '31 "6-54")

7-WINDOW SEDANS ALSO AVAILABLE (AS SEEN ABOVE)

29-30

ROADSTER

70-H.P. DICTATOR 8 JOINS 68-H.P. DICTATOR 6 IN '30, BOTH WITH 115"WB

COMMANDER 6 and 8 IN '29 and '30. '29 6 = 74 HP (GJ) '30 " = 75 HP @ 3000, with 248.3 CID 8 = 80 HP @ 3600 with 250.4 CID BOTH WITH 119½"WB ('29) 120" WB ('30)

BROUGHAM

'30 MODEL has SMALL SETS of VERTICAL HOOD LOUVRES, INSTEAD of ONE LONG ROW.

COUPE

STROMBERG CARBURETOR STANDARD ON ALL (1929 THROUGH '36)

new '29 COMMANDER 8 (FD) has 5.50 × 19 TIRES, AS ON CMNDR. 6 and all '30 DICTATOR, COMMANDER MODELS.

CONVERTIBLE CABRIOLET

'29 PRESIDENT 8 (FE, FH) has 114 H.P. @ 3200 RPM, new 336.7 C.I.D.

TOURER ('30 ONLY)

125-135" W.B. PRESIDENT 8 4.08, 4.31 G.R.

115 H.P. ('30)

'29 HAS LANDAU IRONS

6.50 × 19

VICTORIA COUPE

STUDEBAKER

31

6 (6-54)

205.3 C.I.D. SIX (114" W.B.)
HAS 70 H.P. @ 3200

114"- W.B.
DICTATOR
IS 8 ONLY,
IN '31.

1931 MODELS
HAVE NEW
GRILLE,
"OVALOID"
HEAD-
LIGHTS

COMMANDER 8
BROUGHAM
124"
W.B.

101 H.P.

new = "FREE WHEELING"
(AVAIL. TO '35)

ROLL-UP WINDOWS

PRESIDENT 8
CONVERTIBLE
RDSTR.

122 H.P. @
3200 RPM (THROUGH '32)

32

1932 MODELS : SIX
DICTATOR 8 (62)
COMMANDER 8 (71)
PRESIDENT 8
(91)

NEW CIRCULAR GAUGES IN OVAL PANEL
(REPLACE FORMER UPRIGHT-
RECTANGULAR GAUGES IN
HORIZONTAL RECTANG.
PANEL.

new
ST. REGIS
COUPE

'32 6 (6-55)
has 117" W.B.
(THROUGH '33)
230 C.I.D.
(THROUGH '33)
80 H.P. @
3200 RPM

DICT. 8 has 117" W.B.
81-85 H.P. @ 3200
(221 CID AS IN '31)

CMDR. 8 has
new 125" WB
BUT 101 HP @ 3200
and 250.4 CID as BEFORE.

Studebaker Free Wheeling is controlled
by a touch of a lever on the dash. There
is no necessity for keeping your foot con-
stantly on a button.

To start the Triumphant New Studebakers you simply switch on the ignition
with a key. The engine instantly responds
—and even should it stall at any time,
it automatically starts again.

PRES. 8
has 135" WB
4.31 G.R.

'32 tire sizes = 5.50 × 18 (6 and DICT. 8)   6.00 × 18 (CMNDR. 8)   6.50 × 18 (PRES. 8)

33

MODELS : SIX, COMMANDER 8, (117" WB)
PRESIDENT 8 and
SPEEDWAY PRESIDENT 8
(125", 135" WB)

110-H.P. PRES. 8 (82) USES 250.4 CID
STR.-8
ENGINE
FORMERLY
IN '32
CMNDR.

6 (56) has
85 HP @
3200 RPM

CMR. 8
(73) has
236 CID,
100 HP
@ 3800
RPM

SPDWY. PRES. 8 (92) is
FINAL USER OF THE 336.7 CID STR. 8 (132 HP @ 3400)

"DICTATOR"
MODEL
SUSPENDED,
RESUMED
'34.

17" WHEELS ('33-'34)   117, 117, 125, 135" WHEELBASES,
AS IN 1932.

STUDEBAKER

34

SEDAN REAR

BENDIX POWER BRAKES
(MECH. BRAKES ON DICTATOR 6)

CMNDR. 8 has 221 CID, 103 HP @ 4000 RPM 119" WB

'34 DICT. 6 has 205.3 CID (THROUGH '35) 87 H.P. @ 3600 RPM 113" W.B. 4.55 G.R.

new STREAM-LINED "LAND CRUISER" REAR ('34)

NARROW GRILLE FOR 1935

PRESIDENT LAND CRUISER ('35)

35

88-H.P. DICTATOR new 6 114" WB

HYDRAULIC BRAKES (ALL)

120"- W.B. CMNDR. 8 has 107 HP @ 3800 RPM

"REGAL" has FENDERWELLS

DICTATOR 6

new 116" wb (THROUGH '37)

6.00 x 16

217.8 CID, 90 HP @ 3400 (THROUGH '40 CMNDR.)

(4.55 G.R. BECOMES STANDARD ON ALL.)

PRESIDENT 8

new 125" WB (THROUGH '37) 250.4 CID ('33 THROUGH '42) 115 H.P. @ 3600 (THROUGH '37)

36

6.50 x 16

'36-'37 COUPE REAR WINDOW.

STATE PRESIDENT 8

37

DICTATOR 6 USES CARTER CARB. DURING 1937.

new 1-PIECE HOOD is HINGED AT BACK.
VENT PANES IN FRONT DOORS.
EMERGENCY BRAKE LEVER HUNG AT LEFT.

COMMANDER 6
8-A

2-PIECE REAR WINDOW →

PRESIDENT 8
4-C

FIRST COMMANDER SINCE '35 "8"

38

"DICTATOR" MODEL NAME ABANDONED, IN FAVOR OF "7-A" SIX (SAME SPECS. AS CMNDR.)

INTERIOR

STATE PRESIDENT 8 CLUB SEDAN

NOTE FENDER PARKING LIGHTS

(OPTIONAL) "MIRACLE SHIFT" BELOW DASH

STROMBERG CARB. ON ALL '38s, AND ON '39s EXCEPT CHAMPION

COMMANDER 6 (9-A)
226.2 C.I.D., 90 H.P.
@ 3400 RPM, 116½" W.B.
(SINCE '38)
6.00 x 16 TIRES (SINCE '38)

AUTO-LITE IGN. ON SIXES, DELCO-REMY IGN. ON EIGHTS (SINCE '33)

CHAMPION →

PRES. INTERIOR

EXCLUSIVE! REVOLUTIONARY!
Studebaker's new Central
CLIMATIZER

PRESIDENT 8 (5-C)
250.4 C.I.D. ENGINE
(INTRO. '29 IN CMNDR.)
110 H.P. @ 3600 RPM
(SINCE '33)
122" W.B.
(SINCE '38)
6.50 x 16 TIRES
(SINCE '36)

39

CHAMPION 6 (G)
(NEW)
110" WB

164.3
C.I.D.
78
H.P.

PRESIDENT 8
(COMMANDER 6 SIMILAR)

DASH
(CHAMPION)

264

5.50 x 16
TIRES

"CHAMPION" INTRODUCED THURS., APRIL 20, 1939. (CARTER CARB.)

19-20

STUTZ — THE CAR THAT MADE GOOD IN A DAY

(1912 - 1934)

STUTZ MOTOR CAR CO. OF AMERICA, INC., Indianapolis, U.S.A.

"H" SERIES
AVAIL. IN VARIOUS BODY TYPES.

130" WHEELBASE (4-CYL. MODELS and '25 "6 95")

STROMBERG CARB. (THROUGH '25)

PRESSURE FUEL FEED (ON 4-CYL. MODELS THROUGH '24)

3.5 GEAR RATIO

STUTZ factory

IGNITION: DELCO (4-CYL.)
REMY (6-CYL., 23-25)
DELCO-REMY (AFTER '25)

"BEARCAT"
STUTZ' MOST FAMOUS SPORTS MODEL.
(AVAIL. AS "SUPER BEARCAT" ON SHORT WHEELBASE, IN EARLY 1930s.)

4 CYL., 360.8 C.I.D. T-HEAD ENGINE (TO '24)

BEARCAT

21-22

(LEFT-HAND DRIVE)

"K" and "H" MODELS

FINER HOOD LOUVRES; HORN REMOVED FROM RT. SIDE

"KLDH" 1922 MODEL HAS NEW "DH" ENGINE and COMPENSATING SPRINGS.

KLDH "SPEEDWAY 4" 2-PASS. ROADSTER (3.75 G.R.)

23

268 C.I.D. NEW VACUUM FUEL FEED ON 6.

"690" 6 CYLINDER (NEW)
5-PASS. SEDAN

120" W.B.
(ALSO ON '24 "690" and '25 "693," "694" "694-HB" SERIES

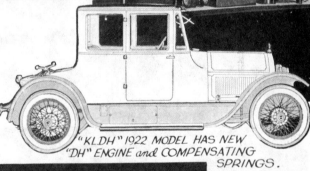

SPEEDWAY 6 "695"

"SPEEDWAY 4" (FINAL YEAR FOR 4-CYL. MODEL WAS 1924.)

24-25

1925 IS FINAL YEAR FOR STUTZ 6
(BOTH THE 130"-W.B. SPEEDWAY 6
AND 120"-W.B. SPECIAL 6 [694-HB
LATE MODELS AVAIL. WITH LOCKHEED HYD. BRAKE

SAFETY STUTZ

32 × 6.20 TIRES (THROUGH '28)
NEW HYDRAULIC BRAKES

Six body styles, designed and constructed under the supervision of Brewster of New York. All closed bodies automatically ventilated.

TOP
50"
70"
20"

131" W.B. (THROUGH '28)

The symbol of Safety

SAFETY CHASSIS New

NEW ZENITH CARB.
92 H.P. @
3200 RPM

The first and only automobile to provide safety-glass all around without extra charge to the buyer ✱

✱ = STUTZ' EARLY SAFETY GLASS RE-INFORCED BY FINE HORIZONTAL WIRES, VISIBLE TO THE EYE. ILCO – RYAN THICK-LENSED HEADLIGHTS ADOPTED, 1927 →

WORM DRIVE

287.3 C.I.D. STRAIGHT - 8 (NEW)
(298.6 C.I.D. IN '27 and '28)

STUTZ SAFETY 8 CHASSIS

26-27

5.0 G.R.
(THROUGH '28)

MODEL "AA"
"AA" SERIES

28
"BB"
115 H.P. @
3600 RPM

32 × 6.20
OR
32 × 6.75
TIRES

VACUUM and OTHER FUEL FEEDS AVAIL.

266

STUTZ

'29-30 BLACKHAWK L-8 has FUEL PUMP

WITH WEYMANN FABRIC-PANELED LIGHTWT. BODY

BODIES BY HALE KILBURN LE BARON WEYMANN

BLACKHAWK "L-6" has 6 CYLS., 241.5 C.I.D. 85 H.P. @ 3200
"L-8" has STRAIGHT-8 ENG., 268.5 C.I.D. 88-90 H.P. @ 3100-3200 RPM

BLACKHAWK

"MONACO"

('29)

SOME EARLY '29 BLACKHAWKS HAVE DART LOUVRES AT REAR OF HOOD.→
127½" W.B. ON ALL BLACKHAWKS. 4.75 G.R. ('29)

All engines have overhead camshaft.

'29 FLEETWOOD TOWN CAR ALSO AVAIL.

"M" SERIES

6.50 x 20

134½-145" W.B. (TO '34)
STRAIGHT-8, 322 CID ENG. (TO '34)

115 H.P. @ 3600 RPM

4.5 G.R., EXCEPT ON '29 BLACKHAWK

29-30

FRONT DETAILS

BODIES BY LE BARON, WEYMANN, ROLLSTON, BRUNN, ETC.

STRAIGHT-8
6-CYL. "LA, LAA" SERIES (THROUGH '33) (CONTINUES BLACKHAWK 6 SPECS.)

VENT DOORS ON HOOD

DASH

('31)

31-34

NEW "CHALLENGER" SERIES JOINS "CUSTOM" IN 1933.

"SV-16", "DV-32"

SOME 1933-1934 STUTZES HAVE NEW STREAMLINING BUT RETAIN FLAT RADIATOR.

7.00 x 18

267

AUTO. CHOKE and CLUTCH, LARGER COWL VENTS IN 1933

TEMPLAR (1917-1924)

TEMPLAR MOTORS CORP., CLEVELAND, OHIO
with "VITALIC TOP-VALVE MOTOR"
(4 CYL., O.H.V.)
C.I.D.
43 H.P. @ 2100 RPM
118" W.B.

SPOTLIGHT MOVED LOWER DURING 1919.

ONLY 3 LUG-BOLTS BEFORE 1920.

TEMPLAR "SPORTETTE" ('21)

ROADSTER ('22)

6-CYL. AVAIL. BEFORE TEMPLAR DISCO

('24)

(THE FINAL TEMPLAR)

TERRAPLANE

(1933-1938)

BUILT BY HUDSON
(REPLACES THE 1932
ESSEX. TRANSITIONAL
MODELS OF 1932-1933 NAMED
"ESSEX-TERRAPLANE.")

33

106"(6) OR 113"(8) W.B.

8
HAS HOOD
VENT DOORS

6 CYL.
193.1 C.I.D.
70 H.P. @ 3200
8 CYL.
244 C.I.D.
94 H.P. @ 3200

Terraplane

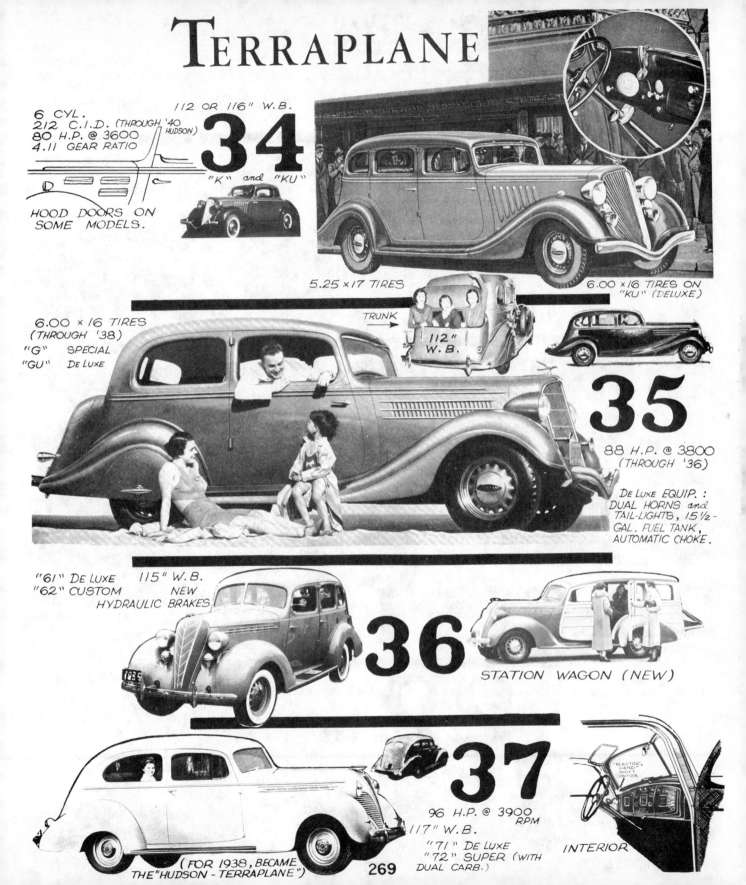

6 CYL.
212 C.I.D. (THROUGH '40 HUDSON)
80 H.P. @ 3600
4.11 GEAR RATIO

HOOD DOORS ON SOME MODELS.

112 OR 116" W.B.

34
"K" and "KU"

5.25 x 17 TIRES

6.00 x 16 TIRES ON "KU" (DELUXE)

6.00 x 16 TIRES (THROUGH '38)
"G" SPECIAL
"GU" DE LUXE

TRUNK

112" W.B.

35
88 H.P. @ 3800 (THROUGH '36)

DE LUXE EQUIP.: DUAL HORNS and TAIL-LIGHTS, 15½-GAL. FUEL TANK, AUTOMATIC CHOKE.

"61" DE LUXE   115" W.B.
"62" CUSTOM   NEW
HYDRAULIC BRAKES

36
STATION WAGON (NEW)

37
96 H.P. @ 3900 RPM
117" W.B.
"71" DE LUXE
"72" SUPER (WITH DUAL CARB.)

"ELECTRIC HAND SHIFT CONTROL"

INTERIOR

(FOR 1938, BECAME THE "HUDSON-TERRAPLANE")

269

TEXAN

TEXAS MOTOR CAR ASSN.,
FORT WORTH, TEXAS

(1918-1922)

4 CYLS.   115" W.B.
"A-38" has LYCOMING ENGINE
"C-12" has HERSCH.-SPLMN. ENGINE
3½ × 5" is BORE and STROKE of EACH
(192.4 C.I.D.)

33 × 4 TIRES

TULSA 4

← EMBLEM

33 × 4 TIRES
('20-22)

TULSA AUTO MFG. CO., TULSA, OKLA. (1917-1922)

MODEL "E"
('20-22)
117½" W.B.
4 CYL.
192.4 C.I.D.
HERSCHELL-
SPILLMAN
ENGINE
4.5 GEAR RATIO

ZENITH CARB.
CONNECTICUT
IGN.

VELIE

VELIE MOTORS CORPORATION,
Moline, Illinois

(1908 TO 1928)

MODEL "34"
112" W.B.
(THROUGH '22)

6 CYLINDERS
(ALL BUT '28 "8-88")

MODEL "48"

195.6 C.I.D. O.H.V.
FALLS ENGINE

20-21

ATWATER KENT IGN. (TO '24)

RAYFIELD CARB. ('20)   STROMBERG CARB. ('21-'29)

115" W.B. (THROUGH '23)
(224 C.I.D. CONTINENTAL
L-HEAD ENGINE)
(THROUGH '22)

"34" and "48"
MODELS AVAILABLE ALSO

22

(WITH VELIE-BUILT 195.6 C.I.D.
ENGINE IN NEW 115"-W.B. "58")
(OVERHEAD VALVES) 4.66 G.R. (THROUGH '23)
32 × 4 TIRES (THROUGH '23,
AND ON '24 "56")

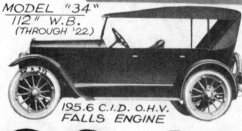

FINAL YEAR FOR
FALLS ENGINE
(ON MODEL "34")

FINAL YEAR FOR
CONTINENTAL ENGINE
(ON MODEL "48")

new MODEL "58"

"SPORT CAR"

270

Velie

Velie Model 58, five-passenger Touring; beautifully finished and equipped; all Velie cars are powered with the remarkable vibrationless six-cylinder, valve-in-head Velie-built motor.

Velie Silver Swallow, five-passenger Sport with satin-aluminum body; equipment includes two extra cord tires, disc wheels, bumpers, spotlights, trunk, two suitcases, hat box, and many other items.

Velie Model 58, three-passenger Sport Roadster; specially painted; extra cord tire, disc wheels, bumpers, spotlights. We also furnish a similar roadster with standard equipment.

4.66 GEAR RATIO IN 1923

115" W.B. (THROUGH '23) 118" W.B. ON BOTH "56" and "58" MODELS, 1924.

WESTINGHOUSE IGNITION (LATE '24 THROUGH '25)

2 - WHEEL MECHANICAL BRAKES

('24)

The new Velie five-passenger Four-Door Brougham; a most desirable roomy car; trunk contains two suitcases and hat box; interior equipment includes vanity case, flower vase and smoking set.

Velie Model 58, five-passenger Sedan; all Velie enclosed cars are upholstered in a choice grade of taupe mohair velvet, with carpets and trimming of harmonizing colours.

('24)

The new Velie four-passenger Coupé, luxuriously upholstered and lined with taupe mohair velvet—with a spacious package compartment back of driver's seat and roomy luggage space beneath rear deck.

23-24

NEW 118" W. B. IN 1924 ; NEW ('24) 203.5 C.I.D.; 4.7 OR 5.1 GEAR RATIO

"60" IS ONLY SERIES OF VELIE FOR 1925 and 1926.

25

MODEL "60"   6 CYLINDERS
OVERHEAD VALVES   204 C.I.D.
48 H.P. @ 2600 RPM

5.10 GEAR RATIO
118" WHEELBASE

new HYDRAULIC 4-WHEEL BRAKES (TO '29)

THE SMARTEST CAR ON THE HIGHWAY

Four Door Coach

VELIE ROADSTER

VELIE

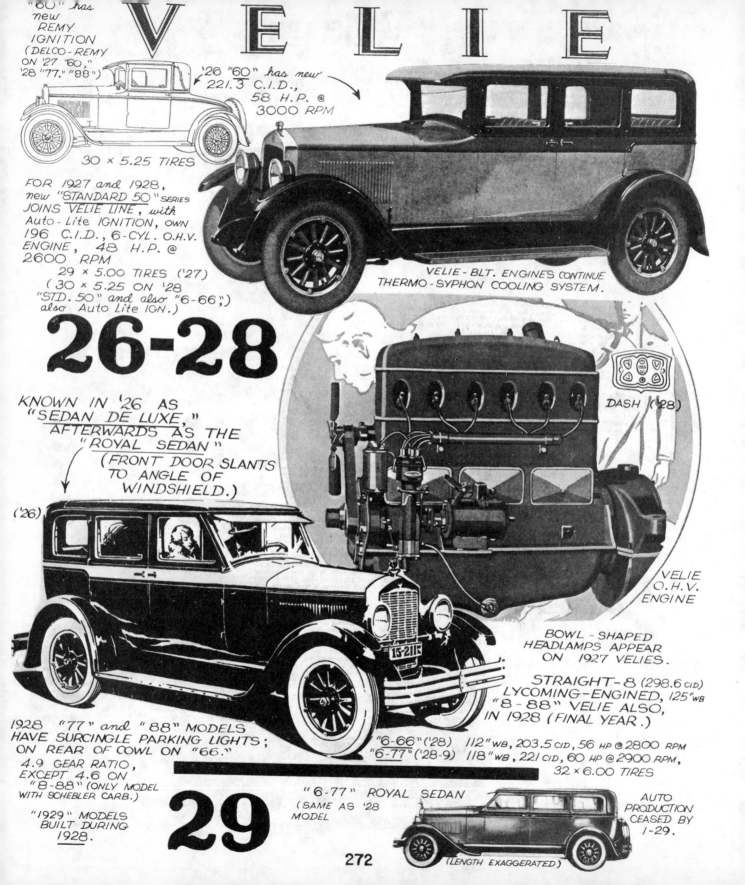

"60" has new REMY IGNITION (DELCO-REMY ON '27 "60," '28 "77." "88")

'26 "60" has new 221.3 C.I.D., 58 H.P. @ 3000 RPM

30 × 5.25 TIRES

FOR 1927 and 1928, new "STANDARD 50" SERIES JOINS VELIE LINE, with Auto-Lite IGNITION, OWN 196 C.I.D., 6-CYL. O.H.V. ENGINE, 48 H.P. @ 2600 RPM
29 × 5.00 TIRES ('27) (30 × 5.25 ON '28 "STD. 50" and also "6-66";) also Auto Lite IGN.)

VELIE-BLT. ENGINES CONTINUE THERMO-SYPHON COOLING SYSTEM.

26-28

KNOWN IN '26 AS "SEDAN DE LUXE," AFTERWARDS AS THE "ROYAL SEDAN" (FRONT DOOR SLANTS TO ANGLE OF WINDSHIELD.)

('26)

DASH ('28)

VELIE O.H.V. ENGINE

BOWL-SHAPED HEADLAMPS APPEAR ON 1927 VELIES.

STRAIGHT-8 (298.6 CID) LYCOMING-ENGINED, 125" WB "8-88" VELIE ALSO, IN 1928 (FINAL YEAR.)

"6-66" ('28) 112" WB, 203.5 CID, 56 HP @ 2800 RPM
"6-77" ('28-9) 118" WB, 221 CID, 60 HP @ 2900 RPM, 32 × 6.00 TIRES

1928 "77" and "88" MODELS HAVE SURCINGLE PARKING LIGHTS; ON REAR OF COWL ON "66." 4.9 GEAR RATIO, EXCEPT 4.6 ON "8-88" (ONLY MODEL WITH SCHEBLER CARB.)

"1929" MODELS BUILT DURING 1928.

29

"6-77" ROYAL SEDAN (SAME AS '28 MODEL

AUTO PRODUCTION CEASED BY 1-29.

(LENGTH EXAGGERATED)

272

VIKING

PRODUCT OF GENERAL MOTORS

BUILT 1929 – 1930 BY GM's OLDSMOBILE DIVISION

29

(INTRODUCED APRIL, 1929)

EMBLEM

V-8 ENGINE
259.4 C.I.D.

80 H.P. @ 3200 RPM

125" WHEELBASE
(THROUGH '30)

30 × 6.00 TIRES

30

81 H.P. @ 3200 RPM

6.00 × 18 TIRES

273

WALTHAM

6 CYLS.
45 H.P.

WALTHAM
MOTOR MFRS., INC.,
WALTHAM,
MASS.

REPLACES
"METZ" CAR
(1922 ONLY)

22

WASP

('20)

MARTIN-WASP CORP.,
BENNINGTON., VT. (1919-1925)
4 AND 6 CYL.
"2611" ('21) has 132" W.B., 4-CYL., 389.9 C.I.D.
WISCONSIN T-III AD ENGINE
BOSCH IGNITION   3.70 G.R.
STROMBERG CARB.   33 × 5 TIRES

WESTCOTT

The Car with a Longer Life

(1912 - 1925)

THE WESTCOTT MOTOR CAR CO.
SPRINGFIELD, OHIO

TWIN OVAL REAR
WINDOWS IN TOP
CONTINENTAL ENGINES (ON
ALL BUT
'24
"60")

C-"38" (224 CID THROUGH '22)
LIGHTER 6 (5.09 G.R.)
(118" W.B.)
C-"48" (303.1 STD THROUGH
(4.45 GR) LARGER 6   '24)
(125" W.B.)

19-20

(A) ↘   (C)
(38)   (48)
33 × 4 OR 32 × 4½
TIRES
(THROUGH
'22)

"C-38"

'19 MODEL
SHOWN. '20 HAS FULL-LENGTH
BODY-HOOD BELT CREASE JUST
ABOVE DOOR HANDLES, ALSO A
NEW COWL VENT.

DELCO IGNITION ON ALL
RAYFIELD CARB.
(THROUGH '24)

21 ←   "C-48"

1922 "A-44" LIKE '21 "C-38," BUT
HAS 120" W.B., 4.66 G.R.

NON-REMOVABLE CYLINDER-HEAD ON 303.1 CID ENG. → "D-48" for '23)
("C-44 and

"CLOSURE" IS NEW ENCLOSED TOURING CAR
FOR 1923

The Closure   81795
Special Closure   1995
Brougham (including trunk) 2490
Sedan   2490
Special Sedan   2690

23

32 × 4½
TIRES ON ALL
'23-'24
WESTCOTTS

C-44-241.5 CID, 4.9 GR
D-48-303.1 CID,
4.45 GR

The Car with a Longer Life

"6-60"
5-PASS.
SEDAN
('24)
("OWN
ENGINE)

Interior of The New Westcott Model
The Closure

24
('25 has
4-W. BRKS.,   32 × 6.20 TIRES,
STROMBERG CARB., 56 H.P. @   2300 RPM

OVERLAND

Whippet
FOURS SIXES

28 × 4.75 TIRES (19") (THROUGH '29)

4-CYL. "96" (INTRO. 7-26)
134.2 C.I.D. (THROUGH '29)
30 H.P. @ 2800 RPM
4.5 G.R.
100 1/4" W.B. (THROUGH '28)

27

6-CYL. LANDAU

6-CYL. "93-A"
169.6 C.I.D. (THROUGH '28)
40 H.P. @ 2800 RPM

109 1/2" W.B. (THROUGH '28)

29 × 4.75 TIRES (6 INTRO. 1-27)

WHIPPET MASCOT →

VACUUM FUEL FEED, TILLOTSON CARB. and AUTO-LITE IGN. (THROUGH '30)

BOTH SERIES have 4-WHEEL MECHANICAL BRAKES.

RAISED PANEL ON '27 FENDERS

FISK

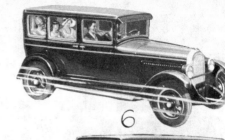

WHITE

CLEVELAND, OHIO
(SINCE 1900)

1922 MODEL "15-A" 4 CYL.
"UTILITY" MODEL ("BUSINESS CAR," ANNOUNCED 11-21)

BETWEEN 1918 and 1936, CARS ON SPECIAL ORDER ONLY. TRUCK PRODUCTION CONTINUES.

WILLS SAINTE CLAIRE (1921-1927)

DELCO IGN. (THROUGH '27)   65 H.P. @ 2700 RPM ('22)
4 TO 1 STD. GEAR RATIO

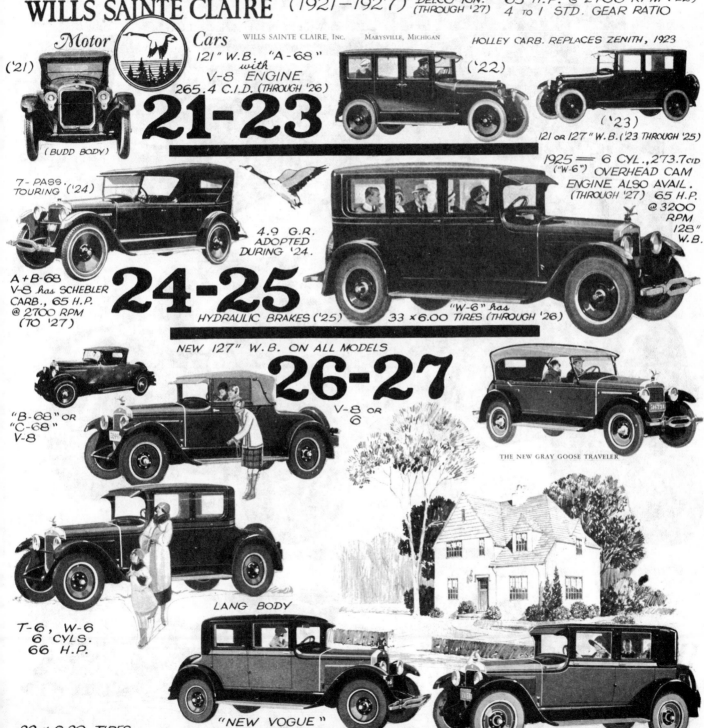

Motor Cars   WILLS SAINTE CLAIRE, Inc.   MARYSVILLE, MICHIGAN

HOLLEY CARB. REPLACES ZENITH, 1923

121" W.B. "A-68" with V-8 ENGINE 265.4 C.I.D. (THROUGH '26)

('21)

(BUDD BODY)

('22)

('23)

21-23

121 OR 127" W.B. ('23 THROUGH '25)

7-PASS. TOURING ('24)

4.9 G.R. ADOPTED DURING '24.

1925 = 6 CYL., 273.7 CID ("W-6") OVERHEAD CAM ENGINE ALSO AVAIL. (THROUGH '27) 65 H.P. @ 3200 RPM 128" W.B.

A+B-68 V-8 has SCHEBLER CARB., 65 H.P. @ 2700 RPM (TO '27)

24-25

HYDRAULIC BRAKES ('25)   "W-6" has 33 x 6.00 TIRES (THROUGH '26)

NEW 127" W.B. ON ALL MODELS

26-27

V-8 OR 6

"B-68" OR "C-68" V-8

THE NEW GRAY GOOSE TRAVELER

T-6, W-6 6 CYLS. 66 H.P.

LANG BODY

32 x 6.20 TIRES ON '27 "T-6" 4.9 G.R. ('27)

"NEW VOGUE" BROUGHAM

DISCONTINUED 1927

WILLYS

SIXES AND EIGHTS

WILLYS-OVERLAND, INC., TOLEDO, OHIO

WILLYS 8 SEDAN DE LUXE

Eight

8 HAS 120" W.B., 245.4 C.I.D., 80 H.P. @ 3200 RPM, 5.50 × 19 TIRES (THROUGH '31)

Six 30

6 HAS 110" W.B., 192.9 C.I.D., 65 H.P. @ 3400 RPM, 5.00 × 19 TIRES (THROUGH '31)

REPLACES "WHIPPET" 6

"6-97" and 113"-WB "6-98-D" SHARE '30 "6" SPECS.

NEW NAME USED FOR 1931

HORIZONTAL HOOD LOUVRES ON SIX

"6-97," "6-98-D," and "8-80-D"

INSTRUMENT PANEL (6)

"8-80-D" SAME SPECS. AS '30, BUT 121" W.B.

HOOD VENT DOORS ON EIGHT

WILLYS·OVERLAND

31

SIDE VIEW SIMILAR TO 1931-1932 WILLYS-KNIGHT "95." (SEE "WILLYS-KNIGHT.")

70-80 M.P.H.

WILLYS 8 and WILLYS-KNIGHT INSTRUMENT PANEL

278

WILLYS

6

1932 "SILVER ANNIVERSARY" MODELS
with "SILVER STREAK" ENGINES

32

('32 6 DASH IS SAME DESIGN AS '31 6, BUT HAS WOOD-GRAIN EFFECTS)

('32 HAS RADIATOR FILLER UNDER 2" LONGER HOOD, AND TRUMPET HORN IN PLACE OF 1931 DISC-SHAPED VIBRATOR HORN.) "6-90-A" and "8-88-A" (AFTER 6-32) IS "1933" MODEL.

The Six Coach, $530

'32 "8-88" and "6-90" have SAME SPECS. AS CORRESPONDING '30-'31 MODELS, BUT 5.50 × 18 and 5.25 × 18 TIRES

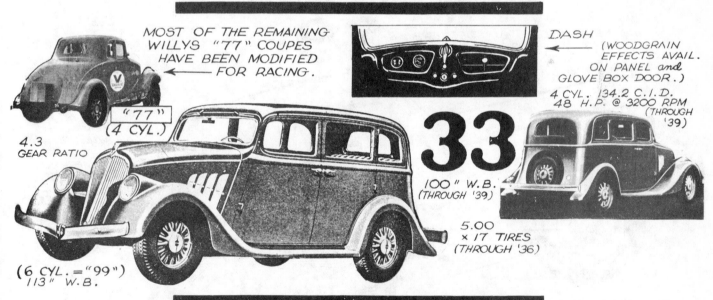

MOST OF THE REMAINING WILLYS "77" COUPES HAVE BEEN MODIFIED FOR RACING. ←

DASH ← (WOODGRAIN EFFECTS AVAIL. ON PANEL and GLOVE BOX DOOR.)

4 CYL. 134.2 C.I.D. 48 H.P. @ 3200 RPM (THROUGH '39)

"77" (4 CYL.)

4.3 GEAR RATIO

33

100" W.B. (THROUGH '39)

5.00 × 17 TIRES (THROUGH '36)

(6 CYL. = "99") 113" W.B.

34

NEW WIRE WHEELS

NEW SEMI-HORIZONTAL LOUVRES

WILLYS

35

(BUBBLE - SHAPED
HOOD VENT PORTS)
'35 HAS WIRE WHEELS.

36

'36 HAS STEEL-SPOKE
ARTILLERY WHEELS.

INTERIOR

EARLIEST '37
MODELS (BUILT
FALL, 1936,) HAVE NO
VERTICAL BUMPER GUARDS.

5.50 × 16 TIRES

37-38

39

THIS NEW MODEL "61" DEVELOPS
61 H.P. @ 3600 RPM,
HAS HYDRAULIC BRAKES,
4.3 - 4.55 GEAR RATIO,
102" WHEELBASE.

DASH
(61)

MODEL "48"
WILLYS HAS
100" W.B.,
MECHANICAL
BRAKES,
4.1
GEAR RATIO,
5.00 × 16
TIRES,
1938
STYLING.

5.50 × 16 TIRES ON "61"

Slip-stream
A DESIGN OF SUPERB
BEAUTY

SHELL

DURING 1939, WILLYS "61"
KNOWN AS
OVERLAND   (4 CYL.)

WILLYS-KNIGHT

(1914 – 1932)

4- CYLINDER
SLEEVE - VALVE
ENGINE

185.8
C.I.D.
(THROUGH
'25)

40 H.P.
@
2600 RPM
('21 -'22)

118" W.B.
(THROUGH '25)

WILLYS-OVERLAND, INC., *Toledo, Ohio*
WILLYS-OVERLAND, LIMITED, *Toronto, Canada*

20-21

5.00 GEAR RATIO
(THROUGH '22)

DIAGRAM OF A CYLINDER,
ILLUSTRATING
THE SLEEVE -
VALVE
MECHANISM →

22

40 H.P. @ 2400 RPM
MODEL "64"   118" W.B.
and 32×4 TIRES

23-24

"COUNTRY
CLUB"
TOURING

'23 MODEL
"67" HAS
124" W.B.
and
32×4½
TIRES

4.44
GEAR
RATIO
('23)

4.44
and
5.12
('24)

Coupe-Sedan
Standard

281

WILLYS-KNIGHT

33 × 4.95

42 H.P. @ 2200 RPM

4

4

25

"66"

NEW 6 HAS 236.4 C.I.D. (THROUGH '27) and 60 H.P. @ 2800 RPM

FISK BALLOON 32 × 6.20

126" W.B. (UNTIL '28)

6 (NEW)

WILLYS-KNIGHT

113¼" W.B. (THROUGH '28)

"70" (6 CYL.)
177.9 C.I.D. (THROUGH '32)
53 H.P. @ 3000 RPM

26

GREAT 6
60 H.P. @ 3000 RPM

27-28

ROADSTER

WITH TOP UP

TOP DOWN

CABRIOLET

"70" Six

The Only Motor-Car Engine That Improves With Use.

53 H.P. @
3100 RPM (3000 RPM, '28-9)

1928 "70"
KNOWN AS
"SPECIAL 6"

WILLYS-KNIGHT

27-28
(CONT'D.)

MASCOT

("56")

109½" New
W.B. Standard Six
157.6 ("56")
C.I.D. ('28)

45 H.P. @ 3000 RPM

"GREAT 6"
"66" (1927)
"66-A" (1928)   DASH
NEW HORIZONTAL HOOD LOUVRES
('27½-'28)

One of the many new beautiful color combinations now available on the Willys-Knight Great Six. Upper body, black; lower body and wheels, spruce-green. Striping, ivory and red. Upholstered in fine quality gray-green mohair.

'28 "66-A" HAS
255 C.I.D.
(ENGINE SIZE RETAINED
THROUGH '32)

INSTR.
PANEL

('29)

29-30
"70-B"

('29)

6 CYLS., 177.9 C.I.D.
53 H.P. @
3000 RPM
4.89 G.R.
29 x 5.50
TIRES (5.50
x 19 IN '30)

112½" W.B.

WILLYS·KNIGHT

29-30
(CONT'D.)

GREAT SIX
"66-B" 6 CYLS., 255 C.I.D.

72 ('29)
87 ('30)
H.P. @
3200 RPM

120" WHEELBASE
"GREAT 6" CAB. CPE., 7-PASS.
SEDAN AND LIMOUSINE have
ROBBINS BODIES.
WILLYS-OVERLAND BODIES
ON OTHERS.

GREAT SIX →

The artistically designed instrument panel, with instruments grouped in a setting of beauty and dignity.

('30)

"87" (1930)

The door interiors are upholstered in broadcloth, with a center strip of Bedford Cord, topped by an artistic panel in needlepoint.

31-32
(FINAL WILLYS-KNIGHT IS 1932 MODEL.)
"66-D" 87 H.P. @ 3200

"95"
(1932)
177.9
C.I.D.
60 H.P. @ 3400
(SINCE '31)

(1929-1930) WINDSOR 8

MOON MOTOR CAR CO.,
ST. LOUIS, MO.

1929 "WHITE PRINCE" has
STRAIGHT-8 CONTINENTAL
"15-S" ENGINE (268.6 C.I.D.)
88 H.P. @ 3100 RPM
125½" W.B.
★ 4.8 and other GEAR RATIOS
31 × 6.00 TIRES ("8-82")
31 × 6.50 " ("8-92")
★ 4.88 GEAR RATIO ("8-82")
3.93 " " ("8-92")

'29 DASH

6-CYL. '30 MODELS ALSO ('29)

1930 "6-69" has 6-CYL. CONT.
"37-L" ENGINE (185 C.I.D.)
47 H.P. @ 2600 RPM,
5.25 × 19 TIRES

1930 6-CYL.
"6-69" and "6-75"
have 120" W.B.,
4.9 GEAR RATIO

→ "6-75" ('30)

"6-75" has 6-CYL. CONT.
"11-E" ENG.(214.7 C.I.D.)
66 H.P. @ 3100 RPM, 5.50 ×19 TIRES

WINDSOR HAS MOON-STYLE
RADIATOR
(PAINTED, ON MOST TYPES)
"8-82" BECOMES "8-85"
FOR 1930, has 4.63 G.R.,
6.00 × 19 TIRES

"8-92" CONT'D. 1930, with
6.50 × 19 TIRES, 3.9 G.R.

WINTHER 6 (1920-1923)

MODEL "61" ('21)
has
120" W.B.,
4.45
GEAR RATIO

RADIATOR
DESIGN

WINTHER MOTORS, INC., KENOSHA, WIS.
HERSCHELL-SPILLMAN ENGINE (248.9 C.I.D.)
(TRUCKS ALSO)

(DISC WHEELS ALSO AVAIL.

WINTON SIX (1897—1924)

THE WINTON COMPANY   CLEVELAND

has 132" W.B.,
OWN 6-CYL.
L-HEAD ENGINE
(347.9
C.I.D.)

('22)

4.90 G.R.
(THROUGH
'21)

WINTON-BUILT
BODY

NEW "40" 4-PASS.
SPORT CAR

DURING 1922, MODEL "25"
REPLACED BY MODEL "40"

('23)

('23)

"40" 7-PASS.
SEDAN

STROMBERG CARB.
REPLACED BY
RAYFIELD CARB.,
and NEW 4.58 G.R.
FOR 1923 and 1924.

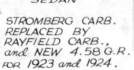

('24) 5-PASS.
COUPE

YELLOW CAB (1921—1936)

'21

Manufacturing Co.
Chicago, U.S.A.

BUILT BY GENERAL MOTORS
AFTER MID-1920s.
KNOWN AS GENERAL CAB
FROM 1936 TO 1938.

Part Two: Airway to Willys 1940-1965

Introduction to Part Two

This book is intended as a helpful tool. But first of all, it's for you to *enjoy!* Browsing leisurely through the pages is like a nostalgic 'time capsule' trip through the 1940's, 1950's and early 1960's.

They're all here, those fascinating, chrome-plastered, bright-colored American dreamboats from the jukebox era—all the four-wheeled friends you remember so well, plus many you may never have seen until now!

And you'll want to keep this collection around as a handy reference book and peaceful 'argument settler' when it comes to positively identifying one year model or make from another. All of the pictures are arranged alphabetically by make, and chronologically by year, with helpful notes on what identifying characteristics to watch for.

Some time ago this writer assembled a hand-made, personal 'car spotter' in a large scrapbook. It was bulky and crude compared to the book you have here, but any time it was carried along to car shows, club meetings, etc., others were anxious to borrow it and check out items of particular interest. "You really ought to make this into a book we could all buy," many suggested. There was a need for such a book, so I then prepared the original edition of the *American Car Spotter's Guide 1940-1965.*

Notice the many better pictures and close-up views in this new edition, as well as the additional written facts. Though this is a spotter's guide and not intended as an encyclopedia, there is helpful information concerning horsepower, wheelbase, tire size, original price, etc., of many of the cars shown here. Available space doesn't allow us to include all prices, specifications, and illustrations for all body types of every individual model in every case.

You'll see many favorites here: the Kaisers and Frazers, the Studebakers, Hudsons, Packards, Fords and Mercurys, the durable Chrysler products and choice goodies such as the beautiful 'woodies' . . . and, of course, many beautiful Lincolns, Cadillacs, Buicks, the Chevies you love, and much, much more. This new edition even includes many rarities such as the fabulous '48 Tucker and others that did not get into full production but which have aroused your curiosity over the years!

Most cars were big and flashy in the era covered here. But if you like compacts and minicars, the Metropolitans and others are presented, plus many Crosley pictures not seen in the old edition.

Concerning the prices included in some cases: they are f.o.b. (freight on board) factory prices. In other words, they are the prices you would have paid had you taken delivery of the car at the factory, and without the added taxes, license and delivery fees. And then there were charges for various accessories or extras included. And prices were always subject to "change without notice," so that a new car might cost more than it had a few weeks or months previously.

Thank you for your interest! I'd certainly enjoy hearing from you if you have comments or suggestions about the book, and if you wish a personal reply, please enclose a self-addressed stamped envelope. And meanwhile, may this book be a handy tool you can use often.

Acknowledgements

With deep gratitude to the following individuals, whose kind help in rounding up certain hard-to-find pictures or facts will always be appreciated! Bill Adams, Ronald C. Adams, David, Roger & John Allen, Jim Allen, Jeff Anderson, Bill Babich, Warren J. Baier, Larry Blodget, Jim Bollman, Paul Bridges, Edwill H. Brown, Emmett P. Burke, Swen H. Carlson, Steve Cifranic, John A. Conde, Virginia Daugert, Howard De Sart, Jim Edwards, Jim Evans, Fred K. Fox, Will Fox, Norm Frey, Jeff Gibson, Bruce Gilbert, Mark Gresser, Dick Grove, W. B. Hamlin, H. Gordon Hansen, Albert R. Hedges, Larry C. Holian, Corinne James, Alden Jewell, David Johnson, Elliott Kahn, Lenny Kellogg, John C. Kelly, Bruce Kennedy, Mark Kubancik, Mike Lamm, June Larson, Rick Markell, Keith Marvin, Larry Mauck, Carl Mendoza, Jim Miller, Harry Mosher, Bruce Newell, Dave Newell, Al Newman, Raymond B. Petersen, Tim Ressler, Walter F. Robinson, Lewis B. Scott, Jay Sherwin, Dave Sibert, Mark Simon, Kirk Slater, Craig Steele, John Stempel, Tom Terhune, R. A. Wawrzyniak, Paul Wehner, Kenneth Wilson, Bob Winke, and Robert Zimmerman.

Thanks are due, also, to the following corporations or associations for either making little-known facts public or for making direct contributions of pictures and/or information: American Motors Corp., Antique Automobile Club of America, Buick Club of America, Cadillac-La Salle Club, Chrysler Corp., Contemporary Historical Vehicle Assn. (CHVA), Corvair Society of America (CORSA), Crosley Automobile Club, De Soto Club of America, Edsel Owner's Club, Fabulous 50's Ford Club of America, Ford Motor Company, General Motors Corp. (& Divisions), Harrah's Automobile Collection, Hudson-Essex-Terraplane (HET) Club, International Edsel Club, Kaiser-Frazer Owner's Club (KFOC), Metropolitan Owner's Club, Milestone Car Society, Oldsmobile Club of America, Society of Automotive Historians, Studebaker Driver's Club, and the WPC/Chrysler Product Restorer's Club.

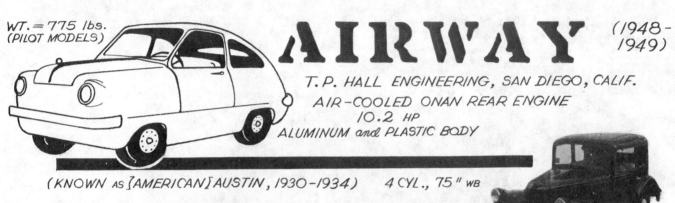

WT.= 775 lbs.
(PILOT MODELS)

AIRWAY (1948-1949)

T.P. HALL ENGINEERING, SAN DIEGO, CALIF.

AIR-COOLED ONAN REAR ENGINE

10.2 HP

ALUMINUM and PLASTIC BODY

(KNOWN AS [AMERICAN] AUSTIN, 1930-1934)   4 CYL., 75" WB

AMERICAN BANTAM

(1935-1941) AMERICAN BANTAM CAR CO., BUTLER, PA.   (OTHER BODY TYPES ALSO)

MODEL
4-65
(1940-1941)
MECH. BRAKES

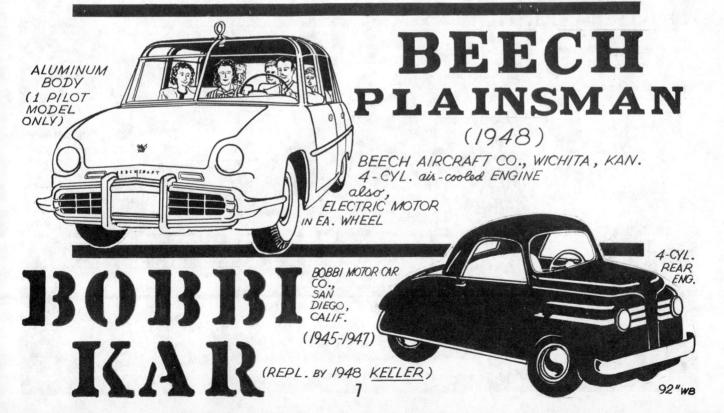

ALUMINUM
BODY
(1 PILOT
MODEL
ONLY)

BEECH
PLAINSMAN

(1948)

BEECH AIRCRAFT CO., WICHITA, KAN.

4-CYL. air-cooled ENGINE

also,
ELECTRIC MOTOR
IN EA. WHEEL

4-CYL.
REAR
ENG.

BOBBI
KAR

BOBBI MOTOR CAR
CO.,
SAN
DIEGO,
CALIF.

(1945-1947)

(REPL. BY 1948 KELLER)

7

92" WB

(ESTAB. 1903)

Buick

BUICK DIVISION OF GENERAL MOTORS

"Best buy's Buick!"

SPECIAL

SUPER

STRAIGHT-8 O.H.V. *engines* (SINCE '31)

1940

LIMITED

Not a six but an EIGHT for **$895** and up

SUPER 51

WHEN BETTER AUTOMOBILES ARE BUILT, BUICK WILL BUILD THEM

MODELS :
40 SPECIAL
50 SUPER
60 CENTURY
70 ROADMASTER
80, 90 LIMITED

248 OR 320 CID
107 HP @ 3400 OR 141 HP @ 3600
(SINCE '38)

6.50 x 16

with

Body by Fisher

Found *only* on CHEVROLET · PONTIAC ·

OLDSMOBILE · BUICK · CADILLAC

121, 126, 133 OR 140" WB

new SAFETY-UNIT SEALED BEAM HEADLIGHTS — brighter, longer-lasting filament in one weatherproof unit with lens and reflector—better lighting over a longer period.

40

RUBY KEELER JOLSON

Here she is with her Buick Estate Wagon, smart, comfortable, useful in no end of ways, and a bargain at $1242, plus $19.50 for white sidewall tires. *

SUPER 59

VARIOUS TIRE SIZES

EIGHT

ON DISPLAY FRIDAY
AT BUICK SHOWROOMS EVERYWHERE

8

BUICK

118, 121, 126 or 139" WB

SPECIAL 4-door Sedan,
Model 47, $1021.

115, 125 OR 165 HP

41

"Buy Buick's Best!" LIMITED

SPECIAL

('41 and EARLIER CONV'TS.
HAVE NO REAR QUARTER
WINDOWS)

DASH

118, 121, 124, 126, 129 OR 139" WB
110, 118 OR 165 HP

42-45

new
"FADE-AWAY" FENDERS BLEND INTO DOORS

"Better Buy Buick"
EXEMPLAR OF GENERAL MOTORS VALUE

SPECIAL

VERTICAL
BARS IN
new
LOWER,
BROADER
GRILLE

CVT., 2-DR. ROADMASTER
has FULL-LENGTH
FRONT
FENDERS

9

BUICK

PRICE RANGE: **$1391.** TO **$2149.**

DASH

CLOCK

CLOSE-UP OF SPEEDOMETER

EASILY-RESETTABLE 2ND ODOMETER RECORDS TRIP MILEAGE

ESTATE WAGON (SUPER)

SUPER

new GRILLE

46

40 SPECIAL   121" WB
50 SUPER   124"
70 ROADMASTER 129"

SUPER

REAR VIEW **10**

ROADMASTER

MODEL 51

SUPER

CONVERTIBLE has POWER-OPERATED TOP, SIDE WINDOWS and FRONT SEAT

When better automobiles are built BUICK will build them

47 $1497. TO $3030.

POSTWAR "BOMBSIGHT"-STYLE HOOD ORNAMENT (SINCE '46)

SPEC. and SUPER have 248 CID, 110 HP @ 3600 RPM

RDMSTR. has 320 CID, 144 HP @ 3600 RPM

MEDALLION MOVED LOWER; NOW IN TOP SECTION of GRILLE.

USA 1947

Super

SUPER

SPEC.-SU.-RDMSTR. PRICES: $1735. TO $3433.

'48 SUPER and ROADMASTER NAMES ALSO APPEAR ON FRONT FENDERS.

48

ROADMASTER

SPECIAL (CONT'D. INTO '49)

OPTIONAL: new Dynaflow AUTO. TRANS.

7.00 × 15

MODEL NAME

11

BUICK

Super
has 3 "PORTHOLES"

49
TOTALLY RESTYLED
(EXCEPT SPECIAL)

ROADMASTER
has 4 "PORTHOLES"
150 HP

BACK SEAT
(SHOWING FOLDING
ARM REST)

ROADMASTER
with Dynaflow Drive

$1787. TO **$3734.**
PRICE RANGE

new DASH

"RIVIERA" (new H/T)

CVT. TOP REAR DETAIL

LATE '49 CONVERTIBLES
and RIVIERAS *have*
new "SWEEP-SPEAR"
SIDE TRIM (AS ILLUSTRATED.)

12

BUICK $1856.

115 HP SPECIAL

SPECIAL INTRODUCED EARLY (IN AUG., '49)

121½" WB EXCEPT ON "52" SUPER SEDAN (125½") and ON 126½" and 130¼" RDMSTRS.

SPECIAL RETAINS 2-PC. WINDSHIELD

STARTLING new "BUMPER-GRILLE"

50

128 HP **Super**

DASH (SPC.)

THE ESTATE WAGON is yours on either SUPER or ROADMASTER chassis. Three power ranges to choose from.

BACK SEAT (SEDAN)

152 HP **ROADMASTER** RIVIERA

130¼" WB ON "RIVIERA & SEDAN"

ELONGATED "PORTHOLES"

BUICK

SPECIAL   SPECIAL DE LUXE

('51)

120 TO 128 HP

ESTATE WAGON

('51)

SUPER 128 HP

51-52

DASH ('52)   ROADMASTER

152 HP

170 HP

('51) ROADMASTER ('52)

SUPER

('51)

Buick Eight

'52 has BROADER HUBCAP MARGINS, FULL-HEIGHT VERT. BUMPER GUARDS, NO CHROME STRIPS ALONG REAR FENDERS.

'51 BUMPER GUARDS DO NOT RUN DOWN FRONT OF BUMPER, BUT REST ON TOP.

Equipment, accessories, trim and models are subject to change without notice.

14

BUICK

FINAL STRAIGHT-8 IN SPECIAL

SPECIAL (125 HP @ 3800 RPM)

53

1903-1953

121½" WB (ALL MODELS EXC. 125½ WB RIVIERA SED.)

SPORT WIRE WH. AVAIL.

SUPER

164-170 HP

new **V8**

322 CID ENGINE IN ALL BUT "SPECIAL"

LIMITED-PRODUCTION "SKYLARK" CVT.

ROADMASTER RIVIERA

ROADMASTER (188 HP @ 4000)

15

BUICK

143 or 150 HP
SPECIAL

ALL V8s

195 or 200 HP
CENTURY

DASH

54

264 or 322 CID V8s
(THROUGH '55)

SKYLARK
$**4483**.

ROADMASTER

SUPER

177 or 182 HP
SUPER

ROADMASTER

200 HP @ 4100 RPM

16

BUICK

150 TO 236 HP

ROADMASTER

TOP TO
BOTTOM: SPECIAL,
CENTURY, SUPER

55

DASH
(SUPER)

BUICK

MEDALLION
GIVES
1956
DATE

SPECIAL

SPECIAL *has* 220 HP @ 4400 RPM
OTHERS, 255 HP @ 4400 RPM

CENTURY

SUPER

ROADMASTER

122 OR 127" WB (SINCE '54)

56

322 CID V8s

new
V-GRILLE (FINE HORIZ. PCS.)

17

BUICK

SPECIAL

WAGON

CVT.

4-DR. H/T

H/T

MODEL NAME ABOVE DIP IN SIDE CHROME TRIM (EXCEPT ON SPECIAL, WHICH HAS NO NAME HERE, OR ON SUPER (with 3 CURVED CHROME PCS. HERE.)

$3354.

CENTURY

ALL WITH new 364 CID ENGINE (CONT'D. IN SPECIAL and LE SABRE MODELS THROUGH 1961)

new CENTURY CABALLERO WAGON (H/T STYLE)

SUPER

CVT.

57

H/T

122" OR new 127½" WB (THROUGH '58)

4-DR. H/T

ROADMASTER

note UNUSUAL REAR DOOR TREATMENT on THIS MODEL

300 HP @ 4600 RPM (EXCEPT SPECIAL, WHICH has 250 HP @ 4400) (THROUGH '58)

new CONVEX GRILLE with FINE VERTICAL PCS.

18

BUICK

1958

new BLOCK-STYLE GRILLE

HEAVY USE of CHROME TRIM

58

SIDE "PORTHOLES"
DISCONTINUED
(UNTIL '60) 250-HP
SPECIAL

$2820.

300 HP IN CENTURY,
SUPER,
RDMSTR.,
LIMITED

$2636.

$4557.

SPECIAL

THE
AIR BORN ✦ B-58 BUICK

SPECIAL CENTURY

CENTURY

ROADMASTER

$5125.

new
LIMITED
(NAME
REVIVED)

19

CVT.

BUICK

ALL-*new* MODEL NAMES FOR 1959:
LE SABRE, INVICTA, ELECTRA, ELECTRA 225

364 CID, 250 HP @ 4400 RPM

LESABRE 123" WB

PACE CAR AT 1959 INDY 500 RACE

LE SABRE
ALL BUT (SPEC.) have
325 HP @ 4400 RPM
401 CID

INVICTA 123" WB

59

(TOTALLY RESTYLED)

DASH

new SQUARED REAR ROOFLINE ON 4-DOOR H/T.

ELECTRA 126.3" WB

CANTED HEADLIGHTS

TOP-OF-LINE ELECTRA 225
IS ILLUSTRATED.

10.5 COMPR. IN 1959

BUICK

$3145.

$2915.

LE SABRE
has 210, 235, 250 or 300 HP

364 CID = LE S.
401 CID = OTHERS
(SAME CHOICES IN '61)

60

A RETURN
TO VARIOUS "PORTHOLE" TYPE SIDE
DECORATIONS AS USED ON
1949-1956 BUICKS

new
"Mirromagic"
INSTRUMENT
CLUSTER
LETS DRIVER SEE
GAUGES IN A
MIRROR THAT
CAN BE TILTED
TO SUIT DRIVER'S
OWN
EYE LEVEL.

INVICTA

INVICTA

1960 BUICK INVICTA 4-DOOR HARDTOP IN MAGIC-MIRROR TAHITI BEIGE AND CORDOVAN

123" WB = LE S., INVICTA
126.3" WB = EL., EL. 225

HEADLTS. PLACED HORIZONTALLY,
new GRILLE
WITH CONCAVE
VERTICAL
PIECES
and new
3-SHIELD
BADGE

INVICTA and
ELECTRAS have
325 HP @ 4400 RPM

ELECTRA

ELECTRA 225

$4300.

21

BUICK

(TOTALLY RESTYLED)

61

126" WB
ELECTRA
225

325 HP

(new ROOFLINE)

123" WB
250 HP
LE SABRE

SPECIAL-SIZE
BUICK SPECIAL
new COMPACT SERIES,
STARTING 1961
SEE SPECIAL

INVICTA

22   123" WB   325 HP

BUICK

2-DR.

4447

LE SABRE

4-DR. H/T

4439

62

$3567.

401 CID V8s (IN all FULL-SIZED MODELS)

ADVANCED THRUST

LE S. 265 HP @ 4400
INV. 280 HP @ 4400
ELEC. 325 HP @ 4400

H/T

4-DR. H/T

INVICTA

CVT.

$3815.

INVICTA ESTATE WAGON

EL. 225 CVT.

$4034. (6-PASS.)

ELECTRA 225

4635

4-DR. H/T

H/T

ELECTRA has 126" WB (OTHERS 123")

SEDAN

Close-up of Wildcat! shows you new medallion and unique fabric overlay (available in black or white).

new 325 HP WILDCAT! H/T

BR 3950

$4125.

BUICK

4647

23

BUICK

SEDAN

280 HP

63 **LESABRE** MODELS

$3298.

2-DR.

CVT.

WAGON *with* REAR-FACING 3RD SEAT

CLOSER VIEW OF LE SABRE DASH *and* ADDITIONAL '63 MODELS ILLUSTRATED ON NEXT PAGE.

24

new V-SHAPED FRONT

BUICK

DASH

$ **4167.**

INVICTA (FINAL YR.)

325 HP (ON ALL BUT LE SABRE)

note =
WILDCAT *has*
ITS OWN UNIQUE
GRILLE

WILDCAT

63 (CONT'D.)

$ **4047.**

Electra 225

$ **4141.**

ELECTRA TAIL-LIGHT
DETAIL

25

BUICK

ESTATE WAGON

210 HP

LE SABRE

64

$3458.

$3593.

WILDCAT
325 HP

THE WILDCAT CONVERTIBLE

THE WILDCAT 4-DOOR SEDAN

WILDCAT (CLOSE-UP)

$4357.

THE ELECTRA 225 CONVERTIBLE

ELECTRA
225

THE ELECTRA 225 4-DOOR HARDTOP

325 HP

BUICK

LE SABRE

H/T
(VINYL TOP)

123" WB
300 CID
210 HP
8.15×15 TIRES

LE SABRE
400

123 OR 126" WB
(SINCE '59)

65

$**3345.**
TO
$**4530.**

4-DR.
H/T

H/T

8.45×15
TIRES
126" WB
401 CID
325 HP

WILDCAT

SEE ALSO:
RIVIERA

CVT.

ELECTRA 225

8.85×15 TIRES

H/T

(INTRO. WED., OCT. 5, 1960, AS SEPARATE COMPACT SERIES OF BUICK)

SPECIAL-SIZE BUICKSPECIAL
THE BEST OF BOTH WORLDS

(and SKYLARK)

NEW!

BUICK'S REVOLUTIONARY ALUMINUM V-8. This hot 155 HP Fireball V-8 weighs just 318 pounds for a .487 horsepower to weight ratio — highest in the industry!

3 VIEWS OF SPECIAL (SEDAN)

61

WAGON has 1-PIECE SWING-UP REAR DOOR

PRICES START AT **$2659.** (STD. CPE

SPECIAL WAGON

THE CLEAN LOOK of action

$3091.

112" WHEELBASE

BUICK skylark

SKYLARK IS new LUXURY 185-HP MODEL of SPECIAL

$2949.

SKYLARK IS AVAILABLE IN TWO-TONE OR SOLID COLORS (AS ILLUSTRATED)

note THAT SKYLARK has OWN REAR STYLING

112" WB and 6.50 x 13 TIRES (THROUGH '63)

28

BUICKSPECIAL

SPECIAL
2-DR. CPE.

4-DR. SEDAN

SPECIAL

SPECIAL
DLX.

3-SEAT
WAGON
$3136.

WAGON

62

185-HP V8
OR *new* V6
ENGINE

SKYLARK

SPECIAL DE LUXE

SPECIAL
2-DR. SPORT COUPE

6.50 × 13 TIRES
(SINCE '61)

WAGON

SPECIAL
DE LUXE

SEDAN

$2682.

63

H/T

SKYLARK
29

CVT.

BUICK SPECIAL
DELUXE 4-DOOR SEDAN

Special 2-seat Station Wagon

SPEC.

SPEC. DLX.

210 HP

SKYLARK

SKYLARK

new 6.50 × 14 TIRES

new SPORTS WAGON

64

(9-PASS.)
$ **3562.**
(CUST.)

new 115 " WB

new RAISED PANORAMIC ROOF WINDOWS, AS ALSO FOUND IN new OLDS "VISTA-CRUISER" WAGON.

REAR FENDER TRIM (WAGON)

Skylark

INTERIOR VIEWS

Skylark

This is the new Buick Skylark Sports Wagon. It has a raised roof so you can sit tall, and a new kind of shaded glass so you can look up and out, and a **forward-facing third seat.** 30

120 " WB (WAGON)
300 CID "WILDCAT" V8

SPECIAL CVT.

BUICKSPECIAL

SKYLARK GRAN SPORT

SPECIAL SED.

SKYLARK GRAN SPORT

65

$2690. TO $3561.

SKYROOF SPORTS WAG.

SPECIAL 2-DR.

SKYLARK WITH NEW FULL-WIDTH TAIL-LIGHTS

H/T

1965 BUICK Skylark HARDTOP COUPE

(SINCE 1902)

(DIV. OF **GENERAL MOTORS**)

Cadillac **40**

8 OR 16 CYL.

COUPE

62

129" WB

V8 has 346 CID (SINCE '36)
135 OR 140 HP @ 3400 RPM
(SINCE '38)

DUAL DIVIDING STRIPS IN BACKLIGHT

127" WB

60 SPECIAL

V8 AND V-16 PRICE RANGE OF $1685. TO $7175. V-16 PRICED FROM $5140.

INTERIOR

THE NEW
Seventy-Two

CADILLAC-FLEETWOOD

138" WB

FLEETWOOD 75 MODELS ALSO (141" WB)

Illustrated is the Touring Sedan for Five Passengers.

32

Cadillac
Standard of the World

40 (CONT'D.)

185 HP @ 3600

V-16
90 SERIES

V-16 has 431 CID (SINCE '38)

$1240. and up final
LA SALLE

LA SALLE WAS A LOWER-PRICED CADILLAC SUBSIDIARY, AVAILABLE 1927 TO 1940.

FINAL 16-CYLINDER CAR BUILT IN U.S.A.

MODELS 50, 52 have 322 CID V8 (SINCE '37) 130 HP @ 3400 RPM 123" WB 7.00×16 TIRES

MODEL 61 (REPLACES LA SALLE)

$4230.
60 SPECIAL

FLEETWOOD 75

new TAIL-LIGHTS

41

62 CONVERTIBLE CP.
$1645.

CONVERTIBLE COUPE HAS A BACK SEAT INSIDE THE CAB. →

new FRONTAL STYLING, with BROAD, LOW GRILLE

33

Cadillac Standard of the World

ROUND GRILLE LIGHTS IN '42 ONLY

60-S

new HOOD RUNS TO WINDSHIELD

62

SMALL VERTICAL STRIPS ON FENDERS IDENTIFY 60-S.

42-45

Fleetwood

MODEL "75" DOES NOT HAVE ↑ "FADE-AWAY" STYLE FENDERS (THROUGH '49.)

61

62

62

46

FLEETWOOD 60-S

(60-S *has* 5 SLOPING CHROME STRIPS ON REAR QUARTER PANEL.)

75

AS IN 1942, A TOTAL OF 6 HORIZONTAL GRILLE MEMBERS, BUT WITH *new* RECTANGULAR GRILLE LTS.

FRONT VIEW

Cadillac
Standard of the World

61 — 126" WB

62
129" WB

TOTAL OF 5
HORIZONTAL
MEMBERS IN
1947 GRILLE.

47 $2060. TO $4590.
PRICE RANGE

Cadillac NAME ON FENDERS
IS NOW IN
SCRIPT STYLE.

CHROME STRIPS
IDENTIFY 60-S
133"
WB

346 CID
150 HP @
3600 RPM

136" WB
ON 75 (THROUGH '49)

new HEAVY FLANGES ON
1947 HUBCAPS.

TOTALLY RESTYLED (EXCEPT "75.")

62

61

has CHROME
ROCKER PANEL
STRIP

126" WB ON
BOTH 61 and 62

$2357.
TO
$4590.
PRICE RANGE

new
"FISHTAIL"
REAR FENDER
FINS

PLAIN ROCKER PANEL ON "61."

48

FLEETWOOD 60-S
133" WB

60-S
REAR FENDER
HAS UNIQUE
CHROME TRIM.

35

Cadillac Standard of the World

61

$2840.
49

IMPROVED V-8 ENGINE NOW HAS OVERHEAD VALVES.

160 HP (THROUGH '51)

...The world's newest engine—for the world's finest car!

$3103.

126" WB (61, 62)

62

$3549.

EXCEPT ON 75, 1949 GRILLE has ONE LESS HORIZONTAL PIECE THAN 1948. new CHROME WRAP-AROUNDS EXTEND GRILLE AT EITHER END.

62

new "COUPE DE VILLE" HARDTOP CONVERTIBLE

$5253.

133" WB FLEETWOOD 60 SPECIAL

$3891.

75

"75" RETAINS OLDER STYLING. 136¼" WB

36

Cadillac
Standard of the World

61

122" WB

AS ILLUSTRATED, NO REAR QUARTER WINDOWS ON 61 SEDAN

50

62

126" WB

$**2761.**
TO
$**4959.**
PRICE RANGE

62 CVT. $**3654.**

new 1-PIECE WINDSHIELD

new GRILLE

60-S (130" WB)
60-S NOW has CHROME STRIPS (LOUVRES) HERE

ALL MODELS RESTYLED, INCLUDING "75."

75
(146 3/4" WB)

37

Cadillac
Standard of the World

FINAL "61" MODEL

61

62

PRICE RANGE:
$2917.
TO
$5405.

160 HP

60-S

75

51

new "WAFFLE" EXTENSIONS AT EITHER END OF 1951 GRILLE

38

GOLDEN ANNIVERSARY

Cadillac Standard of the World

BEAUTIFUL NEW INTERIORS IN ALL MODELS

62 (NOW THE LOWEST-PRICED SERIES)

1902 52

STANDARD OF THE WORLD

"V" INSIGNIA NOW COLORED GOLD, TO COMMEMORATE CADILLAC's 50TH ANNIVERSARY.

THESE new DECORATIONS FOUND ON 1952 MODELS ONLY

52

PRICE RANGE : $3452. TO $5572.

147" WB 75

60-S

★ NEW 190-HORSEPOWER ENGINE
★ NEW HYDRA-MATIC DRIVE
★ NEW FRONT AND REAR END APPEARANCE
★ NEW CADILLAC POWER STEERING
★ NEW DUAL EXHAUST SYSTEM

Cadillac
Standard of the World

62

126"
WB

EL DORADO
CVT. (new)
(has WRAP-AROUND
WINDSHIELD)
$7750.

60-S has
MORE CHROME
ALONG LOWER
EDGE, PLUS THE
CHARACTERISTIC
VERTICAL STRIPS.

60-S $4341.
130" WB

$4144.
62
CVT.

53

PRICE RANGE (EXC. EL D.)
$3571.
TO
$5621.

(THROUGH 1955)
331 CID
ENGINE
210 HP @
4150 RPM

LIMOUSINE

75

146.75" WB

40

Cadillac Standard of the World

62   new 129" WB

$4261.
CPE. DE VILLE

DASH
(CONVERTIBLE)

60-S

new 133" WB

new PANORAMIC WINDSHIELD

54

230 HP @ 4400 RPM

75 LIMOUSINE
new 149.75"WB

EL DORADO CONVERTIBLE

41

Cadillac
Standard of the World

129" WB

62

55

250 HP @ 4600 RPM

HIGHLIGHT FEATURE
of CADILLAC and OLDSMOBILE for '55!

AUTRONIC -EYE®

REAR VIEW

1956

AUTOMATIC LIGHT 'TROL

PADDED DASH DETAIL →

8.00 x 15

BRIGHT

DIM

BRIGHT

Automatically AT NIGHT!

60-S (133" WB)
('75 HAS VERTICAL CHROME STRIP RUNNING TO BOTTOM OF REAR FENDER.)

$6286.

EL DORADO

270 H.P. @ 4800 RPM

with IMPORTED, HANDCRAFTED LEATHER UPHOLSTERY

42   129" WB

Cadillac Standard of the World

CONVERT.

COUPE DE VILLE

62

60-S

PRICES START AT $4146.

(ACTUAL PHOTO)

LENGTH OFTEN EXAGGERATED IN ADVERTISING ART

new 365 CID (THROUGH '58) 285 HP @ 4600 RPM

56

FINER MEMBERS IN GRILLE

LIMOUSINE

75 $6773.

SEVILLE

Eldorado

BIARRITZ CVT.

$6501.

FOR EITHER MODEL OF EL DORADO

305 H.P.

43

Cadillac Standard of the World

$4677. TO **$13,074.** PRICE RANGE (new EL.D. BRGH. IS COSTLIEST MODEL.)

60-S

new SQUARED-OFF TAIL-FINS with LOW, ROUND TAIL-LIGHTS

REAR BRIGHTWORK PANELS ON 60-S

57

EL DORADO BIARRITZ (325 HP)

62

300 HP

EL DORADO (BROUGHAM- 4 DR.) (SEVILLE- 2 DR.)

new GRILLE

ALL '58 MODELS have BACK-SLANTING FINS, AS SEEN ON '57 EL DORADO.

129½ WB

310 HP

58

FOUR HEADLIGHTS

new LOWER, BROADER GRILLE

1958

MORE 1958 MODELS ON NEXT PAGE

44

Cadillac
STANDARD OF THE WORLD

60-S CONTINUES LOWER BRIGHTWORK PANELS ON REAR FENDERS. 133" WB

AS IN 1957, EL DORADO BROUGHAM HAS ITS OWN UNIQUE FRONT END STYLING. **$13,074.**

$7500.

FOR SEVILLE OR BIARR.

EL DORADO SEVILLE

(335 HP, 129½" WB ON EL DORADOS)

EL DORADO BIARRITZ

58
(CONT'D.)

note ROUNDED-DOWN REAR FENDER/DECK PANELS ONLY ON THESE 2 EL DORADO TYPES.

(149¾" WB ON 75)

45

Cadillac
STANDARD OF THE WORLD

ENORMOUS TAIL-FINS!

new "DOUBLE-DECK" GRILLE

DETAILS OF THE UNIQUE REAR END DESIGN IN 1959

CLOSER VIEW OF TRADITIONAL "V" ON REAR DECK.

GRILLE MOTIF IS ALSO CARRIED ON AT REAR

59

325 HP   130" WB
(THROUGH '63)

2 DR. H/T

DE VILLE

NOTE THE ROOFLINE DIFFERENCES BETWEEN THESE 4-DOOR HARDTOPS

1959 PRICES START AT
$**4892.**

'59 HP FIGS. @ 4800 RPM
new 390 CID V8s

FLEETWOOD 75 (149.87" WB)

LIMOUSINE
$**9748.**
(CONT'D.)

46

59
(CONT'D.)

Cadillac
STANDARD OF THE WORLD

FLEETWOOD
60 SPECIAL
(note ITS
OWN UNIQUE
SIDE and FENDER
TRIM)

$6233.

note "FLEETWOOD" NAME
ON FRONT FENDER PANEL. (60-S)

DASH

345-HP
EL DORADO MODELS BELOW:

("ELDORADO" NAME
on FRONT FENDER
PANELS of
BIARRITZ and
SEVILLE ONLY.)
$7401. (EITHER MODEL)

BIARRITZ

BROUGHAM →

EL DORADO
BROUGHAM STYLING
DIFFERS FROM
OTHER 1959
CADILLACS.
$13,075.

SEVILLE

47

Cadillac
STANDARD OF THE WORLD

62

new 1-PC.
GRILLE

PICTURED AT
BOCA RATON HOTEL and CLUB,
FLORIDA

60

PRICES START AT
$4892.
FOR 2-DR. 62
H/T (ILLUSTR.)

$6233.

60-S

62

62

SEDAN
DE VILLE

TAIL-FINS REDUCED FOR '60,
IN STYLE of '59 EL DORADO BROUGHAM.

48

(CONT'D.)

Cadillac STANDARD OF THE WORLD

FLEETWOOD 75 LIMOUSINE

FLEETWOOD 75
9-PASS. SEDAN

$9533.

60 $9748.

PRICE OF 75
LIMO. (ILLUSTR.
AT LEFT)

(CONT'D.)

EL DORADO
BROUGHAM

(SAME PRICES AS IN 1959
ON ALL 3 EL DORADOS)

EL DORADO
SEVILLE

FINAL H/T EL DORADOS UNTIL 1967,
AT WHICH TIME EL DORADO BECOMES A
SPECIAL FRONT-WHEEL-DRIVE 2-DR. H/T.

note
THAT THE
EL DORADO
BROUGHAM
has
SIDE TRIM
DIFFERENT
FROM
THAT OF THE
OTHER
EL DORADO
MODELS
OF
1960.

EL DORADO
BIARRITZ

(EL DO. CVT.
CONT'D. THROUGH '66)

375 HP

62

new
LOWER SIDE FIN,
TO BALANCE
EFFECT OF
UPPER TAIL FIN

61

new 129½" WB
RESTYLED, SLIGHTLY DOWNSIZED *and*
LIGHTENED

new
CONVEX
GRILLE

62

$4892.
TO
$9748.
PRICE
RANGE

CHROME BANDS NEAR
END OF REAR FENDER
IDENTIFY 60-S.

FLEETWOOD 60-S

$6233.

Cadillac
STANDARD OF THE WORLD

DASH

RADIO, CLOCK DETAIL

62

SEDAN DE VILLE

62

$5752.

COUPE

$5189.

Fog Lamps (OPT.)

$10,100.

FLEETWD. 60-S

BACK SEAT

FLEETWOOD 75 LIMO.

REAR COMPARTMENT (75)

$6529.

51

note CONVERTIBLE-TOP STYLING ON HARDTOP.

62

PRICE RANGE: $5191. TO $10,104.

FLEETWOOD 75

9-PASS.

FLEETWOOD 60-S

62

DASH

"FLEETWOOD" ON 60-S FENDER

REAR CLOSE-UP

EL DORADO BIARRITZ

63

HEAD-ON DETAIL OF LIGHTS IN RELATION TO GRILLE

new 340 HP (62 SERIES ONLY)

new GRILLE EMPHASIZES "DOUBLE-DECK" STYLING.

Cadillac

52

Cadillac
STANDARD OF THE WORLD

DASH AND INTERIOR VIEWS

new "COMFORT CONTROL"

new CONVEX GRILLE

64

ALL MODELS NOW HAVE 340 HP @ 4600 RPM and new 429 CID

75

"62" PRICES FROM
$5191.

Comfort Control
combines heating and air conditioning in a single unit, the interior weather never changes. Even humidity is under perfect control. This system now available as an extra-cost option.

53

Cadillac

CALAIS
(REPLACES 62 SER.)

DE VILLE

FLEETWOOD BROUGHAM

65

new TAIL-LIGHTS

PRICE RANGE:
$5224. TO $10,125.

new LARGE 1-PC. GRILLE

new VERTICALLY-PLACED HEADLIGHTS

1965

DASH

RADIO DETAILS

54

CHECKER

CHECKER MOTORS CORPORATION
Kalamazoo, Michigan

SINCE 1922

1947 TO 1955 STYLE →

1956 TO 1958 STYLE →

TAXIS, COMMERCIAL ONLY (THROUGH '58)

Checker Aerobus Limousine

CHRYSLER V8 ENGINE IN PRE-'64 AEROBUS

6-CYL. CONTINENTAL ENGINE USED (UNTIL '63.) STARTING 1964, CHEVROLET 6 OR V8.

DASH ('68)

Checker Marathon Deluxe Limousine

59 ON

NO YEARLY STYLE CHANGES. OCCASIONAL MINOR MODIFICATIONS.

120" WB

Checker Marathon 4-door sedan

SAFETY-BUMPERS (ENERGY-ABSORBING) ADDED IN MID-1970s.

INTERIOR ('69)

Checker Marathon 4-door station wagon 55

CHEVELLE
(NEW)
by Chevrolet

(2-DR. WAGON ALSO AVAIL.)

INTERIOR (MALIBU)

64

194 or 230 cid 6 (120 or 155 HP @ 4400 RPM)

ALSO 283 cid V8 (195 or 220 HP @ 4800 RPM)

300

300 DELUXE

MALIBU →

115" W.B.

300 2-DR.

300 2-DR. 6-PASS. WAGON (MALIBU 4-DR. WAGON has CHROME STRIP ALONG SIDE.)

MALIBU SS

new HORIZONTALLY-SPLIT GRILLE

65

MALIBU SS

194 or 230 cid 6 (120 or 140 HP @ 4400 RPM)
ALSO:
(283 cid V8 avail. only with 195 HP @ 4800 RPM)
3 new 327 cid V8s (250, 300, or 350 HP)

56

CHEVROLET

HEADLIGHTS SUNKEN FURTHER INTO FENDERS

INTERIOR

90 HP @ 3300 RPM

AG, AH
41

PARKING LIGHTS MOVED DOWN

new 116" WB (THROUGH '48)

COUPE

new 2-SPOKE STEERING WHEEL

| 90-H.P. ENGINE | YES | VACUUM-POWER SHIFT AT NO EXTRA COST | YES | UNITIZED KNEE-ACTION | YES | ORIGINAL FISHER NO DRAFT VENTILATION | YES |
| CONCEALED SAFETY-STEPS | YES | BODY BY FISHER WITH UNISTEEL TURRET TOP | YES | BOX-GIRDER FRAME | YES | TIPTOE-MATIC CLUTCH | YES |

"BLACKOUT" MODELS have PAINTED TRIM IN PLACE OF CHROME.

BG, BH
42-45

STYLEMASTER, FLEETMASTER, FLEETLINE ARE new MODEL NAMES (THROUGH '48)

FLEETMASTER (BH)

PARK. LIGHTS IN new GRILLE

'42 MEDALLION

new "FADEAWAY" FENDERS

CAR RATIONING RULES

recently announced by O.P.A. now make it much easier for eligible buyers to get delivery of new Chevrolets

1942

FLEETLINE MODELS ON NEXT PAGE

(AS OF JUNE, 1942)

$880.

CHEVROLET

The² "FLEETLINE" (BH) MODELS

NEW CHEVROLET *Fleetline* AEROSEDAN

EASILY IDENTIFIED BY 3 HORIZONTAL CHROME STRIPS ON EACH FENDER (THROUGH '48)

42 - 45 (CONT'D.)

NEW CHEVROLET *Fleetline* SPORTMASTER

SLOGAN: "THE FINEST CHEVROLET OF ALL TIME"

$920.

DK "FLEETMASTER" HAS CHROME TRIM AROUND WINDOW MOULDINGS

PRICE RANGE: $1022.

DJ, DK

46

TO $1614. *new* GRILLE

DJ "STYLEMASTER" (NO CHROME ON WINDOW or WINDSHIELD MOULDINGS.)

$1194.

SPORT SEDAN

'46 MEDALLION

STYLEMASTER

CHEVROLET

$1255.

216.5 CID
90 HP @ 3300 RPM

116" WB

EK FLEETMASTER

new GRILLE has PROTRUDING CENTER SECTION

EJ, EK 47

$1775.

new MEDALLION

FLEETMASTER CVT.

EK FLEETLINE AERO

EK FLEETLINE SPORTMASTER

$1525.

FK 1948 CHEVROLET "FLEETMASTER" Four Door Sedan

$1340.

FJ STYLEMASTER

FJ, FK 48

new "T"-SHAPED PIECE ADDED AT CENTER OF GRILLE

FK FLEETLINE AERO

PRICE RANGE: $1160. TO $1890.

PACE CAR AT 1948 INDY 500 RACE

60

CHEVROLET

FLEETLINE

2-DR.

4-DR.

METAL-BODIED WAGON

PRICES START AT $1339.

GJ, GK

49

TOTALLY RESTYLED

2-DR. TOWN SEDAN

GJ = SPECIAL
GK = DE LUXE

1949 TRUNK LID has SMALL "T" HANDLE WHICH TURNS.

STYLELINE

4-DR. SPORT SEDAN

SPORT CPE.

VERTICAL PIECES in LOWER HALF of GRILLE

new SHORTER 115" WB (THROUGH '57)

6.70 x 15

1949 HUBCAP has RED CENTER.

PONTOON-STYLE REAR FENDERS

all-new INTERIOR (LEFT AND RIGHT VIEWS)

DLX.
MODELS have CHROME AROUND WINDOWS and on FRONT FENDERS

CHROME (DLX.)
BLACK RUBBER (SPEC)

61

CHEVROLET

$1741.

new "Bel-Air" 2-DR. HARDTOP has WIDE BACKLIGHT →

DASH

1950 TRUNK LID has new RE-DESIGNED HANDLE.

STYLING SIMILAR TO 1949, EXCEPT FOR MINOR DIFFERENCES AS NOTED.

HJ = SPECIAL
HK = DE LUXE

new AUTOMATIC TRANSMISSION AVAILABLE

HJ, HK

50

new 1950 GRILLE WITHOUT VERTICAL LOWER CENTER PCS. SEEN IN '49.

First low-priced car with **POWER**Glide No-Shift driving *

PRICE RANGE:
$1329. TO $1994.
* = POWERGLIDE SOMEWHAT LIKE BUICK'S "DYNAFLOW." (NOT INCLUDED IN ABOVE PRICES)

BACK SEAT (4-DR.)

The Styleline De Luxe 2-Door Sedan

1950 HUBCAP has YELLOW CENTER.

CHEVROLET

FLEETLINE

BEL-AIR $1914.

STYLELINE DE LUXE

STYLELINE PRICES START AT $1460.

JJ, JK
51

GRILLE CHANGED

DE LUXE

NEW Safety-Sight Instrument Panel

INTERIOR VIEWS

NEW Modern-Mode Interiors

STYLELINE DE LUXE

new CHROME TRIM STYLE.

63

CHEVROLET

$1696.

STYLELINE SPECIAL
(has MINIMUM OF
CHROME TRIM)

FLEETLINE DLX.
(NO MORE FLEETLN. SPECIAL)

NEW

26 Exterior Colors
and two-tone color
combinations to
choose from.

New Softer, Smoother
Ride with new and
improved shock
absorber action.

Improved Carbure-
tion with Auto-
matic Choke in
Powerglide models.

New Centerpoise
Power is smoother
— "screens out"
engine vibration.

Color-Matched Two-
Tone Interiors bring
new beauty to De
Luxe models.

52

KJ, KK

STYLELINE
DE LUXE 2-DR.

new 5 RIDGES RUN
DOWN CENTER HORIZ.:
MEMBER OF GRILLE.

new MEDALLION

$1519. TO $2281.
PRICE RANGE

STYLELINE DE LUXE
SPORT COUPE (ABOVE)

(2 VIEWS)

$1992.

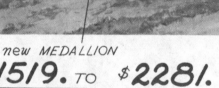

BEL AIR (IN STYLELINE DLX. SERIES)
H/T

FINAL YEAR FOR STYLELINE and
FLEETLINE MODEL NAMES.

64

CHEVROLET

150

AT RIGHT: 210 SEDAN
(IN SAN FRANCISCO, CALIF.) →

210
2-DR.

BEL AIR SEDAN (INTERIOR)

53
(TOTALLY RESTYLED)

"Handyman"
(two of them) 6-PASS. 150 station wagons

210

235 CID ENGINE
(THROUGH '62, ON 6-CYL.)
108 OR 115 HP @ 3600 RPM)

WITH IMITATION
WOODGRAIN
TRIM

BEL AIR
(note
EXTRA
TRIM and
CONTRASTING
COLOR STRIP on
REAR FENDER.)

BEL AIR now
TOP-OF-LINE SERIES
WHICH INCLUDES 2-DR. SEDAN,
4-DR. SEDAN, CONVERTIBLE (ILLUSTRATED)
and H/T SPORT COUPE (ILLUSTRATED)

65 Townsman 8-PASS.

CHEVROLET

new MEDALLION
new TAIL-LIGHTS

54

Push Button Window Controls*
Push Button Door Latches*
Push Button Door Locks (Keyless Locking)
Automatic Dome Light Switches†
Pull Knob Light Switch
Pull Knob Ventilation Controls
Turn Knob Windshield Wiper Control (Push Button Washer®)
Push Button Headlight Dimmer
Toe-Touch Power Brake Pedal®
Extra-Easy Power Steering®
Lever Action Direction Signal Control (Automatic Return)®
Powerglide Automatic Transmission*
Push Lever Heater Controls*
Push Button Radio Controls*
Push Button Glove Compartment Lock (Automatic Light†)
Finger-Touch Horn Blowing Ring†
Key-Turn Starter (Automatic Choke)
Toe-Touch Accelerator Treadle
Push Button Automatic Seat Adjustment Controls®

Advanced Chevrolet Engineering brings
CYBERNETIC CHEVROLET
(Cybernetic = Automatic Control)

210 DELRAY COUPE

BEL AIR

115 HP @ 3700 RPM
OR 125 HP @ 4000 RPM

new OBLONG PARK. LIGHTS

new GRILLE has 5 VERTICAL PCS. INSTEAD OF 3

66

CHEVROLET

150

$1593.

"ONE-FIFTY" HANDYMAN

2 VIEWS OF DASH

210 HANDYMAN

BEL AIR

THE "TWO-TEN" 4-DOOR SEDAN in Skyline Blue.

(TOTALLY RESTYLED)

55

new V-8

ALSO AVAIL. (265 CID, 162 HP @ 4400 RPM
OR 180 HP @ 4600 RPM)
6 CYL. has 123 HP @ 3800
OR 136 HP @ 4200 RPM)

210 "TOWNSMAN" WAGON

THE BEL AIR BEAUVILLE

new "NOMAD" 2-DR. WAGON

(CHROME STRIPS RUNNING DOWN TAILGATE.)

CVT. IS PACE CAR AT 1955 INDY 500 RACE

67

$2472. (6)

CHEVROLET

56

THE "ONE-FIFTY" HANDYMAN
2 doors, 6 passengers, versatile and thrifty.

THE "TWO-TEN" HANDYMAN
2 doors, 6 passengers, all-vinyl interior.

THE "TWO-TEN" BEAUVILLE
4 doors, 9 passengers.

THE "TWO-TEN" TOWNSMAN
4 doors, 6 passengers, loads of cargo space.

BEL AIR 4-DOOR HARDTOP and interior

AIR COND. DETAIL

Now in the low price field...

$2329.

All components are located "up front"... out of sight and out of the way! Harrison air conditioning is available on four great GM cars—Chevrolet, Pontiac, Oldsmobile and Buick.

AIR CONDITIONING!

BEL AIR BEAUVILLE 9-PASS. WAGON

new SMALL ROUND LENSES IN TAIL-LIGHTS

210

AA-1956

6.70 x 15 TIRES

BEL AIR SEDAN
140, 162, 170, 205 OR 225 HP

CORVETTE

NOMAD

new FULL-WIDTH GRILLE

BEL AIR 2-DR.

68

CHEVROLET

PRICES START AT **$1885.**

new 7.50 × 14 TIRES

150

210

BEL AIR

1957 IS 3RD AND FINAL YEAR THAT THE NOMAD IS A SUPER-DELUXE 2-DOOR SPORT WAGON.

$2757. (6)

NEW TRIPLE-TURBINE TURBOGLIDE*
It's the last word in automatic drives. Super-smooth— and there's even a HILL RETARDER position on the selector, for safer control on the steepest down grades!

57

4-DOOR WAGON

NOMAD and BEL AIR have new ANODIZED REAR FENDER PANEL.

new GRILLE COMBINED *with* BUMPER

2-DR. H/T

BEL AIR

HEADLIGHT-HOOD AIR VENTS

COMMAND POST CONTROL PANEL

$2464.   4-DR. H/T   69

140, 162, 185, 220, 245, 250, 270 or 283 HP (new 283 CID V8 joins 265 CID)

CHEVROLET

NOMAD 6-PASS. 4-DR.

DASH

BEL AIR

4-DR., 6 OR 9-PASS. BROOKWOOD

new 117½" WB (1958 ONLY)

BISCAYNE

235 CID 6 has 145 HP @ 4200 RPM

58

2-DR. 6-PASS. YEOMAN

1958

CROSS-SECTION OF "TURBO THRUST" V8 ENGINE

283 OR 348 CID V8s (TO '62) (185 TO 280 HP)

new IMPALA

$2693.

new WAGON TAILGATE

IMPALAS have 6 REAR LIGHTS, AND EXTRA "AIR SCOOP" DECORATIONS.

IMPALA

CHEVROLET

1—*Biscayne Utility Sedan.* Chevy's prices start right here—a handy, handsome 2-door with 31 cu. ft. of cargo space behind front seat.

2—*Brookwood 2-Door,* Chevrolet's lowest priced wagon, is as dutiful as it is beautiful. Seats 6, holds up to 92 cu. ft. of cargo.

3—*Impala 4-Door,* most elegant family sedan in the line, makes you wonder why anyone would want a car that costs more.

4—*El Camino* combines stunning passenger car styling with the load space of a pickup. Good looks never carried so much weight!

5—*Impala Convertible.* Chevy's got a special formula for carefree top-down fun.

6—*Biscayne 2-Door.* This beauty's the lowest priced 6-passenger Chevy you can buy!

7—*Nomad 4-Door,* 6-passenger station wagon—finest of Chevrolet's 5 wonderful wagons.

8—*Bel Air 4-Door.* As luxurious as it looks, yet priced just above Chevy's thriftiest sedans.

9—*Brookwood 4-Door.* Chevy's lowest priced 4-door wagon seats 6, holds 92 cu. ft. of cargo with rear seat down.

10—*Bel Air 2-Door,* distinctively styled inside and out, carries a price tag just a notch above Chevy's thriftiest 2-door sedan.

11—*Impala Sport Sedan.* Here's a 4-door hardtop with the kind of looks and luxury you'd expect only on the most expensive makes.

12—*Kingswood 4-Door,* 9-passenger station wagon, offers rear-facing third seat and power-operated rear window at no extra cost.

13—*Impala Sport Coupe.* It's one of Chevy's full series of elegant Impalas for '59. And you won't find a handsomer hardtop anywhere!

14—*Parkwood 4-Door,* 6-passenger station wagon, distinctively trimmed inside and out, priced a shade above the thrifty Brookwoods.

15—*Bel Air Sport Sedan.* It's Chevy's lowest priced hardtop—and it makes beautiful sense!

16—*Corvette.* Take the wheel of America's only authentic sports car and treat yourself to the snappiest, happiest driving you've known.

17—*Biscayne 4-Door,* thriftiest 4-door sedan in the line, is another big reason

BROOKWOOD

135 TO 315 HP

PRICE RANGE $2160. TO $3009.

BEL AIR

NOMAD 4-DR., 6-PASS.

HUGE *new* TAIL-LIGHTS

59
(TOTALLY RESTYLED)
new 119" WB (THROUGH '70)

BIG "GULL WING" REAR DECK

1959

11 IMPALA SPORT COUPE (H/T)

CHEVROLET

BISCAYNE

NOMAD

60

KINGSWOOD

PRICE RANGE: $2230. TO $2996.

BEL AIR

BEL AIR

new GRILLE

IMPALA SPORT CPE.

Impala 4-Door Sport Sedan

135 TO 335 HP

MODIFIED "GULL-WING" REAR STYLING, *with* *new* ROUND TAIL-LIGHTS

72

CHEVROLET

BROOKWOOD

BISCAYNE

NOMAD

135 TO 360 HP

1961

new ROOFLINE (SPT. CPE.)

(HT) SPT. CPE.

BEL AIR

IMPALA

(RESTYLED)

61

$2230. TO $3099.

PRICE RANGE

new ROOFLINE→

BEL AIR SPT. SED.

DASH

IMPALA

LIGHT CONTROL SWITCH   CIGARETTE LIGHTER AND ASH TRAY   RADIO CONTROLS

LEFT VENT CONTROL   WIPER AND WASHER CONTROL   HEATER CONTROLS   RIGHT VENT CONTROL   IGNITION SWITCH   GLOVE BOX AND LOCK

73

BISCAYNE

CHEVROLET

FINAL 235 CID 6 has 135 HP @ 4000 RPM

DASH

BEL AIR SPT. CPE. ROOFLINE

BEL AIR

1982

new GRILLE

M·1042

IMPALA

283, new 327 or new 409 CID V8s (170 to 409 HP)

IMPALA has ALUMINIZED PANELING AROUND TAIL-LIGHTS.

AG·1400

OUTER-EDGE TAIL-LTS. DO NOT OPEN WITH TRUNK.

IMPALA

62

(IMPALA I.D.)

JET-SMOOTH RIDE

74

BISCAYNE

DASH

IMPALA SPORT SEDAN

BEL AIR

63

PRICE RANGE: $2558. TO $3417.

new 230 CID 6 (140 HP @ 4400 RPM.

IMPALA

note CONVERTIBLE-STYLE "CREASES" STAMPED INTO STEEL ROOF of THIS IMPALA SPORT COUPE.

V8s have 195 HP @ 4800 TO 425 HP @ 6000

new DIP IN MIDDLE OF DECK LID ON 1963 MODELS.

75

1964 JET-SMOOTH **CHEVROLET**

BISCAYNE

BISCAYNE

BISCAYNE

BEL AIR

new STRAIGHT-ACROSS DECK LID *with* CENTER RIDGE

2-DR. BISCAYNE **$2590.,**

64

283, 327, 409 CID V8 ENGINES, SAME SIZES AS IN '63   6 = 140 HP
V8s = 195, 250, 300, 340, 400 OR 425 HP

3.08 TO 4.56 GEAR RATIOS

SPT. SEDAN 4-DR. H/T

9-PASS. WAGON

IMPALA

H/T

IMPALA SS

new IMPALA SS **$3185.,**

ONE OF VARIOUS 1964 UPHOLSTERY PATTERNS

new GRILLE

DASH

CHEVROLET

$2669..
4 DOOR
BISCAYNE

7.35 x 14 TIRES

BEL AIR

IMPALA

IMPALA
3-SEAT
WAGON

$3444..

8.25 x 14
TIRES ON
WAGONS

IMPALA DASH

LIGHTS

VENT | WIPER WASHER | LIGHTER | RADIO | GLOVE BOX | VENT
IGNITION SWITCH | ASH TRAY | HEATER

POPULARLY REFERRED TO AS
THE "COKE BOTTLE" PROFILE

H/T

IMPALA
SUPER SPORT

65
(TOTALLY RESTYLED)
AVAIL. with VINYL TOP

with SPORT WHEEL COVERS →

77

← **$3210..**

Chevy II 4 or 6 CYL. 110" WB

100

300

300

COMPACT CAR
by Chevrolet

(STARTS 1962)

REAR DETAILS

Nova

WAGON

Wagon

6.50 × 13 TIRES
ON
WAG.,
6.00 × 13
ON OTHERS

CONVERTIBLE
(SHOWING DASH,
INTERIOR DETAIL)

NOVA 400

POWER STEERING AVAIL.

PRICE RANGE: **62** $2051. TO $2793.

Nova

REAR and FRONT FENDER and WHEEL COVER DETAIL (NOVA 400)

DASH

(AS SEEN FROM REAR OF WAGON)

CHEVY II

100

$2313.

300

$2395.

$2710.

63

NOVA 400

CHEVY II NOVA 400 SUPER SPORT CONVERTIBLE

new GRILLE

120 HP
(6 CYL.)
(SINCE '62)

NEW V8 POWER
(OPTIONAL)

64

4, 6, or V8

79

MORE '64s ON *NEXT PAGE*

CHEVY II

INTERIOR

64
(CONT'D.)

SPT.
CPE.

NOVA SS
(has THIS EMBLEM)

NOVA

SEDAN

Super Sport

(TAILGATE OPEN)

NOVA

(TAILGATE CLOSED)

65

SEE ALSO: Chevrolet

80

CHRYSLER

CHRYSLER CORPORATION

(EST. 1924)

DASH

FLUID DRIVE'S MAGIC

new GRILLE (9 HORIZ. PIECES)

ROYAL and WINDOR 6 have 241.5 CID (THROUGH '41) 108 HP @ 3600 RPM

122½" WB (ROYAL + WND.)

ROYAL 6 (C-25 S)

C-25 (6-CYL.)

40 **$895***

3-PASS. ROYAL COUPE

C-26 (8-CYL.)

Traveler 8 (C-26 K) (MADE IN 1940 ONLY)

AMERICA'S FIRST FLUID DRIVE!
The vanes of the driving member force the fluid against those of the driven member, thus transmitting the power without a rigid metal connection. Incredibly smooth!

ONLY **$38** EXTRA

ALSO AVAILABLE ON THE NEW YORKER AND SARATOGA MODELS STANDARD ON CROWN IMPERIAL

HIGHLANDER (6 OR 8) has SCOTTISH PLAID UPHOLSTERY

TRAVELER, SARATOGA and NEW YORKER 8   128½" WB 323.5 CID (THROUGH '50) 135 HP @ 3400 RPM (THR. '49)

Be Modern — Buy Chrysler !

ROYAL 6
(C-28-S)

CHRYSLER

3-WINDOW BUSINESS COUPE
$945.
41
new GRILLE (6 HORIZ. PCS.)

new (LARGER BODIES, BUT WHEELBASES 1" SHORTER.)
AVAIL. WITH OR WITHOUT RUNNING BOARDS

SPECIAL "THUNDERBOLT" PHAETON IS PACE CAR AT 1941 INDY 500 RACE

Chrysler includes a Safety Clutch with Fluid Drive!

BE MODERN
Buy Chrysler!

1941 STEERING WHEEL and DASH

—WITH FLUID DRIVE AND VACAMATIC TRANSMISSION

$1096.

WINDSOR 6
(C-28-W)

SPITFIRE ENGINES!

Chrysler offers dozens of combinations in exterior colors and interior tailoring!

(SARATOGA 8 IS C-30-K)

CLUB COUPE INTERIOR (2-TONE)

82

CHRYSLER

41 TOWN and COUNTRY (new)
(CONT'D.)

$2795.

NEW YORKER HIGHLANDER 8 CONVT. (C-30-N)

PLAID UPHOLSTERY OPTIONAL @ EXTRA COST

WHEEL COVER

CROWN IMPERIAL 8 LIMOUSINE (C-33)

$1495.

42-45

ENGINE

C-34 (6)
C-36 (8)

TOWN and COUNTRY

DASH

New Yorker

new "WRAP-AROUND" GRILLE

(CROWN IMPERIAL is C-37.)

new "BEAUTY RINGS"

Fluid Drive and Vacamatic Transmission!

83

CHRYSLER

ROYAL 6 (C-38-S)
WINDSOR 6,
TOWN and COUNTRY 6
(C-38-W)
SARATOGA 8 (C-39-K)
NEW YORKER 8,
TOWN and COUNTRY 8
(C-39-N)
CROWN IMPERIAL 8
(C-40)

EMBLEM

PRICE RANGE:
$1415. TO $4767.

46-48

(new "HARMONICA" GRILLE)

6 CYL. has 250.6 CID
(1942 THROUGH 1951)
114 HP @ 3600 RPM (THROUGH '49)

8 CYL. has 323.5 CID
(1935 THROUGH 1950)
135 HP @ 3400 RPM (THROUGH '49)

CHRYSLER CARS CONTINUE USE OF ADD-ON WHITE "BEAUTY RINGS," THUS MAKING UNNECESSARY THE USE OF HARD-TO-OBTAIN WHITE SIDEWALL TIRES.

(FINAL '48s SOLD AS "EARLY 1949" MODELS, UNTIL
RESTYLED MODELS AVAIL. FEB., 1949.)

121½" WB (6)
127½" WB (8)
145½" WB (CROWN
IMPERIAL 8, THROUGH '54)
139½" WB (6-CYL.
8-PASS., LIMO.)

CHRYSLER

TOWN + CNTRY. H/T (ONLY 7 BUILT)

CONVENTIONAL CONVERTIBLE INTERIOR →

(T + C FASTBACK SEDANS ONLY, 1941-1942)

TOWN and COUNTRY

$3123. ('48)

ONE-OFF 2-DR. BROUGHAM (EXPERIMENTAL)

46-48 (CONT'D.)

'46 - EARLY 1947 "TOWN and COUNTRY" MODELS have GENUINE WOODEN PANELS of ASH and MAHOGANY. (DK. PANELS ON LATER MODELS ARE DECALS)

CHRYSLER

WINDSOR 6

CLUB COUPE

NEW YORKER 8

(C-45) 125½" WB (THROUGH '54)

(LENGTH EXAGGERATED)

$3206.

ACTUAL LENGTH

NEW YORKER 8

NEW YORKER 8 (C-46) 131½" WB (THROUGH '52)

49
(TOTALLY RESTYLED)

PRESTOMATIC FLUID DRIVE* TRANSMISSION
*gyrol Fluid Drive

PRICE RANGE: $2114. TO $5334.

$3970.
TOWN and COUNTRY 8 CONVERTIBLE (SAME SPECS. AS NEW YORKER)

CROWN IMPERIAL 8 LIMO. (C-47)

CHRYSLER

(FINAL YEAR FOR CHRYSLER STRAIGHT-8.)

ROYAL 6, WINDSOR 6
(C-48)

SARATOGA 8,
NEW YORKER 8,
TOWN and COUNTRY 8
(C-49)

50

PRICE RANGE

$2114. TO **$5334.**

TOWN and CNT. 8
AVAIL. ONLY AS
H/T.

new GRILLE

NEW *LOW* LOOK!
NEW *LONG* LOOK!
NEW *LOVELY* LOOK!

NY 8

$4003.

Crown Imperial

LIMOUSINE
(C-50)

CRN. IMP. REAR COMP. has QUARTER WINDOWS.

8-CYL. MODELS NOW DEVELOP 135 HP @ 3200 RPM.

SARATOGA V8 (C-55)
125½" WB

NY V8
(C-52)
131½" WB

IMPERIAL V8
(C-54)
(CRN. IMP. IS C-53)

WINDSOR 6
(C-51-1)

new 331.1 CID O.H.V. V8 REPLACES STRAIGHT-8 (180 HP @ 4000 RPM) (THROUGH '53.)

51

new WIN. DLX. 6 IS C-51-2

87

(CVT.) IS PACE CAR AT 1951 INDY 500 RACE

K-310 CUSTOM-BUILT COUPE

CHRYSLER

CUSTM BLT.

125 ½ " W.B.
(ITALIAN GHIA BODY)
(WINDSOR 6 ENG. CHANGES FROM 250.6 TO 264.5 CID. 116 TO 119 HP @ 3600.)

Imperial

BY CHRYSLER

PHAETON   147½ " W.B.
(FOR PARADE USE, ETC.)

A VARIETY OF ROSE WAS NAMED "CHRYSLER IMPERIAL."

IMPERIAL V8
(C-54)

52

(SIMILAR IN MOST RESPECTS TO 1951.)

(C-53)

$**6994.**

CROWN   IMPERIAL   LIMOUSINE   88

CHRYSLER

WINDSOR 6 (C-60-1) WINDSOR 6

WINDSOR DELUXE 6 (C-60-2)

ALL EXCEPT IMPERIAL *have* 125½"WB (THROUGH '54)

$2555. UP

NY

NEW YORKER V8 (C-56-1)

(NEW YORKER DELUXE V8 IS C-56-2) (new)

53 (new 1-PIECE WINDSHIELDS)

CUSTOM IMPERIAL V8 (C-58) new 133½"WB

CROWN IMPERIAL V8 (C-59)

Imperial

BY CHRYSLER

IMPERIAL (STYLIZED EAGLE) HOOD ORNAMENT (new)

FOR 1954 TO 1965 IMPERIALS, SEE: IMPERIAL

89

CHRYSLER

WINDSOR DELUXE 6 (C-62)
264.5 CID
119 HP @ 3600 RPM

NEWPORT H/T
↖ $2831.

NY 331.5 CID V8s have 195 OR 235 HP @ 4400 RPM

NEW YORKER (C-63-1)

WINDSOR DELUXE TOWN and COUNTRY WAGON 6
$3321.

54

(FINAL 6-CYL.)

DASH

NEW YORKER DELUXE (note SMALL EXTRA HORIZONTAL CHROME PIECE ON REAR FENDER)

NEW YORKER DELUXE V8 (C-63-2)

SEE ALSO "IMPERIAL" SECTION

WINDSOR DELUXE (C-67)

ALL CHRYSLERS 126" WB, NOW V8-POWERED.

WINDSOR DLX. V8 has 301 CID, 188 HP @ 4400 RPM.

55

(RESTYLED)

TOWN and COUNTRY

NEW YORKER DE LUXE (C-68) (331 CID, 250 HP @ 4600 RPM)

$4109.

300 HP @ 5200 RPM
126" WB

new **300** (C-300) 331 CID

90

CHRYSLER

New Pushbutton PowerFlite!
(Illustrated at right)

WINDSOR NEWPORT

DASH

(C-71) WINDSOR

56

126" WB

(C-72) NEW YORKER

N.Y. TOWN and COUNTRY

331 CID OR new 354 CID V8
(225 HP @ 4400 ; 250 OR 280 @ 4600)

NEW YORKER GRILLE NOW DIFFERENT FROM OTHERS.

NEW "PowerStyle" CHRYSLER FOR 1956

(C-72-300) 300-B

NEW YORKER INTRODUCES VERTICAL CHROME STRIPS ON REAR FENDER (THROUGH '62.)

354 CID V8 (340 OR 355 HP @ 5200)

CHRYSLER

SEDAN $3088.

WINDSOR (C-75-1)

WINDSOR TOWN and COUNTRY WAGON

2-DR. H/T

57
(TOTALLY RESTYLED)

WND. and SAR. have 354 CID V8 (285 OR 295 HP @ 4600)

4 HEADLIGHTS ON MOST MODELS

4-DR. H/T

(C-75-2) SARATOGA

(C-76) NEW YORKER

2 DR. H/T

SEDAN

note ONLY 2 HEADLTS.

4-DR. H/T

NEW YORKER has new 392 CID V8 (325 HP @ 4600 RPM)

$4259.

H/T

300-C (C-76-300)

300-C has new HIGH and NARROWER GRILLE, also new 392 CID V8 (9.25 OR 10 COMPR.) TWO 4-BBL. CARBS.

CVT. $5359.

THE MIGHTY CHRYSLER

300 C

300-C ENGINE 375 HP @ 5200 OR 390 HP @ 5400 RPM

92

America's Most Powerful Car!

CHRYSLER

300-D (LC3-S) →
380 OR 390 HP
@ 5200 RPM

58

126" WB
(new
SHORTER 122" WB
ON WINDSOR)

WINDSOR
(LC1-L)

WINDSOR
has
290 HP
@ 4600 RPM
(354 CID)

WINDSOR DARTLINE

note DIFFERENT SIDE TRIM ON '58½ "DARTLINE" (ABOVE)

NEW YORKER

SARATOGA
(LC2-M)

310 HP @
4600 RPM (354 CID)

NEW YORKER
(LC3-H)
345 HP @ 4600 RPM (SAME
SIZE V8 [392 CID] AS 300-D)

new ENGINES: 383 OR
413 CID

59

MC
SERIES

305, 325, 350 HP @ 4600,
OR 380 HP @ 5000 RPM

MORE 1959 CHRYSLERS
ON NEXT PAGE

93

CHRYSLER

(MC2-M)   SARATOGA

(MC1-L)
WINDSOR

LION-HEARTED
CHRYSLER '59

59

(CONT'D.)

(MC3-H)

N.Y.
TOWN and COUNTRY
WAGON

NEW
YORKER

CHRYSLER   300   (REAR FENDER BAND)

300
E

The international classic   ...made in America

300-E
(MC3-H)

$5749.

94

300-E

CHRYSLER

4-DR. H/T

WINDSOR CVT.

SARATOGA (PC2-M) has 383 CID V8 (325 HP @ 4600 RPM)

60

has 383 CID V8 (305 HP @ 4600 RPM)

SAR. SEDAN

SARATOGA has GRILLE LIKE WINDSOR (ABOVE)

NEW PUSHBUTTON DASH PUTS ALL THE CONTROLS AT YOUR FINGERTIPS

NEW YORKER (PC-3-H has 413 CID V8 (350 HP @ 4600 RPM

NEW YORKER TOWN and COUNTRY WAGON

WINDSOR T+C

WNDSR.

NY CVT.

300/F BY CHRYSLER

The 300F medallion is molded like a gear wheel to express the rugged spirit of the car.

The open grille gives the 300F a "Pure automobile" look.

413 CID V8 (375 HP @ 5000 OR 400 HP @ 5200 RPM)

(300-F)

(PC3-H)

CHRYSLER

wagon

(RC2-M)
FINAL 1961
WINDSOR
MODEL

$3303.

new
NEWPORT
LOW-PRICED
SERIES 122" WB
(RC1-L)

$3025.
(NPT. H/T)

61

new GRILLES,
CANTED HEADLIGHTS

NEWPORT
has new
361 CID V8
(265 HP @
4400 RPM)
(OPTIONAL 413 CID V8
has 350 HP @ 4600 RPM)

413 CID V8 with
350 HP @ 4600 RPM
IN
RC3-H
NEW YORKER

NY
TOWN and
COUNTRY

(FRONT
END OF
300-G
ILLUSTR. ON
NEXT
PAGE)

NY

$4133.

96

NEW YORKER SEDAN

CHRYSLER

300-G (RC4-P) has SAME ENGINES AS IN 1960

FINAL YR. of 126" WB for 300 SERIES

61 → (CONT'D.)

300-G new GRILLE CLOSE-UP

NEWPORT

(SCI-2) NEWPORT

361, 383, 413 OR new 426 CID V8 ENGINES

300

62

265 HP @ 4400 RPM TO 421 HP @ 5400 RPM

300-H (SC2-M)

N.Y.

N.Y. 4-DR. H/T

126" WB

NEW YORKER (SC3-H)

ALL 122" WB (EXCEPT NY)

CHRYSLER

PAINTED in ACRYLIC ENAMELS

NEWPORT (TC1-L)

ALL MODELS NOW have 122" WB. (THROUGH '64)

ROUND TAIL-LIGHTS in 1963.

63 TC SERIES

(RESTYLED in new "KNIFE-EDGE" [CREASE] BODY DESIGN.)

PACE CAR at 1963 INDY 500 RACE is 300-J.

SAME 4 V8 SIZES AS IN 1962, BUT TOP "300" HP FIGURE NOW IS 425 @ 5600, with new TOP 13.5 COMP.

DASH

NY TOWN and COUNTRY

SALON (INTRO. 2-14-63)

(TC3-H) 1963 NEW YORKERS have VERTICAL LOUVRES ON FRONT FENDERS.

NEW YORKER

CHROME BANDS JOIN ENDS of GRILLE with EDGES of HOOD. (NY and 300)

300

NEW YORKER

(TC2-M) 300

98

CHRYSLER

6 OR 9-PASS.

Chrysler Newport   Hardtop Town & Country Wagon

NEWPORT

Chrysler Newport Convertible
(VC1-L)

VC1
SERIES

64

361, 383 or 413 CID V8s
(265 HP @ 4400 RPM
TO 290 HP @ 4800)

COMPRESSION RATIOS
NOW RUN FROM
9.0 TO 10.1
TO 1.

NEW YORKER
(VC1-H)

NY SALON

VINYL TRIM
ON ROOF

note
GRILLE and
SIDE TRIM
VARIATIONS BETWEEN
"300" CVT. and H/T
MODELS
ILLUSTRATED

WAGON

300 (K)

300
(VC1-M)

INTERIOR
300

Chrysler Newport Convertible (AC1-L)   NEWPORT   7-W. SEDAN →

5-W. SEDAN

REAR INTERIOR (7-W. N.P. SEDAN)

N.Y.

NEWPORT CVT. (SHOWING DASH)

CHRYSLER MOTORS CORPORATION

CHRYSLER DIVISION

NEW YORKER (AC1-H)

65 AC1 SERIES

300-L

'65's ONLY ENG. CHOICES ARE 383 OR 413 CID V8s (270 HP @ 4400 TO 360 @ 4800)

(AC1-M) 300-L's V8 has SPECIAL CAM. 413 CID $4716. (CVT.)

NEWPT. PRICES START AT $3442.

300 has LARGE RED CROSS IN CENTER OF GRILLE →

300 (AC1-M) $4061.

100

COMET (compact)   LINCOLN-MERCURY DIVISION *Ford Motor Company*

(INTRO. 3-60)

FROM $1998.

60

6 CYL. OHV   90 HP   114" WB

two- and four-door wagons (109½" WB)

COMET

DASH SIMILAR TO 1960

61

new FRONT FENDER TRIM

new GRILLE

"*Comet*" NAME MOVED TO REAR FENDER

new ROUND TAIL-LIGHTS

NAME RETURNS TO FRONT FENDER

new GRILLE

CUSTOM

S-22

62

VILLAGER

Comet

63

COMET *SPORTSTER* hardtop

tach, bucket seats,

Vinyl covered roof optional.

DASH
(CYCLONE)

THE COMET CYCLONE.
Super 289 cu. in. V-8,
chrome engine parts,
competition-type
wheel covers.

*(MIDSEASON
MODEL)*

64

CALIENTE

Comet

CYCLONE H/T

CALIENTE H/T

65

404

VILLAGER

202

REAR FENDER DETAIL

40 days from Cape Horn to Fairbanks

Cord

(SHORTER 100" WB REPLICA OF ORIGINAL 1936-1937 CORD)

DASH

150-180 HP CORVAIR 6 ENGINE

(STARTS 1963)

FIBERGLASS TYPE BODY OF "ROYALEX"

OTHERS SUBSEQUENTLY INVOLVED IN PRODUCING THESE REPLICARS.

MFD. BY GLENN PRAY, BROKEN ARROW, OKLA.

103

corvair

DASH

569 SEDAN

500
(NO CHROME BELT TRIM)

WITH THE ENGINE IN THE REAR

60

AIR-COOLED 6-CYL.
REAR ENGINE-TRANSAXLE UNIT
140 CID
80 HP @ 4400 RPM
6.50 x 13
TIRES 108" WB

700

GENERAL MOTORS
(1960-1969)

COMPACT CAR
by Chevrolet

$1984. and up

CLUB COUPE and INTERIOR (727)

SEDAN

BACK SEAT FOLDS, FOR CARGO.

$2103.
(769 SEDAN)

104

corvair

500

CLUB COUPE

700

700 INTERIOR

spunkier 145-cu.-in. air-cooled rear engine

4-DOOR SEDANS

new OPTION. ELECTRIC HOT AIR HEATER

note UNIQUE WHEEL COVERS ON NEW MONZA →

new CORVAIR MONZA CLUB COUPE and INTERIOR →

61

CORVAIR GREENBRIER SPORTS WAGON

SWINGING SIDE DOORS 95" WB

2 new WAGON TYPES and 2 SUB-TYPES

$2651.

GREENBRIER (STD.)

$2331.

LAKEWOOD 500 (535)

700 (735)

LAKEWOOD STATION WAGONS

SMART, DURABLE INTERIORS—Shown here: the 700's rich fabric-vinyl upholstery, offered in three color-keyed choices. 500 all-vinyl interior also comes in three color-keyed blends. Check the push-button locks on rear doors.

700

105

ENGINE UNDER REAR FLOOR.

corvair

500

GREENBRIER

62

MONZA

MONZA WAGON (ABOVE)
(FINAL YEAR FOR THIS
"LAKEWOOD" STYLE WAGON.
GREENBRIER VAN-TYPE
WAGON AVAIL. THROUGH
1965.)

DASH (ALL BUT SPYDER)

new
CORVAIR SPYDER
(150 HP)

63

MONZA

corvair

STD. ENGINE RAISED TO 95 HP.

DASH

64

MONZA

MONZA SPYDER (ABOVE) has 150 HP. $3008. (667 CVT.)

500

←DASH has CIRCULAR GAUGES.

MONZA

This year, all the coupes and sedans have hardtop styling

FROM $2281. 65

new LARGER BODIES

(ONLY MAJOR CORVAIR RESTYLING)

New power choices, too. There's a new 140-hp engine that's standard in Corsa models and can be ordered for all others—and a 180-hp power plant that you can specify for your Corsa.

MONZA SPORT SEDAN

140 HP (CORSA IS new TOP OF LINE MODEL.)

107

CORVETTE
Sports Car **by CHEVROLET**

6-CYL. CHEVROLET ENGINE (TO '55)

53

STARTS 1953 $3512.

FIBERGLASS BODIES (ON ALL)

('54)

SPEAR on SIDE EMBLEM NOW POINTS UP.

ILLUSTRATED with DETACHABLE TOP

54-55

FULL-LENGTH SIDE TRIM

V-8 ENGINE ALSO (1955)

PRICE CUT 1955

('55)

new TOP

56-57

$2900. ('56)

$3437. ('57)

new SIDE TRIM

V-8s ONLY

102" WB 230 HP

DASH

58

4 HEADLIGHTS

$3631.

new BUMPERS

new VENT LOUVRE GROUP ON TOP OF HOOD (1958 ONLY)

59-60

$3872. (IN '60; $3 LESS THAN '59)

108

CORVETTE

$4272. **61** new GRILLE

new 250 HP **62** **$4375.** new SIDE-SCOOP DESIGN

new "STINGRAY" **63** new SIDE-SCOOPS AGAIN

new GRILLE, CONCEALED HEADLIGHTS, new 98" WB

$4589.

new 1-PC. BACKLIGHT → **64**

Corvette Sting Ray Convertible in Saddle Tan

Corvette Sting Ray Sport Coupe in Riverside Red

$4627.

$4723. 327 CID V-8 has 250, 300, 350, 365 OR 375 HP @ 5500 RPM

65 **$4508.**

4-WHEEL DISC BRAKES

new VERTICAL LOUVRE DESIGN

425 HP 396 CID V8

1965½ CORVETTE "396"

109

CROSLEY

(1939 – 1952)

MFD. IN MARION, IND.

39-42

2-CYL. AIR-COOLED WAUKESHA ENGINE (THROUGH '42)

12 HP

PRICE CUT TO $**299.** IN 1941.

$**412.** IN 1942

80" WB
4.25 × 12 TIRES

CVT. (OTHER MODELS ALSO AVAIL.)

"*a FINE car*" new 4-CYL. WATER-COOLED "COBRA" (COPPER-BRAZED) STAMPED-BLOCK 44 CID ENGINE (26½ HP @ 5400 RPM)

new BODY SIDES COMBINE *with* FULL-LENGTH FENDERS

WAGON

CVT.
$**1035.** ('47)

$**931.** = SEDAN
('47) *new* GRILLE, BUILT-IN HEADLIGHTS ABOVE

(TOTALLY RESTYLED)   80" WB

47-48

(POSTWAR PRODUCTION RESUMES DURING JUNE, 1946)

CROSLEY SPORTS-UTILITY

PICKUP

PANEL DELIVERY

110

CROSLEY

48½

new GRILLE
ON MID-YEAR
"NEW LOOK" SERIES

FOR 1949, COPPER-BRAZED, 58-lb. STAMPED ENGINE
REPLACED BY IMPROVED CAST-IRON VERSION (CIBA.)

49- 50

new GRILLE, "SPEEDLINE"
STYLING

SEDAN

new "HOTSHOT"
SPORTS
ROADSTER

new
HYDRAULIC
DISC
BRAKES (BY
GOODYEAR-
HAWLEY)

CVT.

WAGON

new BENDIX
9" HYDRAULIC
BRAKES

Crosley Hotshot

SUPER

51-52

new 2-BLADED GRILLE *with*
CENTER "SPINNER"

DISCONTINUED DURING 1952

111

DART

Dodge Division of Chrysler Corporation

SENECA

(STARTS 1960)

FULL-SIZED
LOWER-PRICED
new COMPANION
TO DODGE

PIONEER

PHOENIX

$2283. UP

118" WB (WAGONS 122")
(THROUGH '61)

60

PD3 (6 CYL.)
PD4 (V8)

225 CID SLANT 6 has
145 HP @ 4000 RPM
318, 361 and 383 CID V8 have
230, 255, 310, 325
or 330 HP.

DODGE DART	CAR F	CAR P	CAR C
SENECA	Fairlane	Savoy	Biscayne
PIONEER	Fairlane 500	Belvedere	Bel Air
PHOENIX	Galaxie	Fury	Impala

THE DODGE DART IS PRICED MODEL FOR MODEL WITH OTHER LOW-PRICE CARS.

1960

WAGON
with
TAILGATE
OPEN

New Economy Slant "6" Uses
Exclusive Semi-Ram Intake Manifold!

New design
features
inclined block
with new
Equi-flow fuel
induction, over-
head valves,
for greater
fuel economy.

112

DART

145 HP 6-CYL.
CONTINUES

SENECA

SENECA STATION WAGON 6 OR V8,
6 PASSENGER

SENECA 4 DOOR SEDAN 6 OR V8

PIONEER STATION WAGON 6 OR V8,
6 OR 9 PASSENGER

PIONEER 4 DOOR SEDAN 6 OR V8

PIONEER

RD3 (6 CYL.)
RD4 (V8)

61

318, 361, 383 *and*
new 413 CID V8s
(230 TO 375 HP)

PHOENIX 4 DOOR HARDTOP 6 OR V8

PHOENIX

DART 330 2-DOOR HARDTOP 6 OR V8

DART 330 4-DOOR 6-PASSENGER WAGON 6 OR V8

DART 330 2-DOOR SEDAN 6 OR V8

DART 440 9-PASSENGER WAGON V8

new 116" WB
('62 ONLY)

SAME DISPL. AS '61
145 TO 380 HP

62 (TOTALLY RESTYLED)

SD SERIES

DART 440 CONVERTIBLE V8

MODELS

DART 6 === (SD1-L)
" " 300 (SD1-M)
" " 440 (SD1-H)
DART V8 === (SD2-L)
" " 330 (SD2-M)
" " 440 (SD2-H)

1962 IS FINAL YEAR
THAT DART IS
DODGE-SIZED.

113

THE NEW LEAN BREED OF DODGE

DART

SEDAN 170 (RESTYLED)

WAGON

63 TL1 SERIES

8.2 COMPR.

DASH

2-DR.

WHEELBASE REDUCED AGAIN, TO 111" (106" WB ON WAGONS)

$2288. UP

270

CVT.

GT

H/T

ALL 1963 DARTS ARE 6-CYL.
170 CID   101 HP @ 4400 RPM
OR 225 CID   145 HP @ 4000 RPM

H/T

TWO SLANT SIXES AS IN '63
new 273 CID V8
(180 HP @ 4200)

64 VL1 (6) VL2 (V8)

GT

(270 STILL AVAIL.)

170 SEDAN

ENGINES AS IN 1964

65 AL1 (6) AL2 (V8)

Dodge Dart 4-door station wagon. 2-seat model only. 6 and V8 power.

Dodge Dart 270 convertible. 6 and V8 power.

270

$2310. UP

GT

Dodge Dart 2-door sedan. 6 and V8 power.

Dart GT two-door hardtop.

DART, DART 270, DART GT MODELS

114

DAVIS

DAVIS MOTOR CO., VAN NUYS, CALIF.

4 CYL.   3-WHEELER

(NO CONNECTION with the DAVIS CAR MFD. BEFORE 1930)

(1947-1949)

(17 BUILT)

---

4 CYL. CONTINENTAL ENGINE

63 HP

(FEW BUILT)

(1949)

DEL MAR

DEL MAR MOTORS, INC. SAN DIEGO, CALIF.

---

100 HORSEPOWER @ 3600 RPM 6 CYL.

DE SOTO

228.1 CID (SINCE '37)

DASH

COACH

40

S-7

4-DOOR

DeSoto
AMERICA'S FAMILY CAR
De Luxe Coupe **$845** | De Luxe Sedan **$905**

A PRODUCT OF THE CHRYSLER CORPORATION

6.00 x 16 TIRES

122½" WHEELBASE

115

DASH

new "ROCKET" BODIES

CUSTOM

1941 DeSoto

FLUID DRIVE WITH *Simplimatic Transmission* (OPT.)

DLX.

41

S-8

121½" WB (THROUGH '48)

100 HP (6.5 COMPR.)
105 HP (6.8 COMPR.)

DE LUXE COUPE **$898**†

new 236.7 CID (THROUGH '50)
115 HP @ 3800 RPM

42-
45
S-10

NEW AIRFOIL LIGHTS

OUT OF SIGHT EXCEPT AT NIGHT

PERSONALIZED **INTERIORS**

6.25 × 16 TIRES (6.50 × 16 ON 139½" WB MODELS)

COLOR-MATCHED TO YOUR TASTE

DE SOTO APPROVED SERVICE PLYMOUTH

CUSTOM

TOP DISTORTED IN ARTIST'S VIEW

(AN ACTUAL PHOTO ON NEXT PAGE)

116

(1942-45 (THIS IS ONLY SERIES *with* CONCEALED HEADLIGHTS.)

WARTIME DE SOTO
PRODUCTION of PARTS,
ASSEMBLIES FOR GEN.
SHERMAN TANKS
(ILLUSTRATED,)
BOFORS ANTI-AIRCRAFT
CANNON, MILITARY
PLANES, ETC.

42-45
(CONT'D.)

"Styled to Stand Out
...Built to Stand Up!"

DeSoto

ONLY 24,771 1942 DE SOTOS
PRODUCED AUG., '41 TO JAN., '42.

(ACTUAL PHOTO OF 1942 MODEL)

ALL '48-STYLE
CHRYSLER CORP. CARS
CONT'D. TO 2-49.

SINCE LATE 1935, LONG-WHEELBASE DE SOTO
7-PASS. OR 8-PASS. SEDANS and LIMOUSINES
AVAIL., MANY SOLD IN FLEETS TO BIG-CITY
TAXICAB COMPANIES
139½" LONG W.B. AVAIL.
(FROM 1940 THROUGH 1954.)

9-PASS. SUBURBAN SED. ALSO

CUSTOM

S-11

46-48

109 HP @ 3600 RPM

TIRES : 6.50 × 15 , 6.50 × 16 L.W.B. ('46-47)
7.00 × 15 , 7.50 × 15 L.W.B. ('48)

CONVENTIONAL
HEADLIGHTS
RESUMED

LARGER DIE-CAST
GRILLE

"8 out of 10
say DeSoto again*"

117

*=SLOGAN BASED ON POLL WHICH
INDICATED HOW MANY WOULD BUY ANOTHER DE SOTO.

De SOTO

DE LUXE
(has NO EXTRA CHROME FENDER STRIPS.)

CUSTOM

S-13 **49** (TOTALLY RESTYLED)

new '25½" WB (THROUGH '54)

CARRY-ALL SEDAN

112 HP @ 3600 RPM (THROUGH '50)

CLOSER VIEW OF 1949 GRILLE →

new SPORTSMAN H/T

RE-DESIGNED LIKENESS OF HERNANDO DE SOTO, HISTORIC SPANISH EXPLORER FOR WHOM CAR WAS NAMED

1950 GRILLE has PAINTED SECTION IN CENTER, with new EMBLEM.

new ROUND PARKING LIGHTS

S-14 **50**

Drive a De Soto before you decide!

118

DeSoto

SPORTSMAN H/T

S-15-1 (DE LUXE)

S-15-2 (CUSTOM)

51

6-CYL. DISPLACEMENT RAISED TO 250.6 CID 116 HP @ 3600 RPM (THROUGH '54)

AS ON OTHER '51 CHRYSLER CORP. CARS, *new* "ORIFLOW" SHOCK ABSORBERS

new LOWER, SIMPLER GRILLE

1951 MODELS *have* SCRIPT LETTERING ABOVE GRILLE

new Full Power Steering

S-15 MODELS CONTINUE CUSTOM 6

52

1952 MODELS *have* BLOCK LETTERING ABOVE GRILLE

new FIRE DOME V8 (BELOW and RIGHT) (S-17)

S-17 CARS *with* AIR SCOOP HOOD ORNAMENT HAVE *new* "FireDome" 276.1 CID V8 ENGINE

Power Braking

160 h.p. @ 4000 RPM

V-8

119

DeSoto

new MODEL NAMES

POWERMASTER 6
(S-18)

FIREDOME V8
(S-16)

V8
CONTINUES 276.1 CID
(THROUGH '54)

160 HP @ 4400 RPM

new
POWER BRAKES
and OVERDRIVE
AVAILABLE

53

6 has a BROAD SHIELD
EMBLEM on HOOD;
V8 has "V"
BELOW a NARROWER
SHIELD (THROUGH '54)

SPORTSMAN

7.60 × 15

V8 has new
170 HP @ 4400 RPM

THE FINAL 6-CYL.
DE SOTO

POWERMASTER
6

(S-20)

"POWERFLITE" A.T. AVAIL.

CORONADO
SEDAN

FIREDOME V8
(S-19)

54

GRILLE MODIFIED
new SIDE TRIM
and TAIL-LIGHTS

DASH

De SOTO — The *Forward* Look

new 126" WB

V8s ONLY
(1955 ON)

FLITE-CONTROL gear selector lever is mounted on De Soto's smart, new instrument panel—out of your way. Yet at your finger tips."

(TOTALLY RESTYLED)

55

new 291 CID
FIREDOME (S-22)   185 HP @ 4400 RPM
FIREFLITE (S-21)   200 HP @ 4400 RPM

DRIVE A DE SOTO BEFORE YOU DECIDE

(PUSH-BUTTON A.T.)

DASH
(MINOR CHANGES FROM 1955)

230 HP @ 4400 RPM
FIREDOME
(S-23)

new 341.4 CID
ADVENTURER (S-24)
320 HP @ 5200 RPM

"HIWAY HI-FI" BLT.-IN RECORD PLAYER AVAIL.

new 330 CID

new MESH GRILLE

TRIPLE TAIL-LIGHTS with OVERLAPPING FIN

56

255 HP @ 4400 RPM
FIREFLITE
(S-24)

7.60 x 15

PACE CAR AT 1956 INDY 500 RACE

new 12-VOLT ELEC. SYS.

121

DE SOTO

new LOWER PRICE **FIRESWEEP** (S-27)
(has OWN FRONT END STYLING)

4-DR. H/T

(S-25)
FIREDOME

SEDAN

(TOTALLY RESTYLED) **57**

new 325, 341 OR 345 CID

245, 270, 295 OR 345 HP

2-DR. H/T

ADVENTURER

(4 HEADLIGHTS, ANODIZED GOLD TRIM)
(S-26)

FIREFLITE
(S-26)

new 122" WB ON FIRESWEEP; 126" ON OTHERS (THROUGH '59)

4-DR. H/T

EXPLORER WAGON
(3 SEATS)

SHOPPER (2 SEATS)

FIREFLITE SEDAN

122

DE SOTO

(LS2-M) FIREDOME

(LS1-L) FIRESWEEP

16 MODELS, 4 SER.

new "TURBOFLASH" V8
(350 OR 361 CID)

280 TO 355 HP

FIREFLITE
(LS3-H)

CLOSE-UP

58

LS SERIES

LARGE *new* "CONTROL TOWER" WINDSHIELD

DASH

(LS3-S)
ADVENTURER
has ANODIZED SIDE TRIM

DE SOTO — *the exciting look and feel of the future!*

123

'59 DE SOTO

(MS1-L) FIRESWEEP

8.00 x 14 TIRES

361 OR new 383 CID V8
(THROUGH '60)
295 HP @ 4600 RPM
TO 350 HP @ 5000 RPM

FIREFLITE SHOPPER

(ALL BUT FIRESWEEP HAVE
8.50 x 14 TIRES.)
(SINCE '57)

(MS3-H)
FIREFLITE

(MS2-M)
FIREDOME

ADVENTURER
(MS3-H)

DASH

124

1960 DE SOTO

DASH (*with RAISED INSTRUMENT CLUSTER*)

(PS1-L)
FIREFLITE

(PS3-M)
ADVENTURER

H.P. CHOICES :

295 @ 4600 ; 305 @ 4600 ; 325 @ 4600 OR 330 @ 4800 RPM

10.0 TO 1 COMPRESSION

BUILT-IN 45-RPM RECORD PLAYER OPTIONAL AGAIN (AS IN PLYMOUTH)

ALL 1960 and 1961 DE SOTOS ON 122" WB and 8.00 × 14 TIRES

1961 DE SOTO

ITS QUALITY SETS IT APART, ITS PRICE KEEPS IT WITHIN YOUR REACH

FROM $3102.

(THE FINAL DE SOTO CAR, AVAILABLE ONLY IN 2-DR. OR 4-DR. H/T BODIES)

4-DR. H/T

2-DR. H/T

ONLY THE 361 CID V8 IS AVAILABLE, with COMPRESSION REDUCED TO 9.0

265 HP @ 4400 RPM

ODD "SHARK-NOSE" TAIL-LIGHTS

PRODUCED 8-60 TO 12-60

DASH

The highly unusual instrument cluster, with the reel type clock below the speedometer center. Not all options are shown.

2-TIERED GRILLE

DISCONTINUED

125

DODGE DIVISION — CHRYSLER CORPORATION

DODGE

(EST. LATE 1914)

LUXURY LINER DE LUXE **$825** and up

new 119½" WB (THROUGH '48)

DASH

40

D-17 = SPECIAL
D-14 = DE LUXE

87 HP @ 3600 RPM (SINCE '34)

1940 Dodge 2-door Sedan $815, delivered in Detroit*
12-038

3-WINDOW BUSNS. COUPE (new)

Slogan: "DODGE ENGINEERING COSTS NOTHING EXTRA" ('40)

FLUID DRIVE TRANSMISSION AVAIL.

6 CYL.

217.8 CID (SINCE '34)

91 HP @ 3800 RPM

D-19 S = DELUXE
D-19 C = CUSTOM

41 (RESTYLED)

DODGE SEDANS **$815** AND UP
COUPES, $755 and up

new LARGE, WIDE GRILLE

HOOD FOLDS "BUTTERFLY" STYLE

new Safety-Rim WHEELS

INTERIOR

126

DODGE

new 230.2 CID
(TO '54)

new 6.7 COMPR.
105 HP @
3600 RPM

new GRILLE
with VEE
CENTER
SECTION

"THE NEW and the FINEST DODGE"

D-22 S = DE LUXE
D-22 C = CUSTOM

42-45

7-WINDOW SEDAN

DASH and INTERIOR VIEWS

new
7.10 × 15
TIRES IN
1948

D-24 S = DE LUXE
D-24 C = CUSTOM

46-48

102 HP @ 3600 RPM

"FADEAWAY"
FENDERS

5-WINDOW SEDAN
(ALL DOORS FRONT-HINGED)

127

Dodge

SMOOTHEST CAR "AFLOAT"

ROADSTER (new)
(TOP UP)

3-WINDOW COUPE

2-DOOR

((ACTUAL
PHOTO)
(TOP DOWN)

LOWER PRICED
NEW DODGE *WAYFARER*

The Daring New
DODGE
gyrol Fluid Drive plus GYRO-MATIC
Frees You from Shifting
OPTIONAL ON CORONET MODELS

49

D-29 = WAYFARER
(115" WB)

D-30 = MEADOWBROOK
and CORONET
(123½" WB)

(SAME WBs
THROUGH
'52)

(ABOVE) WAYFARER ROADSTER (ARTIST'S CONCEPTION)

New Dodge **CORONET**

CORONET WAGON

103 HP @
3600 RPM
(TO '53)

new
SWITCH KEY STARTING

128

LONGER on the inside ... SHORTER outside!
WIDER on the inside ... NARROWER outside!
HIGHER on the inside ... LOWER outside!

DODGE

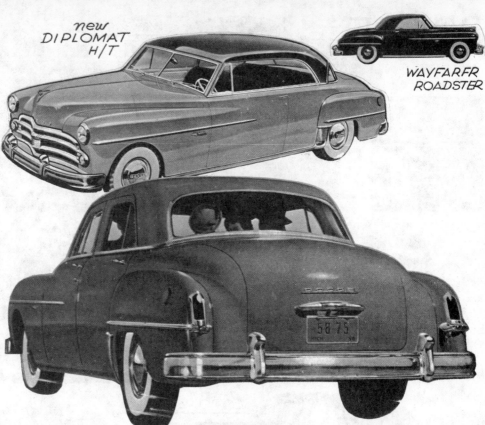

new DIPLOMAT H/T

WAYFARER ROADSTER

INTERIOR

BACK SEAT

SUPER-SIZE LUGGAGE COMPARTMENT!

50

D-33 = WAYFARER
D-34 = MEADOWBROOK ; CORONET

new GRILLE with FEWER and HEAVIER PIECES

DODGE

DODGE

WAYFARER

DASH

FEATHER-TOUCH BRAKING!
Big Safe-Guard Hydraulic Brakes stop smoothly, surely, safely. Cyclebond linings, with their larger braking surface, last up to twice as long. New feather-touch parking brake holds securely on even steep grades . . . easily released with a twist of the wrist.

51

D-41 = WAYFARER

D-42 MEADOWBRK.
      CORONET

SHOWN IN
SAN FRANCISCO,
LOOKING EAST
TOWARD OAKLAND.

CORONET

D-41 and D-42 SERIES
CONTINUE with LITTLE CHANGE

CORONET SIERRA
WAGON

new HUBCAPS

1952 SERIAL NOs. START AT:
WAYFARER   MEAD./CORONET

37175001 (Detroit)   31867601
48009901 (San Leandro) 45090601
48507601 (Los Angeles)
45527501 ═
MD., COR., (L.A.)

LOWER PART OF GRILLE is PAINTED.

52

CORONET
"DIPLOMAT" H/T

FINAL YEAR FOR
WAYFARER MODEL;
REPLACED
IN '53 BY
MEADOWBROOK SPECIAL

130

DODGE

MEADOWBROOK 6
D-46

MEADOWBROOK SEDAN
MDBK. V8 IS D-47

D-48 (114"WB)
D-44 (119")
CORONET V8

new 241.3 CID
V8 (THROUGH '54)

140 HP
@ 4400
RPM

Sensational New
140 Horsepower RED RAM V-8 ENGINE!

INTERIOR →

CORONET SEDAN

6
OR V8

53

(RESTYLED)

WIRE WHEELS,
CONTINENTAL SPARE
AVAIL. →

ABOUT 56%
OF 1953 DODGES
SOLD WERE
V8s.

CORONET
H/T

V8 MODELS
have
DODGE V EIGHT
BELOW
RAM HOOD ORNAMENT

114" OR 119" WB
(THROUGH '54)

131

DODGE

CORONET 6

6-CYL. NOW HAS
110 HP @ 3600 RPM

D-51, D-52 (6 CYL.)

54 D-50,
D-53 (V8)

new GRILLE   ROYAL V8

ROYAL 500 CVT. IS PACE CAR AT 1954 INDY 500 RACE.

ROYAL V8
SEDAN

H/T

V8 has 140
OR 150 HP @ 4400 RPM
(7.1 OR 7.5 COMPR.)

VARIOUS INTERIORS
(JACQUARD FABRICS)

DEPENDABLE
NEW '54 **DODGE**
Elegance in Action

Fully-automatic PowerFlite and full-time
Power Steering—yours at moderate extra cost.

DODGE

FLASHES AHEAD IN '55

CORONET

REAR

CORONET V-8 2-DOOR SUBURBAN

ROYAL V-8 4-DOOR 8-PASSENGER SIERRA

V8 ENGINE NOW 270 CID

CUSTOM ROYAL V-8 4-DOOR SEDAN

new 3-TONE PAINT JOBS AVAIL.

55

D-56 (6 CYL.)
(123 HP @ 3600 RPM)

H/T

new CUSTOM ROYAL LANCER

D-55 (V8)
(175, 183 OR 193 HP @ 4400)

CUSTOM ROYAL LANCER SEDAN

THE FORWARD LOOK ▶

new 120" WB
(ON ALL, THROUGH '56)

6 CYL. NOW HAS 131 HP @ 3800 RPM (230 CID)
V8 has 189 TO 340 HP
(270, 315 OR 354 CID)

D-62 (6 CYL.)
D-63 (V8)

56

The look, the feel, the power of success: New '56 Dodge Custom Royal Lancer 4-Door

new FINS and EMBLEM IN GRILLE
new SIDE TRIM
DIPS AT REAR
new BUMPERS
HIGHER REAR FENDERS

In all the world no car like this

The New Dodge Lancer goes  *4 door!*

MORE 1956 DODGES ON NEXT PAGE

133

New '56 DODGE
(CONT'D.)
VALUE LEADER OF THE FORW...

SIERRA

CORONET LANCER

ROYAL

CORONET

DASH

8-PASS. CUSTOM SIERRA

CUSTOM ROYAL CONVERTIBLE

$2121. UP

PUSHBUTTON POWERFLITE, greatest advance in driving ease and control. Proven by years of successful testing!

new TYPES OF PUSH-BUTTON TRANSMISSION CONTROL

CUSTOM ROYAL LANCER

REAR CLOSE-UP

134

'57 Dodge *SWEPT·WING* (TOTALLY RESTYLED) D-72 (6) D-66, 67, 70 (V8)

new 325 or 354 cid V8s

2-DR. SUBURBAN (D-70)

4-DR. SIERRA (D-70) (D-71 IS CUSTOM SIERRA)

CORONET (6 or V8) (D-72 or D-66)

ROYAL LANCER (D-67-1) 2-DR. H/T

CUSTOM ROYAL LANCER (D-67-2)

new 7.50 × 14 TIRES (8.00 ×14 WAGON, CVT.)

138 TO 340 HP

new 122" WB (ON ALL MODELS, THROUGH '59)

ADDED LOWER "TEETH" IN GRILLE OF ABOVE LATER MODEL.

REAR FINS "OVERLAP" FENDER

new COMPOUND-CURVED WINDSHIELD

138 TO 333 HP 325, 350 or 361 CID V8s

CORONET

CUSTOM ROYAL LANCER

ROYAL

EARLY 1958 MODELS ABOVE

LD-1 (6) LD-2, LD-3 (V8)

58

SPRING SWEPT-WING *by* **Dodge**

58½ MODEL *with* IDENTIFYING CHARACTERISTICS

PAINTED HEADLIGHT AREA, *also new* GRILLE MEDALLION ON 58½

135 *new colors* *new interiors*

'59 DODGE

Coronet 2-Door Sedan, V-8 or "6"

SIERRA

FINAL L-HEAD
230 CID 6
REDUCED TO 135 HP
@ 3600 RPM

326, 361 or 383 CID V8s
have 255 HP @ 4400 RPM
TO 345 HP @ 5000 RPM

59½
Silver Challenger
two-door sedan

6 or V8

CUSTOM ROYAL

new TAIL-LIGHTS

SWIVEL-
SEATS
AVAIL.
(new)

INTERIOR (CUSTOM
ROYAL CVT.)

59

MD1-L
(6)

MD2-L,
MD3-M,
MD3-L,
MD3-H (V8)

PUSH-
BUTTON
SHIFT
PLAN

DASH

136

'60 DODGE

new O.H.V. SLANTED 6-CYL. ENGINE AVAIL. ONLY IN new SUBSIDIARY DART.

361 or 383 CID V8s (THR. '61) IN ALL DODGES EXCEPT new DART or '61-2 LANCER

(295 or 330 HP)

122" WB ON LARGE DODGES (THROUGH '61)

MATADOR·POLARA

POLARA has BRIGHTWORK ON LOWER REAR FENDER.

PD1 and PD2 SERIES

new DART LISTED SEPERATELY

60

POLARA has HEAVY BAND ATOP FENDER

UNIBODY CONSTRUCTION

137

DODGE

265 TO 330 HP

122" WB

POLARA CONVERTIBLE VR

DASH

POLARA 2 DOOR HARDTOP V8

61

POLARA HARDTOP WAGON V8, 6 OR 9 PASSENGER

POLARA V8 IS ONLY LARGE SERIES

SEE ALSO DART, OR LANCER

Dodge Polara 500—2-dr Hardtop

Dodge Polara 500—4-dr Hardtop

D-1962

POLARA 500

POLARA 500

361 OR 413 CID V8 305 OR 380 HP

62

(SD2-P) POLARA MODELS TOTALLY RESTYLED 116" WB (AS ON DART)

D-1962

CUSTOM 880

(CONSERVATIVE OLDER TYPE STYLING) 122" WB

(SD3-L)

361 CID V8 265 HP @ 4400 RPM

1963 DODGE

330 SERIES

440 SERIES

116" OR 119" WB

225 CID 6 (145 HP @ 4000)

318, 383 OR 426 CID V8 (230 TO 425 HP)

DASH

POLARA SERIES

POLARA 500 SERIES
BUCKET SEAT

TD SERIES
63

CUSTOM 880
361 OR 383 CID V8 (265 OR 305 HP)

139

122" WB

REAR VIEW OF CUSTOM 880 WAGON

'64 Dodge

225 CID 6 OR 318, 383 OR 426 CID V8

440 (VD-2) 7.00 × 14 TIRES

330

POLARA

SPORTSMAN WAGON

145 TO 425 HP

POLARA DASH

A - PARK. LOCK ; B - TRANSMISSION BUTTONS ; C - SPEEDO. ; D - CLOCK ;
E - HEATER CONTROLS ; G - RADIO ; H - GLOVE BOX ; I - ASHTRAY, LIGHTER ;
J - IGNITION ; K - WIPER CONTROL ; L - LIGHTS ; M - PARK. BRAKE RELEASE

note THAT POLARA DASH (ABOVE) DIFFERS FROM 880 DASH (SEE 880 CVT., BELOW)

880 WAGON

CONCAVE GRILLE ON 880

WRAPAROUND TAIL LIGHTS ON 880

(VA-3)

8.00 × 14 TIRES

880

FINAL YR. OF '61-STYLE ROOFLINE ON 880

64

140

Dodge

AW1 (6)   AW2 (V8)   **Coronet**

Dodge Coronet 440 2-door hardtop. *6 and V8 power.*

7.35 × 14 TIRES

116" and 117" WB

Coronet

CORONET DASH

Dodge Coronet 440 Station Wagon
(3-seat model also offered)

7.75 × 14 TIRES

145, 180, 230, 265, 270, 315, 330 340, 365 or 425 HP.

Polara 4-door hardtop. *V8 power.*
(AD2-L)

V-8 CHOICES INCLUDE 273, 318, 361, 383, 413 or 426 CID

new 121" WB

Monaco two-door hardtop.

Dodge Monaco. Limited edition. 2-door hardtop. *V8 power.*

65 Monaco
(AD2-P)

MONACO DASH

8.25 × 14 TIRES

Dodge Custom 880 4-Door Hardtop

Custom 880

880 (AD2-H)   141   **Wagon** *has 8.50 × 14 TIRES*

EDSEL $2519. UP

MFD. BY FORD MOTOR CO. (1958, 1959, 1960 MODELS ONLY)

ROUNDUP 2-DR. WAGON

WAGONS HAVE SPECIAL TAIL-LIGHTS

note "HORSECOLLAR" CENTER GRILLE

SLOGAN: "THIS IS THE EDSEL" (OTHER SLOGANS ALSO)

"Teletouch" AUTO. TRANS. CONTROL BUTTONS in STEERING-WHEEL HUB. (OPTIONAL) (1958 ONLY)

58

DASH → (with REVOLVING SPEEDOMETER)

VILLAGER 4-DR. WAGON

V-8s 361 CID, 303 HP OR 410 CID, 345 HP

BERMUDA 4-DR. (DELUXE WAGON with WOODGRAIN)

RANGER (LOWEST-PRICED)

(has MINIMUM of SIDE CHROME)

CITATION

PACER

CITATION (TOP OF LINE) has INSET PANEL SET WITHIN REAR FENDER TRIM LOOP.

CORSAIR

W.B.s: 116" (WAGONS)

118" (RANGER, PACER)

124" (CORSAIR, CITATION)

142

EDSEL

RANGER

PACER, CITATION, ROUNDUP and BERMUDA MODELS NO LONGER AVAIL.

223 CID 6-CYL. ENGINE ALSO AVAIL. STARTING 1959. (145 HP @ 4200 RPM)

$2629.UP

3 V8 ENGINES:
Ranger 292 CID (200 HP @ 4500 RPM)
Express 332 CID (225 HP @ 4600)
or Super Express 361 CID (303 HP @ 4600)

CORSAIR

new ROUND TAIL-LIGHTS

1959

VILLAGER

1959

new DASH

CORSAIR CHROME has VERTICAL STRIPS

59
(RESTYLED)

SLOGAN: "MAKES HISTORY BY MAKING SENSE"

INSET ANODIZED TRIM PANEL IDENTIFIES 1959 CORSAIR.

new 120" W.B. (ALL MODELS, THROUGH '60)

new GRILLE INCORPORATES HEADLIGHTS, with HORIZONTAL MEMBERS IN CENTER SECTION.

EDSEL

CORSAIR NO LONGER AVAIL.

RANGER and VILLAGER ARE ONLY MODELS OFFERED FOR EDSEL'9 BRIEF 1960 SEASON.

new TAIL-LIGHTS PICK UP VERTICAL OVAL THEME FORMERLY DISPLAYED IN EDSEL GRILLE.

FROM
$2635.³⁰

1960 MODEL PROD. :
WAGON, 6-PASS. (216)
WAGON, 9-PASS. (59)
2-DR. SEDAN (777)
4-DR. SEDAN (1,288)
2-DR. HARDTOP (295)
4-DR. HARDTOP (135)
CONVERTIBLE (76)
   TOTAL = ONLY
2,846
1960 EDSELS (TOTALLY RESTYLED)
BUILT !

RANGER

60

VILLAGER

new SPLIT GRILLE

new DASH

3 ENGINE CHOICES :
Economy 6 223 CID
   (145 HP @ 4000 RPM)

Ranger V8 292 CID
   (185 HP @ 4200 RPM)

Super Express V8 352 CID
   (300 HP @ 4600 RPM)

EDSELS DISCONTINUED NOV., 1959

FAIRLANE
BY
(FORD)

new COMPACT / INTERMEDIATE 6 or V-8 for 1962; FORMERLY A FULL-SIZED FORD SERIES

62

$2392. UP

500

new CONCAVE GRILLE

SQUIRE

63

63½ AVAIL. WITH new VINYL ROOF

H/T INTERIOR

145

FAIRLANE

"289" V-8 option

Fairlane wagons:

A PRODUCT OF
Ford
MOTOR COMPANY

FAIRLANE CUSTOM RANCH WAGON

64

SEE ALSO:
FORD

optional features. 4-speed stick. Overdrive. Tachometer.

271 solid-lifter horsepower high-shift underlined automatic!

$2474. UP

HEADLIGHTS
PAIRED IN
PLATES

NO MORE
RAISED "AIR
SCOOP"
EFFECT
ON
HOOD

65

*new
OBLONG
TAIL-LIGHTS*

FALCON (compact)

BY FORD

$ **1912.** and up   (1960 – 1970½ MODELS)

60

CHOICE OF 2-DR. OR 4-DR WAGONS

109½" WB
6.00 × 13 TIRES

6 CYL. 144 CID
OVERHEAD VALVE ENGINE
90 HP

Ford MOTOR COMPANY

A CHOICE OF TWO SURGING "SIXES"!
STD. 144 CID OR
new 170 CID

2-DR.

4-DR.

85 HP (STD.)

4-DR. WAGON ALSO AVAIL.

Falcon Tudor Wagon

new FUTURA CONSOLE

FORD *Falcon* '61
WORLD'S MOST SUCCESSFUL NEW CAR

Futura

1961

$ **2202.** UP

FUTURA has 3 DARTS on REAR FENDERS, and SPECIAL HUBCAPS.

147

Falcon '62
BEST SHAPE ECONOMY'S EVER BEEN IN

FUTURA

FALCON SPORTS FUTURA

FUTURAS HAVE SPECIAL
FRONT FENDER TRIM,
AS ILLUSTRATED.

DELUXE

2-DR.

4-DR.

DELUXE

new SQUIRE

STD. 2-DR.

STD.

new 164 HP V8
ALSO AVAIL.

63

DE LUXE

SQUIRE

FUTURA

new CONVERTIBLE

148

FALCON

Lively new Sprint

THESE MODELS INTRODUCED IN MID-SEASON

63½

new scatback hardtop

Squire

new wider tread

64

(RESTYLED)

$2211. UP

new '260' cu. in. V-8 power option

new longer springs

Squire

New battery-saving alternator.

65

13" or 14" WHEELS

new 170 cu. in. standard Six with optional 3-speed Cruise-O-Matic transmission

new GRILLE

DASH

149

(SINCE 1903)

V8 L-HEAD ENGINE
(SINCE 1932)

STANDARD
has VERTICAL
BARS IN
NARROW
GRILLE

Ford
FORD Division of FORD MOTOR COMPANY

DE LUXE

1940
STANDARD
GRILLE SOMEWHAT
RESEMBLES THAT
OF 1939 DE LUXE

4-PASS. COUPE has 2
FACING BACK SEATS

112" WB

NEW BODY TYPE.

40 60 OR 85 HP
(SINCE '37)

WITH 22 IMPORTANT
IMPROVEMENTS

PRICES
START AT $**650.** (STD. CPE.)

"STEP UP TO THE V·8 CLASS"

new GRILLE

FINGER-TIP GEARSHIFT on steering post. All models, no extra cost.

TRANSVERSE SPRINGS
CONTINUE
(THROUGH '48 MODEL)

new
SEALED-
BEAM
LIGHTS

new

V·8 1940

DE LUXE

FORD "Get the facts and you'll get a FORD!"

TUDOR SEDAN

new 90 HP V8
new L-HEAD 6 also

41

(RESTYLED)

NEW Massive Beauty
NEW Room Throughout
NEW Vision All Around
NEW Faster Acceleration
NEW Stronger, Rigid Frame
NEW Longer Wheelbase
NEW Longer Springbase
NEW Soft, Slower-action Springs
NEW Soft Seat Cushions
NEW Stabilizer Ride Control

CVT.

FORDOR SEDAN

MODELS

SPECIAL (REPLACES STANDARD.

DELUXE

SUPER DELUXE

PRICES START AT
$665. (V8 OR 6 SPECIAL CPE.)

new GRILLE

new 114" WB
6.00 x 16 TIRES

SUPER DE LUXE

FORDOR SEDAN

Steel Stampings for Die-Castings

V8 OR 6 $780.
(SPECIAL 6 CPE.)
new RECTANGULAR PARKING LIGHTS

42-45

"America's Most Modern 6...America's Lowest-priced 8"

Plastics Replace Metal for Interior Trim

DASH

new BROAD, LOW GRILLE with CURVED VERTICAL PCS.

"V8" OR "6" ON new EMBLEM

$930.

151

FORD

PRICES START AT **$1003.** (6 CPE.)

V8 Six

NEW OVERSIZED BRAKES

CLUB COUPE

TUDOR

FORDOR

There's a *Ford* in your future

46

1946 MODEL STARTS JULY, 1945

new GRILLE

NEW 1946 FORD SPORTSMAN'S CONVERTIBLE (V8) (*with* GENUINE WOODEN BODY)

$1865.

Outside and inside, there never was a car like this before! The new Ford Sportsman's Convertible is really *two* cars in one! Ford designers have combined the paneled smartness of the station wagon and the touch-a-button convenience of the convertible!

ALL–METAL CVT. MORE COMMONLY SEEN (ILLUSTR. ON NEXT PAGE)

152

FORD

EARLY 47

(SIMILAR TO 1946)

Ford's out Front

(1947 SLOGAN)

CONVERTIBLE (METAL)

... new stainless steel body molding
newly fashioned door handles ...

... new body colors ...

47½-48

1948 has
new
STEERING
COLUMN
LOCK.

$1517.*
V8 WAGON

There's a FINER *Ford* in your future

A newly styled instrument panel with big new dials for easy reading

*=RAISED
TO
$1855
IN
'48

new HOOD MEDALLION
IDENTIFIES 6 OR V8

MODIFIED GRILLE
NO LONGER has
RED INDENTATIONS.

new
ROUND
PARKING
LIGHTS
PLACED
BELOW
HEADLIGHTS

new wheel rims and hub caps

153

new heavier bumper guards—And many other new features!

FORD

COUPE

TUDOR

PRICES START AT
$1333.
(DLX. COUPE)
(6 CYL.)

CVT.

FORDOR

NEW! '49
STARTS SPRING, '48
(TOTALLY RESTYLED)

Overdrive

Engine speed 42 m.p.h. — Car speed 60 m.p.h.

(OPTIONAL)

57% more luggage space

Wagon

new "Hydra-Coil" FRONT SPRINGS

CHOICE OF COLOR

Hard Tops
1. BLACK
2. COLONY BLUE
3. BAYVIEW BLUE
4. SEA MIST GREEN
5. ARABIAN GREEN
6. MIDLAND MAROON
7. BIRCH GREY
8. GUNMETAL GREY
Convertibles
9. FEZ RED
10. MIAMI CREAM

New "Flight Panel" dash ...

(new CUSTOM SERIES REPLACES SUPER DE LUXE)

"6" OR "8" IN GRILLE "SPINNER" INDICATES NUMBER OF CYLINDERS.

FORD

"Double Duty"

"Country Squire" STATION WAGON

(8-PASS.

C.VT.

50

CHASSIS (V8)

new MID-SEASON 2-DR. "CRESTLINER"

FORD

new EMBLEM ON HOOD (ALSO ON DECK LID)

"TEST DRIVE" A '50 FORD

155

THERE'S A Ford IN YOUR FUTURE WITH A FUTURE BUILT IN!

FORD

CRESTLINE

51

DUAL SPINNERS IN GRILLE

new VICTORIA

VICTORIA INTERIOR

SQUIRE

new DASH

You can pay more but you can't buy better!

VICTORIA H/T with WINDOWS OPEN

156

REAR (SEDAN)

1951

FORD

new **MAINLINE**
(has LEAST AMOUNT of CHROME TRIM)

PRICES START AT **$1526.**

COUNTRY SQUIRE
4-DOOR METAL WAGON *has* IMITATION MAHOGANY PANEL DECALS, FRAMED *with* REAL MAPLE *or* BIRCH TRIM.

new **RANCH WAGON**

Station Wagons

new **COUNTRY SEDAN**

New Flight-Style Control Panel

52
(TOTALLY RESTYLED)

Ford's new Center-Fill Fueling cuts down spillage.

CUSTOMLINE 2-DR.

new **SUSPENDED PEDALS**

DASH

"TEST DRIVE" A FORD TODAY
YOU CAN PAY MORE BUT YOU CAN'T BUY BETTER

HUGE, curved, one-piece windshield and car-wide rear window to match. You can really see what's ahead and what's behind!

CRESTLINE SUNLINER V8
CRESTLINE VICTORIA

101 h.p. High-Compression
Mileage Maker Six

"Only V-8 in its field"!

new **GRILLE** *has* APPEARANCE *of* 3 "SPINNERS"

$2104.

Full-Circle Visibility

110 h.p. High-Compression
Strato-Star V-8

157

FORD

CVT. IS PACE CAR AT 1953 INDY 500 RACE

PRICES START AT
$1537.
(MAINLINE 6 CPE.)

MAINLINE 2-DR

DASH

FORD 50TH ANNIVERSARY

1953

53

ONLY ONE "SPINNER" IN *new* GRILLE.

SUNLINER

FORD-O-MATIC (SINCE '51)

COUNTRY SQUIRE

2-DOOR RANCH WAGON **$2019.** (6)

4-DOOR COUNTRY SEDAN

COUNTRY SQUIRE

NO SHIFTING...NO CLUTCHING

Ford Skyliner (CRESTLINE SERIES)

$2199. (V8 $134 EXTRA) with PLEXIGLASS ROOF WINDOW

54

New 130-h.p. Y-BLOCK V·8

239 CID V8 ENDS '54

MAINLINE

New Ball-Joint Front Suspension

New 115-h.p. I-BLOCK SIX

223 CID (THR. '64)

4. Four-Way Power Seat.

UP DOWN FRONT AND BACK

CUSTOMLINE

5 optional power assists*

★ Master-Guide power steering does up to 75% of steering work . . . ★ Swift Sure Power Brakes do up to one-third of your stopping work . . . ★ Fordomatic Drive does *all* your shifting . . . ★ Power-Lift Windows open and close at a button's touch. And ★ 4-Way Power Seat adjusts up or down, forward or back, at a touch of the controls. *At extra cost.

159

FORD

PRICES START AT
$1606. (MAINLINE 6 CPE.)

SEDAN
MAINLINE

new GRILLE

new FAIRLANE SUNLINER CVT. (ABOVE)

CUSTOMLINE

new "WRAP-AROUND" WINDSHIELD

120-H.P. 6 OR V8s with 162 OR 182 H.P.

55

RANCH WAGON

CUSTOM RANCH WAGON

6-PASS.

COUNTRY SEDANS

COUNTRY SQUIRE

8-PASS. (with FAIRLANE SIDE TRIM)

"Y" SYMBOLIZES Y-BLOCK V8 new 272 CID

FAIRLANE VICTORIA

FORD
SIDE EMBLEM (ON FAIRLANE TYPES)

FAIRLANE CROWN VICTORIA (note BAND WRAPPED OVER ROOF)

new FAIRLANE MODELS IDENTIFIED BY SWEEP SIDE TRIM

FORD

MAINLINE

6 NOW 137 HP @ 4200 RPM

CUSTOM RANCH WAG.

V-8 h.p. upped

The 272-cubic inch Ford V-8, the standard eight for all Customline and Mainline Fords. Has modern dual carburetor, automatic choke, single exhaust.

FAIRLANE FORDOR

1956

new 2-DR. LUXURY PARKLANE WAGON (INTRO. to COMPETE with CHEVY's NOMAD.)

CTY. SQUIRE

The 292-cubic inch Thunderbird V-8, the standard eight for all Fairlanes and Station Wagons, is now available in all Customline and Mainline models, too. Has 4-barrel carburetor, dual exhausts.

202 H.P.

CUSTOM COUNTRY SEDAN

56

CUSTOMLINE VICTORIA

SKYLINER   CROWN VICTORIA

The 312-cubic inch Thunderbird Special V-8,

225 h.p.

new 4-DR. H/T (FAIRLANE FORDOR VICTORIA)

1956 INTERIOR

161

FORD

6 CYL. INCREASED TO 144 HP

CNTRY. SED.

SQUIRE

CUSTOM TUDOR

RANCH WAGON

LADDER-TYPE CONTOURED FRAME

4-way ball-joint front suspension

CUSTOM (REPLACES MAINLINE)

CUSTOM 300 FORDOR

FAIRLANE (note UNIQUE SIDE TRIM)

New deep-offset hypoid axle

FAIRLANE 500 MODELS BELOW

UP TO 245 HP with "SILVER ANNIVERSARY" V8s."

57

FAIRLANE 500 4-DR. TOWN VICTORIA H/T

LOW-SILHOUETTE CARB.

new V8 SKYLINER has RETRACTABLE HARD TOP (POWER-OPERATED)

SUNLINER CVT.

$2942.

REAR

new FRONT END

162

FORD

6 CYL. NOW 145 HP (THROUGH '60)

CUSTOM 300

FAIRLANE 500 SKYLINER (SHOWN *with* TOP IN MOTION, and *with* TOP IN PLACE.)

NOTHING NEWER IN THE WORLD

RANCH WAGON (4-DR. ALSO AVAIL.)

DEL RIO RANCH WAGON

DASH

COUNTRY SEDAN

COUNTRY SQUIRE (2 VIEWS)

NEW INTERCEPTOR V-8

A TRUE AIR RIDE

FINE-CAR DETAIL

new ROOF GROOVES

58 (TOTALLY RESTYLED)

4 HEADLIGHTS

4 TAILLIGHTS

Versatile Cruise-O-Matic Drive! Set selector in D_1 position for brisk, solid-feeling take-off. Select D_2 for gentle, sure-footed starts. What's more, when new Cruise-O-Matic Drive is teamed with a new Interceptor V-8 engine it can give you up to 15 per cent more gasoline mileage.

V8s = 292, *new* 332 *and new* 352 CID (THROUGH '59)

Up to 300 h.p. with new Precision Fuel Induction.

FAIRLANE 500

F-1958

163

FORD

CUSTOM 300

$2132. (6)

note "F O R D" LETTERING ON HOOD

WINDSHIELD DOGLEG DETAILS

Fairlane 500

FAIRLANE 500 VICTORIA ROOFLINE (CLOSE-UP)

note EMBLEM ON HOOD

new GRILLE

FAIRLANE REAR FENDER

(TOTALLY RESTYLED AGAIN)

59

145 TO 300 HP

NEW FORD GALAXIE CLUB VICTORIA—THUNDERBIRD STYLING IN A 6-PASSENGER, 2-DOOR HARDTOP

new 1959½ TOP-OF-LINE GALAXIE MODELS ADDED, with T-BIRD ROOFLINE.

THE FINAL SKYLINER (GALAXIE)

164

FORD

wagons

(INTERIOR VIEW EXAGGERATED)

4-DOOR and 2-DOOR RANCH WAGONS

FENDER CHEVRONS ON THIS '59½ RANCH WAGON

ROOMY NEW FORD RANCH WAGON... LOWEST PRICED WAGON OF THE MOST POPULAR THREE

59 (CONT'D.)

COUNTRY SQUIRE
$3076
*

Country Squire

1959 DASH (ILLUSTR. with FACTORY-INSTALLED AIR CONDITIONER UNIT)

*WAGON PRICE SHOWN APPLIES TO V-8 9-PASSENGER 6 CYL. or 6-PASS. MODELS also avail.

Country Sedan

1959

COUNTRY SEDAN
$2947. *

FORD

FAIRLANE 500

FAIRLANE PRICES START AT $2170. (6-CYL. 2-DR.)

TUDOR

GALAXIE

(TOP UP)

SUNLINER CVT.

(TOP DOWN)

new STARLINER $2723. (V8; 6 ALSO AVAIL.)

ARCHED TAIL-LIGHTS ONLY ON 1960 MODELS →

GALAXIE FORDOR

NEW SLOPING HOOD GIVES INCREASED VISIBILITY

60 (TOTALLY RESTYLED FOR 3RD SUCCESSIVE YEAR!)

145 TO 300 HP

DASH

RANCH WAGON

COUNTRY SEDAN →

9-passenger Country Squire

Beautifully built to take care of itself...

FORD WHEEL COVER

2-DR.

FAIRLANE

FAIRLANE 500
(6 CUT TO 135 HP)

4-DR.

new GRILLE IS CONCAVE, BISECTED HORIZONTALLY

61

$2261.
(6)

GALAXIE 4-DR.
TOWN
VICTORIA
H/T

(CLOSER VIEW OF GALAXIE WHEEL COVER AT UPPER RIGHT)

SQUIRE

RANCH WAGON

STATION WAGONS

CNTRY. SEDAN

292, 352 OR new 390 CID V8s (175 TO 401 HP)

1961

GALAXIE VICTORIA H/T

(CLOSE-UP and DASH)

STARLINER H/T

ROUND TAIL LIGHTS RETURN

1961

FORD

RANCH WAG.

6-PASSENGER COUNTRY SEDAN
(9-pass. model also

COUNTRY SQUIRE

SLOGAN :

Live it up with a Lively One from FORD

Galaxie

new BLUNTED REAR END

62

138 TO 405 HP
(THR. '63)

POWER STEERING

GALAXIE 500/XL.

DENOTES 405 HP THUNDERBIRD ENGINE

GALAXIE 500 and XL have ← GRILLE MEDALLION

Galaxie 500

BUCKET SEATS and FLOOR CONSOLE IN new *Galaxie* 500/XL!

1962 TAIL LIGHTS

new * SIDE TRIM

*=ON 500, XL

Galaxie 500/XL

168

Galaxie 500
(SEDAN and CVT. ILLUSTR.)

FORD

GALAXIE

SQUIRE

note INDENTATION ALONG UPPER BORDER OF WOOD-LIKE "COUNTRY SQUIRE" SIDE TRIM.

1963

63

new GRILLE with SHIELD EMBLEM, AND STEP-UP ALONG LOWER EDGE

new SIDE TRIM

DASH

BACKGROUND: MONACO, ON THE RIVIERA

PRICES START AT $2563.

6-CYL. "300" 2-DR.

UP TO 425 HP IN new '63½

new

Presenting the 63½ Super Torque Ford Sports Hardtop —brand new hardtop that looks like a convertible!

169

new SWING-AWAY STEERING WHEEL AVAILABLE

CLEAR GLASS BACKLIGHT IN CVT.

CUSTOM RANCH WAGON

FORD

SQUIRE

138 TO 425 HP

GALAXIE 500 4-DR. H/T

1964

GALAXIE 500 XL

64 new GRILLE

PRICES START AT $2586.

($2600 IN '65)

(CUSTOM 6 2-DR.)

1964

new GRILLE

(RESTYLED) 150 TO 425 HP (THROUGH '67)

65

CUSTOM 500

P R N DRIVE L CRUISE-O-MATIC

new VERTICAL STACKED HEADLIGHTS

1965

new DIP IN WAGON ROOF

Convenient face-to-face rear seats add passenger space

SQUIRE

GALAXIE 500 XL

GALAXIE 500 LTD

170

TAIL LIGHT SHAPE 19 new

1965

FRAZER

KAISER-FRAZER CORPORATION
· WILLOW RUN, MICHIGAN

(1946-1951)

123½" W.B.
(THROUGH '51)

(REPLACES PRE-WAR
GRAHAM.)

47

F-47

EARLY
FRAZERS
(BLT. 1946)
have PAINTED
GRILLE.

LATER MODEL,
with CHROME
GRILLE →

EMBLEM

JE SUIS PRET

100·HP @ 3600 RPM   7.3 COMPRESS.

6 CYL., L-HEAD CONTINENTAL
ENGINES   226.2 CID
(USED IN ALL
FRAZERS)

SEE ALSO:
KAISER

3 5/16" × 4 3/8" BORE and STROKE
(KAISER SPECS. SIMILAR)

FRAZER
REAR VIEW

47½-48

F-485 ; (MANHATTAN SEDAN
IS NOW F-486)

$**2152.** OR $**2550.**
(SINCE '47)

ILLUSTRATED
ON FAMOUS "17-MILE-DRIVE,"
AT PEBBLE BEACH, CALIF.

ALL
FRAZERS
ARE
4-DOOR
MODELS.

FRAZER

48 (CONT'D.)

JOSEPH W. FRAZER (left) and HENRY J. KAISER (right,) STANDING BY THE 200,000th CAR (A 1948 FRAZER) TO BE BUILT BY THE KAISER-FRAZER CORP.

200,000th

J.W. FRAZER   H.J. KAISER

112 HP

49-50

1949 = F-495 OR F-496 MANHTN.

VAGABOND

new LARGE GRILLE *and* PARKING LIGHTS

PRICED FROM **$2321.**

F-505 *and* F-506 MANHATTAN *are* 1950 MODELS.

MANHATTAN SEDAN *has* HEAVY BAND *of* SIDE CHROME

(1950 MODEL ENDS 2-50)

4-DOOR CVT.

new "MANHATTAN" LOOKS LIKE THE 4-DR. CVT., BUT *has* STEEL PAINTED OR NYLON-PADDED TOP SECTION.

VAGABOND

115 HP

51

(RESTYLED) F-515 OR F-516 MANHATTAN

DASH (SIMILAR TO 1949)

STARTS 2-50

172

EXPERIMENTAL SAFETY CAR BLT. 1945 TO 1947 BY
H. GORDON HANSEN,
AT SAN LORENZO, CALIF.

FORD V8
ENGINE

GORDON DIAMOND

156" WB BETWEEN FRONT REAR
SINGLE WHEELS. ANOTHER PAIR OF
WHEELS "AMIDSHIPS."
PURCHASED BY HARRAH'S AUTOMOBILE COLLECTION

GRAHAM (and HUPMOBILE)

6 - CYL.
L - HEAD
ENGINES

115"
WB

40-41

'41 GRAHAM:
$895. and up

'40 HUPP:
$1145. and up

FORMER CORD
BODY DIES
USED

GRAHAM "HOLLYWOOD" and
HUPMOBILE "SKYLARK" LOOK ALMOST ALIKE!

(FURTHER DETAILS OF GRAHAM, HUPMOBILE INCLUDED IN "AMERICAN CAR SPOTTER'S GUIDE, 1920-1939")

GREGORY

(1949)   (ANOTHER EXPER.
MODEL, 1952)

BEN GREGORY, MFR.,
KANSAS CITY, MO.

4-CYL. Continental
REAR ENGINE
FRONT-WHEEL-
DRIVE

49

PRODUCTION ATTEMPTED

40 HP
94" WB

$1050. (PROPOSED
PRICE)

(1948-1949)

HOPPENSTAND

HOPPENSTAND MOTORS, INC., GREENVILLE, PA.

2-CYL. FLAT, AIR-COOLED, REAR ENG.

48-49

(1950-1954)

Henry J

PRICED FROM
$**1299.**
(WITH PERIODIC INCREASES)

4 OR 6-CYL.
"SUPERSONIC"
ENGINES

(2-DRS.
ONLY)

THIS
GRILLE
STYLE
RETAINED
ON 1952
HENRY J

513 = 4 CYL.
514 = DELUXE 6 CYL.

51
(INTRO. 1950)

KAISER-FRAZER CORPORATION, WILLOW RUN, MICHIGAN

GIVEN
THE
FASHION
ACADEMY
GOLD MEDAL
AWARD

52-54

('52)

ALLSTATE CAR = SPECIAL SERIES
OF HENRY J, SOLD EXCLUSIVELY
BY SEARS, ROEBUCK and CO.

CORSAIR
('53-
'54)

Henry J

new
GRILLE
ON
'53-54

new
VAGABOND
has REAR
"CONTINENTAL" SPARE
TIRE / WHEEL

Vagabond

('52)

174

HUDSON MOTOR CAR CO., DETROIT

HUDSON SIX

(1909-1957)

$670 COUPE (6)

SERIES (6-CYL.)
40 = TRAVELER; DELUXE (113"wb)
41 = SUPER (118" wb)
43 = COUNTRY CLUB (125" wb)
48 = BIG BOY (125" wb)

92 HP @ 4000 (174.9 CID 6)
OR
102 HP @ 4000 (212 CID 6)

INTERIOR (6)

TOTAL OF 86,865 BLT.

new GRILLE

40

SERIES (8-CYL.)
44 = SUPER
45 = DELUXE (118" WB)
47 = COUNTRY CLUB (125" WB)

OVERDRIVE AVAIL.
4.11 STD. GEAR RATIO
6.50 × 16 TIRES

DASH →

H.P. RATINGS CONTINUE THROUGH '47

(CVT.) SUPER 8

STRAIGHT 8 (254.5 CID 8)

128 HP @ 4200

SHOULD HYDRAULIC BRAKES FAIL, EMERGENCY MECHANICAL SYSTEM TAKES OVER (SINCE '36)

HYDRAULIC — MECHANICAL RESERVE

"AUTO-POISE" FRONT WHEEL CONTROL WITH COIL SPRINGS

NEW HUDSON EIGHT PRICES START AT

INTERIOR (8) **$860**

175

HUDSON

PRICES START AMONG AMERICA'S LOWEST

$695

79,529 BLT. 1941

SUPER 6 (SERIES 10)

"SYMPHONIC STYLING"

41

116," 121," OR 128" WB

"AMERICA'S SAFEST CAR"

new COMMODORE 8

• COMMODORE SERIES (Sixes and Eights)

ONLY 5,396 BLT. IN 1942

42-45

new EXTRA SIDE CHROME

SUPER 6

COMMODORE 6 is new

6

CIVILIAN PROD. ENDS 2-5-42

1942

SOME '42s NO LONGER have FRON. HOOD CHROME

POSTWAR PRODUCTION RESUMES 8-30-45. 5,005 BLT. 1945; 93,870 BLT. 1946

SUPER 6

46

COMM. has 2 VERT. STRIPS on REAR WINDOW

121" WB ON ALL (THROUGH '47) PRICED FROM

$1379.

COMMODORE (has HUDSON TRIANGLE EMBLEM AT FRONT END OF CHROME BELT STRIP)

$1379. UP

new GRILLE with RECESSED CENTER SECTION

PRICED FROM

$1421.

SUPER 6

47

103,310 BLT. 1947

COMMODORE

$1421. UP

SIMILAR TO 1946, BUT has HEAVIER CHROME MOULDING MARGIN AROUND MEDALLION OVER GRILLE.

HUDSON

CVTS. NOW HAVE MORE METAL ABOVE WINDSHIELD

142,454 BLT. 1948

new "Step Down" BODIES SURROUNDED BY FRAME

INTERIOR ('49)

48-49

(TOTALLY RESTYLED)

new 124" WB ON ALL

"This time it's *Hudson*"

new PACEMAKER 6 is LOWER-PRICED SERIES (119" WB)

50

COMMODORE 8

REAR SEAT VIEW

ROAD CLEARANCE

INVERTED "V" ON new GRILLE

143,586 BLT. 1950

92,859 BLT. 1951

51

PACEMAKER 6

$2642.

SUPER 6

COMM. 8

$2543.

new HEAVIER, ARCHED GRILLE

$2568.

new HORNET 6

177

PACEMAKER 6

COMMODORE 6

CVT.

new **HUDSON WASP** with 6-CYL. "H-127" ENG.
Hollywood H/T (new)

HUDSON WASP TWO-DOOR BROUGHAM

HOLLYWOOD WASP

CLUB CPE.

new lower-priced running mate

52

HUDSON HORNET

HORNET CLUB CPE.

SEDAN

HORNET

HUDSON

B-W ENGINEERING PRODUCTION

equipped with
B-W OVERDRIVE!
(OPTIONAL)

79,117
BLT. 1952

HYDRA-MATIC DRIVE
available for all '52 Hudsons
at extra cost.

Hudson-Aire Hardtop Styling
at standard sedan and coupe prices

178

COMMODORE 8

FINAL YEAR FOR STRAIGHT 8

HUDSON

SUPER WASP   1953 : 17,792 WASPS, 27,208 HORNETS   HORNET

6-CYL. MODELS ONLY (THROUGH 1954)

53

new HOOD "AIR-SCOOP" and new GRILLE w/o INVERTED "V."

(The JETS SHOWN ON "JET" PAGE)

The **WASPS** in the low-medium price field

SUPER WASP

new HIGH TAIL-LIGHTS

HUDSON DIVISION OF AMERICAN MOTORS
(RESULT of MERGER with NASH, 5-1-54)

new 1-PC. WINDSHIELD

The **HORNET** in the medium price field

CLUB COUPES

new FRONT END DESIGN

54
(RESTYLED)

NEW HORNET SPECIAL
available in Four-Door Sedan, Club Sedan and Club Coupe—all at new low prices

2-DR. CLUB SEDAN

4-DR. SEDAN

HORNET has 160 HP

(170 HP with "Twin H" Power)

INTERIOR of HOLLYWOOD (CAR ILLUS. NEXT PAGE)

new CHROME PC. ON SIDE

179

HUDSON
54
(CONT'D.)

HORNET HOLLYWOOD H/T

32,293 HUDSON CARS BLT. 1954

52,688 BLT. 1955 ("HUDSON" NAME also USED on SOME Ramblers and Metropolitans)

CUSTOM WASP SEDAN

new ENGINE CHOICES

V 8

CHAMPIONSHIP 6

55

(TOTALLY RESTYLED with NASH BODY DESIGN)

HOLLYWOOD H/T

PACKARD V8 USED

new PEAKS OVER HEADLIGHTS

22,588 BLT. 1956

HOLLYWOOD H/T

BIG new DIAMOND-SHAPED GRILLE

56

SEDAN

DASH

180

HUDSON

$2750.

HORNET
SUPER

Lower outside by 2 full inches

DASH
with new Hydra-Matic

new
SIDE TRIM
MOULDINGS

Hornet V-8

IS ONLY AVAIL.
MODEL (SUPER
OR CUSTOM)

327
CID

World's newest V-8 ... 255 hp

57

new "V" EMBLEM
ON GRILLE

ONLY 4,080
BLT. 1957

HORNET HOLLYWOOD H/T
(APPEARS LONGER IN
← PHOTO AT LEFT
THAN IN PHOTO ABOVE)

Slim outside for easy maneuvering

(DISCONTINUED
JUNE 25, 1957)

... way up in power, way down in price!

(1949 - 50)

IMP

INTERNATIONAL MOTOR PRODUCTS
CO., GLENDALE, CALIF.

49-50

FIBERGLASS BODY
63" WB   APPR. 475 lbs.
1-CYL., 7-H.P. GLADDEN *engine*

SOME REPORTS
LIST FINAL DATE AS 1955.

IMPERIAL

54

CUSTOM
(C-64)
133½" WB

331.1 CID V8 (3¹³/16 × 3⅝)
235 HP @
4400 RPM

(EARLIER MODELS ILLUSTRATED
WITH CHRYSLER.)

CROWN (C-66)   145½" WB   7.5 COMPR.
(SINCE '51)

55

new
331 CID V8 (3.81 × 3.63)
250 HP @
4600
RPM

IMPERIAL (C-69) 130" WB

CROWN IMPERIAL (C-70)
149½" WB (THROUGH '56)
(IMPERIAL CONSIDERED AN
INDIVIDUAL MAKE, AS OF 1955.)

new 8.5 COMPRESSION

IMPERIAL
(C-73)
new 133" WB

354 CID; 280 HP @
4600 RPM

56

35 39

CROWN IMPERIAL
(C-70)

182

IMPERIAL

(IMI-1) $**5598.**

new 129" WB
(THROUGH '66)

new 392 CID (THROUGH '58)
325 HP @ 4600 RPM
new 9.25 COMPR.

57

new 129" WB
(THROUGH '66)

note DIFFERENCES IN
NUMBER OF HEADLIGHTS

CROWN
(IMI-2)

LE BARON
(IMI-4)
$**5743.**

LE BARON
SOUTHAMPTON

new 10.0 COMPRESSION
345 HP @ 4600 RPM

FENDER-GRILLE
DETAILS

LYI SERIES $**5969.**

58

IMPERIAL
NAME (NON-
LE BARONS)

IMPERIAL

CUSTOM SOUTHAMPTON (MYI-L)

LE BARON
SOUTHAMPTON
(MYI-H)

59

LE BARON

new
413 CID, 10.1 COMPR. (THROUGH '65) 350 HP @ 4600 RPM (THROUGH 61)
CROWN (MYI-M)
'65

(PY2-M)
CROWN

60

(PYI-L)
CUSTOM
SOUTHAMPTON

$**4933.**
TO
$**6318.**
PRICE
RANGE

CUSTOM 4-DOOR
SOUTHAMPTON

new
8.20 × 15 TIRES
(THROUGH '64)

(PY3-H) LE BARON 184

IMPERIAL

CROWN
(RYI-M)

SOUTHAMPTON

new "FREE-STANDING HEADLIGHTS (THROUGH '63)

61

(RYI- SERIES)

America's Most Carefully Built Car

ORNAMENT at HOOD
FRONT; new
SPLIT
GRILLE

IMPERIAL LE BARON 4-DR. SOUTHAMPTON (SYI-H)

(CUSTOM
IS SYI-L)

CROWN
(SYI-M)

62

RAISED
TAIL-LIGHTS

HP REDUCED TO
340 @ 4600 RPM
(THROUGH '65)

two-door Southampton

4-DR.
SOUTHAMPTON

185

IMPERIAL

CROWN
(TYI-M)

WHEEL COVER

HIGH, NARROW TAIL-LIGHTS

DASH

(FINAL YEAR FOR "CUSTOM" SERIES.)

(TYI-L) CUSTOM

(TYI-H)

63
(TYI SERIES)

(HAND-BUFFED ACRYLIC ENAMELS)

IMPERIAL Le BARON

The LeBaron cloisonné crest on the roof makes this the only car on which this federal jewelry excise tax is paid.

FREE-STANDING HEADLIGHTS FOR 3RD AND FINAL YEAR

IMPERIAL

CROWN COUPE
(VYI-M)

(VYI-M)

Imperial Crown 4-Door Hardtop

LE BARON
(VYI-H)

DASH

(VYI SERIES)
$5865. TO $6740. 64

(TOTALLY RESTYLED; new DESIGN
SOMEWHAT RESEMBLES LINCOLN CONTINENTAL.)

EAGLE CREST ON
LE BARON VINYL TOP →

AUTO PILOT (left)
AM/FM RADIO (above)

HEADLIGHTS MOVED INTO
new SPLIT GRILLE.

The Incomparable IMPERIAL

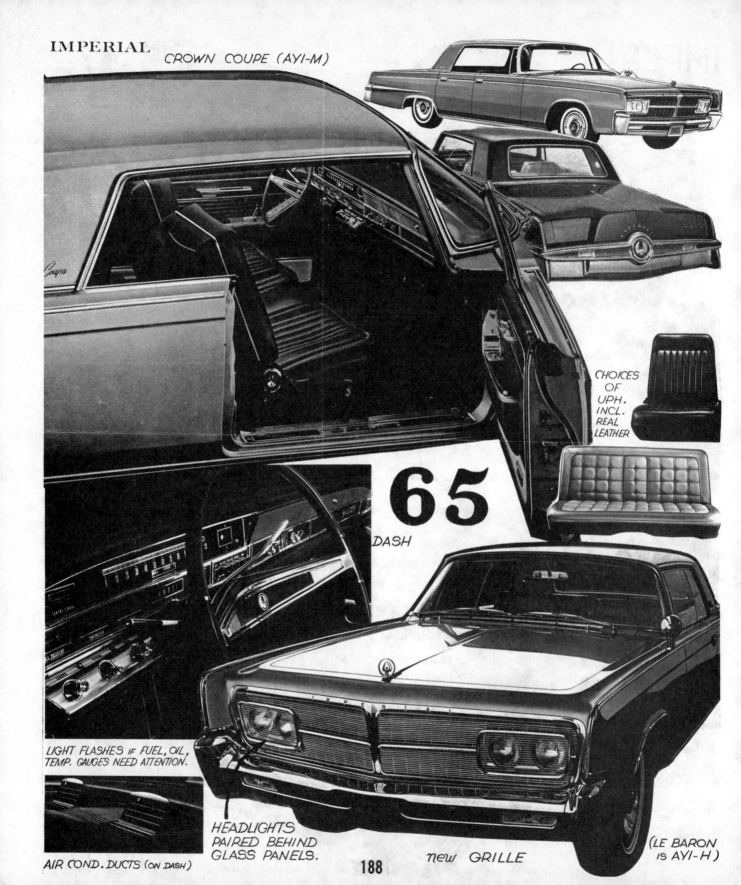

IMPERIAL

CROWN COUPE (AYI-M)

65

DASH

CHOICES
OF
UPH.
INCL.
REAL
LEATHER

LIGHT FLASHES IF FUEL, OIL,
TEMP. GAUGES NEED ATTENTION.

AIR COND. DUCTS (ON DASH)

HEADLIGHTS
PAIRED BEHIND
GLASS PANELS.

new GRILLE

(LE BARON
IS AYI-H)

188

(new "D" SERIES STARTS SPRING, 1937.)

INTERNATIONAL

INTERNATIONAL STATION WAGONS

113" WB

39-40

"D" SERIES
6 CYL.

INTERNATIONAL

"K" LINE SERIES

41-46

See the New Green Diamond Engine

47-49

"KB" SERIES

INTERNATIONAL

new OVERHEAD VALVE ENGINES (SILVER DIAMOND, SUPER BLUE DIAMOND, SUPER RED DIAMOND TYPES)

50-52

ALL-STEEL TRAVELALL WAGON

('52)

new GRILLE and 1-PIECE WINDSHIELD

Motor Truck Division
INTERNATIONAL HARVESTER COMPANY
180 North Michigan Avenue   Chicago 1, Illinois

INTERNATIONAL

53-55

→

56 "S" LINE

CONT'D. INTO EARLY '57; REPLACED BY "GOLDEN ANNIVERSARY" MODELS.

←

57-58

NEW

Golden Anniversary

MODEL

→

the TRAVELALL

59-60

GRILLE (TRUCK)

F904-860

The Travelall

730-114

INTERNATIONAL **61-62**

Scout

The Travelall®

SCOUT is *new* FOR 1961.

63-64

(SCOUT ALSO CONTINUES)

THE TRAVELALL®

65

THE *Scout* BY INTERNATIONAL®

22,089 JETS BLT. 1953

53 $1858. and up **JET** 6 CYLS. (1953–1954)

BY HUDSON

104 HP

105" WB

SUPER JET · DASH

IN ALL THE WORLD NO OTHER CAR LIKE THIS!

JET $1885. **54**

5.90 × 15

SUPER-JET $1933.

DASH

ITALIA

(ONLY 26 BUILT, ON SUPER-JET CHASSIS)

JET-LINER $2057.

note THAT EACH SERIES IS QUICKLY IDENTIFIED IN '54 BY AMOUNT OF CHROME SIDE TRIM.

192

SEE ALSO: Hudson

KAISER

KAISER-FRAZER CORPORATION
● WILLOW RUN, MICHIGAN

(1946 – 1955)

EARLY MODEL, BUILT 1946

KAISER SPECIAL

with CORRUGATED BUMPER

SPECIAL = $1868.

CUSTOM = $2547.

AS IN FRAZER, 6 - CYL., L-HEAD CONTINENTAL ENG. (ON ALL)

6.50 × 15" TIRES

123½" W.B.

EMBLEM

47

K-100 or K-101 CUSTOM

KAISER 6

with PLAIN BUMPER

ALL OVER THE MAP — YOU'LL FIND EXPERT KAISER AND FRAZER SERVICE

47½ - 48

K-481 or K-482 CUSTOM

$1967.

$2557.

SEE ALSO : FRAZER

□ K-F Distributors and parts warehouses   ● K-F Dealers, parts and service stations

ILLUSTRATED AT CAPE COD, MASS.

MA·1232

new 7.10 × 15" TIRES

note 4 VERTICAL BUMPER GUARD ARRANGEMENT ('47½-'48 ONLY)

TRAVELER MODELS FEATURE FULL-OPENING REAR "HATCHBACK."

new 4-DOOR CONVERTIBLE

49-50

new 112 HP

2-cars-in-one

$2088*

Kaiser Traveler
(new)

"TRAVELER" MODEL NAME IN SCRIPT

SEDAN

REAR 3/4 VIEW OF VIRGINIAN

new GRILLE

new VIRGINIAN 4-DOOR HARDTOP

GEAR RATIOS: 4.09; 3.91; 3.73 (OR 4.27 with OVERDRIVE)

194

Kaiser

new 2-door sedan

SEE ALSO: **"HENRY J"**

new HORIZONTAL BLADE GRILLE →

K-511 = SPECIAL
K-512 = DE LUXE

1951
(TOTALLY RESTYLED)

115 HP @ 3650 RPM

new HIGH, ARCHED TOP *with* <u>HUGE</u> WINDOW AREA

new 118½" WB

The **newest** *car in America!*

Anatomic Design*

HOOD ORNAMENT ADDED (ON <u>ALL</u>)

new "<u>GOLDEN DRAGON</u>" (*with* "ALLIGATOR" TYPE UPH., *etc.*)

HUBCAP VARIATION

Hydra-Matic AUTO. TRANS. OPTIONAL (THROUGH '55; *also* OPT. ON 1951 FRAZER)

Built to Better the Best on the Road!

195

MODELS
SPECIAL
VIRGINIAN
DE LUXE
MANHATTAN

'52 Kaiser *Manhattan*

new 1-PIECE WINDSHIELD

new BUMPER-BRIDGE PROTECTS 1952 GRILLE.

118 HP

PRICES START AT $1992.
(SPEC. COUPE)

Kaiser's Anatomic Engineering...

world's safest front seat!

1. Slant-back corner posts—narrower—no "blind spots"!
2. One-piece Safety-Mounted Windshield— designed to push *outward* upon severe impact!
3. Safety-Cushion Padded Instrument Panel!
4. Right hand emergency brake!
5. Recessed instruments—no protrusions!
6. Safety-level seat balances you more safely!
7. Extra front legroom—you sit in a *safer* position!

COMMENDED BY PARENTS MAGAZINE

INTERIOR DETAILS

New

K-521 = VIRGINIAN SPECIAL ; DE LUXE
K-522 = VIRGINIAN DE LUXE ; MANHATTAN

196

KAISER

PRICED FROM $**2313.**

new "V" FIGURE ADDED TO LOWER PART OF FRONT and REAR EMBLEMS.

(new)

CAROLINA 2-DR. (K-538)

REAR DETAILS

53

118 HP
118½" WB

DE LUXE TRAVELER
(K-531 IS DE LUXE SERIES)

MERGES with WILLYS-OVERLAND, TO FORM KAISER-WILLYS.

(LENGTH EXAGGERATED)

MANHATTAN (K-532)

(DRAGON IS K-530)

KAISER-DARRIN
WITH (fiberglass body)
DKF-161

OPTIONAL SUPERCHARGER GIVES 140 HP @ 3900 RPM (STD. HP 118) '55

$**3668.**

new LIGHTS and CONCAVE GRILLE

W. 6 CYL. 161 CID WILLYS F-head ENGINE

('54)

'55 SIMILAR, BUT with HIGHER CHROME FIN TIP on HOOD ORNAMENT (SEE ARROW)

54-55

1955 PRICES START AT $**2503.**

SIMILAR MODELS CONTINUED BY KAISER IN ARGENTINA (I.K.A.,) UNDER THE NAME OF CARABELA. (1955 TO 1962.)

REAR ALSO RESTYLED

KING MIDGET

(1946-1970)
MIDGET MOTORS
ATHENS, OHIO

1 CYL.

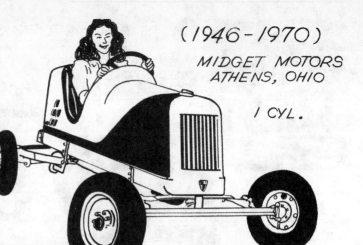

46-50

('55)

EARLY

51-57

(TOTALLY RESTYLED FOR 1951)

(RESTYLED EARLY '57)

LATER

57-70

30% HP INCREASE (TO 12 HP) FOR 1966

KOHLER ENG.

DISCONTINUED
1970
$1095. IN '69

(1949-1950)

CHOICE OF V-8
ENGINES
100"
WB

KURTIS

KURTIS-KRAFT, INC.
LOS ANGELES and GLENDALE, CALIF.
(FRANK KURTIS, founder)

KURTIS
CONTINUED TO
BUILD OTHER TYPES OF
SPORTS and RACING CARS, AFTER
EARL MUNTZ BEGAN PRODUCING "JET"*

* BECOMES MUNTZ JET IN '51,
new 116" WB and ENLARGED TO 4-PASS.

LANCER

COMPACT

[DODGE]

Lancer 170 Two-Door Sedan $2312.

WAGON

6 CYL. INCLINED O.H.V. ENGINE 170 CID with 101 HP @ 4400 RPM or 148 HP @ 5200 RPM

INTERIOR

LARGER 225 CID 6 ALSO AVAIL., with 145 HP @ 4000 RPM OR 196 HP @ 5200 RPM

61

RWI-L , RWI-H

AIR COND., POWER STEERING and POWER BRAKES AVAIL.

1961

106½" WB

H/T COMPACT DODGE LANCER

LANCERS BUILT 1961 and 1962 ONLY. UNITIZED BODY SIMILAR TO PLYMOUTH VALIANT.

LANCER 170 2-DOOR SEDAN 6
$2256   (SLI-L)

LANCER 170 4-DOOR SEDAN 6

ANCER 770 4-DOOR SEDAN 6

$2562.

new GT

LANCER 170 6-PASSENGER WAGON 6   LANCER 770 2-DOOR SEDAN 6

62

SLI

770 (SLI-H)

new GRILLE

1962

(SLI-P)

DISCONTINUED AFTER 1962

199

LARK BY STUDEBAKER
COMPACT SERIES
(1959 - 1963)

2-DR.
PLAY WAGON

6-CYL. OR V8 ENGINES

59

note LOCATION OF GRILLE MEDALLION ON 1959 MODEL

1959 LARK CARRIES "STUDEBAKER" NAME

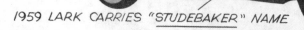

LUXURY Reclining seats that let all the way down are an optional touch of sublime comfort. Seats are pleated, appointments tasteful. Colors are harmoniously keyed to exteriors.

60

GRILLE MEDALLION MOVED TO LOWER CENTER

4-DR. WAGON and CONVERT. ARE new

"LARK" NAME AT REAR END OF FRONT FENDER

"LOVE THAT LARK BY STUDEBAKER"

200

LARK

4 HEADLIGHTS ON new 113" WB CRUISER

180 TO 225 HP

6 has 112 HP

61

GRILLE EMBLEM MOVED; new PARK. LIGHTS; "LARK" NAME MOVED TO FORWARD END OF FR. FENDERS

"You have to drive The Lark to believe it!"

6 has 112 HP

PACE CAR AT 1962 INDY 500 RACE

DAYTONA CVT.

"LARK" IN CAPITAL LETTERS

DETAILS OF new GRILLE

new ROUND TAIL-LIGHTS

62

VIEWS OF DASH

SUNROOF OPTIONAL ON new 225 HP **DAYTONA**

LARK NAME USED ONLY 1959-1963

SLIDING REAR ROOF SECTION ON new REGAL LARK WAGONAIRE

63

new GRILLE AGAIN

REGAL LARK

SEE ALSO Studebaker

LINCOLN V·12

LINCOLN CARS INTRODUCED LATE '20 (FOR 1921.) PRODUCT OF FORD MOTOR COMPANY (LINCOLN MOTOR CAR DIV.) SINCE 1921.

$1360.

V-12 ENGINES (THROUGH '48)

40

-ZEPHYR

new 120 HP @ 3900 RPM

new 292.1 CID (THROUGH '41)

LINCOLN-ZEPHYR SERIES RUNS FROM 1936 THROUGH 1942 MODELS.

new 1-PIECE BACKLIGHT →

125" WB (SINCE '38)

$1400.

new SEALED BEAM HEADLIGHTS

LARGE, OLD-STYLE 150-HP "K" SERIES DISCONTINUED DURING 1940 SEASON, ALONG WITH ITS 414.1 CID ENGINE.

$2783.

CONTINENTAL COUPE

UNITIZED CONSTRUCTION OF BODY-AND-FRAME (IN CLOSED ZEPHYRS)

new CONTINENTAL

(FIRST FULL YEAR AVAIL. AS A REGULAR PRODUCTION MODEL)

CONTINENTAL has LOWER, BROADER BODY STYLING, AND SPARE TIRE IS MOUNTED OUTSIDE of REAR DECK.

CONTINENTAL CABRIOLET

$2840.

7.00 × 16 TIRES
(SINCE '36)

COUPE

CLUB COUPE

LINCOLN
41

SEDAN

4.44 G.R.
(SINCE '38)

new CHROMED BORDER AROUND GRILLE and new PARKING LTS. ATOP FRONT FENDERS

CONTINENTAL

$2700.

$2675. CUSTOM (SEDAN OR LIMO.)
(LIMO.) SPECIAL 138" WB

new AUTOMATIC OVERDRIVE

BUTTON DOOR OPENERS now ON ALL

CONTINENTAL

new 305 CID
new 130 HP @ 3800 RPM

new TALL HOOD MASCOT

42-45

new CHROME DECORATIONS AT EDGE OF REAR FENDERS (USED THROUGH '48)

new GRILLE

new 7.00 × 15 TIRES

"The Finest Lincolns Ever Built"

203

LINCOLN

CONTINENTAL (PACE CAR AT 1946 INDY 500 RACE)

HEAVIER NAMEPLATE ON SIDES OF 1946 HOOD

46

66-H

PRICE RANGE: $2178. TO $4205.

new HEAVIER GRILLE has BOTH HORIZ. and VERT. PCS.

125" WB AS BEFORE, BUT "ZEPHYR" NAME NO LONGER USED.

RAISED HEXAGON AT CENTER OF 1946 HUB CAPS

new LARGER BUMPERS

CONVENTIONAL DOOR HANDLES RETURN, ON STD. TYPES

"Nothing could be finer"

"Lincoln" NAME IN CHROME ON SIDES OF HOOD and ON new PLAINER HUBCAPS

FINAL LINCOLNS with V-12 ENGINES (1948)

7-H   8-H

47-48

CONTINENTALS CONTINUE USE OF BUTTON DOOR OPENERS

CONTINENTAL

FINAL CONTINENTALS UNTIL 1956 MODEL

$4380. ('48)
($200. INCR. FROM '47)

204

new 2-PC. WINDSHIELD (ON STANDARD LINCOLNS ONLY)

(EL) $2527.

$3948.

new COSMOPOLITAN (EH)

49 (TOTALLY RESTYLED)

BACK SEAT AREA (COSMO.)

The "custom touch" adds luxury to the 1949 Lincoln Cosmopolitan!

ALL WITH new V8 ENGINE (L-HEAD)

COSMOPOLITAN

new GRILLE IS LOWER

50

SOME MODELS PRICED ONLY $2 HIGHER THAN LAST YEAR'S

121" WB LINC. "LIDO" CPE. IS NEW

COSMO. "CAPRI" CPE. IS NEW

new FULL-LENGTH CHROME MOULDING ALONG BODY SIDES OF COSMOPOLITAN MODELS (AND CONT'D. ON STD. LINCOLNS)

121" WB

final COSMOPOLITAN

125" WB

51

new GRILLE

LINCOLN SPORT SEDAN

COSMO. SPORT SEDAN $3182.

205

LINCOLN

new 123" wb — $3198.

COSMOPOLITAN

H/T

CAPRI

COSMO. is NOW LOWER-PRICED SERIES, BELOW CAPRI.

52 (TOTALLY RESTYLED)

CVT. $3665.

8.00x15

"Lincoln" NAME IN SCRIPT LETTERING, ABOVE new GRILLE

$3226. COSMOPOLITAN

COSMOPOLITAN LETTERING DETAILS

53

CONV'T. DETAILS

CAPRI LETTERING DETAILS

CAPRI $3549.

new BLOCK "LINCOLN" LETTERING, ABOVE GRILLE WHICH NOW CONTAINS STYLIZED "V" and SMALL EMBLEM

LINCOLN

new FENDER TRIM

54

new GRILLE

"LINCOLN" NAME NOW IN SCRIPT, and MOVED TO FRONT FENDER PANELS.

CONV'T.

CUSTOM IS LOWER-PRICED SERIES, PRICED from $3563.

CAPRI

225 HP

new GRILLE with ALL HORIZONTAL PIECES

55

new 126" WB, new 285 HP

56

new PREMIERE

new PANORAMIC WINDSHIELD

CAPRI H/T

FRENCHED HEADLIGHTS, and new PARK./DIRECTIONAL LIGHTS IN GRILLE

new CHROME SIDE SPEAR

ALSO, A REVIVED **Continental**

(SEE NEXT PAGE)

LINCOLN

Continental

Mark II

Continental Division · Ford Motor Company

$ **9538.** ('56)

($157. MORE IN 1957.)

56-57

300 HP

126" WB

new CONTINENTAL STYLING DIFFERS FROM CAPRI, PREMIERE MODELS (THROUGH '60)

NON-CONTINENTAL 1957 TYPES :   CAPRI PRICED FROM

$ **4649.**

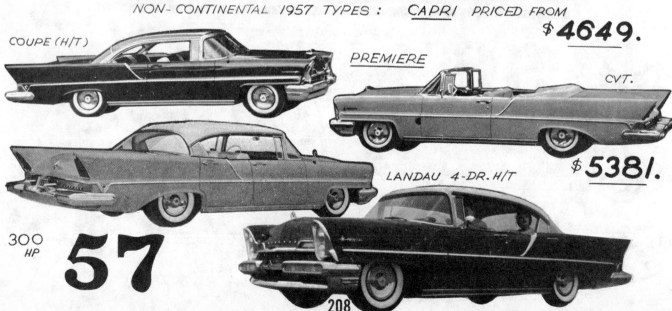

COUPE (H/T)

PREMIERE

CVT.

$ **5381.**

LANDAU 4-DR. H/T

300 HP   **57**

208

CAPRI

new 131" WB (THROUGH '60)

PREMIERE

H/T $**4803.**

CONTINENTAL MARK III

Unmistakably . . . the finest in the fine car field

58

(TOTALLY RESTYLED)

new 375 HP

CONT'L. HAS NEW CRISS-CROSS GRILLE PATTERN

CONT'L. NO LONGER HAS "SPARE TIRE BULGE" IN REAR DECK

9.00 × 14 TIRES

$ **6283.**

(CVT.)

PREMIERE

(CAPRI ALSO AVAIL.)

59

new GRILLE NOW ENCOMPASSES THE CANTED HEADLIGHTS

CUT TO 350 HP

CONTINENTAL MARK IV

$ **7056.**

9.50 × 14 TIRES

209

LINCOLN

PREMIERE

2-DR. H/T

4-DR.

430 CID

HORSEPOWER CUT TO 315 @ 4100 RPM
(new CARBURETOR)
LEAF SPRINGS REPLACE
COILS AT REAR

TYPICAL
UPHOLSTERY
(LEATHER
and
FABRICS)

new HOODED INSTRUMENTS

DASH
and
INSIDE
DOOR
HANDLE

60

CONTINENTAL MARK V

2-DR. H/T

$**5253**. TO $**10,230**.
PRICE RANGE

LANDAU
4-DR. H/T

FINAL YEAR FOR 2-DR.
CONVERTIBLE

TOWN CAR

LIMOUSINE

$**9208**.

9.50 x 14 TIRES

LINCOLN CONTINENTAL

61

(TOTALLY RESTYLED)

$ 6067.

new DASH

REDUCTION OF WHEELBASE to 123" (THROUGH '63) and CUT IN H.P. to 300 @ 4100 RPM (THROUGH '62)

DECK LID OPENS WHEN TOP MOVES

new Four-Door Convertible

REAR

$ 6713.

ALL MODELS NOW KNOWN AS *Lincoln Continental*

new GRILLE and REAR END OF HARMONIZING DESIGN

62

LINCOLN (CONTINENTAL)

63

DETAIL OF
CENTER-OPENING DOORS

4-DR. CONV'T.
with TOP UP

new 320 HP
(THROUGH '65)

The luggage
compartment is larger.

LIMOUSINE

greater

64

(SLIGHTLY ENLARGED)
new 126"WB (THROUGH '69)

interior spaciousness

3" LONGER THAN BEFORE

LIMO-ROOFLINE

DASH

CONV.
(CONTINUES
THROUGH '67)

$6938.

65

new
GRILLE
with
HORIZONTAL
MOTIF

320 HP

430 CID

212

LINCOLN *Continental*
America's most distinguished motorcar.

Marlin BY RAMBLER – Newest of the Sensible Spectaculars (1965 – 1967)
(ANNOUNCED 2-65)

65

116" WB
232 CID 6 (155 HP)
OR
287 CID V8 (198 HP)
OR
327 CID V8
270 HP @ 4700 RPM

POWER DISC BRAKES STANDARD

10,327 '65 MARLINS BLT.

WIRE WHEEL DETAIL

EASILY IDENTIFIED BY UNIQUE FASTBACK "KNIFE-EDGE" REAR STYLING

7.35 OR 7.75 × 14 TIRES

$ **3143.** f.o.b. and up

Marlin GRILLE and SEATS (RECLINING)

Introducing excitement!
The swinging new man-size sports-fastback – MARLIN!

INTERIOR, THROUGH LONG SIDE WINDOW AREA

SEE ALSO:
RAMBLER

213

MERCURY DIVISION OF FORD MOTOR COMPANY

MERCURY 8

SEDAN-COUPE

STARTS *with* 1939 MODEL

116" WB (SINCE '39)

CVT. SEDAN ('40 ONLY)

40

DASH is BLUE *and* SILVER

L-HEAD V8 ENGINE

OVERDRIVE AVAIL.

$930.

new SEALED BEAM HEADLIGHTS

new VENT WINGS

CONTROLLED ALL-WEATHER VENTILATION

new 118" WB (THROUGH '51)

—THE AVIATION IDEA IN AN AUTOMOBILE

new GRILLE

RESTYLED

41

ENGINE

SPARE TIRE *and* WHEEL STOWED VERTICALLY AGAINST WALL →

new 1-PC. BACKLIGHT

214

CONT'D. NEXT PAGE

MERCURY

41 (CONT'D.)

$920.

MORE ROOM — Wherever extra size contributes to comfort, Mercury is big. More head, leg and seat room enables passengers to relax and rest in perfect comfort as they ride.

SMART NEW STATION WAGON is a brand-new Mercury body type this year. Front end and driver's compartment follow the sedan styling. Body is of selected maple and birch. Choice of tan, blue or red hand-buffed leather upholstery. Large luggage capacity. White sidewall tires extra.

THE BIG CAR THAT STANDS ALONE IN ECONOMY

More Power Per Pound

new 6.50 × 15 TIRES

new 2-TIER GRILLE

42-45

NEW *Liquamatic Drive* (OPT.)

DOUBLE CHROME BANDS on FENDERS

$2078.

WOODEN BODY PANELS ON new SPORTSMAN

new GRILLE

new INTERIORS

46

new GRILLE

$1412.

215

CONT'D NEXT PAGE

MERCURY 46 (CONT'D.)

$1390. "COUPE-SEDAN"

"STEP OUT WITH MERCURY"

ALL-STEEL CONVERTIBLE $1604.

INTERIORS ('47)

BORDER OF GRILLE IS NOW CHROME-PLATED

WAGON $1676.

47-48

MORE OF EVERYTHING YOU WANT

WITH Mercury

White sidewall tires at extra cost, when available

216

MERCURY

new 2-DR. WAGON

49

TOTALLY RESTYLED

110 HP

1949

Make your next car *Mercury*

FROM $1997.

new EMBLEMS AT EITHER END

"Better than ever"

50

PACE CAR AT 1950 INDY 500 RACE

LARGE PARK. LIGHTS AT ENDS OF GRILLE

Nothing like it on the *Road!*

new GRILLE and new EMBLEMS

new VERT. TAIL- LIGHTS

51

new OPTIONAL **MERC·O·MATIC**

AUTO. TRANS. 217

LARGER BACKLIGHT

for "the buy of your life!"

MERCURY

Merc-O-Matic Drive ... or B-W Overdrive

CUSTOM

MONTEREY hardtop H/T

NEW 125 H.P. HIGH-COMPRESSION V-8

new DASH

52 (TOTALLY RESTYLED)

1952

MERCURY

new HOOD SCOOP

FROM $**1987**.

new BUMPER-GRILLE

new SHORTER 115" WB

new DECK-LID MEDALLION

DASH

POWER STEERING

POWER BRAKES

1953

new HORIZ. REAR FENDER TRIM

3 new POWER OPTION CHOICES

53

new GRILLE, 118" WB

4-WAY POWER SEAT

218

(CONT'D.)

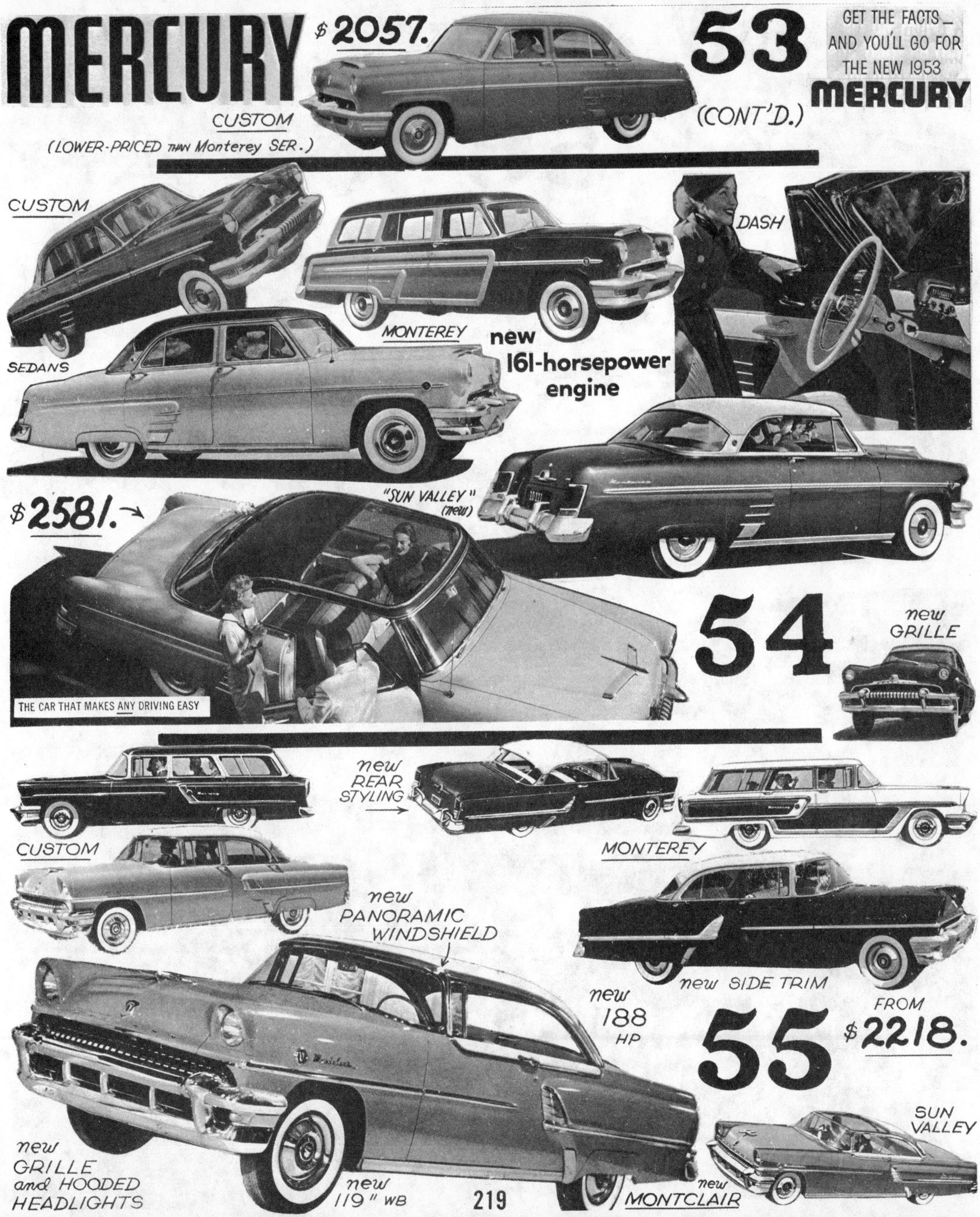

MERCURY
$2057.
53
GET THE FACTS – AND YOU'LL GO FOR THE NEW 1953 MERCURY
CUSTOM
(CONT'D.)
(LOWER-PRICED THAN Monterey SER.)
CUSTOM
DASH
MONTEREY
SEDANS
new 161-horsepower engine
"SUN VALLEY" (new)
$2581.
54
new GRILLE
THE CAR THAT MAKES ANY DRIVING EASY
new REAR STYLING
CUSTOM
MONTEREY
new PANORAMIC WINDSHIELD
new SIDE TRIM
new 188 HP
55
FROM $2218.
SUN VALLEY
new GRILLE and HOODED HEADLIGHTS
new 119" WB
new MONTCLAIR

MERCURY

MEDALIST (new)

For 1956_the big move is to THE BIG MERCURY

MONTEREY

56

CUSTOM

VOYAGER
(IN Montclair SERIES)

"PHAETON" 4-DR. HARDTOP

$2507.

REAR 3/4 DETAIL

MONTCLAIR

new 210 HP

new GRILLE (CLOSE-UP)

interior

MERCURY

BIG M for '57

HIGH BEAM

LOW or HIGH BEAM

QUADRI-BEAM HEADLAMPS (LATER MODELS)

(EARLY) MONTCLAIR

MONTEREY

PACE CAR AT 1957 INDY 500 RACE

with DREAM-CAR DESIGN

(LATER)

57 (TOTALLY RESTYLED)

new 122" WB 255 HP

CONVENTIONAL STATION WAGON

NEW BIG M STATION WAGON

FRONT ROOF VENTS on TURNPIKE CR. (290 HP)

MERCURY ELIMINATES THE LIFT GATE, LOWERS THE TAIL GATE — COMMUTER

new **TURNPIKE CRUISER**

THERE'S ONLY ONE SIDE PILLAR IN THE NEW MERCURY

VOYAGER

2 and 4-DR. WAGONS

THE OPEN-AIR FEELING OF A HARDTOP—

ONLY 2 HEADLIGHTS on EARLY MODELS

COLONY PARK

$3677.

6 wagons

BIG *new* WEDGE TAIL-LIGHTS

CENTER OF BACKLIGHT OPENS, on TURNPIKE CR.

5-7. NEW MONITOR CONTROL PANEL, TACHOMETER, AVERAGE SPEED COMPUTER

221

MERCURY

PRICED FROM $2547.

THE ALL-NEW PARK LANE

1958

58

WHEEL COVER

122" WB (126" ON Park Lane)

20th ANNIVERSARY
'59 MERCURY

"BUILT TO LEAD
_ BUILT TO LAST"

59

new GRILLE VARIES IN APPEARANCE, DEPENDING ON ANGLE FROM WHICH IT IS VIEWED (SEE ALSO NEXT PG.)

ENGINE

new ENLARGED WINDSHIELD AREA

222

(CONT'D.)

MERCURY

MONTEREY SEDAN

MONTCLAIR

59 (CONT'D.)

1959

FANCIER REAR STYLING ON MONTCLAIR

PARK LANE
4-DR. H/T
CRUISER
(ABOVE)
has SPECIAL
REAR SIDE
TRIM

WHEEL
COVER

126" WB
(128"
ON
Park Lane)

VOYAGER

COMMUTER

COLONY PARK
$3932.
(6-PASS.)

$3330. (9-PASS.)

COMMUTER

WAGON DETAILS

SLIP THE THIRD SEAT UNDER THE FLOOR

223

MERCURY

FROM $2631.

2-DR. H/T (MONTEREY)

MONTCLAIR

MONTEREY

(RESTYLED) 60

4-DR H/T (MONTEREY)

9-PASS. COMMUTER $3240.

9-PASS. COLONY PARK $3950.

$3858.

$4018.

PARK LANE 4-DR. H/T

126" WB ON ALL MERCURYS (1960 ONLY)

PARK LANE CVT.

CHROME PCS. IDENTIFY MODEL SERIES

224

MERCURY

METEOR 600

new series
V8 or new 6

METEOR 800

the better low-price cars

61

MODEL NAME at FRONT END of DOOR →

Meteor 800

MONTEREY

MONTEREY

COLONY PARK

COMMUTER

METEOR 62

S-33 DASH

METEOR

MONTEREY CUSTOM

new GRILLES

S-33 WHEEL COVER

MONTEREY

new TAIL-LIGHTS AT TOP OF FENDERS

225

MERCURY

METEOR

FINAL METEOR. 6-CYL.
MERC. ENG. ONLY IN COMET AFTER '63.

METEOR S-33

MONTEREY

new OPENING "BREEZEWAY" BACKLIGHT →

H/T

4-DR H/T

CONSOLE (S-55)

63

S-55 and INTERIOR ←

MONTRY. CUSTOM MARAUDER ('63½)

METEOR CUSTOM

COUNTRY CRUISER

COLONY PARK and INTERIOR →

226

MERCURY

V8s ONLY

No finer car in the medium-price field

MONTEREY

FROM **$3202.**

120" WB (ALL MOD.)

2-DR. H/T

Commuter station wagon

COLONY PARK

250 HP V8

64

4-DR. MARAUDER H/T **$3567.**

MONTCLAIR

2-DR. H/T (BREEZEWAY ROOFLINE)

CLOSE-UP OF DOOR— (PARK LANE) SHOWN ABOVE

$3799.
4-DR. MARAUDER H/T

PARK LANE (300 HP) INTERIOR

2-DR. H/T (BREEZEWAY ROOFLINE)

-227-

DASH

MERCURY

NOW
IN THE
LINCOLN
CONTINENTAL
TRADITION

TOTALLY
RESTYLED
65

MUSTANG

(1947-1949)

ROY C. McCARTHY,
MUSTANG ENGINEERING CO.,
SEATTLE AND RENTON, WASH.

4-CYL. HERCULES ENGINE
59 H.P.   65 M.P.H.
NO DEALERSHIPS; FACTORY ORDERS ONLY

49

ALUMINUM BODY
102" W.B.
5.50 × 15" TIRES

MUSTANG *Ford*

(STARTS APRIL, 1964)

65

6 OR V8
(170 CID)   (260 CID)

standard-equipment

STD. TYPE w/o
GRILLE LIGHTS →

(bucket seats, full carpeting, vinyl interior,
floor-mounted transmission)

Surprisingly spacious trunk

REAR

CVT. IS PACE CAR AT
1964 INDY 500
RACE.

WHEEL
COVER

STANDARD DASH (ABOVE)

$**2368**$* f.o.b. Detroit

AND UP

ALL CIRCULAR GAUGES ON
DE LUXE DASH
(BELOW)

New luxury instrument panel

options *INCLUDE* :

a 289 cu. in. V-8. Four-on-the-floor. Tachometer and clock
combo. Special handling package. Front disc brakes—

STANDARD
SIDE
EMBLEM →

NOTE
MESH
GRILLE
ON '65.

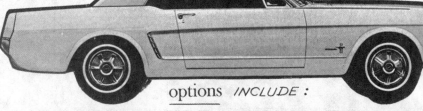

MUSTANG

Unique Ford GT stripe — badge of America's greatest total performance cars!

New integral arm rests — courtesy lights

INTERIOR VIEWS (ABOVE)

"2+2"
FASTBACK

NOTCHBACK HARDTOP

Mustang
GT

CONVERTIBLE

65
(CONT'D.)

EXTRA (FOG)
LIGHTS IN
GT GRILLE

IDENTIFYING
RACING STRIPES
ON GT →

MUSTANG

(VINYL-COVERED ROOF AVAIL.)

NASH MOTORS—Division of Nash-Kelvinator Corporation, Detroit

Again... IT'S THAT NEW **NASH**

6 CYL. OR STRAIGHT-8

SEDAN

(1917 — 1957)

(ALSO BLT. LAFAYETTE LOWER-PRICED MODELS, 1934-1940)

$795. and up

1940 IS FINAL YEAR FOR 2-PIECE BACKLIGHT IN CLOSED NASH CARS

(THE FINAL) LAFAYETTE 6

117" WB
4.1 GR

40

OVERDRIVE AVAIL.

COACH

4013

AMBASSADOR 6 AVAIL. (121" WB)

"BUSTLE-BACK" SEDAN, SHOWING BACK SEAT BED AVAILABLE →

AMBASSADOR 8
125" WB

COUPE
4085

4081
CABRIOLET

"Weather Eye"

HEATER-COOLER AVAIL. (SINCE '38)

63, 617 BLT. 1940

DASH

"SPECIAL" ROADSTER

231

NASH

600

80,408
BLT. 1941

GILMORE-GRAND CANYON RUN
Nash Ambassador 600
Nash California Co. Distributors

Now—coil springs on rear wheels, too!

4149

$745 BUYS

Nash
IN RED LETTERING
ON BUMPER and
HUBCAPS

41

"Go NASH
AND SAVE MONEY EVERY MILE"

AS BEFORE, FIRST 2
DIGITS IN MODEL NO.
SIGNIFY THE YEAR
(SINCE '35)
AMBASSADOR

4183 (8)

CLUB
COUPE
KNOWN AS
"BROUGHAM"

REAR

SINCE '41 "600s,"
UNITIZED
BODY—AND FRAME
CONSTRUCTION

31,700
BLT.

4240

1942

42-
45

NASH

FINAL
STRAIGHT
8 NASH
MODELS

232

NASH

NOW 6-CYL. ONLY
(THROUGH '54)

600 DLX.

112" WB L-HEAD ENG.

121" WB 112 HP OHV

4663

new MEDALLION and PK. LITES

4640

46

AMBASSADOR

PROD.
6148 (LATER '45)
98,769 (DURING '46)

MODEL 4664 AMB. SUBURBAN SEDAN with WOODEN PANELING

new GRILLE

AMBASS. SEDAN IS PACE CAR AT 1947 INDY 500 RACE

4740 (600)
4760 (AMB.)

EL SEGUNDO, CALIF. and TORONTO, ONT. BRANCH PLANTS PURCHASED THE PRECEDING YR.
MEXICO CITY PLANT OPENS 6-18-47.

4748 (fastback)
4740 (bustle-back)

"You'll be Ahead with Nash"

47

new CHROMED EXTENSIONS AT EITHER SIDE OF UPPER GRILLE PORTION

PROD.: 113,315

600

4842

COUPE

48

EXCEPT ON "600," new HIGHER BELT LINE CHROME FOR 1948

SUPER

"FASTBACK" SEDAN

4868

new CVT. (1,000 BLT.) AMBASSADOR

4871

"BUSTLE BACK" SEDAN

4840

4863 OR 4843

DASH (MORE DETAILS NEXT PAGE)

MORE '48 DETAILS ON NEXT PAGE **233**

NASH

48 (CONT'D.)

118,621 BLT.

FULL VIEW OF INTERIOR

You'll be Ahead with **Nash**

Great Cars Since 1902

"SUPER" and "CUSTOM" are NEW

AMB.
SUPER (MODEL NAME ON SIDE OF HOOD.)

4860

---

600   82 HP

4949

has "600" in CHROME, ON FRONT FENDER PANEL.

EL SEGUNDO, CALIF. PLANT OPENS 10-48

49

TOTALLY RESTYLED *new* *Airflyte*

PHANTOM VIEW

MODELS (NO CVTS.)

142,592 BLT.

ONE SINGLE WELDED UNIT!

with Girder-built Unitized Body and Frame ...Airliner-styled interiors... Cockpit Control...Uniscope... Matched Coil Springs on all Four Wheels...Twin Beds... Uniflo-Jet Carb

AMBASSADOR   112 HP

234

NASH

BACKLIGHTS ENLARGED

WITH *HYDRA-MATIC DRIVE*

191,865 BLT.

The Ambassador Custom 115 HP

50

The Statesman 85 HP

(REPLACES 600)

...NEW SUPER-POWER ENGINES!

new SLIDING GLOVE DRAWER
THICKER BUMPER GUARDS

new **Rambler** *also avail.* AT NASH DEALERS

Airflytes for 1951

5148

STATESMAN

New sky-flow fenders

TRUNK DETAILS

51

5159

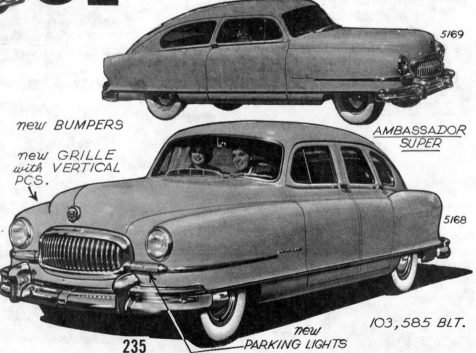

5169

AMBASSADOR SUPER

new BUMPERS

new GRILLE with VERTICAL PCS.

5168

RECLINING SEATS
(*with* BODY CENTERPOST NOT SHOWN, IN ORDER THAT SEAT DETAIL CAN BE SEEN.)

235

new PARKING LIGHTS

103,585 BLT.

NASH

50TH ANNIVERSARY (OF RAMBLERS)

Golden Airflytes

Pinin Farina, STYLIST

(TOTALLY RESTYLED FOR 1952)

('52)

new 88 HP

5255

new 114¼" WB
STATESMAN CUSTOM

AMBASSADOR CUSTOM
← 120 HP

5275

new 121¼" WB

7.10 × 15

52-53

152,141 BLT.*   153,753 BLT.*   *= INCL. RMB.

5355

('53)
100 HP

'53 WITH new STRIPS OF CHROME ON VENT

DASH ('53)

('53)
AMBASSADOR COUNTRY CLUB
5377

Ambassador Country Club

110 HP
STATESMAN SUPER

67,192 BLT.

54

130 HP
AMBASSADOR SUPER

5465

5446

new BORDERS AROUND MODIFIED GRILLE

5475

ST. OR AM. CUST. MODELS have REAR-MOUNTED "CONTINENTAL" SPARE TIRE.

AMERICAN MOTORS CORP. FORMED BY MAY 1, 1954 NASH-HUDSON MERGER.

AMBASSADOR CUSTOM

STATESMAN SUPER
5545-1

CNTRY. CLUB 5547-2

'55 NASH

5585-1

(RESTYLED) Scena-Ramic WINDSH.

AMBASSADOR SUPER

new "INBOARD" HEADLIGHTS

5585-2

57,619 BLT.

AMB. CUSTOM
208-HP V8
PACKARD ENG. OPTIONAL

STATESMAN SUPER

5645-1

Ambassador Special

130 HP

56

5665-1 (6)

AMBASSADOR SUPER 6

AMBASSADOR CUSTOM V8

5657-1

5655-2

Torque-Flo V-8

THE NEW
Ambassador Special
WITH new A.M.C. - BUILT V8
190 HP
250 CID
(INTRO. 4-56)

237

NASH

AMBASSADOR COUNTRY CLUB

PHOTOGRAPHED IN DISNEYLAND

56 (CONT'D.)

DELUXE, SUPER, or CUSTOM 6
REPLACE
STATESMAN 6
MODELS

AMBASSADOR SUPER

V·8

5785-1

255 HP

new GRILLE and SIDE TRIM

57

THE FINAL NASH

5787-2

AMBASSADOR CUSTOM

121½" WB

5785-2

- New wider front tread for surer footing
- New sharper, easier turning
- Airliner Reclining Seats
- All-Season Air Conditioning
- Choice of Hydramatic, Overdrive or Standard
- Twin Travel Beds

new STACKED HEADLIGHTS

238

SUPERSEDED BY RAMBLER

JOIN THE SWING TO THE TRAVEL KING
'57 Nash
World's Finest Travel Car

OLDS F-85 →

BY OLDSMOBILE
(COMPACT)

(STARTS 1961)

155 STD. HP

ENTIRE REAR DOOR RAISES, ON WAGON

61

112" WB
6.50 x 13 TIRES
3.36 GEAR RATIO

F-85 *Cutlass*

Above: F-85 Cutlass Sports Coupe. Also available: new F-85 Club Coupe . . .

new
ROCKETTE 185 Engine
(ALUMINUM BLOCK)

185 HP V8

10.25 COMPR.
4 BBL. CARB.

F-85 SEDAN

$ 2713.

OLDSMOBILE

F-85·61

" ...it's every inch an OLDSMOBILE "

239

OLDS F-85 →

F-85 COUPE

CUTLASS COUPE

CUTLASS

$2949.
(SAME PRICE AS
LAST YEAR)

62

F-85 COUPE

CUTLASS H/T

CVT.

WAGON

JETFIRE H/T
(note HEAVIER SIDE TRIM)

new SHAPE OF
TAIL-LIGHT

TO 195 HP with
ALUMINUM V8

DELUXE
SEDAN

63

new GRILLE with
"OLDSMOBILE" NAME
ACROSS CENTER STRIP

OLDS F-85 →

240

There's "Something Extra" about owning an OLDSMOBILE!

WAGON (DLX.)

OLDS F-85

CUTLASS

new 230 HP

F-85 V-6 SPORTS COUPE

VISTA-CRS.

WHERE THE ACTION IS!

F-85-64

WIRE WH. COVERS AVAIL.

64 V8 OR V6

new VISTA-CRUISER WAGON has ROOF WINDOWS

CVT.

new ECON-O-WAY V-6

SEDAN PROFILE

an all-new transmission

JETAWAY DRIVE

JETFIRE ROCKET V-8

Vista-Cruiser

AC 207

CUTLASS

65

4-4-2 has 400 CID V8

442

VISTA-CRUISER has FOLDING, FORWARD-FACING 3RD SEAT
Roomy cargo area—holds over 100 cubic feet!

1965

The Rocket Action Car!

CUTLASS

241

Product of **GENERAL MOTORS**

OLDSMOBILE

(SINCE 1897)

OLDS PRICES START AT

$807 up,

FOR "60" BUSINESS COUPE

(PAINTED HORIZ. PCS. IN GRILLE OF "60")

GM GENERAL MOTORS

6 OR 8-CYL. L-HEAD ENGINES

40

new SEALED-BEAM HEADLAMPS

116" WB 6.00×16

"Bigger and Better in Everything!"

WITH *Hydra-Matic Drive*

AUTOMATIC TRANSMISSION (OPT.)

124" WB

NO GEARS TO SHIFT!

CUSTOM 8 CRUISER (90)

7.00×16

70

120" WB

229.7 CID 6 (SINCE '37) 95 HP @ 3400 RPM

OR

257.1 CID 8 (SINCE '37) 110 HP @ 3600 RPM

"BEST LOOKING CAR ON THE ROAD!"

THE CAR *Ahead!*

STYLED TO LEAD — BUILT TO LAST

new 238.1 CID 6 (100 HP @ 3400)

41

new 119" OR 125" WB

SPECIAL 60

new "SPECIAL 60" TOWN SEDAN (66 SER.)

$852., and up, f.o.b.

242

(CONT'D.)

41
(CONT'D.)

HYDRA-MATIC

ABOVE PLATE IDENTIFIES CARS *with* AUTO. TRANS.

STRAIGHT-8 ENGINE SPECS. AS IN '40.

PROVED AND IMPROVED FOR "42"!

HYDRA-MATIC DRIVE*

THE GENERAL MOTORS CONTRIBUTION TO SIMPLER, SAFER, MORE EFFICIENT DRIVING!

119", 125", OR 127" WB

"B-44"

SERIES

42

NEW
4U·4·42

(CONT'D.)

OLDSMOBILE

SPECIAL 66

$960., f.o.b.

42 (CONT'D.)

ENGINE SPECS. AS BEFORE

INTERIOR

OLDSMOBILE IS TURNING OUT CANNON FOR FIGHTING PLANES — SHELL FOR THE ARTILLERY

DYNAMIC CRUISER

"YOU CAN ALWAYS COUNT ON OLDSMOBILE —

— IT'S QUALITY-BUILT TO LAST!"

CHROME TRIM ELIMINATED

WARTIME "BLACKOUT" MODEL →

42 ½ - 45

244

OLDSMOBILE

76

A NEW AND FINER

GM GENERAL MOTORS HYDRA-MATIC DRIVE

NO CLUTCH PEDAL — AUTOMATIC GEAR SHIFTING

INTERIOR

66

46

98

125" WB

CLUB SEDAN

119" WB

$1290. and up, f.o.b. (66 CL. CPE.) ($95. MORE IN '47)

66

ENGINE SPECS. (6 and 8) AS SINCE '41

$2305. f.o.b.

66

STATION WAGON

98 CUSTOM **$2160.**, f.o.b. CRUISER CVT.

119", 125" OR 127" WB (THROUGH '48)

47

LONGER RED SECTION AROUND "OLDSMOBILE" NAME IN FRONT FENDER CHROME STRIP

It's *Smart* to own an Olds

CENTER SECTION OF BUMPER NO LONGER GROOVED AT TOP

245

OLDSMOBILE

$1385. and up, f.o.b. (66 CL. CPE. or 2-DR.)

76 (6-CYL.)

119" OR 125" WB ON OLD-STYLED 6 and 8

48

RETAINS 1947-STYLE BODY, BUT *has* "OLDSMOBILE" NAME and *new* CIRCLE EMBLEM ABOVE GRILLE, and NEW-STYLE CHROME SIDE TRIM.

new FUTURAMIC

"98" MODELS TOTALLY RESTYLED

127" WB

98 (OLDSMOBILE'S FINAL CARS *with* STRAIGHT-8 ENGINE)

"FUTURAMIC" NAME BEGINS WITH *the* 8-CYL. RESTYLED 1948 OLDSMOBILES, AND IS USED FOR A FEW YEARS AFTERWARDS.

$1740., f.o.b. 2-DR. CLUB SEDAN

98 CONVERTIBLE *has* *new* HYDRAULICALLY OPERATED POWER SIDE WINDOWS *and* AUTOMATIC FRONT SEAT ADJUSTER

$2160., f.o.b.

246

FUTURAMIC

OLDSMOBILE

$1732., *and up, f.o.b.*
(76 CL. CP.)

76

New
NEW *ROCKET* ENGINE!
(O.H.V V8)

105 HP
119½" WB
6

135 HP
(TO '52)

49

new AIR SCOOPS
BELOW HEADLIGHTS

98
(125" WB)

new "HOLIDAY" H/T $2973. f.o.b.,

You've got to drive it to believe it!

"88" DESIGNATION USUALLY
ON REAR FENDER

UNLIKE "98," THE new '49½ "88" has
CURVED
LOWER
EDGES
OF
WINDSHIELD.

NEW "88" (49½ INTRO. AFTER SEASON UNDER WAY)

LOWEST-PRICED CAR
WITH "ROCKET" ENGINE

$2375.,
f.o.b.
88 DLX. SEDAN

119½" WB

"88"

THIS
IDENTIFIES
V8 MODELS

CVT. IS PACE CAR AT
1949 INDY 500 RACE

"The New Thrill"

247

OLDSMOBILE ROCKETS AHEAD

FINAL 6-CYL. "76" has NO CHROME STRIP ON FRONT FENDER

$1761., and up, f.o.b. (76 2-DR.)

"88"

OLDSMOBILE 88

50

88

88 CVT.
$2294., f.o.b.

98

8.20 × 15 TIRES on 98 CVT.

7.60 × 15

Make a Date with a "Rocket 8"!

V8s ONLY

(119½" WB ON 88 ONLY)

NEW! "88" SUPER 51

135 HP

7.60 × 15 TIRES (88, SU-88)

$1970., and up, f.o.b. (88 2-DR.)

248

(CONT'D.)

CVT. **$2673.**, f.o.b.

SUPER "88" 120" WB

2-DR. **$2265.**, f.o.b.

51
(CONT'D.)

"ROCKET" 98 122" WB

New Room Inside!

DLX. HOLIDAY H/T **$2882.**, f.o.b.

$2610., f.o.b.

88

$2262., f.o.b. 2-DR. 120" WB

$2462., f.o.b. SU-88 SEDAN

The "Rocket" Oldsmobile's New Power Steering* makes driving so easy you can...

Park with just 1 finger!

SU-88 H/T

HORIZ. GROOVES ON SU-88 FENDER PAD; VERTICAL GROOVES ON 98.

new VERTICAL "TOOTH" AT CENTER OF GRILLE

52

SUPER

new SIDE TRIM (SEE DETAILS)

98 TAIL-LIGHT

Ninety-Eight
SEDAN
$2786., f.o.b.

124" WB   160 HP
new "SUPER" RANGE in Hydra-Matic

$3229., f.o.b. CVT.

OLDSMOBILE

REAR QUARTER DETAILS (SEDAN)

Ninety Eight
H/T

new SIDE TRIM DESIGN IDENTIFIES '52

250

OLDSMOBILE

88

2-DR.

88 has 150 HP @ 3600 RPM

$2262., f.o.b.

FINAL YR. FOR 303 CID V8s

53

H/T

DETAILS OF SUPER 88 HOLIDAY H/T

DETAILS OF THE 1953 ENGINE

SUPER 88

SEDAN

SU-88, 98 have 165 HP @ 3600 RPM

CVT. 3229., f.o.b.

Ninety-Eight

AIR COND. AVAIL.

Holiday

H/T

$3022., f.o.b.

POWER BRAKES and POWER STEERING ORDERED with MOST UNITS.

OLDSMOBILE

$ **2237.**, and up,
_f.o.b._

88

new PANORAMIC
WINDSHIELDS
ON ALL

SUPER
88

HOLIDAY COUPÉ

170 HP @ 4000 (88)

185 HP @ 4000
(SU-88, 98)

ALL *with*
new
324 CID V8s.
(THROUGH '56)

54
(RESTYLED)

98

122" WB (88, SU-88)
126" WB (98)

98 STARFIRE CVT.

Ninety-Eight

REAR DETAILS (98)

$ **3248.**,
_f.o.b._

INTERIOR
OF
NEW
"Starfire"
185 HP

LARGE,
BOXY
DECK AREA

1954

252

OLDSMOBILE
55

SEDAN $ **2362.,** f.o.b.

7.10 x 15

88

185 HP

OLDSMOBILE'S ENTIRELY NEW

INT.

SUPER 88

7.60 x 15

A HARDTOP...WITH 4 DOORS!

Holiday Sedan

IT'S A HOLIDAY... with Sedan convenience!
IT'S A SEDAN... with Holiday smartness!

Ninety Eight

7.60 x 15

NEW!

NEW!

ALL-AROUND *new* 202 HP ENG. (SU-88, 98)

56 88

FINAL YR. FOR 324 CID V8 (230 OR 240 HP @ 4400 RPM)

INTERIOR

(CONT'D. ON NEXT PAGE)

"Holiday" *new* BISECTED GRILLE

88 2-DR.
$ **2338.,** *and up,* f.o.b.

253

OLDSMOBILE

SUPER 88

$2484., f.o.b.
SU-88 2-DR.

98 4-DR. H/T DLX. HOLIDAY SEDAN

56
(CONT'D.)

$3456., f.o.b.

GOLDEN **ROCKET**

GOLDEN ROCKET

f.o.b. PRICES START AT
$2691. (88 2-DR.)
277 HP @ 4400 RPM
WITH *new* 371 CID V8
(371 CID AVAIL. THROUGH '60)

57
(RESTYLED)

new TAIL-LIGHTS and SIDE TRIM

8.50 x 14 TIRES (THROUGH '58)

SUPER **88**

new SUPER 88 FIESTA

$3499., f.o.b.

new GRILLE

122" WB (126" ON 98)

SUPER

$3887., f.o.b.

← note 3-PC. BACKLIGHT on H/T (new)

new **Starfire 98** H/T

254

OLDSMOBILE

88

FIESTA 88

**DYNAMIC 88
SUPER 88
NINETY-EIGHT**
16 models to choose from!

(TOTALLY RESTYLED)

122½" OR 126½" WB

SUPER 88

265, 305 OR 312 HP

58

BADGE ON SU-88 and 98

98

for '58

New Rocket Engine is more powerful, gives greater performance than ever before. In addition, carburetion advances provide you with an opportunity for improved fuel savings, as much as 20%!

THE "CHROME KING" OF ALL CARS!

"OLDSmobility"

$2772.., and up, f.o.b.

→ DASH DETAILS

New Trans-Portable®—a transistor radio that serves as your regular car radio, operating on car's built-in circuit, can also be unlocked and carried from car as a compact, lightweight portable.

New Safety-Vee Steering Wheel, with modern two-spoke, safety recessed design, allows unobstructed view of vital instrument panel gauges. New twin horn buttons are located within easy reach.

Dual-Range Power Heater® gives the exact amount of heat or ventilation exactly where you want it . . . when you want it. You merely touch a button . . . power does all the work for you!
*Optional at extra cost.

4 HEADLTS. ABOVE new GRILLE

new "LINEAR" LOOK
LTS. SEPERATED WITHIN new GRILLE

371 CID (270 HP @ 4600) OR new 394 CID (315 HP @ 4600)

59

(TOTALLY RESTYLED AGAIN)

$2837., and up, f.o.b.

(CONT'D.)

OLDSMOBILE

4-DR.

DYNAMIC 88

2-DR.

DY-88 HAS NO ROCKER PANEL CHROME

(LENGTH EXAGGERATED)

DYN. 88 HOLIDAY SCENICOUPE H/T

FIESTA

SUPER 88

59 (CONT'D.)

4-DR. H/T HOLIDAY SPORTSEDANS

new 9.00 × 14 TIRES ON SU-88, 98

98

ninety-eight 4-door sedan

98 CVT.
$4366.,
f.o.b.

98 HOLIDAY SCENICOUPE H/T

DASH

1959

$2900.,f.o.b.
88 CELEBRITY 4-DR. SEDAN

DYNAMIC 88

FIESTA WAGON

SUPER 88

OLDSMOBILE
60
PACE CAR AT 1960 INDY 500 RACE

98

with *Roto-Matic Power Steering*

240 OR 315 HP @ 4600 RPM (FINAL YR. FOR SMALLER (371) V8)

GO OLDS '60!

DASH

SU-88 FIESTA WAGON

OLDSMOBILE

WINDOW SWITCHES

RADIO

WONDER BAR

power features and accessories for your driving pleasure

Other Oldsmobile Options include such convenience features as: Guide-Matic Power Headlight Control, Safety Sentinel, Swivel Dome and Reading Lamp, Deck Lid Power Lock Release, Electric Ventipanes, De Luxe Wheel Discs, Trim Rings and Air Conditioning.

POWER HEATER

MANUAL HEATER

Starglo Morocceen interiors—optional at no extra cost in both Dynamic 88 Holiday Sedans and Holiday Coupes. And this long-wearing, easy-to-clean all-vinyl trim is as handsome as it is durable.

THIS REAR-END STYLING IN 1961 ONLY

$**3359.**, f.o.b.

DYNAMIC **88** 123" WB 250 HP

POWER ANTENNA

61

(TOTALLY RESTYLED)

DYNAMIC 88 FIESTA (AVAILABLE IN 2 AND 3-SEAT MODELS)

KEEPS YOU ON THE LEVEL!

Super **88**

OLDSMOBILE 123" WB

Skyrocket PERFORMANCE!

DISTINGUISHED... DISTINCTIVE... DECIDEDLY NEW!

new "Skyrocket"

ENGINE (394 CID V8) 325 HP @ 4600 RPM 10 TO 1 COMPRESSION (USED IN SU-88, 98; OPTIONAL IN DY-88)

DASH

S-88-61

"OLDSMOBILE" NAME BELOW new GRILLE (ON 88s)

258

Foam-padded pattern cloth, handsomely accented with lustrous Jeweltone Morocceen, adds brilliant new sparkle to this Super 88 Holiday Sedan. Five harmonizing color choices are available.

(98 MODELS ON NEXT PAGE)

OLDSMOBILE

61
(CONT'D.)

V8

INTERIOR

CLASSIC 98 SPORT SEDAN

STARFIRE

(new)

CLASSIC *98*
126" WB

98

WHEEL
COVER
(98)

CLASSIC 98 TOWN SEDAN

REAR QUARTER
DETAIL

CLASSIC 98 HOLIDAY SEDAN

(LENGTH
EXAGGERATED)

H/T

DYNAMIC
88

4-DR. H/T

WAGON *has*
UNIQUE REAR
FENDER DESIGN

62
(RESTYLED)

new
SIDE
SCULPTURING

$3404.,
and up, f.o.b.
260 TO 345 HP (THROUGH '63)

new UPRIGHT GRILLE *with* "OLDSMOBILE"
NAME *ABOVE*

259

(CONT'D.)

SUPER 88

98

HOLIDAY
SPORTS
SED.
(98)

62
(CONT'D.)

STARFIRE

98 WHEEL
COVERS

new HARDTOP CPE.
IN STARFIRE
SERIES

$3423.,
and up, f.o.b.

63

DYNAMIC 88

DYNAMIC 88 CONVERT. AVAIL.

(CONT'D.)

260

SU-88 GRILLE LIKE DYNAMIC 88

SUPER 88

SU-88 FIESTA

OLDSMOBILE

STARFIRE

REAR ROOFLINE

63 (CONT'D.)

98 TOWN SEDAN

STARFIRE REAR

WHEEL COVER

98-LS (LUXURY SEDAN)

(98 DETAILS)

4-DR. H/T $4238., f.o.b.

There's "Something Extra" about owning an

OLDSMOBILE

NINETY-EIGHT · SUPER 88 · DYNAMIC 88 · F-85 · STARFIRE · JETFIRE

$339¹., f.o.b.

Jetstar 88

New full-size "88" series at a new lower price!

'64 OLDS WHERE THE ACTION IS!

new 330-cubic-inch Jetfire Rocket V-8

JETSTAR 88 CELEBRITY SEDAN

JETSTAR 88 HOLIDAY SEDAN

Jetstar 88

FIESTA STATION WAGON (2- or 3-seat)

DYNAMIC 88 HOLIDAY COUPE

CELEBRITY SEDAN

DYNAMIC 88

SUPER 88

394-cubic-inch Starfire V-8 Engine

J 1964

Brilliant new sports coupe in the medium-price class! **Jetstar I**

TOWN SEDAN

98

64 Starfire

S-1964

NINETY-EIGHT

1964

Ninety-eight

O-64

262

REAR FENDER (98)

65

330 CID V8   260 HP 123" WB
7.75 × 14 TIRES
Jetstar 88 $**3334.,** f.o.b.

DYNAMIC 88 LINE
JOINED BY
new **DELTA 88** →

$**3504.,** f.o.b.
DYNAMIC 88
↓
H/T

123" WB

425 CID
SUPER
ROCKET
V8
360 HP
(TO 370 IN DELTA 88)

Delta 88.

$**3697.,** f.o.b. ↗

8.25 × 14
TIRES

new GRILLE

OLDSMOBILE

DELTA 88 DASH

note THAT STARFIRE and 98
have OWN GRILLE
DESIGNS

370 HP
STARFIRE →

$**4761.,** f.o.b.

CVT.

H/T

$**4334.,** f.o.b.

98 (126" WB)

98
LUXURY
SEDAN

$**4237.,** f.o.b.

Ninety-Eight

WITH
VINYL
TOP ↓

↗

8.55 × 14 TIRES

HOLIDAY
SPORT
SEDAN

NINETY-EIGHT

263

'65 OLDSMOBILE
The Rocket Action Car!

98 DASH

PACKARD

(1899–1958)

PACKARD MOTOR CAR CO., DETROIT

SIX-CYL. OR STRAIGHT-8 L-HEAD ENGS.

DETAILS OF COWL VENT, ETC.

INTERIOR DETAILS

110 SIX $975.

40

(1800 SERIES)

120 EIGHT $1095.

CVT.

$867 TO $6300

delivered in Detroit, State taxes extra. *Prices subject to change without notice.*

Air Cool-ditioning is available on closed models of the Packard 120, Super-Eight 160, and Custom Super-Eight 180 at extra cost, installed at the factory.

AIR CONDITIONING INTRODUCED FOR FIRST TIME!

OVERDRIVE OPTIONAL

ASK THE MAN WHO OWNS ONE

GRILLE GUARD ON 160 and LARGER MODELS

160 SUPER 8 and ENGINE

Model illustrated is Packard Super-8 One-Sixty Touring Sedan $1632* (white sidewall tires extra)

264

(CONTINUED)

DARRIN SEDAN

THIS DARRIN MODEL (RARE) has TOP and BODY DESIGN ENTIRELY DIFFERENT FROM OTHER PACKARDS

PACKARD

180 CUSTOM 8 BY DARRIN

4570.

127" WB

138" WB

$6100.

40 (CONT'D.)

DARRIN CONVERTIBLE

LIMOUSINE

180 CUSTOM 8

FORMAL SEDAN

$2825.

HEADLIGHTS SUNK DEEPER INTO FENDERS, with PARKING LIGHTS SET ON TOP

$1436. $1024.

110 SIX

120 WAGON

DLX. SEDAN INTERIOR (110)

DASH

new 1-PIECE BACKLIGHT

"the Class of '41"

41 (1900 SERIES)

6 lines of cars — 41 body styles
$907 TO $5550

120

261 AVAIL. TRIM COMBINATIONS!

180 DARRIN

265

PACKARD

new **CLIPPER** 8 CYL.

(STARTS 4-41)

41½

(1951 SERIES)

$1375.

OTHER 1941 MODELS CONTINUE ALSO

Clipper

new 2-DR. CLIPPERS NOW ALSO AVAIL.

110

180

INTERIOR

LOOKING AHEAD? SKIPPER THE CLIPPER

42-45

(2000 SERIES)

new CHOICE OF 6 OR 8-CYL. CLIPPERS

ELECTROMATIC DRIVE

SIMPLIFIED DRIVING WITH NO JERK·NO SLIP·NO CREEP

SUPER 8 *has* 148" WB

CUSTOM SUPER CLIPPER

$1746. DELUXE CLIPPER

46-47

(2100 SERIES)

(BIG CITY PACKARD SHOWROOMS MORE LUXURIOUS THAN THIS RURAL OUTLET)

$3161.

STATION SEDAN
(new)

EIGHT

NEW SMOOTH SIDE BODIES

←

SUPER-8 CVT.
IS FIRST OF
1948 PACKARDS
TO BE INTRODUCED

SUPER 8
130 HP

$2529.

EARLY

48-49

(RESTYLED) (2200 SERIES)

$2990.

$3461.

CUSTOM 8
160 HP

127" WB

$3866.

1948 - EARLY '49 DASH
ILLUSTR. ON NEXT PAGE

CUSTOM 8 has
CRISS-CROSS PIECES
IN GRILLE.

ASK THE MAN
WHO OWNS ONE

267

PACKARD

CLOSE-UP
VIEW OF
DASH

(2200 SERIES)

$2383. ('50)

135 HP (8)
150 HP (SU. 8)
160 HP (CUST. 8)

DELUXE 8

EIGHT
(120" WB)

SUPER 8
new
127"
WB

DASH
and
BACKLIGHT
DETAILS

Ultramatic Drive
AVAIL.

"*Golden Anniversary*" new LARGER BACKLIGHTS
MODELS ON 4-DOOR SEDANS

49½-50

(2300 SERIES)
77 MAJOR IMPROVEMENTS

CUSTOM 8
127" WB

268

Prestige car of the medium-priced field: Packard "200" Club Sedan—$2366
—one of nine exciting new models for '51

200 (145 HP)

250 CVT.

"NEW, ALL-NEW"

PRICE RANGE
$2302.
TO
$3797.

51-52

(TOTALLY RESTYLED 2400 SERIES)

(2500 SER.)

122" WB

250 MAYFAIR

300

REAR SIDE DETAILS

1952 MODEL (left) SIMILAR, BUT has new HOOD ORNAMENT and MEDALLION ON GRILLE

Ultramatic

400 PATRICIAN

COSTLY MODELS CONTINUE CORMORANT FIGURE AS 1951 ORNAMENT

1951 MODELS have "PACKARD" NAME ABOVE GRILLE

New Armor-rib body construction!
New Tele-glance instrument panel!
New Safeti-set brake!

269

—the one for '51!

$2588.

CLIPPER DELUXE

New Packard **CLIPPER**

160 HP

new HOOD ORNAMENT and SMOOTH HORIZONTAL GRILLE PIECE (ON CLIPPER ONLY)

53 (2600 SERIES)

CLIPPER SERIES RETURNS (PREVIOUSLY AVAIL. 1941 – 1947)

new CAVALIER 127" WB

$3234.

MAYFAIR

MAYFAIR H/T ALSO, W/O 3 CHROME REAR FENDER PLAQUES SEEN ON ABOVE CVT.

400 PATRICIAN

new GROOVES IN HORIZONTAL GRILLE PIECE (EXCEPT ON CLIPPER)

$5209.

new CARIBBEAN

270

PANAMA

CLIPPER
DELUXE

SUPER CLIPPER

122," 127" OR 149" WB
150, 165, 185 OR 212 HP

54

(5400 SERIES)

DASH

CAVALIER

PATRICIAN

FINAL STRAIGHT-8 ENGINES
(288, 327 OR 359 CID)

STUDEBAKER-
PACKARD
MERGER

122" WB

CLIPPER

FIRST MAJOR
RESTYLING
SINCE 1951

new V8
ENG.
with
O.H.V.
(320 OR 352 CID)

PATRICIAN

PRICE
RANGE:
$2586. TO $5932.

225, 245 OR 260
HP @ 4600 RPM

55

(5500
SERIES)

127" WB

400

CARIBBEAN

271

PACKARD

2731.

CLIPPER DELUXE

CLIPPER _SUPER_ also avail.

$3069.

CUSTOM CLIPPER

CUSTOM CLIPPER
CONSTELLATION H/T
3164.

MEMBERS of CLIPPER
GRILLE NOW
HORIZONTAL.

122" WB
(CLIPPERS)
OTHERS, 127" WB

56
(5600 SERIES)

New DISPLACEMENT
OF 374 CID ON
ALL PACKARD V8
ENGINES. ALL BUT
CARIBBEAN *have*
290 HP @ 4600 RPM.

3483.

EXECUTIVE

H/T
$3658.

WIDER-SPACED
GRILLE PIECES
with MESH
BACKGROUND

$4160.

PATRICIAN

$4190.
400
H/T

"ASK THE MAN WHO OWNS _the New_ ONE"

$5995.

CARIBBEAN
has 310 HP @ 4600 RPM

272

PACKARD

57 (57-L SERIES) *new* 120½" WB

$3212.

new SMALLER DISPLACEMENT OF 289 CID

HP REDUCED TO 275 @ 4800 RPM

CLIPPER SEDAN and WAGON are ONLY CHOICES LISTED DURING 1957.

new 116½" WB BODIES LIKE STUDEBAKER (THROUGH '58)

275 HP (THROUGH '58)

WAGON

$3384. (AS IN '57) (58-L SERIES)

58 THE FINAL PACKARDS

ENG. SPECS. AS IN 1957.

See the all-new '58 Packards:
- The panoramic Packard Hardtop
- The supercharged Packard Hawk
- The luxurious Packard 4-door Sedan
- The versatile Packard Station Wagon

Studebaker-Packard
CORPORATION
Where pride of Workmanship comes first!

SEDAN

FRONT END DETAILS

new HAWK H/T

4 HEADLIGHTS (EXCEPT ON HAWK)

HAWK has 2 HEADLIGHTS, LOWER GRILLE

$3995.

PLAYBOY

48 HP with 133 CID HERCULES ENGINE OR 40 HP with 91 CID CONT. ENG.

STEEL RETRACTABLE TOP

97 BLT. 4 CYL.

PLAYBOY MOTOR CAR CORP., BUFFALO, N.Y. (1946-1951)

48

3.73 OR 4.1 GEAR RATIO 90" W.B.

$985.

INTER.

273

PLYMOUTH DIVISION

CHRYSLER
CORPORATION

Plymouth   (SINCE JUNE, 1928)

DASH

6 CYLINDERS
(SINCE 1933)

new 117½" WB
(THROUGH 1948)
6.00 × 16 TIRES (TO 1947)

new 1-PIECE
REAR WINDOW

2-DR.

ROAD KING

COUPE

WAGON

DE LUXE

201.3 CID
(SINCE '34)

new
84 HP @ 3600 RPM
(87 HP *with*
ALUMINUM
CYL. HEAD)

new
ROTARY DOOR LATCHES

WIPERS NOW
FASTENED
BELOW
WINDSHIELD

40

CVT.

PLYMOUTH
BUILDS GREAT CARS

ROAD KING MODELS DO NOT
HAVE ADDITIONAL ROTATING
VENT-WINDOWS IN
FRONT
DOORS.

P-9   ROAD KING
P-10   DE LUXE

COUPES START AT | SEDANS START AT
$645 | $699
DELIVERED IN DETROIT, MICH.

SEDAN

new GRILLE
and SEALED-BEAM
HEADLIGHTS

274

Plymouth

DE LUXE

SPEC. DLX.

$685. 41
AND UP

P-11   DE LUXE
P-12   SPECIAL DE LUXE

2 VIEWS OF DASH

87 OR 92 HP @ 3800 RPM

"BUY WISELY – BUY PLYMOUTH
THE CAR THAT STANDS UP
BEST"

new CLUB
COUPE (5-PASS.)

4-DR., 5-WINDOW
TOWN
SEDAN ('42 ONLY)

95 HP @ 3400 RPM

(RESTYLED)

42

P-14C
SPEC. DLX.

P-14S DE LUXE

275

FRONT DETAIL

Plymouth

SPECIAL DE LUXE *has* CHROME EFFECT on WINDSHIELD FRAME

1946 *has* FLAT BUTTON TYPE DOOR LOCK COVERS.

1948 *has new* 7.50 x 15 LOW-PRESSURE TIRES.

46-48*

P-15S DLX. or P-15C SPECIAL DLX.

* = CONT'D. TO 2-49

95 HP @ 3600 RPM

REAR (SEDAN)

CLUB COUPE

$1075. TO $2068.
(PRICE RANGE, 1946 TO EARLY 1949)

CONVERTIBLE DASH IS PAINTED IN BODY COLOR, INSTEAD OF *being* WOODGRAINED.

SEDAN INTERIOR

276

SPECIAL DE LUXE *has* RADIO GRILLE

DE LUXE

Plymouth

new ALL-METAL 2-DR.
SUBURBAN WAGON

P-17

SEDAN
REAR DOORS
NOW
FRONT-HINGED

6.40 x 15
OR 6.70 x 15
TIRES
(THROUGH '52)

SPECIAL DELUXE
4-DOOR WAGON has
WOODEN PANELS.

P-18

97 HP @ 3600 RPM
(THROUGH '52)

CLUB COUPE

new
"Double-Size"
CVT. BACKLIGHT
has REMOVABLE,
ZIPPERED CENTER
SECTION

49

P-17 (111" WB)
P-18 (118½" WB)

(TOTALLY
RESTYLED)

HORIZONTAL
CREASES ON
BUMPERS
('49 ONLY)
new
SWITCH-KEY
STARTING

SLOGAN: "The car that likes
to be compared"

277

Plymouth

DE LUXE

3-WINDOW BUSINESS COUPE

SPECIAL DE LUXE

PRICE RANGE: $1371. TO $2372.

50 *new* EMBLEM

P-19 DE LUXE (111" WB)

P-20 DE LUXE; SPEC. DLX. (118½" WB)

DASH

new SMOOTH BUMPER SURFACE

new GRILLE *has* FEWER PIECES.

Plymouth

P-22 CONCORD

111" WB

1951 MODELS ILLUSTRATED UNLESS OTHERWISE NOTED.

1951 BELVEDERE is new H/T.

SHIELD BADGE REPLACED BY CIRCLE ON '52.

MODEL NAME IN SCRIPT ON 1952 FRONT FENDER

P-23 CAMBRIDGE and CRANBRK. have 118½" WB

51-52

new CONCORD, CAMBRIDGE, CRANBROOK MODEL NAMES

('51)

DASH

'50 PLYMOUTH TAXI

1952 BELVEDERE (BELOW) has new REAR COLOR SWEEP

('52)

Plymouth

100 HP @ 3600 RPM

SAVOY WAGON

CRANBROOK BELVEDERE

new SPORT WIRE WHEELS OPTIONAL

53

(TOTALLY RESTYLED)
P-24-1 CAMBRIDGE
P-24-2 CRANBR.

A 21769

CRANBROOK

new 114" WB (THROUGH '54)

6.70 x 15 TIRES (TO '56)

P-25-3 BELVEDERE

P-25-1 PLAZA

LATE '54 has new 230.2 CID and 110 HP @ 3600 RPM

P-25-2 SAVOY

$1618. UP

54

EARLY 1954 BELVEDERE H/T DOES NOT HAVE THIS COLOR BAND ON SIDE

BELVEDERE

280

Plymouth

230 CID 6 CYL. OR new 241 CID or 260 CID V8s.

new AUTOMATIC TRANSMISSION CONTROL on DASH

PLAZA

SAVOY

PRICED FROM $1639.

55

6 = 117 HP @ 4000 RPM

V8 = 157 OR 167 HP @ 4400 RPM

(TOTALLY RESTYLED with new "FORWARD LOOK")

new 115" WB (THROUGH '56)

CLUB COUPE

new PANORAMIC WINDSHIELD

BELVEDERE

H/T

6-CYL. has STRAIGHT EMBLEM ABOVE GRILLE →

new FRENCHED HEADLIGHTS

1955

V8 has ABOVE TYPE OF EMBLEM

281

Plymouth

SUBURBAN

6.70 × 15 TIRES (ALL BUT new FURY)

CUSTOM SUBURBAN

SPORT SUBURBAN

PLAZA

BELVEDERE

SEDAN (ABOVE)
4-DR. H/T (BELOW)

PUSHBUTTON POWERFLITE:

SAVOY

56 P-28 (6) P-29 (V8)

125, 180, 187, 200, 240 or 270 HP

H/T

new **Fury** (WITH 303 CID V8) 7.10 × 15 TIRES)

new SHARPLY- PEAKED TAIL FINS

new MESH AT GRILLE CENTER

1956

Plymouth

PLAZA

EARLY '57 (6 OPEN SLOTS BELOW BUMPERS)

BELVEDERE

SAVOY

BELVEDERE

LATE '57 (EXTRA VERTICAL MEMBERS BELOW BUMPERS)

318 CID V8 IN FURY

new 118" WB (122" WB ON WAGONS) (THROUGH '61)

new 8.00 × 14 TIRES ON FURY H/T

SPORT SBN. (BELV.)

TAILGATE WINDOW DETAILS

SECRET LUGGAGE COMPARTMENT. Almost 10 cubic feet of locked space for safe, out-of-sight storage of luggage, cameras and other valuables. On all 6-pass. models.

132, 197, 215, 235 OR 290 HP

new 7.50 × 14 TIRES (ALL BUT FURY)

57

(TOTALLY RESTYLED)

P-30 (6)
P-31 (V8)

$1899. UP

DASH

283

Plymouth

58

LP-1 (6)
LP-2 (V8)

The De Luxe Suburban—2-door, 6-passenger

The Custom Suburban—2-door, 6-passenger

The Custom Suburban—4-door, 9- or 6-passenger

SPORT SUBURBAN

The Plaza 2-door Business Coupe

The Savoy 4-door Sedan

The Savoy 4-door Hardtop

The Belvedere 4-door Sedan

The Belvedere Convertible

Star of the Forward Look

INSTRUMENT CLUSTER

7.50 × 14 TIRES
BELVEDERE

(8.00 × 14 ON
9-PASS. WAGONS
and FURY H/T)

FURY

4 HEADLIGHTS

230 CID 6 (132 HP @ 3600)
318 CID V8
(225 OR 250 HP @ 4400)
350 CID V8
(305 OR 315 HP
@ 5000 RPM)

newest engine—"Golden Commando V-8"
(WITH ELECTRONIC FUEL INJECTION)

SILVER SPECIAL (RARE!)
(PLAZA)

284

Plymouth

CUSTOM SUBURBAN

SAVOY

4-door Sedan, V-8 or 6.

BELVEDERE

2-door Sedan, V-8 or 6

OPTIONAL *new* SWIVEL SEATS (STD. IN SPORT FURY)

59 MP-1 (6) MP-2 (V8)

7.50 × 14 TIRES

DASH

SPORT SUBURBAN

new SPORT FURY H/T

FINAL USE OF L-HEAD DESIGN IN PLYMOUTH SIX

new "CONTINENTAL BULGE" ON DECK LID

FURY

230 CID 6 (132 HP @ 3600)
318 CID V8 (230 OR 260 HP @ 4400 RPM)
361 CID V8 (305 HP @ 4600 RPM)

285

Plymouth

SAVOY

BELVEDERE

V8s have 318, 361, or 383 CID (230, 260, 305, 310, 325 or 330 HP)

new SLANTING O.H.V. 225 CID 6 (145 HP @ 4000 RPM) (TO '71)

note THE REAR FENDER ORNAMENTS WHICH IDENTIFY EACH INDIVIDUAL MODEL SERIES.

CUSTOM SUBURBAN

FURY

4-DR. H/T

2-DR. H/T

WITH SEMI-RECTANGULAR STEERING WHEEL

WITHOUT GRILLE GUARD

WITH GRILLE GUARD

60

PP-1 (6 CYL.)
PP-2 (V8)

SHOWN with ROUND STEERING WHEEL

DASH

7.50 × 14 TIRES

CLOSER DETAILS OF WAGON

286

Plymouth

Battery-saving Alternator keeps battery charged when generators can't. Many police and taxi fleets pay extra to get special Alternator installations. Yet the amazing new Alternator is standard equipment on all 1961 Chrysler Corporation cars.

7.00 × 14 TIRES (6)
7.50 × 14 ON 6-CYL. WAGONS and V8s.
8.00 × 14 ON 9-PASS. V8 WAGON

ALTERNATOR TEST DETROIT to CHICAGO

PLYMOUTH — This car traveled 328 miles without a battery. Alternator, standard on 1961 Chrysler Corporation cars, provided all necessary electrical energy.

SPT. SBN.

61
RP-1 (6)
RP-2 (V8)

145 TO 375 HP

$2260. UP

FURY

LARGEST OF 4 PLYMOUTH V8s IS new 413 CID ENGINE (UP TO 375 HP @ 5200 RPM)

118" WB (WAGONS 122")

GRILLE GUARD AVAIL. ON SOME 1961 MODELS

new GRILLE   287   ...SOLID BEAUTY

Plymouth

Look at Plymouth now!

SAVOY

PRICED FROM
$2531.

SAVOY

6 = 6.50 × 14 TIRES
V8 = 7.00 × 14

BELVEDERE

Plymouth Belvedere 2-dr Sedan

62
(TOTALLY RESTYLED)

SP-1 (6)
SP-2 (V8)

New Forward Flair Design

FURY

new 116" WB

FURY

145 TO
410 HP

TURBO-
FURY (SPECIAL)

NEW SPORT FURY

Special red, white and blue insignia, new wheel covers and new rear deck design tell you that this one is the real thing! There is no mistaking a new Sport Fury—hardtop or convertible.

Action! Fly to 60 mph in 8.5 secs. with optional 305-hp Golden Commando V-8 engine.

288

Plymouth

SAVOY

BELVEDERE

7.00 x 14 TIRES

FURY

FURY

V8 OPTIONS

318 CID (230 HP @ 4400)
361 CID (265 HP @ 4400)
383 CID (320 to 330 HP)
426 CID (370 HP @
4600 to 425 HP
@ 5600 RPM)

1963 IS ONLY YEAR
with UNUSUAL
FRONT CORNER
PARK./DIRECTIONAL
LIGHTS

FURY

MB·2560

with a 5-year or 50,000-mile warranty

63

TP-1 (6 CYL.)
TP-2 (V8)

new GRILLE
new TAIL-LIGHTS
new FULL-LENGTH SIDE TRIM

Get up and go Plymouth!

new
426 CID V8 ENGINE
KNOWN AS
"Super Stock"

DASH

- **A** Transmission Drive Selector (optional)
- **B** Transmission Parking Lock
- **C** Clock (optional)
- **D** Turn Signal Indicator
- **E** Heater Controls (optional)
- **F** Headlights and Panel Lights
- **G** Defroster Outlets
- **H** Windshield Wiper Control
- **I** Ignition Switch
- **J** Cigarette Lighter
- **K** Ash Receiver
- **L** Glove Compartment Lock
- **M** Radio (optional)

N·1558

SPORT FURY

PLYMOUTH'S ON 289 THE MOVE

Plymouth

7.00 × 14 TIRES

BELVEDERE

Savoy 2-Door Sedan

SAVOY

Savoy 6- or 9-Passenger Station Wagon

318, 361, 383 and 426 CID V8s

FURY

230 to 425 HP

64

VP-1 (6 CYL.) (V8) VP-2

BELV.

FURY wagon

REAR OF FURY WAGON

$3/95.

SPORT FURY

new H/T ROOFLINE

new CONVEX GRILLE

290

Plymouth

BELVEDERE II

116" WB

Belvedere Satellite

1965

Belvedere I

new BELVEDERE SATELLITE IS AVAIL. WITH TOP-OF-LINE 426 CID V8 WITH 425 HP @ 6000 RPM.

BELV. has 7.35 x 14 TIRES (EXC. WAGON)

EU-6778

Fury I

273 CID BARRACUDA V8 ENG. NOW AVAIL. IN BELVEDERE I (180 HP @ 4200 RPM)

PACE CAR AT 1965 INDY 500 RACE

SPORT FURY

Fury II

DASH

Fury III

7.75 x 14 TIRES
8.55 x 14 (FURY WAGON)

FURY III

145 TO 425 HP

65

AR-1 (6-CYL.)
AR-2 (V8)

ALL FURY TYPES GET *new* 119" WB (WAGONS 121")

Fury III 4-Door Hardtop

THE ROARING '65s

PONTIAC MOTOR DIVISION of
GENERAL MOTORS CORPORATION

Pontiac
AMERICA'S FINEST LOW-PRICED CAR

SINCE 1926

6.00 × 16 TIRES
(SINCE '35;
6-CYL.)

SPECIAL 6

Pontiac's sealed chassis is where Pontiac's amazing durability begins. Rugged, powerful, yet with micromatic precision in every vital unit, the Pontiac chassis is engineered to serve well long past the point when the average car is past its prime.

AMERICA'S FINEST
LOW-PRICED CAR

DELUXE 6

40

SPECIAL 6

DELUXE 8

TORPEDO 8

"Silver Streak" CHROME STRIPS ALONG HOOD, REAR DECK,
A PONTIAC
CHARACTERISTIC
SINCE
1935.

ONLY
$783*
FOR THE
SPECIAL SIX
BUSINESS
COUPE
OTHER MODELS
SLIGHTLY HIGHER
*PONTIAC FOR PRICE AND PERFORMANCE

A-11214
1940

"HA" SPECIAL 6 MODEL 25
has 117" WB

"HB" DELUXE 6 MODEL 26
and "HA" DLX.8 MODEL 28
have 120" WB

"HB" TORPEDO 8 MODEL 29
has 122" WB

TRIPLE-TIERED
BUMPER
GUARD
AVAIL.
ALSO

292

Pontiac Torpedoes

PONTIAC PRICES BEGIN AT
$828*
*FOR DE LUXE "TORPEDO" SIX BUSINESS COUPE

CUSTOM TORPEDO

STREAMLINER TORPEDO

DELUXE TORPEDO

CUSTOM TORPEDO

[ONLY $25 MORE FOR AN EIGHT IN ANY MODEL!]

41

NEW INTERIOR LUXURY is exemplified by this attractive new 1941 Pontiac instrument panel. Electric clock (except on some models) and radio at extra cost.

DETAILS OF new GRILLE and EMBLEM

THE FINE CAR Pontiac WITH THE LOW PRICE

293

Pontiac

Finest of the Famous "Silver Streaks"

TORPEDO

STREAMLINER

46

WHAT'S NEW AND IMPROVED IN THE 1946 PONTIAC

New, beautiful exterior appearance ... New instrument panel ... Heavier chrome finish ... Improved, rust-resistant bodies ... New interior trim ... Improved clutch ... New, wider wheel rims ... Longer-life muffler and tail pipe ... Improved cooling.

STREAMLINER

TORPEDO

47

NO VERTICAL PIECES IN 1947 GRILLE

TORPEDO

TORPEDO DELUXE

48

STREAMLINER DE LUXE

DE LUXE MODELS have CHROME STRIP ON SIDE of FRONT FENDER, and CHROME REAR FENDER PADS

295

PONTIAC

49

(TOTALLY RESTYLED)

ALL-STEEL WAGON

50

VERTICAL "TEETH" NOW ADDED TO UPPER SECTION OF GRILLE

WHEEL COVER →

REAR FENDER PAD DETAILS

51

L-HEAD 6 CYL. and STRAIGHT-8 ENGINES CONTINUE (THROUGH '54)

('52)

Dollar for Dollar you can't beat a
Pontiac

1952 WHEEL COVER

52

SIDE VIEW OF MASCOT

New High-Performance Economy Axle

More Power

New *Dual-Range*
Hydra-Matic Drive*

new SIDE TRIM

297

PONTIAC

CHIEFTAN SPECIAL

new "DUAL STREAK" RESTYLING
FEATURES TWIN GROUPS of
CHROME BANDS ALONG HOOD
and DECK, with new BODIES

CHIEFTAN DE LUXE

53

new
1-PIECE
WINDSHIELD

WAGONS *with* GRAIN-DECORATED
UPPER PANELS (ABOVE) ARE PRICED
$80. ABOVE SIMILAR WAGONS
of ONE SOLID COLOR ONLY.

new 122" WB

$ **1956.**

$ **2774.**

PRICE
RANGE

The experimental Parisienne stands only
56 inches high. Inside and out it is a
designer's dream of how one "car of the
future" might be styled and equipped.

PARISIENNE
(SHOW CAR)
PUBLICLY DISPLAYED, BUT
NOT A PRODUCTION BODY
TYPE

De Luxe Catalina

Dollar for Dollar you can't beat a
Pontiac

298

PONTIAC

CHIEFTAN SPECIAL 6
(ALSO AVAIL. as 8)

CHIEFTAN DELUXE
(6 OR 8 CYL.)

A BRIEF (1 YR.) RETURN TO SINGLE GROUP OF CHROME STRIPS ON HOOD and DECK

54

new GRILLE with EMBLEM PLACED ABOVE

STAR CHIEF CUSTOM 8
(AT RIGHT and BELOW)

THE NEW *Star Chief*

8-CYL. SERIES IDENTIFIED BY THESE "STARS" ON SIDE OF REAR FENDER

STAR CHIEF DE LUXE 8 (BELOW) COSTS LESS THAN CUSTOM 8

CVT.

FRONT END and WHEEL COVER DETAILS

PONTIAC

(TOTALLY RESTYLED)

55

CHIEFTAN 860

Pontiac leads in station wagon value with four models — the beautiful 860, left, in two- and four-door models, the spectacular 870 four-door and the fabulous Safari.

new PANORAMIC WINDSHIELD →

CHIEFTAN 870

CHIEFTAN ═ 122" WB

STAR CHIEF ═ 124" WB

CHIEFTAN 870 CATALINA H/T (2 VIEWS)

new DASH

PRICE RANGE: $2105. TO $3128.

ALL MODELS *with new* "STRATO-STREAK" O.H.V. V8 ENGINE → 180 OR 200 HP

STAR CHIEF CUSTOM CATALINA (CVT. ALSO AVAIL.)

new STAR CHIEF CUST. SAFARI 2 DR. LUXURY WAGON

Pontiac's flair for years-ahead styling was never more evident than in the fabulous all-new Safari.

BUMPER GUARDS AVAILABLE (RARE)

300

CHIEFTAN

SAFARI

STAR CHIEF

new 4-DR. H/

56 Pontiac

TO 227 HP

STAR CHIEF *Custom Convertible*

PLASTIC "JR. STAR CHIEF" CHILD'S ELECTRIC CARS ALSO, FOR DEALER PROMOTIONAL PURPOSES

REAR DETAILS

301

PONTIAC

CHIEFTAN
252 HP

SUPER CHIEF
270 HP

STAR CHIEF
270 HP

SAFARI WAGON

57

SU. CHIEF WAGON DOOR

PONTIAC
1957

BONNEVILLE
(new)

(LIMITED PRODUCTION)

STAR CHIEF has HEAVY CHROME BAND PLACED WITHIN COLOR CONTRAST PANEL on REAR FENDER

1957

AMERICA'S NUMBER 1 ROAD CAR!

new FRONT END (NO LONGER USES "Silver Streak" CHROME BANDS)

STAR CH. 2-DR. H/T

302

PONTIAC

CHIEFTAN

3 STAR-LIKE FIGS. ON REAR FENDER of CHIEFTAN; 4 on SUPER CHIEF. (EACH MODEL CAN BE IDENTIFIED BY FENDER DECOR., AS ILLUS. BELOW)

SUPER CHIEF

USA·1958
AMERICA'S NO.1 ROAD CAR

58
(RESTYLED)

STAR CHIEF

BOLDEST ADVANCE IN 50 YEARS

BOLD NEW **Bonneville** BY PONTIAC

PACE CAR AT 1958 INDY 500 RACE

BONNEVILLE

303

PONTIAC

CATALINA

new "WIDE-TRACK"

59

(TOTALLY RESTYLED)

122" WB (CATALINA SERIES and on BONNEVL. WAGON)
124" WB on OTHERS

new BONNEVILLE VISTA 4-DR. H/T

"BONNEVILLE" NAME on BONNEVL. GRILLE

CATALINA SAFARI WAGON

(WIDTH EXAGGERATED)

"PONTIAC" NAME ON GRILLE OF CATALINA and STAR CHIEF. STAR CHIEF has STAR-LIKE FIGURES ALONG SIDE OF REAR FENDER.

DASH

8.00 × 14 TIRES

245 HP (280 w. Hydra Matic)
BONNEVL. has 260 HP (300 w. Hyd.)

304

PONTIAC 1960

STAR CHIEF

THE ONLY CAR WITH WIDE·TRACK WHEELS

WAGON AND VISTA DETAILS

BONNEVILLE

60

VENTURA H/T

CATALINA
2-DR.

SAFARI

61
(RESTYLED)

BONNEVILLE
(STAR CHF. TAILLIGHTS
SIMILAR)

305

PONTIAC

STAR CIHEF

61
CONT'D.

BONNEVILLE
OFTEN *has*
"BONNEVILLE"
NAME ON GRILLE
AS ILLUSTR.

VISTA 4 DOOR HARDTOPS

STAR CHIEF

STAR CHIEF VISTA

Wide-Track Pontiac
WIDEST STANCE ON THE ROAD

62

Bonneville

CATALINA

CATALINA 9-PASSENGER SAFARI

306

(CONTINUED)

STRATO - CHIEF
(SOLD ONLY IN CANADA)

WAGONS

LAURENTIAN
2 - DOOR

PONTIAC

62
(CONT'D.)

LAURENTIAN
(SOLD ONLY IN
CANADA)

SPORT COUPE

SPORT COUPES

1962

GP

PARISIENNE
(SOLD ONLY IN CANADA)

SEDAN

GRAND PRIX
New →
DETAILS

MANUAL
SHIFT
CONSOLE

BUCKET
SEATS

TACH.

AUTO.
SHIFT
CONSOLE

303 HP
4 BBL. CARB.

$3917.

307

PONTIAC

CATALINA

9-PASSENGER SAFARI

STAR CHIEF 4-DOOR SEDAN

CATALINA SPORTS SEDAN

BONNEVILLE SPORTS COUPE

BONNEVILLE VISTA

CATALINA / ST. CHIEF

CATALINA

BONNEVILLE

63

2 VIEWS OF G.P.

GP
PONTIAC GRAND PRIX

'63 WIDE-TRACK PONTIAC

308

PONTIAC 120" WB CATALINA

STAR CHIEF
(FRONT SIMILAR TO CATALINA)
123" WB
235 HP

64

CATALINA SEDAN

BONNEVILLE

BONNEVILLE

123" WB

WHEEL COVER

BONN. BROUGHAM
w. VINYL TOP (BELOW)

INTERIOR

$3995.
(CVT.)

306 HP

PRESTON CLOTH-and-MORROKIDE INTERIOR

G.P.

120" WB

WAGON
(BONNEVILLE)

309

PONTIAC

CATALINA

CATALINA 2+2

note LOUVRES ON COWL OF 2+2

BON. BROUGHAM INTERIOR

BONNEVILLE

BONNEVILLE (325 HP)
BROUGHAM 4-DR. H/T

65

G.P.

CAT. 2+2 INTERIOR

Pontiac for 1965
The year of the Quick Wide-Tracks

new GRILLE

Grand Prix

310

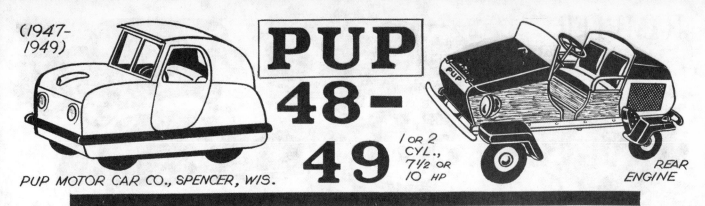

(1947-1949)

PUP 48-49

PUP MOTOR CAR CO., SPENCER, WIS.

1 OR 2 CYL., 7½ OR 10 HP

REAR ENGINE

AT NASH DEALERS

Rambler 6 CYL.

TOP DOWN
TOP UP

$1808., f.o.b.
(CVT. OR WAGON)

100" WB
82 HP

MODEL 5021
New Rambler Convertible Landau
(CUSTOM SERIES)

50

"RAMBLER" NAME REVIVED BY NASH FOR THIS NEW COMPACT SERIES.
CVT. INTRO. 3-50; WAGON 5-50

51-52

new "SUPER"

MODEL 5127 (5227)
"COUNTRY CLUB" HARDTOP
INTRO. 6-51

SUBURBAN MODEL 5114 (5214)

FIRST 2 DIGITS OF MODEL NUMBER INDICATE YEAR OF CAR

57,555 RAMBLERS BLT. 1951;
53,055 RAMBLERS SOLD IN 1952

CONVERTIBLE CONTINUES

RAMBLER

85 HP
(90 with
Hydra-Matic)

5321
CVT.

CUSTOM

53

5327
COUNTRY
CLUB H/T

GREENBRIER

SUPER 2-DR.
SUBURBAN IS LOWEST-
PRICED : $ **2003.**, f.o.b.

5406
CLUB
SEDAN

new DE LUXE

SUPER

5417

$**1550.**, f.o.b.

5414

Nash Motors, Division of
AMERICAN MOTORS CORP.
DETROIT, MICH.

54

100" and
108" WB

5425

5427

CUSTOM

note LUGGAGE RACK
AND DIP IN REAR
ROOFLINE

REAR
DETAILS
(CROSS-
COUNTRY)

312

new 4-DR.
"CROSS-COUNTRY" WAGON (5428)

RAMBLER — a Whole **New Idea** in Automobiles

DELUXE

5514

5515

SUPER

NEW IDEA! *Touch this knob—and it will always be springtime in your Rambler. No cold in winter! No heat in summer! No dust or traffic roar! You breathe only fresh, filtered air. It's American Motors' All-Season Air Conditioning*—greatest health, comfort, safety feature of fifty years. Needs no trunk space. And you buy a Rambler so equipped for less than the price of an ordinary car!* *Patents applied for*

PRICES START AT

$1585., f.o.b. (DLx. 2-DR.)

5517 COUNTRY CLUB

CUSTOM

new GRILLE *with* CRISS-CROSS PIECES

ON 9-22-55, FINAL AMC CAR ASSEMBLED AT EL SEGUNDO, CALIF. BRANCH FACTORY, *with* "DC-" SERIAL NUMBERS. KENOSHA, WIS. FACTORY CONTINUES *with* "D-" SERIAL NUMBERS AS USUAL.

55

83,852 BLT.

CROSS-COUNTRY

5518

INTERIOR (H/T)

HUDSON RAMBLER

NASH RAMBLER

(DETERMINE BY NAME-PLATE ON GRILLE)

NOW AT *Nash* DEALERS AND **HUDSON** DEALERS EVERYWHERE

American Motors 313

RAMBLER

You'll make the Smart Switch for '56

Product of American Motors

AMERICAN MOTORS MEANS [logo] MORE FOR AMERICANS

See Disneyland—great TV for all the family over ABC network.

DE LUXE 5615

SUPER 5618-1

$2230 America's lowest-priced 4-door station wagon, delivered at the factory, including federal taxes. State and local taxes (if any), white wall tires and optional equipment (if desired), extra.

YOU SAVE ON FIRST COST. Model for model, Rambler is lowest-priced of all, with similar equipment, yet you get luxuries that rival the $5,000 cars—Power Brakes standard on custom models!

YOU SAVE ⅓ ON GASOLINE. New Typhoon OHV engine, with 33% more power, delivers up to 200 more miles on a tankful than other low-price cars.

new 120-HP SIX *with* OVERHEAD VALVES

79,166 BLT.

new BROADER GRILLE ENCOMPASSES HEADLIGHTS

56

(RESTYLED) 108" WB ON ALL

Box-Girders All Around Passengers — Box-Sections Absorb Impact — The Old Way — SEE THE DIFFERENCE

Make the Smart Switch to Double Safe Single Unit Car Construction. All-welded, twice as rigid with "double lifetime" durability—means higher resale value.

NOTE VARIATIONS IN UPPER SIDE TRIM →

CUSTOM

Make the Smart Switch to the car that out-corners, out-parks them all. Entirely new ride—first low-priced car with Deep Coil Springs on all four wheels.

"Make the Smart Switch to Rambler!"

new COLOR SPEAR SIDE MOULDINGS ON CUSTOM

2 VIEWS OF *new* 4-DOOR H/T 5619-2

Make the Smart Switch to Airliner Reclining Seat luxury. You have a nap couch to keep children fidget-free on trips, relax grown-ups. Even a chaise longue!

new ROLL-DOWN REAR DOOR WINDOW → 5618-2

New Rambler Cross Country Station Wagon! Enjoy more fun per mile and per dollar in America's lowest-priced four-door Custom Station Wagon.

FLASH! RAMBLER TOPS MOBILGAS ECONOMY RUN FOR 2nd STRAIGHT YEAR! 24.35 m.p.g. with Hydra-Matic Drive!

OVERDRIVE AVAIL.

314

RAMBLER

CUSTOM

Rambler 6 or V·8

new 190 H.P. V·8
And Economy 6

5718-1 (6)
5728-1 (V8)

5718-2 (6)
5728-2 (V8)
CROSS-COUNTRY

GEORGE ROMNEY
PRESIDENT, AMERICAN MOTORS
(UNTIL 2-62)

SUPER

new REBEL V8

5739-2

255 HP
327 CID V8

AVAIL. AS REGULAR
OR HARDTOP
WAGON

5723-2 (V8)

SIDE MOULDINGS
CHANGED

Rambler Custom

6.70 x 15

5729-2 (V8)

315

57

20 MODELS

SMALL EXTRA PIECE
ADDED, IN TOP SECTION
OF GRILLE

114,084
RAMBLERS BLT.
1957

RAMBLER

5802 or 5806

DE LUXE

$1775., f.o.b. and up

new AMERICAN 6 (100" WB) 42,196 SOLD

127 HP 6 SUPER

58

new GRILLES

new TAIL-FINS (ON ALL BUT AMERICAN)

MORE THAN 100 IMPROVEMENTS! 22 MODELS

CUSTOM

INTRODUCED for 1958, new AMERICAN and AMBASSADOR MODELS have OWN GRILLES, DIFFERENT FROM THOSE OF OTHER RAMBLERS.

215-HP REBEL V8

REBEL V8

5829-2

DASH

5888-1 or 2

new AMBASSADOR V8 117" WB

new = 4 HEADLIGHTS

270 HP (THROUGH '59)

5889-2

$2822., f.o.b.

316

186,227 RAMBLERS SOLD 1958

new "DEEP-DIP" RUSTPROOFING

RAMBLER

5902
5906

STATION WAGON

New 100 inch wheelbase
Rambler American

AMERICAN

$1835 Suggested delivered price at Kenosha, Wisconsin, for 2-door sedan at left. State and local taxes, if any, automatic transmission and optional equipment, extra.

SUPER

5915-1

5904-1
AMERICAN WAGON
IS *new*
90 HP

PUSH-BUTTON TRANS. AVAIL. ←

CUSTOM

5915-2

REBEL
108" WB

CROSS-COUNTRY
5928-1 OR 2

REBEL

AMBASSADOR

5985-1 OR 2

5929-2
COUNTRY
CLUB

117" WB

270 HP V8

AMBASSADOR
CUSTOM

59

5989-2

$2822..
f.o.b.

DASH   317

RAMBLER

6005

90 HP **AMERICAN**

6004

DOORS NOW OPEN WIDER (75° INSTEAD OF 55°)

ROOF RACKS NOW ON *ALL* WAGONS

6002 $1781., f.o.b. and up

60

6015

6
DELUXE
108" WB
127 HP

6018 WAGON

SUPER

6015-1 (6)
6025-1 (V8)

SEDAN

6015-2 (6)
6025-2 (V8)

CUSTOM COUNTRY CLUB
6019-2 (6)
6029-2 (V8)

REAR DETAILS ↓

6018 or 6028 (-2 or 4)

CUSTOM

new REAR FENDERS

V8 = 200 HP

3 WIDE SEATS, 5 BIG DOORS. The tailgate is a fifth door with outside key lock so children can't open from inside. Rear seat passengers step in—no scrambling over seats or tailgate.

new "COMPOUND WRAP-AROUND" WINDSHIELD *on* AMBASSADOR

WAGON (6 or 8-PASS.) 6088-1 TO 4
2881., f.o.b., and up

434,704 RAMBLERS SOLD 1960

AMB. CUSTOM COUNTRY CLUB 6089-2

AMBASSADOR V-8
BY RAMBLER

The New Standard of Basic Excellence in Luxury Cars

RAMBLER

6104

6105

6/08 4-DR. WAGONS *also*

6107-2
" -5

$2369.,
f.o.b., *and up*

All New! A Convertible

"THE NEW WORLD STANDARD OF BASIC EXCELLENCE"

AMER. PRICES
START AT
1831.,
f.o.b.
(6/02)

AMERICAN 6
L-HEAD
90 OR
125 HP
OHV

AMERICAN
WAGON
REAR
DETAILS

new Ceramic-Armored Muffler

61
(RESTYLED)

CLASSIC 6 OR V8
127 OR 138 HP
6
OR
200 OR 215 HP
V8

CLOSE
DETAIL
OF CLASSIC FRONT END ↑

RAMBLER

1961

CLASSIC
DELUXE

CLASSIC
CUSTOM
6/08-2 (6)
6/28-4 (V8)
(CLASSIC 2-DR. WAGONS *also*)

...New! First acoustical ceiling
of molded fiber glass

AMBASSADOR V8
↙ 250 OR 270 HP

6188-1,2 OR 4

CUSTOM 400 SEDAN JOINS
AMBASSADOR LINE

6185-5

Rambler
World Standard of Compact Car Excellence

319

RAMBLER

6206

90 HP 6

1962 RAMBLER AMERICAN
DELUXE 2-DOOR CLUB SEDAN
(Also offered in Custom and "400" series)

62

1962 RAMBLER AMERICAN
DELUXE 4-DOOR SEDAN
(Also offered in Custom series)

6205

6208

RAMBLER AMERICAN DELUXE 4-DOOR STATION WAGON
(Also offered in Custom series)

6208

RAMBLER AMERICAN "400" 4-DOOR STATION WAGON
(Also offered in Deluxe and Custom series)

6207-5

AMERICAN "400" CVT.

6216-2

new

1962 RAMBLER CLASSIC CUSTOM 2-DOOR CLUB SEDAN
(Also offered in Deluxe and "400" series)

new DOUBLE SAFETY BRAKES with
TANDEM MASTER CYLINDER

6215-5

CLASSIC 400

6218-5

RAMBLER CLASSIC 6 "400" CROSS COUNTRY STATION WAGON

454,784
RAMBLERS BLT.
1962

1962 RAMBLER AMBASSADOR
CUSTOM 4-DOOR STATION WAGON

6288-2

WB CUT TO 108"

250 OR 270 HP
AMB. V8s

AMBASSADOR 400
AND INTERIOR

6285-5

RAMBLER

6302
← **220**

TOP QUALITY AT AMERICA'S LOWEST PRICE! **$1846**
Manufacturer's suggested retail price for the '63 Rambler American "220" Two-Door Sedan. Optional equipment, transportation, and state and local taxes, if any, extra. An award-winning Rambler value!

AMERICAN 6
100" WB

220 → **6304**

6305

6309-7

440-H H/T
(with 138-HP OHV 6)

440 CVT.

6306-5 **440**

6307-5

63

(CLASSICS and AMB. TOTALLY RESTYLED)

DASH

6315-2

660

CLASSIC
6 or V8
new 112" WB

OPTIONAL 198-HP V8 (STARTING 3-1-63)

770

770

6315-5

6318-5

The New Shape Of Quality

New! Hidden storage compartment in wagon!

250 or 270 HP AMBASSADOR V8
new 112" WB

880 CROSS COUNTRY

6388-2

New! Curved glass side windows ... far easier entry!

990 WAGON SIMILAR

990

6386-5 2-DR.

321

AMBASSADOR has LOWER BODY BAND

6385-5 SEDAN

WINNER OF MOTOR TREND AWARD
CAR OF THE YEAR

RAMBLER

new AMER. WAGON RESEMBLES A SEDAN with GRAFTED-ON REAR SECTION

6406

220

6408

220

6407-5

AMERICAN

6.00 x 14 TIRES (15" OPT.)

330

6405-2

440-H

6409-7

YT. TOP IN BLK., WHITE, GOLD OR TURQ.

440

TO 138 HP

AMERICAN

TOTALLY RESTYLED (new 106" WB)

6418

6418-5

770

660

2-DR.

6416-2

550

CLASSIC (6 has 127 OR 138 HP)

64

770

4-DR. 6415-5

393,863 RAMBLERS BLT. 1964

6489-5

990-H (INTERIOR BELOW)

6488-5

990

DASH (WITH AIR CONDITIONING)

FRESH NEW SPIRIT OF '64!

DASH (W/O AIR CONDITIONING) →

990

250 OR 270 HP

AMBASSADOR

RAMBLER 220

6506

6508-2   6509-7   American 440-H

AMERICAN

American 6

330

New! 3 different sizes of cars
New! 3 different wheelbases
New! 7 spectacular powerplants:
New Torque Command Sixes—
most advanced engines! Big V-8's

6507-5

AMERICAN GRILLE NOW VERTICALLY SPLIT INTO 4 HORIZ. SECTIONS

L-HEAD 195.6 CID 6 STILL AVAIL. IN AMERICAN (90 HP @ 3000 RPM)

65

DASH (AMERICAN)
412,736 RAMBLERS SOLD 1965

CVTS. NOW IN ALL 3 LINES

440

195.6 OR 232 CID OHV 6s with 125 OR 155 HP

6518-5
Rambler Classic 770 Station Wagon

SEE ALSO: MARLIN

6517-5

770

CLASSIC

199 OR 232 CID 6
(128, 145, 155 HP)
198 HP
with 287 CID
V8

6519-5
Rambler Classic 770 Hardtop

CLASSIC
770 SEDAN   DASH

GRILLE CLOSE-UPS

CLAS.

ALSO AVAIL. with 327 CID, 270-HP V8 ALSO USED IN AMB.)

6515-5

6587-5

AMB. (new HEADLIGHTS VERTICALLY STACKED)

CLASSIC 112" WB CONT'D., BUT AMBASSADOR WB INCREASED TO 116".

990

AMBASSADOR V8

6589-7

SLOGAN:

DASH

AMBASSADOR

1965

65-990H

THE SENSIBLE SPECTACULARS

RIVIERA
(by Buick)

(STARTS 1963)

401 CID V8
325 HP @ 4400 RPM

117" WB

(DASH)

7.10 x 15 TIRES

63

America's bid for a great new international classic car

64

ADVENTURE IS A CAR CALLED RIVIERA — AND IT'S A BUICK

'64 DASH

(VINYL TOP ALSO AVAIL.)

new TAIL-LIGHTS IN BUMPER

65

new CONCEALED HEADLIGHTS

WIRE WHEEL OPTION

Wouldn't you really rather have a Buick?

324

(CARS = 1902-1966)

STUDEBAKER

STUDEBAKER CORP., SOUTH BEND, IND.

$660. up (CHAMP.)

116½" WB (SINCE '38)

COMMANDER 6
226.2 CID
90 HP @ 3400 RPM

CLUB SEDAN

CHAMP. 6 has 164.3 CID 78 HP @ 4000 RPM

40

CHAMP. 2-DR. IS PACE CAR AT 1940 INDY 500 RACE.

250.4 CID 122" WB
PRESIDENT 8

110 HP @ 3600 RPM

Lowest priced CHAMPION

110" WB

new WIDER GRILLES

new 169.6 CID, 80 HP (CHAMP.)

You seldom use the clutch!
That's due to Studebaker's famous gas-saving, engine-saving Economatic Shift with Overdrive—available on all Champion models at moderate extra cost.

PRICES BEGIN AT
$690
for a Champion Business Coupe
Champion Club Sedan with trunk . . $730
Champion Cruising Sedan with trunk . $770

COMMANDER
94 HP @ 3600 RPM

119" WB

41

new BAND TAPERS ALONG SIDES (EXCEPT ON SKYWAY)

Distinctively smart, new SKYWAY PRESIDENT 8

Land Cruiser

AVAILABLE ON COMMANDER SIX OR PRESIDENT EIGHT CHASSIS

117 HP @ 4000 RPM
125" WB

325

STUDEBAKER

CHAMPION 6 has 170 CID (SINCE '41 and THROUGH '54)

HIGHEST QUALITY CAR IN LOWEST PRICE FIELD

4-G

Champion 6

PRICES BEGIN AT **$810***
for a Champion Business Coupe

110" WB
5.50 x 16 TIRES

42-45

119" WB
6.25 x 16 TIRES

12-A
The Commander * 6

Studebaker is building an unlimited quantity of airplane engines, military trucks and other matériel for national defense . . . and a limited number of passenger cars which are the finest Studebakers ever produced.
The Studebaker Corporation

CHAMPION . . . $810 and up
COMMANDER . . $1108 and up
PRESIDENT 8 . . $1242 and up

f.o.b.

SKYWAY **COMMANDER** LAND CRUISER 6

PRESIDENT IS FINAL STRAIGHT-8
(FIRST PRES. 8 was 1928 MODEL)
124½" WB

8-C

World's first cars with Studebaker's new, perfected
Turbo-matic Drive
NO CLUTCH-PEDAL   NO CREEP   NO CLASH
Fluid coupling — with controlled gear selection — and automatic overdrive — available on President and Commander models at extra cost.

The President 8

OVERDRIVE AVAIL.

SKYWAY CHAMPION IS ONLY SERIES AVAIL.

"DOUBLE DATER" COUPE

DASH

EARLY **46**

RARE!
(AVAIL. ONLY TO MAY, '46)

$916.. *f.o.b.*

110" WB

326

BODIES AVAIL. = 3-PASS. COUPE;
5-PASS. "DOUBLE DATER" CPE.;
2-DR. CLUB SED.; 4-DR. CR. SEDAN

ALL-NEW 1947 MODELS START MAY, 1946

$1447.

new 112" WB ON CHAMPION 6-G

First by far with a postwar car!

THE NEW 1947 STUDEBAKER

$1442. f.o.b.

47

(TOTALLY RESTYLED)

Starlight COUPES

CHAMPION STRLT. CPE. (ABOVE) *has* 1-PC. WINDSHIELD, UNLIKE OTHER CHAMPION MODELS

$1752.

(SAME HP FIGS. SINCE '41) 14-A COMMANDER 119" WB

SEDAN

COMMANDER REGAL DE LUXE

$1910.

REGAL DE LUXE LAND CRUISER

DETAILS OF 2-DOOR SEDAN (CHAMP. REGAL DE LUXE)

123" WB

CONVERTIBLE (new)

3-W. CPE. CHAMPION

new HORIZONTAL PIECE ACROSS EITHER END OF CHAMPION GRILLE

$1535., f.o.b.

New 1948 Studebaker
First in style

CHAMPION

SEDANS

$2077. COMMANDER

48

new HORIZ. CHROME ABOVE CMNDR. GRILLE

327

" *First in style...first in vision...first by far with a postwar car* "

$1762

CHAMPION (8-G)
NOW has 2
HORIZ. STRIPS
ACROSS
GRILLE

$1757.

$2135.,
f.o.b.

VERTICAL
CHROME CENTER
STRIP ADDED TO
CMNDR. GRILLE

STARLIGHT CPE.
and INTERIOR

49

STUDE. "STARLIGHT"
CLUB COUPES ARE AMONG
THE MOST UNUSUAL and
ATTRACTIVE BODY
STYLES EVER PRODUCED!

LAND CRUISER
INTERIOR

REAR

lowest price

new 113" WB (CHAMPIONS)   85 HP

50

new
"BULLET-NOSE"
FRONT END
STYLING

CHAMPION
CUSTOM 6-PASS.
2-DOOR SEDAN
AS SHOWN

$**1487**50

the "next look" in cars

new 6.40 x 15
TIRES

(CONT'D.)

$1676.

CHAMPION REGAL DE LUXE 6

CHROME ALONG ROCKER PANEL

Studebaker

50
(CONT'D.)

2-DR.

$1566.

CHAMPION DLX. (9-G)

has RUBBER PAD ON REAR FENDER, BUT NO CHROME ALONG ROCKER PANEL.

CVT.

America likes Studebaker's new driving thrill—Every 1950 Studebaker handles with light-touch ease—rides so smoothly it almost completely abolishes travel fatigue. A new kind of coil spring front suspension.

COMMANDER (17-A)

$2024.

$2013.

LAND CRUISER

$2187.

America likes this "next look" in interiors—Fabulously fine nylon cord upholstery, introduced into motoring by Studebaker, is standard in the 1950 Land Cruiser and regal de luxe Commander. Land Cruiser is shown.

CHAMP. CUSTOM HAS NO HOOD ORNAMENT

SEDAN

Studebaker Champion

3-WINDOW BUSINESS COUPE $1643.

51

232.6 CID IN *new* O.H.V. V8 ENGINE ALSO AVAIL.

CHAMPION DE LUXE 6 (10-G) 85 HP

$1744.

(REGAL CHAMP. *has* LEATHER TRIM INSIDE DOORS.)

A brand new V-8 (233 CID) *Commander*

CVT.

has

120 h.p. @4000 (THROUGH '54)

STATE CMNDR. SEDAN

$2143.

"BULLET NOSE" GRILLE SOMEWHAT MODIFIED FROM '50.

new GRILLE IS FLUSH WITH FRONT END

COMMANDER LAND CRUISER

$2289.

"STUDEBAKER...THE THRIFTY ONE FOR '51"

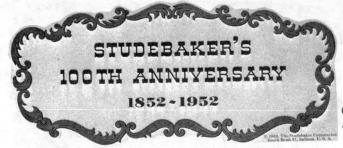

STUDEBAKER'S 100TH ANNIVERSARY
1852~1952

© 1952. The Studebaker Corporation
South Bend 27, Indiana, U. S. A.

CHAMPION
PRICES START AT
$ **1735.**

REGAL COMMANDER

REGAL CHAMPION OR
STATE COMMANDER
CONVERTS.
AVAIL.

PACE CAR
AT 1952 INDY 500 RACE

LAND CRUISER

52
FRONT END
RESTYLED

BODY DESIGN
BASICALLY
AS BEFORE,
BUT
CONTROVERSIAL
"BULLET NOSE"
DISCONTINUED
IN FAVOR OF
A MORE
CONVENTIONAL
(BUT EXTREMELY
BROAD)
GRILLE

"STARLINER"
H/T IS new

* EDITED PHOTO (FROM AD) CAUSES
THE WOMAN DRIVER
TO APPEAR
UNUSUALLY
SMALL, IN
COMPARISON
TO CAR.

STATE COMMANDER

* = A
TRICK TO
MAKE CAR
APPEAR LARGER

See and drive the Studebaker Starliner—It's America's smartest
"hard-top"—available either as a Champion or a Commander V-8.

Studebaker

H/T

53

(TOTALLY RESTYLED)

CHAMPION PRICES START AT
$**1735**.

85 HP @ 4000 RPM

170 CID 6 (THROUGH '54)

MEANS CHAMP. 6 H/T

↑ *new* DESIGN WINS FASHION ACADEMY AWARD

new 116½" WB (120½" ON CPE., H/T and LAND CRUISER)

MEANS CMNDR. V8

NO MORE CONVERTIBLES AVAILABLE (UNTIL '60 LARK)

VERTICAL PIECES ADDED TO GRILLE FOR 1954.

STUDEBAKERS, SINCE LATE 1930s, ARE Styled by *Raymond Loewy* →

CHAMPION PRICES START AT $**1758**.

54

332

CHAMPION CUSTOM

6 CYL. *has* 101 HP @ 4000 RPM (*new* 186 CID THROUGH '58)

A *BIG NEW* CHAMPION
America's No. 1 economy car!
Now more marvelous than ever!

CHAMPION PRICES START AT $ 1741.

55

CHAMPION DE LUXE

INTERIOR (CMNDR.)

COUPES

COMMANDER

(6-CYL. OR V8 WAGONS)

Now in the low price field!
A sensationally high-powered
NEW COMMANDER V-8

CONESTOGA

SPEEDSTER

STATE PRESIDENT

COMMANDER H/T DETAILS

NEW!
AMERICA'S SMARTEST TWO-TONING!

PRESIDENT

The first dynamic headliners of the great Studebaker-Packard alliance! Sensationally powered '55 Studebakers! Amazingly low introductory prices!

224 OR *new* 259 CID V8s *have* 140, 162, 175 OR 185 HP

333

CHAMPION PRICES START AT
$1841.

Studebaker

PELHAM 6

CHAMPION 6

wagons

Craftsmanship with a Flair

PARKVIEW V8

FLIGHT HAWK 6

CMNDR. V8

POWER HAWK V8

FRONT DETAILS OF COMMANDER V8

NEW DUAL EXHAUSTS · Built into the bumper for more style, more class than you've ever seen in a low price car. Ready for 4-barrel carburetion to boost mileage and power.

Hawks

SKY HAWK V8

The Golden Hawk

GOLDEN HAWK V8 (275 HP)

56

SEDAN

PRESIDENT V8

CLASSIC SEDAN has ROCKER PANEL TRIM

"CLASSIC" SEDAN

259, 289 OR 352 CID V8s

PRESIDENT V8 195 HP * @ 4500 RPM

new 12-VOLT ELECTRICAL SYSTEM

NEW CYCLOPS-EYE SPEEDOMETER

* 210 HP with 4-BBL. CARB.

334

PRESIDENT PINEHURST V8

Studebaker

CHAMP. SCOTSMAN IS A *new* BUDGET-PRICED MODEL *with* MINIMUM *of* CHROME *and* PLAINEST INTERIOR

101 HP

W-1 SEDAN

2-DR., 6-CYL. WAGONS
SCOTSMAN (116½" WB)
PELHAM (118½" WB)

PLAIN, PAINTED HUB CAPS, 6.40 x 15 TIRES

57-G
CHAMPION SCOTSMAN 6 (new)
PRICES START AT
$1776. (2-DR.)

CHAMPION DE LUXE 6

STUDEBAKER
1957

57
(RESTYLED)

116½" WB ON MOST

57-G (6 CYL.)
57-H (8 CYL.)

PROVINCIAL 4 DR. WAGON
P-4

1957
D-4
PARKVIEW 2-DR. WAGON

$2561.

COMMANDER
F-2 (CUSTOM)
F-4 (DELUXE)

$2407.
PRESIDENT
W-6

$2246. (DLX.)

Studebaker-Packard
CORPORATION

Where pride of Workmanship comes first!

335

P-6
BROADMOOR 4-DR. WAGON

289 CID (275 HP @ 4800 RPM)
V8 GOLDEN HAWK

C-3 SILVER HAWK
186 CID 6 (101 HP)

K-7

$3185.

57 (CONT'D.)

OR 210, 225 HP V8s (289 CID)

Golden Hawk

58

4 HEADLIGHTS ON SOME MODELS

Studebaker Commanders and Champions

101 TO 275 HP

(SAME HP AS '57) THE FINAL GOLDEN HAWK

180-HP CMNDR.

"Studebaker cars take on a completely new luxury look for 1958!"

SCOTSMAN 6 PRICES START AT $1795.

NOTICE STRIKING DIFFERENCES IN APPEARANCE BETWEEN THE LT.-OVER-DK. AND DK.-OVER-LT. HARDTOPS

REAR DETAILS (SEDAN)

Studebaker President

1958

The Hawk-inspired PRESIDENT STARLIGHT for 1958

Studebaker-Packard CORPORATION
Where pride of Workmanship comes first!

336

STUDEBAKER

59

HAWK 6 PRICES START AT **$2360.**

170 CID 6 (90 HP @ 4000) OR 259 CID V8s (180 OR 195 HP @ 4500)

6 OR V8

SILVER HAWK (C-6)

1959

120 ½" WB

SEE ALSO:
LARK
(STARTING 1959, LOWER-PRICED MODELS USE LARK NAME)

3 new STRIPS ON SIDE OF REAR FENDER

60
new 289 CID V8 RETURNS TO HAWK AS ONLY AVAIL. ENG. (210 OR 225 HP @ 4500 RPM)

$2650.

C-6 HAWK

6.70 × 15 TIRES

61
new TRIM DESIGN ALONG REAR FENDERS

HAWK

$2677.

(C-6)

new HAWK GT

new ROOFLINE

62 (RESTYLED)
new CLASSIC-STYLE GRILLE with HEAVY CHROME BORDERS

$3424. (UP $27. IN '63)

(K-6)

new GRILLE DESIGN with DECORATIVE CRISS-CROSS STRIPS ADDED

63

new AVANTI

HAWK GT

$4759.

AVANTI INTRO. DURING '62   109" WB
289 CID V8

337

STUDEBAKER

6.00, 6.50 OR 6.70 × 15 TIRES

AVANTI V8

113" WB

109" WB

64

109" WB COMMANDER

CHALLENGER (109" WB)

(AVAIL. 1964 ONLY)
112 HP 6 OR
180 HP V8

$2417.

113" WB ON
CRUISER V8

120" WB

1964

FINAL
GRAN TURISMO HAWK

STUDE. PRODUCTION CONTINUES ONLY AT THE CANADIAN BRANCH FACTORY, FOR '65-66.

DETAILS OF WAGONAIRE ILLUSTR. AT RIGHT

TOPSIDE LUGGAGE RACK (OPT.)

Wagonaire

BRAKE RELEASE

65

TAILGATE STEP

6 CYL. OHV ENG. (V8 ON NEXT PG.)

COMMANDER

"the Common-Sense Car"

(UNFOLDS AND LOWERS)

$2581. (6 CYL.)

INTERIOR 338 (CONT'D.)

Studebaker
THE COMMON-SENSE CAR

CRUISER INTERIOR FEATURES

Exclusive Beauty Vanity in glove compartment—(opt.).

Daytona Sports SEDAN

65
(CONT'D.)

DAYTONA INTER.

CLOSER DETAIL OF DASH

V8 NOW has 195 HP

← FINAL YEAR OF 4 HEADLIGHTS

$2985.

Cruiser

S = 6
V = V8

PRICES START AT $2465. (COMMANDER 6 2-DR.)

194 CID, 120-HP 6 OR 283 CID, 195-HP V8

LAST

Studebaker
AUTOMOTIVE SALES CORPORATION

66

Cars BY ST.-P.

109" OR 113" WB (SINCE 1962, ON LARK and LARK-BASED MODELS)

FINAL STUDEBAKERS HAVE THIS GRILLE.

3-66 = DISCONTINUED

339

TEMPEST
BY PONTIAC!

new COMPACT CAR

new 4-CYL. ENG. ADAPTED FROM THE RIGHT HALF OF A PONTIAC V8!

FROM **$2329.**

new FOR
61

STD. *and* CUSTOM COUPES INTRO. IN MIDYEAR

112" wheelbase
(THROUGH '63)

(STD.)
(194.5 CID)

4
OR
V-8 (215 CID)

Independent suspension at all wheels

THE HOT TOPIC IS THE NEW TEMPEST BY PONTIAC

TROPHY 4 ENGINE

FOUR CYLINDERS

to **155 h.p.** (Or buy the 155 h.p. aluminum V-8 option.)

FRONT ENGINE ⟷ REAR TRANSMISSION
PERFECT ▲ BALANCE

PONTIAC'S TEMPEST
PICKED BY MOTOR TREND MAGAZINE AS
CAR OF THE YEAR

WITH
340 PONTIAC POWER STEERING (OPT.)

TEMPEST

62

STANDARD TEMPEST COUPE *has* BROAD BACKLIGHT, MINIMUM CHROME

CUSTOM COUPE *has* "TOWN CAR" BACKLIGHT

4 CYL. WITH 110, 115, 120, 140, OR 166 HP. 185-HP ALUMINUM V8 ALSO AVAIL.

new LE MANS

The gas-saving "4" with Pontiac Punch!

LE MANS

4 CYL. 195.4 CID (115-166 HP) TEMPEST (NAME RETURNS TO FRONT FENDER)

CVT. WITH TOP DOWN

LE MANS

326 CID V8 ALSO AVAILABLE (260 HP)

LE MANS *has* RECTANGULAR TAIL-LIGHTS, "LE MANS" ON FRONT FENDER.

63

LE MANS WITH TOP UP

341

Wide-Track Pontiac Tempest

64
(RESTYLED)

Tempest

new 115" WB

new 215 CID 140-HP IN-LINE O.H.V. 6

Tempest CUSTOM

SAFARI WAGON

326 CID V8 ALSO AVAIL.
(250 OR 280 HP)

LE MANS

GTO ("GTO" APPEARS ON GRILLE) (new)

1964

LE MANS

342

TEMPEST

1965: The year of the Quick Wide-Tracks

TEMPEST

SAFARI WAGON

Tempest **65** FROM $2618.

H/T (new)

140-HP 6
OR
250-285 HP V8

TEMPEST CUSTOM

Le Mans

FRONT-END COMPARISON
OF LE MANS (left) and GTO (right)

SEE
ALSO:
Pontiac

OFFICIAL **PACE CAR·MOTOR TREND RIVERSIDE "500"**
COURTESY OF
HURST

GTO

343

THUNDERBIRD

(INTRO. FALL, 1954, FOR 1955)

(Ford)

(MODEL 40)

55

"CLASSIC" T-BIRDS AVAIL. with REMOVABLE HARD TOP OR CVT. TOP (THROUGH '57)

ALL with V-8 O.H.V. ENGINES

193 HP

102" WB (THROUGH '57)

$2944.

6.70 × 15 TIRES (THROUGH '56)

40-B   H/T has new PORTHOLES (EXCEPT EARLY MODELS)

56

40-A

202 HP

new 7.50 × 14 TIRES

57

NAME MOVED TO FRONT FENDERS

212 HP

GRILLE, BUMPERS, TAIL-LIGHTS MODIFIED

$3408.

new WHEEL COVERS

344

new DASH

THUNDERBIRD

Exclusive "Panel Console"

DASH

63-A

76-A

new 113" WB

58
(TOTALLY RESTYLED)

300 HP
(THROUGH '65)

The car everyone *would love to own!*

CVT.
76-A

HORIZONTAL
PCS. ON
GRILLE *and*
BETWEEN
TAIL-
LIGHTS

H/T
63-A

new
8.00×14
TIRES

59

new
SIDE TRIM
EACH YEAR

9 VERTICAL CHROME BANDS on EA. REAR FENDER

(1960
ONLY)

6 TAIL-LIGHTS
IN 1960

60

$4222.

new GRILLE

sliding sun roof (new)

'60 THUNDERBIRD
THE WORLD'S MOST WANTED CAR 345

'61 THUNDERBIRD
UNIQUE IN ALL THE WORLD

$ **4637.**

PACE CAR AT 1961
INDY 500 RACE

61
(TOTALLY
RESTYLED.)

(OPTIONAL) ←

Swing-Away Steering Wheel glides out of
your way for easier, more graceful entrances
and exits—yet locks safely in place before
you can drive.

$ **4170.**

unmistakably New, unmistakably Thunderbird

new BODY TYPES and MODEL NUMBERS in 1962

HARDTOP

CVT.

$ **5552.**

LANDAU
(new)

$ **4511.**

with
VINYL
TOP and
DECORATIVE LANDAU IRONS

Thunderbird
Sports Roadster
(new)

new GRILLE

62

| H/Ts = MODEL 83 |
| CVTS. = MODEL 85 |

new SPTS. RDST.
has TWIN TONNEAU
CAPS (as illustrated)

346

unique in all the world

THUNDERBIRD

$4529. TO $5648.

H/T 83

63

INTERIOR (OFFERING WOOD-GRAIN EFFECTS)

LANDAU 87

CVT. 85

final SPORT ROADSTER 89

113.2" WB

64 (RESTYLED)

new DASH

new 8.15 x 15 TIRES

new WIDE TAIL-LIGHTS with T-BIRD EMBLEM

PRICED FROM $4486. (IN '64 and '65)

65

5 new VERTICAL STRIPS ON EACH TAIL-LIGHT

INTERIOR with new WOOD-GRAIN EFFECTS

347

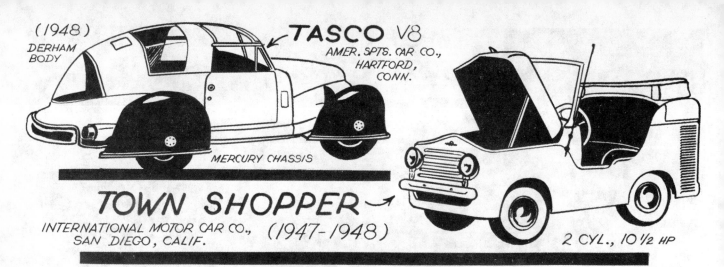

(1948)
DERHAM BODY

TASCO V8
AMER. SPTS. CAR CO.,
HARTFORD, CONN.

MERCURY CHASSIS

TOWN SHOPPER ↝
INTERNATIONAL MOTOR CAR CO., (1947-1948)
SAN DIEGO, CALIF.

2 CYL., 10½ HP

Tucker '48

THE TUCKER CORP., 7401 S. CICERO, CHICAGO, ILL. (1946-1949)

PRINCIPAL OUTPUT
PRODUCED DURING
1947, BUT KNOWN AS
1948 MODELS.

PRESTON TUCKER
(FOUNDER)
(1903-1956)

6 - CYL.
HORIZ. OPPOSED
FRANKLIN/TUCKER
REAR ENGINE

TURNING (CENTER)
"CYCLOPS EYE"
HEADLIGHT

CRASH COWL

RARE!
ONLY 53 BUILT, INCLUDING PILOT MODELS.

SYMBOL OF SAFETY

348

Valiant
NEW FROM CHRYSLER

106½" WB
(THROUGH '62)

V-100

INCLINED
6-CYL.
170 CID
O.H.V.
ENGINE
101 HP @ 4400 RPM
OR 148 HP @
5200
RPM

$2053.
and up
V-200

V-200s have EXTRA
SIDE CHROME TRIM.

1960

V-200

60

QX1-L
OR
QX1-H

V-100

225 CID PLYMOUTH 6 CYL.
ENGINE ALSO AVAIL.
(145 HP @ 4000 RPM)

V-200

V-200

1961

new H/T

DASH

V-200

61

RV1-L OR RV1-H

note GRILLE CHANGE

FINAL
YEAR FOR
148-HP VERSION
OF SMALL ENGINE

V-200

349

VALIANT

$2590.

V-100

V-200

62

SVI

SVI-L (V-100)
SVI-H (V-200)
SVI-P (SIGNET)

new SIGNET *(has* FRONT BUCKET SEATS)

$2538.

SIGNET *has* INSIGNIA ON DARK GRILLE

(*new* 18-GALLON FUEL TANK)

Valiant V-100 2-door sedan/metallic green

ENGINE

new CONVTS.

TRANSMISSION PUSHBUTTONS

106" WB

63 TVI

(TOTALLY RESTYLED)

13M-82

350

Valiant V-200 4-door station wagon/dark metallic blue

VALIANT

note THAT THIS LATER SERIES CONVERTIBLE has LESS REAR BRIGHTWORK and DIFFERENT DECK EMBLEM FROM "SIGNET" ILLUSTR. ON PRECEDING PAGE

63 (CONT'D.)

Valiant presents

AMERICA'S LOWEST-PRICED CONVERTIBLE...$2340*

$2215.

V-100

Valiant V-100 2-Door Sedan

Barracuda (new) (INTRO. 4-2-64)

6 CYL. OR V8

64

V-200

$2670.
(6)

VVI-L (V-100)
VVI-H (V-200)
VVI-P (SIGNET 200)
VVI-P29 (BARRACUDA)

new 273 CID V8 has 180 HP @ 4200 RPM

$2549.

SIGNET

AJ·6830

new GRILLE with "PLYMOUTH" NAMEPLATE ABOVE

Valiant/64 style
Best all-around compact

351

$2766.

VALIANT

BARRACUDA

$2801. (V8)

65

6 and V8 ENGINE SPECS. AS BEFORE, EXCEPT THAT new OPTIONAL 10.5 COMPRESSION VERSION of V8 IS ALSO AVAIL., with 235 HP @ 5200 RPM

ALL-VINYL SEATS IN "100."

100

Plymouth Valiant 200 4-Door Station Wagon

200

6 CYL.:
AVI-L (100)
AVI-H (200)
AVI-P (SIGNET)
AVI-P29 (BARRACUDA)
(V8s have "AV2" PREFIXES)

200

The Roaring '65s*

DASH

Valiant Signet

new FLAT-PROFILE AIR CONDITIONER

$2234. TO $2932.

352 *= SLOGAN APPLIES TO PLYMOUTH ALSO.

COUPE

(WILLYS NAME SINCE 1917)
(ALSO WILLYS-KNIGHT, OVERLAND, WHIPPET)

WILLYS

WILLYS-OVERLAND
MOTORS, INC.
TOLEDO, O.
PRICED FROM $495.

DE LUXE

4 CYL. ONLY (SINCE '34 and THROUGH '47)

40 "4-40"

FLAT-BACKED LOWER-PRICED "Speedway" MODEL DOES NOT HAVE THE EXTRA STRIPS (HORIZONTAL) ALONG FRONT END OF HOOD.

102" WB
4.3 GEAR RATIO

new = REAR QUARTER WINDOWS (SEDAN)

RED-LETTERED "AMERICAR" NAME ON HOOD STRIP

new 1-PC. VERTICAL-BARS GRILLE ON '41.

41 "4-41"

new 104" WB

new PLAINSMAN MODELS (AT TOP OF LINE) OFFER OVERDRIVE and ALUMINUM HI-COMPR. CYL. HEAD AS STD. EQUIP.

new 4.4 GEAR RATIO

5.50 x 16

AMERICAR

new BISECTED GRILLE

FROM $695.

42 "4-442"

ALSO

Jeep

(SEE FOLLOWING PAGES)

5.50 x 16

353

WILLYS 'Jeep'

UNIVERSAL JEEP (4-W-D)

MILITARY STYLE ('46)

$1146.

EARLY MODEL ('46)

Station Wagon

CLARK & COMPANY

All-Steel Station Wagon (new) ENGINE

MILITARY JEEPS INTRO. '41

46-47

CJ-2A SERIES

('47)

$1565.

"Jeep Station Wagon" ON HOOD

104" WB

new 6-CYL STATION SEDAN

has IMITATION WICKER PANELS

(PHOTOGRAPHED IN PORTLAND, ORE.)

4 CYL. (6 CYL. IN STA. SED.)

48

JEEP LT. TRUCKS ALSO AVAIL.

EXPORT MODEL (note PLAIN BUMPER SOMETIMES USED)

354

(CONT'D.)

WILLYS 48 (CONT'D.)

the Jeepster $1765.

JEEPSTER CVT. PRODUCED TO 1953; RE-INTRO. BY KAISER-JEEP, 1967.

4 OR 6 CYL.

New

JEEPSTER $1595.
(FOR 4 CYL.)

THE 'Jeep' Station Wagon

6-CYL. ENGINE NOW AVAIL. ALSO IN WAGON OR JEEPSTER. 4-CYL. ALSO CONTINUES. 63 HP

49

'Jeep' Station Sedan
6 CYL. only

DEEP UPHOLSTERED SEATS, interior roominess and road-leveling wheel suspension add to the smooth, luxurious riding comfort of the 'Jeep' Station Sedan.

6.70 × 15

$1890.

355

WILLYS 'Jeep'

('50)

JEEPSTER

new GRILLE (EARLY '50 has '49-STYLE GRILLE.)

('51)

50-51

MILITARY JEEP

FIRST NON-JEEP WILLYS CAR PRODUCED SINCE 1942 MODELS:

The Revolutionary New *Aero Willys*

108" WB

AERO-WING ('52 ONLY)

AERO-ACE

52

AERO-LARK has 6-CYL. L-HEAD engine; WING, ACE, EAGLE have HURRICANE 6 F-HEAD. JEEP WAGONS, JEEPSTERS also

356

DETAILS OF F-HEAD COMBUSTION CHAMBER →

New Hurricane 6 Engine, F-head design with 7.6 compression, one of the world's most efficient power plants.

Willys Aero

AERO LARK

NO HOOD ORNAMENT ON LARK

2-DR.

AERO-LARK DELUXE ↗

FIFTIETH YEAR
ANNIVERSARY OF
WILLYS-OVERLAND
53

AERO-ACE

4-DR.

AERO-FALCON
(REPLACES '52 AERO-WING) (AERO-FALCON 2-DR. RESEMBLES LARK DLX.)

AERO-ACE 2-DR.

ACE H/T ALSO AVAIL. (ILLUSTR. AT LOWER RIGHT)

AERO-EAGLE H/T

AERO ACE H/T →

Station Wagon

JEEP 4 (4-W-D)

JEEP 6 DELUXE

357

Willys Aero

AERO FALCON NO LONGER AVAIL.

REAR SPARE TIRE

AERO EAGLE CUSTOM

LARK, ACE, EAGLE MODELS

54

KW

Kaiser-Willys Sales Div.
Willys Motors, Inc.

H.P. INCREASED

90 OR 115 HP

WIDER OPENING TOP DOOR GIVES **WIDEST OPENING OF ANY STATION WAGON IN ITS FIELD**

WAGON has new GRILLE

CUSTOM

4 OR 6 CYL.

4-W-D

all-new GRILLE, TAIL-LIGHTS and TRIM

55

BERMUDA H/T

FINAL WILLYS CARS BUILT IN U.S.A., BUT JEEP PRODUCTION CONTINUES. KAISER JEEPS BLT. 1963 TO 1969. AMERICAN MOTORS CORP. BEGAN BUILDING JEEPS (SINCE START OF 1970 MODEL SEASON.)

358

Part Three: American Motors to Thunderbird 1966-1980

American Motors   6
Buick   39
Cadillac   79
Chevrolet   97
Chrysler   162

Dodge   182
Ford   224
Imperial   267
International   271
Jeep   277
Lincoln   284
Mercury   293

Oldsmobile   322
Plymouth   362
Pontiac   387
Thunderbird   425
Miscellaneous   431

Introduction to Part Three

Over the years, I've often been asked to do a book on the American cars that have appeared *since* those illustrated in the 1940-1965 *American Car Spotter's Guide*. And certainly, such a book is needed. Many auto buffs know their older cars, from the early '60's on back . . . But many have despaired of being able to correctly identify the myriad post-1965 models. "They all look alike," many have complained. That isn't really true, though, as there's a rich treasure of interesting, distinctive and unusual cars in this part, waiting to be explored.

The luxurious V-8 dreamboats and scrappy 'muscle cars' of the late sixties and early seventies are now becoming of interest to car collectors; they are unusual, yet they can be driven at freeway speeds. And a pre-1975 car has the advantage of not needing unleaded fuel.

We come all the way up to 1980 in this book, so now you'll be able to identify almost any car on the street if you use this book and the others in this series.

A year ago, when I compiled the *Imported Car Spotter's Guide* (1946-1979) I'd said that many readers may find it "a tool in helping them select" a used car. The same applies with this book. It's not only for your enjoyment and edification, but it's useful as an illustrated catalog of the domestic used cars currently for sale. Most of the cars on these pages can be seen on the streets anywhere, and as time goes by, many may become collector's items.

I'd like to remind you that in this book you'll find the many sub-makes listed with the parent make of which they are a division.

Some technical details are included in this book, such as many original prices, engine sizes, horsepower figures, etc., which we hope will add interest to the illustrations. In most cases, the listed prices are f.o.b. (meaning the original price if delivered at the factory without tax, license, delivery charges). However, most of the prices shown *do* include the cost of some basic accessories, so they are sometimes higher than so-called 'sale' prices quoted for cars with no extras. As for engine specifications, in some cases the standard available engines are listed but there were also additional engines that were optional at extra cost.

This is the longest yet of the books in this series, because of the vast complexity of sub-divisions of makes which abounded since the 1960's. Chevrolet, for example, has many spin-offs such as Camaro, Corvette, Chevy II/Nova, Corvair, Monte Carlo, and so on. This holds true in nearly all other makes as well, and while it adds interest to the automotive scene, it adds confusion, too. Each of these sub-makes is an individual car in itself, and all must be illustrated.

In some cases I included all body styles available from a given make or sub-make in one year. However, showing the full line of body types of all cars (all the coupes, two- and four-door sedans, hardtops, convertibles and wagons for each and every year) would be prohibitive.

Your interest in *American Car Spotter's Guide 1966-1980* is deeply appreciated. There was an old slogan, "Every time we sell a car we make a friend." I like to feel that way about your having bought this book. I'll enjoy hearing from you should you have comments, questions or suggestions about the book. Please send along a self-addressed stamped envelope if you'd like a personal reply. I hope this will be a book you'll want to browse through or take along with you often, and that it will come in handy many, many times!

Acknowledgements

I'm very grateful to my wife Sandy and daughter, Tammy, for all the help they provided with the clipping and filing of thousands of car ads from old magazines. And special thanks to my mother, Wallea B. Draper, for obtaining many new car brochures for me.

For many years I've been saving both new and old car ads, as well as brochures, books, etc., but this new project was greatly helped when Dave Anderson, a teacher at my daughter's elementary school, kindly told me about a treasure of discarded magazines of the 1960's and 1970's that I could have if I would contact another teacher he knew, who was "up to her ears" in old magazines she no longer needed for her art class. So I'm also grateful to Lynn Nygard, and the Pacific Grove, California, Middle School for providing many magazines with helpful car ads.

Much gratitude is due to Alden C. Jewell, Ken Wilson and R. A. Wawrzyniak, each of whom graciously supplied some original literature from their collections! And my thanks, also, to each of the following individuals and organizations for certain ads, pictures or details they helped to gather: Bill Adams; Roger, David and John Allen; American Motors Corp.; Jeff Anderson; Harold and Lillian Atherly; Warren J. Baier; John Bergquist; Scott Boettcher; Paul Bridges; Buick Club of America; Emmett P. Burke; Swen H. Carlson; Chrysler Corp.; Elegant Motors, Inc.; Ford Motor Company; General Motors Corp.; Highway Aircraft Corp.; Lawrence C. Holian; International Harvester Corp.; Robert L. Jiminez; Sue Johns; Elliott Kahn; William F. Kosfeld; Paul Lewis; Kathryn Lincoln; Dale R. Long; Keith Marvin; Larry Mauck; Rev. Wayne McMillen; Bruce B. Mohs; Dave Newell; Oldsmobile Club of America; George Reichow; Tim Ressler; Lewis B. Scott; Ben Shealey; Mark Simon; John Stempel; George Stilwell; Bob Sutherlin; Jack Tinsley; Jim Van Nortwick; Don Watson; Paul Wehner; Rev Elroy Weixel; and the W.P.C. (Chrysler Product Restorers') Club.

AMERICAN MOTORS

AMBASSADOR

232 CID (155 HP) 6 OR 3 V8s, UP TO 327 CID
STD. V8 (287 CID)/98 HP)

* (TO 1974)

990

66

Six or V8

CVT. $3337.

116" WB (THROUGH '66)

$3354.

wagon

* "AMBASSADOR" NAME ORIG. INTRO. 1927 BY NASH.

(880 MODELS PRICED FROM $2878.)

INTRO. 10-7-65

new **DPL.**

$3230.

H/T COUPE and DPL INTERIOR

(note THE UNIQUE BLACK-AND-WHITE CHECK PATTERN ON FABRIC SEAT AND DOOR SIDE COVER-ING.)

American Motors...where quality is built in, not added on.

6

AMERICAN MOTORS *AMBASSADOR*

From $2515 to $3143*

990

AMBASSADOR WAGONS

$3435.

880
2-DR.
$2971.

The Red Carpet Ride.

67

new
118"
WB

990 SEDAN
$3/28.

DASH

HOOD
ORNAMENT
ADDED

DPL
$3310.

DPL GRILLE
BEARS 2
RALLY LIGHTS

1967

AMBASSADOR DPL CONVERTIBLE AND HARDTOP
(DPL CVT. AVAIL.
ONLY IN 1967.)

THE **NOW** CARS FROM THE
1967 AMERICAN MOTORS

7

AMERICAN MOTORS AMBASSADOR, DPL, OR SST MODELS; NO MORE 880 OR 990 SERIES)

SEDAN $3065.

DASH

new DOOR HANDLES

new SIDE SAFETY LIGHTS

new GRILLE

DPL (INTRO. 9-26-67) **68** AIR COND. NOW STD. EQUIP.

SST (ABOVE) has RALLY LIGHTS ON GRILLE.

WAGON (DPL) $3452.

DOOR OPENS SIDEWAYS OR SWINGS DOWN

68 DPL

NO MORE HOOD ORNAMENT UNTIL 1974.

8

AMERICAN MOTORS AMBASSADOR

69

AMBASSADOR SEDAN, DPL and SST SEDANS, WAGONS and H/Ts AVAILABLE. new 122" WB

"Ambassador" NAME ON new GRILLE; HORIZONTAL ROW OF HDLTS.

new HORIZONTAL SHAPE FOR FRONT SIDE SAFETY LIGHTS.

AMBER LTS. NOW IN NARROWER SLOTS.

SST $3570.

$3,165 (SALE)

REAR

(INTRO. 10-1-68)

To make an appointment for a test ride visit your American Motors Dealer. A number of them have chauffeurs available.

(INTRO. 9-25-69)

70

PLAINER GRILLE

FROM $3295.

'71 FROM $3706. (INTRO. 10-6-70)

BROUGHAM, SST WAGONS AVAIL.

STATION WAGON HAS A V-8 ENGINE AIR-CONDITIONING, AUTOMATIC TRANS AS STANDARD EQUIP

DPL has new 258 CID, 150 HP 6 CYL. ENG. (STD.)

BROUGHAM SERIES ADDED

71
new GRILLE

9

AMERICAN MOTORS *AMBASSADOR*

(DPL MODEL DISCONTINUED)
SST IS NOW LOWEST-PRICED, STARTING AT $3889.

(4-DR.)

72

AMERICAN MOTORS 1972 BUYER PROTECTION PLAN.

3 HEAVIER HORIZONTAL PIECES IN GRILLE.

AMC
We back them better because we build them better.

WAGON $4645.

SEDAN, H/T OR WAGON AVAIL.

new SAFETY BUMPERS

new HEAVIER VERTICAL PCS., AS WELL AS HORIZONTAL, IN GRILLE

73

(FINAL H/T PRICED AT $4261.)

SST DISCONTINUED; BROUGHAM IS ONLY REMAINING SERIES IN AMBASSADOR LINE (PRICED FROM $4245.

SEDAN $4245.

2-SEAT WAGON $4960.

3-SEAT, $5068.

HOOD ORNAMENT ADDED, (AGAIN) AND *all-new* GRILLE

DASH

The new Ambassador woodgrained instrument panel with AM/FM stereo radio, Adjust-O-Tilt wheel and Cruise-Command speed control.

GRAINED PANEL NOW GOES *HIGHER* UP BODY SIDES.

74

FROM $4559. (SEDAN)

(THE FINAL AMBASSADOR)

AMC American
AMERICAN MOTORS CORPORATION

(TO 1969)

compact car
ALSO KNOWN AS
Rambler
440

AMC DEALERS ADVERTISED AS THE "FRIENDLY GIANT KILLERS"

CVT. $2704.

$2588.

new
Rogue H/T

RACING STRIPES ALONG HOOD ARE *NOT* INCLUDED AS STD. EQUIPMENT.

GRILLE NOW SPLIT INTO JUST 3 HORIZONTAL SECTIONS.

106" WB (THROUGH '69)

66

199 CID 6 (128 HP) OR ROGUE 290 CID V8 (200 HP) 6.45/6.95 × 14 TIRES

220

(STANDARD MODEL) DOES NOT HAVE CHROME STRIP ALONG SIDES.

2-DR. $2235.

11

AMC American

DASH

$2306.

440

QUALITY BUILT IN — SO THE VALUE STAYS IN

$2591.

RAMBLER AMERICAN WAGON

$2665.

ROGUE

H/T

new FRONT FENDER GROOVES ON ROGUE MATCH THE GRILLE.

THIS '67 ROGUE IS THE FINAL CONVERTIBLE IN AMERICAN MODEL LINE.

67

$2489.

HORIZONTAL GRILLE PCS. ARE NOW UNBROKEN, (AS THEY WERE IN 1964.)

220

2-DR.

$2062.

THE NOW CARS

12

AMC American

440 →
CHROME ALONG SIDE

220 ↑
4-DR.
$2257.

ROGUE
$2477.

68 ROGUE

68-440

ROGUE and 440 (ABOVE) have BRIGHT METAL BETWEEN TAIL-LTS.

2-DR.
$2179.

68
(INTRO. 9-26-67)

new SINGLE HEAVY HORIZONTAL CHROME STRIP ACROSS GRILLE (OTHER HORIZ. PCS. ARE BLACK)

RAMBLER

68-220

13

AMC American

(FINAL USE OF "RAMBLER AMERICAN" NAME)

69 (INTRO. 10-1-68)

STD. 199 CID 6 (128 HP)
290 CID V8 (200 HP)

"RAMBLER" NAME NO LONGER APPEARS ON GRILLE. SOME VERTICAL PCS. NOW ALSO VISIBLE.

THIS MODEL REPLACED BY:

new TRI-COLOR HOOD EMBLEM

Rambler $1,998 (SALE PRICE) (RAMBLER 220, 440 and ROGUE RANGE IS $2231. TO $2710.

American Motors' Hornet
$1,994 to $3,589

(NEW NAME, TOTALLY RESTYLED) (INTRO. 9-25-69)

70

SLOGAN: "THE LITTLE RICH CAR"

new ALUMINUM GRILLE
new 19-GAL. FUEL TANK

1970

ENGINES:
199 CID 6, 128 HP
232 CID 6, 145 HP
232 CID 6, 155 HP
OR
304 CID V8, 210 HP

SST, WITH VINYL TOP

1970

HORNET

new 108" WB

LOW-PRICE HORNET *has* LESS TRIM, PLAIN SMALL HUB-CAPS

SEE ALSO AMC "HORNET"

14

American Motors AMX (new)

(INTRO. 2-24-68)

(ASSOCIATED WITH JAVELIN SERIES THROUGH '74)

97" WB

$3485. ('68)
$3571. ('69)

EA. AMX CAR'S PRODUCTION NUMBER IS SET IN DASH.

V8 ENGINES
290 CID (225 HP)
343 CID OR
390 CID (315 HP)

1969 MODEL INTRO. 10-1-68.

READILY IDENTIFIED BY UNIQUE DUAL WEDGES ON HOOD, EACH BEARING 5 PARALLEL LOUVRES.

68-69

E70 × 14 TIRES

A-8 SERIAL # PREFIX

A-9 PREFIX FOR 1969, MORE STRIPE COMBINATIONS.

new STD. 360 CID V8 (290 HP) (INTRO. 9-25-69)

70 $3677.

new E78 × 14 TIRES

new BODY STRIPE

new ROCKER PANEL DECORATION

new GRILLE and HOOD SCOOP

PRICES
$3861. ('71)
3505. ('72)
3555. ('73)
4073. ('74)

360 (OR 401 CID V8s OPTIONAL)

('72)

GRILLE, SPOILER ('71)

JX-1971

71-74 (NO 1975-76 AMX)

BUMPER GUARDS

AMERICAN MOTORS **AMX** HORNET-AMX

108" WB

77

(AMX BECOMES OWN
SERIES IN 1978.)

258 CID 6
(95 HP) OR
304 CID V8
(120 HP)
(V8 AVAIL.
THROUGH '79)

AMX-citement.

A higher level of excitement.

1979 MODELS ILLUSTRATED

WHEELBASE
SHORTENED TO
96" ('79)

78-80

6-CYL.
PRICES = $5624. ('78)
7019. ('79)
6766. ('80)
'78 V8 = $5391.
'79 V8 = 6769.

16

American Motors Classic (1961 to 1966)

("RAMBLER CLASSIC")

intermediate size car

112" WB

WAGONS FROM $2888.

AVAILABLE IN "550," "770" OR "REBEL" SUB-MODELS.

770 CVT. $3065.

66

2 SIXES and 3 V8s AVAILABLE. STANDARD ENGS.: 287 CID V8 (198 HP) OR 232 CID 6 (145 HP) 6.95/7.35×14 TIRES

(THE FINAL "CLASSIC" LINE)

new GRILLE

(WHITE VINYL TOP ALSO AVAIL., 3-66)

new "CRISP-LINE" ROOF (Rebel/H/T)

$2972.

(MARLIN ALSO IN CLASSIC LINE, '65-'66.)

(SEE AMC MARLIN)

Rebel (INTRO. 10-7-65)

(AVAIL. ONLY AS 2-DR. H/T)

(CLASSIC REPLACED BY THE **AMERICAN MOTORS 1967 Rebel**)

17

AMC Concord

(REPLACES HORNET)

(SINCE 1978)

78 NEW

232 CID 6, (90 HP) OR 304 CID V8 (120 HP)

D/L. 2-DR. SALE = $3949. (REG. $4700.)

DASH

108" WB

(HATCHBACK, 4 DR. and WAGON AVAIL.)

121 CID 4-CYL. ENGINE and 258 CID 6-CYL. ENGINE ADDED; OTHER 6-CYL. and V8 STILL AVAIL. (FINAL CONCORD V8)

D/L 4-DR. $5701.

D/L WAGON $5901.

4 new RECTANGULAR HEADLIGHTS

79

new GRILLE

LIMITED 4-DR. $6459.

$5701.

D/L HATCHBACK

1980 PRICES = $5868. TO $7323.

80

new WRAP-AROUND TAIL LTS.

151 CID 4 OR 258 CID 6

18

American Motors Gremlin

standard 6-cyl. engine.

(1970 TO 1978)

1970 SALE PRICES :

Gremlin
$1,879 2-Passenger
$1,959 4-Passenger

('70) "GREMLIN" FIGURE

INT. ('71)

96" WB

('71)

199 OR 232 CID 6 (128 OR 145 HP)

('70)

HATCH WINDOW OPENS

"GREMLIN" FIGURE ON FENDER

(INTRO. WED., 4-1-70)

6.00 x 13 TIRES (THROUGH '72)

70-71 (INTRO. TUES., 9-15-70)

GREMLIN "X"

('71) has STRAIGHT-LINE BODY STRIPE

THIS HUBCAP STILL AVAIL. 1971.

BUMPER GUARD

19

AMC Gremlin

AMERICAN MOTORS
BUYER PROTECTION PLAN

(INTRO. WED., 9-22-71)
new V8 OPTIONAL

72

"THE BEST PUT-TOGETHER CARS OUT OF DETROIT THIS YEAR MAY COME OUT OF WISCONSIN.

THAT'S WHERE AMERICAN MOTORS MAKES THEM." —Popular Mechanics

FROM $2287.

Gremlin X

"5-LITRE V8" DESIGNATION INDICATES new 304 CID 304 CID V8.

new LEVI's UPHOLSTERY AVAILABLE (OPT.)

73

FROM $2325.

new SAFETY BUMPERS
new 6.45 x 14 TIRES

GREMLIN X
new CURVE IN BODY STRIPE. $2610.

AMC Gremlin
We back them better because we build them better.

74

FORMER HORIZONTAL MOULDINGS IN UPPER REAR QUARTER PANELS NOW ELIMINATED

new GRILLE, MINOR RESTYLING

FROM $2887.

GREMLIN X has new UP-CURVE AT REAR END OF BODY STRIPE (AS ILLUSTRATED)

Six or V8

AMC Gremlin

FROM $3127.

(ADD $169. FOR BUCKET SEATS)

STD.
232 CID
6 (100 HP)

258 CID 6
OR 304 CID V8 OPTIONAL

VINYL INTERIOR

DASH

6-CYL. ENGINE →

Levi's® Gremlin in H1 Deep Blue Metallic.

LEVI'S GREMLIN (ABOVE) and LEVI'S INTERIOR

See all the '75 economy cars from AMC and you'll see why people call AMC dealers

'75

THE ECONOMY EXPERTS

X

Levi's®

21

AMC Gremlin

232 CID 6 (100 HP)
304 CID V8 (150 HP)

6-CYL. PRICED FROM $3216.

(CUSTOM - $3325.)
6.45 × 14 TIRES

76

FINAL YEAR FOR "Gremlin" NAME AT FRONT OF RAISED CENTER SECTION OF HOOD

new GRILLE

"Gremlin is America's lowest priced car." ($162. LESS FOR V8)

There's more to an AMC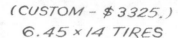

INTRODUCING BUYER PROTECTION PLAN II
('77)

note STRIPE PATTERN
('77)

6 CUT TO 90 HP

new 4 CYL. ENGINE ALSO AVAIL. (121 CID, 57 HP)

new GRILLE

77-78

THE FINAL GREMLIN

('78) LEVI'S INTERIOR STILL AVAIL.

the only full 2 year, 24,000 mile warranty on engine and drive train.

('78)

X

SPECIAL NOTICE
All benefits of BPP II are also available on all new 1976 AMC models purchased on or after Sept. 1, 1976.

FROM $3499. ('78)

(REPLACED BY **SPIRIT**)

EPA MPG: 22 CITY, 35 HWY. (4 CYL.)

22

AMC ▟█ Hornet (FORMERLY American)

(1970 HORNET LISTED WITH AMERICAN)

232 CID 6 (135 HP @ 4000 RPM)
258 CID 6 (150 HP @ 3800 RPM)
304 CID V8 (210 HP @ 4400)

(INTRO. 10-6-70)

71

SC 360 (new)

↑

WITH 360 CID V8 (245 HP @ 4400 OR 285 HP @ 4800)

$2853.

DASH

(new)

THE SPORTABOUT. STATION WAGON

ALSO AVAIL. WITH WOOD-GRAIN TRIM →

Spring Special ↙

1971½

"SPECIALLY EQUIPPED" MODELS IN SPRING, 1971 INCLUDE

Free sunroofs

Hornet

new 3-SPOKE STEERING WHEEL AVAIL.

AMERICAN MOTORS BUYER PROTECTION PLAN ▟█

72

(INTRO. 9-22-71)

new IMPROVED "TORQUE-COMMAND AUTO. TRANS. AVAIL.

FROM $2465.

HORNET

SPORTABOUT

23

AMC ▟▊ Hornet

AS ALSO USED IN GREMLIN, LEVI'S JEANS MATERIAL AVAIL. FOR INTERIOR (SPRING, 1973)

SPORTABOUT
station wagon

$2903.
UNGRAINED SPORTABOUT ALSO AVAIL.

Introducing the Hornet Hatchback.

new GRILLE

73

AMC ▟▊ Hornet
We back them better because we build them better.

HATCHBACKS FROM $2715.

(new)

HORNET HATCHBACK $3665.

$3865.
UNGRAINED

new 1974 ENERGY ABSORBING SAFETY BUMPERS

74

WITH GRAIN

HORNET SPORTABOUT

24

AMC Hornet

1975 HORNETS PRICED FROM $3902.
1977 HORNETS FROM $4343.

FINAL 3 YEARS
FOR HORNET.
FEW VISIBLE
CHANGES FROM
1975 – 1977 EXCEPT
FOR BUMPER IMPROVEMENT
NOTED (1976.)

HORNET
Sportabout

Hometown AMC

Service ↓

AMC BUYER PROTECTION PLAN.™

new
GRILLE

('75)

HORNET D/L
2-DR.

75 - 77

HATCHBACK "X"

('76)

('75)

1976 has THIN RUBBER STRIPS at BUMPER EDGES

STD. AM RADIO

(AM / FM
ALSO AVAIL.)

(REPLACED BY
CONCORD,
1978)   ('75) 4-DR.

25

AMERICAN MOTORS
Javelin
68

(1968 TO 1974)

(INTRO. 9-26-67)

(56,462 BLT.)

**brand new,
8 cylinder, 280 horsepower**
343 CID (290 CID V8 ALSO)

(232 CID 6 ALSO)

109" WB (THROUGH '70)

6.95/7.35 × 14 TIRES (THROUGH '69)

DASH HAS DEEPLY-RECESSED ROUND GAUGES and CONTROLS

$2743.

SST = $2848.

AMERICAN MOTORS *JAVELIN*

(INTRO. 10-1-68)

69

SCRIPT "JAVELIN" NAME NOW ABOVE GRILLE.

SPECIAL

Big Bad Javelin

IN "BIG BAD ORANGE," "BIG BAD BLUE" OR "BIG BAD GREEN," WITH PAINTED FRONT and REAR BUMPERS, OTHER OPTIONS.

new "BULL'S EYE"

new "MARK DONOHUE" REAR SPOILER AVAILABLE

WITH OPTIONAL DUAL EXHAUSTS and CHOICE OF 360 CID OR 390 CID V8s.

(INTRO. 9-25-69)

70

new GRILLE INCLUDES HEADLIGHTS UNDER A COMMON UPPER BORDER.

27

AMERICAN MOTORS *JAVELIN*

STD. JAVELIN $3386.

(INTRO. 10-6-70)

SST $3506.

71

(TOTALLY RESTYLED)

new 110" WB

IF YOU'RE GOING TO BUY A SPORTY CAR, BUY ONE THAT'S BEEN PLACES.

new GRILLE $3296.

72

(INTRO. 9-22-71)

(1974 IS FINAL JAVELIN.)

$3347. ('73)

$3867. ('74)

73-74

new MESH GRILLE WITH RALLY LTS.

28

AMERICAN MOTORS

MARLIN

(1965 - 1967)

6 CYL. OR V8

IN 1965, 1966, A PART OF THE CLASSIC LINE

112" WB (THROUGH '66)

66 (INTRO. 10-7-65)

(ONLY 4547 BLT.)

SALE $2601.

REG. $3051.

SOME WITH CORRUGATED ROCKER PANEL TRIM

232 CID 6 (145 HP @ 4300 RPM) OR 287 CID V8 (198 HP @ 4700 RPM) 2 OTHER V8s AVAIL., TO 327 CID)

NOW A PART OF AMBASSADOR LINE FOR '67. new 118" WB

ROUND MEDALLION REMOVED FROM REAR DECK

6 CYL. has new 155 HP @ 4400 RPM; STD. V8 with new 290 CID (200 HP @ 4600 RPM) OR 2 new 343 CID V8s (TO 280 HP @ 4800 RPM)

67 (ONLY 2545 BLT.)

$3315.

new SIDE LT.

new SMOOTHER BODY SIDES, RECTANGULAR GAS FILLER DOOR

RALLY LTS. IN GRILLE

THE FINAL MARLIN

29

AMERICAN MOTORS Matador

(1971 TO 1978)

(INTRO. 10-6-70)

232 CID 6 (135 HP)
OR STANDARD 304 CID V8
(210 HP)

(REPLACES **Rebel**)

If you were to compete
against G.M., Ford and Chrysler,
what would you do?

71

118" WB
E78/G78×14
TIRES

TAIL LIGHTS

4-DR. SEDAN $3277.

H/T (ABOVE) $3306.

ROOF RACK and
WITH WOODGRAIN

THE MATADOR STATION WAGON

2-SEATS = $3680.
3 " 3798.

UNGRAINED WAGON
AT LEFT, AS VIEWED
FROM REAR INTERIOR
OF WAGON.

AMERICAN MOTORS

A CAR YOU PROBABLY NEVER HEARD OF.
THE MATADOR.

(INTRO. 9-22-71)

WAGONS FROM $3652.

72

new GRILLE

STD. 304 CID V8 HP CUT TO 150

H/T = $3330.

The L.A. Police Department discovers the Matador.

POPULAR AS POLICE CARS IN VARIOUS WEST COAST CITIES and ELSEWHERE.

WAGONS = 2 SEAT $3652.
3 " 3760.

73

new GRILLE

FINAL MATADOR 2-DR. H/T PRICED AT $3261.

SEDAN $3227.

$3985.

WAGONS $4311. UP

74

SEDAN and WAGON = 118" WB
new COUPE (NEXT PG.)
has 114" WB

(CONT'D. NEXT PAGE)

31

AMERICAN MOTORS

PRESENTING THE ONLY ALL-NEW MID-SIZE CAR FOR 1974

AMC ▼ Matador

BLACK TUFTED NYLON-KNIT FABRIC WITH COPPER BUTTONS IN ILLUSTRATED "OLEG CASSINI" INTER. OPT.

REAR

ONLY COUPES ARE TOTALLY RESTYLED.

OLEG CASSINI MODEL BEARS A SIDE MEDALLION. $4428. ('74)

('75)

('74)

STRIPE, BLACK GRILLE ON "X"

Matador **X** $4289. ('74)

74-78

1974 COUPES PRICED FROM $4029. $5660. IN 1978.

('75)

SEDAN $5302. ('77)

MATADOR SERIES ENDS 1978.

COUPE(ONLY) GETS *new* GRILLE, 1976.

('76)

('75)

32

American Motors

AMC Pacer (1975-1980)
75-76

6 CYL. 232 CID

22-GAL. FUEL TANK 100" WB

$3,299*

AMERICAN MOTORS

$3,499 WITH A/C ('76)

The first wide small car.

2-DR. HATCHBACK CONTINUES

57.1"   60.7"

$4153.   Wagon (new)

77

There's more to an AMC ◢◼

33

INTERIOR

AMC ⧄ Pacer

78

304 CID V8
ALSO AVAIL.
('78-'79)

new
GRILLE

6 CYL.
90 HP
new
V8
120
HP

WAGON
$4519.

2 SERIES
NOW AVAIL.:
DL *and*
LIMITED

LIMITED
HATCHBACK
$6222. ('79)

(1979
EXAMPLES
ILLUSTR.)

DL INTERIOR (IN
CABERFAE CORDUROY)

6 HAS
new 258 CID

new WHEELS →

LIMITED WAGON
$6372. ('79)
6974. ('80)

DL WAGON
(DL
HATCHBACK
ALSO
AVAIL.)

79-

80

new UPRIGHT
HOOD ORNAMENT

(THE FINAL PACER)

34

$5456. ('79)
5980. ('80)

◢ **AMERICAN MOTORS**

REBEL

(1967 TO 1970)

(FORMER CLASSIC MODEL)

DASH

$2863. SED.

770
WAG.

$3049.

REBEL SST HARDTOP

114" WB
232 CID 6
(145 HP)
OR
STD. 290 CID
V8 (200 HP) "550" FROM $2739.

67

UN-GRAINED

REBEL WAGONS $3155.

GRAINED

7.35/7.75 × 14 TIRES

↗
new "VENTURI"-STYLE GRILLE

SST CVT. $3227.

new SST "INTAKE" AHEAD OF REAR WHEELS (ALSO IN '68)

AMERICAN MOTORS Rebel

ANCHOR DECOR ON UPHOL.

VARIOUS UNIQUE WOODGRAINS and INTERIORS FOR REBEL WAGONS (SPRING, '67)

67 1/2

MARINER WAGON

WITH "TYPHOON" V8 ENGINE

BLEACHED TEAKWOOD PLANK WOODGRAIN EFFECTS ON BODY

550 (6 CYL.) WAGON

(550, SST ARE ONLY AMC CONVERTS. STILL AVAIL.)

SST (290 CID Typhoon V8)

6-CYL. 770

DASH

SST

(INTRO. 9-26-67)

68

SQUARE, RECESSED DOOR HANDLES (new)

SST "INTAKE" AHEAD of REAR WHEELS

new SAFETY SIDE LIGHTS

68 SST

new 3-PIECE TAIL-LIGHTS

SST (OWN GRILLE) 36

Rebel SST

AMERICAN MOTORS

An intermediate-sized car for the price of a compact.

Rebel $2,484[1] (SALE)

69

new GRILLE
new TAIL-LTS.,
WIDER TRACK (INTRO. 10-1-68)

(REG. $2944.)

Rebel Wagon

(INTRO. 9-25-69)
(THE FINAL REBEL. REPLACED BY 1971 MATADOR)

70

new GRILLES

$2,766.* sale price

FRONT SAFETY LIGHTS NOW HORIZONTAL

(*new*)

the "Machine".

Up with The Rebel Machine

WITH 390 CID V8 (340 HP)

37

AMC SPIRIT (STARTS 1979)

(REPLACES AMC Gremlin)

79 INTERIOR

LIFTBACK

4 CYL. (121 CID)
6 CYL. (232 OR 258 CID)
OR V-8 (304 CID)

96" WB

G.T.

$5420.

LIMITED

RELATIONSHIP TO FORMER GREMLIN CAN BE SEEN.

SEDAN

DL

$4504.

DASH

(V-8 NO LONGER AVAIL.)

80 $4687.

IN 1980, AMERICAN MOTORS WILL BE THE ONLY CAR MAKER IN AMERICA WITH...

ZIEBART
RUST PROTECTION

AMERICAN MOTORS 5-YEAR NO RUST-THRU WARRANTY

AMERICAN MOTORS BUYER PROTECTION PLAN

ALL THIS AT NO EXTRA COST.

BUILT FOR TODAY.. BUILT TO LAST FOR TOMORROW.

LIFTBACK

GENERAL MOTORS

BUICK (full-sized)

(SINCE 1903)

(SEPARATE SECTION FOR
SPECIAL, SKYLARK, CENTURY, REGAL,
SPORT WAGON.)

LE SABRE (BELOW) 123" WB

WILDCAT (325 HP)
(GS-340 HP)
126" WB

WILD.
CUSTOM
$4037.

WILDCAT has
UNIQUE GRILLE

$4421.

Electra 225

(and ELECT. 225
CUSTOM)

126" WB
401 CID V8
325 HP

ELECTRA
225 CUSTOM
SPT. CPE.
$4300.

66

(CUSTOM MODELS IN
EACH SERIES ARE
HIGHER-PRICED.)

1966 Buick.
The tuned car.

Electra 225 has 4 CHROME SEGMENTS,
LE SABRE has 3, and
WILDCAT has NONE.

39

BUICK

LE SABRE

220 HP

CUST. H/T $3560.

DASH

(INTRO. 9-29-66)

67

WILDCAT

new SLANTING SCULPTURED LINES RUNNING LENGTH OF BODY SIDES

430 CID 360 HP V8 (THROUGH '69)

Electra 225

430 CID V8

ELECTRA 225 LIMITED

WILDCAT

68

(INTRO. 9-21-67)

H/T $3951.

WILDCAT CUSTOM H/T $4172.

(CONT'D. NEXT PAGE)

BUICK

LE SABRE

(SHOWN WITH and WITHOUT VINYL TOP)

LeSabre. $3771.

68 (CONT'D.)

INTERIOR

(ELEC. 225 LTD.)

ELECTRA 225 LIMITED

$4597.

ELECTRA 225

SEDANS FROM $4288.

feeling in an
your living room. 'My
s me that feeling. The interior
ot a bit gaudy."

like a puff of wind. And it takes a hill like a
solutely devoted to the Electra Limited."

ents get in the car and say, 'I didn't
y're building a car like this today."

Wouldn't you really rather have a Buick?

41

BUICK

No wonder Buick owners keep selling Buicks for us.
Wouldn't you really rather have a Buick?

LE SABRE

350 CID V8

4-DR. H/T FROM $3740.

69

(INTRO. 9-26-68)

LE SABRE GRILLE *has* 5 HORIZONTAL PCS.; (ILLUSTR. WILDCAT GRILLE *has* JUST ONE.)

WILDCAT

430 CID V8

ELECTRA 225

(ELECTRA GRILLE AT LOWER LEFT)

430 CID V8

LE s. CUSTOM 455 $4570.

1970 BUICK
SOMETHING TO BELIEVE IN.

HUB OF LE SABRE STEER. WH. DIFF. FR. OTHERS

LeSABRE

new 124" WB (THROUGH '76)

LeSabre 4-door Sedan.
FROM $4169.

LeSabre Custom Convertible.

$4532.

LeSabre Custom 4-door Hardtop.
FROM $4403.

LE SABRE CUSTOM 455 IS ADDED, TOPPING 3 LE SABRE LINES.

(INTRO. 9-18-69)

70

WILDCAT CUSTOM IS NOW ONLY WILDCAT LINE.

(CONT'D. NEXT PAGE)

$4892.

Wildcat Custom 4-door Hardtop.

BUICK

$4974.

WILDCAT CUSTOM
(CONT'D.)

Wildcat Custom Convertible

Something to believe in.

DASH
(Elec. 225)
(EST. WAG.,
WILDCAT,
LE SABRE.
SIMILAR)

$5272.

70 (CONT'D.)

ELECTRA
225
CUSTOM
SPT. CPE.
(H/T)

124" WB

ESTATE WAGON
(new)

(new
127" WB
ON ELECT.)
(THROUGH '76)

$5709.

Electra 225 Custom Convertible

Electra 225 Custom Limited 4-door Hardtop

new 455 CID V8
(370 HP)
(SAME
ENG. IN
ESTATE
WAGON)

$5312.

44

BUICK

LE s. CUSTOM
4-DR. H/T $4744.

WILL RUN ON
UNLEADED GAS,
BECAUSE OF
1971 ENG.
MODIFICATIONS

LE SABRE
SPT. CPE
(2-DR. H/T) $4592.
CUSTOM LE SABRE 4680.

1971

new
LOW
OBLONG REAR
SIDE LTS.
(THROUGH '73)

LE SABRE

"Something to believe in."

71 (INTRO. 10-3-70)

124" WB
(127" ON
ELECTRAS,
ESTATE WAGON)

GRILLE

"BUICK"

CENTURION

REPLACES
WILDCAT

(CVT.
ALSO
AVAIL.)

CENTURION (new)

455 CID
V8
315 HP

FROM $5170.

FROM
$5465.

ELECTRA 225

(ELECTRA 225 CUSTOM, LTD. also)

45

BUICK

Something to believe in.

$4596.

1972 Buick LeSabre.

350 CID V8
150 HP

CENTURION GRILLE IS SIMILAR, BUT has ALL-VERTICAL PCS.

LE. S. CUSTOM SPT. CPE.
$4624.

LeSabre.

72

(INTRO. 9-23-71)

FROM $5427.

1972 Buick Electra 225.

455 CID V8
STD.
225 HP

(SAME V8 AS IN CENTURION)

73

new SAFETY BUMPERS

$4624. (CUST. SPT. CPE.)

1973 LeSabre.

LeSABRE

(CONT'D. NEXT PAGE)

46

DASH

REAR END DETAIL

1973 Centurion.

BUICK.
The solid feeling.

CVT. $4993.

Centurion

$4803.

(FINAL YEAR FOR CENTURION)

73 (CONT'D.)

Electra 225

Electra 225
FROM $5428.

Estate Wagon
$5551.

DASH CLOSE-UP

47

BUICK

LeSabre Luxus Convertible

$5256.

LeSabre FROM $4915.

GRAINED 3-SEAT WAG. $6043.

Estate Wagon

74

new STYLE OF REAR QUARTER WINDOWS ON COUPES

Electra 225 FROM $5428.

$6425.

1974 Electra Limited

Low-fuel indicator. Available on all Electras. The red light warns you when the fuel level drops to approximately 4½ gallons.

HIGHER BUMPER GUARDS ON SOME CARS

48

BUICK

BUICK ELECTRA PARK AVENUE.
$7584.

75

LeSabre.

SPT. CPE.
$5413.
LUXUS SPT. CPE.
$5634.

FINAL
BUICK
CVT.
(LE SABRE
LUXUS)
AVAILABLE,
AT
$5706.

BUICK *Dedicated to the Free Spirit in just about everyone.*

LeSabre
231 CID V8
105 HP
$5350.

LeSabre CUSTOM.
350 CID V8
155 HP

76

new
GRILLES

$7874.

PARK AVE.
Electra 225
455 CID
V8
205 HP

EL. 225 CUST. PRICED
FROM $6970.

Electra 225
INTERIOR

BUICK

SPT. CPE. $6449.

LeSabres.

new SHORTER 116" WB

REAR (WRAP-AROUND TAIL-LTS.)

'77 Le SABRE CUSTOM.

$6122.

DASH (LE S.)

VARIOUS ENGINES:
231 CID BUICK V6 (105 HP @ 3400 RPM)
350 CID V8s (2)
CHEVROLET = 160 HP @ 3800
OLDS = 170 HP @ 3800
403 CID V8 (OLDS) 185 HP @ 3600

ELECTRA 225

77

BUICK SALESMEN'S 1977 SALES CAMPAIGN BADGE

I'M OPEN TO OFFERS

ELCTR. WITH new SHORTER 119" WB

Electra 225

new SMALLER 350 CID V8 IN ELECTRA

BUICK. Dedicated to the Free Spirit in just about everyone.

FROM $7303.

50

America's only turbocharged production automobile engine.

BUICK
A little science.
A little magic.

OTHER ENGS.
231 CID STD. V6
301 CID V8
305 CID V8
350 CID V8
403 CID V8

TURBO.
V6 (231 CID)
(151/175 HP) AVAIL. IN $6890.
SPT. CPE.

There are four turbocharged production cars in the entire world.
Two of them are Buicks.

The other two cars are the Porsche Turbo Carrera and the Turbo Saab.

Buick LeSabre. Under $5800.

SALE PRICE ABOVE ; REG. PRICED FROM $6259.

ESTATE WAG. $7399. w. GRAIN

78 new GRILLES

THE NEW ELECTRA:

22 HIGHWAY   **15** CITY   **18** COMBINED*

ELECTRA 225 ; ELECTRA LTD. OR
ELECTRA PARK AVE. MODELS
WITH 350 CID V8 (153 HP)
(405 CID V8
ALSO AVAIL.)

ELECTRA SEDANS $7996. UP

ELECT. CPES. PRICED FROM $7821.

ELECTRA

FRONT DETAILS

ELECTRA INTERIOR

51

BUICK

SPT. CPE.
$7657.
LE SABRE

Buick LeSabre 4-door
$6110, 18 EPA-estimated mpg,

79

BUICK
After all, life is to enjoy.

Electra

FROM
$8877.

(EST. WAG.
(NOW has ONLY 3
HOOD PORTS, LIKE
LE SABRE)
('79 ONLY)

3-SEAT WAGON W.
GRAIN $8360.

ESTATE
WAGON

52

BUICK

Buick Diesels AVAIL.

LE SABRE MODELS NO LONGER BEAR IDENTIFYING HOOD PORTS.

LeSabre

LeSabre

$8530.

80

The new 4.1 Liter Electra. America's first and only traditional luxury car powered by a V-6 engine.

AS BEFORE, LE SABRE SPT. CPE. has DIFFERENT GRILLE.

ELECTRA PARK AVE. has WIRE WHEELS, FULL-LENGTH CHROME BELT

FIC. LTD. CPE.

Electra
LIMITED SEDAN $9816.

ELECTRA
EPA EST. MPG=17
HWY=23

$10,717.

LeSabre and Electra Estate Wagons

$10,513.

BUICK COMPACTS

(COMPACT LINE OF BUICKS STARTS 1961)

(SPECIAL IS LOWEST-PRICED MODEL, FROM $2783.)

(GS)

Buick Sportwagon FROM $3390.

DASH (GS)

225 CID 6 (155 HP) OR 300 CID V8 (210 HP)

← GS WITH 401 CID, 325-HP WILDCAT V8 ENG.

115" WB

66

SKYLARK GS (GRAN SPORT) H/T $3384.

1966 Buick. The tuned car.

new GS-340.

GS-400. $3563.

SPECIALS FROM $2844.

67 new GRILLES

54

Skylark

BUICK
COMPACTS

SPORT WAGON FR. $3711.

Skylark (SKYLARK CUSTOM)

WAGON *and* SEDAN *have* 115" WB ; CPE. *and* CVT. *have* 112" WB.

$3326.

2-DR. W.B. SHORTENED TO 112"

GS-400 WITH 400 CID V8
(340 HP)
← $3528.

(RESTYLED)
68

7.75 x 14 TIRES

350 CID V8 (280 HP @ 4600 RPM)

GS-350
(GS-400 LOOKS SIMILAR)

$3295.

new 230-HP V8 (STD. IN SKYLARK CUST.) RUNS ON REGULAR GAS

55

BUICK COMPACTS

Sportwagon

WITH *new* "DUAL ACTION" TAILGATE →

FROM $4195.

350 CID V8
3 SIDE PORTS LIKE SPECIAL (DLX.)

GS-350

"350"

350 CID V8
(280 HP)

$3810.

GS-400

400 CID V8 (340 HP)

H/T $3954.

"400" LETTERING

69

new GRILLES

MODIFIED STAGE I
GS-400 has "STAGE I" LETTERING INSTEAD, ALSO HI-LIFT CAM, 3.64 GEAR RATIO, ETC.

SKYLARK

H/T FR. $3739.

350 CID V8 STD. ON SKYLARK CUSTOM; AVAIL. ON OTHER SKYLARKS.

No wonder Buick owners keep selling Buicks for us.

Wouldn't you really rather have a Buick?

56

BUICK
COMPACTS

"SPECIAL"
MODEL NAME
DISCONTINUED

Skylark

$3737.
SKYLARK
350

WITH 350 CID
V8 (260 HP)

SPORTWAGON.
FROM $3977.

70

4-door Sedan.
$3614.

(SKYLARK
CUSTOM
4-DR. SED.
IS SIMILAR)

SKYLARK

$3563.

(VINYL
TOP
EXTRA)

1970

(CONT'D.
NEXT
PAGE)

2-door Sedan.

57

BUICK COMPACTS

$3899.

$3868.

SKYLARK CUSTOM

CVT. $3987.

70 (CONT'D.)

GS-455 STAGE I H/T

(360 HP)

Introducing automobiles to light your fire.

(GS H/T $3865.)

GS-455

455 C/D V8 (350 HP)

GS 455 Convertible. $4257.

58

BUICK

COMPACTS

1971 Buick. Something to believe in.

GS

$4259.

71

SKYLARK CUSTOM →

$4100.

WILL RUN LOW-LEAD OR UNLEADED FUELS.

(SKYLARK CUSTOM, GS ARE FINAL CONVERTIBLES (IN COMPACT SERIES.)

Skylark 350.

72

(FINAL USE OF SKYLARK NAME UNTIL 1975)

1972 Buick Skylark. Something to believe in.

Buick Bargain Days.

73

new NAME = **CENTURY**

(TOTALLY RESTYLED)

(CONT'D. NEXT PAGE)

$4073.

Century Luxus Colonnade Hardtop Coupe

59

BUICK COMPACTS

Century 350 Colonnade Hardtop Coupe

Wouldn't you really rather have a Buick?

PRICE OF $3811. FOR EITHER BODY TYPE

Century 350 Colonnade Hardtop Sedan.

gran sport

Gran Sport Colonnade Hardtop Coupe.

Century **73** (CONT'D.)

"BUICK" NAME ABOVE GRILLE ON **CENTURY 350**

(WAGONS ON NEXT PAGE)

Regal instrument panel.

VERTICAL PCS. IN REGAL GRILLE

CENTURY REGAL

$4210.

REGAL IS new TOP MODEL IN new CENT. LINE.

Regal Colonnade Hardtop Coupe.

60

BUICK COMPACTS

73 (CONT'D.)

Century Station Wagon.
$4222. UP

WOODGRAIN OPTIONAL AT EXTRA COST

Century *LUXUS*

$4385. UP

Introducing Apollo. By Buick.

111" WB
250 CID 6 (100 HP) OR
350 CID V8 (150 HP)

instrument panel with wood-grain vinyl accents.

Custom interior available.

73½

(INTRO. APRIL, 1973)

4-DR. $2883.

2-DR. HATCHBACK $3009.

2-DR. CPE. $2860.

E78 × 14 TIRES

BUICK COMPACTS

Apollo

GRILLE MODIFIED

FROM $3877.

Space-saver spare tire.
Standard with the Apollo Hatchback Coupe is a space-saver spare tire. If it's needed, the included inflation cylinder pops the folded spare into a full-size, functioning emergency tire.

Apollo $3900.

1974 Apollo INTERIOR

Century Regal

new SEDAN (JOINS CPE) $4734.

Gran Sport

74

DASH

Century 350

$4622.

Century Luxus

$4303.

1974 Buick Station Wagons *also*

$4602. 62

new TAIL-LIGHTS

REAR BUMPER of Station Wagon

FROM $4160.

BUICK
COMPACTS

HATCHBACK (REGULAR OR "S" MODELS) 97" WB

Skyhawk

(new) 231 CID V-6 (110 HP)

Buick Dedicated to the *Free Spirit* in just about everyone.

BR 78 × 13 TIRES

SKYLARK S/R

SKYLARK

RETURNS TO JOIN (AND THEN REPLACE) APOLLO SERIES.

$5122.

75 (CENTURY LUXUS REPLACED BY CENTURY CUSTOM.)

V-6 Buick Century
SPECIAL
$4665.

REGAL $5098.

According to E.P.A. figures,

Century Wagons

In dynamometer tests recently conducted by the Environmental Protection Agency, a Buick Century equipped with a 3.8-litre V-6 got 24 miles per gallon in the highway tests. (And 16 mpg in the city test.)

GM MARK OF EXCELLENCE

Be there am BUICK

BUICK COMPACTS

SKYHAWK FROM $4217.

SKYHAWK

coupes

'76

COUPES, HATCHBACKS and 4-DOORS IN SKYLARK, SKYLARK S/R LINES. ("S" COUPE ALSO)

(LOWEST-PRICED SKYLARK IS "S" COUPE, $4359.)

(CONT'D. NEXT PAGE)

SKYLARK S/R $5060. HATCHBACK (ILLUSTR. ABOVE) (LENGTH EXAGGERATED)

BUICK Dedicated to the Free Spirit in just about everyone.

SKYLARK S/R.

BUICK COMPACTS

UNUSUAL ROOF of REGAL TYPE (SINCE '73)

76 (CONT'D.)

CENTURY

CENTURY SPECIAL PRICED AT $4836.

note GRILLE DIFFERENCES

$5366. REGAL

coupes

A LIMITED NUMBER of "INDIANAPOLIS 500" CENTURY V-6 PACE CAR REPLICAS (IN SPECIAL SILVER, RED and BLACK PAINT COMBINATION) AVAIL. at BUICK DEALERS.

PACE CAR REPLICA (RARE)

OFFICIAL PACE CAR

BUICK Free Spirit

BUICK
COMPACTS

Nighthawk.

SKYHAWK FROM $4299.

SKYHAWK

(NIGHTHAWK → has SPECIAL PAINT)

SKYLARK

V-6

2.56 GEAR RATIO

MPG. 27 HWY., 17 17 CITY

77

REGAL

OPT. SUN ROOF

SALE $5115.05

(REG. $5739.)

Century

4-DR. FROM $5390.

CENTURY

REGAL

W/O GUARDS

W/GUARDS

Regal

CENTURY SPECIAL
$5197.

new BUMPERS

66

BUICK
COMPACTS

CENTURY SPECIAL
PRICED FROM
$5754.

A little science. A little magic.

Wagon Century

$6461.

231 CID V-6

MPG.= 27 HWY.
19 CITY

CENTURY

new FASTBACK REAR

new 2-door or 4-door

$6098.
(4-DR.)

note DIFF. BETWEEN ROCKER PANEL / LOWER DOOR TRIM ON CENTURY — AND CENT. CUSTOM

Century Custom

"3.2 Litre" on COWL

(TOTALLY RESTYLED)
all-new
BODY
SHAPES
108"
WB

"CENTURY CUSTOM" on REAR FENDERS

196 OR 231 CID V6 (86/102 HP)

305 CID V8 (145 HP)

231 CID V6 TURBO (151/175 HP)

78

TURBO REGAL

$6480.

STD. WH. CVR.

REGAL

CLOSE VIEW OF REGAL FRONT END

BUICK

Regal

REGAL DASH has GRAINED STRIP

REGAL FROM $6197.

67

BUICK COMPACTS

Skyhawk. FROM $4855.

79

HATCHBACK $5543.

Skylark.

SEDAN $5493.

turbocharged
Regal. $7144.

Century Special. $6497.

Century Limited and Century Custom.

Century Sport Coupe $6928.

$7154.

Century Wagons.
(UNGRAINED CENT. SPEC. ALSO)

BUICK
COMPACTS

Skyhawk
WITH ROAD HAWK OPTION PACKAGE

EPA EST. MPG	EST. HWY	EST DRIVING RANGE	EST HWY RANGE
15	24	277	444

FROM $5313.
FINAL **SKYHAWK**
(DISCONT'D. 1-80)

80

(SOME 1980 MODELS AVAIL. SPRING, 1979)

SKYLARK FROM $6525. (2-DR.)

Skylark is equipped with GM-built engines produced by various divisions. See your dealer for details.

Skylark

DASH

new 104.9" WB 4 CYL. or V6

(CONT'D. NEXT PAGE)

EPA EST MPG	EST HWY	EST DRIVING RANGE	EST HWY RANGE
24	38	336	532

new SPORT COUPE $7140. (SPORT SEDAN ALSO

69

BUICK
COMPACTS

BLACK DASH and ROUND-HUB STEER. WHEEL WITH STANDARD

SKYLARK INTERIOR →

with standard engine and available automatic transmission, it offers the following EPA estimates.

EPA EST MPG	EST HWY	EST DRIVING RANGE	EST HWY RANGE
20	27	362	488

← SPT. CPE. $7292.

Century CUSTOM

new **Century Limited Sedan** $7566.

CPE. $6776.

$7601.

80 (CONT'D.)

Regal Limited

EPA EST MPG	EST HWY	EST DRIVING RANGE	EST HWY RANGE
20	27	362	488

↗ 2-TONE PAINT ON new **Regal Somerset**

PY-6809

Regal $7182.

Century Wagon $7331.

WOOD-GRAIN OPTIONAL AT $316.

Century Estate Wagon $7629.

BUICK *RIVIERA* (OWN SEPARATE SERIES SINCE 1963)

425 CID V8 (360 HP)
8.45 × 15 TIRES

luxury cars.

new 119" WB FROM $4513.

new GRILLE

66

Riviera GS

GS MODEL

1966 Buick. The tuned car.

TAIL LIGHTS

HAZARD FLASHERS AT ALL CORNERS, *and* ENERGY-ABSORBING STEERING COLUMN

new 430 CID V8 (360 HP)

CENTER CONSOLE AVAIL.

67

(INTRO. 9-29-66)

$4557.

71

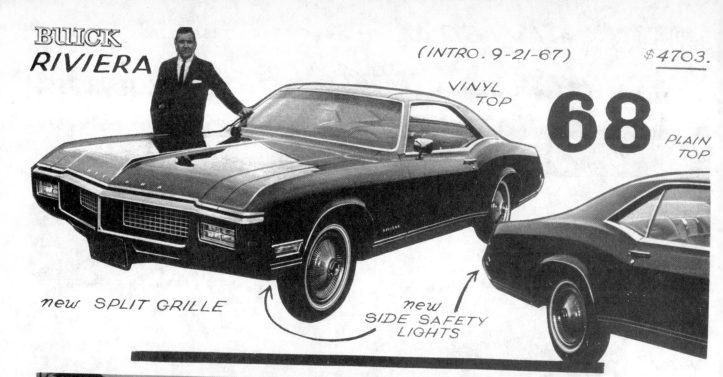

BUICK RIVIERA

(INTRO. 9-21-67) $4703.

VINYL TOP

68

PLAIN TOP

new SPLIT GRILLE

new SIDE SAFETY LIGHTS

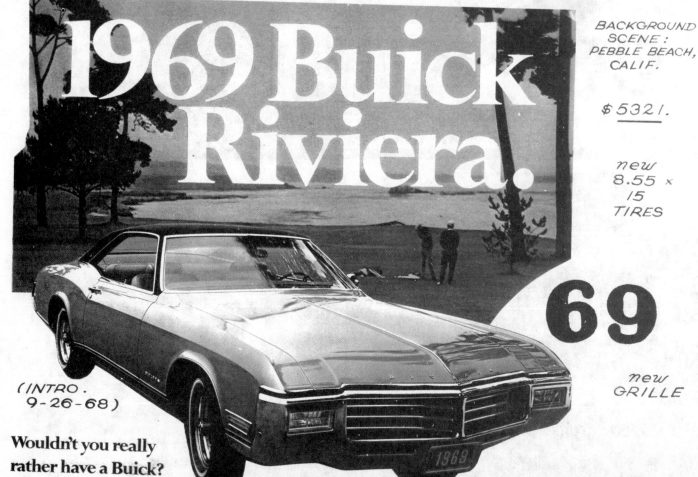

1969 Buick Riviera.

BACKGROUND SCENE: PEBBLE BEACH, CALIF.

$5321.

new 8.55 x 15 TIRES

69

new GRILLE

(INTRO. 9-26-68)

Wouldn't you really rather have a Buick?

72

BUICK RIVIERA

note:
1970 IS THE ONLY MODEL WITH THIS UNIQUE new DECORATIVE MID-SIDE TRIM with DIP

VINYL TOP

new H78 × 15 TIRES

70

new RED ROUND SIDE SAFETY LT. AT REAR, WITH RIVIERA "R" SYMBOL IN CHROME, ACROSS LENS.

new GRILLE
WIDER REAR WINDOW
new TAIL LIGHTS

new 455 CID V8 (370 HP)

PLAIN TOP

Something to believe in.

$5474.

DASH

GS

(INTRO. 9-18-69)

"GS" LETTERING

73

BUICK *RIVIERA*

(INTRO. 10-3-70)

GS

1971 Buick Riviera GS.

(TOTALLY RESTYLED)

71

new 122" WB

ANOTHER
VIEW OF
TAIL ↘

$5917.

3.42
GEAR RATIO

315 HP WITH 455 CID V8

EMPHASIS ON *all-new* POINTED
BOAT-TAIL REAR END STYLING.

Something to believe in.

HP CUT AGAIN TO 250
(455 CID V8)

$5790.

new
SIDE
CHROME

72

new
TAIL-
LIGHTS

(INTRO. 9-23-71)

BUICK RIVIERA

AccuDrive, variable ratio power steering, power front disc brakes, new durable stamped steel rocker arms, new computer-selected chassis springs for superb ride and handling, new windshield washer and radiator overflow coolant reservoirs integrated with the fan shroud, solenoid actuated throttle stop, new Exhaust Gas Recirculation (EGR) and Air Injection Reactor (AIR) emission control systems, evaporative emission control system, integral voltage regulator and Delcotron, brake proportioning valve

$5795.

new GRILLE

73

DASH

↑
new THICKER ROCKER PANEL TRIM COVERS PART OF DOOR

Bravo Cloth and Madrid-grain Vinyl 60/40 Notchback seat available in Riviera in Blue, Sandalwood or Saddle.

Engine, standard: 455 C.I.D. V-8. Carburetion: 4-barrel.

Engine, available: Stage 1 modified 4-barrel 455 C.I.D. V-8 engine with performance ratio, positive traction axle and special ornamentation.

Transmission, standard: Turbo Hydra-matic 400 automatic.

Axle Ratios: with standard engine: 2.93:1; with Stage 1 engine: 3.23:1 with positive traction.

STD. HP 250
REAR LIC. PLATE NOW IN CENTER
FINAL YR. FOR POINTED REAR

Oxen-grain Expanded Vinyl and Madrid-grain Vinyl 40/40 seats available in Riviera in White, Saddle or Black.

INTERIORS 75

Newport Knit Vinyl and Madrid-grain Vinyl 40/40 seats standard in Riviera in Sandalwood or Black.
ALSO:
Oxen-grain Expanded Vinyl and Madrid-grain Vinyl 60/40 Notchback seat available in Riviera in Green, Sandalwood, Saddle, Black or Burgundy.

$6308.
PLAIN TOP

BUICK *RIVIERA*

PARTIAL VINYL TOP

74

RESTYLED
(ALL-*new* ROOFLINE
and REAR)
HP CUT
TO
230
(455 CID
V8)

new
J78×15
TIRES

OPT.
LEATHER
UPHOLSTERY

new
DASH

HOOD
ORNAMENT
ADDED →

new
VERTICAL GRILLE
WITH
"RIVIERA" NAME
ABOVE GRILLE, 1974.

new RECTANGULAR HEADLIGHTS

JR 78×15
TIRES
(THROUGH
'76)

75

$6993.

new GRILLE
new CORNER LTS.
"BUICK" NAME ABOVE GRILLE.
"RIVIERA" ON GRILLE, IN SCRIPT.

76

BUICK RIVIERA

PLAIN TOP

HP CUT TO 205
(FINAL 455 CID BIG V8)

$7401.

76

new GRILLE

VINYL TOP

BUICK Dedicated to
the Free Spirit in just about everyone.

(SLOGAN 1975 TO 1977)

$7988.

new UPSWEPT REAR
QUARTER MOLDING   (DOWNSIZED)

77

new GRILLE
new FRONT and
CORNER LIGHT
DESIGN

SMALLER
350 CID V8
(170 HP)

new 116" WB (THROUGH '78)

GR78 x 15
TIRES
(THROUGH '78)

The Riviera LXXV.

(OPT. SILVER-AND-BLACK
BUICK 75TH ANNIVERSARY
COLOR SCHEME)

$8763.

78

350 OR
403 CID V8

BUICK
LXXV

77

A little science.
A little magic.

BUICK
RIVIERA
After all, life is to enjoy. ('79)

$10,960.¹⁰ (S) ('79)
11,822.¹¹ (S) ('80)
DASH

new 114" WB

79-80

"S" (TOP, LEFT) ('79)
(has BLACK GRILLE and SIDE MIRRORS, OWN WHEEL CVRS.)

RESTYLED and DOWN SIZED

new FRONT-WHEEL-DRIVE

V6 OR V8

$10,683.¹⁰ ('79)
11,491.¹⁰ ('80)

1980 has new INTERIORS and REAR VIEW MIRRORS PLACED FURTHER FORWARD ON DOORS (arrow)

S

('80)

78

(SINCE 1902)

Cadillac

Standard of the World

GM

New elegance, new excellence, new excitement!

Interior
(FLEETWOOD)

9.00 × 15 TIRES
129.5 " WB
(CALAIS, DE VILLE)
133 " WB
(FLTWD. 60 SP.)
149.75 " WB
(FLTWD. 75)

SEDAN de VILLE

$6303.

V-8 ENGINES
(SINCE 1915 MODEL)
(OVERHEAD VALVES
SINCE 1949)
129½ " WB
(FLEETWOODS have
133 " OR 149¾ " WB)

429 CID V8 (340 HP)

66

EMBLEM

FLEETWOOD
60 SPECIAL

BROUGHAM

$7417.

79

Cadillac

H/T COUPE
$5718.

NEW GRILLE
67

CALAIS

SEDAN
$5893.

DE VILLE

SEDAN
$6303.
(SAME PRICE)

$6286.   CVT.

4-DR.
H/T

H/T COUPE
DE VILLE
$6070.

FRONT
DETAIL

(CONT'D.
NEXT PAGE)

80

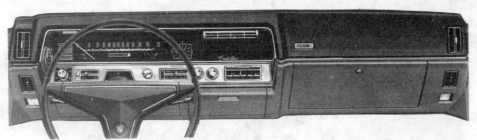

new DASH

EL DORADO
BECOMES SEPARATE
SERIES, 1967 ON.
SEE "CADILLAC
EL DORADO"
SECTION.

VINYL PADDED
↓ TOP ON THE
BROUGHAM

FLEETWOOD
60
SPECIAL

BROUGHAM
$7417.

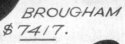

67

(CONT'D.)

SEDAN WITH
PLAIN TOP

$7101.

FLEETWOOD 75

(has
8.20 × 15 TIRES)

SEDAN = $10,522.
LIMOUSINE = 10,733.

75 INTERIOR
(7-PASS.)
IN
LIGHT GRAY
DEVONSHIRE
CLOTH

Cadillac

Brilliant new styling • Dramatic new interiors • Totally new instrument panel • Concealed windshield wipers • Improved variable-ratio power steering • New disc brakes available • Wide choice of eleven luxurious body styles.

new 472 CID V8 (375 HP)

DE VILLE

CVT. $6101.

4-DR. H/T
DE VILLE = $6463.
CALAIS = 6169.

CALAIS CPE. (H/T) $5993.

Elegance in action

68

(RESTYLED)
(INTRO. 9-21-67)

DE VILLE $6463.

new DASH

CPE. DE VILLE (H/T) $6230.

TWILIGHT SENTINEL AUTO. HDLT. CONTROL (LTS. WILL STAY ON 90 SEC. AFTER IGNITION SHUT OFF)

$7577.

FLEETWOOD (60 SPECIAL) BROUGHAM

FLEETWOOD 75 LIMOUSINE (PADDED ROOF OPT.)

$10,930.

82

Cadillac. $7788.

FLEETWOOD 60 SPECIAL

(INTRO. 9-26-68)

4 HEADLTS. NOW IN HORIZONTAL PAIRS

69 *new* GRILLE

↖ *new* REAR STYLING

BROUGHAM

DE VILLE $6399.

$6632.

-a masterpiece from the master craftsmen.

Cadillac presents the Spirit of the Seventies

FINAL DE VILLE CVT. $6772.

4-DR. H/T $6822.

DE VILLE

The elegantly spirited 1970 Cadillac

(INTRO. 9-18-69)

H/T $6588.

new GRILLE **70**

new CORNERING LTS.

new L78 × 15 TIRES (all models)

DF 3379

Fleetwood 75.

$11,227. UP

83

Cadillac

DASH

HORSEPOWER CUT TO 345 @ 4400 RPM (GROSS) OR 220 @ 4000 RPM (NET) 2.93 GEAR RATIO (3.15 ON 75)

$6983.

CPE. DE VILLE H/T

DE VILLE

new 130" WB

new 1-PC. TAIL-LIGHTS

CX-307

4-DR. H/T $7177.

AM/FM STEREO RADIO AND 8-TRACK TAPE PLAYER AVAIL.

new RUBBER-TIPPED BUMPER GUARDS (ON ALL MODELS)

71

new GRILLE new WIDELY-SPACED HEADLTS.

(INTRO. 9-29-70)

SIDE VIEW (60-S)

(CONVERTIBLE MOVED TO EL DORADO LINE, 1971-76)

One of the most appreciated new Cadillac luxuries available is the lamp monitoring system that tells you whether your headlights, rear lights and turn signals are functioning properly. Coupled with the lamp monitoring system is a warning light that tells you when your windshield washer fluid is low.

DETAILS OF ↑ REAR QUARTER OUTSIDE COURTESY LIGHT

133" WB FLEETWOOD 60 SPECIAL BROUGHAM

(note ARCHED WINDOWS)

$8502.

(FLTWD. 75 GETS new 151½" WB)

(27-GAL. FUEL TANK) CAN RUN ON REGULAR OR UNLEADED FUEL

84

Cadillac

FLEETWOOD BROUGHAM

HP CUT AGAIN, TO 220 (THROUGH '73) (INTRO. 9-23-71)

$8843.

AUX. LTS. MOVED UP FROM BUMPER and PLACED BETWEEN HEADLTS.

72

new GRILLE

H/T DE VILLE $6874. CALAIS $6477.

$6477.

CALAIS

DASH

DE VILLE 4-DR. H/T $7096.

AS BEFORE, A WREATH AROUND EMBLEM IDENTIFIES THE FLEETWOOD.

new GRILLE

73

Fleetwood Seventy-Five

INTER. (75)

LIMO. $12,063

Cadillac $7752.

NEW REAR QUARTER WINDOWS

CPE. DE VILLE

← HOOD ORNAMENT ADDED DURING '74, BUT AVAIL. ON EARLY "SPECIAL MODELS."

MOST EARLY '74s BEAR CRESTS ABOVE GRILLE, AS ILLUSTRATED.

AVG. MPG 12 CITY 15.8 HWY.

HP CUT TO 205

74 new GRILLE

new 2-TIER CORNER LTS.; HDLTS. CLOSER TOGETHER (ROUND, IN SQUARE FRAMES)

$9422. UP
FLEETWOOD
BROUGHAM $10,414.

CPE.

$8184. TO $14,557. PRICE RANGE

ELDORADO 500 CID V8 NOW USED, BUT HP CUT TO 190 (THROUGH '76)

W. ORNAMENT ON HOOD

75 new GRILLE, RECTANGULAR HEADLIGHTS

FINAL YEAR FOR CALAIS MODELS

Cadillac

H/T $8629

$9265.

DE VILLE

$9067.

FLTWD. BROUGHAM TALISMAN SEDAN

$12,748

76

new FINER "CROSSHATCH" GRILLE PCS.

new WHEELBASES: DE VILLE, BROUGHAM = 121½" "75" = 144½"

$11,546.

SEDAN DE VILLE $10,020.

(FLEETWOOD) BROUGHAM

new 425 CID V8 (180 HP)

new 77

"DOWNSIZED" MODELS (TOTALLY RESTYLED)

COUPE DE VILLE (2 VIEWS) $9810.

TYPICAL MODERN SHOWROOM

Cadillac

Behind the great name...
...a great car.

78

FLEETWOOD BROUGHAM
$12,292.

"Cadillac"
NAME NOW
ABOVE
GRILLE, IN
CHROME SCRIPT.
(SEE ARROW)

EMBLEM
(HOOD)

(new)

DE VILLE
CPE.
(IN SHOWROOM,
TOP SCENE) PRICED
AT $10,444.

(75 FORMAL LIMO.
PRICED AT
$20,363.)

new
GRILLE
has MORE
VERTICAL and FEWER
HORIZONTAL PCS.

88

Cadillac

(DIESEL ENG. AVAIL.)

new GRILLE has SMALLER and MORE CRISS-CROSS PCS., with "Cadillac" NAME RETURNED TO UPPER BORDER of GRILLE.

'79

DASH

new OPERA LIGHT ON FLTWD. BRGHM.

CPE. DE VILLE $12,401.

AVAIL.

$14,927.

The Fleetwood Brougham

$23,388.

The Fleetwood Limousine

SIMULATED TEAKWOOD TRIM on DASH

new SMALLER 368 CID V8 (150 HP)

80

new GRILLE has MOSTLY VERTICAL PIECES. new WIDE AMBER AUX. LTS. BELOW HEADLTS. and CORNER LTS.

120" WB *Cadillac Eldorado* (OWN SERIES SINCE 1967)

with front-wheel drive.

FLEETWOOD CREST ON REAR QUARTER PANEL

67 New

429 CID V8 (340 HP)

$6955.

ELDORADO...world's finest personal car

Elegance in action!

CONCEALED HDLT. DETAIL

68

new 472 CID V8 (375 HP)

new FRONT CORNER LT. IN FENDER TIP

new REAR SAFETY LIGHT

DIAMOND PATTERN CLOTH AND VINYL

CHOICES of UPHOLSTERY (LEATHER ALSO AVAIL.)

$7283. (VINYL LANDAU TOP $137 EXTRA)

DEAUVILLE CLOTH with VINYL BOLSTERS (CHOICE OF 4 COLORS)

FRONT ST. BACK ST.

Cadillac Eldorado

PLAIN TOP

VINYL TOP

$7389.

69

new GRILLE WITH FINER PCS.
new UNCONCEALED HEADLIGHTS

WITH OPT. SUNROOF

DASH

70

new GRILLE and SIDE TRIM

new 500 CID V8 (400 HP)

new L78 x 15 TIRES

FROM $7607.

1971 DASH

(FIRST EL DORADO CVT. AVAIL. SINCE 1966)

REAR QUARTER WINDOWS ARE *new*

71

new GRILLE
new 126.3" WB

$8468.

NAME JUST BELOW CHROME STRIP

1971

1971

$8098.

Cadillac Eldorado

$8252.

HP CUT TO 235 (THROUGH '73)

72

new GRILLE

$7936.

(SAME PRICES AS '72)

REAR

CORNER LTS. NOW LOWER AT FRONT END

new GRILLE

73

new ENERGY-ABSORBING SAFETY BUMPERS

92

Cadillac Eldorado

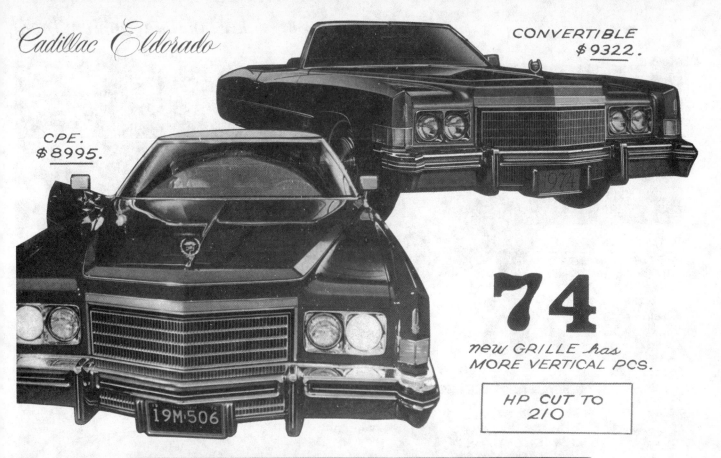

CONVERTIBLE $9322.

CPE. $8995.

19M 506

74
new GRILLE *has* MORE VERTICAL PCS.

HP CUT TO 210

$9935.

HP CUT AGAIN, TO 190

INTERIOR (CVT.)

new GRILLE

NAME NO LONGER APPEARS ON SIDE OF COWL

75
SIDE SAFETY LT. NOW MOVED

new

$10,354

BACK FROM FRONT CORNER

Cadillac Eldorado   *Eldorado Convertible* (BELOW), $11,049.   **Last of a magnificent breed.**

THE FINAL CONVERTIBLE MFD. BY A MAJOR AMERICAN FACTORY!

"Cadillac" NAME NOW ABOVE GRILLE.

76

(CPE. PRICE = $10,586.)

It is the only convertible now built in America. And it will be our last. The very last. Because the Eldorado Convertible will not be offered in 1977.

new SMALLER 425 CID V8 (180 HP)

new GRILLE WITH MORE, FINER VERTICAL PCS. and "ELDORADO" NAME ABOVE.

77

PHANTOM VIEW

Automatic Level Control. Adjusts for changing loads automatically.

Four-Wheel Disc Brakes. Ventilated discs have cooling fins for rapid heat dissipation.

Automatic Climate Control. Redesigned for 1977. Compressor works only when necessary.

COUPE = $11,187.

BIARRITZ CPE. = $12,947)

(CPE. PRICED FROM $11,921.)

QUARTER PANEL LIGHT

Eldorado Custom Biarritz

78

new GRILLE WITH HEAVIER HORIZONTAL PCS.

$13,786.

94

Cadillac Eldorado

$17,043.

BIARRITZ

$14,693.

new BOXY REAR QUARTERS

DOWNSIZED, WITH new SHORT 113.9" WB

79
(RESTYLED)

FUEL-INJECTED 350 CID V8 (170 HP)

CPE. PRICED FROM $15,509.

368 CID V8
(350 CID V8 IN CALIFORNIA)

(160 OR 145 HP)

80

Available for Eldorado

Astroroof Shown with Biarritz.

Eldorado Wire Wheel Covers.

AS BEFORE, note SPECIAL REAR QUARTER PANEL DECOR WHICH IDENTIFIES *Eldorado Biarritz*

$18,003.

1980 GRILLE

20.6-GAL. FUEL TANK

P205/75R15 TIRES
2.19 GEAR RATIO

Digital Electronic Fuel Injection and on-board diagnostics for servicing.

Standard for Eldorado...Available at no extra cost for Seville

FUEL INJECTION

95

new AMBER LIGHTS BELOW HEADLAMPS

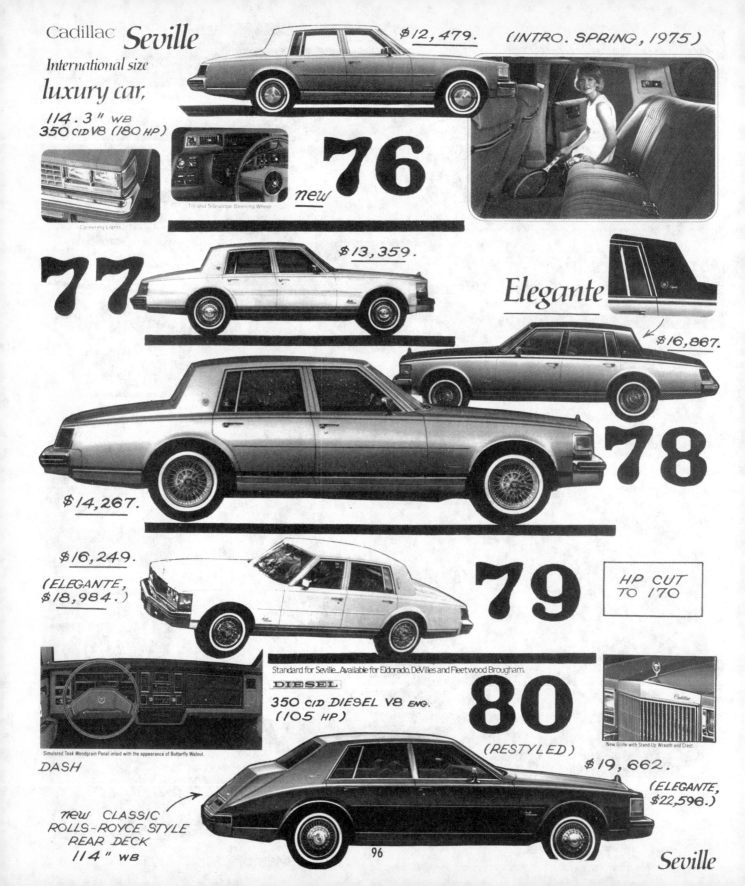

Cadillac *Seville*

International size
luxury car.

114.3" WB
350 CID V8 (180 HP)

$12,479.   (INTRO. SPRING, 1975)

new **76**

Tilt and Telescope Steering Wheel

Cornering Lights

77 $13,359.

Elegante

$16,867.

78

$14,267.

$16,249.

(ELEGANTE,
$18,984.)

79

HP CUT
TO 170

Simulated Teak Woodgrain Panel inlaid with the appearance of Butterfly Walnut.

DASH

Standard for Seville...Available for Eldorado, DeVilles and Fleetwood Brougham.

DIESEL
350 CID DIESEL V8 ENG.
(105 HP)

80
(RESTYLED)

New Grille with Stand-Up Wreath and Crest

$19,662.

(ELEGANTE,
$22,596.)

*new CLASSIC
ROLLS-ROYCE STYLE
REAR DECK
114" WB*

96

Seville

(SINCE 1964) **CHEVELLE** BY CHEVROLET   **MID-SIZE**

FULL COIL SUSPENSION

115" WB

(300 IS LOWEST-PRICED, LITTLE CHROME, $2607 UP. 300 DLX. has CHROME STRIP ALONG SIDE.)

Malibu Wagon
2-SEAT

MALIBU CVT. = $3030.

MALIBU

$3093.

H/T SPT. CPE. $2821.

194 CID 6 (120 HP)
230 CID 6 (140 HP)
283 CID TURBO-FIRE V8
(195 OR 220 HP)
327 CID V8 (275 HP)
396 CID V8s
(325 OR 360 HP)

(300 TYPES have PLAINER REAR DECKS without CHROME ORNAMENTATION)

FLUSH-AND-DRY ROCKER PANELS

66

DASH

OPTIONAL TACH. ←

SS 396 $3219.

SS has Turbo-Jet V8's

(396 CID)

6.95/7.35 × 14 TIRES (OPT. RED-STRIPE NYLON TIRE and MAG.-STYLE WHEEL COVER) 97

(SS CVT. ALSO AVAIL.)

CHEVELLE

$3079.

MALIBU

7.35 x 14 TIRES

H/T $2877.

DASH and CONSOLE

new GRILLES and TAIL-LIGHTS

67

new safety features standard — GM-developed energy-absorbing steering column, four-way hazard warning flasher, dual master cylinder brake system with warning light, folding front seat back latches.

SS 396.

Turbo-Jet V8

SS 396

H/T $3083.

SS 396

SS 396

(F70 x 14 TIRES ON SS-396)

note "SS 396" IN GRILLE CENTER

2-SEAT

CONCOURS

new TOP-OF-LINE WAGON (300 DLX. and MALIBU WAGONS ALSO AVAIL.)

$3269

98

LARGER STD. 307 CID V8
(200 HP) USES REG. GAS
230 CID STD. 6
(140 HP)

CHEVELLE BY **CHEVROLET**

MALIBU

68
(RESTYLED)

AT CENTER:
Chevelle Nomad Custom
WAGON
(new)
$3303.
(3-ST.)

WITH OPT. VINYL TOP

SS-396
H/T = $3249.

BE SMART. BE SURE. BUY NOW AT YOUR CHEVROLET DEALER'S.

new WB
112" 2 DR.
116" 4 DR.
(THROUGH '77)

FRONT VENT WINDOWS ELIMINATED

STD.
230 CID 6
(140 HP)
307 CID V8
(200 HP)

69

new GRILLES

new LOCKING STEERING COLUMN and TRANS. LEVER

MALIBU H/T
$3025.
$3372 WITH OPTIONAL ILLUS.
SS-396 PACKAGE

(also NOMAD, GREENBRIER, CONCOURS, CONCOURS EST. WAGONS AVAIL.)

4530·01

99

WAGONS FROM $3655.

CHEVELLE BY CHEVROLET WITH OPTIONAL Chevelle SS 396 PACKAGE

TOP TO BOTTOM: NOMAD, GREENBRIER, CONCOURS, CONCOURS ESTATE WAGONS

CHEVROLET
On The Move.

new 2-TIER GRILLE

70

new 250 CID STD. 6 (155 HP)

UP TO 400 CID TURBO-JET V8 (330 HP)

MALIBU

H/T $3534.

SS PKG.

new TAIL-LIGHTS RECESSED IN REAR BUMPER

MALIBU

STD 250 CID 6 (145 HP)

STD 307 CID V8 (200 HP)

71

new GRILLE and BUMPERS. new CORNER LTS. new SINGLE HEADLTS.

H/T $3719.

1971. You've changed. We've changed.

100

CHEVELLE

SCENE:
6 FLAGS AMUSEMT. PK.,
ATLANTA, GA.

250 CID 6
(110 HP)
307 CID
V8
(130 HP)
350 CID
V8 (165
OR 175 HP)

400 CID V8 (240 HP)
454 CID
V8 (SS)
(270 HP)

72

new GRILLE

Building a better way to see the U.S.A.

H/T ILLUSTR.
WITH and W/O
VINYL
TOP

H/T
$3683.

MALIBU

4-DR.
SEDAN
FROM
$3486.

"HEAVY CHEVY" SPT. CPE.
has BLACK GRILLE, SPECIAL
STRIPING (INTRO. MID-'71)

DLX.
CPE.
$3599.

DLX. 4-DR. = $3566.

COLONNADE
4-DR.

Malibu

$3711.

100 TO 245 HP
(400 CID V8 DISCONTINUED
'73 ONLY)

(CONT'D.
NEXT PAGE)

73

new
ENERGY-ABSORBING SAFETY BUMPERS

TOTALLY
RESTYLED **DELUXE** COLONNADE CPE.
and 4-DR.
(ABOVE)

Chevrolet. **Building a better way** to see the U.S.A.

CHEVELLE

OPT. WHEEL COVERS

6.

LAGUNA FRONT END IS ENTIRE BUMPER. OTHER *new* TYPE BUMPER AT TOP (GUARDS OPT.)

MALIBU →

MALIBU $3997.

FR.

wagon

DLX. WAGON $3909. UP

DLX. →

MALIBU

5261-CE

CPE. $3743.

OPTION. SWING-OUT (90°) BUCKET SEATS

(MALIBU SS *has* "SS" IN CENTER OF BLACK GRILLE and ON COWL.)

DASH (LAGUNA)

REAR

New Laguna

$4373.

CPE. $3932.

Laguna Estate

IJM-984

102

CHEVELLE BY CHEVROLET

(CHEVELLE DELUXE DISCONTINUED)

$2878* MALIBU 6 COUPE

$2873* MALIBU 6 SEDAN

(MALIBU, CLASSIC and CLASSIC EST. WAGONS AVAIL.)

Malibu Classic

'74

Engines	Power Rating*
Turbo-Thrift 250 Six	100-hp
Turbo-Fire 350 V8	145-hp
Turbo-Fire 350 V8	160-hp
Turbo-Fire 400 V8	150-hp
Turbo-Fire 400 V8	180-hp
Turbo-Jet 454 V8	235-hp

new GRILLES

(DURING 1974, MALIBU 6 CPE. PRICE INCREASED TO $3954.!)

Malibu Classic $4590.

LANDAU CPE.

new HOOD ORNAMENT (MAL.CLASSIC ONLY)

Malibu Classic Sedan

Malibu Classic: (NEW)

Chevrolet makes sense for America.

$4376.

Chevelle Laguna Type S-3.

(note 2 AVAILABLE TOP STYLES)

LAGUNA TYPE S-3

S-3 GRILLE

$4504.

S-3

(GR70 x 15 TIRES ON Laguna)

NEW

103

CHEVELLE
coupe.
$3407.*

MALIBU
Malibu Wagon

The lowest-priced sedan.
$3402.*

$4989.

MALIBU CLASSIC
CPE.

22% higher gas mileage with standard V8

Malibu Classic instrument panel, with new speedometer calibrated in both miles per hour (mph) and kilometers per hour (kph).

$5412. WAGON
(MAL. CLASSIC ESTATE) →
(3-ST.)

(ALSO AVAIL. W/O GRAIN)

SEDAN $4744.

250 CID 6
(105 HP)
350 CID
V8
(145 OR
155 HP)
400 CID V8 (175 HP)
454 CID V8 (215 HP)

new SLOPING FRONT ON

LAGUNA TYPE S-3

catalytic converter.

NEW '75

(RESTYLED FRONT *and* REAR ENDS)

$4867.

LAGUNA TYPE S-3
(ALSO AVAIL. INTO 1976)

DASH

104

'76 Chevelle.
A size whose time has come.

Two roomy Chevelles priced under $3671. (SALE)
26 MPG Highway, 18 MPG City. EPA. *

REG. $4711.

$5185. (LANDAU)

MALIBU CLASSIC

76

new GRILLES
(MAL. CLASSIC *has* OWN 4 HEADLIGHTS, MESH-TYPE GRILLE) →

MALIBU

REG. $4746.

* = WITH 250 CID 6 (105 HP) 20 HWY., 14 CITY
WITH 305 CID V8 (new, 140 HP)

(454 CID V8 DISCONT'D.)

Smart, complete, mid-size Chevelle.

(NO MORE TYPE 9-3)

MALIBU WAGON

$5466.

SALE: $3885.

new GRILLES, FEWER ENG. CHOICES

77

MALIBU

250 CID 6 (110 HP)
305 CID V8 (145 HP)
350 CID V8 (170 HP)

MALIBU CLASSIC

$5651.

DASH (MALIBU CLASSIC)

$5327.

(illustr. LARGE SIDE MIRROR is OPTIONAL.)

TAIL-LT. DETAILS

Chevette

Chevrolet's new kind of American car.

(SINCE 1976)
(SOLD BY 6,030 CHEVROLET DEALERS)

85 CID 4 (52 HP) (97.6 CID, 60 HP AVAIL.)

EPA rating
- 40 MPG highway
- 28 MPG city

13-GAL. FUEL TANK
155×80-13 TIRES

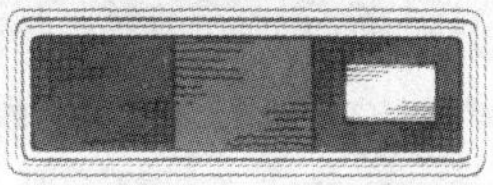

94.3" WB

76

RALLY SPORT OR WOODY TRIM AVAIL.

3.7 OR 4.11 G.R.

INTERNATIONAL TAILLIGHTS. It's the red, white, and amber combination found in most world-type cars. Outside—stop. Middle—signal. Inside—backup.

$3314. SCOOTER has NO BACK SEAT

Bright and happy. That's Sandpiper with the special Custom Interior that features richly patterned "Reef" cloth-and-vinyl upholstery in tones of Yellow, Cream and Gold. Carpeting, instrument panel and seat belts are Yellow Gold. Also included: deluxe door trim, wood-grain vinyl accents, sport steering wheel, day-night rearview mirror, carpeted cargo area and added acoustical insulation.

Sandpiper

43^MPG EPA HIGHWAY

31^MPG EPA CITY ESTIMATE

Shown below is Sandpiper's special interior trim.

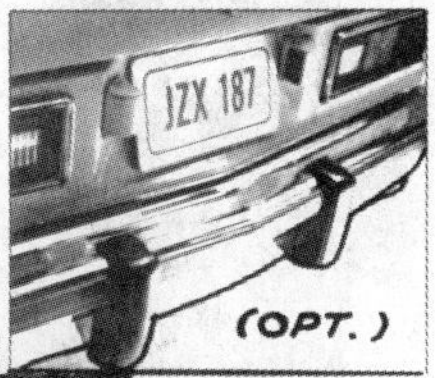

BUMPER RUB STRIPS AND GUARDS. Front and rear. Protect from minor dings. Add styling appeal.

JZX 187

(OPT.)

RALLY SPORT PKG.

new SANDPIPER PKG. OPT.

ZIX 362

It'll drive you happy.

2-DR. $3540.

77

new 57 HP (85 CID ENG.) OPT. SIDE TRIM STRIP AVAIL.

(OPT.)

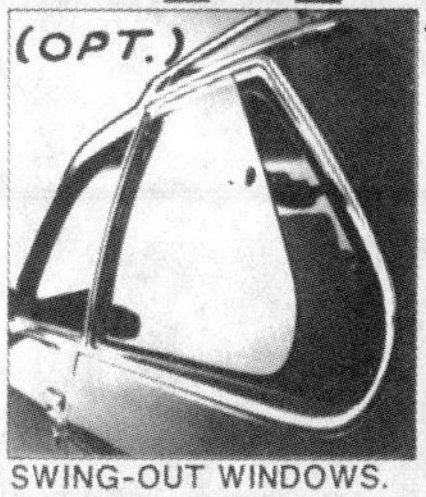

SWING-OUT WINDOWS. SPECIAL INSTRUMENTATION. For the well-informed driver. Has tachometer and voltmeter. Included with available Rally Sport equipment.

107

Chevette

108

SINCE 1918, MFD. BY **General Motors**

CHEVROLET

(EST. 1911) FROM $2832. (BISCAYNE 2-DR.)

Caprice DASH

IMPALA HUB CAP

IMPALA

66

new GRILLE, BUMPER and TAIL-LIGHT

(INTRO. THURSDAY 10-7-65)

119" WB
7.75/8.25 × 14 TIRES

STD. ENGINES
250 CID 6 (155 HP)
283 CID V8 (195 HP)

NEW

↑ REAR VIEW

Caprice Custom Wagon

$3800. (3-SEAT)

CUSTOM SEDAN $3516.

* **CAPRICE**

Custom Series →

note HORIZONTAL BANDS ACROSS CAPRICE TAILLIGHTS (UNLIKE TAILLIGHTS OF BISCAYNE, BEL AIR OR IMPALA MODELS)

*-(CAPRICE INTRO. 1965, AS A $242 OPT. PKG.)

$3453.
CAPR. CUST.
CPE. ROOFLINE (New)

DENOTES A 327 CID V8

109

'67 Chevrolet gives you that sure feeling

Biscayne $3036.

$3469. UP

(INTRO. 9-29-66)

Impala

STANDARD ENGINES
155-hp Turbo-Thrift 250 Six
195-hp Turbo-Fire 283 V8
EXTRA-COST OPTIONAL ENGINES
275-hp Turbo-Fire 327 V8
325-hp Turbo-Jet 396 V8
385-hp Turbo-Jet 427 V8

'67 IMPALA

Impala SS $3350.

67 new GRILLE

$3192.

Caprice Custom Sedan

$3477.

1967

Impala Sport Coupe

new GRILLE IS HORIZONTALLY BISECTED BY BUMPER CROSS BAR

68

$3809. UP

CAPRICE

CUSTOM SEDAN $3621.

new ROUND TAIL LTS. IN BUMPER

CUSTOM CPE.

formal

STD. 250 CID 6 (155 HP)
307 CID V8 (200 HP)

$3371.

Impala coupes

note SMALL new SIDE LIGHTS

Fastback
SPORT CPE. $3318.

1968

(INTRO. 9-21-67)

CHEVROLET

ALL ENGINES
EXCEPT 427 CID V8s
USE REGULAR
GAS.

Impala

$3427.

new
PLASTIC
GRILLE

$3426.

(INTRO. 9-26-68)

ENGINES : 250 CID 6 (155 HP)
327 CID V8 (235 HP)
350 CID V8 (255 OR 300 HP)
396 CID V8
(265 HP)
427 CID V8
(335 OR 390 HP)

69
(RESTYLED)

new
KINGSWOOD
ESTATE
(3-SEAT)
$4019.

new CONCEALED
HEADLIGHTS

Caprice

wagon
new
BROOKWOOD,
TOWNSMAN, KINGSWOOD
and KINGSWOOD ESTATE
WAGONS

Putting you first, keeps us first.

(INTRO. 9-26-68)

note FLARED
REAR FENDERS

111

BROOKWOOD, TOWNSMAN, KINGSWOOD
KINGSWOOD ESTATE WAGONS
(FROM TOP, DOWN)
(119" WB)

70 *new* Wagons MODELS (7)

(INTRO. 9-18-69)
3-ST. $4201.

new V-GRILLE $3812.

2-ST. $4088.

KING9. EST.

Impala

Right Car. Right Price. Right Now.

IMPALA CUSTOM H/T $3607.

2-DR. CUST. H/T

Caprice $3815.

(*new* MONTE CARLO IN SEPARATE SECTION.)

On the move: The Chevrolet '70s. 112

BROOKWD.

Impala

(BISCAYNE 4-DR. SED. FR. $3885.)

(INTRO. 9-29-70)
STD. HP
CUT (6-145)
(V8-245)

new GRILLES

71

new 121½" WB

↓ $4239.

Caprice. ↗ CAPR. CUSTOM SED. 4-DR. H/T $4545.

Caprice TYPE WITH MID-SIDE TRIM SPEAR (TYPE W/O, ABOVE RT.)

1971. You've changed. We've changed.

Impala $4257.

72

FINE HORIZ PCS. IN IMPALA GRILLE ↗

350 CID V8 HP CUT AGAIN, (TO 165)

1972 SLOGAN: "CHEVROLET. BUILDING A BETTER WAY TO SEE THE U.S.A."

(FINAL BISCAYNE 4-DR. PRICED AT $3878.)

$4479.

Caprice 4-Door Sedan.

(new)

WITH 400 CID V8 (170 HP) CAPRICE

FINAL 127" WB

CAPRICE GRILLE DETAIL

↗ SUBURBAN (CARRYALL) FR. $3640.

(INTRO. 9-23-71)

WAGON

WITH DISAPPEARING TAILGATE

113

WHEEL COVER TYPE USED ON 2-DR. H/T

CHEVROLET

LOWEST-PRICED IS NOW THE **BELAIR**

73

4-DR. SEDAN AT $4018. → new GRILLES

$4196.

IMPALA

Impala

350 CID V8 CUT TO 145 HP
G78 × 15 TIRES
(L78 × 15, WAGONS)

New

improved front bumper system that retracts on minor impact and hydraulically cushions the shock.

CAPRICE

DASH

IMPALA CUSTOM CPE. *has* INDENTED REAR WINDOW.

CAPRICE ESTATE WAGON FROM $4784.

OPTIONAL WIRE WHEEL COVERS

$4755.

$4496.

CAPRICE

AGAIN, CAPRICE *has* OWN GRILLE.

CAPRICE 400 CID V8 CUT TO 150 HP

1973 Chevrolet. Building a better way to see the U.S.A.

CHEVROLET

IMPALA

(BEL-AIR 4-DR. SED. PRICED AT $4473.)

IMPALA SPT. CPE. $4675. CUSTOM CPE. $4742.

74

IMPALA SPT. SED. $4728.

new GRILLE TOTALLY ABOVE BUMPER. new FRONT CORNER LIGHTS ADDED.

CAPRICE MODELS FR. $4978. (4-DR.)

DASH (CAPRICE)

Caprice Estate wagon

FROM $5313.

New Flip-Down seats (wagon)

Caprice Classic

note GIANT new RR. QUARTER WINDOW ON **Caprice Classic**

CUST. CPE. $4996.

REAR

CVT. $5258.

Caprice

115

CHEVROLET

FINAL BEL-AIR

BEL AIR 4-DOOR SEDAN

IMPALA

(FINAL CVT.)

IMPALA 4-DOOR

NEW CATALYTIC CONVERTER
(Standard, all '75 Chevrolet cars, and trucks 6,000 GVW and below.)

LANDAU CPE. WITH LARGE QUARTER WINDOWS STILL AVAILABLE

CAPRICE CLASSIC SPORT SEDAN

75

Caprice Classic

(new)
CATALYTIC CONVERTER (SINCE 1975)

Chevy Suburban

$4707. UP
129" WB

CHEVROLET MAKES SENSE FOR AMERICA

FROM $5758.

Now that makes sense

CAPRICE ESTATE

IMPALA TAIL-LTS.

4190 ED

EPA M.P.G.
13 CITY, 18 HWY.
(w. STD. 350-2 V8)

$5068.

$ 5323.

IMPALA 76

NO MID-SIDE CHROME STRIP.

Impala S

SEDAN

(CONT'D. NEXT PAGE)

INTERIOR

116

CHEVROLET 76
(CONT'D.)

$5638.

(FINAL 4-DR. H/T)

$5603.

Caprice Classic

note DIFFERENCES IN WHEEL COVERS

1976. Chevrolet makes room for America.

(TOTALLY RESTYLED)

Now that's more like it.

Impala

IMPALA RR.

The 1977 Caprice Classic Sedan

New

$5967.
116" WB

SIZE

CAPRICE CLASSIC CPE. $5917.

77

Caprice Classic.

| 22 mpg. hwy. | 17 mpg. city |

REAR

CID 6 (110 HP)
STD. 305 CID V8
(145 HP)

DASH (CAPRICE)

20.2-cubic-foot trunk

SUBURBAN $5087. UP

FROM $6427. 117

CAPR. ESTATE

WAGON

CHEVROLET

EST. RANGE **450** CITY **650** HWY WITH 25-GAL. FUEL TANK

18 **26**

EPA EST MPG* HWY ESTIMATE WITH STD. 229 V6 ENG. (115 HP)

IMPALA WAGON FR. $7526.

IMPALA

IMPALA SPT. CPE.

$7105.

IMPALA SEDAN $7214.

new P205/75R×15 TIRES (P225 ON WAGONS)

80

CAPRICE CLASSIC LANDAU CPE. has BRIGHTWORK BAR EXTENDING UP OVER ROOF $7954.

STD. 267 CID V8 (120 HP) 305 OR 350 CID AVAIL.

DASH (CAPRICE CLASSIC)

RICH WOODGRAIN EFFECTS

CAPRICE CLASSIC

SEDAN $7635.

CAPR. $8125. UP ESTATE WAGON

BOTH IMPALA AND CAPRICE CLASSIC GRILLES ARE **NEW**

New engines.

119

CHEVROLET Camaro (1967-1981) (INTRO. 9-29-66)

6 CYL. OR V8 (140 TO 325 HP) 108" WB

NEW

STOCK CAMARO 6 COUPE (FROM $2792.)

RS (RALLY SPORT) WITH CONCEALED HEADLTS. AVAIL.

SS-350 CPE. w. CONCEALED LTS.

67

"SS 350" ON GRILLE

SS-350 WITH 350 CID V-8 ENG. (295 HP) OR 396 CID (325 HP)

SS-350 Interior

Command Performance "The Hugger"

Camaro

SS

(SEE DATA AT LOWER LEFT)

Chevrolet

68

new GRILLE

new "FLOW-THROUGH" VENTILATION
ELIMINATES VENT PANES

new DASH

DUAL ROWS of SQUARE PORTS
ATOP HOOD (SS MODELS)

SS

(STD. CAMARO
H/T FROM
$ 2917.)

230 CID 6
(140 HP)
OR
327 CID V8
(210 HP)
STD.

NOTE new
FRONT and
REAR SIDE
(RECTANGULAR)
SAFETY LIGHTS,
AS REQUIRED BY
LAW

7.35 × 14 TIRES
121

REAR FENDER

V-SHAPE and CRISS-CROSS PCS. IN new GRILLE → (BLK.)

Chevrolet **Camaro** (FINAL CONVERTIBLE AVAILABLE)

SS SPT. CPE. WITH RALLY SPORT EQUIP.

69

(CONTINUES TO FEB., 1970)

140 HP 6 TO 396 CID 325 HP V8

(EARLY 327 CID, 210 HP V8 REPL. BY new STD. 307 CID, 200 HP)

Step on the gas and it steps up performance.

SIDE LOUVRE DETAIL

new E78 x 14 TIRES

(AVAILABLE FOR EITHER SS OR Z-28)

Camaro's new Super Scoop

(IT OPENS ON ACCELERATION, PROVIDING COOL AIR TO CARBURETOR, ETC.)

SS has BIG V8 ENG., POWER DISC BRAKES, WIDE OVAL TIRES, and 3-SPEED FLOOR SHIFT.

Camaro

Chevrolet

DASH

RS (RALLY SPORT) CPE.) (note ROUND INBOARD PARK./DIR. LTS., PROTRUDING GRILLE)

(RESTYLED)

The instrument panel wraps around you. A new invisible resilient bumper surrounds the grille of RS models.
There are four transmissions available. And six power plants up to the 360-hp 396.

'70 FROM $3089.

Super Hugger.

RS

REAR DETAIL

70-71

(1970 (SOMETIMES REFERRED TO AS THE 1970½ CAMARO, BY REASON OF ITS LATE DEBUT.)

(BLUE OR BROWN VINYL TOPS NOT AVAIL. UNTIL '71)

New Camaro. Feb. 26th.

We've never announced a car at this time before. But then nobody's ever announced a car like this before.

STD. 250 CID 6 (155 HP) OR 307 CID V8 (200 HP)

Z-28 PKG.: $573. EXTRA

360 HP V8 AVAIL.

(Z-28 has BROAD DUAL STRIPES on HOOD and DECK)

SPORT CPE. WITH DELUXE BUMPER

FRONT DISC BRAKES NOW STD.

See it. At your Chevrolet Sports Dept.

Chevrolet
Building a better way to see the U.S.A.

Camaro **Sport Coupe**

Sport Coupe / Rally Sport / SS / Z28

STD. 307 CID V8
(130 HP) (6
ALSO
AVAIL.)

DASH

72

FEWER PCS. IN new
STD. GRILLE

FROM
$3580.
(V8)

Rally Sport

Super Sport

"SS 350"

4-SPOKE
STEER. WHEEL

new STD. EQUIP.

"Z28"

Z28

note
"Z-28" ON
GRILLE

(REAR)

124

Chevrolet **Camaro** TYPE LT/Z 28/RALLY SPORT/SPORT COUPE

307 CID V8 CUT TO 115 HP
(6 CYL. AVAIL.)

Z-28

V8 SPORT COUPE $3608.

(NOT AVAIL. ON Z-28) TURBINE I WHEEL

UNIROYAL TIGER PAW F70-14

73

new FRONT BUMPER

LT DASH
(LT = "LUXURY TOURING")
$3884.
(V8)

LT (new)

AVAIL. ONLY FOR SPT. CPE. OR RS

RALLY SPORT ($90. LESS FOR 6-CYL.)

(SS NOT AVAIL.)

125

Building a better way to see the U.S.A.

Chevrolet **Camaro**

CHEVROLET MAKES SENSE FOR AMERICA.

STD. $4091. (LT = $4438.)

TOTALLY RESTYLED

74

Z-28

(6 CYL. $212. LESS)

250 CID
(100 HP)
6-CYL. STILL
AVAIL.; STANDARD
V8 IS 350 CID,
(WITH *new* 145 HP)

DASH

TAIL-LT. DETAIL

$4424. Sport Coupe or Type LT. ($4796.)
(105 HP 6 CYL. $145 LESS)

SPORT COUPE

2-TONE

WITH RALLY SPORT TRIM

('75)

new RECTANGULAR EMBLEM, NOW ON HOOD and REAR DECK

Camaro

75 -76

('75) **TYPE LT**   LT WOODGRAINED   126

Chevrolet

Camaro

Z28

Z-28 SPOILER

$5767.

STD. 305 CID V8 (145 HP) OR 250 CID 6 (100 HP)

SPT. CPE. $5082.

STD. E/FR78 × 14/B TIRES

(Z-28 = GR70 × 15)

SPECIAL PAINT JOB ON Z-28

Z28 77

RETURNS!

Z-28 350 CID V8 has 170 HP
(ENG. AVAIL. FOR "LT" also)

SEE WHAT'S NEW TODAY IN A CHEVROLET.

OVERHEAD VIEW OF new T-BAR ROOF AVAIL.

new ALL-MOLDED FRONT APPEARS "BUMPERLESS"

78

(6-CYL. has new 110 HP)

Camaro Z28

has new SLANTING LOUVRES ON SIDE OF COWL.

$6236.

(STD. $5562. UP)

new T-BAR AVAIL.

DASH

LT FR. $5962.

127

STD. 250 CID 6 (115 HP) OR 305 CID V8 (130 HP.)

Camaro Sport Coupe

$6252.

Camaro Rally Sport

(FULL LINE ILLUSTR.)

79

RS FROM $6661.

WITH T-TOP (OPTIONAL)

Z-28 DASH ILLUSTR. AT TOP OF PAGE

"Z-28" SIDE DECAL NOW ON DOOR

Z-28 GRILLE

new Camaro Berlinetta

Berlinetta

Z-28 has 350 CID V8 (170 HP)

1979 Camaro Z28

$7167.

$6995.

CAMARO. THE HUGGER.

128

Camaro
Chevrolet

SPORT COUPE. $6699.

AVAILABLE OPTION

80

TAIL-LT. DETAILS

BERLINETTA

$7462.

RALLY SPORT

FROM $7116.

AVAIL. FOR RALLY SPT. OR SPT. CPE.

NOT TO BE CONFUSED WITH WIRE WHEELS SHOWN ON BERLINETTA

new STD. ENGINES
229 CID 6 (115 HP)
267 CID V8 (120 HP)
(305 CID V8 AVAIL.)

Z28 DASH

EPA MPG:
20 CITY
26 HWY.
(6)

Z28 FOR 1980.
THE MAXIMUM CAMARO.

WITH 350 CID V8 (new 190 HP) 129

(STARTS WITH 1980 MODEL) **CHEVROLET** Citation
A whole new kind of compact car.

(FRONT WHEEL DRIVE)
TRANSVERSE ENGINE
104.9" WB
P185/80R×13
TIRES

STD. DASH

Club Coupe. →
$6300.

2-DR. HATCHBACK
$6427.
(STD. CPE = $5965.)

(ALSO KNOWN AS "CHEVY" CITATION.)

4-DR. HATCHBACK
$6293.

Custom Interior DASH
(ROUND GAUGES)

(NEW) 80

(INTRO. 4-19-79)

SLIP STREAM STYLING

Full Wheel Covers.

EPA MPG 24 CITY, 38 HWY. WITH 151 CID 4 (90 HP)

173 CID V6 (110 OR 115 HP) ALSO AVAIL.

SPORT PACKAGE - $500.

X-11
WITH SPECIAL PAINT JOB, P205/70R-13 TIRES

X-11 STEERING WHEEL

130

(X-11 CL. CPE. ALSO AVAIL.)

"THE FIRST CHEVY OF THE '80s"

(1960 – 1969)
MONZA

CHEVROLET CORVAIR

rear-engine design with
Independent suspension at all four wheels

H/T $2556.

A most unusual car for people
who enjoy the unusual

$2630.
SPT. SEDAN
(4-DR. H/T)

MONZA
CVT.
$2699.

(FINAL)
CORSA
$2666.
(H/T)

66

$2809.

1966
SALES:
88,951
("500" IS
LOWEST-PRICED
MODEL, FROM
$2289.)

108" WB   6 CYL., 164 CID
7.00 x 13 TIRES   95-140 HP

CORSA
SERIES
NO LONGER
AVAILABLE 1967

1967 SALES:
24,736

500

$2339.

67

New oval steering wheel—This easy-to-grip
wheel sits atop the GM-developed energy-
absorbing steering column—one of many new
standard safety features. Others include 4-way
hazard warning flasher and a lane-change feature
incorporated in direction signal control.

THIS
BEST
IDENTIFIES
A 1967
MODEL.

95
OR
110 HP
ENGINES
ONLY,
DURING
1967.

142D·91

MONZA CVT. $2770.

'67 Corvair
The rear-engine road car

131

CORVAIR

$2457.

a true hardtop.
And it's Chevrolet's
lowest priced hardtop.

Corvair 500

Corvair 500 Sport Coupe

"500" INTERIOR

Corvair Power Teams

ENGINES	TRANS-MISSIONS	AXLE RATIOS
95-HP TURBO-AIR 164 (Standard)	3-Speed (Standard)	3.55:1
	4-Speed (Extra-cost)	3.55:1
	Powerglide (Extra-cost)	3.27:1*
110-HP TURBO-AIR 164 (Extra-cost)	3-Speed (Standard)	3.27:1*
	4-Speed (Extra-cost)	3.27:1*
	Powerglide (Extra-cost)	3.55:1
140-HP TURBO-AIR 164 (Extra-cost)	3-Speed (Standard)	3.55:1
	4-Speed (Extra-cost)	3.55:1
	Powerglide (Extra-cost)	3.55:1

Positraction available for all ratios.
*3.55:1 may be specified.

1968 PRICES
SHOWN. $10
INCREASE, 1969.
SALES:
1968 = 12,977
1969 = 3,102

$2840.

MONZA CONVERTIBLE

new DASH

new SIDE SAFETY LTS.

(DISCONTINUED 5-14-69)

68-69

(FULL 1968-1969 LINE ILLUSTR.)

OPT. LUGGAGE CARRIER

(NO 4-DR. HARDTOPS AFTER 1967)

MONZA INTERIOR

OPT. WIRE WHEEL COVERS

MONZA SPT. CPE.

'68 Standard Safety Features

☐ Energy-absorbing steering column
☐ Seat belts with pushbutton buckles for *all* passenger positions
☐ Shoulder belts for driver and right front passenger with pushbutton buckles and convenient stowage provision on all models except convertibles
☐ Passenger-guard door locks with deflecting lock buttons — all doors
☐ Four-way hazard warning flasher
☐ Dual master cylinder brake system with warning light and corrosion-resistant brake lines ☐ Latches on front seat backs ☐ Dual-speed windshield wipers and washers ☐ Outside rearview mirror ☐ Back up lights. ☐ New side marker lights and parking lights that illuminate with headlights ☐ Padded instrument panel, sun visors, windshield pillars ☐ Reduced-glare instrument panel top, inside windshield moldings, horn button, steering wheel hub, and windshield wiper arms and blades ☐ Inside day-night mirror with deflecting base ☐ Lane-change feature in direction signal control ☐ Safety armrests ☐ Thick-laminate windshield ☐ Soft, low-profile window control knobs, and coat hooks ☐ Energy-absorbing seat backs ☐ Yielding door and window control handles ☐ Energy-absorbing instrument panel with smooth contoured knobs and levers ☐ Tire safety rim ☐ Safety door latches and hinges ☐ Uniform shift quadrant ☐ Snag-resistant steering wheel hardware ☐ Fuel tank and filler pipe security.

$2721.

132

Chevrolet

CORVETTE (SINCE 1953)

STINGRAY CPE.

*98" wb (ALL) V8 ENGINES

OPT. 427 CID (425 HP)
STD. 327 CID (300 HP)

66-67

('66) $4784.

FR. $4573. FR. $4604.

(CVT. and H/T CVT. ALSO)

7.75×14 TIRES

(* – SINCE 1963)

327 CID (300 – 350 HP) OR 427 CID (390, 400 OR 435 HP)

(TOTALLY RESTYLED)

68

OPT. HARD TOP

$5157. CPE.

new F70×15 TIRES

CVT. $4814.

new T-TOP (INTERIOR)

Corvette simulated wood steering wheel and instrumentation.

'69 Corvette CHEVROLET a true American sports car.

note "STINGRAY" NAME ADDED, ON FRONT FENDERS

69

327 CID REPL. BY *new* 350 CID V8 (300 HP)

427 CID CONT'D. (390, 400, 430 OR 435 HP)

STINGRAY COUPE WITH ROOF SECTIONS REMOVED

(350 CID OR *new* 454 CID V8)

70-72

(300, 350, 370, 390 OR 460 HP '70) ('71 270, 330, 365, 425 HP OR 210, 275, 285, 325 SAE NET HP) ('72 200, 255 OR 270 HP)

new VENTS

('71)

new CRISS-CROSS PCS. IN GRILLE; SQUARE PK. LTS.

('71)

FROM $ 5126. ('70)
5548. ('71)
5532. ('72)
(CVT. PRICES)

(1972 CARRIES LIC. PLATE IN GRILLE CENTER, AS DO MANY PREV. MODELS.)

134

Chevrolet Corvette

Building a better way to see the U.S.A.

$5847.

$5621.

73

new GRILLE *and* PARKING LIGHTS *new* RESILIENT BODY-COLORED BUILT-IN FRONT BUMPER

350 CID (190 HP @4400 RPM OR 250 HP @5200)

454 CID (275 HP @ 4400 RPM)

new DOMED HOOD

GR 70 ×15 TIRES

We gave it radials, a quieter ride, guard beams and a nose job.

CVT.

(350 OR 454 CID)

DASH

74

RESTYLED (sloping) REAR END

195,250 OR 270 HP

Chevrolet

Corvette

75-76

(350 CID ONLY FROM 165 HP ('75) 180 HP ('76))

The roll of radials.
Corvette's Efficiency System extends right to the road and those special GR70-15 steel-belted radial ply tires.

IMPROVED BUMPER SYSTEM ('75)

('75)

INTRODUCING A MORE EFFICIENT CORVETTE.

new HIGH ENERGY IGNITION

new CATALYTIC CONVERTER

(1975 IS FINAL CONVERT.)

DASH

The only one.

$ 9504.

new EMBLEM

77

new BLACK WINDSHIELD POSTS

FRONT

SIDE LIGHT LENS

• Soft-Ray tinted glass.
• Black windshield posts give new "thin pillar" look.

180 OR 210 HP

Firestone

500

![Chevrolet] Corvette

350 CID V8 (175, 185 OR 220 HP)

SEE WHAT'S NEW TODAY IN A CHEVROLET.

Silver Anniversary Corvette.

new FASTBACK REAR WINDOW **78**

new

25TH ANNIVERSARY EMBLEM

P225/60R x 15 TIRES

$10,286.

Chevrolet CORVETTE

DASH AND CONS.

79

FIBERGLASS BODIES ON ALL CORVETTES (1953 ON)

P225/70R×15 OR P255/60R×15 TIRES

new REAR SPOILER

$13,104.

new 2-PC. CORNERING LTS.

GOODYEAR POLYSTEEL RADIAL

(GDYR. GT TIRES, 1980)

$11,536.

350 CID V8 STD. (195-225 HP)

(RESTYLED)

80

(new 305 CID V8 ALSO AVAIL.) 180-190 HP

new FRONT END WITH AIR DAM; LOW-PROFILE HOOD

CHEVROLET
Monte Carlo

(2-DR. H/Ts ONLY)

70

(INTRO. 9-18-69)

$3123.
(NEW)
$3464.
(REG.)

116" WB

V-8 ENGINES:
350 CID (250 HP)
350 CID (300
400   265
400   330
454 CID (360 HP) (IN SS MODEL)

G78×15/B TIRES

IMITATION (VINYL)
CARPATHIAN BURLED ELM GRAIN
ON INSTRUMENT PANEL

71
new GRILLE

new RAISED ORNAMENT

$4041.

245,270,
300 OR 365 HP

**1971. You've changed.
We've changed.**

139

DASH

CHEVROLET **MONTE CARLO**

new GRILLE

72

$4009.

STD. 350 CID V8 CUT TO 165 HP

CUT TO 145 HP

new DASH (RESTYLED)

73

new OPERA WINDOWS

3 CPE. MODELS AVAIL., FR. $3827.

STD., S, LANDAU MODELS

CHEVROLET Monte Carlo

Landau

TURBINE II WHEEL

DASH

S or LANDAU TYPES (BOTH ILLUSTR.)

$4858.

new TAIL-LTS.

74

new GRILLE

$4614.

Monte Carlo S

SIMULATED WIRE WHEEL COVER →

new GR70 x 15/B TIRES

CHEVROLET MAKES SENSE FOR AMERICA

LANDAU CPE. $5273.

new TAIL-LTS.

75 new GRILLE

S COUPE $5003.

RALLY WHEEL

DASH

↑ new DLX. WHEEL COVER

141

Monte Carlo

When a car makes you feel good about its looks, that's style. When it makes you feel good about yourself, that's character.

76

DASH

new GRILLE

w/o VINYL TOP $5218.

DELUXE WH. COVER

WITH VINYL TOP $5511.

Wire wheel covers.

Rally wheels. Turbine II wheels. (Std. on Landau.)

new TAIL-LIGHTS

new 305 CID V8 (140 HP)

LANDAU CPE.

Like you, it's an original.

305 CID (145 HP) V8, OR 350 CID (170 HP) V8

new TAIL-LIGHTS

LANDAU CPE. W/VINYL TOP

w/o VINYL TOP

$5539.

RALLY WHEELS

$5869.

77

DELUXE WHEEL CVR.

1977 DASH IS SIMILAR IN MOST RESPECTS TO 1976 TYPE ILLUSTR.

GR 70 x 15 TIRES

new SPORT WHEEL COVER

new GRILLE

new 108" WB

CHEVROLET Monte Carlo

78

RESTYLED

SPORT CPE. $6086.

LANDAU CPE. $6451.

new 205/70R×14 TIRES

DASH

105 HP, 231 CID V-6 IS new STANDARD ENGINE. 305 CID V8 ALSO AVAIL. (145 HP)

The Third Generation Monte Carlo.
A new dimension in affordable luxury.

DASH SIMILAR TO 1978
200/231 CID V6s (94/115 HP)
267/305 CID V8s STD.
(125/160 HP) (350 CID V8 AVAIL.)

T-TOP (OPT.)

79

new FRONT and REAR CORNER LIGHT LENSES
(w. HORIZONTAL STRIPS)

RALLY WHEEL

SPORT CPE. $6711.
(LANDAU CPE. $7561.)

143

CHEVROLET MONTE CARLO

80

WITH T-TOP AND 2-TONE PAINT OPTION ↘

new GRILLE has FEWER PIECES. 4 new RECTANGULAR HEADLIGHTS →

SPORT CPE. $7040.

LOW SIDE LIGHT REPLACES CORNER TYPE. ↗

new DASH

new STYLE OF RALLY WHEEL ↓

LANDAU CPE. $7288.

P-205/70R-14 TIRES STANDARD

115 HP, 229 CID V-6 IS new STD. ENG. (231 CID IN CALIFORNIA) (110 HP) (TURBO V6 AVAIL.)

267/305 CID V8s AVAIL. (120/155 HP)

144

(SINCE 1975)

Chevrolet
Chevrolet makes sense
for America

Monza

97" WB   87 HP
4 - CYL. (140 CID)
   OR
2 V-8s)

THE NEW MONZA "S"
HATCHBACK COUPE
$3946.

Monza 2+2

COWL
LETTERING

18½-
GAL.
FUEL
TANK

75-76

POWER
VENT
SLOTS

$4250.

2+2

TROMPE L'OEIL WHEEL COVERS. That's
French for "fool the eye." Which is what
these standard wheel covers do beautifully.
They look like expensive metal wheels but
they're tough molded polycast.

BR 78
× 13
TIRES

"V8
4.3 LITRE"
PLAQUE
DESIGNATES
A
262½ CID
V8
(110 HP)
(125 HP, 305 CID V8
AVAIL. ALSO)

Chevrolet MONZA

4 **CYL OR** V6

(V8 AVAIL. ALSO)

('78)

WAGON

(1979 FINAL YR., AT $4646.)

↑ NEW ('78)

(ESTATE WAG. ALSO, '78 ONLY)

SALE **$3698**

EPA ESTIMATES **34/24** HWY CITY

WAGON **78-80**

new GRILLES

BODY SIDE MOULDINGS BECOME STD. EQUIPMENT IN 1979.

COUPE

$4080. ('78)
4517. ('79)
5041. ('80)
(4497. SALE)

Monza 2+2
↙↓

('80)

DASH

(1979 MODELS ILLUSTRATED, UNLESS OTHERWISE INDICATED.)

WITH OPT. "SPYDER" PACKAGE

2+2 Sport

147

(1971 – 1977) **Chevrolet** **VEGA**

PANEL EXPRESS

KAMMBACK WAGON

HATCHBACK

71

(NEW)

FROM $2320.

97" WHEELBASE

4 CYL. OVERHEAD CAM 140 CID 90 HP @ 4800 RPM

KNOWN AS 2300 SERIES (BECAUSE ENG. IS IN 2300-cc CLASS)

2.53, 2.92 OR 3.36 GEAR RATIOS

new aluminum engine

STD. 2-DR.

(GTs ON NEXT PAGE)

NAMEPLATE READS: "CHEVROLET VEGA 2300" (ON 1971 and 1972 MODELS ONLY)

25 MPG.   148   **CHEVY'S NEW LITTLE VEGA.**

VEGA
CHEVROLET

WAGON

GT.

2-DR.
HATCH-
BACK

(NEW)

BLACK GRILLE
A-70 × 13 TIRES
110 HP

(OTHER MODELS
CONTINUE FROM '71)

"GT"

71 - 72

INTRODUCING THE VEGA GT.

The Custom Interior

We can show you only so much here. Available GT equipment includes special instrumentation: tach, amp and temp gauges, electric clock, and sport steering wheel.

GT
DASH
(ABOVE)
has ROUND
GAUGES

Swing-out rear side window.

SWING-OUT
REAR
SIDE
WINDOW
(OPT.)

CUSTOM INTERIOR

NO STYLING CHANGE, BUT
SOME IMPROVEMENTS:
EASIER-SHIFTING 3 and
4-SPEED TRANSMISSIONS.
new WINDSHIELD WASHER CONTROL.
NAMEPLATE NOW READS
"VEGA BY CHEVROLET."

Better belts and jack.

73

new
ESTATE
WAGON
$2850.

Chevrolet introduces a neat little woody.

STRONGER
BUMPERS

149

The Vega LX.
It's a deluxe version of the Notchback Coupe, with a vinyl roof cover.

LX

(1975)

VEGA

DASH

GT DASH

VEGA GT.

new GRILLE

new TAIL-LIGHTS

FROM $2788. ('74)

"COSWORTH TWIN CAM" DECAL

('75)

Introducing the Cosworth Vega. ('75)

It's the special Vega with a number of hand-assembled, very expensive components.

The Cosworth engine comes out of Cosworth Engineering of England and makes use of sophisticated developments like twin camshafts and electronic fuel injection. It develops 120 horsepower at 5600 rpm and a torque of 115 lb./ft. at 5200 rpm.

The Cosworth interior has special instrumentation

The only exterior color available is the one shown here black, highlighted by gold decals, pinstriping and wheels.

TWIN CAMS.
$5979.

Vega GT. To stripe or not to stripe?
That's up to you. GT sport stripes can be ordered in black or white.

CHROME "GT" (ON COWLS OF UNSTRIPED GTs)

74-75

VEGA WAGONS

$3031. ('74)
$3314. ('75)

STD. WAGON

GT →

Vega Estate Wagon.
$3259. ('74)

PANEL EXPRESS (NOT IN VEGA LINE AFTER 1975)

(Vega Estate GT. ALSO AVAIL.)

150

VEGA CHEVROLET

OPTIONAL SUN-ROOF

• Soft-rim steering wheel with cushioned center.
• 80 mph in white numbers with metric equivalents in blue.
• Available AM/FM radio and accessory electric clock.

1976 SLOGAN: "built to take it."

DASH

• Inside hood release.

SPORT CPE.

new GRILLE

• Function symbols in headlights, cigarette lighter and radio control knobs.

new LARGER TAIL-LTS.

wagon
$3540. ('76)
$3836. ('77)

HATCHBACK

The 1976 Vega Dura-Built 140 engine is so good it's backed up by a 5-year or 60,000-mile guarantee.

ALSO AVAIL.:
GT WAGON, GRAINED ESTATE, ESTATE GT WAGONS

1977 GT

76-77

(FINAL '76 COSWORTH PRICED AT $6135.)

• Tachometer, temperature gauge and voltmeter.
• Wood-grain vinyl accents.
• Electric clock.
• 80 mph in white numbers with metric equivalents in blue.
• Assist handle built into instrument panel pad.

"Today's Vega"

(1977 SLOGAN)

33 mpg highway/24 mpg city (EPA).

• Inside hood release.
• Four-spoke sport steering wheel.
• Available Four-Season air conditioning and AM/FM radio.
• Cigarette lighter.

151

GT DASH

(1962-1979)

CHEVY II
by CHEVROLET

Station Wagon

DELUXE MODELS KNOWN
AS

Nova

153 CID 4 (93 HP)
194 CID 6 (120 HP)
283 CID V8 (195 HP)
6.50 x 13 TIRES
(WAG. = 6.95 x 14)

110" WB
(1962-1967)

66

new GRILLE;
new TALLER TAIL-LTS.

NOVA H/
SUPER SPORT H/T
$2652.

LOWEST-PRICED
"100" 2-DR. IS $2250.)

STATION WAGON AVAIL. THROUGH '67.
(FROM $2709.)

NOVA SS
H/T
$2708.

4-CYL = 90 HP
6-CYL = 140 HP
V8 = 195 HP

67

1967 GRILLE
DIFFERENCE
ILLUSTR. AT
LOWER
LEFT

NOVA
4-DR.
$2519.

'67 Chevy II
The stylish economy car

152

DASH

Chevy II **NOVA**: The not-too-small car CHEVROLET

(WAGONS NO LONGER AVAIL.)

STD. 4-DR. (w/o SIDE CHROME)

SS

68

(TOTALLY RESTYLED) new 111" WB (THROUGH '79)

153 CID 4 (90 HP)
230 CID 6 (140 HP)
307 CID V8 (200 HP)

UP TO 295 HP AVAIL.
7.35 × 14 TIRES

SS OPTION $210. EXTRA

SALE PR.
all-new Nova at only **$2261.00***
(STD. CPE.)

1968 EASILY IDENTIFIED BY "CHEVY II" NAME ON TOP BORDER OF GRILLE.

SPORT WHEELS

OPTIONAL BUMPER GUARDS

RALLY WHEEL

153

CHEVY **Nova**

(NOVA REPLACES CHEVY II NAME)

new COWL LOUVRES

CHEVROLET EMBLEM NOW APPEARS ON TOP BORDER OF GRILLE.

69

153 CID 4 (90 HP)
230 CID 6 (140 HP)
307 CID V8 (200 HP)
SS OPTION : 350 CID V8 (300 HP)

"307" CID NUMBER ABOVE SIDE LIGHTS

PRICED FROM $2446.
(4-CYL. CPE.)

V8 CPE. $2624.

SS GRILLE

7.35 × 14 TIRES

154

CHEVY Nova 70

SANDWICHES · FRIES · MALTS ·

FROM $2554.
4-CYL. CPE.

1970 IS FINAL YR. FOR COWL LOUVRES.

new E78 x14/B TIRES

new SQUARER SHAPE TO PARK./DIRECTIONAL LTS.

The Nova Coupe.

You didn't want it changed for the sake of change.

So we improved it for the sake of improvement.

$2637. ('71-6) 2613. ('72-6)
$2732. ('71-V8) 2703. ('72-V8)

Nova Sedan

CPES. FROM $2607. ('71) 2585. ('72)

250 CID 6 (145 HP) (110 HP, '72)

307 CID V8 (200 HP) (130 HP, '72)

RATED HP and PRICE CUTS, 1972

STD. CPE. W/O SIDE TRIM

71-72

1972 NOVAS ILLUSTRATED

DASH

155

CHEVY Nova

(RESTYLED)
73

CPE. FR. $2589.
4-DR. FR. $2617.

BACKGROUND SCENE:
HISTORIC PLYMOUTH, MASS.

250 CID 6 (100 HP)
307 CID V8 (115 HP)

Hatchback
(New)
FROM $2738.

new 2-TONE ROOF ACCENT TRIM AVAILABLE (ON CAR ILLUSTR. ABOVE, CENTER)

4 TAIL-LIGHTS (new)

1973 DASH (BELOW)
(1974 DASH SIMILAR)

new GRILLE
WITH PARK./DIRECTIONAL LIGHTS BUILT IN

NOVA/NOVA CUSTOM

156

CHEVY Nova

74

250 CID 6 (100 HP)

new 350 CID V8 (145 HP)

DASH

CPE. FROM $3/01.

CHEVROLET EMBLEM ADDED TO 1974 GRILLE

Nova Hatchback Hutch. This handy camping tent attaches quickly and easily to Nova Hatchback models, transforming them into economy two-sleeper campers.

SEDAN FROM $3131.

new BRIGHT ANODIZED ALUMINUM HUBCAPS

□ **Full wheel covers.** Shown left. □ Rally wheels with bright trim rings (included with SS). Shown right.

CUSTOM SS

SS has OWN GRILLE.

new "NOVA BY CHEVROLET" ON DECK (ALSO ON HOOD ON DRIVER'S SIDE)

HATCHBACK FROM $3225.

157

NOVA SIX.

$3218.*

* REG. $3966.

(RESTYLED)

'75

EPA mileage:
16 city,
21 highway.

HATCHBACK
CPE. $4214.

NOVA

NOVA CUSTOM

$4270.

FR78 x 14
TIRES
(EXCEPT ON
$3966. "S"
CPE. AT TOP,
LEFT)

250 CID 6 (105 HP)
new 262 CID V8
(110 HP)

4.3 LITRE

So we've
distinguished the exterior
of our '75 Nova LN—
front, rear and sides—
with this classic LN
emblem.

NOVA
LN

It appears inside, too
(on the steering wheel),
along with some of the
nicest things that ever
happened to a compact.

$4650.

LN (new)

DASH (LN)

NOVA

LN 4-DR.
$4663.

**CHEVROLET
MAKES SENSE
FOR AMERICA**

158

HATCHBACK
$4366.

Nova

$3283*
Nova 4-Door Sedan
(REG. $4232.)

E78×14/B
TIRES ON
STD.
NOVA

Nova SS Coupe.

250 CID 6 (105 HP)
305 CID V8 (140 HP)

76

(Introducing
Concours.)

note THAT GRILLE
OF NEW CONCOURS
has HEAVY PANEL
OF BRIGHTWORK ABOVE

4-Door Sedan
$4780.

Concours

(new)

Concours Coupe

$4745.

CONCOURS has
HOOD
ORNAMENT
and FULL-LENGTH
SIDE TRIM.
(CONCOURS TIRE SIZE =
FR 78 × 14/B)

CONCOURS HATCHBACK
AVAIL., AT $4922.

NOVA DASH
RESEMBLES
ILLUSTRATED
CONCOURS
DASH, BUT
DOES NOT have
WOOD GRAIN.

• Instrument cluster with rosewood vinyl accents, smoked lenses, bright framing.

• Available electric clock.

• Built-in heater and defroster system.

• Concours identification on steering wheel.

• Available Four-Season air conditioning and AM/FM stereo radio.

• Cigarette lighter.

• Glove compartment light and lock.

• Soft-rim steering wheel with cushioned center.

• Color-keyed steering wheel with wood-grain vinyl accent.

159

Concours

CHEVY NOVA

EXTRA-LG. BUMPER GUARDS ONLY ON POLICE CARS.

SEDAN $4539.

77 new GRILLES

UNIQUE MESH GRILLE ON

NOVA RALLY

(BECOMES THE NOVA CUSTOM RALLY IN '78, WITH SIMILAR STYLING)

CPE. FR. $4489.

new 110 HP (6) 145 HP (V8)

THE FINAL **CONCOURS**

CONCOURS GRILLE

TRIPLE TAIL LTS. (new)

$5073.

Concours: A world class luxury compact from Chevrolet.

26 MPG. HWY., 19 CITY

SEE WHAT'S NEW TODAY IN A CHEVROLET.

GM

CHEVY NOVA 4-DR.
$3823.*

*(REG. $4852.)

2-DR.
$3702.*

*(REG. $4777.)

EMBLEM ADDED ABOVE GRILLE, new BUMPERS (STD. NOVA)

78

HOOD ORNAMENT NOT INCL. ON new CUSTOM

NOVA CUSTOM (FORMERLY THE CONCOURS)

Nova

HATCHBACK $5260.

NOVA

Nova Models.

RALLY WHEELS

RALLY →

(note RALLY INSIGNIA and BODY STRIPES

79

250 CID
6 (115 HP)
305 CID V8 (130 HP) OR 350 CID V8 (170 HP)

new GRILLE
WITH
ALL-HORIZONTAL
PCS.

DASH
(NOVA CUSTOM)

BUMPER RUB STRIP
and GUARDS OPTION.

Nova Custom Models. $5406.

FINAL NOVA.
REPLACED BY
CHEVY CITATION
FOR 1980.

WIRE
WHEEL
COVER

CABRIO-
LET ROOF
COVER
(OPT.)

$5306.

GRILLE TOP BORDER
BEARS "Chevrolet" NAME.

POL

CHRYSLER MOTORS CORPORATION

Chrysler

(SINCE 1924)

H/T $3534.

6-PASS. $4177.
9-PASS. $4283.

Town & Country Wagon

Move up to Chrysler

NEWPORT
383 CID V8 (270 HP)

NEW YORKER
440 CID V8 (350 HP)

NY H/T $4248.

NY 4-DR. H/T $4324.

1966

new GRILLES

66

DASH (NY)

V8s 383 OR 440 CID
124" WB (WAGONS = 121")

"300" has 383 CID V8 (325 HP)

2-DR. H/T $4005.

4-DR. H/T

300

300 has 3 CHROME STRIPS ACROSS TAIL-LIGHTS (AS ILLUSTRATED)

GRILLE

$4081.

162

CHRYSLER

Take Charge...Move up to Chrysler '67

H/T $3639.
NEWPORT

DASH (N.P. CUST.)

NEWPORT CUSTOM 2-DR. H/T $3827.

67

(NEWPORT) TOWN and COUNTRY WAGON FROM $4286.

4-DR. H/T

$4430.

NEW YORKER

new TAIL-LIGHTS WRAP AROUND REAR FENDER.

$4299.

SEDAN

(CONT'D. NEXT PAGE)

163

CHRYSLER

300

You can tell a 300 by its dash.

67
(CONT'D.)

SLOT-
TYPE
TAIL
LIGHTS
(new)

2-DR. H/T
$4134.

Three Hundred.

4-DR.
H/T
$4210.

WHEEL
COVER

OPTIONAL
ROAD
WHEEL

FLOOR CONSOLE WITH
PERFORMANCE
INDICATOR

CHRYSLER
CONVERTIBLES
DISCONTINUED
AFTER
1970.

DISC BRAKE
WHEEL COVER

new
BULGING
GRILLE

CVT.
$4487.

164

make your move
MOVE UP TO CHRYSLER '68

CREASE PATTERN ON REAR FENDER

4-DR. H/T $4271.

NEWPORT

9 PASS. $5022.

TOWN and COUNTRY WAGON

NEW YORKER

68

EASILY RECOGNIZED AS 1968 MODELS BY THE SMALL SIDE SAFETY LIGHTS REQUIRED BY LAW IN '68.

4-DR. H/T $4999.

1968 REAR SAFETY LIGHTS ARE TINY and **ROUND** (300)

H/T

300

note 5 "LOUVRES"

CONVERTIBLE

300 has new CONCEALED HEADLIGHTS WITH CHRYSLER NAME ABOVE HEADLIGHT DOOR

165

CHRYSLER

4-DR. H/T $4568.
NEWPORT CUSTOM

NEWPORT H/T $4323.

WIND DEFLECTOR ON WAGON ROOF

wagon

TOWN and COUNTRY NOW IN NEW YORKER line. 6-PASS. $5193.

Announcing your next car: The great new Chrysler.

NEW YORKER

69 (RESTYLED)

N.Y. 4-DR. H/T $5225.

1969

REAR

300

H/T $4714.

note VERT. PCS. IN 300 GRILLE

166

CHRYSLER

NEWPORT CUSTOM

STANDARD-TYPE NEWPORT DOES NOT HAVE SIDE TRIM AS SEEN ON THESE MODELS.

4-DR. H/T $4705.

Your next car: 1970 Chrysler.

(WITH ANTIQUE GOLD VINYL TOP COVERING, AZTEC EAGLE HOOD MEDALLION)

(ABOVE)
The new Chrysler Cordoba.

(SPECIAL-EDITION H/T)

70

6-PASS. $5349.

TOWN and COUNTRY WAGON

NEW YORKER GRILLE IS SIMILAR, BUT has UPRIGHT RECTANGULAR MEDALLION AT CENTER.

300
(3 VIEWS)

4-DR. H/T $4928.

H/T $4849.

DDA-70

167 REAR DETAIL (300

CHRYSLER

$ 4672.

ROYAL
(REAR)

(NEWPORT)
ROYAL
(new)

NEWPORT
CUSTOM

01-752

1971

71
new
GRILLES

"ROYAL"
NAME
BELOW
"NEWPORT,"
ON COWL
PANEL

ROYAL

DIFFERING
DETAILS

168

(CONT'D.
NEXT PAGE)

Chrysler New Yorker & Town & Country

FROM $5596.

DASH →

$5686.

HEAVY CHROME SIDE STRIP ON NEW YORKER 4-DOOR HARDTOP

SUN ROOF OPT.

NEW YORKER

71 (CONT'D.)

4-DR. H/T $5205.

2-DR. H/T $5126.

Chrysler 300

(CHRYSLER CONVERTS. NO LONGER AVAIL.)

CHRYSLER Plymouth Coming Through.

CHRYSLER

$4863.

Newport Custom

new OUTBOARD TAIL-LIGHTS

Newport Royal

$4630.

new GRILLES

72

Town & Country

NEW YORKER H/T $5552.

FROM $5692.

2-DR. N.Y. BRGHM. $5777.

(300 DISCONTINUED UNTIL '79)

(new) **New Yorker Brougham**

73

Chrysler Newport
Extra care in engineering...it makes a difference.

new GRILLE, *new* FRONT END STYLING. "CHRYSLER" NAME ABOVE GRILLE

new ENERGY-ABSORBING SAFETY BUMPERS

CHRYSLER

Town & Country Wagon
FROM $5885.

73
(CONT'D.)

4-DR. H/T
FROM $5769.

Chrysler New Yorker
Extra care in engineering...it makes a difference.

For generations, an automobile advanced in engineering.
For 1974, a totally new expression of that idea.

(RESTYLED)

new NARROW "CLASSIC" STYLE GRILLE.
NEWPORT TYPES have DIFFERENT
ARRANGEMENT of GRILLE PCS. and VERTICAL
OUTBOARD TAIL-LIGHTS.

74

Chrysler New Yorker

Interior does not display standard safety belts.

AVAILABLE FEB., 1974, NEW YORKER
ST. REGIS COUPE has
new OPERA WINDOWS.

ILLUSTR. 2-DR. H/T : $6288.

171

CHRYSLER

note TUBULAR COURTESY LTS. JUST FORWARD OF OPERA WINDOWS

MEDALLION (BELOW) IS FEATURED IN CENTER OF CORDOBA HOOD ORNAMENT

CORDOBA CPE.

318 CID
V8
150

CORDOBA IS ENTIRELY

$5581.

NEW! 75

WITH SMALL (115") WB
WITH VINYL-COVERED TOP

(TOWN and COUNTRY, NEWPORT, NEWPORT CUSTOM MODELS ALSO AVAIL.)

FINAL 4-DR. SEDAN N.Y. BROUGH. IN 1975, PRICED AT $6851.

ALSO 2-DR. H/T $6908.

← ILLUSTR. 4-DR. H/T $6998.

Chrysler New Yorker Brougham

new DUAL SLOTS IN BUMPER, new BUMPER GUARDS

new CRISS-CROSS PCS. IN GRILLE

172

CHRYSLER

Chrysler Cordoba

$5959.

76

new GRILLE WITH ALL-VERTICAL PCS.

new ELECTRONIC IGNITION "LEAN BURN" ENGINE AVAILABLE EVERYWHERE EXCEPT IN CALIFORNIA.

THE FINAL NEWPORT CUSTOM →

TOWN and COUNTRY WAGON has GRILLE LIKE ILLUSTRATED NEWPORT CUSTOM, BUT STD. NEWPORT DOES NOT HAVE THE HEAVY VERTICAL STRIP NOR 2 HEAVY HORIZONTAL STRIPS ACROSS GRILLE.

$6207.

THE LARGE SIDE MIRRORS ARE OPTIONAL, IN TRAILER TOWING ACCESSORY PACKAGE.

$7368.

The 1976 Chrysler New Yorker Brougham

(NEW YORKER'S new "WATERFALL" GRILLE IS SIMILAR TO TYPE LAST USED ON DISCONTINUED 1975 IMPERIAL.)

CHRYSLER

$6012.

(new STEEL-TOP CORDOBA "S": $5962.)

new T-BAR ROOF OPTION

Chrysler Cordoba

FINE CROSS-PCS. ADDED TO CORDOBA GRILLE.

INTRODUCING CHRYSLER LEBARON.

WITH 318 CID V8, 145 HP
112.7" WB

$5,758.

$5,741. AS SHOWN.

NEW SIZE

LEATHER SEATS OPT. IN LE BARON MEDALLION SERIES.

77

LE BARON GRILLE CLOSE-UP

1977 Newport. $5374.

1977 Chrysler New Yorker.
$7873.

(N.Y. 2-DR. ALSO AVAIL.)

174

CHRYSLER

(w. PAINTED STEEL TOP)

CHRYSLER CORDOBA 'S'. $5550.

1978 Chrysler Cordoba
"The picture of style and taste."

DON'T SETTLE FOR ANYTHING LESS.

NEW 2-TIER RECTANGULAR CORDOBA HDLTS.

LeBARON
TOWN & COUNTRY.

TAIL-LIGHT DETAIL
T+C REAR

$5761. (new)

(WAGON ADDED)

Le BARON

$5270.

SWING-UP STEERING WHEEL

"S" COUPE
$5114

78

25 MPG HWY / 17 MPG CITY

V8; 2 DR NEWPORT AND NEW YORKER MODELS. 4 DR. ONLY AFTER 1978.

FINAL NP 2 DR.
$6432

NEW YORKER

NEWPORT

NY 4-DR.
$8420.

new GRILLE

CHRYSLER

CHRYSLER 300.

(FIRST new "300 SINCE 1971)

79

note UNIQUE GRILLE

DASH

WITH 360 CID V8

("300" SHARES CORDOBA CHASSIS)

DASH

CORDOBA

PRICED FROM $6666.

REAR DETAIL

new GRILLE

2-TONE HOOD PAINT VARIATION

T-TOP

THE CONTEMPORARY CLASSIC.

176

CHRYSLER

LeBARON. $6124.

$6835.

LeBARON MEDALLION 2-DOOR

LeBARON SALON.
NEWEST NAME IN THE LeBARON LINEUP.

$6361.

LeBARON TOWN & COUNTRY

$7055.

T-TOP 2-DR. AVAIL., ALSO SUNROOFS

DASH

28 MPG HWY. / 18 MPG** CITY

79 (CONT'D.)

REAR DETAILS

new GRILLE

GET A LITTLE STYLE IN YOUR LIFE.
ADD A LITTLE LIFE TO YOUR STYLE.

LeBARON MEDALLION 4-DOOR SEDAN.
177
$7063.

CHRYSLER

NEWPORT

225 CID 6
OR
318 CID V8

23 MPG HWY 17 MPG CITY

NEWPORT EMBLEM

**CHRYSLER NEWPORT. $6,089.
NOW YOU CAN HAVE IT ALL...NOW.**

79 (CONT'D.)

Chrysler New Yorker
Fifth Avenue EDITION

$10,596.

note LOUVRES

DASH (FIFTH AVENUE)

NEW YORKER.
$9096.

178

CHRYSLER

IMITATION CABRIOLET ROOF AVAIL.

Cordoba.

new GRILLE and SINGLE HEADLIGHTS

80

DASH

CORDOBA PRICED FROM $7454.

"Cordoba. An American Classic."

REAR DETAILS

GRILLE UNLIKE OTHER 1980 LE BARONS

(CONT'D NEXT PAGE)

LeBaron Salon Two-Door LS Limited.

CHRYSLER

LeBaron

COUPES PRICED FROM $6801.

new PLAIN-SIDED WAGON $7158.

SEDANS ALSO AVAIL.

new GRILLE is CLASSIC STYLE, *has* ALL-VERT. PCS. *new* DIRECTIONAL LTS.

LeBaron Town & Country Wagon. $7747.

80 (CONT'D.)

new PENTASTAR EMBLEM

NEWPORT $7858.

1980 N.P. SLOGAN: "FRIEND OF THE FAMILY."

new LT. ADDED

180

CHRYSLER

THE INCOMPARABLE NEW YORKER.

ALUMINUM ROAD WHEELS OPT. (NEWPORT OR NEW YORKER)

$10,459

new WHEEL COVERS

NEW YORKER.

80 (CONT'D.)

LITTLE DIFFERENCE BETWEEN '79/'80 N.Y. DASH

FIFTH AVENUE.

FIFTH AVENUE

CHRYSLER

$11,759

"THE ONE AND ONLY."

2 new HORIZONTAL STRIPS ON 1980 5TH AVE. FENDER LIGHT

181

DODGE DIVISION **CHRYSLER** MOTORS CORPORATION

DODGE

(SINCE 1915 MODEL)
(MFD. BY CHRYSLER CORP. SINCE 1928)

JOIN THE DODGE REBELLION

$2736.

STD. CORONET SERIES (lowest priced Coronets
(NO SIDE CHROME)

Coronet DELUXE

$3065.

$2737.

(440 WAGONS ALSO)

66

(6 CYL. or V8)

117" WB

Coronet 440 $2891.

Signal when ready. Hidden behind the handsome grille are Coronet's turn signals and parking lights.

1966

CORONET 440

440 H/T INTERIOR (ABOVE)

$3045.

← Coronet 500 →

Coronet 500.

1966

$3261.

CORONET

500 DASH

182

(CONT'D. NEXT PAGE)

DODGE

POLARA

Polara

FROM $3555.

66 (CONT'D.)

$3320.

$3533.

("POLARA 500" MODELS ALSO)

(121" WB and V8 ENGINES IN POLARA, MONACO)

Polara

Slip gracefully and frugally out of the low-price field. It's never been so easy. See what Dodge Monaco and Polara cars offer you as standard equipment. Then slip behind the wheel—and get a kick out of driving!

$3405.

Monaco

MONACO

FROM $3808

wagons

A-60

REAR DECK BEARS "MONACO" NAME, INSTEAD of "DODGE"

$3759.

$2884.

90" WB

CUSTOM SPORTSMAN

Monaco 500 2-door hardtop. 383 4-barrel V8 power, standard.

183

MONACO 500—THE VERY FINEST DODGE OF ALL FOR '66.

($2567. STD. SPORTSMAN ALSO)

DODGE — *Coronet*

$3070.
Dodge Coronet 2-seat station wagon.

$3141.
Dodge Coronet Deluxe 2-seat station wagon.

440 **DLX.**

FRONT CLOSE-UP

COR. DLX.

(INTRO. 9-29-66)

67

new GRILLES

440

$3352.

CORONET R/T
(w. 440 CID V8)

FROM $3666.

Coronet 500

Dodge Coronet 500 SE (Special Edition)

The Dodge Rebellion wants you!

COR. 500 TAIL-LTS. A APPEAR INVISIBLE BY DAY.

1967

Dodge Polara station wagon, available in 2-seat and 3-seat models.

POLARA STATION WAGON
(POL. 500 *has* VERTICAL TRIM STRIPS NEAR FRONT TIP *of* FRONT FENDER.)

POLARA REAR LIKE MONACO

MONACO

$3676.

Monaco 500
BEARS "DODGE" NAME AT REAR

"MONACO" NAME AT REAR, (EXCEPT ON MONACO 500)

$3896.

184

CORRUGATED

DODGE

a two-way tailgate...

CORONET 440

$3072.

Coronet 500 wagon

FROM $3933.

new GRILLES

(INTRO. 9-14-67)

Watch out. You're getting

68 DODGE-fever

CORONET 500

POLARA 122" WB (SINCE '67)

$3483

POLARA 318 CID V8 (230 HP)

POLARA WAGON FROM $4105

MONACO 500 H/T

$4035.

new FULL-WIDTH TAIL-LT. ASSEMBLY ON POLARA, MONACO.

MONACO WAGONS FROM $4469.

383 CID V8 (290 HP)

new SIDE SAFETY LTS. (CIRCULAR)

CUSTOM **SPORTSMAN**

108" WB (AVAIL. SINCE '67)

two sizes— (90" WB
4 models— to choose from! $2887. UP) 185

MONACO

$3815.

DODGE

CORONET

440 H/T $3521.

69 (INTRO. 9-19-68)

White Hat Special Coronet.

The Dodge Coronet White Hat Special comes in a 2-door hardtop or 4-door sedan—with the features listed below—at a special low package price.
■ Vinyl roof in black, white, tan, green—or standard top
■ Whitewall tires ■ Front, rear bumper guards ■ Deep-dish wheel covers ■ Light group ■ Outside, remote-control rearview mirror ■ Bright trim package.

Coronet. 500

$3655.

Coronet 500

note DUAL HOOD SCOOPS ON

CORONET SUPER BEE

STANDARD SUPER BEE EQUIPMENT
• Special 4-bbl. 383-cid Magnum V8 (440 Magnum V8 heads, valve gear, hot cam and manifolds), 335 hp @ 5,200 rpm • Dual exhaust•
• Hurst 4-speed with HD clutch • HD suspension
• HD shocks • HD brakes • Dodge Charger Rallye instrument panel
OPTIONAL
• 426 Hemi—two 4-bbl. carbs—425 hp @ 5,000 rpm
REAR AXLE RATIOS
• 383 Magnum V8—standard: 3.23:1; optional: 3.55:1, 3.91:1
• Hemi—standard: 3.23:1; optional: 3.54 (with 4-speed manual), 3.55:1 (with automatic), 4.10:1 (with manual or automatic)

H/T $3697.
(note BEE FIGURE ON GRILLE)

THIS DECAL and POPULAR ADVERTISING FIGURE IS WELL KNOWN, BUT DIFFERS FROM BEE ON GRILLE.

186

DODGE

a 230-hp V8. Not to mention an all-new instrument panel and concealed windshield wipers.

Polara.

4-DR. H/T
$3996.

69
(CONT'D.)

FINAL YEAR
FOR POLARA
500

This year,
DODGE is turning up the *fever*

Monaco.

MONACO
GRILLE
(left)
DIFFERS
ONLY SLIGHTLY
FROM
POLARA'S.

wagon   **Dodge** CHRYSLER MOTORS CORPORATION

In a test of acceleration, economy, and braking ability, a 1969 Monaco was overall winner, Class II, in the Union/Pure Oil Performance Trials.

FROM $4707.

$4381.

all-new
aircraft-type instrument panel. And ahead
of it all—a big 383-cu.-in. V8. 1969 Monaco.

187

DODGE

(STD. CHALLENGER IS "DEPUTY" COUPE, AT $3562.)

H/T $3670.

Challenger hardtop, showing deluxe wheel covers

SE ↗ WITH FORMAL ROOF, SMALL REAR WINDOW

$3902.

MORE TOPS...MORE MODELS
Three tops available. Standard (shown), a Special Edition (SE) with vinyl-covered formal roof hardtop, and convertible. All nine models feature concealed wipers, locking steering-wheel column, deep-pile carpeting, dual headlights, and more.

Challenger (NEW)

...you could be **DODGE MATERIAL. 70**

(INTRO. 9-23-69)

110" WB
225 CID 6
(145 HP) OR
318 CID V8
(230 HP)
D78/E78 × 14 TIRES

$4249.

DODGE CHALLENGER R/T CONVERTIBLE

Challenger R/T, showing bumblebee stripe (17 colors available)

Challenger R/T

FROM $4007.

note HOOD VARIATIONS ON THESE 2 R/T HARDTOPS. CAR ABOVE has 2 LG. VENT SLOTS; CAR AT RIGHT has SHAKER TYPE AIR SCOOP.

"R/T" EMBLEM ON GRILLE

F70 × 14 TIRES ON R/T

(CONT'D. NEXT PAGE)

188

DODGE

440 $3616.

Coronet Deluxe station wagon. 2-seat model only—Six or V8 power.

Coronet 440 station wagon, 7-seat models—Six or V8 power. 3-seat model V8 power only.

Coronet 440 4-door sedan.

CORONET

Coronet R/T 2-door hardtop. (Convertible also available.)

$3826.

Coronet 500 station wagon, 2-seat and 3-seat models. 318 V8, std.

Coronet 500 2-door hardtop.

Super Bee

1970

$3919.

Coronet 500

70
(CONT'D.)

Polara GRILLE CLOSE UP

1970

$4022.

Polara

Polara 2-door hardtop, with optional Gator Grain roof.

Polara station wagon, 2-seat and 3-seat models. 318 V8, std.

Polara convertible.

$4221.

Polara Custom 4-door sedan. Polara 4-door sedan also available.

$4305.

FROM $4905.

MONACO

A-100 SPORTSMAN

FROM $3207.

1970

4-DR. H/T $4538.

Challenger.

PRICED FROM $3569.

CHALLENGER T/A

(note STRIPES and SPEC. PAINT)

R/T 383 CID V8 (300 HP) $4009.

(INTRO. 10-6-70) CHALLENGER R/T

71

RESTYLED SPORTSMAN

(ILLUSTRATED with OPTIONAL TRAVCO CAMPER TOP)

new SPORTSMAN B-100, B-200 OR B-300 new 109" OR 127" WB

Coronet wagons FROM $3947.

CRESTWOOD $4352. UP

CORONET

(CONT'D. NEXT PAGE)

SEDANS FROM $3649.

190

DODGE

DASH

$4538 AND UP

POLARA

WIRE WHEEL COVER

71 (CONT'D.)

POLARA CUSTOM 4-DR. H/T $4376.

DODGE POLARA

FROM $5105.

DLX. WHEEL COVER

MONACO

H/T $4631.

DODGE MONACO

DODGE MONACO

DODGE

DASH

CHALLENGER.
100" WB

150 HP,
318 CID
V8
(225 CID 6
AVAIL.)

$3634.

7.35 × 14 TIRES

CHALLENGER RALLYE

340
CID V8
AVAIL.

72
(INTRO.
9-28-71)

new GRILLES

F 70 × 14
TIRES

SPORTSMAN
(B-100, B-200, B-300)

9-PASS.
$4451.

↰ CORONET CRESTWOOD

E 78 × 14 TIRES
on all CORONETS
(H78 × 14, WAGONS)

Coronet

↑ $3615.
AND
UP

CORONET CUSTOM
SEDAN
$3766.

118" WB

(CONT'D.
NEXT
PAGE)

DODGE

POL. CST. WAG. $4849.

SED. $4096

POLARA

DASH

PROTECTIVE VINYL-FACED RUB MOLDING ALONG BODY SIDES

POLARA CUSTOM H/T $4308.

72 (CONT'D.)

Monaco.

$5105. TO 5566.

note UNUSUALLY HIGH PLACEMENT of GRAINED PANELING ON MONACO WAGON.

H/T $4631.

ATTRACTIVE MONACO DOOR PANEL

4-DR. H/T $4694.

WITH BUMPER GUARDS (THAT ALSO SERVE AS GRILLE GUARDS) 193

DODGE

'73
new GRILLES

$3752.

Challenger Rallye

(FINAL 1974 CHALLENGER has SHORT SIDE PORTS in COWL, BUT NO STRIPS ACROSS DOOR AS SEEN ON 1973 MODEL ILLUSTR. ABOVE.)

Coronet '73

CORONET SEDAN

STD. CORONET SEDAN $3757.

SEDAN $3907.

Coronet Wagons

Coronet Custom.

wagons

$4358.
(ABOVE)

Coronet
CUSTOM

CORONET CRESTWOOD WAGON, 6-PASS.: $4449.; 9-PASS.: $4569.

(FINAL POLARA TYPES IN 1973)

Polara

Polara 2-Dr. Hardtop
H/T

SPORTSMAN. THE LARGEST SELLING COMPACT WAGON BUILT IN AMERICA.

POLARA 4-DR. SEDAN

Sportsman.

(CONT'D. NEXT PAGE)

194

DODGE

Polara Custom 2-Dr. Hardtop.

Polara Custom Wagon

Polara Custom

73
(CONT'D.)

new
ELECTRONIC
IGNITION
STD. EQUIP.

Polara Custom 4-Door Hardtop

Extra care in engineering makes a difference in Dodge...depend on it.

Monaco

Monaco Brougham 4-Dr. Sedan.

DASH

00409

SHIFT
INDICATOR
ON
SPEEDOMETER

P R N D 2 1

Monaco Wagon

195

DODGE

(CHALLENGER DISCONTINUED DURING 1974; NAME RETURNS 1978 ON JAPANESE IMPORT VERSION.)

CORONET CUSTOM $4333.

(CORONET and CORO. CUST. SEDANS ONLY)

DODGE MONACO BROUGHAM WAGONS (tow up to 7,000 lbs.).

CHRYSLER

WAGON AT LEFT, FROM $5860.

74

(NO POLARA SERIES; DISCONTINUED)

new GRILLES WITH "DODGE" NAME ABOVE, CENTER.

H/Ts FROM $4783.

MONACO

4-DR. H/Ts FROM $5039.

MONACO, CUSTOM and BROUGHAM DIVISIONS WITHIN MONACO SERIES

EXTRA CARE IN ENGINEERING MAKES A DIFFERENCE IN DODGE... DEPEND ON IT.

SPORTSMAN

DODGE SPORTSMAN WAGONS (tow up to 8,000 lbs.).

B-100, B-200 OR B-300 SERIES

note SIDE DOOR VARIATIONS

new GRILLE, WITH DODGE NAME ABOVE

$5011.- 6155.

196

DODGE

Coronet Two-Door Hardtop

2-DR. $5977. ('75)

('75)
FINAL '76 CORONET *has* HOOD ORNAMENT.

SINCE 1975, MOST 6-CYL. MODELS COST MORE THAN COMPARABLE V8s.

75-76

Introducing the Royal Monaco Brougham

DODGE SPORTSMAN WAGON
Extra care in engineering makes a difference.

SEATING ARRANGEMENT →

No wonder we're number one.

MONACO NOW *has* FORMER CORONET WHEELBASE: (2-DR., 115"; 4-DR., 117½")

77

MONACO

REAR

2-DRS. FROM $5061.

(CONT'D. NEXT PAGE)

197

DODGE

BROUGHAM 2-DR. $5297.

PLAID INTERIOR AVAIL.

MONACO

$5818.

MONACO CRESTWOOD WAGON

MONACO WHEEL WITH HOLES

77 (CONT'D.)

$5619.

LOW SIDE LIGHTS ON ROYAL MONACO

CPE. ROOFLINE VARIETIES

Royal Monaco Brougham Hardtop

ROYAL MONACO

BROUGHAM SEDAN

WITH DIPLOMAT ROOF PKG.

$5634.

wagon

$6353.

REAR DETAILS

198

DODGE

standard Diplomat

OR

DELUXE
MEDALLION
MODELS
112.7" WB

77½

"DIPLOMAT.
THAT FIENDISHLY SEDUCTIVE
NEW CAR BY DODGE."

NEW

2-DR.
MEDALLION
$5522.10
AS SHOWN (SALE)

REG.
$5907.

$5569 as shown. More seductive luxury than you ever dreamed of... in a manageable new size from Dodge.

The look is classic. Sculptured.   The smooth V8 is standard.

318 CID
V8
(145 HP)

FR 78 × 15
TIRES

VELOUR
STD. IN
MEDALLION INTERIOR (4-DR.
ILLUSTR.)

DIPLOMAT

(6TH DIGIT IN SERIAL # PREFIX IS
NOW 8 ··· SIGNIFYING 1978 MODEL.)

25/17
MPG HWY   MPG CITY

WITH
T-BAR
ROOF

$5969, AS SHOWN. (SALE)

WAGON
ADDED TO LINE
(FROM $6471.)

MODELS
DRESSED LIKE
SHERLOCK HOLMES and DR. WATSON
CONTINUE APPEARING
IN DODGE DIPLOMAT
ADVERTISING.
(RIGHT, TOP RIGHT)

LOWER-COST
DIPLOMAT
"S" ADDED:
(CPE., $5726.
SED., $5882.)

78

(new
MODELS
ADDED)

(CONT'D.
NEXT
PAGE)

SALE

PRICED AS SHOWN: $5195.*
1978 DODGE DIPLOMAT
FOUR-DOOR

Base price	$ 5147
Six-cylinder engine	Standard
Power front disc brakes	Standard
4-speed manual transmission†	Standard
Deluxe wheel covers	Standard
Power steering	Standard
Transverse torsion-bar suspension	Standard
Vinyl roof	Standard
White sidewall radial tires	$ 48
Total	**$ 5195***

(REG.
$6132.)

199

DODGE

INTRODUCING MAGNUM XE.

78
(CONT'D.)

LOTS MORE VISIBILITY.
We've put more glass area in the side windows behind the front doors. And rear quarter windows in the Maxiwagon wrap right around the corners to make backing up a snap.

Maxiwagon has eight inches more loadspace length this year. Room for more cargo and more fun.

(NEW)

BLT. 1978-1979 ONLY

8. NEW ANTITHEFT MEASURES.
The steering column now locks when you shut off the ignition. And the door vent windows have new latches that click shut for extra security.

SPORTSMAN WAGON

FROM AMERICA'S NO.1 SELLER OF VAN-WAGONS.

ALL-NEW SEATS.

23 MPG HWY/ 17 MPG CITY.
EPA estimates for Dodge Sportsman B100 wagon, with standard 225-cubic-inch six-cylinder engine and manual transmission.

ALL-NEW INSTRUMENT PANEL.
Sedan-type luxury combined with servicing convenience. The combined starter and ignition switch is now on the locking steering column.

DIPLOMAT WAGON 28 MPG HWY/18 MPG CITY *

(WAGON INTERIOR ILLUSTR. ON NEXT PAGE)

79

SPORTSMAN ↓

new GRILLE, new FRONT BUMPER, STACKED RECT. HEADLTS. OPT. (SPTSMN.)

FR. $6869.

"HEY, THAT'S MY DODGE."

FROM $7343.

(CONT'D. NEXT PAGE)

DODGE *Diplomat*

28 MPG HWY/18 MPG CITY

PRICED FROM $6001.

T-BAR ROOFS OPTIONAL

"HEY, THAT'S MY DODGE."

Re-introducing the full-size car. The totally new St. Regis by Dodge.

79 (CONT'D.)

(REAR)
ST. REGIS
$7190. (V8) $7429. (6)

FINAL MAGNUM XE $6380.

NEW

ST. REGIS DASH

118½" WB

St.Regis

A standard two-barrel Super Six provides exceptional mileage. **(225 CID)**

23 mpg highway/17 mpg city

3/8 CID V8 (140 HP) AVAIL.

DODGE

$6485.

DIPLOMAT FOUR-DOOR.

$6334.

DIPLOMAT TWO-DOOR.

Introducing Diplomat S-Type Coupe. A new level of driving

DIPLOMAT 80

new GRILLE
new 108.7" WB ON 2-DRS.

(S-TYPE DASH ILLUS. AT LOWER LEFT)

(112.7" WB CONT'D. ON 4-DRS.)

CLOTH-and-VINYL SEATS IN SALON INTERIOR

$6621.

DIPLOMAT WAGON

$7311.

WITH WOODGRAIN

STD. 225 CID 6 (100/110 HP)
STD. 318 CID V8 (140 HP)

$6772.

OPT. WIRE WH. COVERS

Protective rub strips front and rear (std)

Power brakes—front disc, rear drum (std)

DIPLOMAT DASH (S)

SALON 4-DR.

(CONT'D. NEXT PAGE)

1980 DODGE MIRADA
(REPLACES MAGNUM)

FROM $7217.

new 112.7" WB

"CABRIOLET" H/T AVAIL.

GRILLE

225 CID 6 (100/110 HP)
318 CID V8 (140 HP) OR
360 CID V8

FR.

REAR

Working Gauges
Brushed-Metal Instrument Panel

17 EPA EST. MPG. **25** EST. HWY. MPG.

18 - GAL. FUEL TANK

P195/7R15 TIRES

ST. REGIS

$7733.

80 (CONT'D.)

new SIDE TRIM, BODY STRIPING ADDED

Touring Edition Instrument Cluster.

new
St. Regis Touring Edition.

W. VINYL ROOF

Test drive total performance in a full-size car.

203

ST. REGIS. THE SUBJECT IS LUXURY.

225 CID 6 (100 HP) OR 318 CID V8 (140-150 HP)

DODGE **ASPEN**

(REPLACES DART, 1976)
(REPL. BY ARIES FOR 1981)
"Unbelievable."
(ONE-WORD SLOGAN)

76-77

108½" WB (2-DR.)
112½" WB (4-DR.)

Winner of the 1976 Motor Trend Magazine Car of the Year Award.

Aspen R/T has a bold look. With a blacked-out grille, wide rallye wheels, distinctive stripes.

R/T

6-passenger only

EPA MPG: 30 HWY. 18 CITY

('77)

$4872. ('76)

1976 FROM $4155. TO $4916. 1977 FROM $4515. TO $5216.

(ASPEN, CUSTOM and SPECIAL EDITION MODELS)

(HOOD ORN. ON SPEC. ED.)

new T-TOP AVAIL. ('77)

('76 MODELS SHOWN, EXCEPT WHERE INDICATED OTHERWISE)

204

SMALLER FEELS BIGGER IN AN ASPEN.

Dodge ASPEN

$5684. SPECIAL EDITION

CUSTOM $5513.

CUSTOM 5087.

SPECIAL EDITION $5410.

Aspen Wagon $4294. (REG. $5203.)

25/18 MPG HWY MPG CITY

78 new GRILLE and TAIL-LTS.

DASH

FULL-LENGTH SIDE STRIPE ON CPE. WITH R/T SPORT PAK

AS BEFORE, NO SIDE CHROME ON STD. ASPEN MODELS; SPEC. ED. MODELS have HOOD ORNAMENTS.

the R/T Sport Pak.

SUPER COUPE (BLACKED-GRILLE, SPOILER, ETC.)

SPECIAL EDITION $5262.

NARROWER new GRILLE, WITH FLANKING AMBER AUX. LTS. MOVED UP FROM BUMPER.

(ILLUSTRATED T-TOP IS OPTIONAL AT EXTRA COST)

Dodge ASPEN

WITH SUNRISE → PACKAGE

WITH 2-TONE PAINT and DECOR PACKAGE

Aspen coupe

STANDARD ASPEN SEDAN.
$5201.
(COUPES FROM $5100.)

'79

WITH **Aspen RT.** PKG.

DASH

ASPEN SED. WITH 2-TONE PAINT and DECOR PACKAGE

$5675. →
Aspen Special Edition Coupe

Aspen Special Edition Wagon
$6061.

REAR

SPECIAL EDITION EXT. and INTERIOR PKG.

$5808.

Engines
- Standard 225 1-barrel 6-cyl.
- Optional 225 2-barrel 6-cyl.
- Optional 318 2-barrel V-8
- Optional 318 4-barrel V-8
- Optional 360 4-barrel V-8

206

Dodge ASPEN

INTER. and EXT. OF ASPEN CPE. WITH SUNRISE OPTION PACKAGE

Special.

SALE $4994.

Test drive Total Performance from Dodge.

SPECIAL has MINIMUM of CHROME TRIM.

Optional T-Bar roof
The next best thing to a convertible. Tinted glass panels lift out and store in the trunk to give that fresh air feeling to any Aspen coupe.

ENGINES & TRANSMISSIONS
Federal
- ☐ 3.7-liter (225 CID) 1V Slant Six (std)
- ☐ 5.2-liter (318 CID) 2V V-8 (opt)

High Altitude
- ☐ 5.2-liter (318 CID) 4V V-8 (opt)

California
- ☐ 3.7-liter (225 CID) 1V Slant Six (std)

- ☐ 5.2-liter (318 CID) 4V V-8 (opt)
- ☐ Three-speed manual (std) (N.A Calif. or V-8)
- ☐ Four-speed manual (opt) (N.A Calif. or V-8)
- ☐ TorqueFlite automatic (opt)

SEDAN, CPE., WAGON SHOWN WITH SPECIAL EDITION PACKAGE

(STD. UNGRAINED WAGONS FROM $6141.)

SEDAN WITH CUSTOM PACKAGE

new GRILLE; RECTANGULAR HEADLIGHTS

(FINAL ASPEN)

80

Optional cast aluminum road wheels
Add that sporty road car image to any Aspen with the addition of these great looking optional wheels.

DASH

3-SP. MANUAL TRANS. (3.2 GEAR RATIO) BUT CALIFORNIA-SOLD CARS have 2.9 GEAR RATIO WITH TorqueFlite AUTO. TRANS.

(17) EPA EST. MPG   25 EST. HWY MPG**   207

(REPLACED BY 1981 ARIES)

(1966 – 1978)

Dodge CHARGER

66 *(new)*

$3469.

HDLTS. DISAPPEAR INTO GRILLE

BUCKET SEATS, FRONT and BACK

117" WB (LIKE **Coronet**) (THROUGH '70)

...new leader of the Dodge Rebellion.

V8s: 318 CID (230 HP)
361 (265 HP)
383 (325 HP)
426 CID Hemi (425 HP)

7.35 × 14 TIRES

FASTBACK STYLING (THROUGH '67)

$3482.

VINYL TOP OPT.

new 440 MAGNUM V8 AVAIL.

67

XP-29 MODEL CONTINUES WITH FEW CHANGES

the Dodge Rebellion.

208

$3184. UP

Dodge Charger

new SIDE SAFETY LTS. (ROUND)

68
(RESTYLED)
NO LONGER A FASTBACK

Join the fun... catch **Dodge** *fever*

R/T SE

FROM $3371.

STANDARD CHARGER R/T EQUIPMENT
- 440-cid Magnum (4-bbl.) V8, 375 hp
- Choice of 3-speed automatic or Hurst 4-speed manual • Dual exhausts
- HD suspension • HD shocks • HD brakes
- Dodge Charger Rallye instrument panel • F70x14 wide-treads

OPTIONAL
- 426 Hemi

69
new SPLIT GRILLE

Success Car of the Year

69½-70

Totally new

(RARE)

UNIQUE REAR "TAIL"

Charger Daytona:

(1970 PLYMOUTH ROAD-RUNNER "**SUPERBIRD**" SIMILAR)

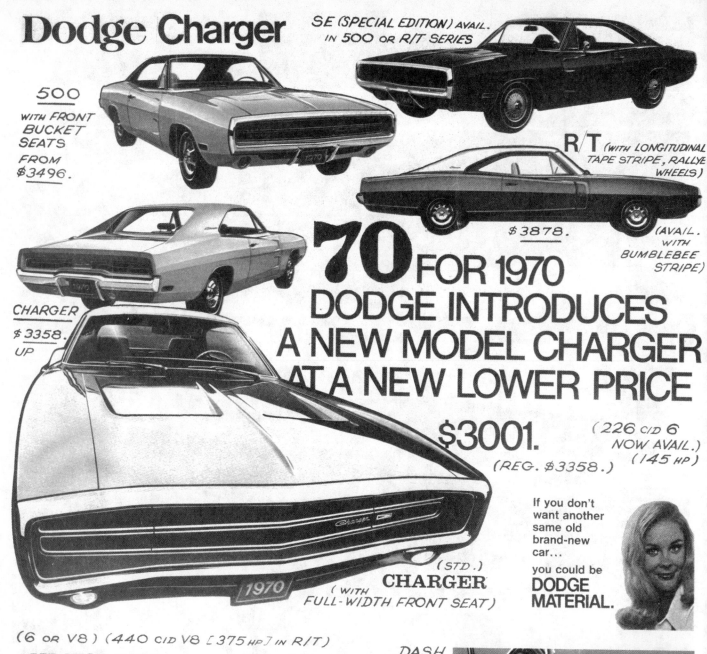

Dodge Charger

SE (SPECIAL EDITION) AVAIL. IN 500 OR R/T SERIES

500 WITH FRONT BUCKET SEATS FROM $3496.

R/T (WITH LONGITUDINAL TAPE STRIPE, RALLYE WHEELS)

$3878.

(AVAIL. WITH BUMBLEBEE STRIPE)

CHARGER $3358. UP

70 FOR 1970 DODGE INTRODUCES A NEW MODEL CHARGER AT A NEW LOWER PRICE

$3001.

(REG. $3358.)

(226 C/D 6 NOW AVAIL.) (145 HP)

(STD.) CHARGER (WITH FULL-WIDTH FRONT SEAT)

If you don't want another same old brand-new car...

you could be **DODGE MATERIAL.**

(6 OR V8) (440 CID V8 [375 HP] IN R/T)

LEFT DECK-SIDE SPORT TYPE GAS FILLER CAP

RACK OPTIONAL

DASH

FUEL

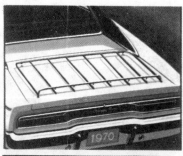

CHARGER R/T

Dodge Charger

$4043.

VINYL TOP

STEEL TOP

300 HP **Super Bee** with a 383 Magnum... regular gas.

PAINTED GRILLE

71 (RESTYLED) new SHORTER 115" WB

Charger SE

CHARGER FROM $3579.

OPEN HEADLIGHTS

CONCEALED HEADLIGHTS SPOILER

new FLAT DOOR HANDLES

$4311.

$4173.

440 CID **R/T** (370 HP)

CHARGER 500

$3973.

note DIFFERENCES IN DETAILS BETWEEN THESE VARIOUS MODELS.

YOU CAN'T AFFORD <u>NOT</u> TO BE DODGE MATERIAL

Dodge CHARGER

dash

CHARGER

FROM $3527.

ROOF DETAILS

72

new GRILLES

Charger Topper
landau vinyl roof.

CHARGER RALLYE

REAR

BULGE ON RALLYE HOOD IS PAINTED BLACK.

WITH CONCEALED HEADLIGHTS, RALLYE DASH, BUMPER GUARDS and SPECIAL TRIM. (note CONVENTIONAL TYPE STEERING WHEEL USED) (arrow)

DOOR SLOTS
(ON RALLYE ONLY)

RALLYE has OWN GRILLE (HORIZONTAL PCS.) and OPEN HDLTS.

SE GRILLE DETAIL

"Special Edition"

SE

DASH

$4017.

Dodge. Depend on it.

Dodge Charger

COUPE

FROM $3700.

CHARGER COUPE WITH LANDAU TOP

SE.

4/53.

new GRILLE

"HALO" TOP

"LANDAU" TOP

73

CHARGER H/T $3949.

new SAFETY BUMPERS; ELECTRONIC IGNITION STD.

E78×14 4 P/R TIRES

225 CID 6
318 CID V8
340, 400 OR 440 CID V8s ALSO
(105 TO 260 HP)

SE WITH new 3-PC. LOUVRED QUARTER WINDOWS

SE

OPT. SUNROOF AVAIL. WITH VINYL TOP

SE INT.

Charger Rallye.

CHARGER RALLYE
The Rallye Package is available on V8 Charger hardtops and coupes, and includes the following items: Rallye Instrument Cluster • Power bulge hood • Body side tape stripe • Hood pins • Front and rear sway bars • F70 x 14 tires with raised white letters.

Rallye Hardtop.

Rallye Coupe.

Extra care in engineering makes a difference in Dodge...depend on it.

Dodge Charger

CHARGER COUPE

$4171.

This year, go Charger style.

(FULL 1974 LINE ILLUSTR.)

74

CHARGER H/T $4370.

SE has HOOD ORNAMENT

E78 or F78 x 14 TIRES

CHARGER SE $4584.

EXTRA CARE IN ENGINEERING MAKES A DIFFERENCE IN DODGE ...DEPEND ON IT.

Introducing Dodge Charger Special Edition '75

HORIZ.- LOUVRED OPERA WINDOWS ARE new AND OPT.

2.45 GEAR RATIO

SE $5412.

318, 360 OR 400 CID V8s (150 TO 235 HP)

"You'll love the change we made."

75

(RESTYLED) (RESEMBLES CHRYSLER'S new CORDOBA)

DASH

GR78 x 15 TIRES, OTHERS

214

Dodge Charger

CHARGER DAYTONA
(new)

75½

(DAYTONA ADDED
IN MID-SEASON)

"CHARGER
DAYTONA"
NAME on SIDE

4 MODELS,
SALE PRICED
FROM

Once you've looked, you're hooked.

$3736.

(BASIC
CHARGER
REG.
$4744.)

new
SPORT=
$5033.

23 MPG. HWY., 16 CITY
WITH 6-CYL. 225 CID (100 HP)

76

SE $5334.

'76
DAYTONA

SE
$5692.

(MOVES TO MONACO LINE)

FINAL CHARGER SE A PART OF 1978
MONACO LINE at $5951.

new
GRILLE

77

318 CID V8
(145 HP) STD.
6-CYL. STILL
AVAIL.

1977½
T-TOP

Dodge Dart

(SINCE 1960; COMPACT-SIZE SINCE 1963)

170 CID 6 (101 HP) 225 CID 6 (145 HP) OR 273 CID V8 (235 HP)

DART

2-DR. $2319.

Dart 4-door sedan. Six or 273 V8 power. $2383.

JOIN THE DODGE REBELLION

66

111" WB (106," WAGONS)

WAGONS

$2661.

6.50 × 13 TIRES

DART 270 SERIES

2-DR. $2439.

270 WAGON $2758.

270 CVT. $2795.

270 H/T $2532.

GT

GT HAS CHROME ATOP FR. FENDERS AND ON ROCKER PANELS

270 4-DR. $2505.

GT H/T $2642. PARTIAL VINYL TOP AVAIL.

GT CVT. $2925.

FULL 1966 LINE ILLUSTRATED

216

$2453. **DART**

$2416.

DART
WAGONS
DISCONTINUED

(INTRO
9-29-
66)

67

(RESTYLED)

new SUNKEN-IN
REAR WINDOW

$2591.

**DART
270**

$2617.

The Dodge Rebellion:
Operation '67

Go '67 Dart!"

$2961.

GT

$2728.

REDESIGNED
RECESSED
INSTRUMENT
PANEL

note "GT"
TAGS

*FULL
1967 LINE
ILLUSTRATED*

217

Dodge Dart

2-DR.
$2556.

4-DR. $2593.

270 4-DR. $2732.

270

(INTRO. 9-14-67)

DODGE fever

68 new GRILLES

270 H/T $2758.

TAIL-LT. DETAIL

PLAIN TOP

GT

GT CVT. $3064.

GTS CVT. $3445.

GT H/T $2860.

VINYL TOP (OPT.)

GT SPORT (GTS.) 340 CID V8

340 CID V8

H/T $3251.

FULL 1968 LINE ILLUSTRATED

This year, DODGE (270 BECOMES CUSTOM) is turning up the fever

DASH

69 new GRILLES

(INTRO. 9-19-68)

Announcing Dart Swinger.

218 $2637.

Dodge Dart

you could be **DODGE MATERIAL.**

DART CUSTOM 4-DR. SEDAN $2972.

4-DR. **DART**

$2807.

CUSTOM H/T $2999.

CUSTOM

OPT. WH. CVRS.

* 60 DAY SWINGER AUTOMATIC SALE!

(NO DART 2-DR. SEDAN AVAIL. 1969 OR 1970)

INCLUDES EXTRAS LISTED AT BOTTOM OF PAGE.

70

(INTRO. 9-23-69) (BUCKET STS. OPT. IN CUST., SW. 340 H/Ts)

SWINGER 340 H/T $3171.

$2790.

SWINGER H/T

Dart Swinger 2-door hardtop. Our lowest priced hardtop.

SHOWING ALL-STEEL RALLYE WHEELS

SWINGER

SWINGER 340 (ABOVE)

SHOWN w. LIGHT COLORED VINYL ROOF

*SALE PACKAGE INCLUDES

- VINYL ROOF
- D78 X 14 WHITEWALL TIRES
- DELUXE WHEEL COVERS
- DELUXE VINYL INTERIOR TRIM
- "RIM-BLOW" STEERING WHEEL

DART, "Swinger"

FULL 1970 LINE ILLUSTRATED

DART SWINGER 2-DOOR HARDTOP

- LEFT, REMOTE-CONTROL MIRROR
- CARPETS
- VINYL BODY-SIDE MOULDINGS
- BUMPER GUARDS (Frt. & Rr.)
- WHEEL-LIP/BELT MOULDINGS

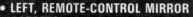

automatic trans.

Dodge Dart

SWINGER $2808.

Dart *CUSTOM* $2856.

(INTRO. 9-15-70)

new GRILLE **71** new BODY (ONLY on new DEMON CPES.)

$3000.

340 CID V8 (275 HP)

DEMON 340

(**new**) DEMON

(108"WB) FROM $2590.

198 CID 6 (125 HP) OR 318 CID V8 (230 HP)

Demon

DODGE DEMON

ALSO AVAIL. SWINGER SPEC. H/T ($2649.) and DART SEDAN ($2697.)

$2665. **72** new GRILLE

DART SWINGER H/T $2773.

(INTRO. 9-28-71)

DART

DART DEMON

DART

$2561.

1972 DEMON REAR STYLING SIMILAR TO 1971.

Dodge. Depend on it.

Dodge Dart

$2898.

NO SIDE CHROME ON **DART SWINGER SPECIAL** H/T

$2702.

$2857.

Dart Custom Sedan & Swinger Hardtop

73 new GRILLE and BUMPERS

Dart Sport.

$2664.

DASH

SPORT (108" WB) MODELS REPLACE DART DEMONS.

REAR CLOSE-UP (DART)

$3124.

SPORT 340

Dodge invents the Convertriple. Three cars for the price of one.

DODGE DART **SWINGER** $3873.

CUSTOM $3915.

the dart dozen

TODAY—more than ever—Dart is right on target.

(SPORT TOPPER, SPORT HANG 10, SPORT RALLYE DELS ALSO)

74

Extra care in engineering makes a difference in Dodge ...depend on it.

$3674.

DART SPORT CONVERTRIPLE '74.

Dart Special Edition. new

1 IT'S A FIVE-PASSENGER COUPE. With the size and features you wouldn't expect from a compact. Features such as torsion-bar suspension, Unibody construction, and the Electronic Ignition System...Dart Sport 1 makes 2 and 3 that much better.

2 IT'S A SUN ROOF CONVERTIBLE. What an option! You get a secure metal sun roof that slides open to give you the sun in the morning and the moon at night. With Dart Sport, the sky's the limit. So sit back, relax, and start to follow the sun.

3 IT'S AN ECONOMY WAGON. With the optional fold-down rear seat, you can flip yourself into a wagon in seconds and have a fully carpeted cargo space that's six-and-a-half-feet long. Dart Sport Convertriple '74. Pack it up and get going.

The new Dart Special Edition is based on the premise that a small car can be a *very* luxurious car. High-backed seats covered in crushed velour

SE

$4349.

1974

Dart Special Edition.

$4565.

Dart "Hang 10."

DASH

new GRILLE

75-76 (EARLY)

1975

(REPLACED BY DODGE ASPEN)

Dodge is right on target

222

DODGE OMNI

4-DR. ('78)
$3981.

SINCE 1978

GRAINED SIDE TRIM OPTIONAL

('78) REAR (OMNI has HORIZONTAL STRIPS ACROSS TAIL-LIGHTS; HORIZON DOES NOT.)

O-24 2+2 FASTBACK (HATCHBACK) STARTS 1979. DE TOMASO VERSION ALSO AVAIL. 1980.

IT DOES IT ALL.

4-DR. 99.2" WB

2-DR. ('79 ON) 96.7" WB

78-80

WITH VOLKSWAGEN 4-CYL. ENGINE 104.7 C.I.D.

155/80 × 13 TIRES

(LENGTH EXAGGERATED)

2+2
('79)-new 2-DR. = $4801.
"   "   5611. ('80)

OPTIONAL SUNROOF WITH GLASS DOOR

('79)

OMNI GRILLE has ALL HORIZONTAL PCS.

PLYMOUTH HORIZON SPECS. SIMILAR

223

FORD

YOU'RE AHEAD IN A FORD

$ 2898.

IMPACT ABSORBING
STEERING WHEEL
WITH PADDED HUB

Custom
and Custom 500

$ 3052.

new
GRILLE *and*
TAIL-LIGHTS

67

(INTRO. 9-30-66)

GALAXIE 500

(SINCE
1952,
RANCH
WAGON *and*
COUNTRY
SEDAN ARE
UN-GRAINED
FORD WAGONS.)

$3212.

COUNTRY
SQUIRE
$ 3816.

LTD
$ 3677.

SelectShift transmission you can use automatically or manually.

225

XL

$3558.

FORD $3048.

CUSTOM (CUST. 500, GAL. 500 ALSO USE THIS GRILLE)

DUAL-FACING REAR SEATS AVAIL.

COUNTRY SQUIRE (LTD) $3977.

(INTRO. 9-22-67)

68

new GRILLES
new 302 CID V8
(210 HP)
6 ALSO CONT'D.

INTERIOR (XL)

$3450.
XL

new CONCEALED HEADLIGHTS (LTD, XL)

OPEN

CLOSED

See the light!
FORD
Ford has a better idea.

(INTRO. 9-27-68)

new Ford Club Wagon

69

new GRILLES
new 121" WB
(THROUGH '78)
(C.W. 105½" OR 123½" WB)

COUNTRY SEDAN
FR. $3741.

standard wagon

RANCH WAGON IS LOWEST-PRICED

FR. $2900.

226

(CONT'D. NEXT PAGE)

C.W. SINCE '65

FORD

new 150 HP IN 6

$3257.

CUSTOM 500
SIDE CHROME STRIP NOT SEEN ON CUSTOM.)

DASH

$3514.

69
(CONT'D.)

LTD

LTD INSIGNIA ABOVE GRILLE

XL

SPRTSRF. H/T
$3536

It's the going thing!

GALAXIE, XL, LTD WITH 351 CID V8 (250 HP)

SPECIAL GALAXIE 500 2-DOOR HARDTOP

70

new GRILLES
new F/G/H
78 × 15 TIRES

FORD GALAXIE 500 SPORTSROOF

$3522.

COUNTRY SQUIRE

$3573.

Take a Quiet Break in a FORD.

(INTRO. 9-19-69)

LTD
AND INTERIOR

$4199. UP

$3724.

227

FORD

$4530 2-DR. LTD BROUGHAM **LTD**

COUNTRY SQUIRE

(INTRO. 9-18-70)

FROM $4809.

Take a Quiet Break...
'71 Ford.

STD 240 CID 6 (140 HP) OR 302 CID V8 (210 HP)

71 new GRILLE

new BUMPER DIPS, TO FOLLOW CONTOUR OF POINTED GRILLE.

DASH

LTD FINAL CVT. CVT. $4517.

COUNTRY SQUIRE FROM $4792.

(INTRO. 9-24-71)

72 2 SLIGHTLY DIFFERING new GRILLES

302 CID V8 (140 HP)
351 CID V8 (153 HP)

Quiet Plus.

GALAXIE 500

H/T $4161.

new STRAIGHT-ACROSS POINTED BUMPER

LTD

FORD

The closer you look, the better we look.

FROM $4550.

$4206.

G78 x 15 TIRES

COUNTRY SEDAN

(RANCH WAGON LOOKS SIMILAR)

GALAXIE 500

(CUSTOM 500 4-DR. SEDAN HAS NO CHROME SIDE STRIP.) ($4014.)

(6 and 302 CID V8 NOT AVAIL. IN FULL-SIZED LINE)

351, 400, 429 OR 460 CID V8s, J78 x 15 TIRES ON WAGONS

73

(RESTYLED)

DASH

AVAIL. POWER-OPERATED SUN ROOF

FROM $4356.

LTD

new INSIDE HOOD LOCK, and FRONT DISC BRAKES STANDARD

LTD BROUGHAM PILLARLESS 4-DOOR H/T also available, AND 2-DR. H/T, 4-DR. PILLARED H/T

PILLARED 4-DR. H/T FR. $4364.

CLOSER REAR DETAILS (LTD)

229

FORD

FROM $5399.
LTD Country Squire

DASH

LTD
BROUGHAM 2-DR.
$5170.

74

new GRILLE; LTD has HOOD ORNAMENT

($4483 CUSTOM 500 4-DR. IS LOWEST-PRICED LARGE FORD.)

(FINAL YR. FOR GALAXIE 500)

LTD REAR →

new

LTD
AND
LTD
BROUGHAM

$5649.

DASH
3-SEAT
$6115.

75

HOOD ORNAMENT

FRONT
RESTYLED

COUNTRY
SQUIRE

CONCEALED
HDLTS. RETURN

LTD.
LANDAU
(new)

(FINAL YEAR FOR
CUSTOM 500)

$6003.

FORD wagon

4-SEAT COUNTRY SQUIRE WAGON $6213.

(4-DR. STD. LTD IS LOWEST-PRICED, AT $5316.)

76

FEW NOTICEABLE CHANGES FROM 1975

note new WHEEL COVERS

LTD

$6177.

(ABOVE) '76½ COUNTRY SQUIRE

NO LONGER SHOWN WITH CHROME STRIP WHICH FORMERLY RAN ALONG GRAINED PANEL

351, 400 OR 460 CID V8s

LTD LANDAU NO LONGER HAS BODY-PAINTED SECTIONS BETWEEN THE 3 AMBER LENSES.

LTD Wagon

FR. $6464.

FR. $6012.

77

LTD. The full-size car

(LTD GENERALLY SIMILAR TO 1976 MODEL)

WITH STD. 351 CID V8 (161 HP)

LTD LANDAU 4-DR. $6340.

new LTD II has 302 CID V8 (130 HP) and HR78 × 14 TIRES

BROUGH. 5698.

Now, in addition to the full-size Ford LTD, Ford also offers LTD's kind of quality and luxury in a sportier, trimmer car that's priced and handles like a mid-size.

the new trimmer, sportier LTD II

(REPLACES TORINO)

FROM $5156. (S)

114"/118" WB
2-DR. 4-DR.

$5362. UP (STD. 2-DR.)

231

(RANCHERO NOW IN LTD II SERIES)

FORD
(E-100 124" WB)
138" WB
CLUB
WAGON
TYPES:
E-150,
250
OR
350

Built Ford Tough

SUPER WAGON

CL. W. INT.

FROM $6756.

LTD DASH

FORD LTD
LANDAU (REAR)

FINAL LARGE (121" WB) LTD

78

FORD LTD
FORD DIVISION
75" ANNIVERSARY

LTD, LTD II
NOW SHARE STD. 302 CID V8 (134 HP)

LTD

2-SEAT: $6848.

Ford LTD Country Squire

$6127.

LTD II

LTD LANDAU $6614.

LTD (REAR)

LTD II DASH

NOW 2
LTD II
COUPE STYLES

$6027.

new WHEELS

232

LTD II
LTD BROUGHAM has
MID-SIDE TRIM.

FORD

CAPTAIN'S CLUB

Wagon

300 CID 6
OR 302, 351, 460 CID
V8s IN CLUB WAGONS
(FR. $7086.)

LTD II

"It's like they made it for me...
sporty and practical"

LTD II 2-door Brougham in Pastel Chamois

(FINAL LTD II = ABOVE)

1979
NEW AMERICAN
ROAD CAR

STD. LTD

LTD DASH

CNTRY. SQ.
FR. $7291.

FORD LTD

LANDAU

302 CID V8
(134 HP)
351 CID V8
(144 HP)

LTDs
DOWNSIZED, WITH
new
114.4"
WB

(TOTALLY
RESTYLED
LTD, LANDAU)

79

note:
1979 has TALL,
NARROW HOOD
ORNAMENT

1979

FORD

DETAILS OF STD. LTD
2-DR.

233

FORD
DIFF. GRILLE ON
LOW-PRICED
LTD "S" →

$7019.

DASH

new
HIGHER
BELT
STRIPING
FOR
1980

80

(LTD "S" WAGON
ALSO)
new P205, P215 75R x 14
TIRES

$7769.

(G)

(new)
FORD LTD
CROWN VICTORIA
SEDAN DETAILS IN
CIRCLE AT LOWER
LEFT)

2-DR.
$7248.

LTD.

$7706.

new WIDER
HOOD ORN.
(CNTRY. SQ.
and CRN.
VICT.)

$8125.
(6-PASS.)
**LTD COUNTRY
SQUIRE**

NO
HOOD ORNAMENT
ON STD. LTDs

$7900.

CROWN VICTORIA SEDAN

(new)

234

Ford FAIRLANE / TORINO

(A SEPARATE COMPACT/INTERMEDIATE SERIES SINCE 1962)
(TORINO INTRO. 1968; FINAL FAIRLANE, 1970.)

116" WB
200 CID 6 (120 HP)
289 CID V8 (200 HP)
OR 390 CID V8 (335 HP) (IN GT)

500-XL

Fairlane re-invented...for 1966

H/T $3201.

The Wizard of Aah's 1966 Fairlane

NAME ON REAR FENDER

Fairlane GT —

(GTA has AUTO. TRANS.)

Special GT and GTA identification

convertible $3426.

GT DASH

66

new GRILLE, new VERTICALLY-STACKED HEADLIGHTS, new TAIL-LTS.

new GRAINED SQUIRE WAGON (113" WB) $3229.

new "MAGIC DOORGATE" SWINGS OUT OR DOWN.

FAIRLANE 500
H/T $2976.

FORD *Fairlane* / TORINO

FAIRLANE CLUB CPE. $2741.

Fairlane

500

CLUB CPE. $2821.

CVT. $3289.

SQUIRE $3347.

Fairlane 500

500/XL

H/T $3063.

Fairlane 500 Wagon

$3163.

67 *new GRILLE*

INTERIOR (500/XL)

Fairlane 500/XL Interior

390 INDICATES A 390 CID V8 IN CAR.

GT H/T $3178.

(note SIDE PAINT STRIPING ON GT)

That GT feeling is contagious: every Fairlane has it.

SHOW YOUR STRIPES!

(INTRO. 9-30-66)

FORD *Fairlane* / TORINO

TORINO. *(new)*

GT

FORMAL H/T
$3156

CVT.
$3359.

TORINO
INT.

TORINO
GT

302 CID V8
(210 HP) OR
390 CID V8

FASTBACK
$3105.

Torino Squire

ALSO 289 CID V8
(195 HP) OR 200 CID 6 (115 HP)

FAIRLANE
500 $3011.

68
(INTRO. 9-22-67)

FAIRLANE

FAIRLANE
SEDAN

$2962.

H/T $2909.

FORD *Fairlane* / TORINO

note:
REAR SIDE SAFETY LIGHTS SMALLER, MOVED FORWARD AND DOWN.

FAIRLANE

$2941.

(INTRO. 9-27-68)

$2952.

69 *new* GRILLES

302 CID V8
4 OTHER V8s,
OR 428 CID 4V
COBRA JET V8 (335 HP)

The 1969 winning streak rolls on. The Ford victory at Martinsville makes it six big wins for Torino over all the other specially modified stock cars.

DATE	EVENT	DRIVER
February 1	Riverside 500	Richard Petty
February 16	ARCA 300	Benny Parsons
February 23	Daytona 500	Lee Roy Yarbrough
March 9	Carolina 500	David Pearson
April 13	Richmond 250	David Pearson
April 27	Virginia 500	Richard Petty

With a roaring start like this the Torinos are well on their way to a repeat of last season's Grand Slam when Torino took the NASCAR, USAC and ARCA championships.

1969

TORINO GT

SPORTSROOF (FASTBACK) $3203.

Torino Talladega

IS '69½ SUPER STOCK SPORTSROOF MODEL. HAS SMALL RECTANGULAR SAFETY LTS. AT LOWER SIDE OF FRONT FENDER.

428

HOOD SCOOP

TORINO SEDAN $3186. (ALSO AVAIL: CONVERTIBLE)

(CONT'D. IN FORD TORINO SECTION)

238

Ford Fairmont

Ford Motor Co. (SINCE 1978)

105½" WB
$4754. ('78)
5773. ('80)

2-DR.

(new) $5474. ('78)
6577. ('80)

Squire Wagon
REAR

78-80

140 CID 4 (88 HP); 200 CID 6 (85 HP)
302 CID V8 (139 HP)(THROUGH '79)
255 CID V8 (1980)

CR78×14 TIRES
(PLAIN-SIDED
WAGONS ALSO,
FROM $5109. ('78) TO
$6059. ('80)

FUTURA
SPECIAL
COUPE has
OWN GRILLE

$5209. ('78) 6/78.
('80)

BR78×14 TIRES

1978 CARS
ILLUSTRATED,
UNLESS NOTED
OTHERWISE

('80)

4-DR.

$4754.
('78)
5157.
('79)
5890. ('80)

DLX. WOOD-TONED
DASH ('80)

2-TONE COLOR BANDS
AVAILABLE ON
1980 MODELS

239

Ford **Falcon** (1960–1970)

$2669.
($2781., FUTURA)

FUTURA

SPT. CPE. WITH VINYL TOP $2555.

new THINNER SIDE TRIM

66

new GRILLE

DASH

1966

(FALCON RANCHERO PICKUP ALSO AVAIL.)

111" WB
170 CID 6 (105 HP)
200 CID 6 (120 HP) IN
SPT. CPE., WAGON
289 CID V8 (180-200 HP)

6 CYL. OR V8 (SINCE '63)

2-DR. $2284.

FUTURA SPTS. CPE.

$2663.

2 new COWL INDENTATION ('67 ONLY)

67

(INTRO 9-30-66)

new GRILLE

REAR (STD.)

240

Ford **FALCON** WAGON

('69)

EARLY
68-70

('68)

('70)

FUTURA SEDAN

170 CID 6 (100 HP)
289 CID V8 (195 HP)
200 CID 6 AVAIL. '69-
'70 (115-120 HP)
302 CID V8 (220 HP) '69-70

FALCON. 7 MODELS. MORE
THAN ANY OTHER COMPACT.

111" WB
(WAGONS 113")

FALCON
PRODUCTION
SUSPENDED
BECAUSE OF HIGH
COST OF ADDING
LOCKING STEERING
COLUMNS, IN
COMPLIANCE WITH
GOVT. SAFETY REGULATIONS.

('69)

INTERIOR ('69)

new E78/G78 x 14 TIRES

FALCON TEMPORARILY REVIVED, AS A
BUDGET-PRICED MODEL OF
TORINO.

2-DR.

70½ **NEW**

LARGER 117"-WB
TORINO SERIES
(WAGON-
114")

3
FINAL
FALCONS
2-DR.
$2827.
4-DR.
$2867.
4-DR. WAGON
$3163.

(DISCONTINUED
SUMMER,
1970)

STD.
ENGINES:

new 250 CID 6
(155 HP)
302 CID V8
(220 HP)

AVAILABLE
351 CID V8 (250 OR 300 HP)
429 CID V8 (360 OR 370 HP)

241

FORD Granada

(INTRO. 1975)

...elegance in a new efficient size

109.9" WB

$3698*...2-Door
($4860., '77)

STANDARD GRANADA

200 CID 6

250 CID 6 IN CALIF.-
SOLD CARS and GHIA

ENGINE

$3756...4-Door

GRILLE

DR 78 × 14 TIRES

14-18† mpg: city / 18-26† mpg: highway

75-77

(302, 351 CID V8 ALSO AVAIL.)

2-DR. $5025.

On the Inside, Ghia
Offers More Luxury

$5083. '75
5232. '76
5368. '77

GRANADA GHIA

(MORE SIDE TRIM and
VINYL TOP)

(1975 EXAMPLES, UNLESS
OTHERWISE INDICATED)

REAR DETAIL

■ Odense Vinyl Trim High-
lights — appear in the roof
center pillars — the
bodyside moldings which are
both protective and decorative — and on the distinctive
lower back panel applique.

DASH

■ Steering Wheel with Downswept Spokes —
permits excellent driver visibility of the
instrument panel controls and gauges.

SPORT COUPE
('76)

SALE:
$4189.

note
SPECIAL WHEELS

242

Ford Granada

$5390.

STD. GRANADA
250 CID 6 (97 HP)
302 CID V8 (139 HP)
new 255 CID V8 also, 1980

new
2-TONE PAINT AVAIL. ON
1979 GHIA

('79)

2 DR. **GHIA**

$5556.
('78)

4 DR. $5635.
('78)

note HEAVY
SIDE TRIM ON
GRANADA GHIA

$5878.

('78)

('80)

('80) ESS

DASH ('79)

1980 WHEEL
COVERS

78-80

new GRILLE and
ESS MODEL
INTRO. 1978

ESS
('78) SEDAN

$5821.

('80)

note UNIQUE RR.
QUARTER WINDOW
ON **ESS** CPES.

$5936.
('79)

('79) TYPE OF ESS COWL LETTERING
DETERMINES YEAR. 243

1980 GAS
MILEAGE →

| 19 EPA EST. MPG | 28 EST. HWY. MPG |
| 342 EST. RANGE | 504 EST. HWY. RANGE |

Ford Motor Company

FORD MAVERICK

(1970 - 1977 MODELS)

(compact)

For $1995...
it's a little gas.

(2-DR. ONLY)

70

(new)

(REG. $2257.)

INITIAL (1970) MAVERICK
INTRO. APRIL 17, 1969.

(SEE NOTE AT LOWER LEFT)

103" WB
6 CYL.
170 CID
105 HP @ 4200 RPM
OR
200 CID
120 HP @ 4000 RPM
16-GAL. FUEL TANK

← STANDARD DASH

6.00 x 13 TIRES (14" OPT.)

For a little more...
it's a Grabber.

Here's what you get:
- 200-cubic-inch Six
- Bodyside tape stripes, black-painted hood and grille
- White sidewalls, 14" wheels and trim rings
- Deck lid spoiler, dual racing mirrors
- 3-spoke woodtone steering wheel, black all-vinyl seat trim
- Choice of five hot Grabber colors

GRABBER MODEL ADDED FEB., 1970

MAVERICK GRABBER

note:
CARS SOLD ON OR AFTER 9-19-69 ARE THEN CONSIDERED "OFFICIAL" 1970s, AS OTHER '70 FORDS AVAIL. THEN.

244

GRILLE EMBLEM

GAS CAP

FORD MAVERICK

new 6.45 × 14 TIRES (THROUGH '74)

MAVERICK
The Simple Machine

STD. 2-DR.
$2419. ('71)
2414. ('72)

Grabber $2598. ('71)
            2583. ('72)

CHOICE OF
3 SIXES OR
V8 ENGINE
SINCE
MID-1971
SEASON.   (1971
            MODELS
            INTRO.
            9-11-70;
            1972
            MODELS
            INTRO.
            9-24-71)

new GRILLE and
HOOD SCOOPS on
GRABBER

71-72

new 4-DR. $2479. ('71)
ADDED   2469. ('72)

DASH (LUXURY DECOR TYPE)

Maverick is available now with optional 250-six automatic or 302-V8 engines.

73

$2,695.*
WITH new
VINYL TOP

new
GRILLE

FORD MAVERICK

FORD DIVISION Ford

MAVERICK

new
BUMPERS

245

FORD MAVERICK

WITH SHOULDER HARNESSES

Energy absorbing bumper for '74.

74

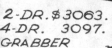

2-DR. $3063.
4-DR. 3097.
GRABBER 3196.

note MAVERICK NAME ON DELUXE REAR QUARTER VINYL PANELS

MAVERICK
Grained vinyl roof.

cushioned bench seats trimmed in random stripe cloth and Vinyl.

2-DR.

GRABBER

In order to achieve the emisssion standards established for 1975, catalytic converters will be installed on all 200 CID engines. On the optional 250 and 302 CID engines, it will not be required.

interior is available in a choice of blue, black, tan or a new light green.

4-DR.

2-DR. === 103" WB
4-DR. === 109.9" WB

DASH

new RADIAL-PLY TIRES BR/CR 78×14 (DR 70×14 - GRABBER)

75

The Ford 200 CID 1V 6-cylinder engine is standard with all 1975 Mavericks. (The 250 CID 6-cylinder engine is standard in California.) This durable engine is designed to provide reliability and economy. The 250 CID Six and the 302 CID V-8 continue as Maverick optional engines.

new 1975 OPTION

DECK LID-MOUNTED LUGGAGE RACK.

76-77

new FLOOR-OPERATED PARKING BRAKE

MAVERICK DISCONTINUED 1977

OPTIONAL ALPINE PLAID ON SEATS

EPA MPG: 30 HWY. 22 CITY

new SPLIT GRILLE

('76)

'77 4-DR. $3719.

246

FENDER BADGE ON GT

(FORD) **Mustang**

108" WB
200 CID 6 (120 HP)
289 CID V8 (200 HP)

Ford Motor Co.

(INTRO. 4-64, FOR '65)

2+2
$2924.

2+2 $2924.

66

MESH IN GRILLE REPLACED BY HORIZONTAL STRIPS FOR 1966.

CVT.

$2970.

SIDE EMBLEM: CHROMED HORSE WITH RED, WHITE and BLUE VERTICAL BARS

DASH

Mustang's new instrument panel groups five easy-to-read dials

VARIATION

MUSTANG! MUSTANG! MUSTANG!

(SLOGAN)

REAR 6.95 × 14 TIRES

$2734.

DASH

FROM $2791.

TYPE WITH PLAIN REAR PANEL 2+2

new GRILLE

67

$2921.

SPORTS SPRINT

GT 2+2 $3242.

247

SLOGAN :

Take the Mustang Pledge.

FORD MUSTANG

Carroll Shelby Presents _The Road Cars..._
G.T. 350 and G.T. 500 for 1967

500

67
MODIFIED
(SHELBY TYPES)

SHELBY G.T.

350

SHELBY
COBRA
DASH

Shelby Cobra

68
new GRILLES

new
SIDE
TRIM

$33/2.

GT
2+2

STD.
2-DR.
H/T
PRICED
FROM $2938.

STD. 6 and
V8 REDUCED 5 HP

FORD MUSTANG

FORD DIVISION *Ford*

GT H/T $3129.

69
new GRILLE

Ford's Exclusive "Shaker" scoop actually protrudes through the hood — rams air directly into the carburetor under full throttle.

MACH I

$3480.

MACH I
SPORTSROOF

(MUSTANG "E"
SPORTSROOF
IS $3078 WITH
250 CID 6,
155 HP)

MACH I ENGINE: 351 CID V8
(250 HP)

GT SPORTSROOF
(FASTBACK) →

GRANDE

$3329 GRANDE has LOW
REAR-FACING "SCOOP"
LIKE GT MODELS.

STD. ENGINES:
200 CID 6 (115 HP)
302 CID V8 (220 HP)

SHELBY CARS
STILL CUSTOM-
CRAFTED WITH
FORD PARTS, BUT
NO LONGER
BEAR A CLOSE
RESEMBLANCE
TO
MUSTANG.

GT CVT.
$3343.

FORD MUSTANG

$3628.

GRANDE

$3876.

$3283.

70

MACH 1

WITH 428 COBRA JET V-8 (E70×14 TIRES)

new GRILLE

Boss 302

6 OR V8, 9 ENGINE CHOICES FOR 1970.

BOSS 302 USES 302 CID, 290-H.P. V-8, F60 × 15 TIRES. (new E78×14, MOST OTHER MODELS)

$4046.

MACH 1

MACH 1 WHEEL DETAIL

7 ENGINE CHOICES FOR 1971 STD. 250 CID 6 (145 HP) STD. 302 CID V8 (210 HP) H/T $3783.

new 109" WB (RESTYLED)

71

MACH 1 GRILLE

GRANDE SIMILAR, BUT has VINYL-COVERED TOP ($3989.)

250

FORD MUSTANG

A PRODUCT OF *Ford*

For Spring Only. A Mustang of a New Stripe.

A New Mustang Hardtop. It's a Special Spring Value at your Ford Dealer's. Now.

REAR WINDOW

71½

STYLED LIKE MACH 1, BUT has BLACK VINYL-COVERED TOP, BLACK SIDE STRIPES; BODY and BUMPERS ARE RED.

FORD MUSTANG *

72

SPORTSROOF $3557.

H/T

HP CUTS
250 CID 6 (99 HP)
302 CID V8 (141 HP)

$3500.

* = FORD PREFIX ADDED IN MUSTANG ADVERTISING, 1972.

MACH 1 $3737.

CVT. $3785.

GRANDE

DASH

$3686.

Control and balance

251

FORD MUSTANG

THE FINAL MUSTANG CVT. $3839.

DASH
STD. 302 CID V8 (141 HP)
(6 CYL. AVAIL.)

Convertible

$3500.
Hardtop

$3557.
SportsRoof

5 MODELS IN 1973
(ALL ILLUSTRATED HERE

* LAST OF THE
"BIG" MUSTANGS

MACH 1
$3737.
E70 × 14
TIRES

new GRILLE
73

new BUMPERS,
COLOR-KEYED TO
BODY COLOR

* FINAL
109" WB
TYPES

FRONT DETAILS

(new)
CRISS-CROSS
GRILLE

CLOSER DETAIL
of GRILLE CENTER

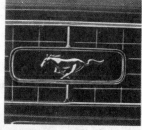

NOTE new
SHOULDER
HARNESSES IN
ABOVE CAR

GRANDE
$3686. E78 × 14 TIRES
(EXC. MACH 1)

252

Ford Mustang II. A new class of small car: First Class.

DASH

HATCH-BACK

B78/BR78/BR70 × 13 TIRES (new)

Mach 1. $4444.

$4327.

3-Door 2+2.

FRONT CLOSE-UP (GHIA)

139 CID 4-CYL. OR V-6 (169 CID)

74

WINDOW DEFR.

ALL-NEW SMALLER THAN PREVIOUS MUSTANGS (96.2" WB)

Ghia $4479.

$4133. Hardtop.

THIS MEDALLION USUALLY SEEN ON GHIA (FULL LINE ILLUSTRATED)

253

FORD MUSTANG II
The closer you look, the better we look.

GHIA '75 MODELS have new ROOFLINE and new UPRIGHT RADIATOR ORNAMENT

Silver Ghia. (new)

GHIA FR. $4514.

new 1975 STEERING WHEEL WITH DOWNWARD-CURVED SPOKE

STD. TYPE H/T

75

$4105.

new HUB CAPS

BR 78 × 13 TIRES
139 CID 4 (83 HP)
169 CID 6 (97 HP)

3-Door 2+2. $4394.

CARS WITH new CATALYTIC CONVERTER
HAVE UNLEADED FUEL WARNING DECAL OVER GAS FILLER CAP.

Mach 1. $4492.

302 CID V-8 JOINS 4-CYL. and V-6.

LATE IN 1975 MODEL YEAR, SIMPLIFIED MPG MODELS JOIN OTHERS, AS LOW-PRICED ECONOMY LEADERS. $3529. (SALE PRICE)

Official U.S. Government Environmental Protection Agency tests:
28mpg (4-speed manual) highway...18mpg city.
26mpg (automatic) highway...18mpg city.
New Mustang II MPG

GHIA MPG

NO HOOD ORNAMENT, new HUB CAPS, FEWER "FRILLS."

75½

254

Mustang II MPG $3,529*

FORD MUSTANG II

MPG

**EPA estimates:
Mustang II MPG.
34** mpg highway **24** mpg city

FROM $4101.

DASH

(INCLUDES TACHOMETER)

140 CID 4
(new 92 HP)
new 171 CID V6
(100 HP)
302 CID V8
(134 HP)

The score for '76:

76

STALLION (new)

AVAIL. AS 2+2 OR H/T, with BLACK GRILLE and WINDOW MOLDINGS. STALLION DECAL ON COWL

$4519.

MACH I

new AIR-SCOOP UNDERNEATH FRONT BUMPER.

COBRA II

Mustang II. Boredom Zero.

MACH I

$4645.

16½-GAL. FUEL TANK

H/T (SPECIAL PAINT OR DECALS OPTIONAL)

3.18 GEAR RATIO WITH 4 CYL.; OTHERWISE 3.0

$4496.

3-DOOR
2+2

77

(HP CUTS)

ENGINES =

4-CYL. (140 CID)
V-6 (170.8 CID)(93 HP)
V-8 (302 CID)(139 HP)

COBRA II

SuperCoupe

GHIA 2-DR.
$4538.

140 CID 4 (88 HP)
171 CID V6 (90 HP)
302 CID V8
(139 HP)

FORD MUSTANG II

DASH

78

STD.
H/T
FROM
$4121.

COBRA

(COBRA FIG.
ON GRILLE)

3-DR.
SPORT

MUSTANG
1979: The New Breed.

$5158.

new
100.4"WB

DASH

2-DR. SPORT

79

STYLING
ALL-
NEW

$5364.

GHIA

(GHIA. SPT.
FASTBK. AVAIL.)

$4793.

FR.
$5846.
3-DR.

$5536.

2-DR.

140 CID 4
200 CID 6
225 OR NEW
255 CID V8s
(TURBO
4 AVAIL.)

80

HOOD
SCOOP WITH
TURBO
ENG.

(23) EPA EST MPG (38) EST HWY MPG

($7474. COBRA
3-DR. SPT.
FASTBACK ALSO
AVAIL.)

(1971–1980)

Pinto
Ford Motor Co.

94" WB, 4 CYL.

Hello world.

$2298.

3-DOOR HATCHBACK

97.6 CID (75 HP @ 5000 RPM) OR 122 CID (100 HP @ 5600)

2-DR. $2155.

new 71

(INTRO. 9-11-70)

Put a little kick in your life.

BLACK OR WHITE VINYL TOP AVAIL.

MULTI-PURPOSE KEY

Do it yourself and save. Pinto is designed to be so simple you can do most servicing yourself. The owner's manual shows you how. And the free Do-It-Yourself Key (above) helps you do everything from gauge the spark-plug gap to adjust the headlight beam.

6.00 x 13 TIRES

$2494.

new **Wagon**

ALSO AVAIL. W/O GRAIN PANELS

new SPORTS ACCENT TRIM

122 CID 4 CUT TO 86 HP

$2708.

72

(INTRO. 9-24-71)

DASH

new **Sprint** DECOR IN WHITE and BLUE, WITH RED STRIPING

new SUNROOF AVAIL.

3-DOOR HATCHBACK

$2355.

257

FORD PINTO

FORD DIVISION **Ford**

73

UNGRAINED WAGON: $2572.

SQR. WAG. $2809.

3-DR. $2422.

DELUXE BUMPER HAS VERTICAL GUARDS and PROTECTIVE BLACK VINYL STRIP (PLAIN BUMPERS CONTINUED ALSO)

2-DR. $2299.

6.00 × 13 / A 78 × 13 TIRES

122 OR 139 CID 4

SQUIRE $3337. ('74)

new BR 78 × 13 TIRES IN 1975

2-DR. $2852. ('74)

new ENERGY-ABSORBING BUMPERS

74-75

$3700.

(1975 139 CID 4 RATED AT 83 HP)

MPG WITH DLX. BUMPERS EXTERIOR DECOR TRIM STRIP

75½

New Ford Pinto MPG 28mpg. $2,769. (SALE)

258

REG. FR. $3329.

FORD PINTO

(*VARIOUS MODELS CONTINUE*)

38 MPG highway, 25 city).

Pinto Pony MPG. More car for the money.

76 new GRILLE WITH CRISS-CROSS PCS.

new PONY MPG (ABOVE) has A MINIMUM OF CHROME TRIM, AND PLAIN HUBCAPS (LOWEST-PRICED MODEL)

Pinto Pony MPG $2,895

(REG. $2966.)

2-DR. PONY $3164. ('77); $3341. ('78)

the best sellers in their class

77-78

1977: 140 CID 4 (89 HP) 171 CID V6 (93 HP) RESPECTIVE HP CUT TO 88 AND 90 IN 1978.

new "ALL-GLASS" HATCHBACK DOOR VARIATION ('77)

$3666. ('77)

A 78 × 13 TIRES

mileage.	
39 mpg highway	27 mpg city
HWY.	CITY

$3861. ('77)

WITH PLAIN SIDES

$4075. ('78)

Wagons

('78)

6. Woodgrain vinyl paneling
7. Roomy cargo area (cargo volume index 57.2 cubic feet)
8. Flipper rear side windows

DuraSpark Ignition. No points or condenser to replace

Critical areas around lights and grille are dent, chip and scratch resistant and absolutely rustproof

9. Low sticker price
10. Electro-dip corrosion protection
11. Sporty suspension system
12. 4-speed floor-mounted transmission (standard), SelectShift automatic (optional)
13. Precise rack and pinion steering.
14. Power front disc brakes.
15. Larger standard engine (2.3 litre 4-cylinder cast iron) than Datsun F-10 Sportswagon, Toyota Corolla and Corona.

SQUIRE WAGON (ABOVE) $4204. ('77)	WAGON	
	33 mpg highway	23 mpg city
	HWY.	CITY

new SLOPING GRILLE, new FRONT-END STYLING ('77)

2-DR. $3550. ('77) 3617. ('78)

259

FORD PINTO *PONY* **wagon**

CRUISING (PANEL/VAN) WAGON

THIS TYPE INTRO. 1977

NEW Design in here

NEW Design up here

FRONT, REAR CHANGES

1979 NEW Design back here

SQUIRE

OLD-STYLE DUAL-CLUSTER ALSO CONT'D.

A78×13 ('79) TIRES   BR78×13 ('80)

79-80

new FRONT END, *new* TAIL-LIGHTS

PONY FROM $3571. ('79) $4121. ('80)

note 3 STYLES of REAR WINDOW

1980

NEW UP FRONT

FINAL PINTO, 1980

FORD

RALLYE

WITH **RALLYE** TRIM

260

1980

2-DR. $4643. ('80)

FORD TORINO
(REPLACES FAIRLANE)

Torino. 14 models

TORINO SPORTSROOF

$3506.
(FINAL
FAIRLANE)

250 CID 6
(150 HP)
OR 302 CID V8
(220 HP)

FAIRLANE 500 2-DOOR HARDTOP

new
117"
WB
(114" ON
WAGONS
and
RANCHEROS)

OFFIAL PACE CAR

Torino GT Convertible.
The Pace Car for all America.

GT CVT.
$3968.

HOOD
SCOOP ON
GT

Torino GT-

(INTRO. 9-19-69)

GT
has
302,
351
OR
429 CID V8
E78/G78 × 14 TIRES
(F70 × 14, COBRA)

(TOTALLY
RESTYLED)

70

(CONT'D.
NEXT
PAGE)

new
PROFILE FOR
SPORTSROOF
→

TORINO
BROUGHAM
(new) $3762.

(FORMAL
ROOFLINE)

VINYL
TOP

SPOILER
DECK
↓

$3861.

(351 CID
V8
USES
REGULAR GAS)

MOTOR TREND
"Car of the Year!"

261

FORD TORINO

LIGHTS CLOSED (BY DAY)

WITH LIGHTS OPEN

FROM $3568.

TORINO 4-DOOR SEDAN

2 COBRA REAR DECK PAINT VARIATIONS

360 HP COBRA (429 CID V8) $3843. (note DUAL PIPES)

RECTANGULAR INSTRUMENTS ON 1970 DASH

70 (CONT'D.)

TORINO COBRA

PLAIN TOP, FORMAL ROOFLINE

TORINO 2-DOOR HARDTOP

$3655.

7" DELUXE WHEEL COVER

WITH CHROME SIDE TRIM

↗ WITH NON-DISAPPEARING HEADLIGHTS

FORD TORINO

$4333.

SQUIRE WAGON

$3812.

1971 Torino 500 SportsRoof

71

new SPLIT GRILLE; EXPOSED HEADLTS.

BROUGHAM 4-DR. HARDTOP

250 CID 6 (145 HP) OR 302 CID V8 (210 HP)

(INTRO. 9-18-70)

$4022.

The first Gran Torino.

SPORT H/T

HP RATINGS REDUCED
250 CID 6 (95 HP)
302 CID V8 (140 HP)

4-DR. PILLAPED H/T $3736.

$3883. (note HOOD SCOOP ON SPORT)

(RESTYLED)

FORD GRAN TORINO

(INTRO. 9-24-71)

72

(CONT'D. NEXT PAGE)

with VINYL TOP

REAR

new GRAN TORINO has THIS new NARROW GRILLE.

GRAN TOR. 2-DR. H/T $3756. UP

with PLAIN TOP

263

More car than you expected.
FORD TORINO

new SHORTER 114" WB
(new 118" WB ON
RANCHERO, WAGONS)

(Standard)
TORINO

has THIS BROAD GRILLE

FROM
$3834.

72
(CONT'D.)

DASH
(CIRCULAR
INSTRUMENTS
CONTINUE, AS
IS USUAL
TORINO STYLE.)

FROM
$4275.

VIEWS
OF
WOODGRAINED
Gran Torino Wagon

INTERIOR

The solid mid-size car.

FORD TORINO

3-SEAT SQUIRE $4339.

STD. TORINO has OWN WIDER GRILLE

GRAN TORINO

114" WB (2-DR.)
118" WB (4-DR.)

73

FINAL TORINO 6 (250 CID)

302 CID V8 STD.

new GRILLES (INTRO. FRIDAY, 9-22-72)

The closer you look, the better we look.

DASH

74

new GRILLES new OPERA WINDOWS IN COUPES

V8s ONLY 302, 351 CID

Gran Torino Squire $5021. (3-SEAT)

$3797. UP

DASH

GRAN TORINO ELITE (new, '74½)

$4752.

DUAL OPERA WINDOWS

265

Ford Torino. Under $4,000.*

(* = REG. $4499.)

with automatic transmission, power front disc brakes, power steering, V-8, steel-belted radials

$5347.

('76)

GRAN TORINO BROUGHAM   2-DR.

TORINO
The solid mid-size.

351 CID V8 (148 HP)
G78 x 14 TIRES

(400 OR 460 CID V8s OPT. IN ELITE)

75-76

(1975 EXAMPLES SHOWN, UNLESS OTHERWISE INDICATED)

INTERIOR DECOR GR. DASH

▲ The Beautiful Standard Elite Interior.

ELITE WHEEL COVERS

▲ Full Wheel Covers. Standard at no extra cost.

▲ Luxury Wheel Covers. Thunderbird inspired, add a nice dress-up touch.

▲ Wire Wheel Covers. Classic styling in the finest European tradition.

▲ Deep-Dish Aluminum Wheels. A sporty look, with bright chrome lugs.

(ELITES AFTER JAN., 1975 DO NOT HAVE SEAT-BELT INTERLOCK SYSTEM.)

Torino
('76)

ELITE HR78 x 15 TIRES

a lot of car for about $4200.*

For about the same kind of money as a little 4-passenger foreign car you can choose a 6-passenger '76 Torino with a standard V-8, automatic transmission, power front disc brakes, power steering, steel belted radials, solid state ignition, and more.

(* = REG. $4728.)

(REPL. BY 1977 LTD II)

$5309. ($5435.-'76)

266

(1926–1975; 1981–) IMPERIAL

BY CHRYSLER CORPORATION

129" WB

$6505. CROWN CPE. (H/T)

V8 ENGINE (SINCE '55)
new 440 C.I.D (350 HP)
9.15 × 15 TIRES

66

CROWN SERIES and
$7158. LE BARON
4-DR. H/T

new GRILLE

CONVERT. AVAIL. AT
$6764.

FR. $6351.
(4-DR. H/T)

THE INCOMPARABLE
IMPERIAL
Finest of the fine cars built
by Chrysler Corporation

IMPERIAL NAME SET IN
new ALL-HORIZONTAL
GRILLE

new CORNER LTS. IN FENDERS

Imperial '67... the newest prestige automobile in a decade.

← new 4-DR. SEDAN ADDED
$5991.

new SHORTER 127" WB

67

(INTRO. 9-29-66)

$6861.

IMPERIAL CONVERTIBLE DISCONTINUED AFTER 1968

REAR DETAILS

IMPERIAL

CROWN
COUPE $6381.

LE BARON
$7599.

(INTRO. 9-14-67)

68

CROWN
4-DR.
H/T
$6774.

new GRILLE

FINAL CVT. ($7156.)

"Imperial" NAME ON
new GRILLE, AND
CREST ON HOOD,
REAR DECK.

LE BARON
4-DR.
H/T $6793.

(new LE BARON 2-DR. H/T ADDED)

BLOCK-LETTER
"IMPERIAL" NAME
IN CENTER OF
REAR BUMPER

HEADLIGHTS
CONCEALED
IN
new
GRILLE

69 (INTRO. 9-19-68)

TOTALLY
RESTYLED WITH
BULGE-SIDED "FUSELAGE" STYLING

(CONT'D. NEXT PAGE)

268

IMPERIAL

$6564. LE BARON
2-DR. H/T
(new)

note TRIPLE OPENINGS FOR SAFETY LT.

VINYL-COVERED TOP BEARS TRADITIONAL IMPERIAL EAGLE MEDALLION

69 (CONT'D.)

('70)

"THE NEW CHOICE"
FROM $6419.
('70)

FR. $6745. ('71)

LE BARON
4-DR. H/T

(INTRO. 9-23-69) new GRILLE (INTRO. 10-6-70)

70-71

FINAL CROWN MODELS IN 1970.

LE BARON MODELS ONLY, IN 1971.
HP CUT TO 335, '71.

$6977. new HEADLIGHT PLAQUES ADDED TO GRILLE OF '71.

1971

269

IMPERIAL (SINCE 1971, REDUCED TO A TOP-LINE MODEL of CHRYSLER, RATHER THAN A SEPARATE MAKE AS SINCE 1955.

"BUTTERFLY" VENT WINDOWS ELIMINATED

72 (INTRO. 9-28-71)

new GRILLE

2-DR. H/T $6795.

HP CUT TO 225

CHRYSLER
Coming through with the kind of car America wants.

L84 x 15 TIRES (SINCE '71)

73

HP CUT TO 215

4-DR. H/T $7305.

2-DR. H/T $7077.

new GRILLE WITH FINER PCS.; IMPROVED BUMPERS WITH VERTICAL GUARDS

IMP'L. PRODUCTION LIMITED ONLY TO LE BARON 2-DR. OR 4-DR. H/Ts, 1971 THROUGH 1975.

RESTYLED FOR 1974. (1975 SIMILAR) FEATURING DRAMATIC new NARROW "WATERFALL" GRILLE; new HEADLIGHT DOORS ARE PLAIN METAL.

74-75

new LR78 x 15 TIRES

HP UP TO 230 (215, 1975)

HOOD ORNAMENT ADDED '74

FR. $8900. ('75)

(NO 1976 TO 1980 IMPERIALS)

$7258. ('74)

new ENERGY-ABSORBING BUMPERS

270

INTERNATIONAL HARVESTER

SCOUT INTRO '61.

4 - CYL.
(SOME WITH
4-WHEEL DRIVE)

66

100" WB

New Scout 800 by International

(SUMMER, '66)
New International Scout Sportop

WITH SLANTING
SOFT TOP OR
HARD TOP

DASH

SALE PRICE
$1777.16   (REG. $2280.)

ROADSTER
OR
PICKUP
STYLE ALSO
AVAILABLE

The home of
McMILLEN PARK
Little League

The Travelall

SCOUT SIMILAR TO
1966, BUT NEW V8
ENGINE IS NOW OPTIONAL.

67

119"
WB
(THROUGH
'73)
(6 CYL.
OR V8)

FROM
$2841.

The new top-powered V-8 SCOUT!

4-CYL.
$2406.
and up

TRAVELALL
has new
GRILLE

INTERNATIONAL HARVESTER

68

Travelall

FROM $3146.

International *Scout*

FROM $2660.

EMBLEM REMOVED FROM ABOVE GRILLE (TRAVELALL)

Travelall. The big-family wagon from International.

new GRILLES *and* SIDE SAFETY LIGHTS ('69)

FROM $3272. ('69) 3502. ('70)

new 800-A SCOUT SERIES

69-70

2 TOP STYLES AVAIL. FOR SCOUT

2-TONE SCOUT "ARISTOCRAT"

(INTRO. SUMMER, '69)

Scout

FROM $2940. ('69)

4, 6, OR V8 SCOUT ENGINES ('70 UP)

71 $3350.

WITH SPECIAL PAINT AND STRIPING

new 800-B SCOUT

NEXT PAGE: 1971 TRAVELALL®

The new Scout Comanche.

272

INTERNATIONAL HARVESTER

DASH

REAR

2 SETS OF VENT SLOTS ATOP COWL

71 (CONT'D.)

STD. $3610.
DLX. 3631.

CUSTOM $3740.

1971

Travelall

new GRILLE

International Travelall
The wagon built to tow.

FROM $3656.

new STD. 6-258 ENGINE

72

new GRILLES; new DASH

ENGINES:
196 CID SLANT-4 (111 HP)
232 CID 6 (135 HP)
304 CID V8 (193 HP)
345 CID V8 (197 HP)

new **Scout II** (INTRO. SPRING '71)

(POWER BRAKES and STEER. OPT.)

DELUXE INTERIOR (Scout II)

$3344.

273

INTERNATIONAL HARVESTER

SCOUT

$3426.

new GRILLE

GEAR RATIOS

3.31
3.73
OR
4.27

19-GAL.
FUEL
TANK

1973

ENGINES: (SCOUT, TRAVELALL)
258 CID 6 (113 HP)
304 CID V8 (137 HP)
345 CID V8 (144 HP)

ALSO AVAIL. (IN
TRAVELALL ONLY 392 CID V8
(179 HP)

73

TRAVELALL

FROM
$3662.

GEAR RATIOS

3.73
4.09
OR
4.56

20-GALLON
FUEL TANK
(15-GAL.
RESERVE AVAIL.)

CUSTOM (ILLUSTR.) = $3790.

INTERNATIONAL HARVESTER

It leads a double life

(FINAL TRAVELALL OF 1974-1975 has 120" WB)

SCOUT II

$3943. ('74)
$4712. ('75)

74-

75

AFTER 1975, ALL PASSENGER MODELS ARE IN

SCOUT

LINE. (new DIESELS AVAIL.)*

new GRILLE ('74)

new TERRA, TRAVELER have 118" WB

76

*-198 CID 6

$5394. (new)

Scout Terra

$5438.

Scout II

new GRILLE

Scout Traveler $5844.

INTERNATIONAL SCOUT

(100" WB CONTINUES ON SCOUT II)

SCOUT THE AMERICA OTHERS PASS BY.

TRAVELTOP $5834.
TRAVELER $6205.

77

new GRILLE

new SS II $5251.

TERRA PICKUP $5720.

275

INTERNATIONAL SCOUT

REAR

('79)

EXTRA CHARGE FOR OPTIONAL 6-CYL. DIESEL ENGINE: $2581. ('78) 2495. ('79)

SS II *has* OWN GRILLE

Scout leads the way.
('78)

78-79

note VARIOUS '79 STRIPING PATTERN TYPES

new GRILLE ('78)

1979 PRICES
SS II $ 6187.
TRAVELTOP   6993.
TERRA PCKP. 7044.
TRAVELER V8 7657.

SCOUT.®
Anything less is just a car.
('79)

TURBOCHARGED DIESEL
AVAIL.

DIESEL ENGINES OPTIONAL (SINCE 1976)

NISSAN (DATSUN) ENG.

80
new GRILLE, VARIOUS STRIPING COMBINATIONS

Our new Turbo-Diesel engine.

Scout Turbo-Diesel fuel economy:
22 EPA EST MPG   **24** EST HWY MPG

100,000-MILE, 5-YEAR ENGINE AND BODY WARRANTY

FIGHT BACK WITH SCOUT.
Anything less is just a car.

KAISER Jeep CORPORATION
Toledo, OHIO

'Jeep'

The Flying 'Jeep' Universal
with 4-wheel drive

4-CYL. "HURRICANE" OR V6 160 HP
(V8 AVAIL.)

66

You've got to drive it to believe it! See your 'Jeep' dealer.

DJ-5   DJ-6   (2WD)
81" OR 101" WB
CJ-5   CJ-6   (4WD)

Wagoneer

REAR

110" WB
6 CYL. OR V8

"Holy Toledo, what a car!"

$2748.

Jeepster

4-CYL. STD.; 101" WB

REAR DETAILS (JEEPSTER)

67

JEEPSTER REVIVED; OTHER MODELS CONT'D.

JEEPSTER AVAIL. THROUGH '72.

4-wheel drive

RDSTR. FROM $2466.

There's a whole family of Jeepsters to choose from...Convertible; Jeepster Commando Station Wagon; Jeepster Commando Pick-up; Jeepster Commando Roadster.

277

Jeep®

UNIVERSAL JEEPS PRICED FROM $2011.

4-wheel drive.

Jeep Wagoneer

68

Flip one simple lever for the extra safety of 'Jeep' 4-wheel drive.

4-DR. FROM $3702.
(2-DR. ALSO AVAIL.)
FOR FINAL TIME IN WAGONEER LINE.)

'Jeep'
4-wheel drive
The 2-Car Cars.

FROM $4145.

WAGONEER

CAMPER EASILY REMOVABLE

Away from the camper.

$3112.

Jeepster Commando

69

WITH V-6 ENG.

New family camper for your 'Jeep' Universal.

CJ-5

NOW MFD. BY

AMERICAN MOTORS

'Jeep'
4 WHEEL DRIVE
The 2-Car Car.

Jeepster
COMMANDO
4 CYL. OR V6
$3207.

FROM $4284.

232 CID HI-TORQUE (145 HP @ 4300 RPM) 6 CYL.

70

OPT. DAUNTLESS 350 CID V8 (230 HP @ 4400)

new GRILLE

FORMER GRILLE STYLE RETAINED ON **Gladiator** PICKUPS.

Wagoneer

278

⫘ Jeep The toughest 4-letter word on wheels.

$3446.

The Jeepster Commando—
it hasn't found a place it can't conquer.

('71)

NOW KNOWN AS **Jeep Commando.** 1973

$3506.
('73)

new COMMANDO GRILLE, 1972

1973 = new
DASH, IMPROVED FRONT
AXLE-AND-PROP-SHAFT JOINTS.
IMPROVED EXH. VALVE SEATS.

1971-72 SLOGAN : "**Jeep guts.**" ('72)

The most famous 4-wheel drive vehicle of them all is now tougher and longer-lasting...believe it or not!

(4-W-D ILLUSTR. ABOVE)

232 CID 6,
258 CID 6,
OR
304
CID V8

CJ FROM $3086

IMPROVED DRIVE TRAIN,
CLUTCH LINKAGE, 1973
ALSO FUEL TANK SKID PLATE.

new 84" OR 104" WB ON 1972 UNIVERSAL

**Jeep Introduces
Automatic
4-Wheel Drive.** ('73)

The Jeep Wagoneer—
the first 4-wheel drive
family wagon.

FROM $4447.

71-73

Jeep Wagoneer.

('71)

REAR
('72)

QUADRA-TRAC—Someday all 4-wheel drive vehicles may have a system like it...Jeep Wagoneer has it now.

WITH GRAINED STRIP

W/O GRAIN
note
EMBLEM ON
FRONT
FENDER
('73) 279

1973 =
new FULLY-PADDED
DASH, new ARM
RESTS (FR. and REAR
DOORS) FROM
$4501.

6 CYL. OR V8

Jeep

New "It's a Jeep and-a-half"

LATE MODEL

FROM $4211.
6 CYL.
109" WB

Cherokee.

EARLY MODEL, w. BUMPER GUARDS and LARGE SIDE MIRRORS.

Jeep CJ-5 "RENEGADE"

WITH ROLL BAR →

6 OR V8 UNIVERSAL

(REPLACES COMMANDO)

74

$3574. STD. CJ-5

standard equipment:
• Automatic Transmission
P R N D 2 1 →

Wagoneer: 4-wheel drive
(V8 ENGINE)

FROM $5466.

FROM $4099.

FROM $6013.

Wagoneer V8
(BROADER GRAIN PANEL)

FROM $4851.

Cherokee

DECORATION *new* ON FRONT END OF SIDE TRIM STRIP ON THE **Cherokee**

75

PHANTOM VIEW OF REAR SECTION (SHOWING LUGGAGE SPACE PROVIDED BEHIND BACK SEAT)

Slogan: "JEEP WROTE THE BOOK ON 4-WHEEL DRIVE."

280

Jeep

Jeep CJ

Who says
economy has
to be dull?

UNIVERSAL JEEP
(RENEGADE
MODEL)

NEW HIGH-EFFICIENCY GEAR RATIOS
Redesigned for 1980 for greater fuel
efficiency without sacrificing the Jeep CJ's high-power
performance capabilities.

note THAT RENEGADE
STRIPING PATTERNS CHANGE
FROM YEAR TO YEAR.

80

15 EPA EST MPG	20 HWY EST MPG

Introducing a feisty, new 4-cylinder
engine and power train that deliver an
EPA estimated MPG of 21 and
a highway estimate of 25*

(4 CYL. PREVIOUSLY
AVAIL. UNTIL
1971)

CJ FEATURES

NEW UPGRADED 4-SPEED TRANSMISSION
Now standard! Four speeds mean greater versatility
on-road and off! And greater fuel economy, too!

FREE WHEELING HUBS
Standard for 1980! Lets you disengage front wheels when
4-wheel drive is not needed—one more way to save gas!

Cherokee

We wrote the book
on 4-wheel drive.

19 HWY EST MPG	15 EPA EST MPG

Jeep Wagoneer *Limited*
The ultimate wagon

new
WHEELS;
POSITION OF COWL
LETTERING CHANGED

283

Lincoln Continental

HOOD ORNAMENT

126" WB
new 462 CID V8
(340 HP)
9.15 x 15 TIRES

(LINCOLN EST. 1920 : '21 MODEL)

Ford MERCURY LINCOLN

BY **Ford Motor Company.** SINCE 1922

4-DR.

H/T (new)

↑ $6118.

$6383.

66

4-DR. CVT. $7016.

Lincoln Continental for 1966: unmistakably new, yet unmistakably Continental

(LEATHER UPH. STD. IN CVT., $111 EXTRA IN OTHERS)

FRONT END DETAILS

FENDER-TIP LTS. DISCONTINUED UNTIL 1968

(INTRO. 9-30-66)

2-DR. H/T (WITHOUT VINYL TOP) $6185.

67

GRILLE SLIGHTLY CHANGED, and EMBLEM REMOVED FROM SIDE OF FRONT FENDER

4-DR. (WITH VINYL TOP)

4-DR., STD. TOP $6427. (VINYL LANDAU TOP $132. EXTRA)

1967 IS FINAL YEAR FOR THE 4-DOOR CONVERTIBLE.

284

2-DR. H/T, BELOW $6400. (STD.) ($6537. w. LANDAU TOP)

A VARIETY OF HUB CAP

new AM/FM STEREO ($244 EXTRA)

Wraparound parking lights and taillights

new coupé roof line.

$6634.

DETAILS OF new GRILLE

RAISED HOOD ORNAMENT ELIMINATED (UNTIL 1972)

EMBLEM REPLACES NAME ABOVE GRILLE, DURING 1968

new SAFETY SIDE LIGHTS

68 (INTRO. 9-22-67)

new BROAD STEER. WH. HUB, DARKER-COLORED DASH

new REAR STYLING

285

2 SERIES NOW AVAIL.

69

(INTRO. 9-27-68) new GRILLE WITH CONTINENTAL NAME ABOVE. (126" WB)

new "COMPUTER DESIGNED" 460 CID V8 (365 HP)

(NO 4-DR. MK. TYPES UNTIL 1980 MK. VI)

$7423.

(NEW)

The Continental Mark III.

(INTRODUCED 4-5-68)
(COMPLETELY new AND UNIQUE FRONT STYLING, and 117.2" WB

4-DR.: $6876.

Continental
(2-DR. $6495.)

(INTRO. 9-19-69)
STD. CONTINENTAL GETS new 127" WB, new GRILLE

2-DR.

4-DR.

Mark III

CONTINUES WITH 1969 STYLING, THROUGH '71.

FRONT SIDE LIGHTS NOW MOVED DOWN TO ENDS OF BUMPER (ON STD. SERIES, THROUGH 1973)

new 225 x 15 TIRES

70

new BROAD GRILLE WITH HORIZONTAL PCS.; new CONCEALED HEADLIGHTS

286

LINCOLN CONTINENTAL

Continental: the final step up.

The Town Car.
(new)

TOWN CAR

GOLDEN
ANNIV.
MODELS

71 new NARROWER GRILLE

(INTRO. 9-18-70)
FR. $7016.

TOWN CAR MODEL CARRIES DESIGNATION ON SIDE

STD. CONTINENTAL STYLING SIMILAR TO ABOVE "TOWN CAR"

new CRISS-CROSS GRILLE PCS.

Continental

$7068 (2 DR.)
7302 (4-DR.)

new GRILLE

72

(INTRO. 9-17-71)

HP CUT TO 224

MK. IV
$8640

(MK. IV REPLACES MK. III)
new 120.4" WB

(new) CONTINENTAL MARK IV
with BIG new GRILLE THAT DIPS INTO BUMPER (1972 ONLY)

HP RATING BACK TO 365 AGAIN

NOTE new SAFETY BUMPERS (ON BOTH MODEL SERIES)

73

CONTINENTAL MARK IV

LINCOLN CONTINENTAL

8832.

$7474.

CONT. NAME ABOVE GRILLE (FIRST TIME SINCE 1969)

287

MK. IV
$9574.
(10,265.
LATER IN
YR.)

REAR

LINCOLN CONTINENTAL

new GRILLE (CONTINTL.)

74

230 R 15
TIRES

MARK IV

DASH

FROM
$7727.
($8309.
LATER IN
YR.)

CONTINENTAL

235 x 15
TIRES

CONTINENTAL TOWN COUPÉ

DASH

CONTINENTAL NAME ON
REAR FENDER

75

460 CID V8
NOW RATED
AT 206 HP

CONTINENTAL TOWN CAR

FROM
$9214.

new
GRILLE

288

LINCOLN CONTINENTAL
CONTINENTAL MARK IV

DASH

new WHEEL COVERS

75

(CONT'D)

MARK IV

$11,082.

new MID-SIDE PROTECTIVE TRIM MOLDING (CONT. and MK. IV)

230R15 TIRES (all MODELS)

new BAND OVER ROOF (CONTINENTAL TOWN MODELS)

76

127.2" WB

CONTINENTAL

STD. 2-DR. $9142. (4-DR. $9293.)

230R15 TIRES

TOWN CAR

CLOSER DETAIL OF COACH LAMPS AND TRIM

289   (CONT'D. NEXT PAGE)

LINCOLN CONTINENTAL
CONTINENTAL MARK IV *(new MK. IV DESIGNER SER. w. SPEC. PAINT and INT. by DESIGNER FOR WHICH NAMED)*

GIVENCHY (BELOW) (TURQUOISE and WHITE)

PUCCI (BURGUNDY and SILVER)

76 (CONT'D)

The Givenchy Edition Mark IV

CARTIER (PEARL GRAY)

BILL BLASS (BLUE and CREAM)

FR. $12,560.

(USUAL $11,060 MK. TYPES CONTINUE ALSO)

Introducing the Mark IV Designer Series

new MARK V

new 400 CID V8 (173 HP)

PUCCI (BLACK and WHITE)

GIVENCHY (DARK JADE and CHAMOIS)

(DES. = $12,996. UP)
(STD. = 11,396.)

BILL BLASS (MIDNIGHT BLUE and PIGSKIN)

CARTIER (DOVE GRAY)

77 (RESTYLED)

new TRIPLE COWL LOUVRES

LINCOLN VERSAILLES *(new)* 110" WB

(VERSAILLES AVAIL. 1977 - 1980)

('79) ('80 VERS. SIMILAR)

('77) 302 CID V8 IN VERSAILLES (351 CID AVAIL. OUTSIDE CALIF. IN '77)

$14,169 IN 1980

VERSAILLES INTERIOR ('77) →

An investment in engineering.

77-79

400 CID V8 CONT.

LINCOLN CONTINENTAL

('78)

STD. CONT'L. NOW USES MARK V-TYPE UPRIGHT GRILLE.

('78) FROM $9974. ('78) 10,985. ('79)

(FINAL LARGE-SIZED MODELS IN 1979)

4 "DESIGNER EDITIONS" CONTINUE, WITH NEW COLORS. $13,899. ('78) 14,592. ('79)

78-79

MARK V

SOME CONT. and MK. V 1979s KNOWN AS "COLLECTOR'S SERIES"

('79)

('78)

$20,099.

1978 DIAMOND JUBILEE EDITION

291

CONTINENTAL WITH EXPOSED HEADLIGHTS 117.4" WB

TOWN COUPÉ

TOWN CAR

302 CID V8

$13,840.

17 **EPA EST MPG 24 EST HWY MPG

30 MPH 252 MILES TO EMPT.

SEAT BELTS BRAKE

UN LEADED FUEL ONLY

OFF ON

RESUME SET/ACCEL COAST

TURN

INTER - LOW

ELECTRONIC DASH

117.4" WB 4-DR.

SIGNATURE SERIES

$21,424.

80 new SIZE 114" WB (2-DR.)

MARK VI

DESIGNER SERIES CONTINUES; BLASS MODEL RESEMBLES A CONVERTIBLE IN 1979 and 1980

FR. $15,236. 292

Mercury

(SINCE 1939)

390 CID V8 (265 OR 275 HP)
410 CID V8 (330 HP)
428 CID V8 (345 HP)

PARK LANE CVT.

$4039.

LINCOLN-MERCURY
DIVISION OF
Ford Motor Co

123" WB
(119", WAGONS)

Dual-Action Tailgate. Swings down like a regular tailgate for cargo. Or swings aside like a door for people.

COLONY PARK WAGON

walnut-toned paneling.

2-SEAT = $3893.; 3-SEAT = $3988.
(UNGRAINED COMMUTER WAGONS ALSO AVAIL.)

66

MONTEREY, MONTCLAIR,
PARK LANE, S-55
MODELS

VINYL TOP AVAIL.

PARK LANE 4-DR. H/T
$3892.

MONTEREY
2-DR.
$3217.

2.8 TO 3.5 GEAR RATIOS
8.15 × 15 TIRES

293

Mercury

Mercury, the Man's Car.

(INTRO. 9-30-66)

67

STD. 390 CID V8 has new 270 HP.

wagon

new PROTRUDING CENTER SECTION OF FRONT END

new BROUGHAM and MARQUIS MODELS. S-55 DISCONTINUED.

FRONT END DETAILS

PRICES START AT $3297.

(uncommon)

PREMIERE CPE.

First hardtop with yacht-deck vinyl paneling.

PARK LANE

new FRONT CORNERING and REAR SIDE LTS.

68

(INTRO. 9-22-67)

new GRILLE

(FINAL YR. FOR COMMUTER WAGON)

Mercury

new 124" WB
(121" ON MARAUDER, WAGONS)

STD. 390 C.I.D V8
(265/280 HP)

COLONY PARK

(new MONTEREY, MONTEREY CUSTOM WAGONS ALSO AVAIL.)

the new MARQUIS. (now INCLUDES ADDITIONAL BODY TYPES)

MARQUIS 429 C.I.D V8 (320 HP)

2-DR. H/T $4098.

69
(INTRO. 9-27-68)

(new MARQUIS BROUGHAM ALSO AVAIL.)

new CONCEALED HEADLIGHTS ON MARQUIS, MARAUDER

8.25/8.55 x 15 TIRES

note OWN REAR STYLING ON new MARAUDER (X-100)

2-DR. H/T 429 C.I.D V8 (360 HP)

Lincoln-Mercury leads the way

$4270.

(MONTEREY and MTY. CUSTOM have ONE-TIER HORIZ. GRILLE and 4 EXPOSED HDLTS.)

Mercury

70

(INTRO. 9-19-69)

Marquis Colony Park

VERTICAL PCS ADDED TO GRILLE

Marquis

G78 × 15 TIRES
H78 × 15, WAGONS

new 351 CID V8 (240 HP)
new 400 CID V8 (260 HP)
429 CID V8 (320 HP)

4-DR. H/T

DETAILS

Marquis

FRONT END CLOSE-UP

GRILLE NOW ENTIRELY ABOVE BUMPER

71

1971

Better ideas make better cars.

(INTRO. 9-18-70)

296

Mercury

DASH (MONTEREY CUSTOM)

MONTEREY $4391.

note SMALL HUB CAPS

REAR (MONTEREY)

← MONTEREY CUSTOM $4530. H/T
(has CHROME STRIP ALONG MID-SIDE)

VARIOUS MONTEREY TYPES have EXPOSED HEADLIGHTS

H.P. CUT:
351 CID V8 (163 HP)
400 CID V8 (172 HP)
429 CID V8 (208 HP)

72

new "WAFFLE" GRILLE PATTERN

(INTRO. 9-17-71)

COLONY PARK
($5045. (2-SEAT)
5167. (4-SEAT)

Better ideas make better cars:

Marquis

4-DR. H/T
$5132.

Mercury's ride rated better than a $34,000 limousine by 36 out of 50 professional chauffeurs.

MARQUIS BROUGHAM PILLARED 4-DR. H/T
$5400.

DASH (MARQUIS BROUGHAM)

3-SPOKE STEERING WHEEL

Mercury

73

new FINER GRILLE PIECES; CORNERING LTS. RETURN TO FRONT FENDERS (USED PREVIOUSLY IN '68)

$5132.

Marquis

(ALSO MONTEREY, MONTEREY CUSTOM, MARQ. BROUGHAM; ALSO MONTEREY, MARQ., COL. PK WAGONS)

new ENERGY-ABSORBING SAFETY BUMPERS

INTERIOR

MARQUIS

74

MERCURY NAME ABOVE new GRILLE (1974 ONLY)

new HEADLIGHT COVERS, new GRILLE, HIGHER CORNER LIGHTS

MARQUIS

MARQUIS WAGON

HOOD ORNAMENT NOW UPRIGHT

75-78

1978 MARQUIS has SIDE TRIM LIKE GRAND MARQUIS

DASH (MARQUIS)

(CONT'D. NEXT PAGE)

298

Mercury

GRAND MARQUIS

GRAND MARQUIS DASH has SWIRLED WOOD-GRAIN VINYL TRIM

75-78
(CONT'D.)

COLONY PARK

GRAND MARQUIS

DASH PLAQUE ('77)

'RIDE-ENGINEERED by LINCOLN MERCURY'

DETAILS OF *new* UPRIGHT HOOD ORNAMENT INTRO. 1975

1979 MARQUIS has EXTRA CHROME STRIP ALONG MID-SIDE

new RECTANGULAR EXPOSED HEADLIGHTS

INTERIOR

all-new 1979 Mercury Marquis
$6755.

79 RESTYLED AND DOWN-SIZED

302 OR 351 CID V8   *new* 114.4" WB

MARQ., COL. PK. WAGONS AVAIL.

GRAND MARQUIS   299 $8186.

Mercury

$7328. MARQUIS $8129. (MR. BROUGH.)

LUXURY WHEEL COVER

15" FULL WHEEL COVER

P205/75R×14 TIRES (P215/75R×14, WAGONS)

80

MINOR TRIM CHANGES IN SOME TYPES, new AUTOMATIC OVERDRIVE TRANS. AVAIL.

COLONY PARK

FROM $8408.

UNGRAINED MARQUIS STATION WAGON ALSO AVAIL.

$8658.

GRAND MARQUIS TWO-DOOR.

4-DR. $8846.

WIRE WHEEL COVERS

RED CENTER ON '79 TYPE, BLACK ON '80 (PERTAINS TO WIRE ONLY)

DASH

GRAND MARQUIS..

note COURTESY LT. and BAND OVER ROOF

CAST ALUMINUM TURBINE SPOKE WHEELS

FRONT DETAILS

"RESUME" SWITCH AVAIL. SINCE 1979

300

MERCURY Bobcat

(1975–1980)

140 CID 4 (92 HP) (ALSO AVAIL., STARTING '76 171 CID V6, 100 HP)

94½" WB

3-DOOR RUNABOUT

24 TO 29 MPG HWY. 17 TO 19 MPG CITY ('75)

(QUITE SIMILAR TO FORD PINTO)

3-DR. FROM $3456. ('75)

('75)

DASH

('75)

FROM $3748. ('75)

VILLAGER WAGON

75-78

1976 = IMITATION CHERRY WOODGRAIN OPT. ON RUNABOUT, AT $3809.

1977 = new EXTRUDED ALUMINUM BUMPERS; new ALL-GLASS HATCHBACK DOOR, MOON-ROOF, 4-WAY ADJUSTABLE DRIVER'S SEAT ARE OPTIONAL

REAR

UNGRAINED WAGON ALSO AVAIL. SINCE 1977.

Bobcat wagons come with all the same standard features

1978 is the year to LOVE THAT BOBCAT. More standard features than last year for a lower sticker price.*

a. Steel-belted radials now standard.
b. Styled-steel wheels with trim rings now standard.
c. Power front-disc brakes now standard.
d. Tinted glass now standard.
e. Front stabilizer bar now standard.

('78)

301

MERCURY BOBCAT

WHEEL and WHEEL COVER CHOICES →

('79)
$4104. UP

3-DOOR RUNABOUT

w. SPORTS ACCENT GROUP ('80)

('79) WITH SPORTS PACKAGE OPTION

new GRILLE **79-80**

WITH SPORT OPTION ('80)

140 CID 4 OR 171 CID V6
BR 78 x 13 TIRES

OPTIONAL SPORTS INSTRUMENTATION DASH

STD. VINYL INT. ('80)

RECTANGLE DASH CLUSTER ←

('80)

BOBCAT AND VILLAGER WAGONS

('79)

VILLAGER
$4519. ('79)
4950. ('80)
(REPLACED BY 1981 LYNX)

302

ROSEWOOD-TONE and WOODTONE GRAIN

MERCURY COMET

Custom Sports Coupe

(1960 – 1977)
(COMET NAME NOT USED IN 1970)

MERCURY LINCOLN
Ford

There are 13 models convertibles, wagons, hardtops, sedans.

new 116" WB
(WAGONS 113")

Completely equipped with white-walls, deluxe wheel covers, vinyl interiors, wall-to-wall carpeting, heater-defroster, seat belts (front and rear), emergency flasher, lots more.

$2908. Comet Caliente

$3168.

'Performance Car of the Year'
Named Pace Car For Memorial Day 500

1966 Performance Car of the year SUPER STOCK

Official PACE CAR   *Mercury COMET* CYCLONE-GT   INDIANAPOLIS 500

6.95/7.35/7.75 × 14 TIRES

66
new GRILLES

$3510.

200 CID 6 (120 HP)
289 CID V8 (200 HP)
390 CID V8s
(265, 275 OR 335 HP) OR
427 CID V8

Cyclone GT

has BODY STRIPES

OPT. DUAL HOOD SCOOPS

CYCLONE H/T $3028.

"Performance Car of the Year"

$3250.

Mercury COMET

Mercury COMET

HORIZ.-GROOVED DASH →

CALIENTE

$2994.

7.35 / x 7.75 x 14 TIRES

Caliente Grandé interior has blue Gossamer nylon or Chambrey nylon in black or parchment. Both framed with crinkle vinyl.

Mercury, the Man's Car.

67 (INTRO. 9-30-66)

202, CAPRI, CALIENTE, CYCLONE, CYCLONE GT

$3386.

CYCLONE GT

$3290.

CYCLONE GT (INTRO. 9-22-67)

(RESTYLED)

68

NOTE new SIDE SAFETY LTS.

new MONTEGO

116" WB

200 CID 6 (115 HP) OR 289 CID V8 (195 HP)

304

MONTEGO MX

$3135.

Mercury COMET

STD. ENGINES: new 250 CID 6 (155 HP) OR 302 CID V8 (220 HP)

69

V8s UP TO 428 CID

(INTRO. 9-27-68)

MONTEGO

H/T $3070. UP

(STD. COMET H/T $2997.)

1969 COMET and MONTEGO SHARE THIS GRILLE.

COMET NAME UNUSED IN '70.

MONTEGO, MONTEGO MX, MONTEGO MX BROUGHAM, CYCLONE, CYCL. GT and CYCL. SPOILER MODELS AVAIL. (INTRO. 9-19-69)

70

new PROTRUDING-CENTER FRONT END WITH ODD new GRILLE

Password for action

(SPOILER GRILLE LIKE GT, BUT has EXPOSED HEADLIGHTS.)

(New)

Cyclone Spoiler.

WITH CJ 429 CID V8 (370 HP) $4365.

351 CID OR 429 CID V8 (360 HP) $3996.

'70 Mercury Cyclone GT. with the accent on action.

(MONTEGO ON NEXT PAGE)

305

STD. ENG. IS 250 CID 6 (155 HP @ 4000 RPM) OR 302 CID V8

H/Ts FROM $3511.

Mercury presents Montego 1970. The action intermediate with the accent on luxury.

70 (CONT'D.)

Montego

2 or 4 doors, "6" or V-8

COMET

170 CID OR 250 CID 6 (100, 115 OR 145 HP) 302 CID V8 (210 HP)

103" WB (2-DR.) 109.9" (4-DR.)

SALE $2217.

SALE $2276.

Comet

RETURNS

COMET DASH

71

(INTRO. 9-11-70)

Comet GT.
SALE $2395.80

(MONTEGO ON NEXT PAGE)

VINYL TOP OPTIONAL

22 MPG (6 CYL., CITY/HWY.)

Better ideas make better cars.
The better small car.

Mercury COMET

Better ideas make better cars:

$2798

Printed electrical circuits in instrument cluster

Energy-absorbing steering column with locking features

Woodgrain vinyl paneling on the dash

Head restraints

Flow-thru ventilation

Dual brake system, self-adjusting brakes

Exhaust emission control system

Front tread 60.5"

Overall length 209.9"

Bias-belted tires

Rear tread 60.0"

(STD. CPE. NO SIDE CHROME)

Montego

71 (CONT'D.)

(REGULAR PRICE, 2-DR. 3694. UP)

117" WB (114" ON WAGONS)

250 CID 6 (145 HP)
302 CID V8 (210 HP)
F78 × 14 TIRES
(G78 × 14, WAGONS)

INTERIOR

REAR

ALL MODEL SERIES AVAIL. IN 1970 ARE CONTINUED. 1971 IS FINAL YR. FOR CYCLONE TYPES.

CENTER OF HOOD PROTRUDES AS BEFORE, BUT MONTEGO has new STANDARD GRILLE WITH CRISS-CROSS PIECES and EXPOSED HEADLIGHTS.

MONTEGO CYCLONE GT

STANDARD CYCLONE ENGINE: 351 CID V8 (285 HP @ 5400 RPM)

GT GRILLE QUITE SIMILAR TO 1970 GT, BUT has new "GT" LETTERING IN CENTER CIRCLE.

1971

Mercury Comet

COMET DASH

A BETTER IDEA FOR SAFETY: BUCKLE UP.

4-DR. (STD.) $2474.
6.45 × 14 TIRES

COMET

Comet GT
$2595.

4-DR. WITH EXTERIOR DECOR GROUP OPTION

72 FRONT RESTYLED ON MONTEGOS

(INTRO. 9-17-71)

Better ideas make better cars.

note GT HOOD SCOOPS

MONTEGO
Mercury Montego 2-Door Hardtop

MONTEGOS: new 114" WB (118" 4-DR.) H/T $3639.

302 CID V8 (140 HP) STD. ENG.

MONTEGO GT FASTBACK 2-DR. H/T $4137.

note GT LOUVRES (3)

Mercury Montego MX Brougham

MX DASH

MX 4-DR. PILLARED H/T

$3742.

$3918.

308

Mercury COMET

MX WAGON (UNGRAINED)
Montego MX

2-SEAT $4055.
3-SEAT $4131.

72 (CONT'D.)

MX VILLAGER
2-SEAT $4229.
3-SEAT 4305.

302 CID V8 STD. ON WAGONS
(ROOF RACK OPTIONAL)

F 78 × 14 TIRES

Built better to ride better.
MERCURY MONTEGO

MONTEGO MX
BROUGHAM 4-DR.
$3928.

73

(FINAL YR. FOR MONT.
GT FASTBACK)

LARGE *new* ENERGY-ABSORBING
SAFETY BUMPERS.

2-DR.
H/Ts:
MONTEGO
$3649.
MONTEGO MX
$3772.
MONTEGO MX
BROUGHAM
$3938.

(COMET PRICES FROM
$3122.)

74

Mercury Montego

GRILLE MOTIF
NO LONGER CONT'D.
AROUND
HEADLIGHTS.

MONTEGO TIRE SIZES :
G/H/HR 78 × 14

MONTEGO 2-DRS.
PRICED FROM $4162.

new
REAR QUARTER
OPERA
WINDOWS ON
MX BROUGHAM
2-DR
$4481.

(INTERIOR ALSO
ILLUSTRATED)

Montego MX Brougham with optional
Custom Trim, radio, remote control mirror,
opera windows, white sidewall tires
and bumper protection group.

309

Mercury COMET

4-DR. $3453.

Mercury Comet with Custom Option

Mercury Comet

200 CID 6 (78 HP)

Mercury Comet standard interior in cloth-and-vinyl

new BUMPER SLOTS

COMET 2-DRS. FROM $3419. (GT PKG. $277.)

75

new DUAL SLOTS IN FRONT BUMPERS

MX VILLAGER WAGON (FROM $5450.)

Mercury Montego MX

MX H/T $4845.

REAR

MX BRGHM. INT.

351 CID V8 (150 HP) IN MONTEGOS

2-DR. H/Ts (4-DR. AVAIL. ALSO)

Custom Trim Option instrument panel for Montego MX Brougham

$4994.

310

Mercury Montego MX Brougham – Custom Trim Option

Mercury COMET

4-DR. $3633.

2-DR. WITH OPTIONAL SPORTS ACCENT GROUP and SPORTS VINYL ROOF

200 CID 6 (78 HP) (250 CID 6 OR 302 CID V8 AVAIL.)

C78 × 14 TIRES

(BASIC 2-DR. PRICE: $3566.)

76

SLIGHT CHANGE IN COMET GRILLE and AUX. LTS.

Comet Custom interior option

COMET WITH CUSTOM OPTION

FINAL COMETS AVAIL. INTO 1977 SEASON.

IMITATION CHERRY WOODGRAIN ON MONTEGO MX VILLAGER

2-SEAT = $5626.
3-SEAT = 5734.

MONTEGO

4-DR. $4904.

MONTEGO DISCONTINUED AT END OF 1976 MODEL RUN.

351 CID V8 (154 HP) (400 or 460 CID V8 OPT.)

MX Villager standard interior

A distinctive note: Opera window (MX BROUGHAM 2-DR.)

MONTEGO MX 2-DR. H/T $5026.

Mercury Cougar (STARTS 1967)

$ 3213.

111" WB
289 CID V8
(200 HP)
7.35 × 14 TIRES
390 CID V8
(320 HP) IN "GT
PERFORMANCE GRP."

New

67

COUGAR ADVERTISING
MASCOT

WITH TRIP
ODOMETER

XR-7 $ 3443.

has GRAINED DASH
and BEARS
THIS SYMBOL

XR7

note EMBLEM
ON HEADLIGHT
COVER SECTION

COUGAR

MERCURY COUGAR

E 70 × 14 TIRES
289 CID V8 STD.
427 CID V8 (390 HP)
IN GT. E

(GT MODEL ALSO)

electric sunroof

$3296.

$3594.

68

XR-7-G has SPORT-STYLE HOOD and RALLYE LIGHTS (G.T.E has HORIZ. BAND ACROSS GRILLE)

new SAFETY SIDE LIGHTS

FROM $3383.

1969½ "ELIMINATOR" (not illustr.) has new FRONT and REAR SPOILERS.

VARIOUS V8s AVAIL., INCLUDING new 351 CID V8 (250 HP @ 4600 RPM) E 78 × 14 TIRES

69

new DOWNSWEPT SIDE SCULPTURE

new GRILLE

(new STD. OR XR-7 CONVERTIBLES ALSO AVAIL.) 313

MERCURY COUGAR XR-7

$4170.

A RETURN OF DOWNWARD EXTENSION OF HOOD AT CENTER, AS IN 1968.

note THAT XR-7 GRILLE DIFFERS FROM STANDARD 1970 COUGAR GRILLE SEEN ON "HOUNDSTOOTH" MODEL BELOW

FROM $3871. '70

new GRILLES.
"ELIMINATOR" has HOOD SCOOP and STRIPES, BODY STRIPES and BLACK GRILLE)

CLOSER VIEW OF HOUNDSTOOTH TOP COVERING

It's wild. It's sophisticated. It's elegant. The sporty look of houndstooth for spring. Cougar sets the trend with houndstooth check vinyl roof and hi-back cloth-and-vinyl buckets. Designer Pauline Trigère comes up with a swaggering houndstooth cape to match. Cougar...far more than just a sporty car. It's styled with European flair. Lean and sculptured, with concealed headlamps and sequential rear turn signals. Powered by a restless 351 cubic-inch V-8. It's the best

INTERIOR

Introducing the Houndstooth Cougar...

"HOUNDSTOOTH" MODEL STARTS SPRING, 1970

with a little something to match by Pauline Trigère.

314

MERCURY COUGAR

351 CID V8
CUT FR. 240
TO 164 HP FOR
1972.
CONVERTIBLE

('72)

DASH

XR-7

new 112" WB

('71)

(RESTYLED)

71-72

315

Better ideas make better cars.

XR-7 ROUND EMBLEM
(OTHERWISE,
EMBLEM IS UPRIGHT
RECTANGULAR.)

MERCURY COUGAR

(PRICED FROM $3821., AFTER 1972 PRICE CUTS)

SUNROOF DETAILS

new GRILLE STYLED LIKE A "RADIATOR"

(FINAL COUGAR CONVERTS.)

DASH

XR-7

$4152.

73

It's not like anybody else's car.

INT.

1974 DASH (1975 has new 2-SPOKE STEERING WHEEL.)

1975 and 1976 have 2 OPENINGS IN LOWER CENTER SECTION OF FRONT BUMPER

new REAR QUARTER OPERA WINDOWS

XR-7

74-76

('74)

new UPHOLSTERY PATTERN XR-7, '74

new ORNAMENT

new AND ENLARGED SERIES

1974, WITHOUT BUMPER OPENINGS

new GRILLE

316

MERCURY COUGAR

PRICED FROM
$5284. ('77)

$5631.
('78)

2 New Hardtops

FOR
1977
ONLY,
2 New Wagons

(351 CID V8, 161 HP IN WAGONS)

77-78

2 New Sedans

2-DRS.
114" WB
4-DRS.
118" WB
302 CID V8
(130 HP)

(RESTYLED)

('77)

**Introducing a new symbol of driving excitement.
The 1977 Cougar XR-7 unleashes 6 new running mates.**

XR-7

79

FINAL COUGAR DASH
WITH ROUND GAUGES

302 OR 351 CID V8

STD.
H/T
$ 6165.

BODY-COLOR TAPE
STRIPS IN XR-7
GRILLE

NEW TAILLIGHTS
WITH HORIZONTAL
CHROME STRIPS

1979

$ 6635.   XR-7

317

MERCURY COUGAR

ELECTRONIC DASH

new STANDARD DASH

255 OR 302 CID V8s

new KEYLESS (OPTIONAL) DOOR ENTRY (PUSH-BUTTON) COMBINATION LOCK

80 FROM $7271.

(DOWNSIZED) (*new* 104.8" WB)

XR-7

new REAR STYLING

P185/75R × 14 TIRES

WHEEL CHOICES (left to right) STANDARD COVER; DECOR GROUP COVER; WIRE WHEEL COVER; CAST ALUMINUM WHEEL.

MERCURY *MONARCH* (1975 TO 1980)

LINCOLN-MERCURY INTRODUCES A NEW PRECISION SIZE LUXURY CAR

REAR ('75)

109.9" WB

STD. MONARCH CPE. FROM $3764. ('75)

HOOD ORNAMENT

GHIA DASH, INTERIOR

Mercury Monarch Ghia instrument panel with optional AM/FM/Multiplex stereo radio and tape player.

ENGINES: 200 CID 6 (78 HP); 250 CID 6 ; 302 CID V8 (130 HP); 351 CID V8

GHIA

GHIA "GRAND MONARCH" SPEC. DELUXE 4-DR. ALSO AVAIL. 1975-1976 (IN ADDITION TO GHIA 4-DR. and CPE.)

$5149. ('75)

75-77

(1975 = GHIA MEDALLION ON SEDAN DOOR POST)

('75) $5207.

(1976 = GHIA MEDALLION MOVED)

319

('76) $5299.

MERCURY MONARCH

RIDE-ENGINEERED

250 C/D 6 OR 302 C/D V8

$5996. ('80)
STD. MONARCH CPE.

CPE. INTERIOR (RECLINING BUCKET SEATS OPT.)

STEER. WHEEL WITH OPTIONAL FINGERTIP SPEED CONTROL

$6552. ('80)

"ESS" INTERIOR (ESS INTRO. 1978)

WITH GHIA OPTION

(1980 EXAMPLES, UNLESS OTHERWISE INDICATED

new HEAD-LTS.; new BUMPERS; "Mercury" NAME IN SCRIPT, LOWER ON GRILLE; CORNERING LTS. MOVED BACK FR. FRONT OF FENDER

78-80 (FINAL MONARCH)

AVAIL. WHEEL COVERS ('78-80)

SEDAN

('79) ('80)

MONARCH ESS

COWL LETTERING READS: "MONARCH ESS" ('78) "ESS MONARCH" ('79) OR "ESS" ('80)

1980

$6505. ('80)

MERCURY ZEPHYR (STARTS 1978)

(QUITE SIMILAR TO FORD FAIRMONT)

WAGONS

STD. ROUND-HUB STEER. WH.

REAR WIPER AVAIL. FOR WAGON

1978 WHEEL CVR. →

1979-1980 WHEELS and COVERS ←

LOWER DASH IS ↑ OPTIONAL SPORTS INSTRUMENTATION GROUP

AVAIL. WITH GHIA OPTION

4-DR.

2-DR.

78-80

ENERGY ENGINEERED FOR MILEAGE: EPA EST. **33** HWY. **23** CITY.

140.3 CID 4 (89 HP), 200 CID 6 (96 HP), 302 CID V8 (130 HP) (255 CID V8 AVAIL. '80)

Z-7 SPORT COUPE.

SPECIAL HOOD and WHEELS WITH TURBO OPTION

(105½" WB) 1980 EXAMPLES ILLUSTRATED

"ES" OPTION ('78-79) has BLACK AREAS AROUND SIDE WINDOWS

ORIG. 1978 PRICES $4700. and UP

$5944. ('80)

RIDE-ENGINEERED

(SINCE 1897)

CUTLASS, STARFIRE ('75 ON) and TORONADO MODELS ILLUSTRATED SEPARATELY

Oldsmobile

GM

GENERAL MOTORS

JETSTAR 88 FROM $3314. DYNAMIC 88 FROM $3442.

123" WB

88

4-DR. H/T HOLIDAY SEDAN $3757.

DELTA **88**

2-DR. H/T HOLIDAY CPE. $3682.

66

123" WB 425 CID V8 (365 HP)

Starfire:

(STARFIRE IS LUXURY H/T WITH BIG V8. NOT TO BE CONFUSED WITH SMALL CAR OF 1975 ON, WITH SAME NAME.)

425 CID V8 (310 HP) STD. (JETSTAR 88 has 330 CID V8 (260 HP)

Ninety-Eight:

126" WB (THROUGH '68)

98 SEDANS FROM $4592.

98 has CRISS - CROSS GRILLE PCS.

365 HP (98)

STEP OUT FRONT IN '66 ...in a Rocket Action Olds!

322

Oldsmobile

(new DELMONT 88 REPLACES FORMER JETSTAR 88)

TOWN SED. 3543.

330 OR 425 CID V8 s

4-DR. H/T $3675.

Aas DELMONT 88 NAME OVER COWL

DELMONT 88
Brand-new 88 series!
Goes to show what Olds can do
with a modest price tag...
and a lot of Toronado inspiration.

DELMONT 88 DASH

$3912.

The Rocket Action Cars are out front again!

(INTRO. 9-29-66)

67 new GRILLES

Engineered for excitement... Toronado-style!
'67 OLDSMOBILE

DELTA 88 CVT.

DELTA 88 4-DR. H/T HOLIDAY SEDAN $3954.

DELTA 88 $3786.

REAR

TOWN SEDAN

(CONT'D. NEXT PAGE)

DELTA 88 HOLIDAY COUPE (2-DR. H/T) $3878.

Oldsmobile

$3951. HOLIDAY CPE.

Delta

↗ CLOSE VIEW OF SIDE TRIM LOUVRES

425 CID V8

DELTA 88 CUSTOM
Two all-new Custom hardtops highlight the Delta 88 line.

1967

$4011.

67 (CONT'D.)

$4736.

Ninety-Eight: HOLIDAY CPE. (H/T)

98 LUXURY SEDAN

$4873.

98 365 HP

note VERTICAL TAIL LTS.

CLOSE-UP (REAR)

(98)

$5020.

$4798.

8.85 × 14 TIRES

98 DASH

Oldsmobile

(INTRO. 9-21-67)

Drive a youngmobile from Oldsmobile

68

V8s UP TO 455 CID

new SPLIT GRILLES

DELMONT **88**

(DELTA GRILLE SAME)

98

LUXURY SEDAN

Tilt & Telescope steering wheel"

(310 HP) 455 CID V8

REAR

Escape from the ordinary in Olds

DELTA 88 *has* 350 CID V8 (250 HP)

Delta 88 Royale

(*new* 124" WB) ➔

(INTRO. 9-26-68)

69

new GRILLES

8.55 x 15 TIRES

OLDSMOBILE NOW SHOWING YOUNGMOBILE THINKING 1969

Delta 88 Royale

note SIDE LOUVRES

98 REAR

Olds Ninety-Eight

(*new* 127" WB)

325

Delta 88 Royale

Oldsmobile: Escape from the ordinary.

$5215.

STD. DELTA 88 USES 350 CID V8 (250 HP) $3969. UP

ROYALE 455 CID V8 (310 HP)

$4350.

88

98
455 CID V8 (365 HP) J78×15 TIRES

ROYALE GRILLE DETAILS

new GRILLES

70 (INTRO. 9-18-69)

H78×15 TIRES

ROYALE COWL LOUVRES

Oldsmobile

Wouldn't it be nice to have an Escape Machine?

71

(INTRO. 9-29-70)

(CONT'D. NEXT PAGE)

FROM $5440.

127" WB

The new Glide-Away Tailgate!

Just turn the key...watch it disappear...out of sight!

Introducing a totally new luxury station wagon for 1971: The Oldsmobile Custom Cruiser.

326

DELTA 88 *Oldsmobile*

THIS TOWN SEDAN IS ONLY DELTA 88 CSTM. WITH CHROME STRIP SHOWN HERE

DELTA 88 CUSTOM

DELTA 88 TOWN SED. $4516.

DELTA 88 and DELTA 88 CUSTOM GRILLE →

DELTA 88 DASH

DELTA (4-DR.) H/T ROOFLINES

ROYALE (2-DR.)

Bumper Guards, Front and Rear—Feature rubber inserts to reduce dings, dents and help protect your investment. (OPT.)

H/T $4953.

DELTA 88 ROYALE

ROYALE GRILLE
ROYALE CVT. $5088.

98 DASH

NINETY-EIGHT 127" WB

71 (CONT'D.)

98s PRICED FROM $5454.
455 CID V8 (320 HP)

Oldsmobile ALWAYS A STEP AHEAD

98 TAIL-LIGHT DETAIL

$5690.

Oldsmobile

350 CID V8 (160 HP)

Delta 88

$4517.

Delta 88 Royale

Not just another pretty car.

$4754.

72

DELTA 88 ROYALE HARDTOP COUPE — 4695.

DELTA 88 ROYALE TOWN SEDAN — 4617.

DELTA 88 ROYALE CONVERTIBLE — 4903.

(INTRO. 9-23-71)

An exceptional new bumper

It gives a little.
Mounted on steel springs, it flexes, then returns to position, to help absorb minor impacts.

new GRILLES

98 REAR

Ninety-Eight

A responsive 455-cubic-inch Rocket V-8 engine that runs efficiently on regular, no-lead or low-lead gasolines.

TIFFANY CLOCK

The Limited-Edition Regency.
A very special Ninety-Eight with the Tiffany touch to mark Oldsmobile's 75th Anniversary.

98 REGENCY INTERIOR

(225 HP)

$5393.

OLDSMOBILE
ALWAYS A STEP AHEAD

FROM $5391.

Custom Cruiser

Oldsmobile

$4517.

Delta 88 Royale.

88 REAR

1973

98 REAR

Not just another pretty car.

73
(RESTYLED)

$5452.

127" WB
455 CID V8
(225 HP)

Custom-Cruiser.
FROM $5356.

98

Ninety-Eight

DASH

$5049.

DELTA 88

$4988

new COUPE
STYLING

DELTA 88 GRILLE

74
new
GRILLES

FROM
$5683.

CUSTOM
CRUISER

(CONT'D.
NEXT
PAGE)

Front and rear bumpers are mounted on
hydraulic cylinders which cushion minor impacts. '74 Oldsmobile Delta 88.

329

Oldsmobile

98s FROM $6003.

instrument panel is now redesigned to provide a new message center which monitors the car and signals you when something is wrong.

NINETY-EIGHT

HOOD ORNAMENT ADDED ←

$6334.

98 REGENCY.

455 CID V8 (210 HP)
J/L 78 × 15 TIRES

74 (CONT'D.)

DELTA 88 ROYALE

FINAL CVT. (DELTA 88 ROYALE) $5772.

98 REGENCY

124" WB
350 CID V8 (170 HP)

$6925.

$5623.

Delta 88 Royale

CUSTOM CRUISER

75 new GRILLES

98 REGENCY $6784.

98:
127" WB
455 CID V8 (190 HP)

98 GRILLE DETAILS

FROM $6134.

It's a good feeling to have an Olds around you.

330

Oldsmobile

Can we build one for you?

DELTA 88

4-DR. H/T $5641.

TOWN SEDAN $5521.

"MESSAGE CENTER"

TOWN SEDAN $5681.

DELTA 88 ROYALE

WITH CROWN LANDAU OPTION →

DASH

350 CID V8
170 HP
HR 78×15 TIRES

H/T $5749.

DELTA 88 ROYALE (REAR)

(UNGRAINED)

(98 ON NEXT PAGE)

76 new GRILLES

127" WB

455 CID V8
190 HP
FROM $6326.

CUSTOM CRUISER

331

(WITH GRAIN)

Oldsmobile
Can we build one for you?

98

LS COUPE

$7294.

$7147.

REGENCY SEDAN

76 (CONT'D.)

98 REGENCY CPE.

EPA MPG 22 HWY. 17 CITY WITH AVAIL. 260 CID V8 (110 HP)

DASH

Delta 88 Can we build one for you?

Delta 88

The 1977 Delta 88.

new 116" WB

$6109.

DELTA 88

231 CID V6 (105 HP) ALSO AVAIL.

98 Regency Coupé

new 119" WB

98 REG.

DOWNSIZED, new GRILLES

98 (REAR)

REAR QUARTERS

77

$7764.

(WAGON ON NEXT PAGE)

→ 98 Regency ←
Can we build one for you?

Oldsmobile

CUSTOM CRUISER 77 (CONT'D.)

NOW has GRILLE LIKE 88 ↓

FROM $6725.

NOW ON 116" WB, LIKE 88 SERIES

(new REAR-FACING 3RD SEAT AVAIL.)

OLDSMOBILE NAME MOVED LOWER

There's a lot of News in Olds today.

Introducing the world's first passenger cars with a diesel V8.

$7918.

Custom Cruiser

| 27 mpg HWY. | 19 mpg CITY | 22 mpg Composite |

FROM $7191.

Ninety-Eight

| 30 mpg HWY. | 21 mpg CITY | 24 mpg Composite |

Delta 88

| 30 mpg HWY. | 21 mpg CITY | 24 mpg Composite |

78

HOOD EMBLEM ON DIESELS ↙

(new)

Oldsmobile
Holiday 88 Coupe
Can we build one for you?

"OLDSMOBILE" NAME MOVED TO LOWER PORTION OF GRILLES IN 1978.

$6311.

DELTA 88
Can we build one for you?

note: CUSTOM CRUISER has OWN UNIQUE GRILLE IN 1979

Custom Cruiser
Have one built for you.

FROM $7651.

79

(CONT'D. NEXT PAGE)

333

Oldsmobile

DELTA 88

$6726.

88 Holiday Coupe
Have one built for you.
$6626.

DIESEL HOOD EMBLEM

Delta 88 Royale

Royale

$6998.

Have one built for you.

DELTA 88 ROYALE (REAR)

79 (CONT'D.)

98 DASH

98 LS

98 REGENCY SEDAN REAR QUARTER PANEL

$8377.

$8579.

98 Regency
Have one built for you.

EPA MPG:
GAS 21 HWY. 15 CITY
DIESEL 29 HWY. 21 CITY

GRILLE EMBLEM

350 CID V8 ENGS.
GAS 160 HP
DIESEL 125 HP

334

Oldsmobile *WE'VE HAD ONE BUILT FOR YOU.*

diesel Delta 88.

| 22 EPA EST MPG | 594 EST DRIVING RANGE |
| 34 HWY EST | 918 EST HIGHWAY RANGE |

DELTA 88 (GAS) PRICES START AT $7382.

HOLIDAY COUPE

DELTA 88

ROYALE

↑ $7641.

DELTA 88 DASH AND STEERING WHEEL

$9741.

98 REGENCY

$9619.

98 MILEAGE

| 17 EPA EST MPG | 425 EST DRIVING RANGE |
| 25 HWY EST MPG | 625 EST HIGHWAY RANGE |

80 (RESTYLED)

Custom Cruiser Diesel

| 21 EPA MPG | 462 EPA Est. Range | 31 Hwy Est | 682 Hwy Range |

UNGRAINED WOODGRAINED

Custom Cruiser. FROM $8410.

98 STEERING WHEEL

88- STYLE GRILLE RESUMES ↗

Oldsmobile **CUTLASS** (and F-85) (SINCE 1961)

with 12 windows.

(F-85 SIMILAR, BUT W/O SIDE CHROME; FROM $2783.)

VISTA-CRUISER (FROM $3300.)

120" WB
330 CID V8 UP TO 320 HP

new REAR →

SPT. CPE. FROM $2998.

66

new GRILLE, WITH "OLDSMOBILE" NAME NOW ON UPPER BORDER

STEP OUT FRONT IN '66 ... *in a Rocket Action Olds!*

115" WB (EXCEPT ON VISTA-CR.)

$3211.

CUTLASS SUPREME

4-DR. H/T (new)

4 bbl. 400 CID 350 HP

442

4-4-2

442

336

Oldsmobile

CUTLASS

new 250 CID 6 AVAIL. (155 HP)

330 CID V8 STD. (250 HP)

67

F-85 $3183.

DASH

Olds 4-4-2

VISTA-CRUISER
(CUSTOM 3-SEAT: $3734.)

4-4-2 CVT.

new GRILLE; AUX. LTS. BETWEEN EA. PAIR OF HEADLIGHTS

CUTLASS SUPREME

Engineered for excitement ... Toronado-style!

'67 OLDSMOBILE

$3265.

320 HP

CUTLASS "S"

new 350 CID V8 (250 HP)
4-4-2 has AVAILABLE
400 CID V8 (325/350 HP)
155-HP, 250 CID 6 ALSO AVAIL.

VISTA-CRUISER

$3910. (3-SEAT)

new 112" WB (2-DR.) 116" WB (4-DR.)

68 (RESTYLED)

WAGON has 121" WB WITH 350 OR 400 CID V8

F-85 FROM $2988.

NOTE *new* SIDE SAFETY LTS.

Drive a youngmobile from Oldsmobile

337

Oldsmobile **CUTLASS**

CUTLASS SUPREME 4-DR. H/T $3486. 3IO HP

350 CID V8

ESCAPE FROM THE ORDINARY.

W·31

Vista-Cruiser:

$3854. (2-SEAT)

$3997. (3-SEAT)

69

GRILLES NOW SPLIT; AUX. LTS. NOW IN BMPR. →

250 CID 6 OR 350 CID V8

Cutlass S.

NOW SHOWING YOUNGMOBILE THINKING 1969

DR. OLDSMOBILE

1969 W·MACHINES W·30/W·31

OLDS "MUSCLE CARS"

PROMOTE IN COMICAL "DR. OLDSMOBILE" ADS (AS ABOVE AND ON NEXT PG.)

W TYPES HAVE LOW AIR SCOOPS

Cutlass

350 CID V8 (250-310 HP) IN **OLDS W·31.**

OLDS 4·4·2 W·30

400 CID V8 (360 HP @ 5400 RPM)

W-31 Models... Available in Cutlass S and F-85 V-8 models.
Wheelbase ....112"

Oldsmobile
CUTLASS

Olds Vista-Cruiser: The all-family Escape Machine. $4095. (3-ST.)

$3953. (2-SEAT)

CUTLASS "S"

CUTLASS SUPREME (FRONT)

70

(RESTYLED)

150 CID 6 (155 HP) 350 CID V8 (250 HP)

"DR. OLDSMOBILE" and HIS ODDBALL ASSISTANT CREW

Cutlass Supreme—

Wouldn't it be nice to have an Escape Machine?

new 2-DR.H/T $3532.

4-4-2
W-30 H/T
455 CID V8
370 HP @
5200 RPM
3.42 G.R.
G70x14 TIRES

RALLYE 350

note "442" AT CENTER

339

SPLIT GRILLE

F-85
SEDAN
$3789.

$4291.

CUTLASS SUPREME.

Oldsmobile CUTLASS

250 CID 6
(145 HP)

71

350 CID V8s
(240/260 HP)

Oldsmobile
ALWAYS A STEP AHEAD

112" WB (2-DR.)
116" (4-DR.)

CUTLASS
CRUISER
$4358.

$4922.
(3-SEAT)
VISTA-CRUISER

CUTLASS
"S"

$3862.

REAR
ROOFLINE
(CUTLASS
SUPR.)

4-4-2 and DASH

SUPER STOCK WHEELS AVAIL. IN 15
COLORS

455 CID
V8
(340 HP)

Oldsmobile **CUTLASS** WAGONS FOR 1972

GM MARK OF EXCELLENCE

VISTA CRUISER (3-SEAT) $4706.

FINAL 121" WB V.C. WITH RAISED ROOF WINDOW SECT. (GRILLE LIKE CUTL. SUPR.)

CUTLASS CRUISER $4296.

CUTLASS 350 CID V8 (160 HP)

new GRILLES

F-85 DASH

F 85 TOWN SEDAN $3756.

Cutlass Supreme 350 CID V8 (180 HP) H/T

Cutlass Supreme Hardtop Coupe

$4046.

new 6-SEGMENT TAIL LTS. (ON ALL BUT WAGONS)

72

4-4-2 DASH

4-4-2 has DUAL EXHAUST PIPES

4-4-2

CUTLASS S

$3825.

4-4-2

now in 4 types: 4-4-2 AVAIL. w. 350 CID OR 455 CID V8

1972 OLDSMOBILE ALWAYS A STEP AHEAD

Meet the 1972 Olds 4·4·2, 4·4·2, 4·4·2, 4·4·2!

Oldsmobile CUTLASS

The brand-new '73 Olds Vista-Cruiser. If you don't see the 9th window right away...

new 116" WB

3-SEAT: $4634.

Cutlass. $3885.

'73 (RESTYLED)

look in the roof.

DASH

new "COLONNADE" ROOFS
new SINGLE HEADLTS.

350 CID V8 (180 HP) (THROUGH '74)

Cutlass Salon. A new Olds in the grand touring tradition.

$4496.

Cutlass Salon

new OPERA WINDOWS

Cutlass Supreme
H/T
$4064.

4-4-2 PACKAGE

(W-29)

"SOFT-SELL" SALES CAMPAIGN BY

The Quiet Men of Olds
We give you a great deal more than just a great deal.

Cutlass S.

342

Oldsmobile **CUTLASS**

H78 × 14 TIRES

SUPREME CRUISER

(NO WOOD-GRAIN)

3-SEAT: $4481.

74

Whatever happens with gasoline, the important thing to you is the car you put the gasoline in.

OLDSMOBILE

CUTLASS "S" COUPE

Recent Proving Ground tests show 17.6 mpg average at 55 mph.

SUPREME

FROM $4143.

VISTA-CRUISER

3-SEAT: $4691.

DASH (CUTL. SALON)

4-4-2 PACKAGE →

CPE. IS new

CUTLASS SALON

Built in the Grand Touring tradition.

new AUX. LTS. QUICKLY IDENTIFY A 1974 MODEL (EXCEPT 4-4-2)

It's a good feeling to have an Olds around you.

Oldsmobile CUTLASS

new TAIL-LTS.

$3756.*
Cutlass
16 MPG CITY
21 MPG HWY.

* REG. PRICES START AT $4583.

75

new GRILLES

250 CID 6 (105 HP) 260 CID V8 (110 HP)
350 CID V8 (170 HP)
FR78 × 15 TIRES

Cutlass S:

SUPREME (4-4-2 has HOOD STRIPES and SLOTS; CHROME IN PLACE OF AUX. LIGHTS)

CUTLASS S

4-4-2 (S)

442

Can we build one for you?

new "WATERFALL" GRILLES

76

FROM $4905.

VISTA-CRUISER

3-SEAT: $5728.

CUTLASS SUPREME CRUISER

3-SEAT: $5610.

(CONT'D. NEXT PAGE)

OLDSMOBILE CUTLASS - 9

344

Oldsmobile
CUTLASS

$5519.

Cutlass Salon

ROCKET 260 V8 STD.

5-SP. TRANS. AVAIL.

76 (CONT'D.)

New
Cutlass S Sedan
(ABOVE)

DASH

T-TOP AVAIL.
(SUPR. and SALON)

$5486.

Cutlass Supreme Brougham

FINAL **VISTA-CRUISER**

$5821 - 5973.

4-4-2

77

new GRILLES

231 CID V6 (105 HP)
260 CID V8 (110 HP)

DASH (S)   Can we build one for you?

S

25 MPG HWY. 17 CITY STD. 231 CID V6

$5256. (SALE = $4811.)

Cutlass Supreme

$5575.

345

Oldsmobile CUTLASS

THE NEW CUTLASS SALON. A CARFULL OF NEW IDEAS.

FROM $5663.

All new bi-level instrument panel

CUTLASS S

23	MPG HIGHWAY
16	MPG CITY
18	MPG COMBINED

Cutlass Cruiser
(new 2-PIECE TAILGATE)
$6356
(REPLACES VISTA-CR.)

Color-coördinated dual mirrors add eye-catching sportiness.

Special paint scheme: White w/ choice of metallic Carmine, Camel Tan, Blue or Green.

Super-stock wheels to give an added flash of color.

$6502.
Supreme Brougham

27 MPG HWY., 19 CITY WITH AVAIL. 260 CID V8

CUTLASS SUPREME

(DOWNSIZED) 108" WB

78

new Cutlass Calais V-6

$6451.

T-TOP AVAIL.

Cutlass Supreme
Can we build one for you?

5-SP. TRANS. AVAIL. IN SALON, CALAIS

$6097.
(T-TOP EXTRA)

Cutlass Supreme

Oldsmobile **CUTLASS**

2-DR. SALON $5985.

$6085.

Cutlass Salon
Have one built for you.

There's a lot of news in Olds today.

$6269.

SALON BROUGHAM

new 90 HP DIESEL V8 (260 CID) AVAIL., 32 MPG HWY., 24 MPG CITY ALSO 231 CID V6 (115 HP) OR 260 CID V8 (105 HP)

$6394.

5.7-litre, 350 CID V8s ALSO AVAIL. (GAS OR DIESEL, 125 HP)

CALAIS DASH

$6853. CUTLASS **CALAIS**

$6425.

CUTLASS SUPREME CPE.

DASH

T-TOP AVAIL.

79 new GRILLES

SUPREME BROUGHAM $6854.

4-4-2

CUTLASS CRUISERS (2-SEAT ONLY)

MOJAVE INTERIOR AVAIL. IN BROUGH.

CUTLASS CRUISER $6266. CRUISER BROUGHAM $6468. (WOODGRAIN OPT.)

350 CID DIESEL AVAIL.

347

Oldsmobile **CUTLASS**

SALON

SALON BROUGH. $7168.

80 new GRILLES

ENGINE CHOICES:
231 CID V6 (110 HP)
260 CID V8 (105 HP)
305 CID V8
350 CID DIESEL V8 (105 HP)

DASH

CUTLASS 4-DOOR

CUTLASS LS SEDAN: $7327.

Cutlass Brougham Sedan.

$7653.

AVAIL. PADDED-GRIP CUSTOM SPORT STEER. WHEEL

(STD. EQUIP. ON CALAIS)

| 20 EPA EST MPG | 360 EST DRIVING RANGE |
| 27 HWY EST MPG | 486 EST HIGHWAY RANGE |

Available instrumentation — with voltmeter, temperature and oil pressure gages, plus trip odometer. Standard on Calais.

CALAIS $7690.

(CONT'D. NEXT PAGE)

Oldsmobile
WE'VE HAD ONE BUILT FOR YOU.

348

Oldsmobile CUTLASS

T-TOP AVAIL. ON CPES.

REAR DETAILS

CUTLASS SUPREME

$7226.

SUNROOF OPT.

20	360
EPA EST MPG	EST. DRIVING RANGE
27	486
HWY EST. MPG	EST. HIGHWAY RANGE

80 (CONT'D.)

AVAIL. 5.7-litre (350 CID) DIESEL V8 ENG. ($960. EXTRA)

(BELOW) SUPREME BROUGHAM

$7568.

CUTLASS CRUISER

$7029.

(V-6 OR DIESEL V8 OPT.)

Cutlass Cruiser Diesel

22	400	34	618
EPA Est. MPG	EPA Est. Range	Hwy Est	Hwy Range

wagon

N. KANARIS

GM

CRUISER BROUGHAM

$7254.

EPA MPG 20	362
EPA EST. MPG	EST. DRIVING RANGE
27	488
HWY.	EST. HIGHWAY RANGE

349

Meet the new Compact Olds— at a compact price.

OLDS OMEGA

111" WB
6 CYL.
250 CID
100 HP

(SINCE 1973)
FROM
$2612.70 (SALE)
($3334. OTHERWISE)

4-door sedan.
TOWN SEDAN

3-door hatchback.

A glove compartment with a door and a lock. Rear windows that roll down.

73

Deluxe interior with new "wet-look" vinyl trim. Full carpeting. Vinyl-grip steering wheel. Chrome trim around the windows and wheel openings.

Your choice of 2, 3 or 4 doors.

Omega

2-door coupe.

LESS BRIGHTWORK ON *new* DASH

FROM $3867.

The soft grip steering wheel is wrapped in vinyl, and feels good underhand. The instrument panel has a good-looking quality to it, too, right down to the grained inlays. Air conditioning is available also.

350 CID V8 (180 HP) ALSO AVAIL. (INTRO. '73 SEASON)

74

new GRILLE

'75 STD. INT.

$4814.

SALON 2-DR.

FROM $3463.05 (SALE)
4-DR

It's a good feeling to have a little Olds around you.

new DASH

75

new "DUTCH ROOF" SHAPE OF GRILLE; *new* TAIL-LTS. 350

Olds Omega

Omega F-85 $4314. Can we build one for you?

(INTRO. DURING 1975 SEASON)

76

new GRILLE (SIMPLER, 4-SECTION ALL-VERTICAL)

(LITTLE CHROME ON F-85)

F-85 INTERIOR IN "RACINE FABRIC"

$4409.

Omega SX

OMEGA

BROUGHAM

(4-DR. BROUGHAM ALSO)

$4599.

SX

(F-85 CONT'D. WITH FEW CHANGES)

BROUGHAM $4913.

OMEGA

77

new GRILLE (CRISS-CROSS PCS.)

BROUGHAM 4-DR. $4973.

$4776.

new DASH

351

Olds Omega

HATCHBACK WITH SX SPORT TRIM

78

ON SALE $4482.
(REG. $5300.)

Oldsmobile
Omega Brougham
Can we build one for you?

(INTERIOR)

new GRILLE WITH MOSTLY HORIZONTAL PCS.

(4-DR. BRGM.)

Oldsmobile
Omega Hatchback '78
Can we build one for you?

28 MPG HWY.
16 MPG CITY (V6)

231 CID V6 (115 HP)
OR 305 CID V8 (130 HP)
(OMEGA'S FINAL V8)

BROUGHAM CPE.

HATCHBACK

BROUGHAM 4-DR.
$5672.

79

new GRILLE WITH ALL-VERTICAL PCS.

Oldsmobile
Omega
Have one built for you.

BROUGHAM CPE.

new 4 CYL. (151 CID, 90 HP)
OR V6 (173 CID, 115 HP)
new 105" WB

80

new DASH

OMEGA

SX

$6455. (TOTALLY RESTYLED)

BROUGHAM 4-DR.

(SX GRILLE ALL-BLACK)

Oldsmobile Omega.

352

Oldsmobile Starfire

(1975-1980)

INTERIOR

FROM $4171. ('75)

1975 DASH

FULL INSTRUMENTS STD. 97" WB

231 CID V6 OR 140 CID 4

2.56 GEAR RATIO

1975 DASH

STD. TYPE ('76)

('75)

B78 × 13 TIRES 18½-GAL. FUEL TANK

75-76

GT ('76)

(SX MODEL *has* THINNER SIDE STRIPE THAN **GT**)

new DASH, 1976, LOOKS SAME AS '77 and FOLLOWING YRS.

FROM $4261. ('77)

JERRY'S ORANGE BURGERS

('77)

140 CID 4 (84 HP) OR 231 CID V6 (105 HP) (145 HP, 305 CID V8 AVAIL. '78)

new GRILLE

77-78

('77) GT

Oldsmobile Starfire

$4095.00

FIRENZA

GT

NO SIDE-STRIPING ON STD. STARFIRE

SPT. STEER. WH.

79

new GRILLE and SINGLE HEAD-LIGHTS

151 CID 4, 231 CID V6, OR 305 CID V8 (130 HP)

REAR VIEW

There's a lot of news in Olds today.

INTERIOR

WHEEL

151 CID 4 (90 HP)

231 CID V6 (110 HP; DOWN FROM 115)

STD. STARFIRE $5294.

TYPICAL 1980 STARFIRE INTERIOR SAME AS 1979 SHOWN ABOVE

GT $5495. (SX)

(THE FINAL STARFIRE)

FIRENZA $5721.

(ORIG. INTRO. DURING '78 MODEL YEAR) (has REAR SPOILER)

new GRILLE WITH MOSTLY HORIZONTAL PCS.

80

STARFIRE
Nifty little road machines built for the long and winding.

Oldsmobile TORONADO (SINCE 1966)

Front-wheel drive

NEW 66

119" WB (THROUGH '70)

FROM $5125.

STEP OUT FRONT IN '66... *in a Rocket Action Olds!* **TORONADO**

V8 ENGINE (ON ALL) 425 CID 385 HP

new GRILLE

new WHEEL COVERS

67

FROM $5182.

(STD. OR DLX. 2-DR HT, 1966 and 1967)

new SPLIT GRILLE

68

new 455 CID V8 375 HP

$5258.

(ONLY 1 MODEL OF 2-DR. H/T AVAIL.)

Toronado. Test drive the front-wheel-drive "youngmobile" from Oldsmobile.

Escape from the ordinary

OLDSMOBILE NOW SHOWING YOUNGMOBILE THINKING 1969

$5344.

69

new REAR DECK

new GRILLE

356

DASH

2-LEVEL
TAIL-LIGHTS
CONTINUE

HP CUT
TO 250

WILL RUN ON
EITHER LEADED
OR UNLEADED GAS
(SINCE '71)

CUSTOM
$5986.
BROUGHAM
$6140.

72

ALL-VERTICAL
GRILLE OPENINGS

OLDSMOBILE
ALWAYS A STEP AHEAD

INTERIOR

73

REAR

new
GRILLE SLOTS ATOP
FR. BUMPER

Oldsmobile **Toronado**

new DASH (new "MESSAGE CENTER" WARNING LTS.)

HOOD ORNAMENT ADDED

74

WITH OPERA ROOF

HP CUT TO 230

CUSTOM $6634.

BROUGHAM $6798.

CUSTOM $7095.

BROUGHAM $7325.

new SQUARE LTS.

75

HP CUT TO 215

A new touch of distinction: Toronado's T-crest hood ornament. Another, the opera roof you can order (seen below).

ORNAMENT

note TOP COVER VARIATIONS

It's a good feeling to have an Olds around you.

358

REAR
DETAILS

DETAILS OF
"MESSAGE
CENTER"
SECTIONS
BELOW
SPEEDO.

new
STRIP ON
REAR
FENDER,
and
HEAVIER
SIDE TRIM
STRIPS,
ARE THE
MOST
OBVIOUS
MEANS OF
DISTINGUISHING
THE 1976
FROM
PREVIOUS
TORONADO.

CUSTOM
$7494.

BROUGHAM
$7740.

76

BACK
SEAT

OTHER
UPH.
STYLES
ALSO
AVAIL.

FRONT
COMPARTMENT

Oldsmobile
Toronado

77

BROUGHAM $ 8287.

DASH

WRAPAROUND
REAR WINDOW (XSR)
WITH CREASED
CORNERS EA.
SIDE

← **NEW**

NEW Toronado XSR
Can we build one for you?

CID CUT TO 403
HP CUT TO 200

new GRILLE

XSR AVAIL. WITH
OR WITHOUT
T-TOP

XS = $10,837.
XSR = $11,285.

TORONADO
HP CUT TO 185

new GRILLE
WITH ALL
VERTICAL
PCS.

78

" CAN WE BUILD ONE
FOR YOU ? " SLOGAN
CONTINUES

FINAL
TORONADO
WITH
THIS TYPE
BODY,
BEFORE
MAJOR
RESTYLING

BROUGHAM
$8899.
XS
$11,599.

360

Oldsmobile
Toronado
Have one built for you.

Announcing the all-new 1979 Toronado...

CID CUT TO 350

HP CUT TO 165

new DASH

ROOF-LINE

(TOTALLY RESTYLED and DOWNSIZED)

$10,112.

79

new 114" WB

"Oldsmobile"
(IN LOWER-CASE LETTERS)

XSC SPORT COUPE

(WITH SPECIAL DECOR)

new STEERING WHEEL DESIGN

BROUGHAM

$11,360.

80

GAS OR DIESEL V8s

GAS = 307 CID
150 HP
DIESEL = 350 CID
105 HP
2.41 GEAR RATIO

new GRILLE

361

Plymouth

(SINCE 6-28 INTRO. OF 1929 MODEL "Q")

6.95/7.35/7.75 x 14 TIRES

$3045.

Satellite — Belvedere
116" WB

Let yourself go... Plymouth
VIP FURY BELVEDERE VALIANT BARRACUDA

STD. 225 CID 6 (145 HP) OR 273 CID V8 (180 HP) OR 3/8 CID V8 (230 HP)

66 new GRILLES

SPT. Fury
119" WB

VIP (new)

(117" OR 121"-WB WAGONS AVAIL.)

FURY WHEEL COVER

$3365.

4-door VIP

$3492.

362

The new 2-d hardtop VIP.

Plymouth

(INTRO. 1-66

DASH

66½ 2-DR. VIP $3429.

$3101.

Belvedere

(SATELLITE)

67 new GRILLES

(INTRO. 9-29-66)

REAR DECK DETAILS (GTX)

Belvedere GTX (new) WITH 440 CID V8 (375 HP)

67

GTX H/T $3330.

(CONT'D. NEXT PAGE)

'67 Plymouth VIP

FRONT DETAIL

2-DR. VIP H/T $3476.

Plymouth is out to win you over this year.

67 (CONT'D.)

FURY I, FURY II, FURY III and SPORT FURY MODELS (SINCE '65)

FURY TOP DETAIL

SPT. FURY $3638. CVT.

2-DR. HARDTOP

4-DR. H/T

Fury

SPORT Fury

SPORT FURY SIDE SCRIPT

new "FAST TOP" $3392.

engine, drive tr. 5-year/50,000-mile warranty

FURY III $3604. (3-SEAT)

Fury wagon

REAR DETAILS, WITH REAR FACING SEAT

Fury

DASH (FURY) WHEEL CVR.

364

Plymouth

new 190 HP FOR 273 CID V8 SATELLITE

H/T $3047.

3-SEAT $3602.

Satellite Sport Wagon

SPT. SATELLITE SERIES has 318 CID V8 (230 HP)

(INTRO. 9-14-67)

68

new CIRCULAR SIDE SAFETY LIGHTS AT EITHER END

FROM $3805.

ROAD-RUNNER (new) WITH 383 CID V8 (335 HP)

$3229.

(FURY) SPORT SUBURBAN

FURY III 4-DR. H/T $3430.

SATELLITE WAGON (FRONT)

Fury

$3623.

VIP

...the Plymouth win-you-over beat goes on ♥

SPORT FURY FROM $3569.

Belvedere

Plymouth CPE. $2967.

BELVEDERE SPORT SATELLITE

1969 $3251.

new AIR VANE VENTILATION FOR WAGON

(RESTYLED) **69** (INTRO. 9-19-68)

Road Runner $3284.

SPORT FURY $3671.

Sport Suburban

(OTHER VIEW ABOVE)

A completely new Fury for 1969.

VIP GRILLE

$4086. (3-SEAT)

STARTING 1969, PLYMOUTH SIDE LIGHTS ARE RECTANGULAR.

DASH (FURY)

VIP FROM $3750.

Look what Plymouth's up to now: 366

Plymouth

FROM $3066.
(BELV. CPE.)

NOBODY MAKES IT LIKE
Plymouth makes it ♥

(SLOGAN)

ROAD RUNNER
FROM $3290.

ROAD RUNNER BIRD FIGURE NOT AVAILABLE.

(USED ONLY IN ADVERTISING TO IDENTIFY ROAD RUNNER)

BELVEDERE GRILLES SIMILAR, BUT WITHOUT BRIGHT VERTICAL POS.

70

(INTRO. 9-23-69)

FURY II 2 DR. $3381.

ANTI-THEFT LOCK ON STEERING COLUMN.

Fury I

SEDAN $3303.

FURY GRAN COUPE

new FULL-LOOP FURY BUMPERS ENCIRCLE LTS. FRONT and REAR.

NOTE new CONCEALED HEADLIGHT FEATURE (ALSO ON SPORT FURY)

FURY III CONVERTIBLE $3788.

(new DUSTER IN VALIANT SECTION.)

367

Plymouth $3535.

SATELLITE TYPES WITH new 3-PC. SIDE LTS.

CHRYSLER Plymouth **Coming Through.**

Satellite

new 115" WB (2-DR.)
117" WB (4-DR.)

SAT. CUSTOM, BROUGHAM have EXTRA LTS. IN GRILLE

new **Sebring**
(CPE., DASH BELOW)

(RESTYLED)

new GRILLES, ETC.

71 (INTRO. 10-6-70)

$3930.
SEBRING PLUS

$4268.

GTX ↑

WITH 440 CID V8 (370 HP)
(note UNIQUE STRIPING, TRIM ON THESE SPECIALTY CPES.)

ROAD RUNNER ↘

DASH (GTX, ROAD RUNNER)

SOME ROAD RUNNERS ADVERTISED WITH CHROME AROUND GRILLE

(RR 383 CID V8 has 300 HP)
(FURY ON NEXT PAGE)

$3918.

Plymouth

FURY I HAS LESS SIDE CHROME $3676.

Fury II $3824.

FURY II and III GRILLE

1971

Fury III Interior

$4030.

Fury III

ALTERNATOR, TEMP. GAS GAUGES SET ABOVE

120-MPH SPEEDO.

$3998.

71
(CONT'D.)

2-DR. FORMAL HARDTOPS

FURY III

Sport Fury

$4086.

Sport Fury

$4140.

(FROM $4494.) SPORT SUBURBAN

GRAN CPE.

3 CHROME TABS ATOP FR. FENDERS OF Sport Fury GT

Plymouth

SATELLITE $3484.

$3553.

SATELLITE CUSTOM $3723.

(INTRO. 9-28-71)

72

SEBRING has CHROME TRIM HERE
STANDARD 318 CID V8 CUT TO 150 HP
(6 AVAIL.)

ROAD RUNNER

$3863.

RR 400 CID V8 (255 HP)

THIS GRILLE ALSO USED BY SATELLITE REGENT WAGON

1972

FURY I
$3915.

FURY GRAN SEDAN
CPE.

FURY III
$4214.

$4438.

$4425.

ALL-NEW FURY GRILLE

FURY SPORT SUBURBAN
FR. $4840.

370

Plymouth

STD. 225 CID 6 (105 HP)
318 CID V8 (150 HP)

Satellite Wagon
FROM $4050.

SATELLITE, CUSTOM, REGENT WAGONS IN SAT. SERIES

73

FRONT RESTYLED $3714.

SEDAN

Satellite

DIFFERING TAIL LIGHT DESIGNS

SATELLITE REGENT WAGON (SAME GRILLE AS SATELLITE CUSTOM)

E/F/H78; F70×14 TIRES (ON VARIOUS SAT. TYPES)

Satellite Coupe
$3645.

DASH

SATELLITE SEBRING

$3893.

$3887.

Road-Runner
(2 VIEWS)

(FURY ON NEXT PAGE) 371

Plymouth
FURY

$4323.

F78×15 TIRES

Fury I 4-Door Sedan

$4032.

Fury III

Fury II

four-door
73
(CONT'D.)

1973

360 CID
V8
(170 HP)
ENGINE in
SUBURBAN,
CUSTOM SUBURBAN,
and SPT. SUB.
WAGONS have
(FURY SERIES)

SPORT SUBURBAN
has GRAB
IRONS
$5056.
(3-SEAT)

FR.
$4521.

FURY
GRAN
note EMBLEMS

wagon

DASH

FR. $4703.372

CUSTOM SUBURBAN

Plymouth

(FINAL)
SATELLITE

(SATELLITE SERIES ENDS DURING 1974)
FR. $3890.

SATELLITE WAGONS
FR. $4042.

SATELLITE CUSTOM $4220. UP

new Voyager

FROM $4060.   109" WB   B100, B200, B300

WITH SATELLITE TYPE OF 225 CID 6 (105 HP)

REGENT FR. $4441.

SATELLITE REGENT
(SATELLITE CUSTOM SED. has SAME new GRILLE DESIGN)

1974

74

DASH (FURY)

PLYMOUTH FURY WAGONS

CST. SUB. FROM $4814.

CUSTOM SUB.

360 CID V8 (180 HP) IN FURY

FURY III H/T $4474.

Fury

SPT. SUBURBAN FR. $5065.

SLOGAN: "EXTRA CARE IN ENGINEERING ... IT MAKES A DIFFERENCE"

400 CID V8 (185/205 HP) IN GRAN FURY, WAGONS.

WAGONS INCLUDE:
Fury Sport Suburban ▪ Custom Suburban ▪ Suburban
Satellite Regent ▪ Satellite Custom ▪ Satellite

373

Plymouth

('75)

The Small Fury.

(new 115"/ 117½" WB)

(ROAD-RUNNER MOVED TO FURY SERIES, 1975)

(RESTYLED)

Plymouth Fury

$3699. (SALE)

GOOD GAS MILEAGE. EVEN WITH AN AUTOMATIC TRANSMIS
23 mpg hwy. 16 mpg city E.P.A. estimates

75-76

('76)

FURY

('76) $6344. Gran Fury Sport Suburban. (124" WB)

FURY

SINCE 1975, NUMBER OF FULL-SIZE PLYMOUTH MODELS REDUCED

(ROAD-RUNNER RE-APPEARS AS A 1977 VOLARE MODEL.)

77-78

('78)

('77) new GRILLE

(NO 121½", 124" WB GRAN FURY TYPES AFTER 1977.)

1980 GR. FY. RETURNS WITH 118½" WB)

(NO 1979 MODEL OF PLYMOUTH FURY)

**1980 PLYMOUTH GRAN FURY.
A MATTER OF FAMILY PRIDE.**

225 CID 6 (100 HP) TOTALLY RESTYLED AND DOWNSIZED

GRAN FURY

80

FROM $6823.

V8s ALSO AVAIL. 318 CID (140 OR 155 HP) OR 360 CID

DASH

P195/75 R15 TIRES and OTHERS

374

PLYMOUTH HORIZON

(SINCE 1978)

WITH VOLKSWAGEN 4 CYL. 104.7 CID ENGINE

99.2" WB FROM $3981.

155/80 × 13 TIRES

$3706 *
38/25 †
HWY / CITY

GRAIN TRIM (ABOVE)

WHEN YOU WANT TO GO ANYWHERE IN COMFORT AND CONFIDENCE.

RELAX. PLYMOUTH HORIZON CAN HANDLE IT.

new **78**

DODGE OMNI SPECS. SIMILAR

THAT'S IMAGINATION. THAT'S PLYMOUTH.

new TC-3 2-DR. 2+2 FASTBACK (HATCHBACK) $4801. ('79)

ORIG. TYPE CONT'D. with VARIED TRIM and OPTIONS

79-80

96.7" WB ON 2-DR.

1980 PRICES:
$5265. (4-DR.)
5611. (2-DR.)

2-DR. has BODY and GRILLE STYLE UNLIKE 4-DR.

DASH (TC-3, 1979)

"SPORT APPEARANCE" TRIM with TC-3

SIDE DECAL, and CAST ALUMINUM WHEELS.

Plymouth Valiant 66

(VALIANT = 1960-1976)
(VOLARE = 1976-1980)

PLYMOUTH DIVISION — CHRYSLER MOTORS CORPORATION

SIGNET H/T $2487.

100, 200 OR SIGNET MODELS

106" WB

6-CYL. OR V8 FROM $2862.

Barracuda (SINCE 1964)

DASH ('67 BARRACUDA INTRO. 11-25-66)

new 108" WB

('67 VALIANT INTRO. 9-29-66)

TAIL-LT.

67

new GRILLE

100 2-DR. $2346.

100 (WITH 200 DECOR OPTION) (NOTE SIDE CHROME)

100 REAR

4-DR. $2537.

SIGNET

2-DR. $2491.

TURN SIGNAL INDICATOR IS VISIBLE TO DRIVER

(200 ELIMINATED AS A MODEL SERIES)

376

Plymouth Valiant

BARRACUDA
FR. $2936.

Barracuda. 4 new engines.

225 CID 6 (145 HP)

318, 340, 383 CID
V8s
(FROM 230 HP)

6.95 × 14
TIRES (ON
BARRACUDA
SINCE 1967)

(INTRO. 9-14-67)

68

new
GRILLES

(FINAL YR. FOR
SPLIT GRILLE ON
VALIANT)

VALIANT SIGNET
2-DR. $2633.

6.50/7.00
× 13 TIRES

VALIANT

new GRILLES

69

SIGNET 4-DR.
$2737.

(INTRO. 9-19-68)

'CUDA
340

('CUDA 383 AVAIL.)

**Barracuda Coupe,
Convertible and 'Cuda**

Plymouth Valiant

Barracuda

$3219.

Barracuda is America's lowest priced sporty car.

Barracuda is so popular that sales are up 53%.

$3543. (CUDA)

(new GRAN COUPE ALSO)

new HEMI-'CUDA WITH "AIR GRABBER" and 426 CID V8

2-DR. RESTYLED VALIANT NOW KNOWN AS

(INTRO. 9-23-69)

VALIANT/ DUSTER DASH

70 new MODELS (RESTYLED)

PLYMOUTH "HEART" NECKTIE USED IN ADVERTISING

Duster

FROM $2172.

(new DUSTER 340 ALSO AVAIL., WITH 340 CID V8 ENGINE, 275 HP)

NOBODY MAKES IT LIKE **Plymouth makes it ♥**

SLOT-LIKE TAIL LTS.

1970

DUSTER CARTOON DECALS

THE GOLD DUSTER

The Gold Duster—Special Version of The Popular Duster

It includes:

- 225 CID ENGINE OR 318 CID ENGINE
- WHITE SIDEWALL TIRES
- UNIQUE DELUXE WHEEL COVERS
- BUCKET-SEAT STYLE TRIM
- DUAL HORNS
- CHROME DRIP MOLDING
- ARGENT PAINTED GRILL
- GOLD DUSTER EMBLEM
- GOLD SIDE TAPE STRIPES
- GOLD REAR STRIPES
- CIGAR LIGHTER

Plymouth Valiant **Barracuda**

$3583. (H/T)

6-PORT GRILLE

$3840.

(THE FINAL BARRACUDA CVT.)

('71 BARRA-CUDA INTRO. 10-6-70)

VALIANT (below)

$3891.

'cuda

$2639.

DUSTER 340 (below)

$2982.

340 SPOILER OPT. →

71 new GRILLES

('71 VAL. INTRO. 9-15-70)

SCAMP 2-DR. H/T (new) (SCAMP has 111" WB. $2808.

ALL OTHER MODELS RETAIN 108" WB.)

$2560.

DUSTER

Plymouth Valiant
'CUDA
BARRACUDA

$3761.

$3554.

'Cuda 2-Door Hardtop

Rallye Instrument Cluster. What you see is what you get on Barracuda and 'Cuda.

Barracuda & 'Cuda

STD. VINYL SEATS

Duster 72
(BELOW, and NEXT PAGE) (new GRILLES)
(INTRO. 9-28-71)

Interiors

OPT. VALIANT BENCH SEAT in VINYL and CLOTH

DUSTER 340

OPT. DUSTER, DUSTER 340, VALIANT BENCH SEAT

$2987.

DUSTER HAS SLIGHTLY ALTERED REAR (DUSTER NAME AT VERY CENTER, PLY. NAME OFF LID.)

SPECIAL TOP ON Gold Duster.

1972

380

Plymouth Valiant

VALIANT
$2608.

Valiant 4-Door Sedan

WITH SIDE STRIPE and "DUSTER" DECAL AT FRONT END OF STRIPE

Twister Package.
A lot of extras for your Duster including rear quarter panel designation and hood paint treatment.

TWISTER

WITH SIDE TRIM STRIP and CHROME "DUSTER" LETTERING ON COWL

Valiant Scamp

72
(CONT'D.)

SCAMP CLOTH- AND-VINYL SEAT (OPT.)

$2773.

STD. SCAMP VINYL SPLIT- BACK BENCH SEAT

BUMPER GUARDS

NAME ADDED

new WH. COVERS

381

Plymouth Valiant

Barracuda

$3675.

'CUDA

$3860.

SCAMP'S GRAINED DASH OPTIONAL IN VALIANT/ DUSTER MODELS.

VALIANT 4-DR. $2687.

vinyl roof **Gold Duster.**

73

new GRILLE

new SAFETY BUMPERS →

Duster 340

$3093.

SCAMP

DUSTER

$2616.

$2857.

Plymouth Valiant

$3352.

DUSTER 360 (below) REPLACES FORMER DUSTER 340. has new 360 CID V8 ENG., BUT HP CUT TO 190.

Duster 360

Space Duster

Gold Duster

Plymouth Duster
Extra care in engineering...it makes a difference.

CHRYSLER Plymouth

FINAL YR. FOR BARRACUDA, 'CUDA (FEW CHANGES FROM 1973.)

74

new Valiant Brougham INTERIOR

Introducing Plymouth Valiant Brougham.

$4014.

WITH new BEIGE CRUSHED VELOUR UPHOLSTERY (SEE ILLUSTR. AT RIGHT, CENTER)

REAR OF SCAMP RESTYLED

$3361.

Plymouth Scamp.

(automatic transmission INCL.)

383

Plymouth Valiant

America's **No.1** selling small car comes from Plymouth.

(SCAMP H/T STILL AVAIL.)

The style of a European sedan. At the price of an American compact.

Valiant Brougham.

More car in a small car. That's par for Duster.

75-76

FINAL VALIANTS and DUSTERS. (REPLACED BY new VOLARE AFTER 1976.)

Plymouth Volaré

The new small car from Plymouth.

RESTYLED, and 1/2" LONGER WHEELBASES:
2-DR.= 108½"
4-DR.= 112½"

76

225 CID, 100 HP 6
OR
318 CID, 150 HP V8

PREMIER WAGON = $4859.

The accent is on comfort... and space.

LG. MIRRORS OPTIONAL, USED WHEN HAULING TRAILERS

VOLARE, CUSTOM OR PREMIER MODELS

PREMIER 4-DR.= $4892.

384

Plymouth Volaré

PREMIER 4-DR.

PREMIER WAGON

Volaré Premier 4-Door Sedan

Volaré. The small car with the accent on comfort.

SPT. CPE WITH OPERA WINDOWS

ROAD RUNNER

The new Volaré T-Bar Roof:
(T-TOP)

77

VOLARÉS 3

new SPORT COUPES ADDED ("FUN-RUNNERS") PLUS new T-TOP OPTION

NOTE THAT SOME 1977 VOLARES DON'T HAVE HOOD ORNAMENTS, IF NOT IN PREMIER SERIES

SUN RUNNER
(WITH SUN ROOF OR T-TOP)

FRONT RUNNER

DUSTER CPE. RETURNS, 1979.

Don't Give Up.
Get a New Plymouth Volaré

19/14*
MPG HWY   MPG CITY
$4427**
Price includes optional automatic transmission.

4-DR. ('78)

new GRILLE WITH "WAFFLE" PATTERN

78-79

(CONT'D. NEXT PAGE)

Plymouth *Volaré*

('78) 25/18* MPG HWY MPG CITY $4362**

** = SALE PRICE

Volaré. America's first choice in wagons.

78-79 (CONT'D.)

PREMIER WAGON $5672.

COUPE WITH "PREMIER" PACKAGE

ROAD-RUNNER

WAGON (CUSTOM PKG.)

(GRAINED PREMIER WAGON AVAIL.)

4-DR. WITH "CUSTOM" PKG.

(LOWEST-PRICED VOLARE IS SPECIAL CPE., AT $5610.)

80
new GRILLE (FINAL VOLARE)

DUSTER CPE.

DASH

FRONT SIDE SAFETY LIGHTS NOW VERTICAL, and AT FENDER CORNER.

(REPLACED BY 1981 RELIANT)

386

full-sized cars.

GM MARK OF EXCELLENCE

PONTIAC

(SINCE 1926)

V-8 ENGINES (SINCE 1955)

$3628.

CATALINA SCRIPT; COWL LETTERING IN OTHER MODELS WITH NAMES IN BLOCK LETTERS

↖ $3240.

Catalina

389 CID V8 (290 HP) 121" WB

new GRILLES **66**

$4011.

"2+2" LETTERING

CATALINA WAGONS FROM $4164.

DASH

2+2

421 CID V8 (338 HP) (356 OR 376 HP AVAIL.) 121" WB

Ventura

389 CID V8 (290 HP)

Star Chief Executive

124" WB

H/T (new) $3590.

INTERIOR (EXEC.)

REAR FENDER TRIM

(CONT'D. NEXT PAGE)

387

PONTIAC

$4385.

WAGONS : 121" WB

Wide-Track Pontiac/'66

"BONNEVILLE" NAME ALSO SEEN ON GRILLE OF

Bonneville
124" WB

BONNEVILLE WAGON $4704.

$4543.

STAINLESS STEEL LOWER SIDE TRIM (BNVL., GP)

66 (CONT'D.)

389 C/D V8 IN BON., GP (333 HP)

BONNEVILLE BROUGHAM OPTION

GRAND PRIX has "GP" and RALLY LTS. ON GRILLE

GRAND PRIX has OWN REAR STYLING, 121" WB

Grand Prix

$4449.

AVAIL. ONLY AS A 2-DR. H/T

UP TO 376 HP AVAIL. (GP)

SIDE DETAILS

GRAND PRIX has OWN GRILLE

WOOD-GRAIN ON GRAND PRIX DASH

PONTIAC

Where did they hide the windshield wipers * on the 1967 Pontiacs?

Only your Pontiac dealer knows. And he's not talking until September 29.

new 400 CID V8 (290 HP)

Catalina

$3274.

* = new WIPERS CONCEALED BELOW REAR END OF HOOD

(new) EXECUTIVE SAFARI WAGON

FR. $4557.

new GRILLES

67

8.55 x 14 TIRES

UP TO 376 HP WITH new 400, 428 CID V8s.

new ENERGY-ABSORBING STEERING COLUMN; new 4-WAY HAZARD FLASHER

BONNEVILLE H/T 400 CID V8 (325 HP)

$4405

(INTRO. 9-29-66)

BONNEVILLE H/T (REAR QUARTERS)

'67 Grand Prix (GP)

GP 400 CID V8 has 350 HP

GP $4770. CONVERTIBLE ADDED TO LINE (1967 ONLY)

new CONCEALED HEADLIGHTS (ONLY ON GRAND PRIX)

Ride the Wide-Track Winning Streak.   389

PONTIAC

400 CID V8
(265 OR 290 HP)

CATALINA
H/T
$3518.

FROM $4723.

EXECUTIVE
SAFARI
WAGON

"MORROKIDE" (IMITATION LEATHER)
and CLOTH UPHOLSTERY AVAIL.

(INTRO.
9-21-67)

68

METAL "NOSE" MORE
PRONOUNCED
THAN BEFORE.

new GRILLES, TAIL LTS.

VENTURA
4-DR. H/T

$4571.

124" WB
BONNEVILLE
H/T (WITH TAIL
LIGHT DETAILS
ABOVE)

DASH
(BONNEVILLE
BROUGHAM)

400 CID V8
(340 HP)

GRAND
PRIX
H/T
$4676.

GP
400 CID
V8
(350 HP)

WAGONS have
400 CID V8
(265, 290 OR 340 HP)

Pontiac announces the great break away!

Pontiac Station Wagons

CATALINA FROM $4496.

$5081. BONNEVILLE

EXECUTIVE SAFARI

FROM $4849.

CATALINA, VENTURA, EXECUTIVE have THIS GRILLE

new GRILLES 69 (INTRO. 9-26-68)

TYPICAL PONTIAC MEDALLION

RECTANGULAR-CLUSTER NON-GP DASH

BONNEVILLE $4733. 428 CID V8 (360 HP)

new 125" WB

GRAND PRIX

new 118" WB

GP NOW has UN-SHROUDED INDIVIDUALLY-SET HEADLIGHTS

GP new "WRAP-AROUND" DASH

$4853.

391 400 CID V8 (350 HP)

PONTIAC

EXECUTIVE
3-SEAT WAGON
$5178.

70

new GRILLES
(INTRO. 9-18-69)

$4034.

122" WB (SINCE '69)

CATALINA CONVT.
(EXECUTIVE has SAME GRILLE)

(NO MORE VENTURA MODELS, BUT AVAIL. AS $106. OPTION IN CATALINA LINE.)

DASH (BNV.)

BONNEVILLE

BONNEVILLE
4-DR. SEDAN $4746.
(DASH ABOVE)

new 455 CID V8 (360 HP) IS PONTIAC'S LARGEST ENGINE.

$4876.

$4961.

This is the way it's going to be.

392

GRAND PRIX AND INTERIOR

PONTIAC

The First Catalina Brougham

H/T $4614.

CATALINA new 123" WB

350 OR 400 CID V8 (250 OR 265 HP)

G/H 78×15 TIRES $5236.

Catalina

H/T $4400.

GR. VILLE

71 new GRILLES

(INTRO. 9-29-70)

The first

Grand Ville ↙ (new)

$5096.

Bonneville RESEMBLES GRAND VILLE, BUT BEARS THESE MARKS

126" WB 455 CID V8 (280 OR 325 HP) IN BNNVLLE., GR. VILLE

Pure Pontiac!

GP H/T $5087.

REAR

Grand Prix

G78×14 TIRES

118" WB 400 CID V8 (300 HP)

note ONLY 2 HEADLTS. ON GP

PONTIAC

SAFARI WAGON (3-SEAT)

$4992.

$5320. (3-SEAT)

(UNGRAINED) GRAND SAFARI

WAGONS WITH 127" WB 400 OR 425 CID V8s (265 OR 280 HP)

Safari

SAFARI GRILLE (ABOVE) IS LIKE THAT OF CATALINA. GRAND SAFARI has CRISS-CROSS GRILLE PCS. (AS BONNEVILLE and GRAND VILLE.)

Grand Safari

3 VIEWS OF TAILGATE, SHOWING HOW WINDOW RETRACTS INTO ROOF, AND DOOR LOWERS UNDER FLOOR.

71 (CONT'D.)

L78 × 15 TIRES

GR. SAFARI 2-SEAT: $5170.
3-SEAT: $5320.

Pontiac

new ENERGY-ABSORBING SAFETY BUMPER

CONVERTIBLE $4596.

350 OR 400 CID V8 (160 OR 175 HP) IN CATALINA →

400 OR 455 CID V8s (175 OR 185 HP) IN WAGONS

Catalina
123½" WB
SEDAN $4229.
G78 × 15 TIRES

'72 Pontiac ...a cut above!

CVT. $5156.

Grand Ville

126" WB

OWN TAIL-LTS., BUT GRILLE LIKE BONNEVILLE

H78 × 15 TIRES, 455 CID V8 (185 OR 220 HP) IN BNVL., GR. VIL.

new GRILLES

72 HP CUTS

(INTRO. 9-23-71)

Bonneville

SEDAN $4685.

BONNE. 4-DR. H/T $4809.

Grand Prix.

GP (BELOW) WITH 400 CID V8 (200 HP)

Grand Prix

$4988.

G78 × 14 TIRES (GP)

REAR 395

118" WB FRONT

PONTIAC 124" WB

CATALINA FROM $4209.

REAR (BNVLLE.)

4-DR. H/T $4716.

LG. SIDE MIRRORS NOT STD. EQUIPMENT.

$4794. CATALINA

400 OR 455 CID V8s (175-225 HP)

BONNEVILLE

$5198.

$5495.

new WIDE GRILLES ON 1973 MODELS ONLY. (ON ALL BUT GP)

new OPERA WINDOW $4974.

(new 116" WB) GRAND PRIX (RESTYLED)

73

350, 400 OR 455 CID V8s (150 TO 215 HP)

124" WB BONNEVILLE (GRAND VILLE GRILLE SIMILAR)

new "COLONNADE" H/T CPE. $4837.

CATALINA SAFARI (GRAND SAFARI ON NEXT PAGE)

$5498.

74 (RESTYLED) new WRAPAROUND PARK./DIR. LIGHTS, ONLY ON GRAND VILLE.

GRAND VILLE

H/T REAR (CONT'D.)

GRAND PRIX and DASH

396

PONTIAC

BONNEVILLE BLOCK TWEED UPHOLSTERY ←

74
(CONT'D.)

3-SEAT WAGON WITH WOODGRAIN $5969.

Grand Safari
Pontiac's full-sized station wagon

Catalina

$5272.

ROUND HEAD-LIGHTS

Beautiful things are happening at your Pontiac dealer's!

Grand Ville Brougham
Pontiac's most luxurious full-sized car.

$6430.

Grand Prix
Pontiac's classic personal car.

GP

"SJ" $6128.

$5867.

Catalina
Pontiac's lowest priced full-sized car.

CATALINA SAFARI (3-SEAT)

new RECTANGULAR HEADLIGHTS

G/H/LR78×15 TIRES
$6468.

$6306.

Grand Safari

75

new GRILLES

123.4" WB

400 CID V8s (170-185 HP)

DASH

Bonneville

$5657.

RTS Radial Tuned Suspension

397

PONTIAC
Bonneville

Bonneville: 19 mpg Highway/13 mpg City (EPA)

CATALINA 4-DR. SEDAN ($5370.) IS LOWEST-PRICED FULL-SIZED PONTIAC.

76

new GRILLES

400 AND 450 CID V8s (170, 185, 200 HP)
STANDARD
GP COUPE $5377.
SJ = $5802.
LJ = $6138.

SJ

CATALINA SIMILAR TO ABOVE CAR, BUT HAS 5 HVY. HORIZONTAL STRIPS ACROSS GRILLE.

DASH

STANDARD
Grand Prix. $4798.*

(* = REGULARLY PRICED AT $5377.)

GP 350 CID (160 HP)

116" WB

new "WATERFALL" GRILLE

(UNILLUSTRATED "LJ" has 2-TONE PAINT WITH SPECIAL STRIPING.)

OTHER MODELS RESTYLED, DOWNSIZED (SEE NEXT PG.)

77

(ON GP, LARGE CORNER LTS. REPL. BY new EXTRA LT. BETWEEN EACH PAIR OF HEADLIGHTS, AS SHOWN)

GRAND PRIX

new GRILLE, WITH PCS. SPACED FURTHER APART.

new WHEELS

new 180 HP (SJ)

$5,109.* (SALE)

GRAND PRIX

REG. $5701. (LJ = $6064.)
(SJ = $6334.)

PONTIAC ▼ THE MARK OF GREAT CARS

(CONT'D. NEXT PAGE)

398

PONTIAC

BONNEVILLE SEDAN
$6089. new 116" WB

new DASH (GAUGES PLACED HIGH)

BONNEVILLE BROUGHAM (VINYL TOP)

$6624.

ALL-METAL TOP

PONTIAC NAME ABOVE LTS.

77 new 231 CID V6 (105 HP)
(CONT'D.) new 301 CID V8 (135 HP)

WITH WOODGRAIN

3-SEAT GRAND SAFARI
$6569.

PHANTOM VIEW, SHOWING HOW REAR DOOR OPENS SIDEWAYS OR SWINGS DOWN.

Pontiac

GRAND **Safari wagon**
$7079.

CATALINA SAFARI FROM $6601.

DASH

Bonneville
$5931.

(REG. $6608.)

1978 Pontiac's best year yet!

(GP RESTYLED)

$7354.

Bonneville Brougham

301 CID V8 INCREASED TO 140 HP (V6 UNCHANGED)

FR/HR 78 x 15 TIRES

Grand Prix

new GRILLES

new DASH

78

$5772.*

(REG. $6185.)

Grand Prix.

25 mpg Highway, 18 City!

108" WB ON GRAND PRIX

GRAND PRIX HOOD ORNAMENT

GP

PONTIAC

$6645.

18 EPA ESTIMATE MPG **27** HWY ESTIMATE

CATALINA and DASH

2-DR. $6909. UP

GP "LJ" (STRIPED) WITH DE LUXE VINYL TOP

BONNEVILLE AND BNV. BROUGH.

SAFARI

79 new GRILLES

V6 INCR. TO 115 HP (V8 UNCHANGED)

CLOSE-UP OF BONNEVILLE GRILLE, FRONT END

LJ $6840.

195/75R14 205/70 R14 (SJ) TIRES

GRAND PRIX

FROM $6530.

231 CID V6 (115 HP) EPA:

19 EPA EST MPG **25** HWY EST

ALSO AVAIL: 301 CID V8 (140/150 CID)

THE 1979 PONTIACS ▼ OUR BEST GET BETTER 401

PONTIAC

CATALINA

GAS MILEAGE =

231 CID V6 (115 HP)

80

OR *new* 265 CID V8 (120 HP)

BONNEVILLE INTERIOR

SEDAN
$7322.

ALL NEW
STYLING
FOR
COUPE →

BONNEVILLE and
CATALINA NOW SHARE
SAME GRILLE DESIGN.

BONNEVILLE
CPE.= $7837.

GRAND (BONNEVILLE)
SAFARI WAGON

$8570.

GRAND PRIX

GP DASH

LJ WITH
OPTIONAL
T-TOP →

GP PRICES
START AT
$7096.

MORE
PONTIAC
PG E**X**CITEMENT
TO THE **G**ALLON

V6
OR
new 265 OR
301 CID
V8 (120 OR
140 HP)

LJ = $7475.
SJ = $7993.

Pontiac COMPACTS

(1961 TEMPEST 4 was FIRST PONT. COMPACT)

medium-priced

TEMPEST OHC SPRINT

(SPRINT PKG.)

(230 CID OHC 6, 165 HP)
207 HP @ 5200 RPM, SPRINT

OR 326 CID V8 (250 HP)

115" WB

CVT. FROM $3093.

LE MANS

$3006. (H/T)

66

(REAR) GTO

(TEMPEST, CUSTOM, LE MANS OR GTO MODELS)

GTO

GTO has RALLY LTS., "GTO" ON GRILLE.

GTO has 389 CID V8 (335 HP)

"GTO" MEANS "GRAN TURISMO OMOLOGATO"

CVT. $3425.

The tiger scores again! Wide-Track Pontiac/'66

Wide-Track Pontiac/67

7.75 x 14 TIRES

LE MANS

GTO CVT. $3547.

HOOD SCOOP DETAIL

SAME HP AS 1966, EXCEPT new 215 HP IN SPRINT

H/T $3317. **Pontiac GTO**

67

has F 70 x 14 TIRES

RALLY I

RALLY II

new GRILLES (TEMPEST FROM $2787.)

403

H/T $3094.

PONTIAC COMPACTS LE MANS (RESTYLED) 68

We've just received our 4th Car of the Year award.

new GRILLES. HEADLTS. NOW HORIZONTALLY PAIRED. 112" WB = 2-DR., 116" = 4-DR.

Wide-Track 1968 Pontiacs

GTO HEADLTS. CONCEALED

HAS 400 CID V8 265 OR 350 HP

GTO

400 CID V8 (366 - 370 HP)

ALL RISE FOR

THE JUDGE

SPOILER

The Judge: a special GTO by Pontiac

H/T $3544.

69

new GRILLES

250 CID 6 (175 HP) STD. 350 CID V8 (265 HP)

DASH (JUDGE)

LE MANS

H/T $3292.

The year of the great Pontiac break away

$3634. (CVT.)

70

New T-37 Hardtop. (TEMPEST)

This is the way fun is going to be.

(CONT'D. NEXT PAGE)

new LeMans Sport

NARROW GRILLES

250 CID 6 (155 HP)
350/400 CID V8s
255-350 HP

LE MANS

PONTIAC
COMPACTS

CPE.
$3187.

70 (CONT'D.)

(FINAL USE OF
TEMPEST MODEL
NAME)

F78/G78
× 14
TIRES

GTO

H/T $3661.

**"This is
the way it's
going to be."**

GTO HEADLTS.
NO LONGER CONCEALED

400 OR 455 CID V8
(350 TO 370 HP)

H/T = $3690.

GTO

$4235.

(CVT. = $4465.)

LE
MANS
T-37

71

(CONT'D.
NEXT PAGE)

250 CID 6 (145 HP)
TO
455 CID V8 (335 HP;
310 NET HP)

405

PONTIAC COMPACTS

LE MANS WAGON

Le Mans

new 2-WAY TAIL-GATE SWINGS ASIDE OR DOWN.

$4216. (2-ST.) $4329. (3-ST.)

71 (CONT'D.)

GRILLE

DASH

4-DR. $2684.

SPRINT CPE. (DISTINGUISHED BY HEAVY SIDE STRIPE)

Ventura II

(new)

(INTRO. SUMMER, 1971)

250 CID 6 (145 HP) OR 307 CID V8 (200 HP)

71½ -72

new LOWEST-PRICED PONTIAC SERIES 111" WB

CPE. $2654.

E78 × 14 TIRES

note DISTINCTIVE 4-PC. GRILLE, SINGLE HEADLTS.

406

PONTIAC COMPACTS

LeMans $3690.

72

GTO

GTO HARDTOP COUPE

LeMANS 4-DOOR SEDAN

GTO

"GTO" on LOWER REAR FENDER

$3598.

LeMANS COUPE

AVAIL. LeMans

LE MANS
(WITH ENDURA FRONT END OPTION)

GT
H/T CPE.
(note SIDE TRIM)

GTO has SAME FRONT AS ABOVE, EXCEPT FOR "GTO" INSTEAD of "PONTIAC" on GRILLE.

$4147.

LeMANS 3-SEAT STATION WAGON

2-SEAT GRAND LE M. (GRAINED)

$4104.

LeMans Station Wagons

(FINAL LeM. CVT.) *LeMANS SPORT CONVERTIBLE*

LeMans Sport

(note THE DIFFERENCES AMONG GRILLES OF VARIOUS LE MANS TYPES ON THIS PAGE)

Luxury LeMans (new)

LUXURY LeMANS 4-DOOR HARDTOP

4-DR. H/T $4077.

STD. 350 CID V8 CUT TO 160 HP.

400 or 455 CID V8s ALSO AVAIL.

VINYL ROOF and CREST DETAIL ABOVE

2-DR. H/T $3954. 407

PONTIAC
COMPACTS

250 CID 6 (100 HP)
new 350 CID V8
(150 HP.)

FROM
$2660.

'73 Ventura.

(VENTURA
CUSTOM
ALSO)

DASH

VENTURA
NO
LONGER
KNOWN AS
"VENTURA II"

new
BUMPERS

73

new GRILLES

new
LOUVRED
REAR
QUARTER
WINDOW
DETAIL

$3867.

Introducing
LeMans
Sport Cpe.

Le Mans.

(LUXURY
LE MANS
has 8
HEAVY
VERT.
GRILLE
PCS.)
→

LUXURY LE
MANS

408   $4129. (CONT'D.
NEXT PAGE)

PONTIAC COMPACTS
73 (CONT'D.)

GRAND AM

CPE.
112" WB

(new)

2-DR.
$4969.

4 DR. $5058.

Introducing the first Grand Am.

400 CID V8 (170 HP)
GR 70 × 15 TIRES

Grand Am

(SIDE INSIGNIA)

The Wide-Track people have a way with cars.

GRAND AM DASH (NOTE THICK, PADDED MERCEDES-TYPE HUB ON STEERING WHEEL) (arrow)

Ventura
Pontiac's low-priced compact car.

Ventura Custom Sprint in Sunstorm Yellow.

250 CID 6 (100 HP)
350 CID V8 ← (150 HP OR 155 HP) →

LE MANS
2-DR. COLONNADE H/T

$3176.

Ventura Custom Hatchback Coupe in Carmel Beige.

$ 3869.

74

VENTURA CUSTOM

new GRILLES

$ 3055.

409

VENTURA GTO
(CONT'D. NEXT PAGE)

PONTIAC COMPACTS

VENTURA CUSTOM 4-DR. $4334

Pontiac strikes again.

DASH

HATCHBACK $4302.

VENTURA

250 CID 6 (105 HP)

Ventura's standard instrument panel. The custom cushion steering wheel is standard on Ventura Custom, Sprint and SJ. It's available on Ventura.

Ventura SJ.

$4699. (CPE.)
4716. (HATCH.)
4824. (4-DR.)

75 (CONT'D.)

$4749.

Grand LeMans

2-DR. COLONNADE H/T CPE.

LeMans Safari

(3-SEAT) $5207.

LeMans

$4605.

Grand LeMans Safari

350 CID V8 (155 HP)

$4627.

$5401. (3-SEAT)

CPE. ROOF LINE

Grand Am.

$5495.

1975

DASH

Grand Am

(NO MORE GRAND AMS UNTIL 1978)

400 CID V8 (170 HP)

PONTIAC

COMPACTS

The Mark of Great Cars.

subcompact Astre

FR. $3377.

VENTURA

250 CID 6
260 CID V8
(BOTH 110 HP)
IN VENT. or
LE M., GR. LE M.

DASH

1976 PONTIAC GRAND LeMANS.

FROM $5106.

Sunbird

(new) 97" WB $3921.

BASIC 140 CID 4 IN SUNBIRD or ASTRE (70 HP)

76

(new GRILLES)

LeMans toppings are available in four flavors. This landau, full vinyl, canopy or padded landau.

ASTRE SAFARI WAGON

37/26

MPG/HIGHWAY   MPG/CITY

ASTRE HATCHBACK

37/26

MPG/HIGHWAY   MPG/CITY

"IRON DUKE"

151 CID 87 HP 4-CYL. ENG. (STD. 140 CID has 84 HP)

SUNBIRD SPORT HATCH

SUNBIRD

$4226
4101.

77

new GRILLES

SPT. CPE.

PHOENIX FROM $5060. (2-DR.)

PHOENIX

(111.1" WB)

(**NEW**)

WITH
151 CID 4 (87 HP)
231 CID V6 (105 HP) OR
301 CID V8 (135 HP)

PONTIAC ▼ THE MARK OF GREAT CARS

412

PONTIAC
COMPACTS
77
(CONT'D.)

THE FINAL Ventura

4-CYL., 231 CID V6 (105 HP), OR 301 CID V8 (135 HP)

$4635.

GRAND LE MANS and DASH

$5520.

Grand Le Mans

$6186.

new 231 CID V-6

85 HP 4 OR 105 HP V6

Sunbird $3541

78
(Resized)

new 108" WB

Pontiac's best year yet!

LE MANS DASH

27 mpg Hwy. 19 mpg City! These are EPA estimates for LeMans with its std. 3.8 litre (231 CID) 2-bbl. V-6 and available auto. trans.

REAR

$5866. UP

LE MANS SAFARI WAGON

GRAND AM 301 CID V8 (140 HP)

413

$6091. UP

LEMANS $4481.

PONTIAC
COMPACTS

A78 x 13 TIRES (SINCE '76)

FROM $4276.

SUNBIRD

DASH

SUNBIRD SPORT SAFARI $4633. (INTRO. '78 @ $4181.)

↑ SUNBIRD "FORMULA" PACKAGE INCLUDES EXTRAS SHOWN (REAR SPOILER ALSO)

note AVAIL. VINYL-COVERED LANDAU TOP on PHOENIX CPE.

SOME MODELS have new GRILLES

79

(CONT'D. NEXT PAGE)

CPE. $5274.

PHOENIX

PHOENIX DASH

LJ GRILLE

LJ $5874.

27

PONTIAC COMPACTS **OUR BEST GET BETTER**

GRAND LE MANS $6410.

231 CID V6 (115 HP)
301 CID V8 (140 HP)

79 (CONT'D.)

LE MANS $6085.

$6222. UP

CPE. $6338.

SAFARI WAGON

REAR

GRAND AM

GRAND AM 1980 GRILLE

80 (new GRILLES) WITH STD. SIDE MIRROR AND WHEEL COVERS

151 CID 4 (86 HP)
231 CID V6 (115 HP)

SUNBIRD STD. CPE. $4915.

A78 x 13 TIRES (SINCE '76)

SUNBIRD

You'll recognize this 'Bird by its distinctive tail feathers. Sunbird Sport Hatch, shown with available Formula Package.

$5274. PLUS FORM. PKG.

SUNBIRD

(CONT'D. NEXT PAGE)

SPT. CPE. $5164.

PONTIAC Firebird

(SINCE 1967)
The Magnificent Five are here!

108″ WB

$3127.

(215-HP) SPRINT
230 CID OHC 6

STD. FIREBIRD
230 CID OHC 6
(165 HP)

E70 × 14 W.O. TIRES

400

67 (new)

(INTRO. 2-23-67)

Firebird HO.

HO (note STRIPE, "HO" LETTERING on SIDES. (HO MEANS "HIGH OUTPUT")

V8 326 CID (285 HP)

400 CID V8 (325 HP)

326 326 CID V8 (250 HP)

Firebird 326

$3705.

(INTRO. 9-21-67)

Firebird 400.

new 250 CID FOR OHC 6 (175 HP)
(SPRINT 6 = 215 HP)
350 CID V8 (265 HP)
400 CID V8 (335 HP)

68 new SIDE SAFETY LIGHTS

(VARIOUS MODELS CONT'D.)

H/Ts FROM $3238; CVTS. FR. $3453

400 H/T $3490. 400 CID V8 (330 OR 335 HP)

417

PONTIAC
Firebird

(INTRO. 9-26-68)

69 *new NARROW GRILLE*

$3588.

Firebird 400 by Pontiac

HOOD - MOUNTED TACH. STILL AVAILABLE (SINCE '67)

400 CVT. $3772.

REAR SPOILER DETAILS

TRANS.-AM DASH

Firebird Trans Am.
(new)

69½

LONG HOOD SCOOPS

400 CID V8 (335 HP) 3.55 TO / GEAR RATIO

418

$4366. ('70 SEASON)

PONTIAC FIREBIRD

TRANS-AM (345 HP)
400 CID V8

FORMULA 400

$4149.

FORMULA 400
400 CID V8
(330 HP)
(note HOOD SCOOPS)

DENT-PROOF PLASTIC "ENDURA" FRONT END

FIREBIRD SYMBOL

(RESTYLED)

70+

new GRILLE
SINGLE HEADLTS.
new RECTANGULAR-SPLIT SIDE LIGHTS

E78 x 14 TIRES

all two-door hardtops

$3999.

ESPRIT
(has BIRD EMBLEM ABOVE GRILLE)

(KNOWN OFFICIALLY AS "1970 +" MODELS. INTRO. 2-26-70)

DASH

TRANS-AM has STRIPE, SPOILER, and AIR DAM BELOW GRILLE

T.A. $4752.

The all-new Firebirds are here.

STD. CPE has NO SPECIAL TRIM.

$3743.

Pontiac announces the beginning of tomorrow.

New, even for Pontiac.

419

PONTIAC FIREBIRD

STD. CPE. FROM $3910.

71 (INTRO. 9-29-70)

335-HP TRANS-AM has F60×15 TIRES; FORMULA has E70×14 (OTHERS, E78×14)

"Pure Pontiac!"

Esprit $4155. new WHEEL COVERS →

A bumper you can knock. And a price you can't.

250 CID 6 (145 HP) OR 350 CID V8 (250 HP) STD.

FROM 3716.

STD. WH. CVR.

STD. H/T

STD. REAR

DASH

(STD. 350 CID V8 CUT TO 160 HP)

ESPRIT $3954.

Formula 400

$3981.

(FORM. 350 and 455 ALSO AVAIL.) (350 CID V8 CUT TO 175 HP)

new MESH PATTERN IN GRILLE →

72 (INTRO. 9-23-71)

Trans Am

$4718

T.A. (455 CID H.O. V8 CUT TO 300 HP)

PONTIAC FIREBIRD

73

$3716. STD. CPE.

new CRISS-CROSS PCS. IN GRILLE.

(OTHER MODELS CONT'D. TRANS-AM OFFERS GIANT "FIREBIRD" DECAL FIGURE ATOP HOOD.)
350 CID V8 cut to 150 HP
T.A. 455 CID V8 cut to 215 HP

$3865. (STD.)

TRANS-AM
$4708.

The Wide-Track people have a way with cars.

FIREBIRD DECAL

GR70 x 15 B/WL TIRES (T.A.)

note HONEYCOMB-TYPE WHEELS

74

RESTYLED, SLOPING FRONT END WITH VERTICAL PCS. IN GRILLE

Part engineering. Part soul.

250 CID 6 (100 HP)
350 CID V8 (155 HP)
170 HP IN FORMULA)
new 400 CID TRANS AM V8 (225 HP) (185 HP IN '75)

DASH

FORMULA HAS GR 70 x 14 TIRES

$4207. FORMULA

$4853.

TRANS-AM

STD. $4584.

6 CYL. NOW 105 HP

$5244.

75

(new AUX. LTS. and HORIZ. PCS. IN GRILLE) 421

T.A. DASH

$4829.

ESPRIT

PONTIAC FIREBIRD

250 CID 6 (110 HP)   350 CID V8 (160 HP)
STD. = $4834.
ESPIRIT = $5090.   TR. AM. = $5514.

76 *new* GRILLE WITH MESH PCS.

FORMULA $5092.

PONTIAC ◆ The Mark of Great Cars

STD. = $5174.
ESPIRIT = 5455.
FORMULA = 5534.

TRANS-AM $6013.

(SE OR SKYBIRD PKG. AVAIL.)

77

new GRILLE WITH *new* QUADRUPLE RECTANGULAR HEADLIGHTS

231 CID V6 (105 HP)
301 CID V8 (135 HP)

TR. AM 400 CID V8 (180 HP)

GR 70 × 15 TIRES (TR. AM)
(OTHERS = FR78 × 15)

1978 ▾ Pontiac's best year yet!

STD. Firebird has 231 CID V6 (105 HP)
$5662.

OPTIONAL T-BAR ROOF

ESPIRIT $5959.

TRANS-AM $6390.

400 CID V8 (403 CID, CALIF.)

GR 70 × 15 TIRES

new BLACK GRILLE

78

FORMULA
305 CID V8 (145 HP) NOT AVAIL. IN CALIF.
$6039.

(SE, SKYBIRD OR *new* REDBIRD PKG. AVAIL.)

PONTIAC FIREBIRD

FORMULA

231 CID V6
(115 HP)
301 CID V8
(140 HP)
(305, 350 CID AV.)
403 CID V8 (TR.AM.)
(185 HP)

$6633.

400 CID V8
(220 HP)
ALSO
AVAIL.

A NEW BREED OF WOW.

(Pontiac, Buick, Chev. and
Oldsmobile ENGINES
USED)

TRANS-AM
DASH

Trans Am.

$6914.

As exciting going as it is coming.

(225/70 R14
TIRES ON TR. AM. OR FORMULA;
FR 78×15 on OTHERS)

79

new
SEPARATELY-
PORTED
HEAD
LIGHTS

(RESTYLED
FRONT and
REAR)

2.41 TO 3.23
GEAR
RATIOS
AVAIL.

CLOSER
DETAILS OF
TRANS-

STD.
FIREBIRD $6046.
(ESPRIT = $6414.)

423

Thunderbird

Ford Motor Company

Highway Pilot Control...

THROTTLE-SET CONTROLS BUILT INTO SPOKE OF STEERING WHEEL (ABOVE)

$5005.
TOWN HARDTOP

TOWN LANDAU
$5105.

TOWN LANDAU TOP DETAILS

SEQUENTIAL TURN SIGNALS IN FULL-WIDTH TAIL-LIGHTS

new GRILLE; new TAIL-LTS.

66

113" WB

FINAL THUNDERBIRD CONVERTIBLE AVAIL. 1966, AT $5400.

390 C/D V8 (315 HP)

Stereo-Tape System...
Overhead Safety Control Panel

THUNDERBIRD 67

(RESTYLED)
(INTRO. 9-30-66)

2-DR. FR. $5144.

DASH

note HOW A SIDE SECTION OF TOP OPENS WITH REAR DOOR

new CONCEALED HEADLIGHTS IN *new* GRILLE

LANDAU 4-DOOR IS *new* $5366.

new 115" WB (2-DR.) 117" WB (4-DR.)

INTERIOR

68

new SIDE SAFETY LIGHTS

(INTRO. 9-22-67)

2-DR. FROM $5263.

new GRILLE

new 429 CID V8 (360 HP)

8.15/8.45 x 15 TIRES

4-DR. LANDAU $5471.

426

OPTIONAL SUN ROOF

2-DR. $5359.
2-DR. LANDAU 5499.
4-DR. LANDAU 5578.

THUNDERBIRD

2-DR. (FORMAL ROOFLINE) LANDAU

(INTRO. 9-27-68)

new 8.55 x 15 TIRES

69

new GRILLE

STD. 2-DR. ROOFLINE

4-DR.

INTERIOR

new 215R15 TIRES

FROM $5498.

70

(RESTYLED) (INTRO. 9-19-69)

new POINTED FRONT END STYLING, WITH HEADLIGHTS NO LONGER CONCEALED

FINAL 4-DR. ($5920.)

EVERY 3RD HORIZONTAL STRIP IN GRILLE APPEARS HEAVIER

WITH LANDAU ROOFLINE $5841.

new H78 x 15 TIRES

71 427

THUNDERBIRD NAME OVER REAR SIDE LIGHT (INTRO. 9-18-70)

HARDTOP ROOFLINE $5698.

THUNDERBIRD

72

INTERIOR

PAINTED DISC WHEEL COVERS ALSO

HP CUT TO 212

new 120.4" WB

215 R15 TIRES

FRONT END TOTALLY RESTYLED

(INTRO. 9-24-71)

2-DR. H/T IS ONLY TYPE NOW AVAIL. = $5730.

ALL-HORIZONTAL GRILLE PCS.

new
OPERA WINDOWS

new ORNAMENT ATOP HOOD

1975 WHEEL CHOICES

Deluxe Wheel Covers

Simulated Wire Wheel Covers

Deep-Dish Aluminum Wheels Standard with Copper Luxury Group

Wide White Sidewall Tires (new)

20TH ANNIV. "SILVER" OR "COPPER" '75 MODELS AVAIL.

INSTR. PANEL ('73)

new 460 CID V8 IN '74

194 HP ('75)

$6170. ('73)
7790. ('76)

CRISS-CROSS GRILLE PCS.

73-76

('75)

('73)

428

('77)

Base sticker price:$5,063*

THUNDERBIRD

new SHORTER 114" WB
STD. new 302 CID V8 (130 HP, '77)
(134 HP, '78)

A new look...

a new size...a new price...

but unmistakably Thunderbird

'77 FROM $5568.

NOT ALL MODELS HAVE THIS LOWER LIGHT

'77 LANDAU has 400 CID V8 (173 HP) ($7990.)

77-78

Among the new Thunderbird's fine appointments is this handsome instrument panel

('77)

INSTRUMENT PANEL

NOTE new PLACEMENT OF SIDE WINDOWS

T-TOP AVAIL.

302 OR 351 CID V8 (134 OR 144 HP)

Heritage

79

new GRILLE

STD. $6439.
TOWN LANDAU = $8866.
HERITAGE = $10,687.

THUNDERBIRD

new 255 CID V8, OR 302 CID V8

DASH

New-Size

SILVER ANNIVERSARY MODELS

(RESTYLED) **80**

WB SHORTER = now 108.4"

WIRE WHEEL COVERS (OPT.)

P185/75R × 14 TIRES

$7003. TO $11,679., PLUS EXTRAS

ALUMINUM WHEELS (OPT.)

LUXURY WHEEL COVER

SLOGAN: **Spread your wings**

1980

430

MISCELLANEOUS RARITIES

INCLUDING
REPLICARS (MODERN COPIES OF FAMOUS CLASSICS)
KIT CARS (TO BE ASSEMBLED BY OWNER, ON CHASSIS OF VW, ETC.)

THESE ARE BUT A FEW EXAMPLES OF THE MANY EXCLUSIVE, LIMITED-PRODUCTION AUTOMOBILES AVAILABLE ON SPECIAL ORDER SINCE 1966. (SOME ARE IN CURRENT PROD.) AN ENTIRE BOOK COULD BE WRITTEN ON SUCH RARE CARS, AS THE CURRENT FIELD IS QUITE EXTENSIVE!

AUBURN ('74)

BRADLEY GT ('76)

AZTEC 7 ('76)

BRICKLIN ('74)

CLENET ('77)

(DATE IN PARENTHESES REFERS ONLY TO YEAR OF SPECIFIC EXAMPLE ILLUSTR., AND DOES NOT MEAN THAT PRODUCTION IS, OR WAS, LIMITED TO A SINGLE YEAR.)

CORD ('66)

LIBERTY ('76)

EXCALIBUR ('79)

GLASSIC ('71)

MIGI ('76)

MOHS ('67)

FASCINATION ('72) (PILOT MOD.)

431